Sara Castro-Klarén
The Narrow Pass of Our Nerves

SARA CASTRO-KLARÉN

The Narrow Pass of Our Nerves
Writing, Coloniality and Postcolonial Theory

IBEROAMERICANA - VERVUERT - 2011

Library of Congress Cataloging-in-Publication Data

Castro-Klarén, Sara.
The narrow pass of our nerves : writing, coloniality and postcolonial theory / Sara Castro-klarén.
    p. cm. -- (Nuevos Hispanismos ; 12)
Includes bibliographical references.
 ISBN 978-1-936353-05-7 (Iberoamericana Vervuert Pub. : alk. paper) -- ISBN 978-8484895916
(Iberoamericana)
 1. Spanish American literature--History and criticism. 2. Latin America--In literature. 3. Colonies in
literature. 4. Postcolonialism in literature. 5. Postcolonialism--Latin America. I. Title.
 PQ7081.C352 2011
 860.9'98--dc22

                                    2011011408

© Sara Castro-Klarén
© of this edition: Iberoamericana

Iberoamericana, 2011
Amor de Dios, 1 - E-28014 Madrid
Tel.: +34 91 429 35 22 - Fax: +34 91 429 53 97

Vervuert, 2011
Elisabethenstr. 3-9 - D-60594 Frankfurt am Main
Tel.: +49 69 597 46 17 - Fax: +49 69 597 87 43

info@iberoamericanalibros.com
www.ibero-americana.net

ISBN 978-84-8489-591-6 (Iberoamericana)
ISBN 978-1-936353-05-7 (Iberoamericana Vervuert Publishing Corp.)

Depósito Legal: SE-6372-2011

Cover design: Carlos Zamora

Printed in Spain by Publidisa.

This book is printed on acid-free paper.

To my family: Peter, Alexandra and David. This book is also dedicated to Sebastián Machaca (Arequipa 1900?-1980?) and Nazario Turpo (Cuzco 1950?-2008). Two curanderos *whose unlettered knowledge and wisdom hovers over the pages of these essays.*

"Truenos"

EN LAS TIENDAS GRIEGAS

Y el Alma se asustó
A las cinco de aquella tarde azul desteñida
El labio entre los linos la imploró
Con pucheros de novio para su prometida

El Pensamiento, el gran General se ciñó
de una lanza deicida.
El Corazón danzaba; mas, luego sollozó:
¿la bayadera esclava estaba herida?

Nada! Fueron los tigres que la dan por correr
a apostarse en aquel rincón, y tristes ver
los ocasos que llegan desde Atenas

No habrá remedio para este hospital de nervios,
para el gran campamento irritado de este atardecer!
Y el General escruta volar siniestras penas
allá. . . . .
En el desfiladero de mis nervios!

"Thunderclaps"

IN THE GREEK TENTS

And the Soul was alarmed
At five o'clock that faded blue afternoon.
The lip implored in between the linens
pouting like a bridegroom to his betrothed.

Thought, the great General, girded himself
With a deicidal lance
the Heart was dancing; then it sobbed:
was the bayadere slave wounded?

Not at all! It was just tigers given to running
So as to post themselves in that corner, and sadly watch
The sunsets arrive from Athens.

There will be no cure for this hospital of nerves,
for the great vexed encampment of this afternoon!
and the General inspects sinister pains spreading swiftly
There. . . . .
In the narrow pass of my nerves!

(From *Los heraldos negros*, 1918. See *The Complete Poetry. A Bilingual Edition. César Vallejo*. Edited and Translated by Clayton Eshleman. University of California Press, 2007, 100-101)

TABLE OF CONTENTS

ACKNOWLEDGEMENTS

Over the course of the years one acquires many debts to colleagues, friends, and family. I cannot here name all the many generous and kind people who in one way or another have made my research possible. However, I want to express a particular debt of gratitude to my Alma Matter, The University of California at Los Angeles, to Dartmouth College, the Woodrow Wilson Center in Washington D.C. and the Johns Hopkins University. Without the intellectual environment and the support I received at these and other institutions of learning my many years of research would not have been possible. I also owe an extensive thanks to two historians of Latin America: Peter Klarén and Franklin Knight. Many thanks are also due to the stimulus of the very large circle of discussants engaged in colonial studies and postcolonial theory. Each meeting became the opening for a large and unsuspected vista. Among these colleagues I need to stress the dialogue with Stephen Greenbaltt, Dipesh Chakravarty, Walter Mignolo, José Rabasa, John Beverley, Ileana Rodríguez, Félix Bolaños, Gustavo Verdesio, Mabel Moraña, Fernando Coronil, Juan Zevallos, Antonio Cornejo Polar, Patricia Seed, Vicky Unruh, Michael Lazzara, Alfonso del Toro, Fernando del Toro, Mario Valdés, María Elena de Valdés, John Chasteen, José Antonio Mazzotti, Julio Ortega, Regina Harrison, Adriana Bergero and Horacio Legras. Many thanks also to the ethno-historian Luis Millones and the archeologist Ramiro Matos. Finally, I want to acknowledge my graduate students at Johns Hopkins for their stimulating dialogue and their dogged pursuit

14

of their projects and ideas. Of course I alone bear responsibility for the arguments put forth in these essays and any errors or mistakes are entirely my own. And I thank Michael Lavers, my editor, without whose generous work, expertise, and keen intelligence this volume would not have been possible.

Preface

I have chosen the closing verse from César Vallejo's poem entitled "Thunderclap" from *Los heraldos negros* (1918) for the title of this collection of essays because, with the figure of the "sinister pains spreading swiftly there / in the narrow pass of my nerves," Vallejo captures the moment when subjects such as Garcilaso de la Vega, Inca, Guamán Poma de Ayala, Sor Juana Inés de la Cruz and even José Carlos Mariátegui realized that their destiny was to write, to write in order to engage in battle, but with a little advantage: positioned at the *desfiladero,* or narrow pass. In Vallejo's poem Alma, at the prospect of battle, "se asustó," while the Grand General Thought ("el Gran General Pensamiento") girded himself with a deicidal lance. My reading of the poem extends the scene from the moment when the battle is contemplated in fear to the moment when a strategy has been devised for coping.

I find this combination of fear and apprehension followed by the decision to write in order to fight to be the core of the prose of the world that post-conquest writers deploy in order to surface from the avalanche of conquest which has literally set their world upside down. The experience of "El mundo al revés," as Guamán Poma decribes it, is not confined in the colonial world to one generation or to one place. The coloniality of power that ensues as a world order, the shifting but always colonial position of the subject, is experienced in different guises over and over again by writers as distant in time and space as the Inca Garcilaso de la Vega and José Carlos Mariátegui as they both search for a *punto de mira.* Outnumbered and overwhelmed by the Eurocentric claims made on knowledge and capacities by the colonial discourse that ensued after 1492, both Alma and the Great General need to move from the plain that gives the advantage to an army onto an elevated point in the terrain from which to see the whole of the field, ascertain the strength of the enemy and plan their mode of engagement while they are, like Kierkegaard, trembling in fear and suffering of "susto," as an Andean healer would tell you. After many years (thirty for Guamán Poma, twenty for the Inca) of inhabiting the "hospital of nerves," the "vexed encampment" that Vallejo figures for this classic Greek battle, the colonial writer crawls up to the top of the escarpment and from there he situates himself above the narrow pass. From there he/she can now see and has modified the terms of the battle. Indeed, he/she has set up the place through which the troops of the enemy can pass. The enemy cannot now come as an overwhelming tumult and overpower him/her in one single attack. It can now pass only a few at time at the risk of being attacked by surprise by the colonial. The enemy has thus been rendered vulnerable to the eye and the understanding of the colonial writer and can now be engaged under the advantage of a good weapon. It is this moment of setting up oneself at the *desfiladero*, at the narrow pass, that I try to capture in these essays.

PART I

WRITING COLONIALITY

"Who is making all that racket, and not even
letting the Islands that linger make a will?"
(César Vallejo. *Trilce* I)

CHAPTER 1
Guamán Poma: Coevalness and the Space of Purity

I. WRITING AND ETHNIC IDENTITY

Mestizaje, as a space of post-conquest mitigation of the physical and cultural trauma that ensued in the Americas after 1492, has been a central trope in the cultural history of Spanish America ever since the Inca Garcilaso de la Vega (1539-1616) theorized the terms of his own ethno-biography and epoch making *Comentarios reales* (1609). However, the dream of recovery of territorial and governmental sovereignty, or at least the hope for an effective separate rule from the Spanish invaders and conquerors, has also animated Spanish American history since the inception of the conquest and colonial rule. The most recent example takes place in Bolivia with the Katarista movement (Catarista) that began in the early 1970's.[1] This history of separatist rebellions has only come to the forefront in the later part of the twentieth century.[2] Despite the delicately complex composition of the "ethnic" factor in post-colonial Spanish

---

[1] The Katarista rebellion in Bolivia, named after the Aymara leader Túpac Katari who in 1781 lead a rebellion and siege of La Paz against the Spanish colonial regime, officially began in Bolivia in 1876 with the appearance of the Ejército Guerrillero Túpac Katari. The Kataristas went on to seize control of the Aymara peasant unions in 1981 and became a rising force in Bolivian politics. Impatient with the slow pace of reform, they spun off yet another organization that claimed autonomy and Indian self-rule with the creation of the Ayllus Rojos (Tenenbaum 280; Stavig).

[2] For a full discussion on the Túpac Amaru II rebellion that rocked the southern Andes in 1780 see Galindo; Stavig; Thurner. More recently, Sergio Serulnikov, in his 2003 book *Subverting Colonial Authority: Challenges to Spanish Rule in Eighteenth Century*

America, historians have in recent years paid greater attention to the many and important Indian and *mestizo* rebellions. These uprisings and rebellions have always expressed a desire for Indian autonomy from the Spanish colonizing cultural and political complex. From the very first rebellion against the Spanish conquerors, led by the Inca Manco Inca (1516-1545) in Vilcabamba (1536-45), to the rebellions led by Túpac Amaru II (1738-81) in Southern Peru (1780-83), and the Aymara leader Túpac Katari (1750-81) in Bolivia (1781), taking arms against the established colonial powers meant the recovery of a territorial space in which ethnic autonomy and self rule would be possible.[3]

Indeed, it is important to remember here that the force of "ethnic" identities and desire for self rule antecedes the conquest in both Europe

Southern Andes, has studied the year 1780 in both Peru and Bolivia paying special attention to the ways in which the colonial project is put into question by the leaders of the Indian rebellions that demand, like Guamán Poma, a separate realm from the Spanish.

[3] Regarding Manco Inca's rebellion, Héctor López Martínez writes that "Cuarenta años que la penetración hispánica en Sudamérica [España] tropezaba con una obstinada resistencia en Vilcabamba y el grupo [Inca] seguía manteniendo la esperanza de recobrar la tierra" (López Martínez 150). The sixteenth century was plagued with a series of *mestizo*, Indian, and Spanish rebellions. For very good reasons each of these groups sought redress outside the civil order and took up arms. Most of their grievances devolved around the issue of proper claims (heirs) to the land. At every turn, the Crown proved to be master of the situation, and most claims remained unsatisfactorily "resolved." For a recent study of the Torote rebellion, see Brown 15-53. In 1737, after a long period of peace, Ignacio Torote, a Pangoa *curaca*, led a war against the Spanish missionaries who were destroying Indian culture and life in the Amazonian area of Peru. With the help of the inhospitable sub-tropical forests of the area, Torote and his followers managed to challenge the Spanish missionaries for a long time. In 1742, in a completely unconnected rebellion, Juan Santos Atahualpa led a huge uprising in the central sub-tropical area of Peru. His intention was to recapture the whole of the territory of the viceroyalty and establish an Indian kingdom. His thousands of followers believed that he was divine. By far the most famous and well organized rebellion was the uprising lead by José Gabriel Condorcanqui, a well known cacique, who in 1780, under the name of Túpac Amaru II, took up arms against Spanish Colonial rule in order to liberate Indians and *mestizos* alike. His new nation would include everyone but the Spanish (Stavig 209). The figure of Túpac Amaru II no doubt inspired Túpac Katari to take part of his name and thus claim alliance to the Incas. Túpac Amaru II is today one of the great heroes of peasant movements and the rebellious left in Latin America. In some places his allure and prestige is comparable only to the position of the mythical Ché Guevara. Perhaps the clearest example of an ethnic separatist movement outside the Andes can be found in the Caste War of the Yucatan ("La guerra de las castas") of 1848. This war was fought by descendents of the Yucatan Mayas in order to overthrow their white and mestizos masters.

and the Americas. Investigating the terms of the articulation of a separate space of "ethnic" identity and autonomy is particularly important in light of the fact that "ethnic" or racial identity became so intricately blurred, confusing and yet primordial in the organization of power and society in the post-conquest Andes.[4]

In what follows I take the term "ethnic" in its original Greek sense of race, people, and culture. For each of these terms there has been much theorizing in the last quarter century, but for my purposes here I need "ethnic" to do simple work at the level of claims to territory, identity, and loyalty. Thus, by ethnic group, I am indicating communities who see themselves in control of a specific geographic territory. In the exercise of that control they also share and venerate a common sense of the past (ancestors) as their specific origin. In turn, these communities articulate these practices and beliefs in a common language, religion, and culture. Further, an ethnic identity demands loyalty to the community from those who share and benefit from its sense of being and solidarity.

The post-colonial struggle for autonomy is first voiced, in lettered form, by Guamán Poma de Ayala (c. 1534-1616), the self styled Andean prince and author, who in 1616, as he faced the end of his life, decided to send his long reflection on colonial rule to the king of Spain.[5] He hoped that his "letter" to the king would bring, if not separate rule for Andeans, as he advocated in his 1090 folio pages, at least some mitigation of the harsh and cruel colonial rule under which he and his fellow Andeans had been placed by the conquest.[6]

In Guamán Poma's articulation for a separate territorial, political, and cultural space, we find the complex art of building an appeal to a dominant, hegemonizing force based on the insightful and penetrating analysis of the dominant force's own idealized principles and/or ideologies. Guamán Poma's appeal for justice, which to him and some of his Spanish

[4] For a discussion of rivalry, stratification, and conflict in the pre-conquest Andes see Stern chapter 1.

[5] References in this essay are to the 1980 Biblioteca Ayacucho critical edition prepared by Franklin Pease.

[6] For the question of disease as one of the formidable allies of the Spanish in the conquest of the Americas, see Crosby; Cook. For the question of conquest and the demographic composition of the armies, see Hanke. He writes that "The army that captured Tenochtitlan was really an army of Indians captained by a few Spaniards" (168). For the case of Peru, see Espinoza Soriano.

contemporaries means nothing less than returning the realm to the Indians, turns upside down the ideology of the conquest as a "civilizing mission." It is this thoroughly original, radical, de-colonizing gesture that situates Guamán Poma's political reflection among the texts of old that speak to the present. The continued importance of the *Nueva corónica y buen gobierno* for our time stems from the capacity to see with a new, postcolonial perspective both his own cultural legacy as well as the architecture of the Spanish colonial machine.

Immediately after the conquest, the only polities that managed to escape the freshly released imperial forces of des-structuration and incorporation were those ethnic communities at the periphery of the great Amerindian empire, such as the Yaqui in Northern Mexico or the Patagonians at the southern tip of the continent. Nathan Wachtel in his *Los vencidos: los indios del Perú frente a la conquista española (1530-1570)*, offers a detailed account of the procedures and processes of des-structuration that the implantation of Spanish colonial rule carried out upon the former structures of the Inca realm. With the term "des-structuration" Wachtel points not only to the destruction of the old structures, but more importantly, to the "supervivencia de las estructuras antiguas o de elementos parciales de ellas, pero fuera del contexto relativamente coherente en el cual se situaban; después de la conquista subsisten restos del Estado inca, pero el cimiento que los unía se ha desintegrado" (135).

In the case of the Andes, the resistance by a faction of the surviving Incas, such as Manco Inca in Vilcabamba, and later Túpac Amaru I, lasted barely forty years (1532-72). Other descendents of the last Inca Huayna Cápac (1488-1527), such as the Inca Paullu (1516-1549), remained allied with the Spanish invading forces. Despite the fact that the rebels managed to improve their army with horses and swords, defeat was written in the wind as the forces of internal betrayals, European disease, a superb Inca system of roads, and food storage all coalesced in favor of the invaders. When Manco Inca met the Spaniards and their Indian allies, the Inca Paullu among them, in bloody and exhaustive battles, despite his guerrilla strategy and the impossibly difficult terrain of his jungle refuge, the young Inca simply did not have the physical resources at hand. The empire crumbled.[7] The Andean (ethnic) polities that the Incas had per-

---

[7] In his chapter "Rise and Demise of Post-Inca Alliances," Steve Stern offers a detailed account of the politics of this period. He describes and analyses the impossi-

suasively or forcibly brought under their rule were in disarray, and the now rebel Incas simply could not secure enough territory to afford the luxury of a separate realm. After Viceroy Toledo sentenced the adolescent Túpac Amaru I to execution in Cuzco in 1572, the Inca royal elite and their allies gave up. Indeed, many of them "collaborated very closely with the interests of the metropolis" (López Martínez 155).

However, if the royal elite stopped trying to recover its power or share in a governing structure with the new winners of the wars of conquest, the legitimacy of the ruling group remained a great source of contention among the Spaniards themselves. Beyond the struggle among the conquered, the conquerors, and the Crown, in a few short years the emerging class of *mestizos* added their voice and agency to the physical and juridical struggle for control of the territory and rule over the Andean people. The *mestizos* argued that they were the legitimate rulers as heirs to their Inca mothers and Spanish conqueror-fathers.

Given the fact that the sixteenth century was plagued by civil wars among the Spanish, Indian and *mestizo* rebellions added even greater instability to post-conquest life. This turmoil permeated the life of Guamán Poma. It is not surprising then to find in his folios a keen awareness of a relentless physical, political, and cultural struggle. And yet it is puzzling to see that he closes his book with a plea for radical separatism and not simple reform, as many of his contemporaries advocated. In his plea he goes beyond all claims adduced in the civil wars by any and all factions. His project is sweeping and it goes beyond the arrangement put in place by Viceroy Francisco de Toledo (1515-1582) with the creation of "repúblicas de indios" and "repúblicas de españoles." Guamán Poma does not at all propose to split up the former Tahuantinsuyo between conquerors and vanquished or between *mestizos* and Spaniards. His far reaching project calls for the complete return of the land and government to the former Andean ethnic lords. Under this plan all non-Indians must leave the former Tahuantinsuyo. Like so many surprising positions of Guamán Poma, this call for radical separation is rooted in his experience, his dedicated thinking on the matter, and his unique understanding of

bility of the Spanish attempt to make the "transition from simple plunder to territorial occupation and finally, to imperial rule. Having captured the Inca empire, the Europeans would now have to learn how to govern it" (27). The European failure to learn how to govern is what Guamán Poma chronicles as a crisis in full swing.

government informed by his knowledge of Inca governmentality as well as utopian Christianity modulated in an Andean post-colonial world. It is precisely because he sees the devastation wrought by the civil wars, together with the cruel and destructive effects of the "pacification" of the land brought on by the viceroys sent to quell and organize the colony that Guamán Poma dares to dream of his plan for separate rule.

We do not know if the "myth" of Incarrí was already in operation at the time of Guamán Poma, but the idea of a return to a time and space unpolluted by Spanish rule is of course expressed not only by Guamán Poma but also by his contemporary followers of the Taqui-Oncoy. At about 1560 the Andes witnessed the rebellion of many Andeans who, led by "priests" of the old religion, claimed that the old gods (*huacas*) were returning to fight against the Spanish and expel them from the land. Restoration of both land and rule to the Andean people was judged to be imminent. The followers of this movement danced frenetically, and that is why the rebellion was called "taqui-oncoy," meaning in Quechua "the sick dance."[8]

The narrative of Incarrí, told and believed among peasants in contemporary Peru, was first discovered by the anthropologist and novelist José María Arguedas (1911-1973). The "myth" of Incarrí (Inca-rey) holds that the head of the last Inca, decapitated by the Spaniards in 1532, remains alive. It is buried somewhere near Cuzco, the ancient sacred center of the Inca realm. The body of the Inca has also been in a process of reconstitution and when it is complete it will join the head. At that moment the Inca realm will be restored. The current owners of the land will be expulsed and the Indians will recover domain over the land. The movement of the Taqui-Oncoy, contemporary with the life of Guamán Poma, predicates the rebellion and return of the *huacas*, the Andean gods and guardians of the land and sources of well being ("sumak kawsay"). The *huacas* will return to vanquish and expulse the Spanish from the land. With the return of the *huacas* there will occur a full restoration of Indian domain over the land and the old way of Andean living well ("sumak kawsay") will also return. As we can see this dream of "ethnic" autonomy and self rule, this

[8] See in this collection my essay on the "Taqui-Oncoy." It was José María Arguedas who discovered the narrative of the Incarrí in the Central Andes around the middle of the twentieth century (Arguedas 173-182). For more on Andean millenarian beliefs and movements see also Ossio.

dream of return, is not Guamán Poma's alone. In fact, it is a recurrent and rather wide spread phenomenon in both time and space in the Andes.[9]

As late as the nineteenth century, Indian rebellions still bore the mark of Guamán Poma's dream of the "sumak kawsay." In 1881 Pedro Pablo Atusparia, former *varayok* of several Indian villages in Huaraz, led a great revolt against the republican government (Herrera; Thurner). Unlike Túpac Amaru II, once defeated Atusparia was not put to death. The Indigenista movement was by then in full swing, Clorinda Matto de Turner (1852-1909) had already published her epoch-making *Aves sin nido* (1889), and the Indian rebel was praised in the local newspapers and at gatherings of the new *letrado* class. Although the question of separation seemed to be rendered mute by the wars of independence, the departure of the Spanish, and the creation of new "modern" republics, the situation of the Indian peoples remained problematic. Colonialist racism was rampant and Indians were in many instances still denied citizenship and even their humanity. The desire for ethnic pride, greater rights, and economic well being continued to fuel the aspiration for government inspired by Inca rule, if only as a distant dream.

Dazzled by the political power of writing as both a technical devise for record keeping and argumentation, and as a structure of juridical might and colonization, Guamán Poma, self fashioned as author and Andean prince in the prologue to his *Corónica*,[10] saw himself bypassing colonial administrative filters and reaching directly to the king (folios 960-63). The collection and summary of more than 30 years of witnessing, learning the Spanish language, learning about Spanish cultural practices on the ground and on paper, and from oral discourses, allows *El primer nueva corónica y buen gobierno* to represent, if in fragmented form, a whole period/world of post-conquest practices and discursive exchanges, negotiations, appropriations, distortions, and mutilations.

As a "letter" to the king, Guamán Poma intended to send the message that he would have liked to deliver in person, for, in one of his (now) most famous drawings, he envisioned himself in the presence of the king, occu-

---

[9] For a discussion of the classic Andean cosmic temporal arrangement into four eschatological ages, see Wachtel, *Sociedad e ideología* 190-91. For a more recent study of Guamán Poma's treatment of the Andean and Christian epochs and calendars, see Cox.

[10] Born after the execution of Atahualpa in 1532, he claims to have spent almost all of his 87 years resisting Spanish abuses (folio 916). Despite exhaustive research scholars have not turned up anything of significance on his life. See Urton 201-208.

pying the very same time and space that the new technology of the "letter" both allows and denies. This scenario in which he speaks with the king directly and in person is of course fed by the two communication legacies that inform his "letter." From the European perspective, the first thing that comes to mind, and this is in fact suggested by Guamán Poma himself, is the oral delivery of a report to the king by one of his trusted advisors or *cronistas*, or even the dialogue that confession makes possible. The other tradition of communication and transmission of knowledge imbedded in Guamán Poma's scene is the tradition of the *quipu*. The *quipukamayoc*, like all other administrators of the Tahuantinsuyo, had to be at the ready to render an account of his state of knowledge to the Inca or one of his trusted *curacas*. There is no question, as Gary Urton and Galen Brokow have suggested, that Guamán Poma not only had access to *quipus*, but also worked with the model of the *quipu* in mind (Urton 205-206; Brokow 111-47). He himself asserts at the beginning of his *Corónica* that much of his data is taken from *quipus*: "no mas por los quipus y memorias y relaciones de los antiguos de muy viejos y viejas sabios testigos de vista, para que de fe de ellos que valga por ello cualquier sentencia juzgada cologado donde varios discursos, pase muchos dias y annios indeterminado hasta que vencido de mi..." (folio 8). The indeterminate spelling and meaning on "cologado" that oscillates between "colgado" and "colocado," tempt the reader of Guamán Poma to imagine him working from and with a *quipu*. There, in his major string, he hangs ("colgar") colored strings and ties knots of different sizes colors and textures in a space ("colocar") that moves both laterally as well as vertically.

Guamán Poma expects that writing, that is to say his letter conceived as the ground for struggle, would accomplish what his physical and legal person had failed to do at the post-colonial courts set up by the Spanish, and with the *corregidores* to whom he had taken his complaints. After reading his long testimonial and historical reflection, Guamán Poma thought that the king could not help but conclude, and order in writing, that the Indians of Peru could and should govern themselves in order to ensure the survival of the Spanish empire itself. Guamán Poma, alone, living in a society in disarray, chooses writing, an individual act, which nevertheless reverberates through the entire network of a lettered society, as the new weapon to use in a redefined battle field.

His writing project was conceived only a few years after the execution of Túpac Amaru I in 1572. Guamán Poma bitterly recriminates Viceroy

Toledo (1515-1582) for the needless and cruel execution of the young Inca (folio 937). Despite the fact that, as a self fashioned Yarovilca prince, Guamán Poma makes his rivalry and resentment of Inca rule perfectly clear in his letter, he nevertheless admires the principles and practices of Inca governance as much as his *mestizo* contemporary writing in Spain, Garcilaso de la Vega the Inca does. Thus he too writes to fight for good government based and modeled on Inca political philosophy. In doing so, he undertakes one of the most detailed and exhaustive accounts of social organization and the production of knowledge under Inca rule. This account, an extraordinary auto-ethnography, offers a full picture of a world capable of functioning entirely—materially and spiritually—by itself. The Andean world under Inca rule was categorically not in need of any civilizing mission from Spain or any other European nation. There-fore, his claim to ethnic autonomy is not a question at all of individual rights. Guamán Poma sets the foundation for arguing for the autonomy of a non-European and completely viable human order.

II. SEPARATION AND AUTONOMY

Separation by force had proven futile. The young Manco Inca had failed at Vilcabamba, and the Spanish civil wars had not managed to split up the territory among the warring factions. It was time to face the invaders within the space they had just inaugurated with the conquest and des-structuration of Andean polities and cultures. By 1564, and especially in view of the millenarian rebellion of the Taqui-Oncoy, there was a general recognition in the Andes that post-conquest Peru was mired in a deep cri-sis. "Native fears that continued cooperation with Europeans would lead to disaster" were wide spread and deeply held (Stern 51). For Guamán Poma, it was time to begin to navigate within the set of rules brought over and blindly implanted in the colony. It was time to navigate in the chaos of des-structuration and to interpelate the very root on which the making of rules was based. Only such a deeply critical perspective could hold a mirror to the Spanish. Deconstruction of the edifice of rule making might show them the unbridgeable gap between the rules as enunciated, their own internal contradictions, and the fraudulent distance between the written rule and its deployment in praxis.

Guamán Poma's writing enterprise entails also a critique of writing that points to a multitude of gaps in the process of meaning making, interpretation, and the weight of power. While it is true that he takes up writing in the hope of using it as a new weapon in his struggle, it is no less true that as he analyzes the workings of the relationship between writing, meaning making, and power, Guamán Poma, gains a critical perspective on writing itself. The appropriation and deployment of the new technology of writing and of the European archive necessary to sustain the proposal made in his letter unfolds by showing many of the hidden aspects of the problem of writing. Under the current lens of post-modern theory, informed by Derridean analysis of writing as well as Foucault's genealogical approach to discourse, we can see that Guamán Poma does not exhibit a naïve "faith" in writing. Rather he shows an awareness of the complexity of discourse and its conflicted relation to "the truth." For one thing, Guamán Poma finds that the written word is as glued to power as the oral arts of memory in the pre-conquest Andes had once been.

In hindsight, the ethnic autonomy project sounds, at best, paradoxical, and at worst, naïve. Yet, an examination of the deft production and manipulation of the data presented in *El primer nueva corónica y buen gobierno* shows that Guamán Poma's intellectual tools, political aims, and challenge to the Christian ideology that made the conquest possible were chosen with great care and intelligence. His chronicle, although disheveled from the perspective of a European book form, is not at all the garbled product of a primitive mind, refusing the light of the European renaissance, as some of his early commentators have written.[11] That the thrust of his project was historically valid was demonstrated by the chorus of Spanish voices that advocated separation, but not separate rule, for the Indians. The many reform tracts denouncing the destruction of the Indians at the hands of colonial rule and the petitions Bartolomé de Las Casas (1474-1566)[12] made to the Crown stand as not the only, but certainly the most dramatic, example of the argument for separation. The

---

[11] See for example "Juicio crítico de R. Pietschmann" in the appendix of Julio C. Tello's *La primeras edades del Perú por Guamán Poma* (84). See also Porras Barrenechea 7.

[12] For an extensive chapter on Las Casas and his actions at court in defense of the Indians, see Brading. For a more detailed account of Las Casas's practical and discursive interactions with indigenous peoples and their rights, see Daniel Castro.

establishment of Franciscan millenarian reserves and the Jesuit utopian states constituted the partial actualization of the dream of separation.[13] Silenced for more than three hundred years, Guamán Poma's post-colonial thinking on the constitution of separate ethnic and political spaces in which the obligations of the conquered to the victors could be drawn down to a minimum, stands in stark contrast with the historical policies that ensued. Nevertheless, the *Corónica* remains a good place for thinking about post-colonial ethnic and nation state relations, since the thrust for autonomy remains an option in many places of post-colonial and neo-colonial struggle. The case in point is the current struggle taking place in Bolivia after the election to the presidency of the Aymara politician Evo Morales. The Kataristas in Bolivia right now would like a realm of their own and this is not because they are fundamentalist, but rather, because as Guamán Poma later came to understand, capitalism and communal organization are not compatible.

More over, while Guamán Poma's refrain, "dios permita que no nos acabemos" (may God not allow our disappearance) speaks of the drama of the Amerindian holocaust, it also raises a voice for those who have suffered similar conditions throughout history. The fear of complete disappearance from the face of the earth wraps up the trauma of physical and cultural conquest. The pain of the loss of identity and the despair of seeing one's world disappear without recourse reverberates in time and space beyond the Andes. In the face of similar catastrophes, people have responded with the idea of achieving a separate realm of their own in order to survive. The phrase "a space of one's own" does not, of course, fail to remind us of Virginia Wolf's own call for a room of her own, a call that not long ago galvanized feminists the world over.

In this regard it is important to understand how Guamán Poma constructs his sense of identity (Andean Prince) and how, based on that construction, he proposes the idea that the post-conquest Andes should be, for the betterment of all involved, including the king, governed by the descendents of the pre-Inca Andean lords. What we know about Guamán Poma is what he has chosen to tell us in his letter to the king. On his

---

[13] For an ample discussion on the existence among the Franciscan missionaries in Mexico of millenarian realms empowered by a vision inherited through St. Francis of Assisi from Joachim de Fiore, see Lafaye 30-33. For a larger treatment of the Franciscan experiment, see Phelan.

father's side he descends from the Yarovilca ruling elite (segunda persona del Inca Cápac Apo Guamán Chaua Yarovilaca Allauca Guanoco) (folio 4-5). His mother was one of the many legitimate daughters of the Inca Túpac Yupanqui (folios 15, 1920-22), the penultimate Inca. Born after the death of Atahualpa in 1532, he claims to have spent most of his 87 years resisting Spanish abuses ("mira cristiano a mi todo se me ha hecho") (folio 916). He also leaves clear traces of his interaction and employment with Spanish priests, such as Cristóbal de Albornoz (1534-1610). These priests were in charge of the campaign for the "extirpation" of idolatries that tried to deal, in the 1560's, with the Taqui-Oncoy, as well as the suspicion that the Andean people had not really converted to Christianity. The self-fashioned Andean prince also worked for Spanish functionaries in charge of collecting the memory of the "history" of the Incas[14] among various polities in the Andes.

In these cases he seems to have worked as a translator. But his association with these functionaries of the Crown and the church does not seem to have merited any favors, for his complaints of mistreatment are numerous and constitute a leitmotif in the long letter. Having been expelled by the *corregidor* from his own province, he says that he "traveled" during the last thirty years of his life. His thirty years of travel amount to a sort of exile from the good graces of the established order and the institutions and resources that they controlled. It means that as a student of the Christian doctrine and court translator he had no place that he could call his own. He was uprooted by the conquest not only from rank and family, but from the essential and existential association with the land that the *ayllu* system literally incarnated in an almost sacred way. He became a *forastero*, an alien everywhere he went. David Brading calls him the "Andean Pilgrim" (Brading 147). As an alien in his own land he managed, among other things, employment as translator with priests and Crown functionaries who did not see in him an intelligent agent, but rather as a mere instrument in a task that they, at the center of discursive powers, performed for themselves and the king. No doubt, he learned much about European legal culture, Christian doctrine, cosmography, and the lettered world in general from the company of the groups that

---

[14] See in this volume my "Historiography on the Ground" on the matter of writing a history of the Incas that would dispute their right to rule according to the Spanish jurisprudence of the moment.

worked for Cristóbal de Albornoz (1534-1610) and Pedro Sarmiento de Gamboa (1530-1608). Sarmiento de Gamboa successfully carried out the assignment he received from the viceroy Toledo and authored his *Historia índica* (1572).

Along with his masters, he too collected evidence, information, and above all made his own observations on both the Indians and the Spanish, their post-conquest interactions and strategies, or lack thereof, for dealing with the post-conquest chaos. In doing so, he authored an auto-ethnography and an ethnography of his others (the Spanish). He became especially aware of the power and role that writing had in the production and administration of colonial rule.

Guamán Poma spent a great deal of his time in reconnoitering the land. Under the directives of his Spanish employers he quizzed the memory of the elders. Maybe he learned, from Sarmiento de Gamboa, (and not unlike our own polls), how to coax a certain kind of answer to a given question. He was certainly intimately involved at the very incipient stages of the making of a narrative that had been teleologically designed. Thus, in the joint and conflicted production of both auto-ethnographies and ethnographies, he came to understand the inherent biases, blindness, and insight underscoring field work based on the "memory" of the "natives." He was indeed deeply involved in the production of self as other. As guide and translator, his discursive positionality, from subject to object and back again, must have hinged on small shifts in the discursive place of enunciation assumed with his every question, and in the translation of every answer given to the conductor of the inquiry. He also observed and noted the brutal physical and discursive violence of the Spanish at every inquiry, court, and *doctrina* in which he was either observer or participant.

III. LEARNING WRITING

His sources were many and varied. Students of Guamán Poma have done a great deal of work in trying to pinpoint his sources, and that work has been very useful. Nevertheless, as Walter Mignolo has pointed out, when the task at hand is "comprender el decir de crónicas andinas o mesoamericanas, indígenas o mestizas, que llevan a cuestas el rumor de la diferencia" that difference is generally "aplastada como fuente, puesto que al hablar de 'fuentes' se pone a todos los cronistas en el mismo nivel, y así sale aventajado el cronista hispano, puesto que es para él y no para el diciente indígena o mestizo, que el concepto de 'fuentes' tiene sentido" ("Decires" 17). I will thus proceed here mindful of the sources that Guamán Poma himself and his students have discussed,[15] but keeping in mind that my focus is to investigate how Guamán Poma appropriates, bends, reorganizes, and in general deploys the discursive means at his disposal in order to challenge the Spanish cosmo-vision that denies Andeans the possibility of self-rule.

For thirty years (folio 1104), Guamán Poma listened, questioned, read, raged, and wrote. Frequently in the privacy of silence, and often in public, the self styled prince fumed about the profound misunderstandings of ignorant and educated Spaniards alike. Throughout his text he decries the physical and cultural destruction wrought about by colonial rule. He writes: "Y anci, dios mio ¿Donde estas?...Todo aca es mentira. Y anci el dicho padre le espanta a los yndios; aun el dicho autor se espanto deste dicho padre. ¿Qué me hará los indios pobres y pucilanimos, encapaces por no uer mas tantas cosas ni hartarse de llorar con los pobres" (folio 1104). With his campaign to correct the misunderstandings and misdeeds of the Spanish, he managed to make himself persona non-grata to many Spanish colonial administrators. The reflections of a whole life-

---

[15] It seems, from Guamán Poma's own account, that he learned a great deal about Catholic doctrine from his half bother. He reports that he was lovingly instructed by the hermit Martín de Ayala, his half bother and protector. We can surmise that his other great source is constituted by the many instances of missionary preaching at churches and at the more informal "doctrinas," or evangelizing preaching sites at which he seems to have been present very often. He seems to have a special fascination for sermons preached at mass and at other rituals of the faith. He also seems quite conversant with the proceedings of the Concilio de Lima (1583). He offers comments about its deliberations in his *Corónica*. And of course his close collaboration and work with preachers and students of Andean culture such as the extirpator of idolatries Cristóbal de Albornoz and the Mercedarian Martín de Murúa, author of the *Historia general del Perú* (finished by 1611 according to Manuel Ballesteros Gaibrois's 1987 edition of Murúa's *Historia*), did bring him into contact with the book world and religious visual culture which constituted the basis of the Spanish evangelization project. Particular sermons stand out in his mind with poignant clarity. As he recollects the occasion of the sermon or the specifics conveyed by the priest, he relives his passionate rejection of the priests' misunderstanding and denigration of Andean culture, and especially the epistemological abuses of the campaign for the extirpation of idolatries. Moreover, his contact with Murúa seems to have been extensive, for the Andean *cronista* warns the reader about priests like Murúa, who attempt to steal the work of assistants and apprentices such as Guamán Poma.

time came to fill and inspire the drama of the 500 drawings, and to empower the broken prose of *El primer nueva corónica y buen gobierno*. His reflections arise not just from intellectual labor but are in fact a labor of pain. He is fully aware of the inseparable condition of suffering and gaining in cognitive capacity. Guamán Poma makes original use of set phrases in Spanish such as "recordar es llorar," "viajar es llorar," and "amar es llorar." In this vein, he states that in his case to write is to cry. However, despite this disclaimer, and despite his refrain that there is no remedy to this hell, the reader knows and even feels the pleasure that Guamán Poma experiences with each denunciation of yet another abuse and cruelty done by priests and *doctrineros* to the innocent Indians.

As with so many other aspects of his biography, almost nothing is known for certain about how he became so conversant with the newly introduced European categories of thought, as well as with the Spanish juridical and theological controversy on the human rights of the Indians. His deft handling of the issue, and the dates of the publication of Las Casas's work (*Del único modo de atraer a todos los pueblos a la verdadera religión*, 1537; *Brevísima historia de la destrucción de las Indias*, 1552), as well as his mention of the Council of Lima (1583) (folio 997), indicate that he was familiar with the content and the scope of the arguments involved (Brading 150-152). Professing not to know Latin, a great disadvantage at the time and in relation with his intellectual ambitions, he also notes that he does not have the benefit of any formal schooling ("no soy letrado") (folio 8). For this salient lack he apologizes. But he also uses the occasion to engage the generosity of the reader, who is asked to forgive him for the blunder he may commit in his writing.

Given the painfully obvious second language acquisition condition of his Spanish, it is superfluous to say that this apology is made in keeping with the customary rhetoric of authorship in Europe (his sources) at the time. This apology is necessary and compelling, not simply rhetorical. Coming from the vanquished culture, a culture already severely criticized for not having "writing" in the European sense of the term at the time, Guamán Poma approaches writing with both anxiety and trepidation, for he will have to bend it and flex it to accommodate not only his pre-conquest oral language arts but also the oral transmission of European culture taking place all around him in the Andes. The immensity and difficulty of approaching writing is only as great and forbidding as the idea of proposing a project of separation and ethnic autonomy.

El primer nueva corónica y buen gobierno, like the Bible, deals with a myriad number of topics and accounts of human events over an ambiguously determined span of time. Perhaps for this reason, it is sensible to argue, as some scholars have done (Brading, Cox, Ossio), that the Andean *cronista* had the Bible in mind as the paramount model for writing about the origins of civilizations and their teleological ends. For his treatment of time before the Incas in which he postulates four ages, he draws on the Biblical division of time into four ages. With respect to this issue, David Brading writes that

> drawing upon standard Biblical chronology, albeit with some deviations, he postulated a million years after the creation of Adam, but fixed the effective beginning of the New World history with the arrival of a descendant of Noah sometime after the great Flood. There then follows four ages covering some 5,300 years, the equivalent of the three Biblical epochs initiated respectively with Noah, Abraham and David. (Brading 150)

However, Nathan Wachtel argues that for a full accounting of how Guamán Poma grafts Christian time onto Andean time, how he cuts makes and correspondences, one needs to consider that the Andean thinker operates in the two temporal series. For Wachtel, Guamán Poma's cuts and splicing of time sequences, "confirman que Guamán Poma percibe el mundo bíblico y occidental a través de la visión indígena y que somete a su orden los elementos que llegan del exterior" (Wachtel, *Sociedad* 203).[16] Thus the model of the Bible, qua model, is not so much linked to content as to its porous and multiple format. In this sense, the Bible's huge span of time, multiple narrators, and hundreds of narratives and prophecies constitutes a sort of mirror image to Guamán Poma's own rendition of a chronology of the world and its most significant events, such as the coming of Christ and the appearance of Inca government in the Andes. Not unlike the

---

[16] Wachtel has shown how Guamán Poma's seemingly confused temporal sequence of the world's time flow, from its creation to the present, that is to say 1612, obey Andean space and time categories. In fact, Guamán Poma manages to graft Christian time and space into the Andean quadripartite divisions of time and space (*pacha*). Wachtel concludes that "todo ocurre como si Guamán Poma yuxtapusiera, o mejor dicho, pusiera las dos tradiciones en serie: 5,000 (las edades indias) + 1,612 (la era cristiana) = 6,612. De este proceso fundamental resulta el enredo cronológico... Es un hecho significativo que Guamán Poma maniobre las cifras para hacerlas encajar, casi a la fuerza, en el esquema de las cinco edades" (*Sociedad* 209).

Bible, Guamán Poma's letter contains a great many details dealing with geography, demography, religious practices, economic organization and the like.

However many parallelisms with the Bible may be found by the reader trained in European written "fuentes," it would be a mistake to neglect the stronger and better-known Andean arts of memory in Guamán Poma's hands. The Bible, given the small numbers of the book circulating in the Andes at the time and the restrictions placed by the Church upon the categories of qualified readers, may have actually never been in the hands of the Andean pilgrim. The *quipu*, on the other hand, was profoundly familiar to Guamán Poma. He not only tells us that he used them in compiling his information, but he shows many Inca functionaries—accountants (folio 3320), *colca* inspectors (folio 335), administrators (folio 320), secretaries (folio 330), "justice indios" or judges (folio 801), and astrologists (folio 883) handling huge *quipus*. More over, when he speaks of his Andean sources ("testigos de vista"), he lists by name at least ten very old *caciques*, who obviously spoke from the memory of the *quipu* and other Andean oral and graphic arts of memory, such as textiles, *tokapus*, and architecture (folios 1078-1081).[17]

It thus seems more sensible to think, like several scholars have by now proposed, that the Andean intellectual was working from at least one great *quipu* (see "Memory and Writing" in this volume). In so doing he was following the epistemology imbedded in that Andean art of memory. Summarizing the most recent scholarship on the *quipu* (Wachtel, *Sociedad*; Zuidema; Bauer; Ascher; Aveni; Solomon; Cox; Brokaw; Urton) we can say that Guamán Poma not only drew much of his information from one or several *quipu*, but that he may have used the system of knowledge and "visible language"[18] of the *quipu* as a determining model for his letter. Moreover, these recent studies on the *quipu* have shown the structural correspondence between the *quipu*, the Andean calendar, and the system of the *ceques*. According to Aveni, the system of the *ceques* can the compared to an enormous *quipu* spread out, like a map, over the entire empire (275-277). Thus, in trying to understand how Guamán Poma deploys Andean categories of understanding into his

---

[17] For more information, see Niles.

[18] For further discussion of this term, see Ascher, "The Quipu" 329-356; Ascher, *Code of the Quipu*; Zuidema; Aveni; Bauer.

appropriation of writing includes the special task of trying to understand his categories for classification, an epistemological consideration that determines how he envisioned the order of a separate realm. Taken as an immense effort to find points of correspondence between two cosmovisions and finding out the irreconcilable differences between them leads me to say that *El primer nueva corónica y buen gobierno* is not a metaphor for the clashing meeting of two cultures, it is rather the ground and constitution of the making of the post-colonial world, one in which, as in the system of the continental plates, the borders and edges engage in constant friction, accommodation, venting, and creation.

The long argument for separatism moves along a road filled with asides, detours, breaches, and leaps. For the greater part of the letter, the idea of a separate Indian realm appears obliquely and intertwined with numerable other topics. Critics have labeled this aspect of Guamán Poma's appeal to the king utopian, and therefore dismissible in the sense that the conditions of possibility just were not there. I think that the distinction that Karl Mannheim makes between utopia and ideology is useful in assessing the historical importance and remaining potential of Guamán Poma's articulation for a separate rule. Mannheim argues that utopia constitutes the "wish images" of existing ideologies, embodied in the actual conduct of groups who try to realize them.

In *Ideology and Utopia* (1936), Mannheim states that:

> Every period in history contained ideas transcending the existing order, but these did not function as utopias, they were rather the appropriate ideologies of this stage of existence as long as they were "organically" and harmoniously integrated into the world view characteristic of the period... Not until certain groups embodied these wish images into their actual conduct, and tried to realize them, did these ideologies become utopias. (173-74)

With this understanding in mind and in anticipation of Guamán Poma's arguments for "good government," it would seem that his letter, due to its colonial power-knowledge situation, constitutes a set of ideological propositions not so harmoniously integrated into the characteristic, let us say in this case, dominant world view of the period (European). It is clear that most of his ideas for good government came from his own summary of Inca governance. However, it is equally indisputable that some of these tenets of governance converged with established Christian ideals for good governance. Guamán Poma, the Inca Garcilaso, and some of the Jesuit missionaries did not hesitate to point out such coincidences. In fact, as an explanatory move that would explain just such coincidences, many colonial intellectuals postulated an earlier preaching of Christianity done by St. Bartolomeo. But the fact of the matter is that both sets of ideas about good governance clashed ("todo es mentira," folio 1104) with Spanish practices.[19]

The existing ideologies (Andean and European) in the post-conquest Andes had not anticipated the clashing reality, and during Guamán Poma's time these ideologies suffered all kinds of contortions and deformations in order to absorb the shock of conquest. Steve Stern writes:

> In the 1560's, the contradictions inherent in the post-Inca alliances imposed themselves more sharply than ever. The growing dependence of Indians upon Europeans to settle disputes; economic shortages or hardships imposes by colonial extraction, emigration or population decline... all eventually would have provoked a reassessment of native policies towards the colonials.[20] (Stern 47)

Guamán Poma's radical proposal endeavors to extract out of both sets of ideologies one discursive space in which they may converge in a coherent way so as avoid the chaos unleashed by the conquest and to put in

---

[19] In the closing pages of the letter, and again deploring the physical and ideological violence that the making of *mestizaje* implies, the author writes: "Y anci como uide tanto tormento de los pobres, y del sermon del padre teatino que todos nos quiere mal, y de auer muerto ochenta indios, me acorde de yr al pueblo de San Christobal a donde alle un indio mandoncillo... Su muger hacia casta de español y su hija legitima... casta de de cholos mestizos. Y esa dicha India la tenia en la cocina el señor lesenciado. Y con otras solteras... Entonces vino un teniente de corregidor. Este dicho padre se quejo al dicho teniente que auia muchas amazebadas indias en el dicho pueblo. Entonces el dicho teniente le desterro tres indias hermosas a la uilla de Guancabilca a que fuesen a servir a su madre, a donde le fornique españoles y hagan casta de mestizos y sea mas bellaca entre español y puta" (folios 1102-1103).

[20] David Noble Cook writes that "within fifty years the original inhabitants of the Caribbean were virtually extinct. Central Mexico's population fell from nearly 15 million in 1519 to 1.5 million a century later, and there was a similar demographic collapse of Andean America. A century after first contact the regions least affected by the disaster lost at least 80 percent of their people, 90 percent or more was more typical and some regions became destitute of people" (Cook 5). Clearly, Guamán Poma's perception of Andean collapse and danger of extinction was not exaggerated.

place Andean rule. This hope and project rests on the undeniable fact that it is the Andeans who have the experience and know-how for good government and not the Spanish.

Furthermore, if we take European "Christian" ideology to be the characteristic world view of the dominant group, and if we see Guamán Poma as the individual member of the vanquished group attempting to turn this ideology into actual behavior, Mannheim's distinction is useful but still leaves unanswered questions. To think in Mannheim's terms one would have to hold that the ideology of the Spanish conquerors and colonizers was uniform, when, in fact we know that the Crown, the missionary orders, the Church in Rome, and the colonizers were often at odds as to their understanding of the goals and the meaning of the Spanish project in the "Indies." One would also have to assume that the dominant Andean group and the vanquished Indians in general formed one single social organism, when in fact we know, to a large extent from the *Nueva corónica* itself, that there were many important, differentiating, and contending pre-Inca polities. Their sense of differences played a significant role during and after the conquest[21] and is never out of sight in Guamán Poma's writing of the pre-conquest past. Despite what the phenomenon of the Taqui-Oncoy shows about the wish and capacity for rebellion, it is not known if any Andean groups were prepared, ideologically or practically, to turn ideology into actual behavior. Therefore we must view Guamán Poma's ideological appeals and blueprint for good government as concomitantly ideological and "utopian" in Mannheim's sense of "utopia."

However, in assessing the impact that the "New World" had on the Old regarding the question of utopian thinking, it appears that Thomas More's (1478-1535) critique of unrestrained economic individualism and private property in favor of a communitarian economic and social arrangement was inspired by what he read about Caribbean and Tupi societies in the letters of Amerigo Vespucci (1501). More published his *Utopia* in 1516. Arthur E. Morgan, in *Nowhere Was Somewhere: How History Makes Utopias and How Utopias Make History* (1946), writes that More went to Flanders in 1514, and that while there he may have

---

[21] For a history of the Inca Empire that plays up the differences and disputes between the Incas and their rivals, see Rostworowski.

received "direct information about Peru" (34). Further, Morgan states that "More's description of the life and social system of *Utopia* corresponds in the main, so closely with ancient Peru...that accidental coincidence seems to be out of the question" (35). Using William Prescott's *Conquest of Peru* (1847), Morgan develops a topic by topic comparison between More's *Utopia* and pre-conquest Peru, showing the close correspondences (39-60) and emphasizing that "this fundamental economic structure...existed nowhere in Europe" (39).

Perhaps because Guamán Poma's blueprint for good government emphasizes a communal economic and social structure, critics not familiar with the *ayllu* structure have been quick to label the separation project of Guamán Poma utopian in the same way in which More's work is understood in its placement within European thought and history. In Europe's legacy, the Golden Age, and any other social structure based on communal arrangements, figures indeed as a non-place. But, such was not the case in the Andes. Thus the term "utopia," as it arises out of Thomas More's European utopia, does not apply in the least to Guamán Poma's project. To speak of Thomas More and Guamán Poma in the same breath is to breed confusion.

Besides a different provenance, there is another very important difference in the thinking of these two men. Guamán Poma departed from his own personal and historical experience of the "utopian" realm as a model for a future close at hand. Moore's dream was imagined in relation to a distant and imperfectly known human order in the case of the reports on the Tupi and a utopian dream in the case, perhaps of Augustine's *City of God*. Because Guamán Poma's model was part of his own lived experience, his blue print did not involve some far off place in space and time (although it was so for the king), nor was it a dubious experiment, such as state sponsored communism turned out to be in the twentieth century.

From Guamán Poma's location, both physical and discursive, his separate realm could have happened right then and there. All that was necessary was to sever the ties with the Spanish world and keep the new space hermetically sealed from the European invaders. Then, after severance, the task of restauration—not experimentation—could begin.[22] With the

---

[22] In Guamán Poma's imagined conversation with the king, he calculates that his powers of persuasion will bring the king to agree with him in that "Que es muy justo y servicio de Dios y de su magestad que los españoles no se puede poblar junto con los

immediate cessation of the aftermath of conquest, the negative effects of
the Spanish invasion could have been absorbed by the Andean society
and it would have been on its way to recovery. The half century of the
post-conquest could be seen as a severe pruning from which the trunk of
the three could have recovered and bloomed again.

The functional opposition in Guamán Poma's mind at the end of the
sixteenth century was not so much the bi-partite organization of the
Andean principles of *hanan* and *hurin*. Instead he sought to take advantage of the European opposition enacted in the Toledo's organization of
the realm into "repúblicas de españoles"—urban centers—and "repúblicas de indios"—Indian communities in the country side. For Guamán
Poma, the tactic was to accept the conquest and to accept the losses. Thus
the practical thing was to leave the towns and cities to the Spanish, their
mestizo brood, and their Black slaves (folios 526-546). The Indians could
then go back to their villages and fields, to the glory of their *ayllu* organization, where they could start to regroup according to their pre-Inca
ethnic identities and polities.[23] The Inca Garcilaso in his depiction of
Cuzco tells us that the *barrios* that surrounded the sacred center of the
navel of the world were arranged as a map that represented all the different polities that constituted the empire. This division dated back to the
time of the Inca Manco Cápac who ordered that the "savages that he had
subjugated should be settled according to their place of origin, those from
the east to the east, those from the west to the west" (Garcilaso 421-22).
Noting the love of order and *quipu*-like categories, the Inca goes on to
note that "The insignia they wore on their heads were a sort of headdress
which served for identification, each tribe and province differing from the
rest" (422). Agreeing with Guamán Poma on the pre-Inca origins, or
rather pan-Andean cultural universe, the Cuzqueño *cronista* notes that

---

indios en las ciudades ni en las villas, aldeas, ni vaya a morar ningun español ni
española ni mestizos ni zabahigo ni cholo.... Que los indios se hacen bellacos y borra-
chos, jugadores, perezosos, ladrones, cimarrones. Viviendo con ellos se alzaran y se
haran traidores" (folio 533).

[23] In this respect Guamán Poma goes much further than Philip II's *cédula* of 1578.
It forbade blacks, mulattoes and *mestizos*, but not the Spaniards, from being in the
company of the Indians in order to prevent the corruption of the "naturales."
Although this kind of segregation was established by law, it was never actually
obeyed. Guamán Poma is aware of both the law and its ineffective application (Gibson
135-36).

"This was not an invention of the Incas, but a costume of the various tribes. The Inca kings ordered it to be preserved to prevent confusion among the tribes and the nations from Pasto to Chile" (422).

Like most Indian or *mestizo* writers of his time, Guamán Poma had experienced a complete loss of power and status. Nicole Villaseñor writes that "Whether they be Indian or *mestizo* there is an undeniable fact that emerges from their life stories: their social failure. Each was ejected from the position that he could have claimed or aspired to given the circumstances of their birth" (98).[24] In this sense, he writes from the fringes of established power. Yet he manages not to write against any properly constituted authority. Nor does he write against the forms of discipline and repression that civilization entails, as the French socialist Charles Fourier (1772-1837) did in this Phalansteries.[25] Were these two dreamers of a new order to meet, they would have very little in common. They would reject each other. Guamán Poma's disciplinary sensibility knows no bounds. He hones closely to Biblical morality in as much as a good deal of its commandments and prohibitions coincide with his Andean sense of ethics. He takes it for granted that his Christian reader agrees with this ethical vision and joins him in decrying all the floggings, rapes, stealing, excessive tribute, and all other depravations of the colonial world inaugurated by the conquest. He is obsessed with a desperate sense of loss and the subsequent urgency to restore a living world before it is too late in the face of the waves of pandemics hitting the post-conquest Andes.

In Guamán Poma's eyes, Fourier and his phalanxes of pleasure seeking individuals would deserve to be cast into hell along with the voracious judges and the licentious priests. Judges, priests, *corregidores*, soldiers, and even viceroys had come to the Andes to contaminate a pure and straightforward order. The world had been set upside down ("el mundo al revés"), and unless the corrupters were expelled from the land there would be no remedy. For the moralist in Guamán Poma, a cult of the

---

[24] "Sean mestizos o indios.... Un hecho innegable surge de la historia de sus vidas: su fracaso social. Cada uno en su órbita, fue arrojado de la posición a la que habría podido pretender por su nacimiento."

[25] For more information, see Fourier. The phalansteries represented a system by which society would be re-organized into units comprising their own social and industrial elements. The buildings occupied by the workers were called phalansteries, from the Greek "phalanx," meaning armed infantry formed in ranks and files.

individual sense of self and desires as the center of the earth, the idea that
he/she is entitled to follow his/her preferences, honor his/her emotions,
be entitled to accumulate all possible wealth, would simply amount to
further perversion, chaos, and demise as a civilization.

IV. SETTING UP SEPARATE RULE

Before proceeding to a description of the organization of the Indian separate
state under indirect Spanish rule, the ideological bases for Guamán Poma's
gambit should be examined a bit further, for they determine the parameters
of the dreamer's imagination. A sense of duality pervades all aspects of the
text. Much of this duality can of course be traced to the Andean dualistic
organization of the cosmos and life as a whole as well as to the system of reciprocity that pervaded Andean understandings. But some of the dual qualities of the letter to the king are simply factual to the organization of the huge
compendium. For instance, a significant part of the text is bilingual. There
are some entries in Aymara, but these are very few. The manuscript is both
written in European alphabet and drawn, although not "illustrated" for
"readers" or decoders familiar with either system of encoding images, or
with both. The letter encompasses an (or a dual) historical account of the
world. This temporal account of human history admits on the one hand to
the separation of two temporal series, and on the other, tries to find points
of convergence of the separate lines in an effort to create a coevalness.[26] By
deploying an Andean reading of the Christian utopia in combination with a
decanted memory of Andean structures of government, the texts produces
a blueprint for future, post-conquest government. Like a Janus, it faces both
the past and the future. The discourses deployed in the 1090 folios posits
two types of readers, the Christian public reader of the published manuscript (folio 7), and the private reader of the manuscript letter, that is to say
the Christian king of Spain. To some extent, the king's reader function is
meant to conflate them both, for Guamán Poma appeals to the private con-

[26] In a manner of speaking we could say that Guamán Poma is keenly aware of the
ideological dispositive of the Judeo-Christian discourse by which coevalness is denied
to those civilizations outside of the European perimeter. The Andean thinker anticipates the meditations of Johannes Fabian's *Time and the Other: How Anthropology
Makes its Object*. Nicole Villaseñor points out that for the Inca Garcilaso, the civilizing work of the Spanish is less brilliant than the work of the Incas.

science of the king as it informs his public performance of his duties as a Christian (not pagan) prince.

Roughly the first part of the folios is addressed to Philip the II (dead by 1598). The second part assumes Philip III to be the addressee. There can be no doubt, as unthinkable as it may seem to us today, that Guamán Poma fully expected the king to read his letter and to order its publication in book form. His imagined, new authorial persona allows Guamán Poma to envision a scene in which he holds forth in dialogue with king. In this scenario, either of the two Philips, qua king, would confer with the Andean prince. The king replies to Guamán Poma's advice just as he does with his most trusted advisors. In this sense Guamán Poma does not hesitate to compare himself to the Duke de Alba. The king would/should be particularly interested in how to put an end to the brutal ravaging of the Spanish petty bureaucrats and the declining population of Peru.

On what grounds did Guamán Poma base his ambition to of an audience with the king? How could a vanquished Indian persuade the king to set up a separate realm with complete Indian rule, when the principle rationale for conquest had been evangelization and the "New World" was already teeming with mestizos, mulattoes, blacks, zambos, criollos, and Europeans? How could the swing of an extraction economy and the birth of modern capitalism be reversed even if such understanding was not yet in place? The answer is very complex, but at least part of it entails Guamán Poma's understanding and/or creative misunderstanding of the ideological struggles of his time.

Confidence in the power of the word as metaphor for the world seems to be strongly determining at the start of the enterprise. Guamán Poma's sense of the coincidence between the written word and the truth is paramount in the early stages of the composition of the letter. Although he argues without using linear, explicit logic, and prefers the accumulation of data to deduction or induction, he ends up constructing a vision of the world by means of a vast net of references that speak to each other at various levels of exposition when the folios are retrospectively considered together. The power of this "descriptive" material is not unlike the intelligent accumulation of data that Clifford Geertz imagines when he conceptualizes ethnography as a thick description. The discriminating accumulation of instances reaches a crescendo, or rather a point of significance when the parallel accumulation (in "calles") of direct or indirect references to the underlining theme achieves full visibility. Every thing in the letter is about the theologico-political controversy on the conquest of the Amerindian societies and the place of the Indians in the newly inaugurated colonial or imperial order.

This Indian writer, operating in a remote corner of the globe now post 1492 centered in Europe, was keenly aware of the fact that to settle political disputes it was necessary to engage religious reasoning. He was also able to recognize the two discourses as indivisible and indistinguishable from one another in as much as they functioned in tandem in questions of colonial governmentality. Paramount on his mind was the rationale given to justify wagging war on Indian peoples and polities. The justification of the conquest by way of evangelization never made sense to Guamán Poma, even when he presented himself as a sincere and devout Catholic. Thus, he sought, either with naïve sincerity or great cunning, the acquisition and use of the same weapons that had declared him and his vanquished people irresponsible children, incapable of ruling themselves.

In response, he would argue that the Spanish were less deserving of ruling the land because they had been evangelized more than a thousand years ago and they still could not behave as good Christians, whereas the Indians had been practicing good government on their own, without the benefit of evangelization for thousands of years. Natural reason had served the Indians quite well. They had managed with out the aid of revelation or evangelization.

Turning the aim of the weapons around and pointing to the Spanish he could show in drawings, short narratives, and related incidents how his majesty's old Christian subjects were in fact bad Christians: sensual, deceiving, uncharitable, greedy, cruel etc. They thus had no right to rule the land and much less the Andeans. Questioning the legitimacy of the Spanish conquest from the vantage point of evangelization made his work not only subversive, but probably also heretical. In fact, Guamán Poma dared to argue, not unlike Rene Decartes (1596-1650), that reason alone (natural light) was enough to devise knowledge and civilization. Thus, it defies the imagination to think that this man, who no doubt was seen as nothing more than an "idolatrous savage" by his contemporaries, managed to live long enough to write his folios, to learn on his own enough theology and other discourses in order to challenge the rationale of the conquest, and to pretend to have an audience with the king.

The repetitious and at times tiresome, but always interesting, description of Spanish sadistic abuses of the conquered people amounts to an undeniable description of inept government, headed by the king. Without mincing any words, the king is informed of his failure to keep up his part of the bargain with the Indian peoples as his vassals and *encomendados*. While it could be argued that it is the *corregidores* and *encomenderos* who fail to administer the laws justly, Guamán Poma makes the point over and over that in the cosmic governmental contract, it is the king who is ultimately responsible to the Pope, and thus to God. Divine rule is thus directly questioned.

Moreover, the underlining supposition in the evangelizing mission in which land and material possessions are "rightfully" accorded to the Spanish in exchange for the salvation of souls, is not being honored in the Andes. Both Philips are reminded that instead of true evangelizers, what they have sent and continue to send is a pack of "rats, cats, lions and vipers" (folio 704). This flesh eating pack not only insatiably devours the flesh of the innocent Indians, but in doing so deprives the king of both labor and tribute. Thus the comparison of the Spaniards to a carnivorous fauna carries more political than literary weight. Their animalization stresses the wild behavior of the "civilizing" agents, and by bringing out this underlining contradiction Guamán Poma challenges the "spiritual" rationale for the conquest and domination. The Indians, seen in many of the drawings as a pure and natural flesh, are capable, he argues, of two of the highest human values in any civilized order: work and organized society. The Spanish, in contrast, have only brought chaos and war. They live off the labor of others and cannot organize the running of the empire for the common good.

With this critique Guamán Poma has not only turned the rationale for European domination upside down, he has also demonstrated to the king that this kind of domination keeps his pockets less full than they otherwise should be given the riches found in the Andes. Having given up the idea that ethics can be a motivating factor in the behavior of the Spanish, he decides to stop pretending, and instead of making a purely moral appeal to the king, Guamán Poma emphasizes the economic interests of the king. He warns the king about the imminent economic disaster to ensue should he allow the continued decline and eventual extinction of the Indians. Thus, in his message to the king he both covers up and unveils the intimate and indissoluble connection between the king's economic interest and the discourse of evangelization. He knows that in order to be heard, he must gamble and pretend that the king actually fears for his soul. The author of the letter proposes the following way out of the impasse: a purely Andean separate realm.

Such space of purity—physical and political—would guarantee the king the two most prized items in European civilization: a constant flow of gold and the salvation of one's soul. With Guamán Poma's proposal, Las Casas, who also proposed some kind of separation, need not fear for the salvation of the Spanish or the Indians any longer. In his more radical proposal, Guamán Poma finds what the logic of the Dominican friar had to continue to deny at all costs: the radical incompatibility of the safety and well being of the Indians with any kind of Spanish rule. The aporia of benign colonial rule is unmasked and the full consequences of a fearless analysis inform the blueprint for a space of purity.[27]

With these cards on the table Guamán Poma places himself in a position of grave danger. He thus cloaks the thrust of his writing under the idea dear to the Inquisition: the reform of all souls. The moral language and intent of his critique of Spanish evangelizers, *encomenderos* and bureaucrats alike is expected to mask and blunt the political objective of his examples and laments.

Ironically, it is at this juncture in his writing that his blueprint for the future ("later") starts becoming history ("then"). In his scheme for total separation and return to Andean culture and rule, there are, however, two European cultural items that he wished to retain: Christianity and writing (folio 792). In both he finds universal values that he would like for everyone to have and master at the same level, without the hierarchies and exclusions with which the mastery of writing and Christianity operate under colonial rule. In this general cleaning up, or decontamination, everything else must go, except perhaps scissors. For Guamán Poma, the best political, economic, and cultural order can be obtained when people remain where fate (God) originally placed them and carry on with their duties and privileges set in place: "el español a España y el negro a Guinea" (folio 792?). Migration across continents, the movement of peoples and goods across oceans, and the conquest of peoples by others of

---

[27] In *Another Face of Empire*, Daniel Castro argues that Las Casas discursive and political efforts to save the Indians from destruction could never really go beyond the necessity of empire and colonial rule for Spain. The many experiments the friar ran and the many laws he inspired were always destined to fail, if the intent had been to save the Indians from the ravages of colonialism.

radically different cultures spell chaos and injustice based on unaccept-able differences. Although he does not mention the *mitimae* status of his family in this regard, it is clear that from his own life experiences as a *forastero* and *mitimae* that he abhors the violent and general uprooting that colonial rule brought onto Andean life.

V. THE FUTURE OF TIME

However accurate and persuasive Guamán Poma's denunciation of the Spanish colonial regime may have been to any reader of his letter, we still need to ask: what was the possibility for such a project to turn into real-ity? By the first quarter of the seventeenth century and after the Toledean reforms, colonial rule seemed firmly implanted in Peru. Further, Guamán Poma's complaints and denunciations were not really new in European circles of power. With the rapid circulation in both the Indies and Europe of the *Brevísima historia de la destrucción de las Indias* (1552), Las Casas had already convinced many of his contemporaries of the Spaniard's moral unfitness to rule the Indians. The Dominican friar had even advanced the unthinkable notion that the people who were entitled to rule were the *mestizos* and not the conquerors or the court appointed officials, and least of all the *encomenderos*.

Las Casas, like others, argued that the fathers of the *mestizos* had con-quered the land and their mothers were the heirs to the vanquished lords. The king was not unmoved by Las Casas's arguments and pleas at court, as well as the power of his many publications and actions. The Crown enacted new laws to protect the Indians from abuse and thus to clean up the moral charges of their failed Christianity in order to defend Spain's right to further exploration, conquest, and colonization. But the Crown remained weary of the contentious, restless, and ambitious *mestizos*. In fact, it moved to strip them of their privileges as well as curtail their ambi-tion for administrative office in both the Church and the government.

In view of this mindset, what else could a man argue who was trying to claim the right of the Indians to rule themselves? Like Las Casas, he had to appeal to the Christian reader's idealized sense of the self, and especially remind Christians of their firm belief in the idea that all human beings were crated equal by the same God. Further, Guamán Poma argues that his fellow Indians have proven to be the equal of Europeans not just by virtue of theological reasons, but because they have demonstrated historically to be capable of establishing a better, and even more Christian, form of government than their European counterparts. Given the European self-centered view of human history, Guamán Poma's reasoning would be nothing but scandalous, for not even the jurist and defender of Indian rights Francisco de Vitoria (1486-1546) could resist the forces that claimed European superiority to all other cultures and polities.

Another route needed to be found, and another chain of reasoning needed to be brought out to show that although the Indians had created different civilizations, the difference did not spell out inspiration by the devil or inferiority of kind, but rather equality and coevalness stemming from a source ignored by European reasoning. The point was not to start one's thinking from the strictures of the Biblical creation story, but rather to open up the narrative to an account of human history in which not all past things are known with total certainty, and new calculations, as Wachtel shows (*Sociedad* 203-212), are possible. Consequently, Guamán Poma starts his long equalization argument by mounting an assault on European uni-linear time, an idea that has not appeared in the West until the work of the anthropologist Johannes Fabian in his path-breaking *Time and the Other: How Anthropology Makes its Object* (1983).

Fully aware that the narrative composite of the Bible is the chief mechanism by which the Spaniards reckon time and the political legitimization of events within its calendric organization, Guamán Poma seeks the soft spots in the constitution of such reckoning. His aim is to seek spaces where he can graft the passage of time in the Andes and his own calendric account of the passage of time[28] into the single flow postulated by Christian time. His pressing need is to show how Indians, and especially his ethnic group, the Yarovilcas, can be thought of as descendents of Adam and Eve. In this regard, he is of course, not original. But it

---

[28] Here I differ from Wachtel. I believe that Guamán Poma's political thrust is to find a place for the Indian in the European cosmos in order to ameliorate the rapid setting of racism. Thus he would be less interested in inverting the operation of time. Further, Wachtel shows in his analysis of Guamán Poma's "mapa mundi" that what Guamán Poma's spatial and temporal categories permit him to do is to integrate the king of Spain and the Pope in the Andean cosmos of the four corners and the high and the low, that is to say the Tahuantinsuyo.

is not his originality that matters as much as his maneuvering of the arguments in order to achieve his effects.

The universal flood seems to him, as it had to many Spanish missionaries and theologians (Lafaye 30-50), to be an event plagued with enough confusion about who and how many were saved, to admit to the theory of a third age of creation in which some of Noah's descendents where brought to populate the New World by God himself. Here Guamán Poma makes use of some of the tenets of the current discussion on the origins of the Amerindian peoples in Spanish intellectual and political circles, a discussion dominated by the unmovable idea of a single divine creation in Biblical geography. The problem at hand then was to "explain" how the Indians got here. If they were to be thought as equal to the other peoples accounted for in the Biblical story, a place for them had to be found somewhere in that narrative.

At times, more concerned with the concrete mechanics of reproduction than with the confusing details of the Bible's account of the begets, Guamán Poma calculates how fast the Andean land could have been populated after the flood. His concern with population growth and decline is no mere cosmographic or theological indulgence. Some earlier commentators have pointed out that he exhibits the peculiar inclination for numbers typical of the statistically minded Incas when he engages in his calculation of years and the relations between the passage of time and demographic growth. This may well be true. However, we cannot forget that what Guamán Poma wants is a separate Andean state in order to stave off the extinction of the Indians ("se despueblan las Indias") and thus attention to numbers and to demographic classification will prove fundamental. Today it is estimated that between 1519 and 1605, the population of central Mexico declined by 95%, and that in Peru, between 1572 and 1620, the decline came close to 50%. During the first decades of the conquest the population of the Peruvian coast also experienced a 95% decline (Sánchez Albornoz 22-85; Cook 5).

Understanding the ways in which the population of the Andes could recover from the holocaust was literally a question of life or death at the very moment when Guamán Poma was writing. Such a desperate understanding of the situation explains the existential nature of his daring in deciding not only to write the letter (keeping written or *quipu* records for more than 30 years), but especially to mount his argument for a separate realm and to make it public. In the motif "que no nos acabemos,"

Guamán Poma welds in a single topos the concrete reality that everyone can attest to with the political ideology that drives both the analysis and the proposal for a solution.

Grafting Andean time onto Christian time by way of the universal flood was indeed effective but it did not clear all the problems standing in the way of self rule. Despite Vitoria's arguments on the Indians' capacity to build civilizations on their own, and thus meet Aristotle's criteria for considering a people civilized (the construction and inhabitation of cities, as well as living according to a set of laws), the Aztecs were disqualified from full equality because of their practice of human sacrifice, and the Incas were also ruled out because of the Spanish report of royal incest.

Not wishing to point out, and thus offend, that at least in the case of Adam and Eve the story of Biblical creation also implies original incest, Guamán Poma looks for another way out. He resorts once more to confusion. He proposes a new interpretation of the conundrum of original universal incest. He suggests that like Adam and Eve, the founders of the third age in the New World must have lived very long lives and also born many sets of twins (Cox 42). There would have been so many people of mating age within such a short period of time that it would have been impossible to keep track of everyone's kinship. With this scenario of uncontrolled mating on both sides of the Atlantic, Guamán Poma believes that he has quelled the incest disqualification. He is so confident of having done so, that pages later he uses the very same argument to disqualify the Incas as a possible post-colonial ruling group and even to show that their claim to divine origin (children of the sun) is (has to be) only a clever invention (folio 51). For Guamán Poma, royal incest was a clever political ploy on the part of the Incas to keep power to themselves. Grafting Andean time onto the opening left by the discontinuity of the flood was indeed a very productive move for Guamán Poma's multifaceted project of establishing equality (coevalness,) and thus the right to self rule.

One of the unintended consequences of this line of argument to disqualify the descendants of the Incas, a group with whom he no doubt wrestled for power and influence, is that he ended up adding his voice to Toledo's own quest to disqualify the Inca's claim to rule the land as established lords and examples of good government (see chapter 5 in this volume, "Historiography on the Ground"). Neither Toledo nor any other Crown official or missionary was apt to make distinctions between different Andean polities unless, of course, such distinctions enabled the colonizers to set one group against another and thus rule more effectively over local factions. Having been an aid and translator of Pedro Sarmiento de Gamboa, who had been charged by Toledo in the 1560's with interviewing anyone whose memory of the Andean past disputed the Inca version in order to disqualify the Incas as the original and just rulers of the land and thus block any claims made by their descendants to any further rule, Guamán Poma should have known what the consequences of his arguments could be for all Indians. But his times were desperate times and the thought that he could make a good case for a realm ruled by the descendants of the old *curacas* was indeed compelling.

If the charge of incest was dispelled from his ancestors, and if he hoped to draw benefits from the clear distinction he made between the Incas and his own ethnic group, all was not yet well. Guamán Poma knew that he must still engage one more argument standing in his way to claim equality. The "discovery" of the New World had thrown most European notions of human nature—neither animal nor divine—into crisis (Lafaye 3-50). Theories on the right to make war and to conquer and subjugate peoples sanctioned the outright taking of the spoils of war as well as the economic, social, political, and cultural "rights" of individuals and the conquered polity. But the fact that the Amerindians were not at war with the conquering Spanish, and did not, like the Turks, contest Christian supremacy, posed a problem in the smooth flow of the standing war and conquest theory. Guamán Poma's writing seems to be steeped in the debates that questioned the Spanish right to wage war on the Amerindians and to despoil them of their economic and cultural possessions. The argument holding that there were some incipient rights to all human beings regardless of their standing in any specific human political arrangement began to emerge out of the controversy of the "discovery" and the condemnation of perennial Spanish warfare against the Indians. The self styled "author" shows a deep familiarity with the terms of the debate ignited by the publication of *Brevísima historia de la destrucción de las Indias* (The Devastation of the Indies: A Brief Account) (1554) by Bartolomé de Las Casas (1474-1566), as well as the debate in which the Dominican friar engaged his nemesis Ginés de Sepúlveda (1490-1573).

Although he does not write at length on the terms of this debate on human rights, it is clear that when he observes and reports on the distraught situation of his fellow Andeans he does so through the prism of the concepts of human (equal) rights and the kind of revolutionary justice that becomes its unspoken corollary. From his observations, it is clear that the Indians' humanity is diminished every day with each new ordinance, with each new practice of subjection and exploitation, and especially with each new rape that not only violates the humanity and rights of each woman so violated, but also destroys the social, and thus human, arrangement of each family and the capacity for survival of the group. Increasingly, and despite Vitoria and Las Casas, Spanish rule turned the Indians into bodies without rights, where every practice of subjection is squeezed out of the human spirit. Thus reform, even though that is what Guamán Poma claims to be advocating, becomes impossible to countenance (Stern 51-79). Complete separation is the only possible way to keep from extinction.

But what guarantees, the Spanish would argue, that Indian rule would in any way be just? Here once again, Guamán Poma brings up the "historical" example of the Incas and the pre-Inca polities. Despite his dislike for the Inca royal house, his admiration and deeply grounded knowledge of the Inca economic, political, and cultural world has filled the pages of the entire first half of the book, and thus constitutes his justification for the idea of a restoration of good government. The solution, once again, does not require invention, debate, or experimentation. It is at hand. It is still alive, on the ground.

But then again, would this also be a return to the pagan ways of old? Would this restoration mean a rejection of Christianity? Guamán Poma deploys yet another argument to quell such fears and to show that Spanish history is not any more providential than any other people's history. To construct this argument, he deploys another calculation designed to rupture the smooth passage of Euro-Christian time and to insert in the break a new and modifying consideration.

In the account of the ages of the world, he figures, making use of the Rodrigo Zamorano's *Cronología y repertorio de la razón de los tiempos* (1594) (Cox 42-52), that Christ was born at about the same time that Julius Cesar was born in Rome and the Inca Sinchi Roca in Cuzco. Thus he superimposes the two cosmological centers of the worlds that were then clashing. With this superimposition he produces the figure that had eluded both Las Casas and Vitoria. If Rome and Cuzco are conflated then there is but one single flow of time in which the Incas fit "neatly." Now that Rome is in the picture, we are reminded that conquest and empire have always found their justification in their "civilizing mission." For

Guamán Poma, Rome's civilizing mission could easily be compared to the Inca's own, and these two were no less virtuous than the Spanish providential claims to conquest. As if this were not enough of a leveling and diffusion of Christianity's special claims into two pagan empires, Guamán Poma goes on to remind his readers that the Spanish had lived under Roman (pagan) rule for a long time. Nobody, he argues, faults the Spanish for their subjugation to Rome. It is only after the apostle Santiago brought them the good news of the gospel that the Spanish became Christians. In fact, Guamán Poma relishes in stating that from this perspective, the Spanish too are but recent converts (*conversos*). In this way the Spanish are all new Christians ("nuevos" and not "viejos cristianos"), and a new level of coevalness has been achieved.

With his deployment of Cuzco and Rome occupying the same temporal notch and the Spanish reformulated as new Christians (converts just like the Indians) everyone is on the same footing: both New World and Old World people are converts to Christianity. No one can make claims to authenticity or special origin. With this leveling argument, there is no longer any need for the Spanish Crown to be presiding over the New World. The Pope in Rome can preside over the Indians just like he presides over all of Christendom, Spain included. It is thus not inconceivable that the Indians could duplicate the faithful conversion of the Spanish and become great defenders of the faith themselves, or even Saints and theologians. Indians could achieve great artistic prowess and powers in honor of God, for they were, like other Christians, capable of achieving all and any great human heights. Proof can be readily found in the saintly life of his own half brother Martín de Ayala, or in retrospect, we might say, in the writing of *El primer nueva corónica y buen gobierno*.

The Yarovilca's daring does not stop with these equalizing moves. While the Pope may oversee the world from Rome, good government requires wise delegation of authority. Mere lip service to religious and political principles simply does not work. In this regard, Christ himself gave the best example. He delegated his authority to St. Peter and the apostle passed it on down to the Popes in Rome. Thus, Guamán Poma invokes a pontifical order for the world. In order to persuade his reader, he embarks in a tedious and seemingly out of place recitation of the names and dates of the Popes, strangely intertwined with the Inca line of descent. It is as if he were reading from a post-colonial *quipu* in which each colored knot contained a name, a date, and a place in a long and integrated genealogy of legitimate rulers. If one bears his equalizing quest in mind, the meaning of the tedious list becomes clear. In the flow of Christian-Pontifical time, there have been many lineages of rulers, all beholden to Rome for legitimization. Here Guamán Poma plunges to the heart of the matter, for he gently and obliquely reminds the king of Spain that his authority is tenable only under the doctrine of divine rule and the Pope's confirmation of such principles and practices. Within this scheme—Christ to Peter, Peter to the Popes, the Popes to the kings—a Yarovilca prince is well suited to be a "segunda persona" of the king of Spain and thus establish a bridge (pontifical) rule in a separate Indian state. Clearly Guamán Poma is not thinking of being an Indian viceroy. That, for him, would be a contradiction in terms.

In his proposal, Guamán Poma is careful to leave the king's position as an empty signifier, unscathed even though the administration of justice that flows from it is quite perverse. The question is not whether Spain should have an empire in the New World, but rather who should rule in the *name* of the chain of authority that flows from Christ to the Pope to the king. This chain does not include the *encomenderos*. Having illustrated the bureaucratic and moral incompetence of the Spanish, Guamán Poma argues that the Indians themselves are the only other logical and historical choice.

The Indians had been proven to be rational and intelligent. As new converts to Christianity they were setting an example for the Spanish. Above all, the Indians were a historical people contemporary to the Romans, and therefore not just "natural" and corporeal beings lacking in spirituality. They had a place in the time of civilization and therefore they were entitled to continue to exist in the Christian/historical flow of time rather than be destroyed for ever.

VI. The Space of Purity

Unfortunately for Guamán Poma the greatest "natural" enemies to his project of separate rule for Andeans were the *mestizos*, in both their physical presence and their imperial classification. Nowhere does Guamán Poma make an effort to disguise his intense dislike for the *mestizos*. Although he does not mount a moral critique of the *mestizos* as he does of the Spanish, he expresses a physical revulsion at the very idea of their presence. He charges the *mestizos* with personal, social and political failings. *Mestizos* are lazy, shiftless, sensual, and arrogant. Only *zambos*, the offspring of Indians and Africans, are deserving of equal or greater loathing. Guamán Poma feels totally alienated from both *mestizos* and *zambos*, for they fail to meet one of the most important requirements in Guamán Poma's idea of a well integrated and well run polity: clarity and purity of descent. Absence of a spotless bloodline and purity of kinship alike provoke in Guamán Poma nothing but disgust, suspicion, and even resentment for *mestizos*, *zambos* and mulattoes. These people of mixed descent pose a challenge to his classificatory scheme as well as to his arguments for separate rule. His rejection of people of mixed descent cannot be thought as racist in the modern sense of racism, even when, as Walter Mignolo has shown, our modern sense of racism stems from the Spanish obsession with "pureza de sangre" ("Preamble" 15-17). For Guamán Poma the question is not differences in skin color or even culture, the question is the mixture. While he does not hesitate to express his disgust for the *mestizos* and the mulattos, he also does not hesitate to feel pity for the black slaves and to condemn slavery, since he feels that Africans are "human too."

Central and overwhelming on his mind is the part *mestizaje* plays in eroding Indian culture and even the sense of physical identity with one's ancestral community. The image of the *mestizos* touches a number of vulnerable spots in Guamán Poma's consciousness. These range from the physical to the moral. *Mestizaje* means that Indian women are being raped and must keep the offspring of fathers who do not even recognize their children. Besides being an economic and social burden to the *ayllus* and Indian communities, these children do not reproduce the material nor the social being of the Indian men, who must accept violated daughters, sisters, and wives as if nothing had happened, when in fact the whole system of Andean social organization and "selfhood" is ripped apart with the violating of the strict kinship marriage rules (Zuidema 27-33). The males of a strong patriarchal culture are indirectly, but in very real ways, being relegated to a barren life. Their line of descent is being choked and annihilated, and this is unbearable in a culture in which ancestor worship and attachment to origin and kinship are as strong as they were in the Andes.

Guamán Poma relates the repeating tragedy of the husband who returns after years of *mita* work, or other tributary labor, to find his home full of "mesticillos." Disgusted and in despair, the man abandons his wife and his village, thus breaking the fundamental bonds for the reproduction of the Andean social organization. This Indian head of household also leaves, self exiling himself from the old order, in order to keep himself from a grater transgression: killing the children of the rapist ("por no matallos"). The normal narcissistic love of the parent for the child, the ego love of the ethnic group for itself, is denied or turned upside down by the post-conquest appearance of the *mestizo*. And what, may we ask of the mother, of her torn relationship to her post-conquest off-spring? For Guamán Poma, there is no greater threat to self-continuity, to self-differentiation, to the hope of stemming ethnic (racial) extinction than the growing *mestizo* population.

Of course, Guamán Poma is speaking not only from the perspective of a social and political analysis but from lived experience as well. In one of his many confidential asides to the reader he states that: "mira christiano, a mi todo se me ha hecho, hasta quererme quitar mi mujer un fraile Mercedario" (folio 916). He adds that "pretenden que fueran los indios bobos, asnos, para acabar de quitarles cuanto tiene, hacienda, mujer, hija" (folio 916). Thus, *mestizaje* means individual and group loss of control over the affective world, as well as the reproductive possibilities of couples, families, and *ayllus*. Guamán Poma knows in the flesh, from first hand observation and lived experience, that no law protecting the Indians can have any effect over the intractable work of *mestizaje. Mestizaje* spells out the indefatigable watering down of Andean bodies and culture.

From the data that Guamán Poma records, it would seem that some of the Indian women he observed did not share the same revulsion at the notion of sexual and cultural intercourse with the Spanish. Although many felt so ashamed and violated when raped, that, like the men, they also abandoned their families and villages, others were not so horrified at the idea of becoming the concubines of Spanish or African men. Guamán Poma condemns and laments this situation because it denies Indian men the possibility of having progeny. He writes that "y se acaban los Indios por no tener mujeres y porque todas las mujeres se van detrás de los españoles" (folio 1018). Worried that this new freedom in mating has affected the Indians at the moral level because it "has unleashed a great sensual desire among the Indians" (folio 888), and even more concerned with the depopulation of the Indian towns, Guamán Poma insults the Indian women who leave the *ayllus* and villages to follow the Spanish into their cities. Furious, he writes that "las mujeres salen, se ausentan, salen de noche, se hacen bellacas, putas" (folio 880). For him, these women are not only whores, but they are traitors as well. However, when one considers the life of toil and submission that he described earlier in the letter as the condition of women in pre-conquest society, it is not so surprising to see that the women may have thought that in the cities they could gain a new freedom from such a regime of work.

And work is the other point of contention Guamán Poma has with the *mestizos*. Although he writes with implacable fury about the Spanish Indian labor abuse in *mitas*, as well as multiple other forms of taking the Indian's labor for free, Guamán Poma cannot bear the fact that by law the *mestizo* population is not required to participate in the same regime of forced labor as that which the Spanish imposed over the Indians. This labor inequality is indeed the world turned upside down ("el mundo al revés"). If the *mestizos* have no labor obligations, let them be barred from the Indian villages. Let them join the world of the Spanish, along with the mulattoes and the *zambos*. Or better yet, Guamán Poma tells the king, deport them to Chile or cast them into the sea. It does not matter what is done with them, just keep them out of Guamán Poma's separate Andean state in which restoration of the old order means organized labor.

The sin of miscegenation is not only linked to the destruction of the Indian families and to the labor regime that excludes the *mestizos* from labor tribute, but it is also posited as the chief reason for the king's decline in revenue. Without Indians, and especially without a quick recovery of the Indian population, the king quickly looses his share of the Indians' labor. Guamán Poma paints a dire picture for the post-conquest Andes:

> Se ha de perder la tierra porque ellos (españoles y mestizos) han causado gran daño y pleitos y perdiciones. Se perderá la tierra y quedara solitario y despoblado el reino y quedará muy pobre el rey por causa del dicho corregidor y demás españoles que roban a los indios sus haciendas, casa, sementeras, pastos, y sus mujeres, por así casadas y doncellas, todas paren ya mestizos y cholos, hay clérigo que tiene ya veinte hijos y no hay remedio. (folio 446)

An Indian separate realm would consequently be dedicated to four main objectives: the recovery of the Indian population, the production of loyal Christian subjects, goods destined to ensure the survival needs of an efficient and skilled labor force and the surplus needs of the state, and the production of an abundant surplus in order to keep the king of Spain with so much wealth as to insure his supremacy in Europe. Guamán Poma has no problem rejecting Las Casas's arguments in favor of *mestizo* rule, for unlike Las Casas, who had never been to Peru, nor lived with any Indian community, Guamán Poma wrote from the incontestable knowledge gained on the ground. Besides, *mestizos* would be the least capable of effective rule for they were truly new to the business of government: they had no history and no cosmos on which to rely for a model.

As Guamán Poma's series of arguments moved along, there was no question that the only viable thing to do was to return to Indian rule. But who would these Indians be? Because Guamán Poma's blueprint for good government was modeled in the past, he proposes a historically tested and proven Indian nobility made up of old men,[29] who would exercise a form of government that mixed, in Alfred Metraux's estimation, despotism with socialist freedom. For Guamán Poma the advantage of having old men in charge is not only that they are wise, but also that they are no longer moved by the ambition and lust for power of younger men. They do not covet goods excessively because in a society with no private property there is no question of inheritance. Worldly honor is no longer a temptation for men so close to entering the kingdom of God. The proximity to death compels them to ethical behavior. These old men compare well with classical ascetics.

VII. The Organization of Purity and the King's Advantage

Guamán Poma, by proposing a return to the past governed by old men free of desire, envisions an ultimate stage of stability marked by purity, coherence, unity and lack of contradictions. For him, a mixture of categories, ambiguity of positions, and an infinite set of pluralities act as destabilizers that eventually produce chaos. Singleness, separation, differentiation (*quipu* calles), and classification foster order, knowledge, planning, and predictability. Every object, every task, every act, and every office must be clearly distinguished from every other one to avoid confusion and

---

[29] Ironically, the king's officials had no use for the *mestizos* either. They suspected their political and cultural loyalty. They found them contentious, pretentious, and rebellious. On the matter of Inca rule and its wisdom, Alfred Metreaux argues that the Incas "combined the most absolute kind of despotism with the greatest tolerance toward the social and political order of its subject peoples" (81).

error. Thus, he would have people dressed in different colors and wearing different ornaments to sign unequivocally their occupations, stations in life, regional origins, and responsibilities in the polity to which they belong. He could then take pleasure in the intellectual and aesthetic existing order: "que bien se ve cada uno en su traje" (folio 797). Here he echoes Garcilaso's own pleasure in the physical arrangement of Cuzco in accordance with the place of origin of each visiting polity and the costume of each polity wearing their own insignia (Garcilaso 423), so that everyone would immediately know their identity and kinship. This exigency for unequivocal distinctions and classifications, I think, may stem from the exigencies of the *quipu* mathematical system for the collection, maintenance and organization of data.

There is no question that division of labor constitutes for Guamán Poma the chief social organizing principle. In this sense, his vision does not fall into the hierarchies of the time with the monarch at the top and the vassals at the bottom. Guamán Poma's emphasis on labor does in fact sound "modern," albeit "conservative." Terms such as "modern," "conservative," "individual," and "freedom" taken from our own "modern" value system do not really provide us with an understanding of Guamán Poma, the world that he faced, the struggle that he waged, and above all his efforts to rescue from the smoldering ashes a livable order for those who, like him, had been totally dispossessed.

Guamán Poma was looking to strike a contract, a bargain between the state and each member of the community. For him, all human relations were cast in terms of work and not in the modern sense of individual rights. The state, for him, guaranteed the universal right to work and to reproduce, creating the next communal generation. Gender, age, physical capacity, and skills constitute the criteria for differentiation based on labor. As in Inca times, children could begin to work for the community and thus for the common good as soon as they could begin to gather fruits, catch birds, and collect feathers. Guamán Poma delights in describing how each member of the community would carry on with his/her work, thus making the community flourish in an abundance of goods and harmony. Work guaranteed the social existence of each member from their birth to their death bed, and that included the physically impaired who never had to worry for their sustenance as they always already belonged. His rivalry and dislike of the Inca royal family fades away in this discussion of the organization and universal benefits of the work order. The Yarovilca prince lavishes as much praise on the Inca as he expresses scorn and contempt for the lazy, avaricious, and heartless Spanish.

Destruction of the family as a result of the introduction of modes of production guided by the principle of private property constitutes Guamán Poma's bitterest complaint (folio 36). He argues that emotional well being, a sense of self-respect, love, charity and other spiritual values have also been destroyed by the principle of private property and the uneven acquisition and holding of wealth (folio 37). The pre-conquest family was the basic unity for the production of goods, as well as the physical, social, and emotional reproduction of the self. Because the family worked primarily for its needs, it was allowed some measure of private property, but the great surplus went to the state so that it may attend to the needs and imperatives of others and of the community as a whole. In a non-monetary economy, state officials are paid in goods destined for consumption and not for personal accumulation. In this economy, waste in the Spanish style of over consumption and private accumulation would not be possible.

Thus the role of the state would be minimal and consequently not very expensive. There could never be "comenderos que gastan largamente como no les cuesta su trabajo, ni sudor, sino que pide a los pobres indios" (folio 559). Besides the Andean people, the other great beneficiary of the return to the *ayllu* system would be the king. He would get his tribute in labor, goods—silver, *coca*, cattle—and of course, gold. Although Guamán Poma did not understand very well what the Spanish did with gold, he knew how much they coveted the yellow metal. The conversion of the goods into values of exchange and personal or imperial uses was of no concern to Guamán Poma, as long as the Spanish kept their wicked system to themselves. Separate rule was the only way, even for the king.

In this world of work, the state would be comparable to a small wart on the smooth epidermis of a giant body of people at work. The state was to be an invisible presence in charge of overseeing a smooth operation of the principles that rule the community and every one of its members. The state was not envisioned to grow in power or multiply its functions or prerogatives. It was not at all the giant state of European communism or liberal capitalism. There were no leaps to be taken by this society. Slow and careful adaptation to change would be Guamán Poma's style of response to the new. There was nothing more abhorrent to him, except the *mestizos,* than the notion of rapid change and experimentation, or even worse, change in one's station in life at the expense of the work of others.[30]

In one of his many tableaus, he ridicules the fantasies of wealth and high status of pauper Spanish families at the expense of the Indians. He does so to great political and emotional effect. He poignantly portrays the calculating conversation entertained by many miserable parents:

> What the Spanish Christians who have many children imagine is all gold and silver. Husband and wife spend their days and nights thinking. Husband tells the wife: "You know I am always thinking that our boys should study for the priesthood. The wife replies: "How well conceived and said by lord and husband, for God has given us these many children in order to enrich us. Yago will be a cleric [Yaguito sera cleriguito] and so will Francis. This way they can earn money and send us Indians to serve us, send us money and gifts: porridge, chickens, eggs, fruit, corn, potatoes, and even the greens the Indians eat. It would be good for our Martin to be a Dominican and for Gonzalo to be a Mercedarian. But it would not be a good thing to join the Franciscans or the Jesuits, because the ones who join those orders forget their parents and stay poor and become saints and make no money.[31] (folio 546)

In order to keep the money making Mercedarians—the reader may recall that it was a Mercedarian, Murúa perhaps (folio 1080), who wanted to take his wife away from him—the king must deploy the full powers of writing and decree the return of the land and government to the Indians. Guamán Poma closes his argument with a final appeal to justice, the ultimate basis, in European political theory for the king's right to rule:

> Es muy justo que se vuelva y restituya las dichas tierras y corrales y pastos que se vendieron en nombre de su majestad, porque de bajo de conciencia no se le puede quitarsela a los naturales lexitimos propietarios de las tierras... Despues que se les vuela a los Indios e Indias les valdra muy mucho a su majestad. (folio 536)
> It is just that the many lands, pastures and holding pens that were sold in the name of your majesty be restituted, because good conscience does not allow for taking them away from the Indians, who are the legitimate owners of the

---

[30] Even though both Inca and Spanish societies are clearly hierarchically oriented, Guamán Poma has no use for the Spanish soldier that wants to be treated as if he were a noble lord, for his concerns are labor equality and organization.

[31] This, and all other translations of Guamán Poma, are mine.

land... After [these lands] are returned to the Indians they will prove to be much more valuable to your majesty.

In this scheme of things, the king can only stand to gain: improved lands, more production, more tribute, the appearance of a just king, and maybe even eternal salvation. Guamán Poma is not unaware of the web of impossible complication that would result from the return of the land to its rightful owners given the dispersal of the Indians by the *encomienda* system and the towns created by Toledo. Therefore, the return would take place not in terms of who occupies and has a "right" to the land now, but who occupied and worked it at the time of his grandfather and the time of the Inca Túpac Yupanqui, even before the wars between Huáscar and Atahualpa (folio 536).

VIII. The Impossibility of Coevalness

No matter how attractive and necessary the separate Indian state may have seemed to the king, he had no chance to read the letter, and abrogation of the rights of conquest was not within his power, especially given the fact that "Spain" had just recently merged as a unified nation and state after conquering and taking the lands occupied by the Arabs. The Crown had too much trouble controlling its Spanish subjects in the New World to risk, even on paper, the economic and political autonomy of the Indians. Even though Guamán Poma dangled in front of the king the idea of true and faithful Christian converts and greater tribute, the forces of exploitation that shaped the making of the colonial world could not be arrested in any way.

El primer nueva corónica y buen gobierno, aside from rescuing in detail a cultural legacy and offering ample testimony of its destruction by conquest, convincingly presents a scheme for a return to a political and cultural order that Christian ideology could accept. Guamán Poma's miscalculation was, of course, to believe, like Las Casas, that the course of history could be changed by a perfectly reasoned appeal to a prince by another prince ("que soy su principe y protector," folio 981) in an extended and daring maneuver to grasp coevalness. Even an absolute ruler like the king of Spain was subject to forces greater that his power. A glimpse of the impossibility of his dream of a space of purity begins to hound him in the last 100 folios of the letter. Like his *mestizo* counterpart in Spain, the Inca Garcilaso de la Vega, the Yarovilca Prince consoles himself with having saved Andean culture not from destruction but from oblivion: "Y asi escribo esta historia para que sea memoria y se ponga en el archivo de la justicia" (folio 981). With this sentence he begins to separate his work and his dreams from the single flow of time he had recovered with his pontifical maneuvers, and to place in the archive of justice, that is to say in a utopian register that might be activated when the Indian population, if ever, recovered enough, the dream of again inaugurating a space in which their cultural wisdom and political practices would once more be dominant and fill the land with abundance and harmony.

Reprinted from Sara Castro-Klarén: "Huaman Poma and the Space of Purity", in Raymond L. Hall (ed.): *Ethnic Autonomy. Comparative Dynamics. The Americas, Europe and the Developing World*, 345-370. © 1979 New York: Pergamon Press. This is an extensively revised version.

Works Cited

ARGUEDAS, José María. *Formación de una cultura nacional indoamericana.* México: Siglo Veintiuno Editores, 1975.

AVENI, Anthony F. *Empires of Time: Calendars, Clocks, and Cultures.* New York: Basic Books, 1989.

BRADING, David. *The First America: The Spanish Monarchy, Creole Patriots, and the Liberal State 1492-1867.* Cambridge: Cambridge University Press, 1991.

BROKAW, Galen. "The Poetics of *Khipu* Historiography: Felipe Guamán Poma de Ayala's *Nueva Corónica* and the *Relación de los quipucamayoc.*" *Latin American Research Review* 38.3 (2003): 111-147.

BROWN, Michael F. and Eduardo FERNÁNDEZ. *War of Shadows: The Struggle for Utopia in the Peruvian Amazon.* Berkeley: University of California Press, 1991.

CASTRO, Daniel. *Another Face of Empire: Bartolomé de Las Casas, Indigenous Rights and Ecclesiastical Imperialism.* Durham: Duke University Press, 2007.

COOK, Noble David. *Born to Die: Disease and the New World Conquest, 1492-1650.* Cambridge: Cambridge University Press, 1998.

COX, Victoria. *Guamán Poma de Ayala: entre los conceptos andino y europeo del tiempo.* Cuzco: Bartolomé de Las Casas, 2002.

GIBSON, Charles. *The Spanish Tradition in America.* New York: Haper and Row, 1968.

GUAMÁN POMA DE AYALA, Felipe. *Nueva corónica y buen gobierno.* Ed. Franklin Pease. 2 vols. Caracas: Biblioteca Ayacucho, 1980.

HANKE, Lewis, ed. *History of Latin American Civilization: Sources and Interpretations.* Vol. 1. Boston: Little Brown and Company, 1973.

HERRERA, C. Augusto Alba. *Atusparia y la revolución campesina de 1885 en Ancash.* Lima: Ediciones Atusparia, 1985.

LAFAYE, Jacques. *Quetzalcoatl and Guadalupe: The Formation of Mexican National Consciousness, 1531-1813.* Chicago: University of Chicago Press, 1976.

LÓPEZ MARTÍNEZ, Héctor. *Rebeliones de mestizos y otros temas quinientistas.* Lima: Ediciones P.L.V., 1972.

MANNHEIM, Karl. *Ideology and Utopia.* New York: Harcourt Brace, 1936.

METREAUX, Alfred. "The Inca Empire: Despotism or Socialism." *History of Latin American Civilization.* Ed. Lewis Hanke. Boston: Little Brown and Company, 1973.

MIGNOLO, Walter. "Decires fuera de lugar: sujetos dicentes, roles sociales y formas de inscripción." *Revista de Crítica Literaria Latinoamericana* 21.41 (1995): 9-31.

—. "Preamble: The Historical Foundation of Modernity/Coloniality and the Emergence of Decolonial Thinking." *A Companion to Latin American Literature and Culture.* Ed. Sara Castro-Klarén. Oxford: Blackwell Publishing, 2008.

MORGAN, Arthur E. *Nowhere was Somewhere: How History Makes Utopias and How Utopias Make History.* Chapel Hill: University of North Carolina Press, 1946.

OSSIO, Juan M. *Ideología mesiánica del mundo andino.* Lima: I. Prado Pastor, 1973.

PORRAS BARRENECHEA, Raúl. *El cronista indio Felipe Guamán Poma de Ayala.* Lima: Ed. Lumen, 1948.

SÁNCHEZ ALBORNOZ, Nicolás. *The Population of Latin America: A History.* Trans. W.A.R. Richardson. Berkeley: University of California Press, 1974.

STAVIG, Ward. *The World of Tupac Amaru: Conflict, Community and Identity in Colonial Peru.* Lincoln and London: University of Nebraska Press, 1999.

STERN, Steve J. *Peru's Indian Peoples and the Challenge of Spanish Conquest: Huamanga to 1640.* Madison: University of Wisconsin Press, 1982.

TELLO, Julio C. *La primeras edades del Perú por Guamán Poma.* Lima, 1939.

TENENBAUM, Barbara A., ed. *Encyclopedia of Latin American History and Culture.* Vol. V. New York: Charles Scribner and Son's, 1996.

THURNER, Mark. *From Two Republics to One Divided: Contradictions of Postcolonial Nationmaking in Andean Peru.* Durham: Duke University Press, 1997.

URTON, Gary. *The Social Life of Numbers: A Quechua Ontology of Numbers and Philosophy of Arithmetic.* Austin: University of Texas Press, 1997.

VEGA, Inca Garcilaso de la. *Royal Commentaries of the Incas and General History of Peru*. Vol. I [1605]. Trans. Harold V. Livermore. Austin: University of Texas Press, 1966.

VILLASEÑOR, Nicole. *Perú: cronistas indios y mestizos en el siglo XVI*. México: SepSetenta, 1957.

WACHTEL, Nathan. *Sociedad e ideología: ensayos de historia y antropología andina*. Lima: Instituto de Estudios Peruanos, 1973.

—. *Los vencidos: los indios del Perú frente a la conquista española (1530-1570)*. Trans. Antonio Escohotado. Madrid: Alianza Editorial, 1976.

ZUIDEMA, R. Tom. *Inca Civilization in Cuzco*. Tran. Jean Jacques Decostes. Austin: University of Texas Press, 1990.

CHAPTER 2
Guamán Poma: Confession, Pastoral Power, and the Order of the Subject

> "It is a form of power that makes individuals subjects. There are two meanings to the word *subject:* subject to someone else by control and dependence, and tied to his own identity by a conscience or self-knowledge. Both meanings suggest a form of power which subjugates and makes subject to." (Foucault, "The Subject and Power" 212)

I. THE ORDER OF (THE) SUBJECT

The Conquest of America by Europe occasioned a great shift in the understanding of the shape of the globe and the location of old and new territories for both Amerindians and the inhabitants of what after 1492 would be known as the Old World. The conquest also brought about a great commotion in the understanding of how and where human beings were located at cosmological and epistemological levels. For peoples on both sides of the Atlantic it was now necessary to think in terms of self and a new other, for the self was now challenged by a heretofore unknown and unanticipated difference. Although the "civilizing mission" that Europe invented for itself was driven by a sense of continuity as both its presupposition and teleology, the conquest of America meant an irreparable break in previous assumptions of historical continuity and self, and if not unity, at least a naturalized self coherence. Nevertheless, the effects of conquest were, by definition, asymmetrical. While European subjects of knowledge such as Bartolomé de Las Casas (1474-1566), and Francisco de Vitoria (1486-1546) asked questions as to the juridical position that Amerindians were to be accorded in a world under their control, their central location did not necessitate that they inquire into the thought of Aztecs or Andeans on similar matters. In order for the thought of people like Guamán Poma (c. 1534-1616) or the Tlatoani Cuauhtémoc to occupy a place in their discourses concerning the governance of the New World a revolution of global proportions would have been necessary.

From the point of view of the vanquished other, a very different perspective emerged, for they had to contend with the thinking and knowledge apparatus that now not only dominated them, but also prescribed their inferiority and incapacity for self rule for the foreseeable future. Subjects like Guamán Poma could no longer assume their previous understanding of self and/or the world was operative. Thus they had to move onto a redefined and redistributed physical and discursive territory. Their location as living beings had totally changed. They now needed to develop a bifurcated and asymmetrical line of inquiry that, in a constant process of ex-change and negotiation, would allow them to look both into the past "self" formed under pre-conquest conditions and the ongoing process of subjectivation under post-conquest conditions. Under these doubled post-conquest conditions of subjectification (Foucault, "The Subject" 212) they were required to understand and emulate the processes of subjectivation and self-emergence of the dominant, conquering regime as well as reflect on their own emerging events of self subjectivation.

The task facing the post-conquest subject was indeed daunting and the composition and writing of the *El primer nueva corónica y buen gobierno* (1616) can be taken as an empirical example of the processes of subjectivation, in Foucault's double sense of the term—making one subject to someone else, and being tied to one's own identity by a conscience or self-knowledge (Foucault, "The Subject" 212). The conundrum inscribed in Guamán Poma's book stems from the need to make sense of the chaos, to return not to an impossible position of control and same-self identity, real or imagined, but to the cognitive possibility of making sense and ordering the "pachakutic" or world turned up-side down ("el mundo al revés") through the production of a discursive subject that, though disheveled, could exhibit the principle lineaments of order and thus intelligibility.

Although I find that Foucault's thinking on the question of the subject provides indispensable critical ground and insightful considerations for pursuing the problematic imbedded in a post-colonial (post-crisis) subject, the intriguing problematic of the disheveled and dislocated subject was first theorized for me when reading Julio Cortázar. In hindsight such a coincidence—Cortázar and Foucault—should not be surprising, since both the artist and the philosopher shared a great many philosophical and artistic interests as well as attitudes and understandings. Consider for instance the shared list of readings and points of inquiry: Heidegger, the French Surrealists, Alfred Jarry, Jorge Luis Borges, Nietzsche, Georges Bataille, Maurice Blanchot, Gaston Bachelard, the Marquis de Sade, and ancient Aztecs (Castro-Klarén; Miller 84-90, 108-113, 224). It thus goes without saying that the subject to be discussed here is not the unitary or sovereign subject of modernity.

Rather, and in keeping with both the textual evidence in the *Corónica* as well as of our present understanding of the chaos brought about by the conquest and processes of colonization instituted in the Andes during the life of Guamán Poma, what I intend to analyze here are the manifestations and tactics of a disheveled subject struggling to wrest order out of his own conflicted, discursive, and historical positions, as well as of the material that he has assembled for that purpose. There is no question, from the earliest words of the text and the very first drawing that the subject of enunciation deploys, that he thinks himself not to be a unified subject. That is to say he does not represent an integrated voice or self speaking at all times from the same position.[1] But an awareness of a conflicted position does not translate into making the subject *mobile* or *masked*. Such a characterization would presume that it is indeed the same (unitary) subject that moves to different locations or dons different masks over a hardened unitary identity. To the contrary, the point stressed over and over in the *Corónica* is that the subject of enunciation has experienced himself and the world for over 30 years in a whirlwind of epistemological and affective shifts and changes that require multiple acts of re-positioning as well as re-thinking self identity.

---

[1] Gayatri Spivak is not happy with Foucault's theory of the subject, nor is she in accord with Gilles Deleuze's theory of "pluralized subject effects." Spivak writes that "some of the most radical criticism coming out of the West today is the result of an interested desire to conserve the subject of the West, or the West as Subject. The theory of "pluralized subject effects" (271) gives an illusion of undermining subjective sovereignty while often providing cover for this subject of knowledge. Although the history of Europe as Subject is narrativized by the law, political economy and ideology of the West, this concealed subject pretends it has "no geopolitical determinations" (271). Further, Spivak sees in Deleuze and Guatari's theory of desire a hidden move to reintroduce a subject that is the equivalent of the individual, that is to say the sovereign subject that Foucault takes to task in his own critique of the subject. See also Foucault's *Discipline and Punish* and *The History of Sexuality*. For a discussion on the subject in Foucault's thinking see Dreyfus. Of particular interest here, on the question of the subject, is Foucault's essay in that volume "The Subject and Power" (208-226).

The three decade duration of the writing of the letter attests to the multiple explorations of positional identities and not to the donning of masks intended to deceive or play, for the rhetoric of the speaker of the *Corónica* is always cast in a dead serious tone. During such periods of turmoil both internal and external to the subject there has occurred a number of transformative changes (Foucault, "The Subject" 212; Dreyfus and Rabinow, 73-78) particular to the aftermath of conquest in the Andes but previous to the post-Kantian formation of the modern European subject of knowledge. These transformative and disordering circumstances have obliged the Andean subject to produce different positions and identities from which to speak (in fact to write), lest he be silenced by the conquest. To speak for Guamán Poma, means of course, *not* to reproduce as a dominant and unquestioned world view the cosmo-vision and the language of the dominant discourse of the colonial regime, and much less to affirm it without contestation. To write for Guamán Poma as a subject of conquest, not unlike Cortázar's own quest of writing a critique of the realistic novel by writing against the grain of narrative discourse, entails first a labor of dismantling the constituted objects of discourse by analyzing the architecture that holds them together. In order to take apart the entire edifice of the dominant discourse and then to reassemble some of the severed and redefined pieces into a *new* and disturbing object, a great feat of analyses and understanding is required.

This new object, the *Corónica*, on the one hand resembles the parameters and characteristics of the previous, dominant discourse, but on the other hand, it appears disturbingly different and even ironic. The false resemblance is indeed at times parodic, as when Guamán Poma constitutes himself into a subject located within the speaking hierarchy that permits the Pope and the king to rule the world from their discursive positions as sovereigns of the Christian world and of Spain and its domains, respectively. The making of the *Corónica* shows that not all subversive or subaltern subjects are located in the same or similar historical circumstances. Therefore not all low ranking subjects are impeded or enabled in the same ways. And thus while it is questionable that the subaltern subject may speak in the modern, post-Kantian world in which Europe is the subject, it does not follow that by the end of the sixteenth century in the Andes, when modern Europe was just beginning to solidify its grip on the world with the birth of the coloniality of power, subjects like Guamán Poma could not speak in difference, from and for an ironic distance. It follows, rather, that each project for speaking from below bears the marks of the times and of its particular locales. These marks cannot be deleted in the interest of theory. To the contrary, such marks interpolate the universalizing impetus of the theory of the subject no matter the academic positions from which the theory emanates.

In order to intervene in the political and historiographical polemics of the time, polemics that for the Indians were literally a question of life or death, Guamán Poma devises a strategy of cracking the armature of the dominant discourse by identifying the gaps, the discontinuities, the soft spots and the hidden assumptions. In order to identify the gaps and enabling assumptions in the porous discourse of the established knowledges of the European subject, he first had to engage in a long protracted period of study so as to know the structure of the edifice well enough.

In his case, he had to deal with the discourse of evangelization and the law. From the doubly disabled subject position of a Indian non-lettered man he had to figure out, very carefully, where to insert another reason, another subject position, that is to say the subject position that was emerging for him as he conducted his observations and thinking. The enterprise of such a post-conquest subject, at a time when Europe itself was aware, if only for a brief time, of its own internal fissures and fractures as seen in the work of Las Casas and even Vitoria, may be seen to coincide today with a subaltern and indeed subversive position that could muster a voice from both outside—Andean culture—and within—a converted Guamán Poma.

I think that it is important here, in considering the notion of the subject in relation to the tactics and maneuvers that Guamán Poma was devising, to stress that despite Gayatri Spivak's critique of Foucault's theory of the subject, for Foucault the formation of the subject is indivisible from experience. Subject formation is not just a matter of what the discursive regime will allow. Lawrence D. Kritzman points out that in his genealogical analysis Foucault underscores the idea of experience. Foucault "was concerned above all else with the idea of experience. This, he defines as three modes of objectivation (fields of knowledge with concepts, dividing practices or rules, the relationship to one self) through which individuals become subjects" (xviii).

Despite the fact that in *The Order of Things* Foucault does not deal explicitly with the subject, the problematic of the subject is already present there. Although he rejects any kind of teleology and stresses instead discontinuity in history (Dreyfus and Rabinow 73-75), together with the desire to be able to write history without reference to the subject (Mills 34), in dealing with what he terms the archeology of modern man, Foucault differentiates between two stages in modern subject formation: the sovereign or unitary subject and the split subject or the subject-in-crisis. Although Foucault aspired to write genealogies without recourse to the sovereign subject or the individual Cartesian subject, "the subject whose existence depends on its ability to see itself as unique and as self-contained, distinct from others, because it can think and reason" (Mills 33), the differences that he establishes between the sovereign subject and the subject-in-crisis are useful in trying to see how Guamán Poma, as a subject-in-crisis (not post-Cartesian of course) navigates the many subject positions available to him at the birth of the colonial world, that is to say a world turned upside down for post-conquest Andeans like him.[2]

Thus, it is important here to stress that the subject conditions that affect and effect Guamán Poma are directly connected to the disappearance of his world after the conquest and in no way am I implying a parallelism between the shifting and precarious subject positions that Guamán Poma inhabits, with the crisis of modernity in the West and the post-structuralist psychoanalytical recognition of a subject-in-crisis that informs Foucault's refusal of the sovereign subject. What is key here is that Foucault's meditation on the subject-in-crisis leaves the door open for considering other historical experiences from which or within which subjectivities other than the sovereign subject have emerged to constitute themselves into subjects of knowledge.

In "The Subject and Power" Foucault clarifies that rather than power the topic of his investigation has been the subject. He writes that his objective has been to "create a history of the different modes by which, in our culture, human beings are made subjects" (Dreyfus and Rabinow 208). In the same essay he adds that his special interest focuses on the

---

[2] Mills adds that Foucault refused to refer to the subject as unitary in part because of post-structuralist psychoanalysis' own questioning of the unity of the subject. From this point of view, individuals inhabit a wide range of precarious positions, "sometimes willfully adopting particular subject roles and sometimes finding themselves being cast into certain roles because of their past developmental history because of the actions of others... A range of shifting and precarious subject positions means that the subject is no longer seen to be in control" (Mills 34).

transformative role of modes of objectivation: "My work has dealt with the three modes of objectivation which transforms human beings into subjects" (208). However, in order to approach the subject, a consideration of power is first necessary in as much as it is relations of power that constitute the subject. It is the microphysics of power—not the essentialized relation of master and slave—that transform individuals into subjects. Thus, neither power nor the subject constitute positivities for Foucault. The subject is the effect of certain discursive modalities made possible by both power and the will to knowledge. In this context, among the most widespread and powerful modalities of discourse, Foucault argues, is the confession.

First instituted by the early Christian church and later redeployed in secular forms of knowledge and governmentality (Dreyfus and Rabinow 212-216), the technique of the confession by which the self speaks itself, once turned into "pastoral power," migrates to the secular modern world to constitute man "around two roles: one, the globalizing and quantitative, concerning the population; the other, analytical, concerning the individual" (215). Of particular interest in the consideration of the spread of the technique of the confession and pastoral power of evangelization, a situation that Guamán Poma studies in detail some 400 years before the French philosopher, is Foucault's assertion regarding the spread of pastoral power from the particular realm of the Catholic Church into the post-Kantian secular modern world. In closing his considerations on pastoral power, Foucault reflects on how this spread of the technique of confession erased rather than separated the realms of the church and the state:

> The power of a pastoral type, which over centuries—more than a millennium—had been linked to a defined religious institution, suddenly spread out into the whole social body; it found support in a multitude of institutions. And, instead of a pastoral power and a political power, more or less linked to each other, more of less rival, there was an individualizing 'tactic' which characterized a series of powers: those of the family, medicine, psychiatry, education and employers. (215)

On the processes and particular techniques and effects of this spread of pastoral power into daily life Guamán Poma would have had a word or two and many examples to share with Foucault.

Thus, inserted in these discursive conditions, man appears as the subject of his own cognitive experiences with a self awareness that problematizes the "natural" continuation between the things and the words. Foucault, as historian of the European world, looked into the classical world of Greek civilization in order to enlarge the scope of his inquiry into modes of subjectivation. Had he looked into the making of the colonial world in the Andes, he would have found raw and painful first-hand evidence of such an ungluing between the things and the words. But in the Andes such a sense of separation between the things and the world occurred as a consequence of conquest and the need of having to learn a new and strange meaning, not just of the words themselves but of signification as a whole. Cataclysmic events such as the loss of Quechua, and the Andean cultural world imbedded in it, brought about knowledge mutations and offered the ground for the emergence of new subjectivities and knowledges. Dreyfus and Rabinow explain what such a break meant for Europe's subject formation as the object of his own knowledge:

> Once the order of the world was no longer God-given and representable on a table, then the continuous relation that had placed man with the other beings of the world was broken. Man, who was once himself a being among others, now is a subject among others. But Man is not only a subject among objects, he soon realizes that what he is seeking to understand is not only the objects of the world but himself. Man becomes the subject and the object of his own understanding. (28)

(Modern) man, as subject and object of his own understanding, is not so far away from Guamán Poma's own considerations as he writes the history of the des-structuration wrought by the conquest. Wrenched out of his inherited understandings of the cosmos and socio-political world of the Inca empire, he realizes that the strange behaviors unleashed by the conquest call for an investigation and analysis of human beings (being human) as the object of his inquiry. In a manner of speaking, at about the same time on both shores of the Atlantic, after an epistemic break in Europe and the conquest of the Americas in the Andes, there appears the birth of a subject in the position of being both the subject and object of inquiry. In the Andean epistemological break, as the bilingual and bicultural José María Arguedas (1911-1969) later writes, things, feelings, beliefs, objectives, experiences, all appear unglued, alienated, solitary, and unhinged in their non-coincidence with the words.

In this break there appears a subject that knows, who at the same time is always aware that he is being observed in his act of cognition by either "them," or himself as partly constituted by "them." This subject is always aware that he must account to the sovereign subject of knowledge for his cognitive practices for the knowledges that he claims to have and has assumed without sufficient critical distance. This colonial alienated subject of knowledge keeps in mind—to obey or to flaunt—the rules and regulations of the dominant discourse and in doing so sees how his discursive practices bend, irrupt, break, and follow the limits set by his colonial location. The break makes visible the limits of one's situation. It positions the self-conscious subject at the edge of the abyss, a situation from which he or she must begin to move away in different directions.[3]

Conceived as a handful of impossibilities and ambiguities, Foucault sees in the modern construction of man an always open mode of existence, in as much as it he is traversed by a number of limitations. At the closing of *The Order of Things*, Foucault emphasizes the paradoxical constitution of the subject:

> If he is that paradoxical figure in which the empirical contents of knowledge necessarily release, of themselves, the conditions that have made them possible, then that man cannot posit himself in the immediate and sovereign transparency of a *cogito*; nor, on the other hand, can he inhabit the objective inertia of something that, by rights, does not and can never lead to consciousness. Man is a mode of being that accommodates that dimension... always open, never fully delimited, yet constantly traversed. (322)

The multiple objectifications of that modality of being thus constitute the production of the subject. The subject is constituted in that gap in which both the thought and the un-thought meet and rub against one another. The events that take place in this space, at times, exceed the discursive structures and regimes of a given moment or culture. This traversed subject may coincide with the subject of European modernity,

---

[3] Dreyfus and Rabinow point out that Foucault seeks to shows that "with man's attempt to fully affirm his finitude and at the same time to completely deny it, discourse sets up a space in which the analytic of finitude, doomed from the start, twists through a series of futile strategies. Each new attempt will have to claim an identity and a difference between finitude as limitation and finitude as source of all facts, between the positive and the fundamental" (31).

but, when it is a subject-of-and-in crisis, due to the conquest, it is not unlike the subject that emerges of the speaking locations deployed in *El primer nueva corónica y buen gobierno*. In fact, the subject of modernity, as we have inherited it, and compared to Guamán Poma, appears a great deal more integrated and unitary than Foucault would have it, and certainly than how Guamán Poma appears in writing his letter to the king.

Thus, to read Guamán Poma from the assumptions of a unitary and sovereign author-subject is a mistake. Conceiving of the subject in the pages of the Andean letter in the sense of a Foucauldian subject-of-crisis, traversed by the limitations of the paradoxical dimensions of his production of knowledge, which at the same time produces him, may be a more suitable frame in which to understand the Guamán Poma post-conquest enterprise of creating a space to write and be heard. Key to this understanding is the notion that subjects do not "express" a pre-discourse condition, knowledge, identity, or interiority. Rather, a subject is constituted by the discourse modalities and modes in which it appears as such. With these preambles in mind, let us now move to a consideration of the order of the subject in the *Corónica*.[4]

II. "Calles" and the Taxonomy of Confession

My objective here is not to operate at the cusp between the second and third millennium, a reading that reconstructs the text at the moment of its inception (30 long years at least), nor the specific intentions of the person known to us as Guamán Poma de Ayala. Such an attempt at a reconstruction of the text would border into serious anachronism. Moreover, with the category of the "author" as a principle of interpretation, seriously questioned by post-modern theory, especially by Michel Foucault in

---

[4] I reserve further discussion of the subaltern subject for the end of this essay. Here I want to note that, while I acknowledge the impediments noted by Gayatri Spivak, her essay does not really lay out an injunction against the capacity of the subaltern subject to speak. The notion that members of the subaltern class cannot represent themselves is valid only if we accept an essentialist reduction of the subject of knowledge to the European subject, a move that relegates all other subjects to a mere otherness from which, of course, they cannot speak to represent themselves. But that is precisely the point that Guamán Poma's text addresses, how not to become or to speak from the reductive position assigned to a colonial like him by the discourse of conquest.

"What is an Author?" (1977), "author" here is taken chiefly as a function in the structure of signification of the text, a function which nevertheless, as discussed above, emerges traversed by the historical moment that imbricates it. This essay takes into account the historical moment when the writing emerges. It is addressed not to the possible contemporary readers of the letter but rather to the more or less contemporary community of interpreters of Guamán Poma that emerges after the discovery of the text by Richard Pietschmann in 1908.

I propose here to re-imagine the *Corónica* and to think of it not so much as a book but rather as an extensive *tabula* on which one sees the myriad elements that eventually come to constitute the more or less successive linear order of the manuscript. This tabula is thus imagined as a space that allows the subject to lay down a huge assortment of facts, ideas, and interpretations on an ever-growing number of folios, to then gaze upon them and begin developing a taxonomic order capable of wresting intelligibility out of accumulation.

The emblematic scene for the imagined act of cognition appears in the *Corónica* in folio 814 with the figure of the "escrivano de cabildo nombrado por su majestad." In this scene an Andean man, recognizable as such because of the style of his hair, headdress, and clothing sits at a table in the act of writing.

Besides the sheet of paper on which he writes, there are on the table four other objects whose referents are not easily or incontestably identified. Touching or surrounding a pen holder on the left side of the viewer, there appears a double rope that ends in a solid object. This could be taken to be a handle for the rope, or for a wrapped *quipu* head. In the middle of the table, there appears a set of strung beads laid out in a rectangular fashion and also dividing the table into two hemispheres. At first sight the set of beads seems to be a rosary, with perhaps a cross at the head of it. However, next to the cross there is another pending object suggesting another interpretation of the object's identity and relations. Maybe it is not a rosary but actually the accountant's one-string *quipu*. On the right side, in one corner, there is a small square object that could be taken to be the inkwell, and in front of it, farthest away from the "escrivano," there is what could be taken to be a rim of paper. The location of the rim of paper is right across from what could be the wrapped-up *quipu*. Inside the frame of the drawing and right next to the head of the man is written "quilcacamayoc." On the other side of the head of the man and across from the space written as "quilcacamayoc" there is a book stand with books arranged in different positions, indicating that it is a library in use. On the outside of the frame of the drawing, in the same right field of viewing, the word "escrivano" appears as a kind of classifying label for the entire scene.

The scene speaks of the "quilcacamayoc-escribano," who, having brought together the material and intellectual instruments necessary for his accounting, is depicted in the process of rendering the world into an order of intelligibility. The obligations of the "quilcacamayoc-escribano" consist of keeping a correct accounting of the existence of things and making sure that justice prevails in the act of distributing goods of all kinds (material, social, symbolic) to people in accordance with the law and the established costume and the "ordenanzas de Dios y de su majestad" (folio 815). Correct and minute accounting of things and acts according to a classificatory order is for Guamán Poma the foundation of the order of the world, and thus harmony and prosperity. Accounting and classification knowledge protects the "quilcacamayoc-escribano" and the system itself from the abuses of all the other Crown officials. His discourse, backed by the indisputable evidence of numbers (*quipu* records) and writing, trumps all other modes of representation. Guamán Poma observes and recommends that:

> ualga su testimonio como de real o publico, que para que dé fe y autorize y de testimonio, para que a los señores excelentísimos bizorreyes y la audiencia real y justicia de su Majestad. I anci no tema del dicho corregidor, ni a su teniente, ni a jues seglares como eglesisasticos, becitaroes, comenderos ni tenga tanta facultad como un jues rreceptor. (folio 815)

Within this exhaustive taxonomic and accounting order brought about by the conjunction of *quipu* techniques of knowledge and the power of alphabetic writing, a subject of knowledge makes its appearance. This subject is not only aware of his position in a new, colonial order of things, but is also willing and ready to manipulate that position and the available discursive positions for himself ("quilcacamayoc-escribano") to speak from a position of power so as to be perhaps rejected, but also heard. The subject in the *Corónica* appears keenly aware that the rules of discourse to which he is subject exist right next to a juridical discourse that both forbids him to speak, given his status as Indian, and at the same time allows him to speak due to his newly acquired Christian identity. This subject can be labeled colonial, post-colonial, subaltern, or subversive. All these labels offer a sense of what takes place in the *Corónica* and its importance for understanding the formation of the colonial-modernity duality, better theorized now under the notion of the coloniality of power. But what I am trying to show here is the play of inversions, the deployment of categories, and the manipulation of discursive modalities and positions that enable the appearance of order out of the material, physical, and epistemological chaos and disorder into which the conquest plunged the Andean world. In short, such an emergence can be called the Andean post-conquest subject.

The frontispiece or "portada" of the *Corónica* manipulates and combines visual (Andean and European) codes of representation with the codes of alphabetic writing, in order to integrate, that is to say organize, in a single scene his conception of how the organization of power, given the irremediable fact of conquest by Christians, should evolve in this new, post-conquest world order.

Looking at the frontispiece from a European perspective on the organization of space, the space of the drawing appears to have been divided into three vertical columns which are at the same time traversed by three horizontal lines. One could think that the space is divided into nine squares (3X3). Inside each of the squares, as in a *tokapu*, there is a figure, but these figures do not fit into the same taxonomic class. Rather, they are a combination of emblematic human figures (Pope, prince, Andean prince, in vertical descending order) and heraldic figures (in vertical descending order also). Further, each human figure appears to be set on a different ground so that the sense of discontinuity between each square (*tokapu*) and its contents comes to dominate the first, and even the second, viewing of the scene of the frontispiece.

However, the eye is clearly drawn to the center of the space where a strong line of division is marked by the three vertically distributed heraldic shields of honor. The up and down movement of this central line allows the viewer to find a correspondence between each shield and human figure next to it at the horizontal level, so that soon an order begins to appear out of the disorder of the nine squares (*tokapus*). The Pope, his shield, and his title (S.C.R.M) appear at the top horizontal line, followed by the European prince, his shield and his crown in the middle. At the bottom of the scene, on a different ground altogether, there appears the Andean prince, his shield, and his everyday hat (not a princely head dress).

Further examination of the shields reveals that indeed what the page shows is the Pope in Rome, his Sacred Majesty, the Spanish King of Castile and Aragon, and a shield that emblematizes Guamán Poma's name conceived and drawn in the European heraldic traditions. This shield presents a space divided into two fields. In the left hemisphere there is a bird of prey (hawk or "huamán") and on the right there is an American lion (puma). The nine *tokapus*, seemingly in disarray due to the fact that they could not be read in a left to right series of continuity or subject matter, become readable once put in place by the top to bottom (*quipu* strands?) series of the heraldic shields. The arrangement of the heraldic shields yields an order that spells out the new juridical and governmental organization that Guamán Poma believes should operate in the new world, or as he labels the scene, "el reino de las Indias." Thus, from the opening page on, what we have is the result of the manipulation of discourses and subject positions that the whole of the *Corónica* makes manifest so as to produce an order of taxonomies capable of organizing the disarray of the conquest.

The alphabetic text of the *Corónica* begins on the back of the frontispiece. It marks the staring point for a series of short texts placed in contiguity by a topical or taxonomic logic that underscores the notion of succession in a series. Each series could in turn be thought of as an accountant's column. Guamán Poma himself calls these series of series "calles," and it is not far fetched to think that each series could stand for a vertically knotted string or category in a *quipu*. The subject of enunciation explicitly situates his text between two discursive types: confessionary and manuals for the performance of the "visitas."[5] Both of these manuals consist of lists of questions as well as lists of topics about which to conduct inquiries in the interest of developing knowledge about other subjects. The *visitador* needed to investigate the contents of the subject's spiritual interiority. The inquiry also focused on the subject's knowledge about the physical and social world. Both are manuals for interrogation. Guamán Poma informs his reader that his *Corónica*, like the manuals for confession, is not only good for preparing for confession—on the part of the confessor as well as on the part of the penitent—but it is especially "provechoso" (useful) for the Indians to do their confessions and thus for "enmienda de sus vidas y herronias, y idulatrias" (folio 1). The *Corónica*, however does not stop here. Its ambition and purposes are greater than being an aid to confession and leading a virtuous life. This text is particularly useful to master the knowledge necessary to administer confession to Indians properly ("para saber confesarlos") and to find out and learn about other things ("para saber otras cosas") as well (folio 2).

In ordering confessional knowledge and its techniques ("saber confesarlos") there appear other discursive objects. Among them juridical knowledge takes a prominent place as it defines the social and subject positions of individuals. With its exhaustive interventions by way of laws, ordinances, prohibitions, and punishments, juridical discourse affects directly the formation and placement of the subject in the postconquest world. What is more, juridical discourse is directly tied to the techniques of confession, punishment, and penitence of the Catholic rites and establishes a direct and indispensable nexus between religion and political life. Guamán Poma introduces the question of confession at the very outset of his huge text because he recognizes that the technique of question-and-answer that yields a panoply of knowledges is crucial to the establishment of the regimes of the new colonial order and the colonial subject that concomitantly emerges.

[5] A "visita" was a special investigation undertaken by an official of the crown to villages and *corregimientos*. A general *visita* focused on a whole *audiencia* or viceroyalty. This inquiry generally resulted in an extensive report to the appropriate authorities and often juridical action in favor of, or against, loyal or trespassing subjects of the crown which ensued after the *visita* (Tenenbaum 428).

The kneeling position of the subject before a higher ranking person repeats itself in various and different stories as the letter begins to gather direction and force. From the first drawing in which both the European and the Andean prince kneel down before the Pope, to the drawing telling the story of the creation of Adam and Eve (folio 12), passing through the scene entitled "como Dios ordenó la dicha historia," that supposedly tells how God ordered the writing of his *Corónica* (folio 14), onto the scene in which "padre Martíin de Ayala" preaches the gospel (folio 17) and then following onto the "ejemplo del padre caecedo, penitencia" (folio 19), all introductory drawings are organized on the discursive principles of the confessional.

Guamán Poma's analysis of the discursive principles of the confessional and the relations of power to discursive formations, in a way, antecede Foucault's own understanding of confession as the cradle for the birth of the subject as well as pastoral power. Foucault characterizes pastoral power as the principle that postulates that "certain individuals can, by their religious quality, serve others, not as princes, magistrates, prophets, fortune-tellers, benefactors, educationalists, and so on, but as pastors...it implies a knowledge of the conscience and an ability to direct it" (Foucault, "The Subject" 214). In Foucault's genealogy, what is born by the transposition of confession into other discursive instances characteristic of the ensuing secular world is the modern subject. Foucault writes that: "Power of a pastoral type, which for centuries—for more than a millennium—had been linked to a defined religious institution, suddenly spread out into the whole social body" (215). This pastoral power "found support" in many social institutions and instead of creating a rival relation between political and religious power, it brought them closer together (215). Evangelization and conquest in the Andes performed a similar coupling of the religious and political power to regulate subjectivity (28).

Of course, like Foucault, but from a very different angle, Guamán Poma sees in the tactic of the confession the birth of something heretofore unknown to him. But since for Guamán Poma such a birth is contemporary with him, and modernity as such had yet to be identified as a historical period, the subject that Guamán Poma sees emerging cannot be called modern. Colonial/modern may be a useful nomenclature from our vantage point. Nevertheless, the point here is that Guamán Poma identifies and analyzes correctly the birth of a discursive subject, a position from which he, as a post-conquest person can speak, due to the nature of the confessional apparatus for inquiry and production. Guamán Poma, unlike Foucault's account of Europe's modern theory, suffers no illusion. He sees clearly the discursive power of the pastoral move that entrusts people for life in the care of those who, as in (modern) therapy, ask questions and thus attempt to direct their lives. Precisely because he understands such pastoral power very clearly he starts the letter by enticing the king, suggesting that his book can be used for better interrogating the Indians. Nevertheless he ends by suggesting that all would be well if the king himself, the sovereign (*pecador*), would submit also and "voluntarily" engage, under the pastoral guidance of Guamán Poma, the same type of pastoral inquiry in order to gain knowledge and understanding of the destruction that he is fostering in the Andes. With this suggestion Guamán Poma has of course reversed the tables, for it is he who will administer the powers of inquiry and care of the pastoral power.

What is more, Guamán Poma seems to have a clear understanding of the productive aspect of confession which, along with the techniques of psychotherapy, constitute, for Foucault, the bedrock of the production of the modern subject. Drawing on his understanding of sin and its connection to the body as a desiring machine, (lust, cupidity, avarice, rage, theft) Guamán Poma informs us that during the Fourth age, there were no "pecadores de conciencia" (folio 56). What Andean ethics and systems of political organization punished was behavior, for if it postulated an interior to each person it was not a space where the gaze of another could enter and interpret. Thus, to criticize the Inca ("murmurar contra el Inca"), steal, and commit adultery were social transgressions that did not need long inquiries into the conscience of the person. People were found guilty or innocent. If guilty, these crimes were severely punished with nothing less than death. Therefore, in Guamán Poma's interpretation of the Andean subject, most people were innocent, as there was really no such thing as sin and thus there could not be spiritual punishments. This argument bears direct relevance to the persecution of people in the 1560's in the Andes, when the evangelizing priests and the state rounded up people, asking that they confess the sin ("herronías") of secretly worshiping the *wakas*. To any Andean, this notion of a secret, sinful self seemed an absurd idea.

Guamán Poma's understanding of the centrality of the technique of confession in the production of new knowledges, but above all new subject positions of power, is thus *his* unique discovery of a key aspect in European political formations that he seeks to harness as the principle for organizing the new colonial world. Confession is deployed by Guamán Poma as an equalizer. It is not just for the colonizer to use. It is a strategy that allows the colonized to gaze into the interiority of the powerful and have them confess, that is, to produce themselves as Christian sinners. Unlike Foucault, Guamán Poma sees how the pastoral move can work both ways and produce in a space of struggle and negotiation, a sort of uncomfortable dialogue.

In the discipline of confession Guamán Poma finds the techniques and the legitimation that the sovereign confers upon him in order to gaze and delve into the newly proclaimed and universalized interiority of all subjects in the world. Thus he empowers himself to bring under his purview everything and subject it to a discursive apparatus that in Europe is producing man as individual and in the post-conquest Andes produces a fragmented, self-discontinuous, contesting subject capable of negotiating and occupying several positions (pluri valences) at the same time. Thus, from the very first scene in which the letter portrays kneeling persons addressing each other in relations of sovereignty and subalternity, the *Corónica* comes to occupy the place of a great general confession. The subject of this ritual says everything he knows, and at times also includes what he does not know, or even the un-thought. He offers a totality of knowledges for the scrutiny of the confessor (reader) who will in turn become the interpreter and thus maker of bridges (pontical) to the truth. But confession should not be confused with stream of consciousness or some other chaotic running of speech acts. Confession is indeed a well articulated order of discourse. The tactics of silence and omission are indeed constitutive of the confession, an order of thinking and speaking marked by its own taxonomy. Transferring the order of confession to his tabula, and informed by the classification categories of the *quipu*, Guamán Poma reclassifies, erases, omits, and repeats as he seeks an all encompassing order for his enunciation.

In his scenes, he represents the pattern of power relations between those who, with books (folio 13), torture, horses (folio 14), clothing, and arms, inquire into the interiority of others and obligate them to say their confession, to tell the "truth" of their possessions, the location of rich *waka* burials along with the true character of their beliefs and desires. Guamán Poma sets forth a series of spectacles with each of his drawings in that each inscribes a story of coercion and vigilance, underscored by the notion that the state is entitled to have as full a knowledge of a person as the very tactics of vigilance and coercion will permit. Confession (folios 592,445-6), "becita," "hechiceros" (folio 252), punishments (folios 277,464,466,510), the banquet (folio 469), the voyeur (folio 467), the punishment of adulterers (folio 280, 287), and obedience (folio 442), are all examples of the deployment of power over the body in order to acquire access to the new interiority brought in by the technique and order of the confession.

In *Discipline and Punish* (1978), Foucault states that the essential techniques of discipline spread from one institution to another in part by the transplantation of minuscule and meticulous methods (139). All these techniques, as Guamán Poma also notes in his own disciplinary scenes, define "a certain mode of detailed political investment of the body" (139). This "micro-physics of power" (139), has, according to Foucault, reached out, since the seventeenth century, "to ever broader domains, as if they tended to cover the entire social body" (139). It is clear, if one follows Guamán Poma's gaze, which in turn reconnoiters the gaze of the evangelizing priests and secular authorities, that such a micro-physics of power is already in full swing in the Andes a full fifty years before the dawn of the seventeenth century. In the Andes, such vigilance has also developed by riding on the shoulders of the technique of confession. Both Foucault and Guamán Poma record and analyze the "mutation of a punitive system" (139). Describing such a mutation, writes Foucault, will require great attention to detail, for "they are the acts of cunning, not so much of the great reason, that work even in its sleep and gives meaning to the insignificant, as of the attentive 'malevolence' that turns everything to account. Discipline is a political anatomy of detail" (139). In this context, it can be said that, avant Foucuault, *El primer nueva corónica y buen gobierno* does indeed carry out a work of great attention to detail, to the rules of taxonomy that allow for the distribution of meaning on the table where the infinite presentations of malevolence have been laid out.

Thus in the *Corónica* Guamán Poma confesses. He lays out the details of all the practices he has observed and considered in order to begin to understand. His confession is only the pre-amble to hearing the king's own and vaster confession. For Guamán Poma to write is to deploy the all enveloping tactics of the confession. To write is also to cry, for the general survey that precedes confession not only reveals the multitude of forgotten or unidentified sins, but also the details of a deeply sinful world. However, to confess is at the same time to have the ability to order, and to order is the beginning of understanding as things become visible and accessible to thinking. In *Discipline and Punish* Foucault writes that the examination previous to confession brings about a "compulsory visibility" on those whom it subjects (187). He further writes: "Their visibility assures the hold of the power that is exercised over them. It is the fact of being constantly seen that maintains the disciplined individual in his subjection" (187).

To order is to begin to understand the many dispositions for doing violence to the body of Andeans and thus disciplining them into the colonial order. Guamán Poma analyzes the practices that classify, locate, divide, and regulate bodies in the fabric of the social organization. Making use of a technique that the sovereign puts in his hands—question and answer—Guamán Poma traces back the logic of the cultural practices that once were considered "natural" and are now demonized and therefore subject to confession, to a sense of sinfulness. Thus, the subject of this general confession reclassifies objects of discourse often in search of new taxonomies that will avoid the Spanish's own ongoing reclassification of cultural practices into sins. For instance, making use of his taxonomic "calles," the Andean philosopher is placed not next to the *amauta* or the *quipucamayok*, but rather next to the "hechicero." Guamán Poma thus places the Andean philosopher in the column of the dark and evil knowledges that the Spanish feared. Once he describes the practices of both the philosopher and the "hechicero," he clearly distances himself from both (folio 252). He further clarifies that he came about such forbidden knowledge when, in his capacity of translator for the extirpator of idolatries Cristóbal de Albornoz (1530-1610),[6] he interviewed some such "hechiceros." As in other confessions, with his confession he also accuses and implicates others in wrong doing.

The precise taxonomic exigencies of confession invite a series of questions for and from Guamán Poma and his interlocutors. Is it a sin to look in on a couple making love (as he describes that some Spaniards have taken to doing, and by implication he and the reader-viewer do)? Is it a sin to touch the body of a woman? How about desiring such a touch? Is

---

[6] For a discussion of the life and activities of Cristóbal de Albornoz in the Andes see Guibovich 23-40.

it a sin to imagine the couple having sex? And how about selling the woman into concubinage with a priest or Crown official (folio 467)?

Guamán Poma does not trust the word alone. Each example must be drawn into a scene where contexts can be made doubly visible. Only the certainty of exact classifications can allow the subject to make the correct confession and thus "descargar" his conscience (folio 1117). Indeed, correcting behavior entirely depends now on the confession properly executed, and such a correction is the ultimate justification for the entire system, not the acquisition of power over the subject of confession. In fact, that erroneous idea itself needs to be corrected.

The strange mixtures of topics that occur in Guamán Poma's table are in part due to the insufficiency of the classificatory parameters available. Such problems are probably also due to the inoperative system of punishments. Since the visibility brought about by the confessional makes everything the object and subject of suspicion (anticipating the modernity analyzed by Foucault), a guide is necessary in order to navigate this new space of sinfulness. In this first analysis of the effects of the technique of confession as a universal approach to knowledge, Guamán Poma demands that the pastoral function of the post-Trent priest and various representatives of the king be properly discharged in order to produce and sustain order. In "The Subject and Power" Foucault spells out the characteristics of pastoral power:

1. It is a form of power whose ultimate aim is to assure individual salvation in the next world.
2. Pastoral power is not merely a form of power that commands; it must also be prepared to sacrifice itself for the life and salvation of the flock. Therefore, it is different from royal power, which demands a sacrifice from its subjects to save the throne.
3. It is a form of power which does not look just after the whole community, but each individual in particular, during his entire life.
4. This is a form of power that cannot be exercised without knowing the inside of people's minds, without exploring their souls, without making them reveal their inner most secrets. It implies a knowledge of the conscience and an ability to direct it. (214)

In view of the scope of the field of operations and objective of pastoral power, it is clear that Guamán Poma not only describes it accurately in his *Corónica*, but also deploys it so as to acquire the ability to direct the conscience of both the conquered Andeans and their Spanish conquerors. That is why his appeal is also both to the Pope and to the king, the highest ranking pastors in the world.

In this context, his daring to portray naked bodies and sexual encounters of various kinds is not at all sacrilegious, but rather part and parcel of the knowledges under the purview of confession and necessary for the pastor to intervene in saving the souls under his charge. The self-styled Andean prince mobilizes the question of sexual practices at the precise moment in the order of his discourse; that is to say at the point where discourse on sex intersects with a discourse on power by way of the punishment allotted for each kind of transgression. In one of the earliest scenes in the *Corónica* Guamán Poma presents the problem of self-castigation (folio 14). There is a man kneeling down, naked to the waist, castigating his body with a set of whips. With a beatific expression on his face, the man carries out his own laceration under the agonizing gaze of a crucified Christ. The two half naked, visibly suffering bodies, make their sacrificial offering before a divinity absent from the represented space, but whose gaze organizes the meaning of the event in the scene. Behind the half naked kneeling man there is another man. This figure is also kneeling. His hands folded in the gesture of prayer and pleading hold a crucifix. This man watches the offering made by the other two. In contrast with the Christ and the self flagellating man, the observer (watchman) is fully clothed. In this scene no one speaks. In contrast with the confession, the ritual of penitence takes place in silence, with the body in full consciousness. It is not enough to "say." Bodily discipline is indispensable for turning knowledge into a thing capable of discharging ("descargar la consciencia") conscience/consciousness.

There is no question that Guamán Poma understands—avant Foucault—that it is the combination of the confession with the discipline of the bodies and souls that engages the processes of subjectivation under way in the post-conquest Andes. Reading Foucault is sometimes to imagine that he had read Guamán Poma, and reading Guamán Poma is to see Foucault's arguments converted into scenes in the *Corónica*. It is astounding to see how both Guamán Poma and Foucault, at a distance greater than the 400 years that separate them, show how confession and discipline are integrated in a vast structure of domination. Dreyfus and Rabinow remind us that for Foucault "power is not strict violence or pure coercion, but the interplay of techniques of discipline and less obvious technologies of the self... the belief that one can, with the aid of experts [in the law, in education, in love] tell the truth about one self" (175).[7] To this list one would have to add not only ethnography, but especially auto-ethnography, as is the case with Guamán Poma and the production of the subject in the pages of his letter.

[7] On the spread of the techniques of the confessional from the Church onto other institutions, Dreyfus and Rabinow write that "As early as the 16th century the confessional techniques unmoored themselves from purely religious contexts and began to spread to other domains, first pedagogy, then the prisons and other institutions of confinement" (176).

III. THE DIALOGIC ORDER OF THE SUBJECT

On his own then, Guamán Poma detaches and unmoors the technique of the question-and-answer that he observes not only in the confession, but also in the collecting of Andean historical memory that Pedro Sarmiento de Gamboa (1530-1608) is asked by the Vicerroy Toledo to carry out in order to write a non-Inca based history of the empire. As the materials issue forth from the interviews and the *quipus*, handled by those *amautas* and *quipucamayoc* interviewed as well as the personal memory of many more *quipucamayoc* and *amautas*, Guamán Poma sets out to find a place for each item in an exhaustive taxonomy. On his tabula, there emerges a globalizing classificatory rationality that allows the subject to switch places back and forth between the position of the subaltern subject that answers the questions and the sovereign subject who posses the questions. In this text, this colonial subject knows how to play the game in both positions. This game, however, is not a simple and closed back and forth. A third, fourth, and even a fifth position of enunciation appear to open as the subject/object of the question learns to anticipate the answer that the sovereign subject is after and thus for his interpellated position proceeds to furnish an answer that could open up a cascade of divergences and, indeed, new questions. In this play, new, unknown topics may come up for scrutiny, and as they do their appearance disturbs the order of the sovereign subject. In this case, the respondent, as in the *Corónica*, has a chance to take the lead, to get ahead of the sovereign and thus escape across the limits imposed on him as subaltern subject by the dominant discourse. Indeed, Guamán Poma's discursive enterprise entails the dismantling of the essentialist reduction of the subject of knowledge to Europe, in order to set in place the building blocks from which to speak as a post-conquest subject whose subalternity he puts into question.

What is more, in his letter Guamán Poma often appears to be furnishing answers to absent questioners, thus leaving the reader to infer the question to which an answer has been formulated. In this instance, the position of the questioner is interdicted by the answer. Thus, the subject who speaks in the *Corónica* appears to wield a good deal of autonomy and initiative. In fact, he appears as the autonomous author and subject of his discourse.

This authorial autonomous subject that emerges out of the technique of the confession and the give and take of the question-and-answer eventually gains the capacity to turn the discourse of self-accusation into a discourse in which it is the sovereign who is not only interpellated, but is in fact accused by the penitent of failing in the production of himself as the pastor. In the dialogic relation Guamán Poma produces by making use of the confession, the Andean self-fashioned "autor" produces the taxonomical list of failures of the pastoral mission by pointing over and over to a deficient juridical and ethical realm of action instituted by the colonial regime. The order that the subject requires demands that, for instance, the Spanish apply to themselves, with the same attention to detail, the same punishments that they codify and indeed apply to the Indians. The Christian claim that as children of God we are all created equal should, for Guamán Poma, start and end with the appropriate juridical order in which both the means of production and material and cultural administration are rendered onto the Andeans, who, for historical reasons, have an understanding of equal access and distribution.

In conclusion, it is fair to say that having scrutinized the workings of the technology of the confession to produce an account of the post-conquest world that envelops his life, the subject that emerges out of the pages of the new *Corónica* is a subject that is made possible by the taxonomic discourses of both the confession and the *quipu*, for in both there is a thrust to classify, to produce stable objects contained in their classes, and to contemplate the possibility of eventual mixings and matchings according to new insights into new classes or the classificatory grid itself. In this self-ascribed task of producing the world by means of taxonomies, the subject appears, not as a dampened and limited subaltern subject but rather as an active and interpolating subject capable of "pontificar" more than one order of discourse. Above all it is the order of the subject, his capacity to identify and manipulate, that enables him to speak, despite the break of the conquest and the injunctions on his subaltern position.

An earlier and smaller version of this essay was originally published in Spanish as "El orden del sujeto en Guamán Poma" in *Revista de Crítica Literaria Latinoamericana* Año XX, No 41. Lima-Berkeley, 1995, 121-134. Another version was published in Sara Castro-Klarén: *Escritura, transgresion y sujeto en la literatura latinoamericana*. Mexico: Premiá, 1989. This is a newly expanded and revised text.

Works Cited

Castro-Klarén, Sara. «Ontological Fabulation: Toward Cortázar's Theory of Literature.» *The Final Island: The Fiction of Julio Cortázar.* Ed. Jaime Alazraki. Norman: University of Oklahoma Press, 1976. 140-151.

Dreyfus, Hubert L. and Paul Rabinow. *Michel Foucault: Beyond Structuralism and Hermeneutics.* Chicago: The University of Chicago Press, 1982.

Foucault, Michel. *Discipline and Punish.* New York: Pantheon Books, 1977.

—. *The Order of Things.* New York: Pantheon Books, 1970.

—. "The Subject and Power." *Michel Foucault: Beyond Structuralism and Hermeneutics* by Hubert L. Dreyfus and Paul Rabinow. Chicago: The University of Chicago Press, 1982.

Guamán Poma de Ayala, Felipe. *Nueva corónica y buen gobierno.* Ed. Franklin Pease. 2 vols. Caracas: Biblioteca Ayacucho, 1980.

Kritzman, Lawrence D. Introduction. *Politics, Philosophy, Culture: Interviews and Other Writings, 1977-1984.* By Michel Foucault. Ed. Lawrence D. Kritzman. London: Routledge, 1988.

Miller, James. *The Passion of Michel Foucault.* Cambridge: Harvard University Press, 1993.

Mills, Sara. *Discourse.* London: Routledge, 1997.

Spivak, Gayatri. «Can the Subaltern Speak?» *Marxism and the Interpretation of Culture.* Ed. Cary Nelson and Lawrence Grossberg. Urbana: University of Illinois Press, 1989. 271-313.

Tenenbaum, Barbara A., ed. *Encyclopedia of Latin American History and Culture.* Vol. V. New York: Charles Scribner and Son's, 1996.

CHAPTER 3
Dancing and the Sacred in the Andes: From the Taqui-Oncoy to Rasu-Ñiti

If we assume that the Andean peoples interpreted the Spanish Conquest of the Inca Empire as a Pachacuti—a cyclical destruction and restoration of the world[1]—we can view the Andean cosmos as a place of articulation, revision, and response to the challenge of Colonial rule. This assumption lets us step outside the European frame of reference for an understanding of cultural formations in the Andes.

There is no question that the arrival of the Spanish in 1532 meant disaster in the lives of the Andeans. But Andean society did not collapse and simply accept Spanish Colonial rule. Resistance and accommodation, even cooperation, marked the complex dynamics that ensued after 1532 in the Inca Empire. Examining Andean responses, the French ethno-historian Nathan Wachtel writes:

> Defeat was experienced as a catastrophe of cosmic dimensions... The clash coincided with the death of the son of the Sun, the Inca. He constituted the mediating point between the gods and men, and he was worshiped as a god. In some way represented the bodily center of the universe. He was the guarantor of the harmony of the universe. Once that center was murdered, the living point of reference in the world disappeared. Universal order is thus brutally destroyed.[2] (*Los vencidos* 58)

---

[1] The cycle of Pachacuti was thought to occur roughly every five hundred years. For a discussion of the Pachacuti in Andean ideology, see Pease. For the ways in which the idea of a Pachacuti intersects with the Christian idea of the Last Judgment, see MacCormack.

[2] This and all subsequent translations from Spanish are mine. The American historian Steve Stern has a similar focus on the Andean response; see his book *Peru's Indian*

Wachtel describes the Taqui-Oncoy, the cult and ritual of the sick dance that sprang up in 1565, as one of several Andean responses to the collapse of the Inca empire. He views the Taqui-Oncoy as a form of social resistance to the imposition of foreign rule and systematic dismantling of the Andean world. Wachtel calls this a period of "destructuration":

> Spanish domination, while making use of Inca institutions, also caused their demise. This decomposition did not, however, mean the birth of a new universe radically different from the old one. On the contrary, it involved *destructuration*, which we understand as the survival of ancient structures or partial elements of these but displaced from the relatively coherent context in which they used to function. (*Los vencidos* 135)

In this chapter I examine the discourse of the sacred implied in the practice and preaching of the Taqui-Oncoy and analyze the semiotic elements by which this cult addresses the experience of destructuration. My use of the term *discourse* is informed by Michel Foucault's *Archaeology of Knowledge*. Discourse is constituted by a group of statements, which in turn are not merely traces but modalities that allow groups of signs to exist "in relation with a domain of objects and [prescribe] a definite position to any possible subject" (Foucault 107). Foucault's principle of dispersion and redistribution of statements in discursive formations is pertinent here. Also, I indicate how the presence and cult of the *huacas*—exceptional features of the visible universe that represent the sacred and its connection to ancestry and descent[3]—continues, though transformed, to the present day as in the case

---

Peoples and the Challenge of the Spanish Conquest, Huamanga to 1640, as well as his chapter in Wachtel's *Sociedad e ideología, ensayos de historia y antropología andina.*

[3] In 1621 the Spanish priest José de Arriaga (1564-1622), in trying to understand the objects and rites of worship in the Andes, listed the sun, the moon, and the Pleiades, then added *huacas*:

They also worship and reverence the high hills and mountains and huge stones. They have names for them and numerous fables about their changes and metamorphoses. Saying that they were once men who have changed to stone... these are all *huacas* that they worship as gods... and every child who has learned to talk knows the name of the *huaca* of his clan. For every clan and faction has a principal *huaca*... and members of the clan take the name of the community *huaca*. Some *huacas* are thought as guardians and advocates of the town. (22-25)

Among twentieth-century sources, María Rostworowski de Diez Canseco comments in her superb study of religious ideology and politics in pre-Hispanic Peru that

of the scissor dancer (*danzak de tijeras*). Finally, I outline the links between the ritual of the Taqui-Oncoy and the ritual of the scissor dancer.

Before delving into the history of the religious cult and ritual dance of the Taqui-Oncoy, we need to examine the meaning of this name. In Quechua *taqui* refers to a variety of songs and ritual dances. There were historical *taquis* as well as *taquis* especially dedicated to the agricultural calendar. *Taqui* makes special reference to song and its contents. *Oncoy* means sick or sickness. It also refers to the Pleiades, who were among the major deities in the Andean pantheon. The complex Andean astrological knowledge associates the cycles of the Pleiades (before the rainy season), with the emergence of certain pestilences. Thus, the association of the Taqui-Oncoy (Oncoy=Pleiades) with sickness. The Andean calendar marked several dates for festivities and ceremonies dedicated to the prevention of sickness or other catastrophes. The rituals of the Ytu and the Situa ceremonies are best known in the prevention of disasters associated with the rise of the Pleiades (Varón Gabai 371-377). Besides fasting and sexual abstinence, the pre-Hispanic ritual demanded the expulsion of all foreigners or outsiders in order to ensure the efficacy of the cleansing ritual (403). It is thus not surprising that the Taqui-Oncoy priests would attempt to revive this ritual in order to cure the sickly *huacas* and restore health to the dying Andeans, who, in paroxysm of the dance were said to receive the reinvigorating force of the *huacas*.

In one of his few references to the *taqui oncoy*, Guamán Poma de Ayala, a convert to Christianity, wrote that false shamans could make people sick by sucking their blood while the victims slept. They also sucked blood from the victims' bodies in order to cure them of "the sickness of the *taqui oncoy*" (Guamán Poma de Ayala 1:253).[4] He listed *taqui oncoy* along with seven other sicknesses that shamans treated by sucking blood in order to draw out disease. These illnesses all seem to exceed the strict dimensions of the physiological in both cause and symptoms, for they involve the psychological phenomenon of utter fright, terror, hyste-

---

Andean beliefs lacked both the abstract idea of God and a word to express it but had a strong sense of the sacred; "the word for this was *guaca*" (9). The glossary to Stern's *Peru's Indian Peoples* defines Waká as a native Andean God; a sacred being or spirit, often thought of as an ancestor, and materialized in the form of hills, waters, stones, or ancestors' mummies" (262).

[4] For a penetrating study of shamanism in Peru, see Chiappi; Rostworowski 10-11.

ria, or hallucination. Their names alone reveal the psychosomatic conception of the illness and the cure. For example, *chirapa uncuy* is the sickness
caused by the vision of rain with sunshine; *pucuy oncuy* is the sickness
caused by a water spring; *cápac uncuy* is the sickness caused by major
calamity; the *uaca macasca* refers to the state of being wounded by a
guaca. It is important to note that these diagnoses rest on the notion of
having been robbed of or hurt in one's vital force (*cama-quen*—an
Andean concept incorrectly translated as "soul" and better understood as
the energizer of life.

The so-called dancing sickness that Cristóbal de Albornoz, an almost
totally unknown Spanish priest and visitor, discovered in 1564 was extirpated in less than three years after more than eight thousand Andeans had
been accused and condemned for "idolatry" by the energy and zeal of the
campaign led by Albornoz (Stern 51). This extirpation of the Taqui-
Oncoy preceded the better-known and more thoroughly destructive
campaigns of 1610 to 1620 by some fifty years.[5] Although the center of
the Taqui-Oncoy was Huamanga, the cult had converts in Cuzco, Arequipa, Lima, and even La Paz. Some Spanish contemporaries of the
Taqui-Oncoy accused the rebel Inca in Vilcabamba, Titu Cusi Yupanqui,
of promoting this "apostasy" (Wachtel, *Los vencidos* 284).

The cult's preachers announced the end of Spanish domination. The
guacas, they said, were alive and were coming back to fight against Dios.
The *guacas* were already expelling the Spaniards and their Dios. These
local deities demanded the allegiance of their people, who must therefore
not go into churches, listen to evangelizing priests, eat Spanish food, or
dress in Spanish clothing, under threat of being turned into animals.

The sixteenth-century Spanish chronicler Cristóbal de Molina called
the Taqui-Oncoy a "sect" and reported:

> They thought that all the *guacas* of the kingdom, all such that the Christians
> had defeated and burned, had come back to life and had divided themselves
> into two groups. One group had gathered around the deity Pachacamac, and

---

[5] Alberto Flores Galindo writes: "Between 1610 and 1660, three campaigns to
extirpate idolatries were unleashed on the peoples of the central highlands after a
criollo (an indigenous person of Spanish descent) priest discovered that behind the
pious celebrations of the Virgin of the Assumption there hid the worship of Pariacaca
and Chaupiñamacc, two ancient pre-Hispanic deities" (90).

the other around Titicay. All of them were going about in the air giving orders to wage battle unto Dios in order to defeat him. [They said] that when they were about to win, that when the marquess [Francisco Pizarro] entered this land, Dios had vanquished the *guacas* and the Spaniards [had defeated] the Indians; but that now the world was turning and thus Dios and the Spaniards would be defeated, and all the Spaniards would be dead and their cities would be flooded, because the sea was going to rise and drown them, and hence that there would be no memory of them. (Wachtel, *Los vencidos* 285)[6]

Although the Taqui-Oncoy was known to the students of the six-teenth century in the Andes, the study of this millenarian movement dates back a mere twenty-five years. Recent publication of chronicles and accounts by Albornoz and others charged with the extirpation of idola-tries provide a good source for our interpretation of the dancing sick-ness.[7] Of particular relevance to discourse analysis are Franklin Pease's essays on the myth of Incarrí and on the Taqui-Oncoy. Pease shows how, after the defeat of the Sun in Cajamarca, older local gods gained a new preeminence:

Evangelistic indoctrination was simultaneous with the Conquest. The Andean peoples had to accept Christianity as the official religion that dis-placed the solar cult of Cuzco. At the same time they had to accept the rup-ture of *the sacred order* of their world. But this substitution of the Christians' Dios for the Sun did not include or affect all other Andean divinities, as the discovery of the Taqui-Oncoy, thirty years after the Spanish invasion, attests. (Pease, *El dios creador* 70)

The demise of the Sun and the subsequent profanation of Cuzco, the sacred center of the cosmos, disarticulated the Andean pantheon. Since the Andean deities were particularly tied to the system of kinship, social structure, and economic production, their demise meant not only the death of God, but the devastation of the visible and invisible worlds

---

[6] Wachtel quotes this passage from the chronicle *El Cuzqueño* (1575) of Cristóbal de Molina. This, and all other translations of Cristóbal de Molina, Franklin Pease, José de Arriaga, Flores Galindo, José de Acosta, Manuel Burga, Flores Galindo, or Guamán Poma are mine.

[7] See the account of Albornoz published by Luis Millones, "Un movimiento nativista del siglo XVI: el Taqui-Oncoy." On Andean deities, see Pease *El dios creador andino*, and *El pensamiento mítico*; Rostworowski.

alike.[8] For this reason, we can also read the myth of Incarrí as a response to the end of the known social order. Most variants of the myth hold that Incarrí's head was hidden in the underground. There it grows, impervious to decay, so that one day the head and the body will be reunited. On that day, when the mutilated body becomes whole again, Incarrí will be restored to life on the surface of the Pachamama, and if Dios allows it, the son of the Sun will reign again. At the same time, the sacred order—that is, justice as harmony and well-being (*sumak kawsay*)—will be restored to the Andeans.

Besides stating the kernel of a utopia, the Incarrí myth signals a clear affirmation of continuity of the Andean cosmos despite the rupture caused by the Spanish Conquest, as Pease points out. But unlike the preaching by the Taqui-Oncoy or a utopian vision of return to the Andean administration by Guamán Poma, this myth of restoration no longer postulates immediate reestablishment of the sacred order of the time of the Incas. The myth of Incarrí, in all its versions—including those collected most recently by field anthropologists—defers restoration to a messianic time. The messianic moment is marked by a pair of ambivalent signs. One the one hand, its inauguration depends on the growth of the Inca's body, which in turn will leave the underground to reign on the Pachamama; on the other hand, this will happen only if Dios permits, a condition not at all predictable. Thus the myth speaks with a forked tongue. While signaling the continuity of the Andean world, it paradoxically asserts its break with the Inca past, the defeat of the Cuzco solar divinity, and its new dependence on Dios.

The invasion of 1532 left Andean people with stark choices: either to accept or resist Spanish rule. They could give up their *huacas* and separate ethnic identities to become generic Indians, as Viceroy Francisco de Toledo (1569-1581) planned, or they could struggle to resist or overthrow Spanish domination and the works of Dios.[9] If the choice was to fight back, the accompanying expectation included restoration, during their lifetime, of the autochthonous gods and reinstatement of themselves as masters of Andean material and social life. Even as late as 1621, when

[8] For detailed discussion of the origins, properties, and function of *guacas*, see Spalding 63-65.

[9] For a substantive account of the conversion of the many Andean ethnic societies and identities into "Indians," see Stern 80-113.

José de Arriaga published his work on the extirpation of idolatries, it was clear that the Andean people clung to the project of preserving their desire "to carry water on both shoulders, to have recourse to both religions at once . . . for they feel and even say that they can worship their *huacas* while believing in God the Father, the Son, and Holy Ghost. Thus what they offer for the worship of Jesus Christ, they generally offer their *huacas*" (Arriaga 72).

By 1564, when Cristóbal de Albornoz detected the Taqui-Oncoy, there had been several responses and forms of resistance to colonial rule. This is not the place to discuss how each mode of resistance came to be; Wachtel and Steve Stern deal extensively with them. The awareness that Spanish rule spelled out the brutal disappearance of the Andeans and their world had become a vivid and even obsessional preoccupation for the inhabitants of the former Inca Empire.[10] Stern writes that the "Taqui-Oncoy expressed the painful truth dawning upon local societies—that conflict between the Andean and European elements of colonial society was at once inescapable, irreconcilable, and decisive" (Stern 56).

At least four serious types of resistance can be documented, all combining acts with discourse and all seeking the continuity of the Andean world. First the survivors from the Inca ruling class took up arms and entrenched themselves in Vilcabamba. Their response was war, a war that they eventually lost. The rebel Inca Titu Cusi Yupanqui spoke for those who fought in Vilcabamba. Second, Guamán Poma de Ayala (c. 1534-1615) embarked on an unparalleled adventure of writing a letter to the king of Spain. The thousand-page autobiography, utopia, ethnography, and deconstruction of European thought is known as *El primer nueva corónica y buen gobierno* (1615). Third, a large number of *curacas*, *caciques*, and other individuals took up resistance and sabotage through their use of the Spanish legal structure. They became the litigant corps of Andean society. In the attempt to save their lives, welfare, and rights to the land, these "native shyster lawyers"—as the Spaniards named them—ensured that Spanish colonial efforts to establish an extractive economy and a clearly Spanish-dominated society would be ensnared for the rest of the sixteenth century and well into the seventeenth century. Finally, the otherwise unknown Juan Chocne and his followers, as preachers and

---

[10] For an up-to-date examination of the demographic ruin caused by the European invasion of the Andes, see Cook.

converts of the cult and its ritual known as the Taqui-Oncoy, struggled to empower the ancient local gods with the force and the discourse necessary to compete with, and eventually to defeat, the invading god, the Spaniards, and the pestilence that followed in their wake.

In the search for continuity of the Andean world, all four forms of resistance were like the myth of Incarrí. The corollary of their resistance was, of course, the expulsion or at least the separation—as Guamán Poma proposed—of the Spanish world from the Andean life and cosmos. It would appear, at first glance at least, that all four forms of struggle failed. The rebels attempting to revive an Inca state capitulated; Titu Cusi, along with what was left of the Inca nobility, converted to Christianity and even accepted Dios. Guamán Poma died (1616) an old and poor man whose last hope was through suffering to attain sainthood, and whose ultimate consolation for relinquishing princely aspirations was authorship;[11] the utopia of his *El primer nueva corónica y buen gobierno* was deferred indefinitely but his keen-edged critique of a world upside down remains. The litigious Andeans did manage to curtail the immediate erosion of their civil and economic rights; yet because they needed money to pay the costs of fighting in the Spanish courts, they actually fell prey to the policies whose demise they sought. Finally, when the Taqui-Oncoy was uncovered by the Spanish bureaucracy, it was quickly extirpated by the inspections of the extirpators of idolatries.

By the last quarter of the sixteenth century the Andean world, with its posture of explicit resistance to and struggle against the new order of Spanish rulers, had come to terms with defeat. The once sacred order of the universe stood forever profaned, and the discourse of the local rebellious gods that once inspired Juan Chocne's preaching and Guamán Poma's writing had to seek refuge, as in the myth of Incarrí, in a sort of underground to avoid its absolute and complete obliteration.

We do not know exactly when the myth of Incarrí began. Some think it appeared after the rebellion of Túpac Amaru II in 1780-1782. However, as Flores Galindo writes, the myth's presence coincided with the particular historical development of Peru's central highlands, the same area where the Taqui-Oncoy flourished:

[11] For a discussion of Guamán Poma and the question of authorship in his work, see Castro-Klarén 139-57.

There exists a clear link between the history of this utopia and the [life of the Indian] communities. If we were to draw a map of the principal manifestations of the utopia, it should include the places where both the myth of *Incarrí* and the story of the three ages of the world have been found in conjunction with communal theatrical representations of the capture of the Inca. (88)

It would seem, however, in light of the several versions of the myth to be found in the Andes today, that once the messianic myth was born, it remained almost unchanged in the oral tradition. The same cannot, of course, be said about the millenarian beliefs of the Taqui-Oncoy, which we understand were extirpated by Cristóbal de Albornoz and other envoys of Toledo. I suggest, however, given the Andean will for continuity and history's abundant evidence of surviving functions and structures in the Andes,[12] that we will not stray far off course if we view José María Arguedas's scissor dancer in the short story "La agonía de Rasu Ñiti" as rearticulating many elements that once constituted the discourse of the Taqui-Oncoy.

Dancing in the texts of Arguedas is not restricted to Rasu Ñiti. Dancers, music, and musicians appear on many critical occasions in Arguedas's fiction: Cámac in *El sexto* (1961), Ernesto in *Los ríos profundos* (1958), Tankayllu in *Yawar fiesta* (1941), and Don Diego in *El zorro de arriba y el zorro de abajo* (1971) all engage in a delirious dance or *taqui* at key moments of dramatic intensity in the narrative.[13] According to my own conversation with Luis Millones in 1989, it may be possible to trace the link between the Taqui-Oncoy and its surviving manifestations today in specific instances of ritual plays (*comparsas*) celebrated in Andean communities (the research remains to be carried out). Manuel Burga's study of these plays as ritual reenactments of the people's sense of history

[12] See for instance Murra; Ossio, "Cultural Continuity" 118-46. See also Montoya; Carrillo.

[13] José María Arguedas (1911-1969) was an anthropologist. His narrative combines a highly original prose style with a realistic rhetoric that captures the world of the Andean people from their own vantage point and experience. Arguedas grew up in an Andean community of the central highlands. The translation of Arguedas's major novel *Los ríos profundos* (1958) as *Deep Rivers* (Austin, Tex., 1978) and the short novel *Yawar fiesta* (1941; trans. Austin, Tex., 1985), *The Singing Mountaineers*, trans. Ruth Stephan, Kate Flores, and Angel Flores (Austin, Tex., 1957), contains *Canto kechua* and *Canciones y cuentos del pueblo quechua*.

(for example, the death of Atahualpa, the last Inca) shows how the symbols and ritual of the sacramental dance are still at work in the Andes (Burga chaps. 1 and 2).

In the sixteenth century preaching of the Taqui-Oncoy neither the Inca nor the Sun occupied any space or function. Juan Chocne's message about the fighting return of the *huacas* seemed to concede the defeat of the Sun as god of the Inca state. In fact, the Taqui-Oncoy departed from the notion that Dios, the state god of the Spaniards, had indeed triumphed over the Sun. It therefore became the function of the numerous *huacas*—deities or culture heroes—to fight and expel the invaders and their god.[14]

According to Arriaga, besides adoring the sun, the moon, the stars, and thunder, the Indians adored the land, the ocean, mountain springs, snowcapped peaks (*rasu*), and their mythical places of origin (*pacarinas*); small things were also part of the sacred order. Arriaga noted that the Indians held their forebears within the category of the *huacas* and that some of these heroes, such as Libiacancharco, were famous for their feasts and exploits. Thus not only did their heroic ancestors literally occupy the earth, but as Arriaga further observed fifty years after the Taqui-Oncoy had been extirpated, Andeans regarded the *huacas* as the guarantors of "life and health and food." The Christian examiner of the *guacas* seemed puzzled by the "fact" that the "Indians never ask for anything concerning the other life" (22-24, 50).

Within this context of the sacred, Dios appeared rather remote, almost irrelevant, were it not that he was allied with the war-making machine of the Christians. The logic of the Taqui-Oncoy—rejecting Dios and with it Christianity as well as the universe that the discourse of the evangelizing priests sought to implant—radically distanced the Taqui-Oncoy from Guamán Poma's blueprint for future government. The author of *El primer nueva corónica* grows tiresome in his repeated embrace of Christianity and the new god. The author and self-styled prince not only willingly discarded the Sun and its cult as mere Inca superstition or error but even denied that Indians had worshiped the now satanized *guacas*: "They

---

[14] In her study of the myths of Huarochirí, Spalding states, "Wak'as were regarded as hero-deities who had performed great exploits (constructing irrigation canals, for instance) and had turned themselves to stone to guard the resources they had created for their people" (63).

neither made devils their masters nor worshiped idols and *guacas*" (Guamán Poma 1:45, 253). What is more, Guamán Poma's utopia—restoration of Andean administration with the king of Spain as the new Inca principle of order[15]—allowed room for two Spanish cultural tools: Christianity and writing. We can easily comprehend that the self-appointed lawyer of indigent "Indians" would have felt a logical aversion to the emotional contents of the actions and preachings of the frenzied dancing of the Taqui-Oncoy inasmuch as they derived from a cult that Guamán Poma, as a Christian convert, rejected.

Guamán Poma preferred a god even more abstract and distant than the Andean creator god(s). Above all Guamán Poma, the Andean writer, opted for a god figured within and through a complex and ancient discourse. The teleology of the Christian discourse not only posited a single origin for the human species but also seemed flexible enough to permit the grafting of Andean time and peoples into its "universal" sacred and historical order. For Guamán Poma, Juan Chocne's advocacy of a return to the cult of the *huacas* suggested an intolerable answer to the burning question of the day: were the Indians the descendents of Adam and Eve, and therefore human, or had they a separate origin and were they thus beasts of some kind? What is more, Guamán Poma's indirect mention of the Taqui-Oncoy included it in his long section on sorcery. To distance himself from all the shamans and sorcerers whose practices he described, he said that he learned about them when he went along as an assistant to Cristóbal de Albornoz who "consumed all the *guacas*, idols, and sorcerers of the kingdom" (Guamán Poma 1:253).[16]

Thus, contrary to Guamán Poma's political dreams, the Taqui-Oncoy rejected not only two state gods but all things belonging to Spain, from discourse to food and clothing. Besides vowing to drive the invaders into the sea, the Taqui-Oncoy promised the restoration of good health and an abundance of foodstuff ("sumak kawsay") for the Andean peoples. Such

[15] "The king of Spain is assimilated to the notion of Pachacuti in the sense of renovator of the world, which to our understanding was the principal attribute of the Inca in the pre-Hispanic past" (Guamán Poma, quoted in Ossio, *Ideología* 200).

[16] Regarding the nature and efficacy of the (oracular) discourse of the Andean gods just before and after 1532, Manuel Burga writes, "Their gods, who spoke through professionals in Andean technology and knowledge, became fallible. They became liars... The gods lost credibility and thus Andean peoples turned more often to an apocalyptic reading of normal events" (58).

promises were eminently practical and took into account local conditions and feelings of despair before the daily agony of the everyday world. The Taqui-Oncoy thus addressed not only the psychological traumas of the Conquest and the defeat of the gods but also the very palpable needs of the body.

By 1565 it had become abundantly clear that the ecological disaster brought on by the European invasion threatened the physical end of the Andean population. Over and over, Guamán Poma begs God to grant him and his people biological continuity, if nothing else. "Let us not disappear" is one of his several refrains. Freedom from the killing epidemics cause by the European diseases—from the common cold to smallpox— was one of the promises the return of the *huacas* signified to the followers of Juan Chocne.[17] The satisfaction of basic needs—healthy bodies and enough food to go on living—required in turn that people obey the injunction not to eat Spanish foods (which were poisons or carriers of disease) or wear Spanish clothing (which transformed the social and religious meaning of being), under threat of final extinction. The people who did not obey the injunctions would surely succumb: they would be turned into animals, losing all contact with culture and reverting to unconscious nature. The *huacas* threatened those who betrayed them with the very destiny that people feared most: the absolute and irretrievable end to self and to life as they knew it. A clear consciousness of facing the dreaded end, the holocaust, thus characterized the preaching of the sick dance.

Contemporaries of the Taqui-Oncoy failed to see its relation to the crisis of everyday life. As Cristóbal de Albornoz reported, the Taqui-Oncoy was dangerous but only inasmuch as it was an "apostasy," a return to the old beliefs. The *Visitador* dedicated a great deal more ink and paper to enumerating the hundreds of hidden *guacas* or ritual objects that he discovered and whose immediate destruction he himself undertook or supervised than to examining the subject matter of the cult. He

---

[17] The steep decline in the sixteenth-century population was so dramatic that the term "holocaust" no longer seems an exaggeration. The records show that between 1520 and 1600 there were twenty epidemics. People were dying at unprecedented rates not only because of diseases but also from forced labor, military conscription, dietary change, and psychological devastation. For a fuller appreciation of this picture of horror, see Hernández, especially "El Taqui-Oncoy, la enfermedad del canto," 111-35.

reduced the Taqui-Oncoy to its bare essentials, elements that enabled him to speak about the destruction of *huacas* to his superiors in the Spanish ecclesiastical bureaucracy (Millones 86).

Today, when we look at the bare semiotic elements that make up the discourse of the Taqui-Oncoy, a closer reading reveals a complex transformation of religious and political structures that formed the world of Juan Chocne, Guamán Poma, Cristóbal de Molina, and Cristóbal de Albornoz. The analysis of the discourse of the Taqui-Oncoy allows us to rearticulate its elements and to rediscover its presence in cultural forms that have survived until today. Somehow, nodal elements of the cult remain active in a secret and nonverbal inscription to be found in the ritual and choreography of scissor dancers in Andean towns of the central highlands, and reinscribed in José María Arguedas's "La agonía de Rasu Ñiti."

The Taqui-Oncoy accepts the sky as the place of a superior divinity that originally the Sun occupied. The solar defeat at Cajamarca—the capture of the Inca by the Spaniards—leaves that space to Dios, another sky divinity. Although the Taqui-Oncoy reclaims the *guacas* as the active divinities at the center of its pantheon, it nevertheless assigns the celestial space—vacated by a (defeated) Dios—to a vaguely conceived aerial divinity. Albornoz says that they speak of "a being who went about in the air in a sort of basket" (Millones 22). Even though "the Inca figures as a large absence," as Franklin Pease notes, the sky is still considered an appropriate place for the supreme divinity (*El dios creador* 80).

If the transformation in the sky divinity goes from Sun to Dios to one who gets about in a basket, a very different movement takes place on the land. Corresponding to the Sun in the sky, the old religion holds the *huacas* on the land. In a sacred (sacralized) universe, the *huacas* are the essence of the power of the divine on a tangible, material level. The *huacas*, inasmuch as they are believed to be or to have become rivers, monoliths, or snowcapped peaks, dot the sensorial world and, therefore, the psychological universe, with their presence. José de Arriaga comes to the conclusion that since even small and insignificant things or places can be held to be *huacas*, these cannot be destroyed in their material existence. Thus the only way he sees to remove idolatry is to wrench it from the hearts of the Indians. The Jesuit José de Acosta confirms the multiplicity and varied origins of the *guacas*. In his *Historia natural y moral de las Indias* (1590) he comments:

The devil was not satisfied when he made the Indians blind, so that they adore the sun and the moon and the stars and nature as a whole. He went on to give them small things as gods, many of them vile... In Cajamarca de la Nazca they showed me a great mountain of sand. It was a principal worship site or *guaca* of the ancients. I asked what divinity they saw in it. They answered that it was indeed a marvelous thing, being such a high sand mountain among so many other peaks of rock. (223-24)

The *huacas* are literally everywhere and are numerous because the people hold them to be not only their place of origin but also their constant companions in life. They intervene daily in human affairs, especially in matters of health. Drawing from José de Arriaga and the myths of Huarochirí, Karen Spalding notes that *guacas* are not only held to provide good fortune and prosperity but also considered to help conquer and protect new territories. *Guacas* wage war on one another: "The capture of *wak'as*—who continued to be honored and served by their new possessors—as well as the lands was part of the oral tradition of Huarochirí" (Spalding 63-65).

Huacas are the object of public worship and their service is the responsibility of the larger lineages and clans. Worship of the *guacas*, numerous as they are, forms part of the preservation and transmission of communal histories. According to Spalding, a large number of priests preserve and interpret the *huacas*.

Christianity holds a parallel arrangement in sixteenth-century Peru. Corresponding to Dios in the sky, the new religion reserves a sacralized space on the land. In place of the ancient, sacred, but now silent or mistaken *huacas* stand the churches filled with the voices of praying converts and preachers who attempt to organize the whole of life under the dictates of God and the saints. In response to the Christian sacralization that envelops the land with its churches, "evangelizing priests," and sacraments, the Taqui-Oncoy proclaims the new powers of an alliance of great *huacas* ready to battle Dios for sovereignty of the Andean universe. From Chimborazo in Ecuador, through Pachacámac in Lurín, to Tiahuanaco in Bolivia, the *huacas* are making ready to fight Dios.

The Taqui-Oncoy's struggle with Christianity hinges on the question of the land. Because the Andean cosmos implies a sacralized nature, the struggle for control and meaning of the land signifies much more than the location and function of the churches or the *guacas* as places of private or public worship. Juan Chocne, his followers, and many others readily understand that the prohibition to worship the site of the *huacas* does not simply nullify the divine but also negates the link between the Andean peoples and their ancestors (the bodies of family members and even *mallquis*, the embalmed bodies of deceased Incas) and thus destroys their right to use and conceptualize the land—for every lineage derives its identity and claim to the land from a recognized ancestor, real or mythical. Not only do the Christians denounce the *guacas* as false gods who speak lies and mislead the people—the Spaniards destroy their sites and punish their priests—but deny the very connection of the people with their sacralized origin and extirpate their "idolatries." Moreover, the relationship between the myth of origin, the present life of the body, and the sense of an everlasting community, synthesized in the cultural formation of the *huaca*, is dashed to pieces in 1551 when the Inquisition's Council of Lima declares that the sacred ancestors of the Indians, the deceased Incas, are in fact burning in hell (Spalding 245). The paroxysms of fright and despair embodied in the Taqui-Oncoy's sick dance re-present the figures drawn in the churches for future converts. They hear that their deceased parents, children, and grandparents, condemned to suffer in hell, are being devoured by thirst and hunger and consumed by illness. Painfully aware of their kin in hell, they take the return of the *guacas* to the domain of the land to be a logical and utter necessity.

The discourse of the Taqui-Oncoy with its prohibition of Spanish food, dress, and systems of beliefs underscores the body as the point of articulation between a universe loaded with symbols and a desacralized and disarticulated—impossible—purely physical realm. In forbidding Indians contact with the new sacred spaces, the Taqui-Oncoy also forbids them the Catholic sacraments, which revolve around eating (Holy Communion), talking (confession), and rites of corporeal cleanliness and renaming of people (baptism). Within Christian discourse, these sacraments preside over and institutionalize all the critical stages of life, giving way to the birth of a new sense of self.[18]

Nowhere is the power over terrestrial space more keenly disputed than at the level of names. The struggle over the hearts and minds of the

[18] The Jesuits even proscribed the name Santiago because the Indians appropriated it to make of the warrior saint of the Spaniards a new representation for their thunder god Illapa, associating the lighting of Santiago's harquebus with Illapa's own aerial manifestations (Arriaga 54).

Andeans waged by the evangelizing priests recognized patronymics as a key element of self-identity. Whereas Taqui-Oncoy forbade the taking of Spanish names, José de Arriaga in his section on prohibitions explained that the Andeans were not to keep their ancient names because these might have secret associations with the *huacas*. The Taqui-Oncoy forbids "Indians" from taking Spanish names, so that they may not answer to a new function or identity. Under the preaching Taqui-Oncoy, the *huacas* are reconnected with the power of speech and, above all, with a public discourse, so that they can once again transmit their sacred word (as Christian churches do). The *huacas* will protect their people, but only under certain conditions of loyalty to the old ways. No longer fixed to their place of wonder—a majestic peak, a breathless precipice, a clear spring—the *huacas*, like Christian deities, now live within the hearts of men and women (in their social and religious imagination). Cristóbal de Albornoz reports that the *guacas* "entered the bodies of the Indians and made them talk" (Millones 37). The gods are no longer restricted to their former function of oracles. They, like the Christian god, inhabit the individual's inner, invisible, nonmaterial space.

The return of the *huacas* is clearly identified with return of a dominant Andean discourse, of health to the Andean people, and of plentiful Andean foodstuff ("sumak kawsay"). This signals a return to life as it was known before the rupture of the Conquest and the coming of a new god. All desires are oriented toward the wholeness and plenitude of the individual body, which in turn has become the site from which the divinity speaks. The Andean body, thus resacralized and reenergized by the force of the *huacas* within, must not be disguised or desecrated under foreign clothing. Spanish clothing not only hides the Andean self but also distorts it. What the body wears must be in accordance with what the body, as a social and religious sign, signifies and contains.

In most religions, the underground is reserved for deities who oppose the being and works of the creators. A bottomless hole of darkness and heat is reserved for the devil in the Christian pantheon. The Andean imagination speaks of magic snakes—*amarus*—and other beings inhabiting holes, tunnels, and caves; but their sign is positive. We lack adequate knowledge to define the underground assigned to the body of Incarrí or explain the meaning of this underground as the place of regeneration for a celestial divinity. According to Luis E. Valcárcel, the cosmos of the ancient Andean peoples contains three elements: water, earth, and fire. The universe (*pacha*) is arranged in tiers: *hanaq pacha* or "above world," inhabited by gods such as the Sun, the moon, or thunder; *kay pacha* or "the world here," populated by living beings and spirits; and *ukhu pacha* or "inside world," inhabited by the dead and bacteria or germs. These three worlds maintain communication by means of channels and tunnels through volcanic craters, caverns, or springs at fixed points of entrance (*pacarinas*).[19]

In the case of the Taqui-Oncoy, preoccupied with a struggle for domination over the territorial plane and hopeful that "*guacas* would make another world" because "the *guacas* had already defeated the God of the Christians since their turn was already over," the underground has little place (Millones 8, 17). Understandably, the cult's discourse is silent in reference to the underground as a space to occupy or mobilize its imagination. Both Millones and Pease show very convincingly how the Inca principle—the principle of order—generally goes underground after 1532. A similar, but more complex, trajectory transforms the discourse of the Taqui-Oncoy with the ritual dance of the scissors dancers.

"La agonía de Rasu Ñiti" (1962) is a short story Arguedas wrote in one of his best moments.[20] The old and sick scissor dancer Rasu Ñiti (he who steps on snow), prepares to dance his last or death dance. As he readies himself for the final rite of passage, a condor, visible only to the dancer and his wife, hovers over the dancer's head. The condor, the dancer tells his daughter, is the *Wamani*, the aerial divinity that protects him and listens to him as it does to the rest of the Andean peoples. The Wamani's hearing is such that it can even hear the growth of Incarrí.[21] From the narrator's explanation we recognize that this divinity belongs to the sky. A silent presence overhead, it listens intently. Other deities live inside mountains or occupy sacred underground sites from which they inspire other scissor dancers in their rituals and celebrations.

[19] See Valcárcel 137-62. A *pacarina* is also the place of origin for each ethic group; its connection with the community's *guacas* is direct.

[20] The connection between the ritual character of the foxes and the dancing in Arguedas's *El zorro de arriba y el zorro de abajo* (1971) and the dancing foxes of Huarochirí myths seems inescapable. Neither Arguedas nor the critics who study his work have linked the scissor dancers to the foxes in the Huarochirí myths and the generally ritual sacred dances, of which the Taqui-Oncoy must be but one in a series.

[21] In speaking of the famous hero-deity Libiacancharco, the Spanish priest José de Arriaga related that it was "in a shelter below a cave in a very steep mountain. It had its *huama* [*waman*, or falcon totem] or diadem of gold on its head and it was dressed in fine shirts of *cumbi*" (16).

In "La agonía de Rasu Ñiti," the body and performance of the dying dancer constitute fluid spaces inhabitable by either sky or underground divinities. The churches, formerly in dispute with the *huacas*, appear in the dancer's world as spaces particularly suited to the feats of his dance because their high towers are connected to the sacred inner sanctum of the churches by dark, snake-like or snail-like, inner stairways that the dancer climbs up and down with extraordinary skill, taken by the whirlwind of his abstracting and mesmerizing music.[22]

The former univocal quality of the sky, land, and underground as divine space delineated in the Taqui-Oncoy has, in the tale of Rasu Ñiti, been diffused or confused. The church has been integrated into the Andean articulation of space. It has lost the forbidden quality that the Taqui-Oncoy conferred on it during the struggles of the sixteenth century. The aerial god of the basket has disappeared, leaving perhaps Dios in its place or the condor as its visible sign. The scissor dancer of Arguedas has continuity with the ritual sick dances of the Taqui-Oncoy because his body is an emblem of the Wamani's active presence in the world. His body mediates between the political sphere and the religious world; between the practical sphere and the mystical realm; between the churches' high towers to which no priest dares ascend and the space where God and his officiating priests secretly and darkly dwell.

While the extirpation campaign had the effect of driving the *huacas* back into their (now desecrated) natural sites, it unexpectedly also created a new space for the dwelling of the Andean deities: the interiority of believers. Whereas the Inca principle was driven underground, the ritual aerial dance of the scissor dancers may have appeared and survived right under the glaring light of the extirpation campaign as a continuation of the sick-dance connected to the aerial divinity. In the aerial scissor dance, one can recognize the same ability to adapt and transform in order to continue the ancient beliefs that Arriaga detected as he cautioned his sixteenth-century

---

[22] In coming to terms with the Christian cosmos, Andean people not only occupied and subverted the new sacred space aboveground (*kay pacha*), the church, but also tried to change cemeteries into places for the expulsed *mallquis*. Flores Galindo quotes evidence from the account of an extirpation campaign: "In 1613, in a town located between Huancavelica and Ayacucho, upon the arrival of the preachers, a bolt of lightning destroyed a church... the Jesuits who were evangelizing the Indians of the locality examined the ruins of the church only to discover behind the central alter a *guaca*, and under the floor a clandestine cemetery" (92).

fellow priests against the Andeans' ingenuity: "The dissimulation and boldness of the Indians has also reached such a point that during the feast of the Corpus Christi they have slyly hidden a small *huaca* on the very platform of the monstrance of the holy Sacrament" (70).

The dance of the Taqui-Oncoy was a space of transition that divided the voyage from sickness to health, from Pachacuti to restoration. A measure of such health was the preaching of discourse that the *huacas* granted to reward their adepts' dancing. In the face of the devastating epidemics and the thorough destructuration of the Andean social and economic system, the restoration of health to a sick and disintegrating world was more than an appropriate metaphor to express the significance of the cult to the gods. But the discourse of the *guacas* was also forced underground, leaving only the splendor of the dance as a sign of the desire for wholesome and harmonious integration.

In Arguedas's contemporary story, Rasu Ñiti gets up from his deathbed to dance for the last time because "my heart is letting me know" (146). In communication with the Wamani, the mountain divinity whose expression is the condor, the dancer tells his wife: "The Wamani speaks. You cannot hear" (146). The gods have been driven underground, or rather, back into the land; they still communicate, but only privately, secretly, with a few select and trusted individuals. The world and discourse that the *huacas* of the Taqui-Oncoy made public appear transformed in Arguedas's tale as a secret space, unattainable for the uninitiated. Its message resists all interpretation, all dissemination. The wife cannot hear the Wamani, but she can sense it. She must be satisfied by what her husband, the scissor dancer, tells her about the Wamani in their house. She perceives only that it is gray and hovers serenely over the dancer's head. Any act of verbal communication is forbidden to her.

Observing a precise and ancient ritual, Rasu Ñiti dresses in his glorious outfit. With religious fervor, he puts on each piece of clothing in a prescribed order. This dancer's costume is outstanding for its colors and its European slant; it does not observe the prohibitions of 1565. The costume's materials display the most precious Andean brocaded ribbons and the luxury of European silks and velvets. The tailoring of the pants and jackets is reminiscent of a bullfighter's; Arguedas calls it a "suit of light and color" (146).

These elements of the dancer's clothing are his signs, his markings, in a semiotic sense. Satisfied with his dress and ritual, "already dressed by his decoration," Rasu Ñiti steps out into the sunlight before the people who have gathered to see him dance his farewell.[23]

Inverting the relationship of the people to the *guacas* in the Taqui-Oncoy, the Wamani does not speak publicly yet *hears* what all the Andean people know and think. One of Rasu Ñiti's daughters is told that she cannot "see" the Wamani because she is not yet *strong* enough to see him, but she can be sure that the Wamani hears her. "'Yes, he hears,' answered the dancer. 'He also hears how our god is growing, how he is going to swallow the eyes of that horse of the master'"(148).

The Wamani listens and takes note, as St. Peter does, of any offenses perpetrated against the social order. And if the Wamani cannot or does not speak, it does communicate its loving presence through the dancer's performance. Discourse is not the privilege of this deity: through yet another transformation, the Wamani communicates with its people through music. In other words, of the fourfold combination of the Taqui-Oncoy (dance-preaching-music-ecstasy), three elements have survived, and one, the preaching, has been lost. The music of the dancer's scissors (two unhinged steel blades "played" by one hand) is the range of sounds of its people. "Do you hear, my daughter? The scissors are not really played by your father's fingers. The Wamani plays them. Your father is only obeying" (148).

Once again we are in the presence of the possessed dancer of the Taqui-Oncoy. The narrator states:

> They dance alone or in competition with each other. The feats they accomplish and the boiling of their blood during the figures of the dances depend on the [Wamani] who sits on their head and heart. While he dances or lifts and throws crowbars with his teeth, or pierces his flesh through with and awl, or walks in the air on a cord stretched between the very top of a tree and the tower of the town. (149)

In this regard, Martin Lienhard insists on the link between the competitive (dialogic) dancing of the foxes and the myths of Huarochirí, translated by Arguedas, and the "dancing delirium that takes possession of the characters and even of language" in *El zorro de arriba y el zorro de abajo* (Lienhard 120).

---

[23] This ritual dressing coupled to Arguedas's care in observing the order of the investiture points to the totemic dances of undoubted pre-Columbian origin. Like the performance of the scissor dancer, these totemic dances are executed by a single masked man whose clothing integrates either feline skin or feathers (Verger 12).

As the anonymous participants in the Taqui-Oncoy did, Arguedas's narrator posits the Wamani not only as a divinity whose site is a place or a thing in nature, but also as a spirit residing within the dancer's body: "The genius of a scissor dancer depends on the spirit that inhabits him. It could be the spirit of a mountain [Wamani], or the spirit of a silent and transparent precipice" (149).

The "spirit" of the *guacas* thus survives in the dance of this possessed artist. However, mere survival is not their best achievement; for even as they cede the space of discourse, the *guacas* give back to the people, through the dancer and especially in his scissor's song, just for an ephemeral moment, the desired health or harmony of the sacred order so ruptured by the Conquest.

Arguedas's narrator remembers the feats of another scissor dancer, Unto: "The voice of the scissors exhausted all feeling... It floated up to heaven only to return to the world as our eyes followed the dancer... The music of the world will never again play so intensely on two blades of shining steel" (149). In this music played by Rasu Ñiti, the world's sacred order is thus restored for all Andeans. The privileged relation of performer with Wamani is, through his dance and music, rendered communitarian.

As in a Pachacuti, Arguedas's story narrates the tale of death and rebirth. Rasu Ñiti gets up from his sickbed to perform his last dance, a dance in whose ritual and music he will pass his relation to the Wamani on to Atok Sayllu, his disciple: "He was born again, with the tendons of a young beast and the fire of the Wamani" (154).

In this transformed version of the Taqui-Oncoy, the divinity perpetuates itself in its people; they, in turn, find their continuity in the divinity. Arguedas's story thus ends with a double affirmation: the old dancer is to be buried and a new one is to be born. The young disciple is to marry, and thus the sorrow of death is mitigated by the promise of life. It is to the collectivity of Arguedas's story that we can attribute these last words: "Wamani is Wamani," words that the adepts of the Taqui-Oncoy also enunciated in order to restore and assert the continuity of their world.

An earlier version of this essay was originally published as Sara Castro-Klarén: "Dancing and the Sacred in the Andes: From the Taqui-Oncoy to Rasu-Niti", in *New World Encounters*, edited by Stephen Greenblatt. © 1993 by the Regents of the University of California. Published by the University of California Press.

WORKS CITED

ACOSTA, José de. *Historia natural y moral de las Indias (1590)*. Ed. Edmundo O'Gorman. México: Fondo de Cultura Económica, 1979.

ARGUEDAS, José María. "La agonía de Rasu Ñiti." In *Amor mundo y todos los cuentos*. Lima: Francisco Moncloa Editores, 1967.

ARRIAGA, José de. *The Extirpation of Idolatry in Perú*. Ed. Clark Keating. Lexington: University of Kentucky Press, 1968.

GUAMÁN POMA DE AYALA, Felipe. *El primer nueva corónica y buen gobierno*. Ed. John Murra and Rolena Adorno. México: Siglo Veintiuno, 1980.

BURGA, Manuel. *Nacimiento de una utopía: muerte y resurrección de los incas*. Lima: Instituto de Apoyo Agrario, 1988.

FLORES GALINDO, Alberto. *Buscando un Inca: identidad y utopía en los Andes*. Lima: Instituto de Apoyo Agrario, 1987.

FOUCAULT, Michel. *The Archaeology of Knowledge*. New York: Pantheon Books, 1972.

HERNÁNDEZ, Max, Moisés LEMLIJ, Luis MILLONES, Alberto PÉNDOLA, María ROSTWOROWSKI. *Entre el mito y la historia: psicoanálisis y el pasado andino*. Lima: Ediciones Psicoanalíticas Imago S.R.L, 1987.

LIENHARD, Martin. *Cultura popular andina y forma novelesca: zorros y danzantes en la última novela de Arguedas*. Lima, Latinoamericana Editores, 1981.

MILLONES, Luis. «Un movimiento nativista del siglo XVI: el Taqui-Oncoy.» *Ideología mesiánica del mundo andino*. Ed. Juan M. Ossio A. Lima: I. Prado Pastor, 1973.

OSSIO, Juan. *Ideología mesiánica del mundo andino*. Lima: I. Prado Pastor, 1973.

PEASE, Franklin. *El dios creador andino*. Lima: Mosca Azul Editores, 1973.

ROSTWOROWSKI DE DIEZ CANSECO, María. *Estructuras andinas del poder. Ideología religiosa y política*. Lima: Instituto de Estudios Peruanos, 1983.

SPALDING, Karen. *Huarochirí: An Andean Society under Inca and Spanish Rule*. Stanford: Stanford University Press, 1984.

STERN, Steve J. *Peru's Indian Peoples and the Challenge of Spanish Conquest: Huamanga to 1640*. Madison: University of Wisconsin Press, 1982.

VALCÁRCEL, Luis E. *Etnohistoria del antiguo Perú*. Lima: Universidad Nacional Mayor de San Marcos, 1959.

VARÓN GABAI, Rafael. "El Taki Onqoy: Las raíces andinas de un fenómeno colonial." In *El retorno de las huacas. Estudios y documentos sobre el Taki Onqoy, siglo XVI*. Ed. Luis Millones. Lima: Instituto de Estudios Peruanos, 1990.

VERGER, Pierre. *Fiestas y danzas en el Cuzco y en los Andes*. Buenos Aires: Editorial Sudamericana, 1945.

WACHTEL, Nathan. *Los vencidos: los indios del Perú frente a la conquista española (1530-1570)*. Trans. Antonio Escohotado. Madrid: Alianza Editorial, 1976.

CHAPTER 4
Memory and "Writing" in the Andes: From Cuzco to Valladolid and Back Again

PREAMBLE

How the past is understood marks indelibly our sense of the present and its possibilities. The idea of discussing memory and "writing" in the Andes during the first century after the Amerindians came into contact with Europeans allows for an all too necessary inclusion of semiotic systems that engage memory but do not engage "writing" in the restrictive sense in which the term has been used in European history. While "writing" sets the introduction of European alphabetic writing as the point of departure for the examination of historiography and all literacy in the Andes, memory opens the possibility of considering other modes of encoding knowledge and memory, such as the *quipu*, *keros* (drinking vessels), the *ceque* system (Zuidema 1990), dance, ritual, and even architecture. In *The Shape of Inca History: Narrative and Architecture in an Andean Empire* (1999), for instance, Susan Niles argues that in "royal architecture, no less than in their narratives, the Incas shaped historical events, giving material form to claims based on victories in battle, encounters with gods, and deeds carried out by their kings" (xvii). In fact it is the numeracy of the *quipu* and the relation of architecture to narrative poetics (2-84) that has recently made Inca history visible. It has been brought forth from the burial that the ideology of alphabetic writing had performed on it.

This chapter attempts to deal with a long century in which some of the major forces that shaped the discursive history of Latin America appeared and bloomed: the right of the Spanish crown, and by extension of other European nations, to conquer other peoples, and the place in the power-knowledge grid of modernity, assigned to Amerindians and their cultures in the world that empire inaugurated. This century also saw the response and resistance that such discourse elicited in the Andes. Although long silenced by the standing historiography of the New World, the voice of the *panacas*—patrilineal descent groups in charge of preserving specific noble Inca houses—is now being repositioned in the «writing» of the Andes. Thus the encoding of information in the *quipu* system merits a full discussion along with the chronicles and letters written by the *letrados*, the Spanish men of letters who wrote or gave shape to the events of the conquest and its aftermath.

I. Timelines

The timeline that accounts for the events that characterize human activity in the territory that we call the Andes today has been moved back and forth many times as modern historians and archeologists try to come to grips with the phenomenon of continuous human habitation and creation in the Andes. Recent archeological findings stretch the timeline for urban life back into the second or third millennia (2400 B.C.) *before* the birth of Christ, making the Andean invention of irrigation, social organization, and urban life contemporary to the pharaohs of Egypt. The remains of various urban centers offer abundant evidence of large populations and complex social and religious life in the valley of Caral situated about 200 kilometers north of Lima.

This push into the ancient past not only underscores the antiquity and originality of Andean civilizations, but also makes the fabled Incas our very recent contemporaries. And yet there is no question that both modern and post-modern citizens of the world consider the distance between them and the Inca empire to be great, if not insurmountable, due to the *difference* that marks the spread of European modernity and ancient Andean societies. Much of this sense of difference is, of course, owed to the Spanish chroniclers, those soldiers, priests, and crown officials who first related the Spanish encounter with Inca civilization, for all that was written then was told from the intellectual and aesthetic conditions of possibility of warriors and sackers furiously engaged in the conquest of the unimaginably wealthy

Inca empire. As the conquest of America constituted the inaugural act in the play of modernity, the ideological and epistemological legacy of these texts remained unchallenged for the better part of 500 years. It is only since the mid-twentieth century that scholars have begun to study, understand, and dismantle the epistemic complexity involved in the construction of the hierarchical difference (colonial difference) that is itself the result and the companion of conquest.

Perhaps the most important *difference* believed to have existed between Amerindian civilizations and Europe was what the Spanish reported and understood as the absence of writing. Among other things, this absence implied a diminished sense of self-consciousness, a questionable memory of the past and poor conditions for the development and accumulation of knowledge. Despite the fact that the Maya priests of Yucatan showed the Friar Diego de Landa (1524-1579) how the Yucatec phonetic syllabarian glyph system worked, he not only went on to burn every Maya book that he came across, but he also denied that the glyph system was "writing." The Aztec books were quickly characterized as pictures only, and the *quipu*, the knotted cords used in the Andes, were found not to have the slightest similarity to writing, for they did not even resemble books or paper in their physical appearance.

Lately, however, great strides have been made in reversing this Eurocentric mistaken appreciation of the modes and techniques of memory and knowledge accumulation and transmission in Amerindian cultures. Semeioticians, anthropologists, linguists, literary theorists, and philosophers have shown that alphabetic writing is neither the only mode of developing and conserving knowledge nor is it the best, most accurate, or all encompassing. A consensus has developed about the need for a more broadly based concept of "writing," one that can go beyond the alphabet-bound phonetic sense of writing and can thus encompass other systems of visuality as well as tactile systems of recording information. The problem, as Elizabeth Hill Boone has pointed out, is how to speak about writing without tying it to language (6). In the introduction to *Writing Without Words: Alternative Literacies in Mesoamerica and the Andes* (1994), Boone grapples with the key problems imbedded in the longstanding, narrow definition of writing that thinks of writing as a graphic system that captures and makes speech visible. Boone opens the way for a more ample definition of writing, one capable of housing Aztec iconographic representations and Maya glyphs. Part of this discussion is supported by the fact that the final decoding of the Maya glyph system came about as scholars were able to overcome inherited ideas about the location of the invention of writing (only in the "Old World") as well as convictions about the alphabetic necessity of any writing system.

The new thinking about the multiple invention of writing, forced scholars to set aside the idea that "natives" did not understand their own cultural systems. Maya scholars first returned to the instructions given by the Maya priest to Landa in the sixteenth century (Coe 145-166), and later to contemporary Maya speakers, for linguistic and ethnographic data and interpretation in order to finally decipher the Maya code. The riveting story of all the misconceptions and racist attitudes that impeded the recognition of the Maya glyphs as writing and the recent interdisciplinary findings that led to its deciphering have given scholars a new impetus for deciphering the codes in Aztec and Mixtec iconography, and as well as the *quipu*.

Boone points out that the assumption that writing is visible speech has been fundamental to the construction of European ideas about writing. This assumption establishes an inextricable link between writing and the voice. It is further assumed that writing was invented only once in the course of human history and that such an invention is constitutive to the singular position of Europe as the place where original cognitive events of the highest order take place. These assumptions normalize and universalize our received ideas about writing and, in doing so, they get in the way of conceiving of writing as other modalities of recording and communicating information (Boone 3). This notion informs, for instance, the Spanish claim that Atahualpa threw the Bible on the floor because he expected to hear the book speak. The Spanish friar who "reported" the event intended to convey the idea that the Inca was not sophisticated enough to know that writing enables one to *see* rather than *hear* speech. His readers, imbued with the same idea of writing, would of course come to the same conclusion without regard for any cultural and epistemological differences in play at the scene in Cajamarca. Contrary to the friar's account of the scene with the Bible, Boone states that for Indigenous American cultures "visible speech" was not always the goal. In Mexico, for instance, what we call "art" and writing were one and the same thing. Aztecs used one single graphic system (3) which does not necessarily record language (5). This system conveys meaning without expressing language (6). In this sense, the Aztec system is not unlike music, mathematics, or visual ideas; systems which express meaning without falling back into language. Boone observes that in the West, the "notational systems of math and science were developed precisely because ordinary language could not express the full import of scientific relations" (9). In fact, structure is generally effectively depicted visually (diagrams), for the eye can take in at once a greater sense of relations than the serial linguistic form allows.

Thus Boone goes on to propose a new definition of writing: "the communication of relatively specific ideas in a conventional manner by means of permanent, visible marks" (15). Under this definition, the glottographic system of Maya writing, and the Mixteca-Aztec semasiographic system (picture writing), find a place as effective means of communication and accumulation of knowledge. This definition also allows for the *quipu* to enter the hall of "writing," for despite the fact that it has no phonetic counterpart, the *quipu* holds and conveys information, separate from language (20), in a system that has been lately compared to the way computerized programming works. *Quipus*, too, function semasiographically, for the elements—color, size, location, texture, complication of the knot, number—are conventional rather than iconographic.

Quipus, like other systems of recording memory and knowledge, indeed like "writing" itself, can be understood as a system of human semiotic interaction inasmuch as *quipus* are produced in "a community and within a body of knowledge in which: a) a person produces a visible sign with the purpose of conveying a message to somebody other than himself; b) a person perceives the visible sign and interprets it as a sign produced for the purposes of conveying a message; and c) the person attributes a meaning to the visible sign" (Mignolo, "Signs" 229). In this definition of writing or conception of the *quipu* as a semiotic system, there is no need to necessarily institute the representation of speech.

Lately scholars have made great strides in decoding the *quipu* system. The question under consideration is whether the *quipu* was simply a mnemonic device that offered "cues" to the *quipukamayuc*, as the Spanish chroniclers claimed, or whether the system can be considered "writing." New incursions have been characterized by a mathematical approach to the tactile-visual system of cords, knots, colors, and textures. Marcia Ascher and Robert Ascher, in *Code of the Quipu: A Study of Media, Mathematics, and Culture* (1981), have led the way. Scholars have also been keenly interested in the idea that *quipus* did not only encode mathematical knowledges, but were also capable of encoding narrative. Gary Urton, in *Signs of the Inka Khipu: Binary Coding in the Andean Knotted-String Records* (2003) characterizes the *quipu* as a "powerful system of coding information that was at home in pre-Columbian South America, and which, like the coding system used in present-day computer language, was structured primarily as a binary code" (1). Urton has examined the largest number of archeological and colonial *quipus* thus far included in any study. His historical and theoretical study leads him to think that the *quipu*—the system of knotted strings—was used for recording both statistical and narrative information. With this claim, Urton's understanding of the *quipu* moves beyond mathematical studies and explores the earlier claims made by the *mestizo* intellectuals like Garcilaso de la Vega, Inca (1539-1616) and Blas Valera (1545-1597) regarding the *quipu*'s capacity to encode and store narrative information. Urton thinks that the *quipu* was constructed with "conventionalized units of information that could be read by khipu masters throughout the empire" (3). So it seems that the type of information stored in the *quipu* was at least of two kinds: statistical and narrative. Thus the *quipu* allowed for accounting and recounting or telling.

Like other modern scholars, Urton draws on the system of conceptualization and organization that is peculiar to the Andes. In an effort to bring to bear the Andean modes of thinking to the discussion, Urton introduces a new analytical idea: binary coding. This enables him to propose a "separation between the recording code and the script, or the 'readable' message, in the khipu" (162). He can thus conclude that the binary coding of the *quipu* "constituted a means of encoding paired elements that were in relationships of binary opposition to each other, and that, at a semantic level, these relations were of a character known in the literature as markedness relations" (162). Urton states that he has "sketched out a theory of interpreting the hierarchical and asymmetrical signs" of non-decimal *quipu* as the "architecture for canonical literatures (e.g. poetry, historical narrative) whose essential components would have been noted by the khipukamayuc and used as the framework.... for constructing narrative recitations" (164).

The guiding idea here is that binary coding was one of the principle mechanisms and strategies for thinking in the Andes. Thus Urton looks for features of cords that apparently mimic Andean logical structures rather than depart from the Indo-Arabic arithmetic as an a priori assumption. Urton privileges binarism because it is widely recognized as the primary category of Andean thought and social organization. He argues that fiber working requires binarism from the very initial stages of spinning to cord and textile making. In this sense, cord-making mimetizes the logical operations that generate Andean order. For Urton the sign that a cord contains is not the cord, but rather the aggregate of binary combinations (left/ right, cotton/wool, single/double, color/neutral) that construct the cord and function as bits of information. Urton's theory is not wedded to a mathematical model and as such leaves open the possibility that the *quipu* cord could encode segments of speech, words, or even syllables. In this way the *quipu* would be capable of registering "writing" in the usual sense of visible signs that correspond to segments of speech.

One of the most important aspects of Urton's research is that his method and arguments might finally put to rest the notion originally put forth by José de Acosta (1540-1600) and Bernabé Cobo (1580-1657) in 1653, and repeated throughout the centuries with respect to the *quipu*. Both argued that the *quipus* were simply a mnemonic device—not a system—that was used as a memory aid by the *quipukamayuc*. Thus, the intellectual capacity of the *quipu* depended entirely on the interpreter's own abilities. This notion may have been developed in view of the fact that the Inca empire was multilingual, and neither Cobo nor Acosta could imagine how a *quipu* knotted in one part of the empire could be "read" in another if the languages spoken were not the same. The conception of "writing" as visible speech impeded the cognitive imagination of both scholars. Despite the fact that neither Cobo nor Acosta managed to explain how the *quipu* was "read' across the many languages spoken in the Inca empire, a problem that would have called for positing the existence of a system rather than simple "cues," nor how the *quipu* served as the primordial tool in the governance of a huge and efficient state, their ideas remained unchallenged through the centuries. In fact they served to manufacture and cement the epistemological violence that characterized the colonization of the Amerindian cultures by Europe.

While *Signs of the Inka Khipu* has been widely regarded as a major breakthrough in Andean studies, Galen Brokaw writes that, despite the fact that Urton presents compelling archeological evidence for the conventionality of the *quipu* system, he nevertheless does not present enough ethnographic evidence to support the argument about the conventionality of the binary features, nor about the computer-style binary code

(Brokaw, "Toward Deciphering" 574). Further, Brokaw argues that Urton "conflates the referential and the poetics" or the structure of cultural interactions (577). For Brokaw it does not follow that "the fact that Andean Cultures organize the world into binary categories... a homologous structure characterized the operation of reference itself" (578). This scholar also finds it hard to imagine how the *quipu* could support two readings, one numeric and one binary. Brokaw believes that the numeracy direction, as pursued by the Aschers, will eventually result in a better understanding of the *quipu* than the binary code model proposed by Urton (586-87). However, in "The Poetics of Khipu Historiography" (2003) Brokaw also attempts to make the case for the *quipu* as a system capable of storing narrative information. By comparing two colonial documents that certifiably claim *quipus* as their immediate source and *quipukamayuc* as their "readers" in the Quechua oral rendition of the contents, Brokaw is able to establish that there existed a *quipu* biographical narrative genre (112).

One of the documents Brokaw examines is *El primer nueva corónica y buen gobierno* ([1615], 1980) by Guamán Poma de Ayala. Contrary to almost all of the interpreters of Guamán Poma who have detected and commented on the European models operating in his work, Brokaw makes the case for a *quipu*-based historiographic genre as the guiding model in the first part of Guamán Poma's extensive letter to the king. Brokaw goes as far as hypothesizing that "much of the information about indigenous Andean history that appears in the *Nueva corónica* was collected either directly or indirectly from khipus" (116). In his study of *quipu* poetics Brokaw concludes that "undeniably the khipu employed a set of highly complex conventions capable of encoding semasiographic or even phonographic information that included highly stable genres of discourse" (141). He thus agrees, if not on the same grounds or with the same methodology, with the claims that Garcilaso de la Vega, Inca, in his *Comentarios reales* of 1609, made for the *quipu*. This revalidation of Garcilaso as a reliable informant is important because the ethno-historian María Rostworowski (1983) found some of her findings at variance with the Inca's, and concluded from there that Garcilaso's work was not to be trusted, especially when it came to cognitive and narrative claims for the *quipu*.

Frank Salomon, in his *The Cord Keepers* (2004) tackles anew the question of the colonial and the ethnographic *quipus*. His book is the most comprehensive study of both archeological and ethnographic *quipu* to

date. Salomon points out that the archeological or pre-Hispanic *quipus*
that have thus far been examined with radiocarbon dating show that by
600 CE Andean peoples were making highly complex *quipus* (11). Thus
the art of *quipu* making is not only Pan-Andean, but also indicates a
deeply-rooted continuous use and development of an art that precedes
the Incas by a millennium (11). In Inca times, Salomon asserts, the
quipukamayuc or royal *quipu* masters used the cords for imperial cen-
suses, the calendar, inventories of all kinds (food, clothing, tribute, arms,
soldiers, game-keeping,), *chanson de geste*, royal chronicles, sacrifices,
genealogies, successions, postal messages, and even criminal trials (11).
The *quipu* was thus not only versatile, but also demotic, as the information managed by the *quipucamayoc* originated in very small or even
remote localities such as the household, the herder, the soldier, or the
chasqui. Salomon writes that the *quipu* developed among peoples who
spoke a multitude of languages and that the art of putting information on
a string may be a branching tree of inventions (13). In view of the fact that
we do not have a graphogenesis for the *quipu* as we do for writing and its
origins, Salomon thinks that it makes better sense not to think of the
quipu as a single code (13). *Quipus* may have been, at the state level, very
conventional and capable of registering maximally comparable accounts
proceeding from different parts of society. But at the local level, *quipus*
may have been more actor-centered (17) and encoded with greater iconi-
cal dimensions.

Salomon is mainly interested in showing, based on his ethnographic
work, that the "khipu's double capability for simulating and document-
ing social action" works as the "hinge for the articulation between kinship organization and political organization" (7). He argues that his
reconstruction is compatible with the structure of ancient *quipu* specimens (7). Salomon also shows that the supposed political demise of the
cord in the early colony constitutes a misreading of the colonial life of the
art of the cord. In the province of Huarochirí, for instance, the *quipu* was
used right along with the lettered culture (21) that entered the Andes with
the introduction of Spanish imperial linguistic policies. Finally, he argues
that his ethnographic study of the Tupicocha *quipu* practices demonstrates a root relationship between inscription and Andean social complexity (7).

Salomon, Urton, and Brokaw are not the only scholars to approach
the *quipu* from an Andean perspective. Thomas Abercrombie (1998)

argues that the Andean ideal of knowledge is itself centered on the metaphor of pathways. The past was imagined as "chronotopography." In this regard John Rowe had suggested earlier that the *ceque* system resembled a *quipu* spread out in the shape of a circle. For Abercrombie, *quipu* cords are paths guiding the hands, eyes, and mind to the trans-temporal, genealogical line of the sources of things. In this sense it is the spatial and not the verbal faculty that organizes recall (Salomon 19).

In his *Royal Commentaries*, Garcilaso de la Vega, Inca writes that the *quipu* also registered poems and narrative (Book 2, chapter 27). Scholars are still searching for the understanding that would allow cord structures to be matched to narrative structures. Gordon Brotherston, in *Book of the Fourth World: Reading the Native Americas Through Their Literature* (1992), argues that *quipus* could record and "therefore transcribe not just mathematics, but also discourse" (78), and he cites as an example the hymn that Garcilaso published in his *Royal Commentaries.* However, Brotherston's best examples and support for his argument are drawn from the post-colonial Quechua alphabetic literary corpus that arises in the Andes after 1532. Brotherston speculates that the presence of *quipus* in burials suggests that they could tell the biographies of persons (78-9). The study of the chronicles by Martín de Murúa (1590) and Guamán Poma also lead Brotherston to think that the *quipu* recorded not only annals capable of reaching deep into the past, like the Mesoamerican *teomoxtli* (78), but also ceremonial cycles, calendars, hymns of worship and kinship dramas (79). From this perspective, Guamán Poma's *Corónica* can be seen as "a complete account of empire based on native-script records and submitted to the Spanish authorities" (80) by the last of the *quipucamayoc* (Mendizábal Losack 91) who drew directly on the taxonomy and the ideology of the *quipu* (decimal system, reciprocity, oppositional duality, *hanan/hurin*, chronotopography).

Brotherston's detailed study of the play *Apu Ollantay* and its inescapable inscription into both Inca literary pastoralism and kinship drama shows convincingly how the story of the forbidden love between the princess Cusi Coyllor and the heroic commoner Ollantay is part of a *quipu* literary corpus performed in Cuzco by courtiers on public holidays (204). Much work is yet to be done on the considerable corpus of postcolonial Quechua drama, which ranges from the overtly pagan, as *Apu Ollantay*, to the Christian, manifesting deep roots in both the Inca artistic legacy and the Spanish secular and religious theater.

But if postcolonial Quechua language texts found conditions of possibility in both secular and religious drama as well as the lyric, alphabetic Quechua did not find its way in almost any other genre, be it precolonial or postcolonial. Scholars who lament the absence of court documents, letters, annals, or even personal life stories in Quechua are equally astonished by the abundant production of visual representation in art and architecture. In the new space of violence, engagement, resistance, and negotiation that the conquest inaugurated for Andean peoples, the life of written Quechua or Aymara registers a puzzling silence. It is difficult to ascertain the shape and dynamics of the arts of communication and thought in the post-conquest Andes if one's vision remains circumscribed to alphabetic scripted Amerindian languages. One must look beyond the alphabet into other means, modes, and conceptions of communication. A more ample sense of colonial semeiosis would allow for the idea of including iconographic signs into a system of communications in which the sign is not always linked to speech. By definition, this colonial cultural space also implies alternative and conflicting literacies and concepts of knowledge, as we have seen above in the case of the *quipu*.

Why did Andeans not engage writing in Quechua in order to memorialize the past or offer witness to their present? It is true that there were many prohibitions and obstacles, but despite them there appeared in the Andes a significant theater production. In tension with Spanish literary canons, Quechua lyrical traditions persisted through colonial times and reached up to the present. This absence of written texts appears in stark contrast with the wealth of images on paper, canvas, and other aesthetic or valuable objects such as *keros*, textiles, and *aquillas* (large silver bowls) that Andeans produced, exchanged, and used during and after the first hundred years after the fall of Cajamarca.

Inquiring into the issue of native Andean visual traditions, the art historian Tom Cummins, in "Let Me See! Reading is For Them: Colonial Andean Images and Objects" (1998), advances the notion that alphabetic writing was a technology and mode of memorializing life too distant from Andean visual and tactile modes of communication (95). Cummins interprets the scene at Cajamarca as an example of the fact that Andean culture relates orality (speech acts) to objects (the book) in an entirely different way from how Europe conceives of writing and thus books as printed speech (142). Cummins thinks that the Spanish explanation of why Atahualpa rejected the book (the book did not speak when

Atahualpa put it to his ear) is completely bogus. The Spanish interpretation of the scene at Cajamarca relies on the Talmudic tradition of close
textual reading that scrutinizes the text in search of an interpretation that
can reveal the meaning of history. In the Western textual tradition all
relationships between the object and a sense of the past are ruptured
(142). In contrast, objects in the Andean world had a greater place as sites
of memory and knowledge. Textiles and *keros* functioned not only as
testimony of the past but provided also a living link to history. They
aided in keeping the memory of the past alive and viable. These objects
constituted a form of inalienable wealth, a material site for the continuation of history, and as such they were venerated and brought out into the
public light at the time of the performance of the highest rituals when
communication with the Apukuna was in order (143).

The will to persist prompted native Andeans to engage with and contest colonial rule in a number of negotiations and exchanges. It is clear
from the *Huarochirí* (1598?) manuscript and the documentation on the
campaign to extirpate native Andean religion that the will to continue
religious practices and social conduct lead Andeans in search of representational spaces in which they could find room for their modes of perceiv-
ing and understanding the world. Cummins believes that the tactile and
visual modes of representation in relation to oral discourse remained for
Andeans the mode through which they preferred to "inscribe" their existence (95). While there appears to be a meeting ground of European and
Andean symbolic representation, it is neither the province of "syncretism" nor the deployment of other sites of writing. The mutual entanglement that defines colonial situations can be ascertained in the Andes in
the maintenance and circulation of costumes, images, and objects of tradition (140). The images found in *keros*, *aquillas*, and portraits, do not
appeal to the written word (134).

This space of entanglement presupposes the fragmentation of Inca
iconography with a subsequent redeployment in a colonial space ruled by
European visual and iconographic understandings. It is best illustrated by
the frontispiece that Guamán Poma chooses for his *El primer nueva
corónica y buen gobierno* (1615). In this image Guamán Poma redeploys
a number of iconographic signs in order to fabricate his "coat of arms."
He breaks up his name into a heraldic syntax in which the symbols of his
"house" are the eagle (*guamán*) and the mountain cat (puma). These mark
the two fields of his "coat of arms." In a descending hierarchical line he

places an image of himself below that of the Spanish king, and the two, in turn, under the Pope. Dividing the two fields of the frontispiece, he lines up the three coats of arms with the Pope's at the top and his at the bottom, thus producing an integration, exchange, and circulation of meanings that speak of a single, if ambivalent, space of signification. In this intellectual feat Guamán Poma has unmoored a number of signs. He redeployed them, creating a space for the inscription of significations that could be decoded by both Europeans and Andeans. The insertion of the *tiana*—traditional Andean seat of authority for *kurakas*—under the *guamán* on the left-hand side of his coat of arms underscores the Andean effort to resignify European spaces of representation with Andean objects and codes (Cummins 101).

The study of objects and images produced around the first seventy years after the fall of Cajamarca shows a strong continuation of native Andean representational practices. Images and symbols taken from a fragmented Inca iconographic canon appear now conjoined to European images and symbols in a representational space now rendered bivalent by their very presence and articulation. The new representational space flows as the images, despite their radical differences, "speak" to one another. This mutual entanglement of Andean images and symbols with European values, signs, and spaces enables the Andean objects and images to express meaning within both sides of the colonial society (94). This tactic for producing bivalent spaces and values of representation would remain in place through out the colonial period and extends into the present.

II. SPACES OF ENTANGLEMENT

From the perspective of the Amerindians, 1492 marks the inauguration of major, violent and irreversible changes in their histories, ways of life, and situation in the world. That year inscribes the establishment of a potent and permanent machinery of war supported by devastating weapons (horses, gods, steel swords), fueled by a providential concept of history and the power of alphabetic writing. The conquest moved along the path of destruction created by ravaging epidemic diseases for which the Amerindians had no defenses. In less than thirty years the peoples of the Caribbean were nearly extinct, while Mexico and Central America began to experience the ravages of the destructuration of their entire cultures by the military, the bureaucracy, and the evangelizing clergy. As the Spaniards moved South of El Darién (Panama) in search of El Dorado (a kingdom made of gold), small pox, colds, measles, and pneumonia preceded them. The death of Huayna Cápac, the last Inca, the father of Huáscar and Atahualpa, is attributed to one of these plagues. Much of this "glorious" march west and south is reported during the early stages of the conquest to his majesty and crown officials in diaries, letters, chronicles, reports (*relaciones*) and later, in local and general histories, as the Spanish *letrados* traveled right next to the soldiers and priests in search of treasure and free labor.

In examining this palimpsestic corpus of materials often written in the immediate aftermath of battle in America or in the midst of the endless struggle over the Spanish rights of possession and authority over the new lands and the Indians, it is clear that the polemic over the humanity of the Indians, and the issue of just war, permeated every page. Had the extinction of the Indian populations not become part of the generalized understanding of the conquest, this debate might not have reached the dominant tone that it acquired at the time and the force with which it thunders through the ages. The writing of the memory of the Spanish invasion, conquest, and colonization of America as available in the texts written by Columbus (ca.1451-1506), Gonzalo Fernández de Oviedo (1478-1557), Francisco López de Gómara (1511-1566), Hernán Cortés (1484-1547), Bernal Díaz del Castillo (1495-1584), Bartolomé de Las Casas (1474-1566), Pedro Cieza de León (1520-1554), Juan de Betanzos (?-1576), José de Acosta (1540-1600), Garcilaso de la Vega, Inca (1539-1616) and Guamán Poma de Ayala (1535-1516) among many others, may vary a great deal in the practice of history that animates them, the kinds of rhetoric that they deploy, and their possible philosophical sources in Spain, but they all drip with blood, and to that extent the idea of reading them as an extended practice of writing violence, as José Rabasa has recently analyzed in *Writing Violence on the Northern Frontier* (2000), does indeed go to the core of these texts. For reasons that cannot be taken up here, this heterogeneous corpus constitutes what Latin American literary critics and historians refer to as "letras coloniales" or "colonial literature." Despite the fact that the great majority of these texts were not intended by their authors as literature, nor were they read by their contemporaries as such (a good number of them were not published until the nineteenth century), critics have studied them under the lenses of literary analysis and have produced more complex interpretations than the first readings accorded to them by social scientists in search of "facts."

However, as the distinction between literary and nonliterary texts has become less theoretically sustainable, and the interpretative power of this distinction has waned under the more general idea of "text," these "letras coloniales" are often now accorded an interdisciplinary approach. Conceived as a cultural object, a text is a highly priced verbal act that plays a significant role in the organization of a given culture. Although most literary corpuses are articulated within the confines of a single language, in the case of the colonial corpus, it is the referent—America—that confers upon them a certain "unity," the corpus includes works in Latin and even Quechua. Walter Mignolo (1982) has classified this corpus into three major components: a) *cartas relatorias*, or letters that tell of some event in some detail often provided by the eye witness; b) *relaciones*, or reports generally, but not always, requested by the Crown in order to obtain extensive and detailed information not intended for publication or book form; c) *crónicas*, or chronicles that usually narrate a series of events. However, the *cronistas de Indias* generally did not write *crónicas* in the medieval tradition of annals. Inasmuch as they tried to recover the past in texts that exhibit certain literary or historiographic characteristics and emphasized discursive organization, the *cronistas* wrote *historias* (Mignolo, "Cartas" 59). These histories are centered on heroic and even exemplary lives (76). *Cronistas* such as Las Casas and Garcilaso de la Vega, Inca were much influenced by Roman historians, Cicero above all.

The consensus of the time held that the writing of history should be in the hands of the lettered (*letrados*) class and not in the hands of soldiers like Bernal Díaz del Castillo or Indians such as Guamán Poma. History writing was itself divided into several kinds: divine, human, natural, moral, and general (Mignolo, "Cartas" 78). History writing during the period of the conquest was practiced by men who were both soldiers and *letrados*. Fernández de Oviedo, who had spent some time in Italy before coming to America and was thus acquainted with Italian humanism, is the first to attempt one of these new histories with his long *Historia general y natural de las Indias* (1535). Oviedo wrote also as an official crown historian. He wanted to be remembered as the Pliny of the Indies. His idea of *historia natural* was to pull away from the Medieval bestiaries and

offer instead descriptions and interpretations based on eye witness observations made in the new lands. The conqueror-historian thought that history should deal with big and important subjects. Like other *cronistas,*
Oviedo was also trying to follow Cicero when he fashioned his *historia
moral* in a temporal frame that organized the reporting of worthwhile
events from various sources. The influence of Pliny in the arrangement of
nature would determine a hierarchical model with which to view America. Thus from the start, the idea of an *historia natural* allowed for the
classification, not just of plants and animals, but also of peoples and civilizations in an ascending ladder in which Europe would figure at the top
and the Amerindians somewhere at the bottom. This classification would
blend the natural with the moral and infuse all reports, letters, histories,
and polemics about the new world from Oviedo to Ginés de Sepúlveda
(1490-1573), to Las Casas and Acosta in *Historia natural y moral de las
Indias* (1590).

The conquest of this continent brought about a profusion of texts
beyond those identified above. Tracts, learned treatises, and even poems
found an avid public in both Europe and the colonial administrative centers. It gave rise to fierce debates about the nature of the Indians, colonial
policy, and the right to wage war on civilian populations. Lawyers, jurists,
academic intellectuals, crown officials, evangelizing and colonizing priests,
official historians, and even Charles V himself participated. The early,
prelapsarian image of the Indians created by the Italian humanists who
either worked in Spain or for the Spanish Crown soon came under attack
by Spanish warriors and colonists in the Caribbean who painted their enemies as fierce anthropophagic societies (Hulme 1986).

The implicit critique of the conquest imbedded in the characterization of Indian societies as fresh versions of Ovid's world by the Italians
(Peter Martyr d'Anghera, Amerigo Vespucci) was not lost on the Spanish
letrados or the Crown. Despite the fact that by 1530 the demographic
catastrophe was universally acknowledged, and despite the evidence that
the Indians were exhausted by famine, slave labor conditions, and disease,
Oviedo and Sepúlveda wrote stinging attacks on Indian societies. For
these two members of the imperial school of *cronistas,* the Indians were
lazy, vicious, lying, traitorous, half-witted beings given to melancholy,
anthropophagy, and sodomy, among other things. The list of phobias
remained expandable, as can be seen in Acosta's rehearsal of the Indian
portrait in 1590 and especially in his *De procurandam indorum salute*

(1557), a manual for the evangelization of the Indias printed in Lima and quickly disseminated in the rest of the empire. Both Garcilaso and Guamán Poma would spend considerable ink and paper in responding to Acosta (see chapter 5 in this volume, "Historiography on the Ground").

Oviedo began making his cunning views public in various polemics and short publications. He arrived for the first time in the New World in 1514 as a notary public, and soon after that he participated in the bloody conquest of El Darién (Panama) in 1517. There he proudly took his booty in human flesh and he himself branded the Indians to be enslaved and placed in his service. In 1532, after having gone to Spain to publish his *Sumario de la natural historia de la Indias* (1524) and to ask for royal favors, he returned to the New World. He then accepted the lifelong appointment as constable of the royal fortress of Santo Domingo and royal chronicler of the Indies. (Brading 33) Oviedo is regarded as one of the principle advocates of Spain's imperial power. His arguments were fundamental to the cynical deployment of the idea of providential history in which Spain figures as the nation chosen by God to make Christianity universally triumphant. Along with the Spanish Neoplatonist theologians, Oviedo believed that the emperor Charles V was indeed the new sun.

Subscribing to the same doctrine of providential history, Las Casas, a colonist and also slave owner, suffered in 1514 a crisis of conscience. This crisis was due in part to his daily witnessing of the Caribbean holocaust, and in part to the preaching of Franciscans monks in Cuba who realized that the conquest ran contrary to almost every Christian principle. In 1531 Las Casas wrote a memorial to the Council of the Indies. There he warned Spain of eternal damnation if it did not stop the slaughter of the Indians. For years he had been intervening on behalf of the Indians as well as preparing a massive treatise in their defense and conservation.

Las Casas came from a family of converses (Jewish people who had converted to Christianity). As an adventurous lad of 18 years, he arrived in Hispaniola in 1502 eager to make his fortune as a colonist. His father and uncle had accompanied Columbus in his second voyage. They brought him an (enslaved) Indian boy as a souvenir from the islands. Between 1502 and 1514 Las Casas fought as a soldier in the conquest of Cuba. In 1510 the Dominicans arrived in Hispaniola and began denouncing the Spaniards' treatment of the Indians. They also noted the demographic collapse. The Friar Antonio de Montesinos gave an impassioned sermon in 1512 in which he articulated the questions and critique that Las

Casas and his followers were to repeat throughout the centuries: "Are they [the Indians] not human? Do they not have rational souls? Are you not obliged to love them as yourselves?" (Brading 59). The response was the official wrath of the Crown and the church. More atrocities followed.

After his conversion, with the support of the Dominicans, he returned to Spain to campaign in behalf of the Indians and to build alliances, most especially with the bishop of Burgos (Castro 63-102). Las Casas's strategy, not unlike the advice Guamán Poma offered the Spanish king almost a century later, was to make the church and the Crown realize that it was in their benefit to keep the Indians in good condition. His proposals were always reform. He wanted to improve the conditions under which the Indians were integrated, albeit more slowly and peacefully, into the strictly hierarchical colonial world that was emerging. The very title of one of this best known tracts, *Memorial de remedios* (1516), indicates that Las Casas's project, heroic as it was in demanding that the power system in place recognize the humanity of the Indias, could not advocate a radical turn away from the policies of conquest and colonization. As one of his most recent analysts has put it: "What differentiates him from the rest, is his willingness to reach out to offer temporary succor to those being victimized so that they could be benevolently converted, peacefully exploited, and successfully incorporated as members of the new subject-colony where existence depended on the dictates of the king in the imperial capital" (Castro 8).

Nevertheless, Las Casas recommended the abolition of the *encomienda*, that is the king's donation of immense tracks of land and thousands of Indians in perpetuity to individual Spaniards who had served in the armies that carried out the conquest. The *encomienda* system and its later modifications stayed firmly in place until the first half of the twentieth century as the coloniality of power, or rather the dependence of the modern world on its colonial underside, never really entirely waned (Mignolo, "Preamble"). The Dominican friar hoped to persuade the king of the evils of the *encomienda* by citing the particulars horrors and grief that accompanied the population collapse. In Hispaniola, he reported, out of two million Indians found in 1492, only 15,000 remained at the time he wrote the *Memorial* (1516).

Las Casas, who had an *encomienda* in Cuba, described the forced labor conditions and wanton killings in wrenching detail. He had lost all confidence in the ability of his compatriots to treat the Indians in a Christian way. By way of remedies he suggested that Indians and Spaniards live in separate communities, a measure that to some extent was later put in place in Peru not so much to protect the Indians as to better exploit their labor. The idea that the Indians should be left in communities of their own was predicated on the notion that they had demonstrable intelligence to rule themselves, even though they needed still the light of Christianity to fully achieve their divinely intended purpose on earth. Thus the Indian communities would be under the care and tutelage of an evangelizing priest. This idea of separate communities was later embraced by Guamán Poma, who also wrote to the king in search of relief from the death toll of the conquest and Spanish rule. Guamán Poma, however, went beyond Las Casas in that he would also expel the priests about whose greed and un-Christian practices he writes a scathing tract in his *El primer nueva corónica y buen gobierno* (1615).

The reforms spelled out in the *Memorial de remedios* constituted the seedbed for many of the attempts made later by the evangelizing orders and even some Crown officials to engage in what Las Casas envisioned as a peaceful conversation. His stance in defense of the Indians against the charges made by the school of Spanish imperial jurists, theologians, and historians (Brading 2-75) has earned Las Casas the title of defender and protector of the Indians. He is also credited as the progeniture of the modern idea of human, that is, universal, rights.

As we shall see below, Las Casas went even further. After the killings of Moctezuma and Atahualpa, he argued that pagan civilizations had the right to keep their governments, and their members were entitled to restitution of the goods and life the conquerors had usurped. All of this swimming against the current earned him the hatred of many people in both the colonies and Spain. During his long life (1474-1566) he was feared, despised, and opposed by many who saw him as the enemy of Spain. Indeed, from the official point of view among Spanish historians, he was and is still regarded as the architect of what they called the Black Legend— the myriad facts and arguments that together question the legitimacy of Spain's right to conquer and govern Amerindian societies, together with the unmitigated and unavoidable condemnation of the destruction of the Amerindians. The polemic that Las Casas's criticism of conquest fueled with his *Memorial* dominated the whole of the sixteenth century, and nowhere was it heard more loudly or did it play a stronger role than in the dynamics of memory and writing of the former Tahuantinsuyo.

Las Casas crossed the Atlantic several times as he sought to obtain changes in policy in Spain and see them implemented in the New World. What he saw in his many journeys to Venezuela, Mexico, and Nicaragua never ceased to astound and shock him. Peaceful conversation was not even an idea in the heads of most of the evangelizing priests. In his *Del único modo de atraer a todos los pueblos a la verdadera religión* (1530-40), he argued that all peoples of the world were endowed with the same human qualities and cognitive faculties and that God had predestined all souls for salvation. This universalist argument could, however, be interpreted in two opposing ways. On the one hand, it could support the idea of a God-given human universal condition to all peoples, but on the other, it made conversion only the more urgent. In order to stem the force of the second reading, Las Casas argued that the Gospel should be predicated slowly and peacefully, that evangelists should seek to persuade and engage the cognitive capacities of peoples who, like all men endowed with natural enlightenment, sought to know the true God. Preaching was thus coupled with persuasion, an appeal to knowledge and love (Brading 64). The violence of the conquest had created impossible conditions for the proper preaching of the gospel, and it should stop, he argued.

The news from the Americas was shocking and alarming to many Europeans and there developed a great deal of pressure for reform. The Pope finally declared the Indians to have souls. Las Casas's most radical denunciation of Spain and proposals for change were published in his summary work *Brevísima relación de la destrucción de las Indias* (1542). In this text he draws stark differences. Resting on the idea that the discovery of America was an act of divine providence, an idea that Garcilaso de la Vega will later exploit also, Las Casas paints the Indians as gentle and humble human beings in virtual expectation of conversion. The Spaniards, in contrast, are nothing but thieves and tyrants. They burn, torture, murder, enslave, and rape at will, as most eyewitness accounts attest. His proposal for radical reform not only recommends the abolition of the *encomienda*, but also the idea that once the Indians are converted and Spain has accomplished its duty as provided by God, the Spanish should retreat from America, a suggestion not lost in Guamán Poma, who not only promises the king good Indians (Christian vassals) but also unimaginable tribute. The restoration of Andean order and wealth would only be possible if the Spanish retreat to the coastal cities and leave the Andeans to govern themselves.

In 1542 the Spanish Crown came out with new legislation for govern-
ing the colonies. Known as the New Laws, and in part influenced by Las
Casas's critique and recommendations for better government, the New
Laws were rejected by the colonists. Civil war broke out in Peru and more
Andeans were compelled to fight and die in the opposing armies of the
Pizarros, Almagros, and other sundry *caudillos*. Las Casas, deeply influenced by Augustine's *City of God* and the difference in the social orders
created by the love of God as against the love of self, continued to question
the entire legitimacy of the Spanish empire (Brading 78). Derived from
Augustine's *On the Predestination and the Gift of Perseverance*, the idea of
the providential discovery of America provides Las Casas with an explanation for the failure of the Spanish to establish the city of God in America.
Carried away by the self-love that rules in the earthly city, the Spanish
acted as if inspired by the devil (Brading 76). The paramount role that providence plays in the polemics and policies of conquest and relations with
other civilizations is only comparable to the extended functions invested in
the devil (Cervantes 5-75) as the chief presider of the construction of
Amerindian "otherness," or colonial difference.

In response to the barrage of questions brought about by Las Casas's
vociferous interventions, Charles V called for a "junta" or meeting of
jurists and theologians. The chief questions to be put to rest in Valladolid
in 1550-51 were the human status of the Indians and the problematic
behavior of the conquerors, never Spain's right to dominion over the
earth. The jury was composed of Dominican theologians and the two
debaters were to be Las Casas, the friar, and Juan Ginés de Sepúlveda
(1490-1573), the lawyer, known as a defender of the imperial rights of the
Spanish Crown. The chief debaters never saw each other over the long
year in which the debate took place. When Las Casas's turn came he took
five days to read his *Apologética historia* to the judges.

In the debate at Valladolid Las Casas had to contend not only with
Sepúlveda, but also with another, absent adversary. Juan López de Palacios Rubios (1450-1524) had been one of the first Spanish jurists to come
to the defense of Spanish lawful right to empire. He based his arguments
on scholastic theology and medieval canon law rather than civil law. As
far as he could reason and, basing himself on Aristotle, the Indians were
"slaves by nature" in need of tutelage and correction before they could be
fit for self rule. This argument, like several of Las Casas's arguments,
would also reverberate through the centuries and can even be found

today when "modern" democracies demand to be regarded and adopted as the universal model.

Palacios Rubios also worked very cleverly in finding an imperial genealogy for the Pope's political authority over the world. He argued that the world had seen four previous, universal "monarchies"—Assyrians, Medes, Greeks, and Romans— before Christ had inaugurated the fifth and last monarchy of the world. Thus the Pope, as the Vicar of Christ, exercised both spiritual and temporal power over the entire world and could indeed delegate such authority on Spain (Brading 80-81). So Palacios Rubios devised the *Requerimiento* (Seed), a document to be read to the Indians upon their first encounter with the Spaniards that would inform them of the hegemony of the Pope and the king over the entire world. It followed that any Indian who did not accept the authority of the Pope was subject to legitimate acts of war and conquest. The *Requerimiento* was used for the first time in the conquest of El Darién in 1517, a campaign in which Oviedo participated. This document made Oviedo's taking and branding of slaves and the atrocities denounced by Las Casas "legal." The stakes in the Valladolid debate could not have been higher.

Another absent interlocutor in Valladolid was the Dominican and professor of theology and philosophy at Salamanca, Francisco de Vitoria (1486-1546). Like Palacios Rubios, Vitoria had never been to America. He did not have the benefit or the authority of the ocular observer. He worked from reports and from his rich library. In 1534, he, like many others, was shocked to hear of the unlawful execution (regicide) in Cajamarca of the Inca Atahualpa and he wrote on the problem of Spain and the Amerindians without being solicited by the Crown to do so (Pagden 64-80). Vitoria was one of the leaders of the Thomist revival in Spain. He followed Thomas Aquinas's reasoning regarding the difference between pagans and Christians. The theory of natural law was the discursive frame within which the theologians at Salamanca analyzed the critical question that Amerindians posed for European epistemology and theology.

In 1537 Vitoria wrote *Relectio de Indis* (1557), a work that circulated widely in manuscript form and had a lasting imprint in all future discussion concerning the Indies. In *De Indis*, the theologian tries to find an answer to the unthinkable question: What if there is no just title to the conquest of America? As Anthony Pagden points out, with this question Vitoria takes the problem of "just title" out of the strict realm of the law and places it in the space of theology, for the problem involved settling the chief question regarding the nature of the Indian *qua* man (66-67). It was clear to Vitoria from the reports received on Mexico and Peru that the Indians were not simple irrational beings, and thus any common-sense discussion could demonstrate that the Indians were not monkeys but human beings. Relying on Aristotle, Vitoria reasoned that the Indians clearly had the use of reason, in their own way. They had order in their affairs, they had properly organized cities, recognizable forms of marriage, magistrates, rulers, laws, industry, and commerce. They also had religion. For Vitoria, as it had been for Aristotle, the city stood for the most perfect unit of society, the "only place where the practice of virtue and the pursuit of happiness" are at all possible (Pagden 69). Man, for both Plato and Aristotle, can only realize himself as a citizen. Christianity transforms the secular, Greek city into a spiritual community (69). Indeed, St. Augustine could only conceive of the world, both celestial and earthly, as urban. People who built cities and lived in them could simply not be thought of as barbarians or natural slaves. By definition they were civilized. Vitoria found that the Indian societies also exhibited two other traits of civilization: they engaged in trade and hospitality, and they had visibly organized religious, social, and spiritual practices.

However, in the second part of *De Indis*, the part that deals with just title to conquest, Vitoria stars to back-peddle and begins to offer the *contra* argument required in scholastic argument (Pagden 80). There he speaks not of what Indian societies practiced but of what they did not, or rather how they did not resemble Europe, whose assumed normative character had underlined the entire discussion on natural and divine law. Vitoria argued that Indian law was insufficiently wise and unsatisfactory. He abandoned the urban model argument and focused instead on the reports of cannibalism, sodomy, and bestiality which he thought violated the natural order. The Indians' dietary and sexual practices showed that they were not only irrational but even mentally defective and thus incapable of governing themselves (Pagden 85-7).

Vitoria's arguments exposed the insurmountable contradictions driving the discourses of the conquest-cum-evangelization. The contradictions imbedded in the theory of natural law itself were brought to their critical limits, for they were being used to account for the simultaneous, but unthinkable, perception of *sameness* and *difference* that the European cognitive complex obtained from contact with the Amerindians. This conundrum, this limitation in European epistemology, has shadowed the history of Amerindian peoples to the present, for "if the natural slave is incapable of participating in a state of happiness, then he must also be incapable of achieving his proper end (*telos*) as a man. If nature never creates anything which is, of itself, incapable of accomplishing its ends—for such a thing would be useless—then the natural slave is not a man" (Pagden 94).

Vitoria managed to cover over this blind spot in his discourse by appealing to the idea that God created man and that the essential characteristic of man is his rational mind. Thus the Indians' faults and deficiencies could eventually be rubbed out with proper education and discipline, a solution that was not that far away from Las Casas's idea of peaceful and slow conversion. Paradoxically this idea translated into the very harsh laws and bodily punishment that Toledo (1515-1582) put in place in the Andes, in part supported by the denigrating ideas that Acosta put forth in the Third Council of Lima in 1579, and earlier in *De Procuranda* (1557). From the clay that Vitoria's hands molded, the Indian came out not a slave, but a child. In this scheme the king of Spain was the tutor of the Indians. When the Indians no longer required tutoring, they would be left to enjoy their proper liberty. Even though Vitoria had paved the way for a pastoral Spanish evangelization, he had also managed to dismantle Palacios' argument on the universal authority of the Pope and by implication Charles' imperial crown. Vitoria had even dared reason that idolatry was not grounds for dispossession of the Indians. He thus offered the grounds for legal challenges to the ongoing wanton dispossession of the Indians by conqueror, Crown, and church. Upon hearing of the scandalous positions, Charles V ordered Vitoria to stop intervening in the question of the Indies (Pagden 106; Brading 84).

Juan Ginés de Sepúlveda was partly educated in Bologna and Rome. He had been a tutor to Philip II, and by 1536 he was appointed imperial chronicler. He published a tract against Erasmus's pacifism in order to defend the European warrior code and social structure (Brading 86). In 1544 he wrote a dialogue, *Democrates Secundus*, in order to defend the Spanish conquest and empire in the world. He drew his information and arguments in part from Oviedo and Gómara. For him the Indians were slaves by nature for they lacked prudence, intelligence, virtue, and even humanity, all the attributes that the Renaissance thought citizens ought to have. He also defined the Indians by what they were not, especially when it came to lacking "writing." From there he surmised that Indians also lacked history, laws, had no sense of self-consciousness, had no notion of private property, and were, in general, ruled by tyrants. Sepúlveda's challenge caused Las Casas to rethink his materials in order to demonstrate that the Indians were *not* different and that they could be both as savage and as civilized as the Europeans (Brading 88-89). The Dominican had to begin moving toward a comparative ethnography with the ancient world, a move not lost on Garcilaso de la Vega, Inca in his later *Comentarios reales* (1609). In the Valladolid debate, Las Casas's job was to prove that the Indians were neither natural slaves, nor "homunculus," as Sepúlveda would have it, but rather normal human beings created by God, even if the Bible did not mentioned them. By and large he accomplished this seemingly impossible task.

The arguments that Las Casas brandished in this fight were garnished from his *Historia de las Indias* (1542) and his later *Apologética historia sumaria* (1551). Probably the best study to date of Las Casas's thought on the matter can be found in David Brading's *The First America*. In order to frame a sense of cultural evolution Las Casas turned to Cicero and his idea of stages in the natural history of humanity. For Cicero, all men in all nations are essentially the same in their nature. For Las Casas, it was not hard to show that the Aztecs and the Incas resembled the Greeks and the Romans. For instance, of Aristotle's six requirements or marks of civilized life, all could be found in the Amerindian societies: agriculture, artisans and artists, a warrior class, rich men, organized religion, lawful government, and city life. Once again he deployed St. Augustine's argument on natural light and the desire of all men to seek and serve God (Brading 90). Las Casas's approach to Amerindian religions required that he really stretch the comparative frame, and while the thickly-populated Greek and the Aztec pantheons could be profitably compared, some of the rituals and practices of Amerindian religions simply had to be attributed to the devil's ability to gain hold of pagans. In the case of the Incas, whose solar-centric religion was not accompanied with either a large pantheon of other divinities or with a fertile set of mythological narratives, as in the case of the Mexican pantheon, Las Casas made a particular point of arguing that the Incas had on their own come very close to reasoning the existence of a single, paramount god (monotheism).

Despite his comparative ethnology and defense of the Indian's humanity, Las Casas still had to devise a reason that would justify the Spanish empire, as he was an advocate of royal authority. He agreed with Vitoria's argument on the natural right to rule of the Indian monarchs. Idolatry alone did not justify deposing or killing them. He attacked Sepúlveda's argument on the natural slavery of the Indians by saying that it was blasphemy against God to say that He had created a brutish and inferior "race" (Brading 95). Therefore, all wars of conquest against the Indians were unjust. At this point, caught in a dilemma, Las Casas had no choice but to follow Vitoria in defining papal authority as only spiritual—not political—a claim that left the king with no right to a universal empire. The Dominican friar pulled out of his blind spot, not unlike Vitoria, by claiming that the very same spiritual authority obliged the Pope and the king to see to it that the Indians were Christianized, that is to say "educated" into being better men. With this (moral) argument he restored all political authority to the Crown. Indeed, "the only way out," as he entitled one of his tracts, was peaceful conversion, which to the conquerors and colonists sounded like more of the same. It proved impossible to find a balance between the right to convert the peoples of the world and the right of the pagan rulers to preserve their independence. How to serve God in the midst of thieves? is the question that hounded Las Casas's life, as he saw the New World fall off a precipice of evil and injustice.

III. From Valladolid to Cuzco, or How to "Write" the Andean Past and Present

It is in the horns of these irreconcilable claims, these epistemological and ethical dilemmas, that the intellectual and political project of all those who wrote about the Andes after the fall of Cajamarca in 1532 are inscribed. The polemic on the nature of the American Indian that took place, as a result of confusing the Bible with world history, reverberated through the centuries causing all kinds of distortions and misconceptions, blocking the ability to produce new learning and even a more or accurate approach to empirical realities. When Francisco Pizarro (1478-1541) decided to execute Atahualpa and march to Cuzco with his Huanca allies, the priest who accompanied him wrote a report, today considered bogus, to justify the regicide. According to the Spaniards, Atahualpa had committed blasphemy. The scene elaborated has the Spanish showing the Inca a book—the Bible—and telling him that that is the word of God, to which the Inca must submit. Atahualpa, receives the book from the friar's hands, puts it to his ear, and upon hearing nothing he shakes it. He still hears nothing.

Then, angered, he throws the book on the floor, saying that it cannot be God because it does not speak to him. Tom Cummins disputes the idea that the Inca would have expected an object to mimic the word because in the Andes, speech and writing were not associated with objects, as they were in Europe ("Let Me See!"). It is clear also from the lack of adequate translators at the moment that the Spaniards could not have conveyed the message they claim to have given Atahualpa about the book-the-Word-divinity. What the fiction of Father Valderde speaks of is the power claims that the written word allows the conquerors to make in their representative relation with the king of Spain. This is the brash and unreflecting power amalgam of ideas and military power that Andeans, and even Spaniards, would have to address every time they took up the pen to tell the story of the conquest, reconstruct the history of the Incas, petition for favors or advancement, or contest the practices and justifications for the injuries wrought upon people by the colonial regime. Again, providential history was the umbrella that protected all, from those who praised the conquest and destruction of the Andean way of life, to those who, like Garcilaso de la Vega, Inca, wrote to correct the Spanish imperial historians, or Guamán Poma, who hoped to tutor the Spanish king into understanding what good government really would be like.

The conquest of Peru is dominated by a fractious engagement of Spaniards and Andean peoples who saw in the arrival of the Spaniards an opportunity to rebel against Inca rule. Starting with Father Valverde, many Spaniards wrote the memory of their part in the conquest in various forms and addressed different publics. The *Crónica del Perú* (1553) by Pedro Cieza de León (1518-1553), a soldier and *letrado*, is the closest thing to a narrative of the conquest. The second part of the *Royal Commentaries* (1609) by the Garcilaso de la Vega, Inca (1539-1616) remains the classical account of the conquest because of its ample view of the events, the clear concept of history that articulates it, and the beautiful style in which it is written. The recent *The Conquest of the Incas* (1970) by John Hemming draws fully on the corpus of reports, letters, memorials, *crónicas*, treatises, and narratives that the conquest of the Andes, the ensuing civil wars, and the campaign for the extirpation of idolatries produced during the sixteenth century. He especially draws on Garcilaso and Cieza. The issues that dominated Las Casas's writings are replayed in the writing of the Andes: *encomienda*, just conquest, evangelization, right to universal empire, providential history, the place of the Indians in the new scheme of things, rights to private property, rights of the Indians to self-rule, and the quality of their culture.

One way of making sense of the proliferation of writings from Peru is to look at the authors of these texts as part of the ongoing Sepúlveda-Las Casas polemic and separate them by the perspective that they had on the Inca Empire. This is more helpful than a generational or referential classification (Porras Barrenecha). Although the edges of all groupings are always blurry, and *cronistas* like Juan de Betanzos (?-1576) are hard to place neatly on one side or the other, the separation in terms of the particulars of the polemic allows for a better understanding of the discursive forces unleashed into modernity by the conquest as well as the problematics of positionality that accompanied writing in the Andes. In general terms we can speak of two oppositional groups: 1) the Toledo Circle, a number of *letrados* who pushed forward, with all the resources of the Crown, the basic principles of a justificatory imperial history and 2) the various individuals who wrote outside of the circle and who, for reasons of their own, resisted and opposed the ideological thrust of imperial history. The Toledo Circle encompasses the chroniclers, jurists, translators, notary publics, priests, and other *letrados* and scholars engaged by the Viceroy to continue the Spanish imperial school of history and provide the Crown with the necessary information and arguments to denigrate and deauthorize Inca rule and culture. In this group one can easily place the *letrados* hired by the Viceroy himself: Juan de Matienzo (1520-79), Pedro Sarmiento de Gamboa (1530?-92), Juan Polo de Ondegardo (?-1575) and others, who, like the Jesuit José de Acosta (1540-1600), had views of their own and were weary of the Viceroy but did nevertheless confirm the normative and "superior" sense of European modes of cognition. They produced a harsh interpretation of Inca history, one in which they basically characterized the Incas as vicious rulers to whom Plato's definition of the tyrant—men ruled by the desires of the lower organs of the body—applied fully (see chapter 5 in this volume, "Historiography on the Ground").

Although very different among themselves and writing at a good distance from one another, the men who contested, in different ways, the discourse of the imperial historians were the *mestizo* Jesuit Blas Valera (1545-1597 Varner 322-26), the Indian Guamán Poma de Ayala and the *mestizo* humanist Garcilaso de la Vega, Inca, the latter writing from Spain. Cieza de León, although holding onto the view of providential history and the superiority of Spanish culture, cannot be aligned with either group as he wrote of the Inca Empire with great admiration, and his work precedes the arrival of Toledo by a long decade. Although considered "reliable chroniclers," their information needs to be corroborated with other sources. Cieza de León, for instance, is noted for his more or less objective descriptions of Andean culture and Inca rule. However, in this respect, his work cannot compare with Betanzos, who knew more Quechua and had direct access to the memory of one of the royal *panacas*. Cieza de León never failed to subscribe to the notion that Inca religion was inspired by the devil, a "fact" that he did not try to reconcile with his extensive reports on and admiration for the exemplary laws and wise statecraft with which the Incas governed the immense Tahuantinsuyo (Pease).

Although hired by Viceroy Antonio de Mendoza and with probably only an elementary education, Betanzos wrote quite a reliable history of the Incas. He had the great benefit of having learned Quechua in the field. This gave him an unusually great power to understand what was being reported to him and to attempt feats of cultural translation. His marriage to Doña Evangelina, one of Huayna Cápac's granddaughters, gave him unparalleled access to the Cuzco elite whose *quipu* and oral memory clearly informs both the contents and the shape of his narrative. In fact there are times when the *Suma y narración de los Incas* (1557) reads as if Betanzos were both transcribing and translating directly from the narrative of a Quechua speaker. It could be that one of his chief sources is Doña Evangelina herself and certainly a good number of members of her family.

Gómez Suárez de Figueroa was born in Cuzco in 1539 and died in Spain in 1616. His mother was the Inca princess Chimpu Ocllo, later baptized as Isabel Suárez, and his father was the Captain and nobleman Sebastián Garcilaso de la Vega. How Gómez Suárez de Figueroa became a canonical "author" in the Spanish language and better known as Garcilaso de la Vega, Inca, is a fascinating story of self-fashioning that involves the most amazing journey through personal and collective memory, the Renaissance, with its revival of Greco-Roman culture, and the will to recover the Inca past for posterity. Garcilaso has been fortunate with his critics. With the exception of a nineteenth-century Spanish critic who failed to appreciate Garcilaso's ethnographic presentation of the Inca empire, and the ethnohistorian María Rostworowski, most of his biographers and analysts have described and brought out the complexity, subtle maneuverings and intelligence of the Inca's task with satisfied admiration (Varner; Zamora; Fernández; Mazzotti).

His attempt, well into the sixteenth century, to write an account of the Inca empire that corrected and contradicted official Spanish historiography, was a monumental project for one man alone. *El Inca: Life and Times of Garcilaso de la Vega* by John Grier Varner (1968) still stands as the best biography and overall study of the political and intellectual milieu in which Garcilaso had to move in order to safeguard his person, arrange for conditions favorable to becoming an intellectual, and see to the possibility of writing and being published. He changed his name several times and each time the changes coincided with a new stage of consciousness and self assurance. From the time of his birth the rights and the social and economic standing of *mestizos* had diminished rapidly. Officers of the Crown considered them dangerous rivals, treacherous allies, and racially inferior (Mazzotti 22-23). *Mestizos* did not fare any better with the Indians. In fact Guamán Poma, for a set of very complicated reasons that included wanting to stop the sexual practices that engendered *mestizos*, almost always illegally, recommended that the existing *mestizos* move to the Spanish towns (see chapter 1 in this volume). Garcilaso wrote to suture the split and the trauma that the conquest brought about. But he never rejected his father. Instead he sought to clear his name from accusations made about his conduct in one of the many battles of the Spanish civil wars in which Spaniards changed sides easily and thus easily accused of betrayal.

For Garcilaso, *mestizaje* did not mean hybridity, as some recent commentators have wanted to label his efforts. Neither did it mean syncretism. Nor did it mean writing in between two worlds as if dangling from the edges that separated them. One of the purposes of his writing was to bring the two worlds together, in a dynamic of double valence, to create an epistemological and aesthetic space where full double voicing was possible. The Inca in Spain practiced a doubled consciousness of wholeness rather than the partialities or paranoias of hybridity (see chapter 1 in part 2 of this volume, "Mimicry Revisited"). From an Andean perspective, in love with the concept of duality, he sought complimentarity and reciprocity as the guiding principles of inquiry and understanding. The binary of the duality of the *quipu*, can also be seen to inspire the Inca's efforts to find a harmonious "new world." Each of the parts was to remain whole, with a logic of its own, and come together in a dance of complimentarity. In a telling gesture of his Andean search for complimentarity and reciprocity he translated from the Italian (1590) the

Dialoghi di Amore by León Hebreo (1535), for this piece from the "Old World" he found not so much inspiration as confirmation for the development of his capacities as a Andean writer and for his philosophical and aesthetic of complimentarity.

As an illegitimate *mestizo* in Spain and despite his Jesuit connections, Garcilaso needed to authorize himself as a subject of knowledge in order to intervene in the ongoing discourse on the Indies. Any cursory reading of the *Royal Commentaries* yields an ample list of the many contemporary and ancient authors that Garcilaso read in order to prepare for his work. Further confirmation of his firm grasp of issues and debates came to light in 1948 when José Durand found the Inca's last will. It included a list of the books he owned, which was considerable (over 300), given the size of private libraries at the time (Durand). The Inca had clearly immersed himself in the Italian renaissance, the Christian theological and philosophical tradition, the rediscovery of Greek and Roman culture, and the literature and political thought of his Spanish contemporaries. He had difficulties in assembling an equally rich bank of sources for his writing on the Incas. Garcilaso relied chiefly on his memory, the memory of friends in Peru who responded to his letters and answered his queries, the chronicle authored by Cieza de León, and the great book that the Jesuit Blas Valera was writing in Latin on Inca history. The Inca seems to have incorporated this massive treatise wholesale into his commentaries. Beyond the efforts to recover the memory of the Inca world, the chief move that Garcilaso made was to claim greater and better authority over all Spanish theologians and historians, based on his knowledge of Quechua, his free access to the *amautas* on his mother's side of the family, and his persistent demonstration of errors incurred by the Spaniards because of their ignorance of Quechua and their misunderstanding of Andean concepts which only a thorough knowledge of the language could prevent. With one single move, Garcilaso authorized himself and deauthorized most of the detractors of the Indians, something that Las Casas would have dearly loved to do, but could not do because he never learned any Indian languages. Garcilaso slyly argued that not knowing Quechua and wanting to understand Andean culture was like not knowing Hebrew and wanting to understand the Bible.

Margarita Zamora (1988) has written at length on how Garcilaso deployed his savvy understanding of philology to institute Quechua as a language of knowledge comparable only to Latin or even Hebrew in the

Christian tradition of exegesis. Antonio Mazzotti and other critics have pointed out that the majority of studies on the Inca concentrate on the humanist aspects that allow for the configuration of his works, an emphasis which does not allow for an analysis of the many features of both content and style that resist the European colored lenses. In *Coros mestizos del Inca Garcilaso* (1996) he seeks to remedy the situation. He posits a reading of Garcilaso in which Quechua narrative modes and understanding of the past, concepts of time and subject, operate as a kind of subtext (28-29). Mazzotti brings out in Garcilaso the presence of the conventions of Quechua oral narrative and especially the discursive tradition of the Cuzco court and all the symbolism that such choral tradition implies (31-32). This kind of interdisciplinary study surpasses the more narrowly conceived literary and philological analysis. It brings to bear the information and methods made available by iconography, archeology, and ethnohistory in order to detect in the Inca's text more than sheer information conveyed by the Cuzco arts of memory. Studies of post-conquest textualization of Andean memory in alphabetic texts and iconographic structures show that Garcilaso's change of names owes as much to Spanish costumes of the time as to Andean practices of naming according to life stages. Christian Fernández (2004) analyses in detail Garcilaso's coat of arms and shows how Garcilaso redeploys the European conventions of fields and arrangement of totems in order to represent his filiations with the Andean *Amaru* (97-111), the symbol of his *panaca* (37).

Garcilaso wrote at the time when the erasure of Amerindian memory and knowledges was already advanced. He wanted to stem the wave of forgetting that the claims of alphabetic writing, as the only site of memory, had already spread over the Amerindians' sense of the meaning of their cultures. Drawing on the organizing principles of Roman historians, in chapter after chapter, peppered with seemingly arbitrary digressions, Garcilaso places the stones that together amount to the rebuilding of the Inca empire and way of life subtly to dispute the hierarchical differences argued by Palacios Rubios and Ginés de Sepúlveda. He systematically affirms the existence of only one world. He then moves from the location of the Andes in a world that is *one* and a human kind that is *one*, to the particulars of the Andean landscape, the agricultural system, social organization, war, legal, religious and communications systems. Garcilaso stages his narrative rhetoric in order to assure his reader of the veracity of the facts and events presented and to distinguish his history from fables and fictions (Fernández 32; Mignolo, "Cartas"). Mignolo has pointed out that the Inca makes clear that he is in charge of writing history, that is to say, he organizes and gives meaning to the materials while his sources simply tell the story (*relato*) as best they remember (90).

The fact that he entitled his book "commentaries" and not history has always puzzled his readers. It has been said that he took Cesar's commentaries as his model (Fernández 26-28). It has also been argued that the Inca had in mind the genre of the philological biblical commentary prevalent at the time (Durand 322-332 qtd. in Fernández 29). Fernández shows that the commentary genre was widely practiced during the middle ages, establishing a heterogeneous legacy (41) of which Garcilaso was well aware (41-47). It would seem that the Inca chose the tradition of the critical commentary as practiced by St Jerome in his *Contra Rufino* because this practice allowed him to gloss, expand, clarify, criticize, correct, and dispute, in collaboration with the subtle reader. For Fernández, the reader in Garcilaso, as in St. Jerome, is the necessary counter part who will bring to full fruition the half-sentences, digressions, allusions, and invitations to draw the appropriate conclusions sprinkled throughout the text (48-55). This thesis is quite persuasive, for it fits Garcilaso's rhetoric. The Inca may have used the commentary genre more suitable than a straight history because his aim is to carry on a debate not only with specific *cronistas* or historians, but with larger issues in European epistemology and its capacity to engage in civilizations that did not resemble their own nor their understanding of their own.

The richness and complexity of Garcilaso's endeavor—to take on the entire panoply of imperial history that denigrated the Inca and by extension other Amerindian civilizations—has not yet been properly assessed. Although the chief villain of his history, the viceroy Toledo, was dead by the time the *Commentaries* appeared, readers understood that this was not a chronicle, but a formidable rebuttal that showed the refined intelligence of the Incas and the creative capacity of Andean culture. The influence that the Inca's work had in shaping the European and American imaginary with respect to Inca society as sort of a utopia can never be underestimated. *The Royal Commentaries* rejoiced and influenced contemporary audiences in Peru, inspired many eighteenth-century encyclopedists and scientists of the Enlightenment, as well as novelists, like Madame the Graffigny, and playwrights such as Voltaire (1694-1778). It has been reprinted many times and the many and rapid translations into all the major European languages made it a best-seller. It accompanied Túpac Amaru II and other Indian rebel leaders (see chapter 1 in this volume) in dreaming of a more ordered and just word. Despite the fact that the circulation of the book was forbidden by the Spanish authorities, it was always to be found in Bolívar's tents and San Martín's luggage. Its readers recognized a monumental recovery of memory and epistemological potential essential to the maintenance of the community of mankind.

By the 1550's it was clear all over the Spanish-American empire that the idea of evangelizing the Indians had failed rapidly. Between 1567 and 1582 the church held a council in Lima to discuss many matters, including the arrival of the new order: the Jesuits. Among other things it was decided to deny the Indians admission to the holy orders and to forbid them from taking communion. The Indians were basically disenfranchised as Catholics. Toledo had put his ordinances in place and the whole Andean world was near collapse, with the demographic catastrophe in full swing. It is conservatively estimated that the population went down from 16 million to 3 million. Exhausted, resistance was no longer possible. Confusion and grief reigned all over. People fled their villages and abandoned their families in search of work in the Spanish towns. Guamán Poma seems to have paid very close attention to the proceeding of the Council as well as to all other matters in Peru, for he rails about the terms of the discussion and the clearly anti-Andean dispositions.

In 1614, when he is about to hand his manuscript to the person who would take it to Spain and hand it either to Philip III or some trusted advisor, Guamán Poma claims to be 80 years old. Most of what we know about him is glimpsed from his own autobiographical presentation as "author" of *El primer nueva corónica y buen gobierno* (1516). He claims to be from Lucanas, to be the son of a *curaca,* or "prince," as he translates the term into Spanish. He casts himself as servant of the king, a noble Andean Christian who has sought to serve the cause of the king and justice, as a defender of poor Indians in court, as translator and advocate of true Christian causes. For such dedication to the king's interests he has only received scorn and unjust treatment from the Spaniards, especially the priests, whose main interest is the spoliation of Indian labor and property, not to mention their compulsive desire for Indian women.

Guamán Poma, not unlike Garcilaso, knew Toledo's work very well. He was surely familiar with Toledo's *Ordenanzas*—the Viceroy's legislation over every aspect of human life in the Andes (see chapter 5 in this volume,

"Historiography on the Ground"). In fact his familiarity with the events of
the extirpation of idolatries as well as the format of the *informaciones*—the
canvassing of the Andean territory for information useful to the Crown—
suggests that Guamán Poma may have been a translator for Spanish extirpators, magistrates, priests, and other *letrados*. His familiarity with Christian
doctrine is firm and well grounded. There is no doubt that Guamán Poma
was endowed with a powerful mind and an indefatigable thirst for knowledge, for he seems to have heard of every argument and bit of information
animating the polemic of the American Indian and his political and intellectual right to rule the land of his ancestors.

His *Corónica* or extended letter to the king is surprisingly critical of
the Incas. He would agree with the Toledo Circle in claiming that the
Incas were only recent rulers who, through conquest and tyranny,
expanded their original Cuzco holdings into the huge territory of the
Tahuantinsuyo. Guamán Poma even denies that the Incas were originally
from Cuzco. With this denial of origins he may have been forestalling all
possible claims by descendants of the Incas to future high office, or even
a co-government as some were suggesting at the time. In a crafty redeployment of Las Casas, Guamán Poma, proposes that the land and government of Peru be given back—restituted—to the Indians, that is to say
to the *curacas* or ethnic lords, like his family, not the descendant of the
Incas. On this other matter he was squarely against the Toledo Circle,
and that included Acosta.

His challenge to Inca claims to original rule are no less surprising that
his account of universal time, as he not only tries to find the point where
to link Amerindian time to biblical unilinear time, but pushes back
Andean time deeply into four pre-Inca epochs. New research into the
differences that account for the passage of time in the Andes and the
events concerning Inca rule and the making of the Tahuantinsuyo, shows
that some of the discrepancies among the *cronistas* are due to the fact that
they interviewed different Inca *panacas* or came into contact with different ethnic accounts (Rostworowski). In this light it is clear that Guamán
Poma offers an account of time and history that not only differs substan-
tially, but is in fact at odds with the Cuzco accounts prominent in Garcilaso de la Vega, Inca and Juan de Betanzos, for instance. The four ages
that Guamán Poma figures preceded Inca times postulate about a million
years after Adam (Brading 150). He begins the history of the new world
with the arrival of Noah sometime after the universal flood. The four ages

tell of a human cultural development that precedes the arrival of Manco Cápac—the first Inca and culture hero—and accounts for most of Andean cultural inventions: agriculture, cities, laws, and the building of fortresses. Brading notes that the evolutionary development in Guamán Poma is reminiscent of that advanced by Cicero and redeployed by Las Casas (150-51).

Guamán Poma's boldness never ceases to amaze his readers, given the climate of orthodoxy and censorship in which both Spain and the colonies lived. Not content with having grafted Andean time into biblical time by having found the common and universal phenomenon of the flood, the *quipukamayuc* advances the notion that Andean civilization is actually a forerunner of Christianity. This idea is also advanced by Garcilaso. Although it is not possible to know how Guamán Poma became knowledgeable of the details of the Spanish controversy on the American Indians (Adorno), it is clear in the text that he nimbly uses the natural law argument developed by Las Casas and Vitoria in order to argue that in pre-Hispanic society, people were organized and governed by the reason of natural law. Andean peoples lead virtuous lives as they followed their own laws and the devil was not anywhere to the seen, except in the person and life of the some of the *Collas*, or Inca queens. There is no doubt that even in this account of Andean pre-Christian virtue, which defies the consensus reached in Spain about the Indian's immaturity (as in Kant's immaturity also), Guamán Poma feels "safe." It may be that he is aware of the fact that his portrayal of the Incas as usurpers and tyrants coincides with the views sought after and propounded by the circle of *letrados* serving the viceroy Toledo in Cuzco and by implication in Valladolid. He must have reasoned that his devastating critique of Spanish colonial rule, coming as it did from a doubly virtuous person, that is, Christian pre-Christian, or a natural intelligence taken to its true *telos* by the enlightenment of Christianity, would gain him an audience with the king.

If his account of universal history would have seemed outrageous to his contemporaries had they had a chance to read it—the manuscript got lost and was not read until 1911—his daring to give advice to the king of Spain on how to govern so as to save his soul is as admirable as it is puzzling, for he inverts all the denigrating claims made by Palacios Rubios and stretches the generous concessions of "natural reason" made by Vitoria. In one his now famous drawings he imagines a scene in which he sits next to the king of Spain who, as his pupil, listens to the information and recommendations that Guamán Poma, the good governor, offers to his majesty. Like Las Casas, Guamán Poma envisions the time when the Indians and Spanish will live in separate towns with the Indians having been given back their lands. In this utopian setup all work would be paid, and the *mita*, and for that matter all daily life, should be modeled on Inca times and Inca ethics, for they, after all, had the best laws and really knew how to govern. Toledo instead is only creating havoc and wanton suffering. His policy to move the Indians to towns, his exigencies of tribute and long periods of work in the mines, together with the neglect of the fields, is bringing the Andes to a catastrophic end, for the world is now upside down and the Indians are becoming extinct. In the end Guamán Poma's *Corónica* is saturated by the grief of seeing an orderly and healthy world come to end, as he says, "without remedy in sight." The pages written by the self-styled prince speak of the terrifying sense of holocaust, for an entire ancient civilization was about to disappear, while debate continued, kings succeeded each other unable or unwilling to overcome the gridding motions of the machine put in place with the Palacios Rubios learning and logic.

How Guamán Poma was able to become conversant with the entire discursive complex of the conquest-cum-evangelization and redeploy it to critique the conquest and colonial rule, as well as offer a plan for good government, is a feat that remains unequalled in the history of colonial or modern letters. Compared to Garcilaso, his disadvantages were greater and his subalternity was extreme. He managed to learn doctrine by attending sermons, law by frequenting the courts, and drawing by apprenticing himself to various churchmen and artists. Adorno also traces Guamán Poma's ecclesiastical rhetoric to written sources that he quotes in his letter. He seems to have been thoroughly familiar, for instance, with Fray Luis de Granada's sermon *Memorial de la vida cristiana* which was printed and widely circulated in the new world for evangelizing purposes (Adorno 57). The new catechisms and *sermonarios* printed in Lima after the meeting of the Third Council of Lima allow Guamán Poma to have a firmer grasp of the problems that preaching Christianity to the Andean people entailed. These texts helped him sharpen his "pose as a preacher" (Adorno 57). No less important are the confession manuals circulating in the Andes, for they offer a model to Guamán Poma for eliciting information and even for inventing the scene in which he instructs the king. Adorno writes that "Guamán Poma's defense of his race is a direct reaction to the biases expressed in [the] doctrinal texts" (66), circulating in the Andes at the time of the Third Council in which the intellectual potential of Andeans is denigrated by none other than Acosta. Compared to Garcilaso, who could sit down in his house in Cordoba and read a book, perhaps take notes and even discuss his queries and ideas with learned friends, Guamán Poma appears alone, rushing from one scene of oral performances (courts, councils, preachings, masses, inquiries, conversations), swimming in a sea of words and struggling to wrest sense and reason out of the whole debate.

There is no doubt that Guamán Poma was also keenly aware of Las Casas's positions regarding the problematic justification for imperial rule and the natural intelligence and ethics of Indian societies. Like Garcilaso and Las Casas, he had no choice but to seek refuge under the umbrella of providential history and thus accept the king's legitimate authority to govern. This move left open the possibility of demanding good government and trying to assemble his notes and thoughts of a lifetime under this guiding principle.

In conclusion, if, as it has been argued by Mendizábal, Brotherston, and Brokaw, Guamán Poma worked from the cognitive order of the *quipu*, from the Andean ontology of numbers and the art of rectification (Brokaw, "Khipu Numeracy" 293), perhaps we could say in his case, as with the Cuzco school of painting, that we are confronting something new (modern) in the history of the world that 1492 inaugurated. Perhaps we could say that in the *Corónica* we witness the first dismantling if the European discourse of colonization as elaborated by Spanish intellectuals of the sixteenth century. Perhaps we could suggest that it is the Andean structure of knowledge that allows Guamán Poma to dismantle European discourses, locate the fragile seems that hold the parts together, break the fragments, and reassemble them into new series with new semiotic relations, as he does in the *Nueva corónica y buen gobierno*. Perhaps we could say that in a perverse way, the urgent need to respond to the destructuration of the self-world, the vital impulse to retreat from agony allowed Garcilaso and Guamán Poma—from their respective subaltern subject positions—to hone the subject position and discursive perspective that would allow them to redefine the polemic for the postcolonial world.

Published in two parts ("Memory and 'Writing' in the Andes" and "Writing the Andes") in Sara Castro-Klarén (ed.): *A Companion to Latin American Literature and Culture*. © 2008 Oxford: Blackwell. It has been minimally revised. Reprinted by permission.

WORKS CITED

ABERCROMBIE, A. Thomas. *Pathways of Memory and Power: Ethnography and History Among an Andean People*. Madison: University of Wisconsin Press, 1998.

ADORNO, Rolena. *Guamán Poma: Writing and Resistance in Colonial Peru*. Austin: University of Texas Press, 1986.

BOONE H. Elizabeth. "Introduction: Writing and Recording Knowledge." In E. Boone and W. Mignolo, *Writing Without Words: Alternative Literacies in Mesoamerica and the Andes*. Durham: Duke University Press, 1994: 3-26.

BRADING, David. *The First America: The Spanish Monarchy, Creole Patriots, and the Liberal State 1492-1867*. Cambridge: Cambridge University Press, 1991.

BROKAW, Galen. "Khipu Numeracy and Alphabetic Literacy in the Andes: Felipe Guamán Poma de Ayala's *Nueva córonica y buen gobierno*." *Colonial Latin American Review*, Vol.11, No 2 (2002): 275-303.

—. "The Poetics of *Khipu* Historiography: Felipe Guamán Poma de Ayala's *Nueva Corónica* and the *Relación de los quipucamayoc*." *Latin American Research Review* 38.3 (2003): 111-147.

—. "Toward Deciphering the Khipu." *Journal of Interdisciplinary History*. 35.4 (2005): 571-589.

BROTHERSTON, Gordon. *Book of the Fourth World: Reading the Native Americas Through Their Literature*. Cambridge: Cambridge University Press, 1992.

CASTRO, Daniel. *Another Face of Empire: Bartolomé de Las Casas, Indigenous Rights and Ecclesiastical Imperialism*. Durham: Duke University Press, 2007.

CERVANTES, Fernando. *The Devil in the New World: The Impact of Diabolism in New Spain*. New Haven: Yale University Press, 1994.

COE, Michael D. *Breaking the Maya Code*. London: Thames & Hudson, 1992.

CUMMINS, Tom. "Let Me See! Reading is for Them: Colonial Andean Images and Objects 'Como es costumbre tener los caciques Señores.'" In Elizabeth Hill Boone and Tom Cummins eds. *Native Traditions in the Postconquest World*. Washington D.C.: Dumbarton Oaks Research Library and Collection, 1998: 91-148.

DURAND, José. "La biblioteca del Inca." in *Nueva Revista de Filología Hispánica* 3 (1948): 239-264.

FERNÁNDEZ, Christian. *Inca Garcilaso: imaginación, memoria e identidad*. Lima: Universidad Nacional Mayor de San Marcos, 2004.

HEMMINNG, John. *The Conquest of the Incas*. New York: Harcourt, Brace, Jovanovich, 1970.

HULME, Peter. *Colonial Encounters: Europe and the Native Caribbean, 1492-1797*. London: Methuen, 1986.

MAZZOTTI, José A. *Coros mestizos del Inca Garcilaso: resonancias andinas*. Lima: Bolsa de Valores de Lima/Otorongo Producciones; México: Fondo de Cultura Económica, 1996.

MENDIZÁBAL LOSACK, Emilio. "Don Felipe Guamán Poma de Ayala, señor y príncipe, último quellcakamayoc," in *Journal of Latin American Lore* 5 (1961): 83-116.

MIGNOLO, Walter. "Cartas, crónicas y relaciones del descubrimiento y la conquista." In *Historia de la literatura hispanoamericana. Época colonial*, ed. Íñigo Madrigal. Madrid: Cátedra, 1982. 57-116.

—. «Preamble: The Historical Foundation of Modernity/Coloniality and the Emergence of Decolonial Thinking.» *A Companion to Latin American Literature and Culture*. Ed. Sara Castro-Klarén. Oxford: Blackwell Publishing, 2008. 12-33.

NILES, A. Susan. *The Shape of Inca History: Narrative and Architecture in an Andean Empire*. Iowa City: University of Iowa Press, 1999.

PAGDEN, Anthony. *The Fall of Natural Man: The American Indian and the Origins of Comparative Ethnology*. Cambridge: Cambridge University Press, 1982.

PEASE, Franklin. *Del Tahuantinsuyo a la historia del Perú*. Lima: Instituto de Estudios Peruanos, 1978.

PORRAS BARRENECHEA, Raúl. *Los cronistas del Perú (1528-1650) y otros ensayos*. Lima: Banco de Crédito del Perú, 1986.

ROSTWOROWSKI DE DIEZ CANSECO, María. *Estructuras andinas del poder. Ideología religiosa y política*. Lima: Instituto de Estudios Peruanos, 1983.

SALOMON, Frank. *The Cord Keepers: Khipus and Cultural Life in a Peruvian Village*. Durham: Duke University Press, 2004.

SEED, Patricia. *Ceremonies of Possessions in Europe's Conquest of the New World 1492 1640*. New York: Cambridge University Press, 1995.

URTON, Gary. *Signs of the Inka Khipu: Binary Coding in the Andean Knotted-String Records*. Austin: University of Texas Press, 2003.

VARNER, John Grier. *El Inca: Life and Times of Garcilaso de la Vega*. Austin: University of Texas Press, 1968.

ZUIDEMA, R. Tom. *Inca Civilization in Cuzco*. Tran. Jean Jacques Decostes. Austin: University of Texas Press, 1990.

CHAPTER 5
Historiography on the Ground: the Toledo Circle and Guamán Poma

> "As regards the question of Peru... nothing that comes my way has caused me greater embarrassment than the corruption of benefices and the affairs of the Indies which freeze the very blood in my veins."
>
> (Francisco de Vitoria, 1534)[1]

> "Power has no essence; it is simply operational. It is not an attribute but a relation: the power relation is the set of possible relations between forces which passes through the dominated forces no less than through the dominating."
>
> (Deleuze, 27)

> "Y no descuidar de miralles siempre las manos y los pensamientos."
>
> (Toledo)[2]

PREAMBLE

My purpose in this essay is to delve into the construction of subalternity of American polities and peoples by the Spanish discourse of discovery, conquest, and coloniality. Focusing specifically on the "writing" of Inca history under the gaze of Viceroy Francisco de Toledo (1515-1582)—the supreme organizer of Andean Colonial rule—I intend to show that the deauthorizing of the Andeans' own narratives of the past relied on the conjugation of at least three discursive operations. First, it was necessary to deploy a systematic gathering of "facts" under the observation of the forces of the Spanish Crown. The "facts" themselves were the result of "observations" conducted by Spanish agents of the Crown who decoded the observed cultural practices in the light afforded by the transportation of the "facts" to a cultural matrix other than their own grid of signification. Second, the confusion, disjunction, and contradiction which resulted from

---

[1] Quoted in Pagden 65.
[2] Quoted in Valcárcel 6.

observational practices were resolved by the juxtaposition of hermeneutic operations in which translation—cultural and linguistic—played a paramount role. Third, when the assumption of European present practices as normative failed to provide sufficient ground for "othering" Andean accounts of the past as foundation for claims to self-government, coded readings of classical Greek and Roman antiquity were deployed in order to estrange Andean discourses of self-knowledge and produce a generalized deauthorization of local knowledges. Such deauthorization of local knowledges—historiography on the ground—became the keystone for colonial governability.

The connection of this essay to the historiographic work of the South Asian Subaltern Studies group is one of affinity and recognition. Inasmuch as Ranajit Guha and others have questioned the discursive and universal capacity of History—a local European modality of dealing with memory and the past—I find my inquiry into the writing of coloniality reaffirmed. The problem of the writing of history was recognized in the Andes from the inception of the deployment of writing as the principle epistemological paradigm. Ever since, Latin American intellectuals—most notably Guamán Poma, José Carlos Mariátegui, Edmundo O'Gorman, novelists, and anonymous writers—have examined the paradoxical positions of postcolonial writing subjects, their modes of cognition, and the conflict-ridden elaboration of the past that ensued. There is then a convergence of postcolonial perspectives encompassed by the problematic of the writing of history and processes of subalternization as expressed by the South Asian group and the thinking of many Latin Americans across the centuries.

INTRODUCTION

By March 1572, Túpac Amaru, the last direct successor of the Incas and head of the reining *panaca*,[3] was dead. The Viceroy Francisco de Toledo had the young man executed, on charges of conspiracy against the Spanish state, in the central plaza of Cuzco before the eyes of most members of the

---

[3] A *panaca* was made up of the descendants of the last reigning Inca. It excluded the person chosen to occupy the throne, who went on to form a new *panaca*. The *panaca*'s charge was to conserve the mummy of the deceased Inca and the memory of

twelve royal *panacas* and thousands of loyal subjects. One of the many roles of the *panacas* was to conserve the memory of their deceased royal ancestors in rhymed songs, narratives, and probably also paintings. Barely a month before, in February of the same year, the viceroy had gathered together the descendants of the twelve *panacas* for a viewing of the:

> Árbol genealógico pintado y se les leyese la *Historia índica* y lo escrito sobre los cuatro paños preparados para enviar al rey como un resumen de los hechos y de la sucesión de los Incas...Y para concretar, se hizo una nueva informa-ción, a la que fueron convocados únicamente los primitivos conquistadores, y a ellos se volvió a pedir testimonio sobre todo lo que sabían y habían oído decir a los indios desde cuarenta años que vivían en el Perú. (Levillier 285)

The lawyer Polo de Ondegardo (?-1575), who had barely completed his *Notables daños de no guardar a los indios sus fueros* (1571), was also to be present at the reading.[4] His task was to lend his expertise on Inca history to the proceedings so that if questions arouse with regard to the truth of the *Historia índica* (1572) by Pedro Sarmiento de Gamboa (1532-

---

his deeds in songs and narratives. Following Zuidema, María Rostworowski writes that "cada Inca nacía en una panaca y pasaba a otra cuando recibía la mascapaycha, de ahí también que tenía que cambiar de nombre. Cambiar de ayllu no signficaría la creación de un nuevo grupo sino el paso de un linaje a otro.... Este hecho daría una enorme importancia al ayllu o panaca de la madre de un soberano y nos hallaríamos ante una práctica particular de los linajes incaicos" (143). Zuidema explains that the word *panaca* derives from "pana" which means "sister of a man." "Panaca" in Cuzco designates noble *ayllus* (55), and means "group descending from a man's sister" (56). The *panacas* have a calendrical function, with each assuming the celebration of monthly rites in the agricultural calendar (65). See Zuidema 23-34 and 51-61.

[4] The text authored by Polo de Ondegardo was not intended for publication. It was found with the papers that belonged to Francisco de Ávila, known for his "mission" among the Huarochirí and his connection to *Ritos y tradiciones de Huarochirí*, ed. Gerald Taylor. Lima: Instituto de Estudios Peruanos, 1987. The *Relación de los fundamentos acerca del notable daño que resulta de no guardar a los indios sus fueros* lay in the Spanish Archivo de Indias until it was published for the first time by Torres de Mendoza as part of the *Colección de documentos inéditos del Archivo de Indias*. (Tomo XVII, Madrid 1872). A year later Sir Clements R. Markham published it in London with a title more descriptive of its contents: *Relación del linaje de los incas y cómo extendieron ellos sus conquistas*. Polo's work was printed along with other texts by the Hakluyt Society in London as part of *Narrative of the Rites and Laws of the Incas*. The most recent edition, based on the manuscript housed in the Biblioteca Nacional in Madrid and which does not differ from the text edited by Torres de Men-

1592), Polo could put them to rest.[5] The version of Inca history composed by Pedro Sarmiento de Gamboa, to some extent gathered and written during the early part of the viceroy's inspection of the Inca Empire (1569-1572), was never questioned by the members of the twelve *panacas*. Some of the members merely uttered (in Quechua?) the noncommittal phrase: "Así será pues." In the presence of the notary public, they heard the history. They listened to the interpreter's rendition of what was being read aloud in Spanish. The reading of Sarmiento's *Historia índica* took two days and the work of many interpreters. When it concluded, the members of the royal *panacas* were asked to declare in public, and to certify before the appointed notary public, that what they had heard constituted a complete and accurate account of the history of their ancestors and the manner of government employed by them in the empire.

Toledo knew that one of the key roles of the *panacas* was to devote their energies to the conservation of the memory of the deeds of their deceased ancestor in songs and narratives. Much of what was known about the past was committed to memory in songs which were sung and acted out in dance-theater processionals in the many ritual celebrations which marked the Inca calendar. The *amautas* and *quipucamayoc,* or intellectuals, were perhaps the most important members of the *panacas* in terms of their historical function. Thus Toledo was pitting one set of intellectuals against another, one set of records against another. He was making sure that the Spanish law, power, and historiography gained, once and for all, the upper hand.

doza, has a new title: *El mundo de los incas*, ed. Laura González and Alicia Alonso (Madrid: Historia 16, 1990).

[5] The *Historia índica* is the title generally used for the manuscript that Pedro Sarmiento de Gamboa (1532-1592) presented to the Viceroy Toledo and which was read to the members of the twelve *panacas*. Sarmiento planed to write three books on the Incas, but it appears that he only put down the *Segunda parte de la historia general llamada índica*. It was sent to Spain along with the genealogical paintings ordered by Toledo. The Council of the Indies buried it in its archives. At the end of the eighteenth century, a manuscript copy was found in the library of Abraham Gronov in Leiden. In 1906 the German scholar Richard Pietschmann published it for the first time in Berlin with a long preliminary study. This same version was later published by Ángel Rosenblat with a long study on the life and works of Pedro de Sarmiento, "nigromántico," poet, censor, captain, Royal cosmographer, and prisoner of the Huguenots en Mont-de-Marsan in 1586. See Sarmiento de Gamboa.

Toledo had asked Sarmiento de Gamboa to draw from the material being compiled in his *Informaciones*[6] a history of the Incas which would prove that they were not "natural lords" of the Andeans but rather usurpers and tyrants.[7] Although the document known as the *Anónimo de Yucay*,[8] sent to Toledo in 1571, had already advanced the same thesis on the illegitimacy and tyranny of the Incas, and Polo's own study on the origin of the Incas could "prove" that the Incas were not autochthonous to Cuzco, Sarmiento's "history" was more highly authorized, inasmuch as its author was part of Toledo's inner circle of intellectuals and the contents were supposedly based on the notarized depositions and answers made by many *curacas* to the questions posed by the *Informaciones*.[9]

---

[6] For a more or less full text of the *Informaciones*, see Levillier, *Don Francisco*.

[7] The *Informaciones* were not published at the time of Toledo. It lay in the Archivo de Indias in Seville. In the nineteenth century, various historians, among them Clements Markham and Jiménez de la Espada, published partial texts from archival sources. Roberto Levillier, in his *Don Francisco*, published summaries from parts of the *Informaciones*. His purpose was to correct the meagerness of the previous partial publications (204).

[8] *El anónimo de Yucay* has left a deep mark on Peruvian historiography. In 1571, the anonymous writer wrote the *Dominio de los Yngas en el Perú y del que su Majestad tiene en dichos reinos*, known as *El anónimo de Yucay*. This text articulates in the clearest way Toledo's own ideology: it was a mistake (*engaño*) to give to the Incas true and legitimate lordship over this kingdom, great damages have already ensued as a consequence of this falsehood, and there is a need to establish that the only true and legitimate domain and lordship of these kingdoms resided in the Spanish king and his successors. The *Anónimo* reasons that the king was given the Andes as a reward for his labors in the struggle against the Moors, and that, at any rate, there had not been any legitimate rulers of the Andes before the Spanish conquest. This *cronista* launches an impassioned attack on Bartolomé de Las Casas. Finally, the *Anónimo* makes a case for the great virtue in killing these Indians "y alancearlos porque [eran] idólatras, [adoraban] piedras, [comían] carne humana, [sacrificaban hombres] y no eran teólogos." See Carrillo, Vol. 4. 15-16.

[9] Roberto Levillier has published the entire body of Francisco de Toledo, *Ordenanzas*. See volumen 8 of *Gobernantes*. In his *Don Francisco de Toledo*, Levillier offers a summary of the questions put either to individual *curacas* or groups of them, which ranged from five to eighty men called to declare before a notary public and with the aid of an interpreter in meetings called by Toledo and which lasted two or three days. The same fifteen questions were asked both of Jauja (ethnic groups friendly to the Spaniards) and Guamanga (long standing enemies and rivals of the Incas). These questions were later modified for the Cuzco and Yucay assemblies. The questions were designed with a linear idea of the past which did not at all coincide

Toledo's decision to mount a whole juridical and historiographic assault on the Incas seems redundant for he had already decided that "conviene acabar este debate por guerra" (Valcárcel 6). His aim was not only to end the debate on the legitimacy of Inca rule but also to remove the Incas physically in order to proceed to the confiscation and distribution among his supporters of the lands, treasures, subjects, and *pallas* still held by the reigning *panaca*.[10] In fact Polo de Ondegardo was accused by the Anonymous Jesuit of having no other motive for writing on Inca religion than to ascertain the location of the tombs of the royal mummies in order to be the first to sack them.

With the scene of the *panacas* signing their names and thus authorizing the historical theses of *Historia índica*, the viceroy—that is, the colo-

---

with Andean temporal concepts nor with the "historical" categories employed by the *amautas* or *quipucamayocs*. The questions had two aims in mind: to determine if the Incas had gained control of those (local) territories by conquest, and if the Incas appointed the *curacas* or if they let the local *ayllus* elect them. The inquiry not only reflected a European concept of the past foreign to the Andean peoples, but it assumed idealized principles of governmentality that not even the most "advanced" European kingdoms practiced. Here is a sample of the fifteen questions: "1. Descendía el testigo de caciques o capitanes antiguos? Cuál era su calidad? 2. Sabían como era el gobierno de los pueblos del Perú, antes de que los Incas los conquistasen y sometiesen? 4. Gobernabase cada pueblo por sí a manera de behetería? 5. A esos capitanes o principales los elegían los pueblos por reconocerles valentía y entendimiento, o tiranizaban ellos mismos a esos pueblos y se hacían mandones? 6. Expiraban el oficio o tiranía de esos capitanes con su muerte? Qué se hacía en esto? 8. Cuándo en la guerra vencía un pueblo a otro, qué señorío adquiría? 10. Cuál fué el primer Inca que señoreó ese reino y cuál su origin y descendencia? 11. Lo recibieron ellos voluntariamente por señor y le dieron obediencia o los conquistó por fuerza, con guerras, muertes y otras opresiones?." See Levillier, *Don Francisco* 206-207. Carrillo notes that often the required answer was to be either yes or no.

[10] There is no question that part of the high motivation of those surrounding the viceroy in the march on Vilcabamba in search of the eighteen-year old and *uti* (retarded) Túpac Amaru—Martín de Loyola and Pedro Sarmiento de Gamboa—was the promise of fabulous riches to be obtained in *encomiendas*, treasure from the royal mummies, and appointments. As "usurpers," the descendants of the *panaca* in Vilcabamba would not have rights to anything. Perhaps the best illustration is provided by the case of Martín de Loyola, nephew of Saint Ignatius de Loyola, who not only sacked the mummy of one of the Incas but eventually married the coveted princess Beatriz, daughter of Sayri Túpac and heir to the *repartimiento* of Yucay. Satisfied of having solidified his relations with the Jesuits, Toledo writes in one of his letters to the King: "Se casó y holgó de ella el dicho capitán García de Loyola, aunque fuese india" (Valcárcel 13).

nizing state—intervened directly once again.[11] The games of truth played by the Spanish crown and its *letrados* were an effort to extract visibilities upon which to lay the foundations of a colonial order (Deleuze, *Foucault* 63). The Spanish conquest of the Andes required, in order for power to traverse and invest the dominated, their "help." The scene in which the *panacas* certify the Spanish interpretation and therefore valuation of their culture constitutes a critical achievement in the production of the Indian in the Andes. As the viceroy sought to acquire a strategic space to position the forces of the nascent colonial state, he seized on the power of discursive formations—law, civil ordinances, dictionaries, university curricula, language policies, population statistics, state intellectuals, the inquisition, and above all, historiography—as a central tactic in his plan to "organize and pacify" the "land."

However, as the viceroy moved about with complete confidence in his ability to defeat the Inca nobility both militarily and legally—spaces and maneuvers which he controlled exclusively—and while he instituted practices by which the Incas were to be watched at all moments, "and their seed to be eradicated for ever" (Valcárcel 9),[12] he seemed unaware of the fact that his understanding of the power/knowledge relation was also being observed, analyzed, and problematized by those *subjected* by the power of writing which he deployed.[13] Toledo had made the Indians subject to his control but, as Foucault has argued, (in Dreyfus and Rabinow 212), that control and dependence appears also tied to the subject's identity, conscience and knowledge. The colonial subject—Toledo, the *letrados*, the *panacas*—appear in the grid of power that subjugates them, makes them subject to and also enables a specific cognitive productivity.

[11] See the account of the debates between Juan Ginés de Sepúlveda and Bartolomé de Las Casas in Brading, and also in this volume.

[12] Toledo's letters provide ample evidence as to the intent of his campaign against the *uti* (retarded) Inca in Vilcabamba. He takes credit for "Haber sacado toda la raíz y pretención de derecho de este reino y fuera de él y crédito; de poder perderlos y castigarlos" (Levillier, *Don Francisco* 28). Toledo also points out to the king, as he must have done to the people who supported him in Peru, that "Don Felipe Quispe Tito y sus hermanos hijos de Tito Cusi se echaron del reino y su hacienda servirá para freno y seguro del reino" (Valcárcel 9).

[13] Foucault explains that "there are two meanings to the word subject: subject to someone else by control and dependence, and tied to his own identity by conscience or knowledge. Both meanings suggests a form of power which subjugates and makes subject to" (Foucault, "The Subject" 212).

Having set the scene, from here on I will analyze the discursive modes, strategies, practices, and disciplines that colonial rule—as epistemic violence—deployed in the Andes when Toledo's forces elaborated the histories of the Andeans as a prelude to his *Ordenanzas*. Toledo authorized a blueprint for a new world organized by the forces of writing, power, and the law that took the form of a panopticom. From the compilation of the *Informaciones* to the minute regulations of everyday life in the *Ordenanzas*, the ensemble of knowledge that Toledo brought together and developed as he entered the land and the consciousness of the Andeans aims at thinking and producing a model of governmentality that will subject the Amerindian population while at the same time transform their cultural constitution into a replica of the Christian novitiate subject.[14] Moreover, the Toledean discursive panoply would be indeed incomplete if it were severed from the objects and objectives of its discursive maneuvers: the Andean subjects.

While Toledo compels the diverse set of *curacas* to speak the "truth" under the force of his questionnaire in order to produce an Inca history with appropriate subjects (tyrants), other members of the Andean polity, touched by and aware of the far-reaching power of Toledo's examination of their past and memory, prepared responses which, in a manner of speaking, took the place of the silence of the *panacas*. As is well known, the most distinguished and "famous" of the post-toledan Andean chroniclers—Garcilaso Inca de la Vega, Guamán Poma, and the mysterious Anonymous Jesuit (Blas Valera?) (1551-1597)[15]—replied, critically, and

---

[14] I use the term "governmentality" in the sense developed by Michel Foucault in his "Governmentality." "The ensemble formed by the institutions, procedures, analyses and reflection, the calculations and tactics that allow the exercise of this very specific, albeit complex form of power, which has as its target population, as its principle form of knowledge, political economy, and as its essential technical means an apparatus of security" ("Governmentality" 102). The conquest of the imaginary in the Andes cannot be understood as a parallel to the situation in Mexico. For an illuminating analysis of the elaboration of the questionnaire that produced the *Relaciones* in Mexico and a study of the capture of Aztec memory by the Spaniards, as well as the harnessing of the Christian supernatural by the Mesoamericans, see Gruzinski.

[15] Blas Valera was born in Chachapoyas in 1551 and is believed to have died in Spain in 1597. He has often been identified as the author of texts otherwise attributed to the Anonymous Jesuit. The *Relación de las costumbres antiguas de los naturales del Perú*, finished in 1578 (Porras Barrenechea 471) was first published by Jiménez de la Espada in 1879 and reprinted in Lima in 1945. Blas Valera is also supposed to be the author of the

with maneuvers of their own, to Toledo's idea of inventing a past, and consequently a future, on the ground.

No response was more vigorous and detailed than Guamán Poma's *El primer nueva córonica y buen gobierno* (1615), for in his pages we find a micro-history of the Andes, together with a utopia for "self" government. Conceived, in a way, to respond to the charges of "tyranny," Guamán Poma's enormous work also registers the historiographic dilemma brought about by the irreparable, and all too visible, rupture of the end of one order and the birth of another. The sense that the new order is based on falsified, deceiving facts elaborated on the ground of governmentality only deepens the post-toledans understanding of the idea that governability is a game that conjugates the tactics of writing institutions in the production of knowledge to an arena that extends the struggle of the battle field. As if anticipating Foucault, one could say that the post-toledan authors understand governability as:

> The ensemble formed by the institutions, procedures, analysis and reflections, the calculations and tactics that allow the exercise of the very specific, albeit complex form of power, which has as its target population, as its principle form of knowledge, political economy, and as its essential technical means an apparatus of security. (Foucault, "Governmentality" 102)

The post-toledan chroniclers contested Toledo's thesis on the Inca models and practices of governability. Their own versions of the histories of Andean empires were based on personal and collective memories as well as what was left of the *quipu* system of "writing." The lost Latin manuscript of Blas Valera is a major source for Garcilaso's *Royal Commentaries* (1609).[16] Together with Guamán Poma's *El primer nueva*

extensive *Historia Occidentalis*, written in Latin and lost during the sacking of Cadiz by the English. Fragments of this manuscript were read and cited by Garcilaso in his *Comentarios reales*. The Anonymous Jesuit shows a great sense of self-identity with Inca culture. He rejects the version of Inca ritual practices established by Polo de Ondegardo and Pedro Sarmiento de Gamboa. He especially attacks Polo for his weak knowledge of Quechua and his inability to understand the ample semantic shadings of the language. The Anonymous Jesuit pointedly rejects the claims made on the practice of human sacrifice, and seriously details the similarities between Catholic belief and rites and Andean religion: confession, belief in the resurrection, bishops, nuns, anachorites.

[16] The Italian scholar Laura Laurencich Minelli has described a manuscript she has found in the family papers of the Neapolitan historian Clara Miccinelli. Laurencich

córonica y buen gobierno (1615), these texts undertake a minute display, a "thick description," of both the Inca and the pre-Inca knowledge and experience in the arts of governing. The most ambitious of these texts dares to offer the Inca ensemble of economic and political measures as a model of governmental rationality, as a structure of practices, worth preserving and even imitating by the Spaniards. As the post-toledan intellectuals wrote the Andean "conduct of conduct," (Gordon 2), they inaugurated a doubled discursive space which infused European categories of governmentality with a sense of alterity that needed to be recognized as it embodied practices which challenged the Idea—Inca, *ayllu, curaca, acllas, hanan/hurin*, reciprocity—and questioned the notion of referent. The post-toledan intellectuals used their study of practices to intensify thought, and, in their hands, the models or ideas that Spanish intellectuals ventured forth suffered certain wear and tear, resembling eventually

Minelli believes the manuscript to be a seventeenth-century Jesuit text which contains detailed information on the coding of the *quipu* and especially on their use for literary purposes. According to the author of the document, Quechua... "is a language similar to music and has several keys: a language for everyone; a holy language [which] was handed [down] by the knots, and another language which was handed down by means of woven textiles and by pictures on monuments and by jewels and small objects" (Domenici and Domenci 52). Included in the document there are three half pages of drawings signed "Blas Valera." They purport to show how a poem was written with woven symbols and knotted strings. This manuscript also tells the story of Blas Valera's "lost" manuscript, and it confirms Blas Valera's double parentage—Spanish and Andean. Laurencich Minelli states that according to Joan Anello, the author of this document, Blas Valera did not die in Spain. He survived the English attack on Cadiz and secretly returned to Peru in 1598. While in Spain, because of his quarrel with Cardinal Aquaviva, he was supposed to live as if dead. During that time he wrote his *Historia Occidentalis* but he could not publish it. So he sent it to Garcilaso de la Vega, who lived in Cordoba, who used it extensively in his *Royal Commentaries* (1609). Back in Cuzco, Blas Valera undertook a plan for the secret publication of yet another version of his book. Always in hiding, he and his friends looked for a ghost writer who would want to lend his name to the book. They settled on Guamán Poma, who boasted titles of Indian nobility and was well known for his pride and vainglory. See Viviano Domenici and Davide Domenci, "Talking Knots of the Inka: A Curious Manuscript that May Hold the Key to Andean Writing," *Archeology* November-December 1996: 48-56. The finding has been received with skepticism. Quechua scholars have raised questions regarding the Quechua used in the manuscript which, is clearly associated with Chachapoyas uses and therefore not consistent with Guamán Poma's writing in Ayacucho usage. No one is advancing any hypothesis until a facsimile is published.

what Deleuze has termed a "philosophy of the phantasm" behind which there does not lurk the real truth (xliii). The challenge that *mestizo* and Indian intellectuals mounted to the power of Spanish colonial historiography wrote in indelible ink the idea that "the law is always a structure of illigalism" (29).

I. THE BOOKS OF THE BRAVE

As soon as Toledo arrived in Peru in 1569 he sought to gather around him a group of intellectuals who could lend the expertise and authority necessary to his project: to end all possibility of shared rule with the Incas, to discredit Andean culture, and to organize "the conduct of conduct" in Peru. In order to do so he needed to counter not only Las Casas's objections to the *encomienda* system and the many arguments advanced in "Las doce dudas" (1552),[17] but even more urgently he needed to defeat the theory of the Incas's right to rule by virtue of their being "señores naturales" (autochthonous lords), advanced a generation earlier by the Dominican theologian Francisco de Vitoria (c.1492-1546) in Salamanca.

Vitoria had argued that being in mortal sin does not detract from the ability to rule in civil matters. Infidelity to the Christian faith was no impediment to legitimate rule as demonstrated by the existence of Protestant and Jewish rulers. Toledo brought under his circle the adventurer Pedro Sarmiento de Gamboa, the *licenciado* (civil lawyer) Polo de Ondegardo, and the jurist Juan de Matienzo (1520-1588), who had a long residence in Peru, and the friar Cristóbal de Molina, el Cuzqueño, who knew Quechua very well and assisted Túpac Amaru on the day of his execution.[18] Toledo also approached José de Acosta (1540-1600), but the Jesuit kept his distance. Whether Toledo and his circle of intellectuals hatched a conspiracy to defame the Incas, or whether the ideological dovetailing of the histories and plans for government of the Andes that they authored were part of the spirit of the times, writing the "history" of the Incas

---

[17] See Bartolomé de Las Casas, *Aquí se contiene una disputa o controversia entre el obispo don fray Bartolomé de Las Casas y el doctor Ginés de Sepúlveda.* (Seville, 1552; qtd. in Pagden, *The Fall of Natural Man*).

[18] Cristóbal de Molina penned three manuscripts. *Historia de los incas y Relación de las guacas*, both lost, and *Fábulas y ritos de los incas*, which survived and was published in 1943 as *Crónicas de los Molinas* (Lima: Francisco A. Loayza).

became a heated polemic during their lifetime and has remained so for many later students of the period.

The publication of the *Informaciones*, along with much of Toledo's correspondence in 1940, has enabled historians to recover the evidence of a well-thought out set of theses that the viceroy wanted to advance, both by discursive as well as practical methods and tactics. Gustavo Gutiérrez thinks that Toledo carried out a campaign among the Indians themselves destined to demonstrate the illegitimacy of Inca rule over the empire. He condemns Toledo for his intent to "falsear la memoria de un pueblo oprimido" in as much as it entails the mutilation of the capacity to rebel and it is thus "an effective weapon for its subjugation" (Carrillo 14). The historian Raúl Porras Barrenechea, an admirer of Toledo and really not partial to Indians, denies that any such conspiracy ever occurred but does admit and identify the existence of five major "tendencies" or ideological determinants which universally mark the historical work of the Toledo circle:

1. The Inca empire came about suddenly. It was the product of violence and force of arms deployed during the reigns of Pachacútec and Túpac Yupanqui.

 2. The Incas were warring tyrants whose culture was based on cruel rites, military structures, and human sacrifice.

3. The Incas developed an admirable economic and social system.

4. The Spaniards should conduct, as they were doing, intensive study of Andean religion in order to forbid and condemn their moral ideas and religious practices.

5. The historiographic assumptions of the Toledo circle rested on the thought of the Spanish intellectuals, theologians and civilians, who argued for the sustained supremacy of the Spanish empire over the entire globe (Porras, in Valcárcel, 39).

In fact, the convictions which animated Toledo and his intellectuals were not really that far away from the theses developed earlier by Ginés de Sepúlveda, the famed "loser" to Las Casas in the Valladolid debates (1550-51) over the Indians' questioned humanity. Like Sepúlveda, Sarmiento, Matienzo, and Toledo proceeded into their inquiry assuming that it was legal to conquer and kill all Indians due to the gravity of their sins and crimes, the crudeness of their mind ("crudeza de su ingenio"), their extensive practice of human sacrifice, and their ignorance of Christianity.

The *Historia índica*, the *Gobierno del Perú*, Toledo's *Ordenanzas*, and many other texts produced then in the Andes entered the various doors of

Spanish imperial bureaucracy but were not to see the light of day until late in the nineteenth century, when scholars searching in archives found them and published them for the first time. The recognition that such historio-graphic practices, while convenient to the state, were also dangerous to Spanish interests, is best expressed in the 1577 decree issued by Philip II. The Spanish king forbade all further inquiry into Amerindian religion and history, and ordered the colonial authorities to confiscate all manuscripts dealing with such topics. It would seem that as soon as the work of the Toledo circle was done, the king forbade any further research, all inter-viewing of Indians, and any writing up of the results of entering such (other) fields of memory and belief in the Spanish imperial records. The possibility of producing and working on a countermemory was officially foreclosed. As David Brading has put it in *The First America*: "The past constituted too dangerous an arsenal to be left open for random or ill-intentioned inspection" (143). And this referred to both the archives, which buried many things, as well as to the minds of the "natives," for they were to be watched, examined, and regulated at all times. It is in this atmosphere of prohibition, discipline, and fear that the post-toledan intellectuals car-ried out most of their rewriting of the Andean past by wresting out of *qui-pus* and *quipucamayoc* a rationality of the past which then lay in shards.

The truth claims in Sarmiento de Gamboa, Juan de Matienzo, and Polo de Ondegardo did not limit themselves to the ruling imperial fami-lies or Incas. After all, with the death of Túpac Amaru, their participation in history was thought to have been cancelled. In their attempt to make history useful for governing the present, to reemploy elements of the liv-ing past into the construction of the present, these *letrados* also produced and placed on the ground a crucial portrait of the common Amerindian population. For Matienzo, the Andeans were timid, melancholic, pusil-lanimous, "born to serve," cruel, given to all kinds of sexual excesses, and not very bright. It did not matter that this portrait did not coincide with the simultaneously drawn warlike and conquering image of the Inca armies and administrators. Above all, Matienzo assured his readers that the Indians were lazy. They had to be compelled to work. "Compeler a los indios a que trabaxen" (19) becomes a leitmotif in his *Gobierno del Perú* for, according to the jurist, they were sworn enemies of work. Matienzo seems unaware of the fact that a few chapters later, when he recommends that the Indians be taught European crafts but be forbidden from making gun powder and using arms and horses, he justifies his recommendations by remarking on the Indians's exceptional cleverness and ingenuity. "Los indios de este reino son tan hábiles que ninguna cosa les enseñan que no aprendan bien, como no sean cosas que requieran prudencia, que esto no cabe en sus entendimientos" (69).

Both Matienzo and Polo feel comfortable in arguing that some of the Incas' great architectonic achievements resulted from a combination of their cruelty and the laziness of the common people. The Incas' greed and cruelty could never cease to exact the labor of their subjects, so they put them to work even in "useless" tasks such as the channeling of rivers, building forts and steps up the great Andean mountains. Furthermore, according to these observers, this is so because if not compelled to work, the Indians would get lost in their love of festivals, drunken idleness, and devilish worship of the *guacas*. The Spanish Conquest, it was thus argued, actually freed the Andeans from the tyranny of the Incas—the tyranny of work and the tyranny of their rites. Endowed with the new freedom that the conquest brought them and characterized by their inclination for idleness, they were now at liberty to enter the world of labor in the mines and the *repartimientos* that the Spanish offered in the name of new Christian pastoral order which Toledo compiled under the title of *Ordenanzas*.

Toledo's order put firmly in place a very durable colonial despotism. But the curious thing is that this plan for governing, or rather incarcerating this new population was convincingly portrayed as the freeing of a population from its native tyrannical and thus "false" rulers by resorting to a new "colonial" reading of Plato. This erasure of the Andean material past, this preparation of a portal for the inauguration of empire, relies on certain angular readings of both Plato's *Republic*, first prepared by Matienzo, the lawyer, and Aristotle's thesis on natural law as commented by Vitoria. This deployment of Plato and Aristotle in the Andes prepared the ground for the pastoral rule of tutelage.

II. On the Pleasure of Tyranny

The Spanish claims to rule America would have been lost (on paper) without the catapult that tyranny, as elaborated by Plato and read by the *letrados* at the Spanish universities, afforded them in surmounting the walls set up by Las Casas and the plain doctrine of natural right.

Arguments on natural law, human rights, and the right to local rule has been stretched dangerously thin, twisted and turned to the point of the risible, in order to justify not just the conquest and subsequent destruction of the people, but also the right to legal enslavement of entire populations. It seemed that somehow, every time the answer on which to rest Spanish claims was found, another problem cropped up and new ground had to be elaborated out of the ensemble of knowledges available. Francisco de Vitoria (c.1492-1546), a theologian and major player in the School of Salamanca, took up the "need to describe and explain the natural world and the place of man within it, in the same rationalistic terms as Aquinas himself had used in the *Summa contra gentiles*" (Pagden 61). In his attempt to understand the place of man in nature, Vitoria, rather than opting for the self-reflection arrived at by Montaigne (1533-1592) in *Des Cannibals* (1580), assumed without question the primacy of Christian behavior.[19] For Vitoria, European social and political institutions were normative. Thus the only comparison possible, as with José de Acosta, would be one of unequal terms. Comparison meant hierarchy.

Blind to his assumptions, Vitoria labored on the exegesis of Aristotle's and Aquinas's theories of natural law. Aquinas's theory of natural law held out great promise as a tool for explaining the "strange" or "depraved" costumes and thinking of the Amerindians because it involved finding a rationality in the laws of nature. For the Scholastics, the "law of nature was the efficient cause which underpinned man's relationship with the world about him and governed every practice in human society" (Pagden 61). Accordingly, the law of nature constitutes a system of ethics. There could not be a doctor of natural law for it is not a codified body of precepts. Natural law, as Toledo and his circle were to learn from Vitoria and utilize in their historiography, was a "theory in part epistemological, in part sociological, about the mechanisms which permit men to make moral decisions. In its simplest form it consists of a number of 'clear and simple ideas,' the *prima praecepta* implanted by God at the creation of *in cordibus hominum*, to enable man to accomplish his end *qua* man' (Pagden 61).

Such simple and clear ideas were, theoretically, granted to all men. They were an instrument of cognition which allows man to "see" the

---

[19] Montaigne begun to revise the *Essays* almost immediately after their first publication in 1580. For *On Cannibals* see: *Essays* 91-98.

world as it is. These primary precepts were later translated into secondary precepts which constitute the basis for all the codes that regulate social behavior. Practically the entire ensemble of patterns of beliefs and behavior—culture—fell within the scope of natural law, and since the normative primacy of European costumes and beliefs was never questioned by the School of Salamanca it followed that all differences were to be identified and interpreted as an insufficiency in the capacity for cognition, and a weakness in the ability to "see the world as it is." Simple and clear ideas functioned, as we shall see later, in a way similar to an uncritical idea of "common sense." Thus Toledo and Matienzo felt on safe and holy ground when they formulated regulations expressing the tutelage theory that colonial labor and religious law affirm and detail. The theory of natural law constitutes the first philosophical step by which it can be held that all men are natural creatures. However, some, due to the "observed" difference of their dress, food, labor patterns, languages etc., constitute an enfeebled breed apart. The Idea that God had created all man equal—the same species—was thus turned on its head by the colonial situatedness in the structure of domination, and it would be several centuries before it could be taken seriously again.

Moreover, Vitoria's disquisition on natural law and the American Indian were not univocal. In fact, while Toledo may have found his thesis on the Indians' feebleness of mind suitable, he found many other aspects of Vitoria's thinking troublesome, and if he sought to prove publicly that the Incas were tyrants, it was in part to bring closure to the multifarious juridical aspects of the natural law exegesis. In 1537 Vitoria authored his *De Indis* (printed in 1557), with which he sought to bring closure to the ever exasperating question of just title to the Americas.

Vitoria argued that the question was not juridical. He reasoned that only theologians were prepared to discuss divine law. The Indian question devolved on the nature of man, and therefore it was a subject for theologians to solve. Although the force of Aristotelian premises would lead Vitoria to conclude that the Incas, as "señores naturales," had the right to rule their land and the people on it—the very notion that Toledo aimed to disprove with the maneuver of the *Informaciones* and the public reading of the *Historia índica*—Vitoria's reasoning ended up giving Toledo and his circle the most efficacious thesis for the charges against the Indians which in turn were used to justify the rigor of the *Ordenanzas*. That Vitoria did not bring a satisfactory end to the discussion is evident in the fact that the Emperor Charles V, upon learning of the substance of Vitoria's arguments, ordered him not to deal with the question any further.

Slipping back onto juridical ground, Vitoria isolated four reasons for thinking that the Indians could legitimately be deprived of their natural rights. Either they were; a) sinners, b) infidels, c) feeble minded (*dementes*), d) irrational, or all of the above. Vitoria found that the first two were not really impediments to rule. Despite much argument to the contrary, Vitoria found that the Indians were not only rational creatures capable of building cities (Aristotle's indispensable test for deserving inclusion in the category of civilization) and establishing commerce amongst themselves. But where they failed was in loving the Spanish. Anthony Pagden explains that for Vitoria, as with Cicero and Aristotle, trade was a means of establishing communication and knowledge, the foundation of the noblest of human virtues: friendship. "One of the just titles for conquering the Indians might be...that by refusing to 'receive' the Spaniards the Indians were attempting to close those natural lines of communication. By so doing they had revealed the full extent of their barbarism" (Pagden 77). Further, by denying the Christians access to their lands without good reason, the Indians were *refusing to be loved* and hence violating the law of nature, for no man may love another without knowing him (Pagden 77).

Despite the all-too-visible elasticity of natural law, or perhaps precisely because of it, in the second part of *De Indis*, Vitoria took back— that is *retracted*—all the empirical, ocular evidence he had mustered to demonstrate that the Indians lived in full civil societies and could not in any way be considered barbarians in the Aristotelian sense of the word (Pagden 79). In the second part of *De Indis*, the part that deals directly with the "just" right to conquest, Vitoria offered the *contra* argument demanded by the Scholastic method *and* most importantly the reality of forces in place. In this text he focused precisely on the perception of absence of certain European—that is *normative*—social and political traits in Indian societies. According to Vitoria, the Indians did not have adequate laws nor magistrates that would enable them to govern their household satisfactorily. Vitoria's idea of the visibility of law was, of course, pegged to the practice of a written, visible archive. Without writing (European script), the materiality of Indian law and rights (*derecho* in Spanish means both "law" and "right") was inconceivable to Vitoria and his contemporaries. It followed, therefore, that not only was Indian law invisible but what there may be of it was inadequate. How then could their rulers be wise or competent? The best visible proof of such absences and inadequacies was, for Vitoria, the Indians' universal human sacrifice and cannibalism. And therefore in *De Indis* the whole edifice of theology's superior qualifications for investigating the nature of mankind collapsed before the force of what Greenblatt has called mimetic blockage and eucharist anxiety (119-151).[20]

Such blockage or theory of irreversible difference ironically puts a stop to the very circulation of communication and exchange that Vitoria faulted the Indians for impeding when they did not receive the Spaniards with love as the Spaniards entered their territories to sack them and convert them. The pliability in the theologian's discourse on the Indian's humanity, and therefore, on their *human* right to self-rule reenacts the modes of cultural blockage operating at the heart of the Spanish conquest. Greenblatt has identified the idea of a principle of blockage,— "the principle by which homologies are resolved into antithesis, brothers into other" (138)—as the agent at work in the misrecognition and destructiveness of the discourse of the Spanish conquest. "The Spanish need to facilitate the improvisational manipulation of the other. They cannot completely dispense with mimetic circulation, a sense of the underlaying strategic intersection of representational forms, while at the same time they are committed to a mimetic blockage, a radical differentiation that is a constitutive feature of the destructive enterprise and of *the text that records and apologizes for the enterprise*" (139, my italics).

In the end, Vitoria provided two contradictory pictures of the Amerindian mind and this is because both the Andean and the Aztec cultures offered a substantial challenge to the hierarchical cultural classification deployed by the Scholasticism of the School of Salamanca. Vitoria's theology held that while the Indians were rational men, they had no right

---

[20] "But if for the Spaniards absolute blockage occurs around the images of cannibalism and idolatry, there still has to be some point of contact for understanding to occur, some basis for communication and negotiation. Otherwise the whole encounter would be a complete blank, a brute clash of bodies, in which the invaders, hopelessly outnumbered, would certainly be destroyed. The Spanish need to facilitate the improvisational manipulation of the other. They cannot completely dispense with mimetic circulation.... while at the same time they are committed to mimetic blockage, a radical differentiation which is a constitutive feature of the destructive enterprise and of the text that records and apologizes for the destruction" (Greenblatt 139).

to rule because of the depravity of their customs: sodomy, cannibalism, human sacrifice. Such depravity, such absence of virtue, could only be explained by the notion that their minds were feeble, degenerate, and could not "see" the world correctly. In an oxymoronic turn worthy of Jorge Luis Borges, the School of Salamanca, "could, in the end, only make the theory of natural slavery logically and morally acceptable by denying the very existence of the creature it was intended to describe": natural man (Pagden 97).

Perhaps, like Philip II, tired and weary of the twists and turns of the discourse of conquest, Toledo chose another, less-apologetic and more-effective set of tactics. His gamble was to leave in place all the suspicion and feelings of self-same/self-other raised by the natural man and slavery discussion while at the same time focus on "tyranny" as the final chapter on the right to rule the Amerindians. His hopes were high, for as we shall see below, Toledo's thesis on tyranny treaded on very solid ground. He writes to Philip II that it is his wish:

> Cese tanta variedad de opiniones en cosa de tan grande importancia por no estar los hechos de estos reinos claros sino fingidos... cada uno como se le antoja para fundar los derechos que desea con tanta turbación y confusión de conciencia así de su Majestad como de sus ministros y moradores de estas provincias tan escrupulisadas que cualquier ignorante ha osado hasta aquí poner la boca en el cielo. (Valcárcel 23)

Toledo had become convinced that the greatest service he could provide the king was to remove all scruples from his/their conscience, so that they could proceed to distribute wealth among his valuable Spanish subjects, place the Indians under the iron rule of fear and obedience, and collect tribute and taxes. All this could be accomplished with a deeply layered psychological portrait: the Incas were tyrants and the Indians lacked prudence. Once this thesis was proven with the assistance of the Indians themselves, caught in yet another instance of their lack of wits, then the king could accept and implement his role as "tutela y defensión de los indios naturales" (Valcárcel 23). Such a plan called for nothing less than Plato's theory of governability in the *Republic* and *Statesman*, and Toledo found that both Matienzo and Sarmiento de Gamboa, obviously familiar with Plato's ideas on geography and governability, had already been advancing the tyranny thesis. Matienzo's opening remarks for his

Gobierno identify the marks of "tyranny" in the Incas: "Otra señal de tiranos... ser pusilámines... son mentirosos y traicioneros... eran tan crueles" (Matienzo 8-10).

From the outset in *The Republic* the reader learns that the dialogues intend to argue that justice is tantamount with life in the city, governed by temperate and wise men who rule in benefit of temperate and prudent citizens. In the course of the dialogue it is shown why tyranny, oligarchy, democracy, and aristocracy are defective forms of government. The central idea is that these forms of government reflect the personality or character of the men who become the state and thus proceed to set up the laws that reflect or resemble their psychology. What is needed, according to *The Republic*, is an arrangement by which the rulers, like physicians, are men specialized in the knowledge and art of governing, men so trained in their art as to be capable of *separating* their character from their craft. These men would be capable of making a key distinction between subject (self) and object (the government) for, as in medicine, which does not consider the interest of medicine, but rather the interest of the body (301), the philosopher king, versed in the rationality of government, would not govern only in his own benefit. But, Thrasymachus, whose job is to object, remarks: "Socrates, you don't know the shepherd from the sheep" (304). While the pastoral model is eventually discarded in the *Dialogues*, the argument continues its movement assuming that if "the states are as humans are [for] they grow out of human character" (402) the objective of Socrates and company is to discover how to distinguish among the various types of men's characters so as identify the marks of the philosopher-king.

The soul is divided into three principles, and one "principle prevails in the souls of one class of men, another in others" (421). The three principles correspond to three classes of pleasures. The first is the faculty to learn, and it corresponds to the love of wisdom and the capacity for self government. It is the intelligent part of the soul. The second principle involves the passions, and it corresponds to the love of honor. Men ruled by the second principle are ambitious and contentious. They love money. The third principle of the soul involves the appetites, and it corresponds to the love of food, drink, sex, money, and all other sensual desires.

The first principle of the soul rules the capacity for self discipline, discretion, order, and prudence. Temperance allows the philosopher to keep *separate* the three principles of the soul. That is why the perfect guardian

of the city must be a philosopher in whose steadfast nature, stoic practices, and love of truth the state can grow as a firmly structured ensemble
of categories of peoples specializing in their various arts and social functions. Such a state would be a reflection of his own disciplined and stable
character. "Until philosophers are kings, or the kings and princes of this
world have the spirit and power of philosophy, and political greatness
and wisdom meet in one, cities will never have rest from evil" (369). This
first principle of the soul corresponds to the perception and cognitive faculties of the head and the face, and pleasures approved by the lover of
wisdom are the truest (422), for they entail the absence of pain. This
higher form of man regulates his body and his mind in order to preserve
the harmony of the soul. As a ruler he will look at the city—an aggregate
of an ethnic population organized by the principle of division of labor—
that is within him and regulate its resources and forces to produce the balance and harmony of civility.

The second principle prevails in the souls of men who rule oligarchies
and democracies. These types of states are both unruly and their citizens
are fed by either the excessive love of money or of freedom, or both. The
second principle of the soul is tied to the faculties that arise from the
organs housed in the trunk of the body, especially the heart and the liver.

The third principle, the appetites, gives rise to tyranny. The third
principle of the soul is associated with the functions of the lower part of
the body, the abominable digestive and sexual functions that place the
body (self) in contact with otherness. The "transgressions of the tyrant
reach beyond the spurious; he has run away from the region of law and
reason and taken his abode with slave pleasures" (424). The state ruled by
the tyrant resembles his person, and he only grows worse with the incre-
ment of his power. The nature and unlawful character of his appetites
cannot be controlled by either the law or reason, for these lower-third
(body) appetites "awaken the wild beast within us, [which] gorged with
meat and drink, starts up and having shaken off sleep goes forth to satisfy
his desires, and there is no conceivable folly or crime.... when he has
parted company with all shame and sense, a man may not be ready to
commit" (416).

Plato's tyrannical man, "purged away from temperance and brought
into full madness" (417), does not of course coincide with the order of
Andean governmentality, which by definition no European ever "saw."
Andean religion, like Christianity itself, addressed the realm of Plato's

third principle. The move that the Toledo circle makes is to posit the tyrannical man generated by drunkenness, lust, obsessive love of feasts, reveling and frenzy, the tyrannical man given to a succession of pleasures, and the eating of forbidden fruits, as the man to be understood by Andean governmentality. The Toledo circle, prepared by Vitoria's exegesis on natural law, conflates the realm of the sacred with the realm of political and economic administration. The "tyrannical" man that Polo de Ondegardo, Matienzo, Cristóbal de Molina, and Sarmiento left dispersed in the pages of their description of Andean belief—"ritos y fábulas de su origen"—represents religious visibilities in Andean cosmology together with what today we understand as the play of desire. The inclinations of the lower third of the body appear indelibly inscribed in their accounts of "idolatries," that is to say, the ground of the sacred.[21]

It is clear that the charges of Inca tyranny went far beyond the defects of an absolutist form of government practiced by a dethroned elite. Perhaps that is why Philip II sought to compensate with a total denial of all pleasures for his own absolutism, or, in the same vein, Toledo sought to acquire the reputation of an ascetic man moved only by political ambition and money.[22] As such Toledo fell within the ranks of the second principle but stayed well away from the very charges of tyranny which many of his contemporaries made upon him.

At any rate the resemblance between the state, the tyrant, and its subjects informed not only the insatiable curiosity of the Spanish for Andean religious practices but also justified the link between them and the thesis on the unredeemable character of the Indians, who could thus never be allowed to wonder away from the vigilant eye of the colonial Christian

---

[21] In *De Procuranda* (1577), José de Acosta argues that it is not licit to punish the "infieles" or destroy them by force, it is indeed legal to make war upon them ("es lícito hacer guerra a los bárbaros") so that they will abandon their idolatries and their abominable sacred rites: "el trato frecuente con el demonio, el pecado nefando con los varones, los incestos con las hermanas, y madres, y demás crímenes de este género" (Acosta II, 3, 432, qtd. in Shepherd 194).

[22] Toledo brought with him from Spain a good number of pages. He remained single throughout his life, but on more than one occasion his enemies in Peru murmured and even brought public charges concerning the homosexual relations of his pages in his household. For sure, one of his interpreters, Gonzalo Jiménez (Jimenillo) was accused of intentionally misinterpreting at the trial of Túpac Amaru, and of sodomy. The viceroy tried to defend him of the misinterpretation charge, but when he learned of the sodomy accusations, he had the page put to death immediately. (Valcárcel 10-11)

state. For Plato, as well as for Matienzo, who often refers to *The Republic*, tyrannical men (or, for Matienzo, the feeble-minded Indians), occupy a place so far away from the king, the aristocrat, or the *letrados* like Matienzo himself, that even the pleasures they crave and their experiences are, as Plato put it, "shadow pleasures" (425). To the Spaniards, the Indians appeared to be ruled by the third principle of the soul: they literally— pun intended—knew nothing. Their cognitive powers were so diminished by the shadowed pleasures of the lower third—sodomy, anthropophagy, incest, "free" sex—that they, as Vitoria argued, "could not see the world as it is," much less arrive at a body of written law. At best they may have seen shadows. These charges were elaborated in the face of the rampant and universal rape of Indian women and men by the conquering men under Toledo, a reality that in Guamán Poma's account questions the ability of Toledo and his circle to "see" the world as it is.

Bartolomé de Las Casas (1484-1566) had succeed in dismantling the Aristotelian globalizing category of "barbarian," and in doing so he proposed the first comparative ethnology by dispersing in time and space an evolutionary, *cultural* set of four types of barbarians, a scheme which accounted for both the diversity of Amerindian cultures as well as their different behavior from Europeans (Pagden 119-145). But Las Casas's *Apologética historia* (written after 1551), as well as his *Argumentum Apologiae* (1550), remained unpublished during his lifetime, and the psychological portrait advanced by Plato continued to be ascendant in the discourse dealing with Amerindian cultural difference. Despite claims to the contrary,[23] the work of José de Acosta (1540-1600), who left Spain for Peru in 1571, affirmed the tyranny and thus the tutelage thesis.[24] Acosta was critical of the evangelizing manner of the orders that had preceded the Jesuits in America. He also did not believe in the use of force against the Indians, and in harmony with the politics of his order, he sought to position himself as a third—neutral—force in the disputes over the Indians'

---

[23] Anthony Pagden's careful study of Acosta argues that *Historia natural y moral de las Indias* (1590) continues the comparative ethnology done by Las Casas in *Apologética historia* (146-197).

[24] Acosta wanted to inaugurate an order that was not based on lies and without the violent destruction of the Indians' persons and their "possessions." But he did not agree with Las Casas's thesis of restitution, nor with the idea of self-rule. He saw the Jesuit mission as an enlightened system of tutelage in which the king could discharge his responsibilities to his Indian vassals (Shepherd 104).

bodies and souls between the Spanish state and the various evangelizing orders. In his calculations, Acosta looked for points where the interests of the state could coincide with those of the Jesuits (Shepherd 104).

Despite Acosta's studied distance from Toledo, his discursive and political connections to the viceroy's enterprise show such a distance to be more apparent than real. In 1577, while in Lima, and before he wrote his more famous but perhaps less influential *Historia natural y moral de las Indias* (1590), Acosta penned his manual for evangelization and indoctrination of the Indians into the Christian faith. Despite the fact that *De procuranda indorum salute* was written in Latin, it made the rounds in the Andes quite quickly. Since his arrival in Lima, Acosta had delivered several major sermons on the ways to indoctrinate and govern the Indians. He had been a prominent voice in the 1576 Councils of Lima and Cuzco. Acosta joined the viceroy's court in Chuquisaca and accepted to act as an adviser. During this time he met Polo de Ondegardo, Juan de Matienzo, and Pedro Sarmiento de Gamboa. Therefore, it should come as no surprise that the ideas informing the pedagogy recommended in his manual assume an Indian subject impaired by very much the same cognitive disabilities drawn by Vitoria, encapsulated in Plato's tyrant, and deployed by all the intellectuals of Toledo's circle. George Shepherd writes that "Many of the programs initiated by Toledo resurfaced in *De procuranda*. Acosta discusses Toledo's social reductions of Indians into villages, the role of the state in religious affairs, the extirpation of idolatry and the concept of mission as opposed to *parroquia*" (198).

De procuranda does *not* deploy a comparative reasoning for understanding the different behavior of the Indians. It recognizes the difference but it does not explain it. In fact, in this work Acosta departs from the Aristotelian claims on the primacy of experience in the making of cognition. Despite the fact that he recommends that "missionaries should attempt to understand Indians in their own terms and not by means of simple comparison with other races" (Pagden 154), Acosta nevertheless falls back into the psychological model of government and cognition and accepts the tyranny category as descriptive of the Amerindians highest capacity for civilized organization and for understanding of the preaching of the gospel. In fact, the tyrant model, unwittingly, turned out to pose a major challenge to the idea of preaching the gospel, for it proposed Indian subjects so blinded by deep cognitive disabilities as to be rendered incapable of *understanding* notions such as God and the Eucharist. The tyrant thesis came dangerously close to bordering onto the erection of a doctrine of complete psychological—cultural—incompatibility between Indians and Europeans. The remedies necessary to bridge the gaping chasm between the third and first principles of the soul needed thus to engage not only the dimension of the soul but the corporeal space, as Toledo and Matienzo recommended. The "care" of the body—disciplined work, food, clothing, movement, sleep, hygiene—needed to be brought within the scope of doctrine.[25] In practical terms, *De procuranda*'s rationality was not that different from Matienzo's *Gobierno del Perú* (1569), and the similarity was not lost on Toledo, who although resentful of the Jesuits for founding universities without his permission, nevertheless claimed Acosta and his ideas as part of his organization.

III. GOVERNMENTALITY: *ORDENANZAS* AND *BUEN GOBIERNO*

Having cleared all the discursive obstacles—scruples—Toledo, relying very heavily on the *Gobierno del Perú* (1567) prepared by Matienzo,[26] preceded to order the chaos brought about by the destructuration of the conquest and the civil wars among the Spaniards and Andean which ensued after the events of Cajamarca in 1532.[27] Nathan Wachtel has proposed the notion of *destructuration*, not simply as the destruction of the

---

[25] Following Aristotle's discussion of incontinence in the *Nicomachean Ethics* in which he identifies "three cause for incontinent behavior; 1) genetics, 2) natural depravity, 3) the influence of habit in one's mental state" (Shepherd 173), Acosta regards the formation of new, bodily habits in the Indians as crucial to his plan for acculturation. Acosta states: "mucha más fuerza tiene la educación y el buen ejemplo, que entrando desde la infancia por los sentidos, modela el alma aún tierna y sin pulimiento, porque le infunde formas vivas en las que, imbuida la mente, es llevada por natural inclinación a apetecer, obrar y rehuir, del modo que cualquiera naturaleza obra según las formas que tiene en sí... que la fuerza de la costumbre hace una segunda naturaleza" (Shepherd 173).

[26] Guillermo Lohmann Villena has shown in great detail the close relationship of *Gobierno del Perú* to Toledo's *Ordenanzas*. Lohmann feels that Matienzo's masterpiece is contained in his recommendations for the readjustment in the tribute that *yanaconas* were to pay and which Toledo adopted. On the whole it is clear that the *Ordenanzas* would not have the range in scope nor the precision and clarity for which they are known without the work of Matienzo. See Lohmann Villena.

[27] For more on the idea of colonial rule as a destructuration of the Inca empire, see Wachtel *Sociedad*.

local order by the colonizing power but rather as "the survival of ancient structures displaced from the relatively coherent context in which they used to function" (*Sociedad* 135), as way to understand the Andean situation in Toledo's hands. The climate of resistance, revolts, accommodation, and even attempts to bring back the Inca order despite the Incas' demise, involved, of course, the whole of the Andean population (Spaniards and Andean) in a collective act of boundless cultural translation and accommodation (see in this volume chapter 3 on the Taqui-Oncoy). The conquest wove in a single if heterogeneous strand the discursive work of evangelization, together with the work of the legal system as the twin forces in the emergence of a new economic system that took over the conception of the body, its labor and its relation to both the means of production as well as the fruits of that production. Therefore, *lenguas*, or interpreters were necessary with almost every step that Toledo took to control the overlapping relations.[28]

Integrating the myriad of official and unofficial, bad and good and even censored translators we find Guamán Poma. By his own account he would like us to think that he was present at all discussions, *informaciones*, map makings, interrogations, Inquisitorial trials, sermons, and civil trials going on the Andes then. Although very little is known about his identity, it is certain that he worked as a court interpreter and that, as he himself tells us, he worked for the zealot Cristóbal de Albornoz in one

---

[28] It has already been noted that in the trial that the Audiencia de Lima set up against the prosecutor Loarte, who had been in charge of Túpac Amaru's own "course and precipitous" trial, that Loarte was accused of employing the services of Gonzalo Jimenez, Jimenillo, known for his inaccurate and even insidiously false interpretations. Upon accusations of sodomy, Jimenillo was put to death by order of the viceroy, despite the fact that he was one of his pages. In Arequipa, in 1575, three years after the execution of the young Inca, Toledo engaged Gonzalo Holguín, expert in Quechua, Aymara, and Puquina with the title of "Lengua General," or Chief Official Interpreter of the State. In this ordinance, Toledo set up a series of regulations on the expertise of interpreters, the quality of the person who may hold governmental position and the mandatory need of the viceroy and other officials to keep interpreters available for all functions. In the stipulations for Holguin's appointment (500 pesos ensayados) Toledo tells his interpreter that "habéis the jurar de guardar ante mí y de usar bien y fielmente el dicho oficio y no dejéis de cumplirlo así por ninguna manera, so la dicha pena y a más quinientos pesos para la cámara de Su Majestad." The interpreter must keep records: "hacer memoria...Que no reciba dávidas, ni cohechos de los indios" (Toledo, *Ordenanzas* 300-302).

of his campaigns "against idolatries" at the time when Albornoz discovered the Taqui-Oncoy movement in 1564 (see in this volume chapter 3 on the Taqui-Oncoy).[29] A comparison of the method, the strategy of the questions in the *Informaciones* (1572), the governmental plan devised by Matienzo in his *Gobierno del Perú* (1567), and the contents and organization of *El primer nueva corónica y buen gobierno* (1615) shows clearly that Guamán Poma had intimate knowledge of the preparation of the Spanish texts and their intent. His own multilingual, "illustrated" letter to the king attempts a total and globalizing response to most, if not all, the tactics and strategies of the Toledo circle and those who had prepared the way for the tyrant (Plato's lower one third of the soul/body) thesis.[30] I cannot here offer the details of the comparison. I will limit myself to identifying three nodal points.

All three proposals for a governmental model are examples of destructuration. Guamán Poma's model would basically keep pan-Andean labor and social institutions intact. The rulers would be a set of illustrated, very temperate, and prudent *curacas*, local Andean lords who, having adopted Christianity and reading and writing, would *continue* the Andean world in behalf of the Spanish king, who would, of course, receive tribute. The chief qualification of the *curacas* was their experience gained in the Andean tradition of good government. As Guamán Poma endeavors to show, they knew how to run an ordered and very productive society. The *curacas* scored high marks in economics, ethics, and common sense. Guamán Poma shows that they had even devised, in practice, a social system which embodied all the chief principles of Christianity as an ethics of living. Thus there was no need for Spanish juridical or political thought. Regarding the "vices" and the "evils" that the Spaniards saw in Andean rites and religion, Guamán Poma formulated a very adept answer. Such "tyrannical" behavior was indeed the work of the devil, a Christian, not Andean, gnoseological category, with which the Spaniards, as he pointed out, had ample experience. Thus the objectionable behavior of the Andeans did not stem from within, from their character or psychology;

---

[29] See Guamán Poma, *El primer nueva corónica y buen gobierno* (1583-1615) 282, 285, 689, 690.

[30] The work of Guamán Poma has received abundant and very serious examination. For his engagement with Andean and European discourses, see Ossio, Wachtel, *Sociedad*; Pease *El dios* and *Las crónicas*; Burga; Adorno; Julio Ortega 198.

the lack of temperance was the work of an external force. The devil and his temptations were omnipresent and thus Guamán Poma was willing to accept that Christianity be preached in the Andes as an antidote, while he rejected the "tyranny" thesis in each and every one of his pages.

Matienzo and Toledo, having perhaps calibrated better the extent to which the interjection of Spanish cultural practices in the Andean world would result in structural changes, devised a model by which to control the Indian population through new and old institutions—*reducciones* (or Indians towns), *encomiendas*, colonial *mita* (or forced labor)—which would also serve as the appropriate vehicle to wear down the Indians' affection for and loyalty to their pan-Andean cultural practices, especially religion and the *ayllu* organization. Following Matienzo's advice, the viceroy's plan was to discipline the bodies and souls of the Indians so completely as to keep them physically and psychologically exhausted all the time.

Toledo and Matienzo differed on the kind and quality of the ruler. Implicit in the *Ordenanzas* is the idea that the ruler, as representative of the king, would be a member, like Toledo himself, of the Spanish nobility. Matienzo had other ideas. He thought that the only appropriate and capable rulers for the colony would be Spanish *letrados*, in his mind the closest thing to a philosopher-king. Quoting Plato, Matienzo writes: "No dexará de haber males y desventuras en la república hasta que la manden y gobiernen filósofos, esto es, hombres sabios" (197).

Assuming the tyranny thesis, Toledo's program, like Acosta's, entailed a two-stage process of conversion: the regulation of the body, building good habits, would in time produce the prescribed and desired mental habits. Thus Toledo's *Ordenanzas* regulated the minutia of the concreteness of the body—twenty lashes to anyone who took away an Indian's cloth that covered his coca basket—as well as the minutia of the social and political order. Toledo drew up regulations on the appointment and duties of the *corregidores*, on the place, quality, and functions of the "casas de cabildo," on the jails, the qualification of the candidates for the office of Indian *alcaldes*, on the specific date when elections were to take place, on the identity and function of the participants in the feast of Corpus Christi, on the appointment of the supervisor of mills, butcher shops, and inns; on the kind of work and pay of the African slaves, the Cañari Indians, the wages that day laborers were to receive, on the silversmiths shops, on the quality and dates for market day, etc. His aim was, as he himself put it, to continue "to specify the punishments needed in order to insure the execution of order...so that each person could carry on with his business" (37).

Toledo goes on to theorize his ideas on the relation of punishment and justice as the foundation of government.[31] Justice is practically synonymous with punishment, for to "punish the evil man is great mercy [*misericordia*] indeed. Justice is the greatest pity [*piedad*] that can be carried out in as much as to forgive a bad man is to be cruel to all others" (38). Toledo states his conviction on the fundamental role of rigorous punishment for small transgression in the constitution of the republic and good government [*buen gobierno*]" (38). Just punishment, or order, depends on the division of the population and behaviors into infinitesimal categories. The detection of the smallest infraction of the law demanded a very large corp of observers and listeners—witnesses, clergy man, *alcaldes, corregidores, auditores*, translators, scribes, confessors, interrogators, visitors, tax collectors—capable of entering their observations in the multilayered archives of punishment that Toledo set up at the heart of all the institutions he regulated.

The proper consideration of the nature of the infraction, and the assignation of the fitting punishment, was both facilitated by and dependent upon the written record. Aware of the Toledan order's dependency on the written word and on the archival system of government it deployed, Toledo set many ordinances requiring the need for *corregidores* to employ *letrados* for the *cabildos* to keep written records of everything, for the scribes and notaries to be present in almost every transaction, and of course for the translators to swear to translate and interpret accurately and to observe the prohibition of receiving gifts from the warring parties (40-66). Toledo is particularly clear in forbidding the use of *quipus* in any official transaction. He ordered the *cabildo* scribes to note "todo lo que los indios suelen poner en quipos, para que sea más cierto y durable, en especial en las faltas que tuvieran de doctrina y entradas y salidas de sacerdotes" (338). Guamán Poma would not destroy the *quipu*, but would indeed agree with Toledo as to the need to keep a

[31] All translations from the *Ordenanzas* of Toledo, the *Gobierno del Perú* by Matienzo, *De Procuranda* by Acosta, *El primer nueva corónica y buen gobierno* by Guamán Poma and from the Jesuit Anonymous are mine.

written record of every transaction, for in Guamán Poma's view only the detailed archival record could keep the Spaniards from cheating on the Indians. Thus both sides understood and sought the manipulation of dimensions of writing as the engine of the law and a relation of power.

Matienzo's observation of Andean social and political practices had furnished Toledo with the main categories for the organization-destructuration of Peru. Acosta had contributed the notion of building a new pastoral order from the ground up, that is, from the smallest corporeal habits onto mentalities. Together with Sarmiento de Gamboa and Polo de Ondegardo, and through the types of questions and the situation of the witnesses interviewed in the *Informaciones*, Toledo had managed to press his own political thesis: that the Incas, as tyrants and usurpers of the "right" of the local lords or *curacas*, had no legitimate claim on Andean government. Toledo, unlike Guamán Poma, had no wish to preserve the native authority of the *curacas*. The study of Andean religion—the *guacas*, origin myths, rites—carried out by Cristóbal de Molina, el Cuzqueño, the civil lawyer Polo de Ondegardo, and the "cosmógrafo del rey" Pedro Sarmiento de Gamboa contained all the necessary information-cum-interpretation to extend the tyranny thesis to the *curacas* and thus place them under the gaze of suspicion and vigilance. Although the *curacas* were deployed by Matienzo as the political link between the old Andean order and the new colonial administration, their authority on a myriad of things had to be drastically curtailed as to produce the appropriate circumstance for conversion in the fields of belief and authority.

With a series of prohibitions Toledo sought to flatten out the *curacas* and to take away all illusion pertaining to the power invested in the ceremony of their persons. For each infraction the *curacas* could receive 100 lashes or be brought to trial, face imprisonment, and loss of their office. They could also be accused, before the Inquisition, of idolatry or relapses into the old religion. Toledo forbade them to offer other Indians any assistance or favors. They could not seek the help of the *Audiencia* or carry on with suits. They could not receive tribute. They could not keep the company of Spaniards in order to curry favor. They could not ride horses or be carried in litters. They could not have banquets at which common Indians were invited, as in the old Andean practice. They could not have a voice in the marriage of Indians under their jurisdiction. They could not hold office if they were suspected or condemned of having any allegiance to the old religion (330-373). More charitable, Matienzo thought that they should be allowed to wear Spanish clothing. In that way they would spend their money on the purchase of Spanish goods and in a perverse echo of Vitoria's objection to Indian self-rule, "learn to love us, for they would love our clothing and begin to look like men" (69).

Conclusions

Toledo's indictments against Andean culture were monumental and they were certified by the studies of his circle of intellectuals and the power of his office. By the time he was finished with the *Ordenanzas*, the viceroy had not only executed the last Inca, but he had placed a historiography on the ground with the full force of the most important knowledge of the time: cosmography, jurisprudence, theology, "informaciones," Renaissance political theory, ocular observation, testimony and verification, and, on the ground, the public assent of the *panacas*. In organizing "the conduct of conduct" in the former Inca empire, Toledo and his circle came up with a potent mixture of the pastoral model—the tutelage of the Christian shepherd over his sheep—with Machiavelli's reason of state. The Anonymous Jesuit, widely believed to be the *mestizo* Jesuit Blas Valera, and Guamán Poma, in separate or perhaps coordinated ways, endeavored to contest the viceroy's claims on the "tyrannical" qualities of Andean culture and government, as well as to device a blueprint in which conversion would take place but only at the level of the Gods. In the plan of the post-toledan Andean intellectuals, the habits of the Andeans, already the product of immense corporeal and mental discipline, would stay in place—as a Christian order *avant-la-lettre*. What would change would be the identity and worship of the divinities. Blas Valera, Garcilaso de la Vega, Inca, and Guamán Poma advanced a revolutionary thesis on which the right to autonomous rule could be based: a *truly comparative ethnology*. Their method and tactics would show that the Andeans' ethics and law, and thus their entire social and political organization, espoused more strictly and consistently the ideal Christian ethics than any observable behavior of any Spaniard, especially that of most of the friars and high bureaucrats that were in charge of the conversion, who in fact engaged in the most libidinous behavior Plato could have ever imagined.

The effect of their writing was, of course, nil on the policymaking of their contemporaries. Garcilaso's *Comentarios reales* (1609) had a tremendous impact both in Europe and the Americas long after his death. For a long time it stood as the only known reconstruction of life in the Inca Empire, and, as Manuel Burga in his *Nacimiento de una utopía: muerte y resurrección de los incas* (1988) and David Brading in *The First America* (1991) show, it was fundamental in the later construction of nationhood in the Andes.[32] Only more recently has the work of Guamán Poma come to join the ranks of the subaltern's disputation with Toledo. I do not have space here to enter into their arguments and rationality of government, suffice it say that they offered an economic and social model—the disposition of things—in a rather "modern" and complex thinking in which the relation of men/women to things was the ground of governmental administration. Guamán Poma seems to have been specially aware of the distinction between government and sovereignty, a distinction which was not made in Europe until the idea of government as economic administration appears in the work of Guillome de La Perrière (*Mirrorir Politique* (1567); see Foucault, "Governmentality," 89-97). Curiously, both in La Perrière and Guamán Poma, government is defined as the right manner of the disposition of things and people and their imbrication with other things such as wealth, resources, and institutions. Government is not the imposition of laws on men, as Toledo ordained, but rather the management of things, and as Foucault has pointed out in the case of La Perrière, it is the arrangement of multiform tactics (95).

In summary, when Toledo arrived in Peru, he understood his service to the king in strictly Machiavellian terms: "The objective of the exercise of power is to reinforce, strengthen and protect the principality, but with this last understood to mean not the objective ensemble of its subjects and its territory, but rather, the prince's relation with what he owns, with the territory he has inherited or acquired, and with his subjects" (Foucault, "Governmentality" 90). Thus his statements regarding the need to protect the Indians from destruction have to be understood in the sense of protecting the king's property and not as humanitarian feelings or poli-

---

[32] To gage some of the *Commentaries* impact on the formation of another historiography, see Burga; Brading. Of course the work of Garcilaso, like the work of Las Casas, provided some of the key information for the main charge of the Spanish "black legend:" the wanton and cruel destruction not only of the Indians but of their civilizations.

cies. In the hands of Toledo, whose mission and measures encapsuled rather neatly Machiavelli's reason of state (the state is a holding-out provision to retain sovereignty, however acquired), governing the Andes took the form of the logical result of the pedagogic and pastoral discourse of Scholasticism (Gordon 9). Such theory of tutelage could only be based on the deployment of a myriad of disciplinary techniques. The Toledan order kept its subjects physically and mentally exhausted at all times: it was a nightmarish version of a limitless and unforgiving novitiate. When Matienzo, Vitoria, Sarmiento, and Acosta speak of making *men* of the Indians (they are not speaking of human rights as some have claimed), they are calling for and justifying a desire for extreme uses of what Michel Foucault has called biopower, or the excessive deployment of power over persons understood as living beings. Toledo's regulations exemplify, anachronistically, the observation that Foucault makes of "modern" man as an "animal whose politics places his own existence into question" (Foucault, *History* 143). The double movement which took place in Europe at the end of the sixteenth century—the state centralization coupled with the dispersion of religious dissidence (Foucault, "Governmentality" 88)—registered in the Andes under colonial rule a level of repression which Europe was spared until later, when the combination of the pastoral model and reason of state would produce the totalitarian regimes of this century.[33]

An early version of this chapter was originally published in *The Latin American Subaltern Studies Reader*, ed. Ileana Rodríguez, 143-171. © 2001 Durham: Duke University Press. All rights reserved. Reprinted by permission.

[33] In his *A History of Latin America: Empires and Sequels, 1450-1930* (1997), Peter Bakewell writes that Toledo's policies on restricting the physical movement of the Indian population largely failed (233). Through a quirk in Toledo's legislation which exempted those living away from their communities from service in the *mita*, Indians found the loophole that enabled them to flee the *reducciones* and dreaded *mita*. They fled into hidden inaccessible places, into the Spanish towns, into the service of *curacas*, into the cash economy. On the matter of population decline, Bakewell reports that the Toledo census of 1570 showed 1.3 million Indians. By 1620 the Spanish authorities reported 700,000. The population continued to decline until the epidemic of 1720. The total estimated decline for the Andes is 48.5% and for Central Mexico is 85%.

Works Cited

BAKEWELL, Peter. *A History of Latin America: Empires and Sequels, 1450-1930.* Cambridge: Blackwell Publishers, 1997.

BRADING, David. *The First America: The Spanish Monarchy, Creole Patriots, and the Liberal State 1492-1867.* Cambridge: Cambridge University Press, 1991.

CARRILLO, Francisco. *Cronistas del Perú antiguo. Enciclopedia histórica de la literatura peruana.* Lima: Editorial Horizonte, 1989.

DELEUZE, Gilles. *Foucault.* Ed. and trans. Sean Hand. Trans. Minneapolis: University of Minnesota Press, 1988.

DOMENICI, Viviano and Davide DOMENCI. "Talking Knots of the Inka: A Curious Manuscript that May Hold the Key to Andean Writing." In *Archeology* November-December 1996: 48-56.

DREYFUS, Hubert L. and Paul Rabinow. *Michel Foucault: Beyond Structuralism and Hermeneutics.* Chicago: The University of Chicago Press, 1982.

FOUCAULT, Michel. "Governmentality." In *The Foucault Effect: Studies in Governmentality: With Two Lectures by and an Interview with Michel Foucault.* Ed. Colin Gordon, Peter Miller, and Graham Burchell. Chicago: University of Chicago Press, 1991. 89-97

—. *History of Sexuality. Volume I: An Introduction.* New York: Random House, 1980.

GORDON, Colin. "Governmental Rationalty: An Introduction." In *The Foucault Effect: Studies in Governmentality: with Two Lectures by and an Interview with Michel Foucault.* Ed. Graham Burchell et al. Chicago: University of Chicago Press, 1991. 1-50.

GREENBLATT, Stephen. *Marvelous Possessions: The Wonder of the New World.* Chicago: University of Chicago Press, 1991.

GUAMÁN POMA DE AYALA, Felipe. *El primer nueva corónica y buen gobierno.* Ed. John Murra and Rolena Adorno. México: Siglo Veintiuno, 1980.

LEVILLIER, Roberto. *Don Francisco de Toledo.* Buenos Aires: Biblioteca del Congreso Argentino, 1935.

LOHMANN VILLENA, Guillermo. "Etude Préliminaire." To *Gobierno del Perú* by Juan de Matienzo, Paris: Institut Francais d'Études Andines, 1967.

MATIENZO, Juan de. *Gobierno del Perú (1567).* Ed. Guillermo Lohmann Villena. Reprint, Paris: Institut Francais d'Études Andines, 1967.

PAGDEN, Anthony. *The Fall of Natural Man: The American Indian and the Origins of Comparative Ethnology.* Cambridge: Cambridge University Press, 1982.

PLATO. *The Dialogues of Plato: The Seventh Letter.* Chicago: Encyclopaedia Britannica, 1952.

PORRAS BARRENECHEA, Raúl. *Los cronistas del Perú (1528-1650) y otros ensayos.* Lima: Banco de Crédito del Perú, 1986.

RABASA, José. "Of Zapatismo: Reflections on the Folkloric and the Impossible in a Subaltern Insurrection." In *The Politics of Culture in the Shadow of Capital*. Ed. Lisa Lowe and David Lloyd. Durham: Duke University Press, 1997. 399-431.

ROSTWOROWSKI DE DIEZ CANSECO, María. *Estructuras andinas del poder. Ideología religiosa y política*. Lima: Instituto de Estudios Peruanos, 1983.

SHEPHERD, George. *José de Acosta: Reading the American Past and Programming the Future toward the Christianization of Amerindians*. Washington, D.C.: Diss. Georgetown University, 1996.

TOLEDO, Francisco de. *Ordenanzas*. Ed. Roberto Levillier. Vol. 8 of *Gobernantes del Perú, cartas y papeles, siglo XVI*. Ed. Roberto Levillier. Madrid: Imprenta de Juan Pueyo, 1925. 14 vols.

VALCÁRCEL, Luis E. *El virrey Toledo, gran tirano del Perú*. Lima: Impr. del Museo Nacional, 1940.

WACHTEL, Nathan. *Sociedad e ideología: ensayos de historia y antropología andina*. Lima: Instituto de Estudios Peruanos, 1973.

ZUIDEMA, R. Tom. *Inca Civilization in Cuzco*. Tran. Jean Jacques Decostes. Austin: University of Texas Press, 1990.

CHAPTER 6
Writing Subalternity: Guamán Poma and Garcilaso, Inca

"Porque en todo sea tragedia a los indios, mestizos, y criollos [del Perú] el Inca Garcilaso de la Vega, su hermano, compatriota y paisano salud y felicidad"

Garcilaso de la Vega, Inca, *Comentarios reales*, 1609, 1616

"Y no hubo conquista"

Guamán Poma de Ayala , *El primer nueva corónica y buen gobierno*, 1615.

PREAMBLE

The postcolonial perspective, as it emerges in the English speaking academy, is situated in a specific historical conjuncture. First, it is important to note that it is an inquiry that departs from, even though it also questions, the post-structuralist challenge to epistemology and the subsequent decentering of the subject with its claims to "truth" and "knowledge." Second, it should not be forgotten that Edward Said's *Orientalism* (1978) is generally acknowledged to lay the theoretical basis for the examination of colonial discourse, that is, the discourse modes in which Europe has constructed its (oriental) others. Said's work has been extended and radicalized in the hands of other former subjects of the English speaking empire and so the postcolonial perspective has come to be associated with the contemporary diaspora and dispersal of postcolonial intellectuals and academics. Third, postcoloniality faces the current crisis of self and national identity in an increasingly transnational world. These three problems are made only more severe and paradoxical by a theory that postulates a split subject always already given in the impossibility of discursive arrest. Finally, this anxious subject of English-speaking postcoloniality writes the world and itself without awareness of a previous, major, if not modular, colonial period and postcolonial experience which is enormously relevant to many of its concerns—the subaltern subject, cultural translations, oral and written traditions, margin-center relations, the question of authenticity, modalities of excess, hybridization, and transgression. Only most recently, for example, has Bill Ashcroft, in "Excess: Post-colonialism and the Verandahs of Meaning" (1994), stated that "post-colonialism does not mean 'after colonialism,' that it begins with the moment of colonization" (34). He makes this statement without any reference at all to the Latin American trajectory of writing, a writing marked by the sign of resistance *ab initio*. What is more, this incisive essay which identifies the excess of insistence, the excess of supplementarity, and the excess of hybridity as three interrelated modes in the phenomenon of postcoloniality, builds its argument in the absence of the long-standing question of *mestizaje* in Latin America, as well as the recent work of Julio Ortega on the literature of excess.

Looking at parallels and divergences between Latin America and the English postcolonial retrospective will probably show that some of the ground being "theorized" now has already been problematized before. This is so if we understand "theory" as not a philosophy or an abstracted system of rules, but rather as a given position from which a questioning of the foundations of the disciplines (power/knowledge) in the humanities, and a voicing of disjunctions with the basic assumptions of philosophy, history, and literature, is undertaken. In the case of Latin America such a questioning or contestatory position has sought to account not only for its own textual production but has also established an "unremitting dialogue with the texts of the continental world about them and with them" (Kadir 41). What is more, self-conscious texts have not, by definition, eschewed the ever-vexing problem of historical context, the link between discourse and society, and the mechanisms of dominance which define colonial situations of all kinds,[1] but have in fact dwelled in and sprung from such difficulty.

It is at the convergence of postcolonial theoretical preoccupations and the question of the subaltern as the subject of another historiography that a consideration of Guamán Poma's intervention into the formation of colonial discourse, and Garcilaso de la Vega, Inca's commentaries on the colonial repertoire whose texts turned the ancient Americas into prime examples of barbarity and otherness, become pertinent. I hope that bringing to bear these heterogeneous works on the present conundrum of the subaltern will prove illuminating, though I am aware of the current bias against visualist language.

---

[1] For a lucid and helpful discussion on the relation of post-structuralism and its contribution to a critical theory capable of thinking such a relation between discourse and historical context see Poster 6-9, 70-86.

But first allow me a few more prefatory remarks. A distinction between colonial texts and postcolonial theory needs to be drawn, if not on theoretical grounds then at least on the basis of important empirical time-space locations and historical identities. Colonial discourse, as Said characterized it in *Orientalism*, and as Peter Hulme has used it in his *Colonial Encounters* (1986), entails:

> an ensemble of linguistically-based practices unified by their common deployment in the management of colonial relationships. . .Underlying the idea of colonial discourse, in other words, is the presumption that during the colonial period large parts of the non-European world were produced for Europe through a discourse that imbricated sets of questions and assumptions, methods of procedure and analysis, and kinds of writing and imagery, normally separated out into discrete areas of military strategy, political order, social reform, imaginative literature, personal memoir and so on. (Hulme 2)

Colonial discourse thus comprises the texts written for and consumed, on the main, by Europe in the process of production of the rest of the world as its other. But taking this far the outline of the problem is insufficient. Once produced, those texts deployed in the management of colonial relations were also read in the colonized localities, and their truth claims were received and interpreted in a variety of modalities. The reception given to these colonial texts, in most cases, corresponded to the class/race hierarchies that the power/knowledge of colonial discourse managed as the colonial social order. For instance, when particular catechisms to Christianize specific colonial subjects (whose subjectivities were assessed in need of particular explanations of Christian doctrine) were developed with the aid of local informants and translators, something else and something more complex than the production of Europe's others was at work; something more that the elaboration of cultural difference as a set of oppositional traits took place in the space of receptivity of the colonial text. The very notion of a diagnosis of the signification requirements of the prospective converts implied a search into the quiescent religious assumptions of the friar in charge of evangelization. In facing and constructing the otherness of his "inferior" and idolatrous charges, the friar also had to take a look, as it were, from the "outside" onto the naturalized superiority and singular truth of his faith. Such moments of cultural alienation rendered different and contrasting responses. In some cases the superior/inferior characterization of the difference became doubtful and dissolved a little. In most, the very doubt engendered greater zeal. Fear intensified the terms of the higher/lower, good/bad opposition with which the spiritual conquest sustained the gains of the military conquest.

Such estrangement, of course, cut both ways. For the colonized, as we see in the writings of Garcilaso, Inca and Guamán Poma—shocked by the version of themselves that the furious workings of colonial discourse was implanting as the basis for future rule, estranged from themselves by the otherness projected onto them—responded also. Their texts are the first that wrote back, in the endless correspondence between Europeans, Indians, *mestizos*, *criollos*, and mulattos that the history of Latin America entails. Because texts like the *Comentarios reales* and *El primer nueva corónica* "write back," they cannot simply be rolled over or simply placed under colonial discourse, as first and most usefully, though insufficiently, categorized by Said.

Two points ought to be stressed here. The first is the need to draw a categorical distinction between the texts elaborated by the colonizer and the texts produced by the colonized. This should be done not so much in regard to the more-or-less European fracture of the text, but rather in relation to the position of subalternity deployed by the subject of enunciation. Even though in "real life" such stark opposition (Colonizer/colonized, sovereign/subordinate) could be almost infinitely shaded and diffused, distinctions which account for the different positionality of the subject are necessary in order to avoid extending theories over practices for which they really cannot yet account for (Mignolo).

For instance, if we were to agree that colonial discourse comprises "the variety of textual forms in which the West produced and codified knowledges about non-metropolitan areas and cultures, especially those under (formal) colonial control" (Williams and Chrisman 5), and critics such as Gayatri Chakravorty Spivak, Homi Bhabha, Aijaz Ahmed, and Ania Loomba to name a few, are postcolonials, what kinds of relocations would we have to perform in order to understand the discursive production of subjects born and settled in the territories known as Latin America? Who, in the great list of "colonial" or "republican" writers, would reenter as a colonial or postcolonial author? An implicit denial of coevalness irregularities such as this is of course the product of a neo-colonial classification which pairs all English language products with the First World (theory) and Spanish language products with the Third world (materials for export?, relays of copies?). I would therefore say that the postcolonial perspective could be of interest to the study of Latin America and of greater use to the English postcoloniality itself if we were to decouple its theoretical explorations from attempting new universalizing coordinates, and renewed focus were placed in locating specific anti-colonial or decolonizing discursive projects. The general aim would be to decolonize knowledge to attempt emancipatory mappings.

The second point has to do with the assumption of stationary and unbreachable constitutions of discursive practices in this colonial situation that produces Europe's other. Almost by definition such production takes place in the Bakhtinian "contact zone," the space of struggle and negotiation in "social spaces where disparate cultures meet, clash, grapple with each other, often in highly asymmetrical relations of domination and subordination" (Pratt 4). One of the problems with Said's *Orientalism,* a problem which he feels lies outside the design of his book, is the absence of an engagement of and with the ideological struggle taking place in the contact zone. Restoring the terms of the response to colonial discourse on the part of the colonized is not, as Said argues, yet another instance of "orientalism," or othering, but rather an opportunity to understand more fully the workings of the constructions of subjects in contexts of oppositional and/or in-between relations. Perhaps then we could move beyond the proposition that those cast as "natives" or subaltern subjects cannot, theoretically, speak. If we see power, as Said does, in terms of a strategic exercise given at all levels of society, or, as Foucault put it in his *The History of Sexuality* (1978), "Where there is power, there is resistance" (95), then we need to assume a paradigm of "colonial discourse" that provides a place for the emergence of subaltern subjects.

The study of Latin America has amply demonstrated that in the contact zone's space of struggle—households, haciendas, the confessionary, school rooms, universities, judiciaries, commentaries, and chronicles—heterogeneous negotiations of subject formation take place on a daily basis.[2] Such exchanges have often been murderous, as Fanon puts it. But they have also been the occasion for the emergence of new twists and new namings in the arts of combat, translation accommodation, resistance, rebellion, mimesis, appropriation, and sub-version.

___

[2] To give just a few examples, see for instance Stern *Peru's* and *Resistance.* See also: Albo and Barnadas; Concordo Morales; Gruzinski; Aguirre Beltrán; Farriss; Klor de Alva; Clendinnen.

I. Writing Interdictions

Post-(modern)colonial critics have highlighted the question of the subject, and especially the impossibility of thinking of an autonomous subject of agency. If the bourgeois idea of the autonomous individual no longer holds, and if Marxism is seen as just one of the several great master (teleological) narratives of the Enlightenment (Young 173),[3] how can an autonomous subject of agency be postulated for the colonial-subordinates who would appear to be doubly traversed by the split subject and the crisis of representation? As a matter of fact, it is worth noting here that the same problem of agency has plagued feminist theory even when it has most productively engaged postmodern theory.

Debates on the subaltern by necessity border debates on the constitution of identity and cultural differentiation. In *Gender Trouble: Feminism and the Subversion of Identity* (1990), Judith Butler has demonstrated the performative constitution of identity so that we no longer can assume identity as either origin or referential substance. Above all, such debate brings up the problem of the intellectual, his or her relation or position in the historic block that he or she would represent in his or her genealogy. Urgent questions are being asked about classes of intellectuals and the kind of knowledge that they attain, produce, disseminate, and authorize. Whether they are posited as universal or local intellectuals (Foucault), or traditional or organic thinkers (Gramsci), it seems that we can no longer assume that a subalternized intellectual, such as Garcilaso or Guamán Poma, can *ipso facto* carry a transgressive or oppositional weight to the imperial (colonial or neocolonial) enterprise due to their insertion in the all-encompassing terms of colonial discourse or the over arching game of language. From the postcolonial perspective, we do not seem to know to what extent a subaltern subject, one who is in the place of the subject but at a rank below, can play a role in the constitution of a separate and contestatory identity. The theoretical impossibilities of positing a subaltern agency, together with the suspicion that such a problem might be just another "attempt to retain the position and influence of

---

[3] Young argues that Marxism is just one more strategy in the West's will to domination. It disables the potential of other knowledges. He feels that Marxism works for both Gayatri Spivak and Fredric Jameson as another transcendentalizing gesture to produce closure.

global centrality" (Adam and Tiffin viii)[4] on the part of Western intellectuals, has been most forcefully put to the question by Gayatri Spivak in the much quoted title of her article "Can the Subaltern Speak?"

Here Spivak takes Deleuze and Foucault to task for stating that European intellectuals can represent the voice of the oppressed. She indicates that the problem stems from the practice of running together the twin meanings of representation: representation as "speaking for" and representation as in art or philosophy (70). These two sense of representation (in the law and in subject predication) "are related but irreducibly discontinuous" (70). Therefore, the "banality of leftist intellectuals' lists of self-knowing, politically canny subalterns stands revealed [because] in representing them, the intellectuals represent themselves as transparent" (70). Spivak calls for a continued critique of the subject and agency in order to keep us from "restoring the category of the sovereign subject within the theory that seems most to question it" (73). More to the point, Spivak states that Guha's historiographic project, as delineated by Subaltern Studies, since it is expressed in a post-representationalist vocabulary, hides an essentialist agenda and a predicament different from the self-ascribed transparency of intellectuals like Deleuze and Foucault (80).

Instead, she finds more promise in a micrological accounting of the texture of power, which calls for further theorizing on the ideology of subject formation (74). Such theories, however, cannot afford to overlook the category of representation in its two senses. They must note how the staging of the world in representation—"the scene of writing. . .dissimulates the choice of the need for heroes, paternal proxies, agents of power" (74). Therefore, we need to go back to the scenes of writing in Garcilaso, in Guamán Poma, in Amaryllis, in the anonymous Tlaxcaltecas, but in doing so we must be wary not to telescope the sovereign, transparent subject onto the enunciatory functioning of the subaltern. If subaltern subjects are to emerge, they cannot do so in a mimetic play with the sovereign subject. Here it is worth advancing that reading both Guamán Poma and Garcilaso constitutes a pedagogy on how not to assume a sovereign subject.

---

[4] Adam and Tiffin feel that postmodernism projects itself as a normative "neo-universal to which 'marginal' cultures may aspire, and from which certain of their more forward looking products might be appropriated and 'authorized'" (viii). This is a position that be came to be recognized by many Latin American critics, though not by all.

In other words, we cannot continue to reduce or explain the heterogeneity of texts authored by subaltern subjects in order to make them conform to academically institutionalized norms of either Renaissance, Modern, or Postmodern modes of readability. This task is a difficult one, because to restore their agency means for us to understand, and to understand is an act that is intertwined with the power/knowledge distributions of the academy and society at large. We are still a long way from reading in a realm outside or beyond "literature." Furthermore, understanding still comes easier in the representational mode.

In Spivak's theoretical considerations there is yet one more danger zone to traverse for the desire to touch the consciousness of the subaltern is fraught with dangers. In that perilous zone there lies in ambush the specter of psychoanalysis. In such dark murkiness, a delirious interior voice, the voice of the other in us, plays the gamble of transforming itself into the voice of the subaltern. (This red alert reminds me of the confessor's warning on the devil's council: one can always confuse one's evil intentions with virtues causes, for it is the voice of the devil within us that simulates desire and clothes it in the language of virtue). Thus, the predicament of the intellectual who would write the subaltern is analogous to Freud's own use of woman as scapegoat in his "continuing desire to give the hysteric a voice, to transform her into the subject of hysteria" (92). And so, the conclusion Spivak leads us to is that the subaltern cannot speak. Representation has withered away, language—the other—is but a ruse. Facing similar interdictions as colonial Indians coming from cultural traditions without "writing," Guamán Poma and Garcilaso embarked nevertheless in a life-long struggle to represent both self and world under the strictures of coloniality.

II. Evocation in a New Mode

But Spivak's weariness does not have to be taken as the final word on the matter. Anthropologists have also had to come to grips with the crisis of representation. Ethnography has seen its object of knowledge consumed in the pyre of post-structuralism. Though ethnography has written whole cultures in whose "descriptions" thousands of informers have participated, and in contrast with the silence that Spivak would keep in reference to the sati widow, Stephen A. Tyler sees the future of ethnography in "evocation." Parenthetically, it should be remembered here that one of the faults found with Garcilaso's "history" of the Inca empire is that it is too evocative, not consistently factual, the sequence of "facts" is often interrupted by evocations of landscapes: a booming red hill of Abancay on Inca Roca's way to the conquest of Charcas, the flight of the pink flammingoes in the bay of Paracas, the toys toddlers played with while in their whole in the floor. Evocation is for Tyler no longer cursed with representation (129). It does not symbolize what it evokes, it does not link two different places in time and space. It avoids the absurdity of describing non-entities. "Evocation—that is to say "ethnography"—is the discourse of the post-modern world, for the world that made science, and that science made, has disappeared, and scientific thought is now an archaic mode of consciousness surviving for a while yet in degraded form without the ethnographic context that created and sustained it" (123).

Tyler chooses to emphasize the participatory and dialogic aspect of discourse in order to free ethnography from mimesis. In evocation he sees the chance to avoid the inappropriate mode of scientific rhetoric that entails "objects," "facts," "descriptions," "generalizations," "experiments," and "truth," all now rendered "into empty invocations" (130). Once delivered from the burden or representation, ethnography no longer needs to conform to the canon of realism,

> promoting, on the one hand, the absurdity of describing non-entities such as "culture" or "society" as if they were fully observable... and on the other, the equally ridiculous behaviorist pretense of "describing" repetitive patterns of action in isolation from the discourse that actors use in constituting and situating their actions, and all in the simple minded surety that the "observer's" grounding discourse is itself an objective form sufficient to the task of describing acts. (This) is the failure of the whole visualist ideology of referential discourse. (130)

Tyler goes on to reminds us that in ethnography there are no "things" out there to be the objects of description. There is discourse and categories of discourse. And this is so despite those who would locate, record, and examine the discourse of "natives" on the presumption that it represents unconscious patterns. For Tyler, such a representation and interpretation of myth "recommits the crime of a natural history of the mind" (131). Thus, the referent (culture) is gone, and the rhetoric that produced the referent (representation) is also gone.

It follows that if we take Spivak's objections to Guha's historiographical project and we put them next to Tyler's farewell to ethnography, we find that the crisis of representation, coupled with the impossible relay of agency of the subject to the subaltern subject, places on the grid of suspicion the very notions of culture as a thing out there and of cultural difference. This difference has been assumed to be the ground from which any subject, sovereign or subaltern, speaks. And it has been the grounding gesture in the work of Garcilaso, Inca and Guamán Poma. Both have sought to authorize their work on the basis of a knowledge that was different, greater, fuller about a world that was correspondingly different and which they knew from the inside, in contrast with the Spaniards' mistaken and superficial appreciations of the "things" they saw but did not quite understand.

III. WRITING BACK IN RECIPROCITY

The awareness of a profound general cultural crisis,[5] a long-lasting change in episteme, if you wish, has probably occurred many times in the world before the end of the eighteenth century in Europe, and it has probably been concomitant with deep and swift population movements. Conquest and diaspora have taken place on repeated occasions before the English imperial expansion and the late twentieth-century movement of English ex-colonials who leave the margins for the metropolitan centers. When, after the conquest of Mexico (1521) and the Andes (1532), Spain became an imperial power, historiography, and what was later to be known as ethnography, struggled to keep intact its biblical teleological sense of time and space in order to reject the opening and possible diatopical understanding of the world. In order to so it had to produce a system of othering.

The recent quincentenary of Europe's conquest of this hemisphere has been the occasion of an important revision of our knowledge about

---

[5] "Science adopted a model of language as a self-perfecting form of close communication that achieved closure by making language itself the object of description. But closure was bought at the cost of descriptive adequacy. The more language became its own object, the less it had to say about anything else. So the language of science became the object of science, and what had begun as perception unmediated by concepts became conception unmediated by percepts" (Tyler 124).

the opening of that contact zone. Besides the emergence of the production of the ancient Americans as Europe's modern other—as the product of the play of Europe's own archive—these studies have confirmed and extended Hyden White's view of the "noble savage" or its inverse "bestial other" as a fetish of Europe's prohibitions (*Tropics of Discourse*, 1978). Comparatively speaking, apart from a few brilliant studies, less has been done on the constitution of the subaltern subject. The field always cites the problem of the lack of adequate sources, bona fide documents, the absence of unsullied Indian verbal representations, and untrustworthy Indian or even *mestizo* voices, even when these have mastered European systems of representation. The absence of alphabetic writing, itself deployed at the time of conquest as the acid test to qualify into the ranks of civilization, continues to dictate the direction of the field. The difficulty of the task can be assessed by the enormous learning required, well beyond what is ordinarily called literature in the academy, in the making of books such as Martin Lienhard's *La voz y su huella* (1989), José A. Mazzotti's *Coros mestizos del Inca Garcilaso: resonancias andinas* (1996), the comprehensive and masterful *Book of the Fourth World* (1992) by Gordon Brotherston, and Luis Millones' *El retorno de las huacas* (1990).

It is thus pertinent to any research on subaltern subjects to consider the conditions of impossibility under and with which two contemporaries, living the full destructuring force of "spiritual" conquest in the seventeenth century, went about the business of authorizing a self and a past (culture), which once (re)constructed could take the place of an original matrix of identity. What follows is a brief re-contextualization, in the light of some key issues in postcolonial theory, of Guamán Poma, writing in his place of bio-cultural origin, and Garcilaso, marooned in the metropolis, witnessing the daily naturalizing and solidification of his difference (skin color, slanted eyes, high cheek bones) into inferior rank and dispossession. In singular ways, but also with similar approaches, both men take on the full deployment of the oppressive powers of representational, colonial discourse. At times they themselves write representations of their own (portraits, anecdotes, monarchy successions, personal memories, autobiographical pieces), and for this readability they have been commended. At times they force new counter-yielding pieces from the rhetoric and genres of representation. When they do they bring established modes of writing to a crisis, they make visual the ideology and the rhetoric occluded in the constitution of "writing" into a naturalized and hegemonic representation of memory as a monotopical past (strange mixes of fragments of genres, questioning of the subject of enunciation, simulating modes of authorization, insertions of other representational modes) (Castro-Klarén). Such counter-writing has more often than not cost the Andean men dearly in the esteem of their Euro-American readers. At best, Guamán Poma is relegated to a source, or explained away as someone who misunderstood the uses of "relación," "sermon," and "history," and Garcilaso to the place of a biased, clever, if elegant, practitioner of the best the Renaissance had to teach him.

Writing representations, counter-representations, and destructuring the established conventions of genre by which meaning is produced entails caution and profound understanding, even when such analysis is not always brought to the level of conscious and rational discourse. It is not just accident. One does not just stumble into the critique of a whole episteme. It is not nonsense. It is a movement in consciousness similar to the critique that avant-guards produce in the face of spent modes of representation. The singular achievement of the work of Guamán Poma and Garcilaso is that these "authors," from a subaltern and self-endangering position, managed to produce a critique of European modes of representation when this colonial discourse was in full power/knowledge ascendancy. Their counter-move takes place not past the colonial period but *ab initio*. And recognizing that is not a move that creates heroes or patriarchies. It is folded right into the production of colonial texts and will continue the production of counter-texts right to the present "post-modern" novel. It is a will to claim ones' own otherness, regardless of its contents and circuitry. It is a praxis of agency designed to achieve a shift in the positions of domination and subordination. It is "un no dejarse." The enterprise that the two Andeans took up, to counter-write self, world, and culture, and the strategies visible in their texts, antecede and yet coincide with the contestatory interrogating, the "sly civility," the mimicry, the doubling of identity that Homi Bhabha believes to be the discursive positions of the colonized subject (see his book *The Location of Culture*, 1994). Colonized subjects such as of Guamán Poma and the Inca Garcilaso wrote from a place of enunciation that they crafted from their perspective and as well as from the debris that they leave behind as they deconstruct European discourse. What is more, they write back in the mode of reciprocity, the Andean discursive practice that permits the co-presence of more than one voice, more than one cultural register in an always already dialogical situation. The Andean contact zone of struggle is always thus dialogic due to the principles of reciprocity and duality.

The work of José Durand on the library that the Inca Garcilaso left at the time of his death in his house shows that Garcilaso seemed chiefly interested in, and fully familiar with, the major debates in renaissance historiography. His financial means to own so many books and to enjoy the leisure time to read and write during the greater part of his adult life, together with his intellectual capacity to read Greek, Latin, French, Italian, and of course his two native languages—Quechua and Spanish—cast doubts onto the portrayal of this intellectual as a marginal, and certainly takes him out of the box of the "natives." Moreover, despite the anti-imperialist thrust of the content of his work, it has been the Spanish "literary critics" and their hispanizing counterparts in Latin America who have exalted the classical qualities of his clean and elegant prose. Though he struggles with controversial and dangerous topics—Inca religion, Royal incest, strange myths of origin which include four foundational couples—which he sought to "domesticate" by astutely and carefully finding them places of contiguity of analogy in the European archive where he could discuss them partially, at a slant, Garcilaso manages to keep a firm reign over the intertextual web—Roman history, Greek mythology, Italian historiography—that he deploys in order to construct the history (evocation?) of his mother's side.

Unlike Guamán Poma, and always aware of the need to entertain his European readership and perhaps even his Andean readers, he does not allow the present—his claims to royal favors, his pain at the news he hears about his motherland—to overwhelm the general plan of the *Comentarios reales*: to find the discursive apparatus by which to write a history of his Andean ancestry capable of bridging past and present and thus attenuate the rupture of the conquest. Moreover, Margarita Zamora, in *Language, Authority, and Indigenous History in the* Comentarios reales de los Incas (1988), has shown in detail how Garcilaso chose among the available historiographical debates and rhetoric and appropriated those best fitted to his enterprise. In his choice of humanist theories of translation and exegesis of the ancient Hebrew Bible in order to authorize the Quechua language as the source for knowledge about the Andean civilization, Garcilaso reaches well beyond the immediate imperialist (oppressive) power and breaks open onto the fresher fields of Italian humanism. Therefore, this subaltern subject is neither a naïve nor a confused, unschooled, "authentic" native, nor does he place himself in the scene of writing as a mindless, responding other in the presence of his master. Displaying uncommon agency, and making dangerous choices, Garcilaso opts for Italian Humanism and not Spanish orthodoxy in his engagement with the field of discursive possibilities. Like Guamán Poma, Garcilaso has sifted carefully the questions that need to be asked and responded to, and the places where it is best to posit the subject that will engage them.

And yet the *Comentarios reales,* like *El primer nueva corónica,* is visibly marked by gaps, moments of intense disarticulation, contiguities that defy all sequential logic, silences, baffling insertions, and contradictions. Above all, both texts, whose titles border on the legal (*crónica*) and historical genre (*comentarios*), open up with unaccustomed self-conscious narrators whose main objective would seem the constitution of their own writing authority. The representation of himself that Guamán Poma attempts remains incomplete to the very last page. And yet it is the incompletion of his grand attempt, his lies about his true identity, and his pretension to be taken by his interlocutor for a prince that somehow seed his text with the intense indeterminacy that only an outsider could bring to the established modes of the power/knowledge complex that subordinates him. As subaltern self portrayals, Guamán Poma's verbal and graphic depictions of self answer questions with further questions. As the *Corónica* grows in topics, in illustrations, in the number of languages that it employs, in the number of readers that it addresses, in the number of "uses" that it claims to offer his heterogeneous public, more means less. More information precludes rather than aides in the putting together, the fitting of Guamán Poma and his "world" into a totalizing representation. The last page arrests the infinite flow of the signs which do not come to closure, for we know that the book will go beyond the pages, it will spill right into the passage of historical time. Unlike Garcilaso's attempt to bridge one heroic past to a heroic, though tarnished, paternal present, Guamán Poma's discursive inconclusiveness bridges the present with the future because "no hay quien le ponga remedio."

Placed by unexpected cataclysmic historical change, Guamán Poma and Garcilaso sit at the cusp, at the point where two branches of a curve, of cultural difference, meet. Like a Janus, each of these men can look back upon a past that is no more and can never be again. Nostalgia, "la memoria del bien perdido" (Hernández 175-210), and anger fuel, in part, the decision to write the past the way it was understood, as horizon. Likewise, when looking ahead, their eyes set upon a myriad of uncertainties, a discursive order that at once denies them their past identity and yet confirms them into the "knowledge" of their otherness from Europeans and from themselves. Both choose a double, overlapping, palimpsestic plan of elaborating—not recovering—an identity of "mezclas" in a space of reciprocity.

By definition "mezclas" interrogate the unified, pure sovereign subject of colonial discourse. Writing Andean culture, manipulating and questioning colonial discourse within its own ethical claims to superiority becomes the foundation of the project. Therefore, both men will claim a "Christianity" *avant la conquête* for their respective ancestries. The corollary they set up reads as follows: if the emerging difference between *us* and *them* is Christianity, then demonstrating that the core of our own "civilization" constitutes a praxis of a christianity *avant la lettre* should dissolve a claimed difference that in fact legalizes a hierarchy of dominance.

Both Guamán Poma and Garcilaso have been read as more or less reliable ethnographic informants. At this level in the discursive hierarchy these subalterns have been found pretentious, naive, funny, cunning, genial, sly, tricky, astute, utopian, confused, untrustworthy, and impossibly outstripped by European rules of knowledge formation and accumulation.[6] Their accounts of Andean cultures—origin, kinship system, government, religion, daily life, fauna, flora, art—appear traversed by many other preoccupations besides the representational requirements of establishing objects, preceding to their description, listing or speculating on their function, and relating them in an overall pattern of custom and belief. While both texts deploy and simulate the discursive rules that allow the West to enter and examine another culture, by producing it, in their case, it produces the paradox of an auto-ethnography. Mary Louise Pratt has coined this most appropriate term, by which she means the instances when "colonized subjects undertake to represent themselves in ways that engage with the colonizer's own terms" (7). And as it has been shown above they also interrogate those very rules and presuppositions.

Therefore, the polemical bent of the texts produced at the very cusp of colonial discourse engages both the contents of cultural difference as well

---

[6] These perceptions of Guamán Poma and Garcilaso bear an astounding similarity to Homi Bhabha's portrayal of the colonized man and the arts of mimicry (Bhabha relies on Fanon) and sly civility with which he faces the colonial master (Bhabha 93-112).

as the rules of formation that enable the invention of culture as difference. In the "Proemio al lector" of the *Comentarios reales* Garcilaso states that his purpose is not so much to contradict what the Spanish "historians" have written on the Inca Empire, as to correct what they misunderstood and thus *serve* them as commentary. Garcilaso could not announce more clearly his subaltern position. However, his commentaries, in as much as they include a full (idealized?) account of the Inca monarchy (diarchy?), a full ethnographic report, a series of biographies, a display of Andean landscape, etc., far exceed the limits of his obviously false presentation. It is clear that by the use he gives to the term *comentarios* he never intended to *serve* the Spanish chroniclers or historians. Quite to the contrary: he meant to make us (*servirse*) of their authority and their foibles (not knowing Quechua) in order to write his own/other version. In this u-turn maneuver Garcilaso separates, classifies, and evaluates his sources (colonial discourse) into knowledgeable and reliable—Cieza de León, Las Casas—and untrustworthy "historians" such as Fernández de Oviedo and Lope de Gómara. This exercise of power/knowledge on the part of Garcilaso is only part of what is required to authorize his knowledge of self and cultural identity. The other is to go beyond commentary, to transgress the bounds of that discursive mode as inhered from Julius Cesar—commentary by participants in current events. By assuming that the production of the past is coterminous with the politics of the present, Garcilaso mounts a sly and very civil polemic on the "knowledge" contained in his sources.

Under the guise of useful but almost inconsequential commentaries lies an acerbic, long-lasting achievement of contestatory knowledge which on several key occasions has played a foundational role in the history of rebellions and independence movements in Latin America (Túpac Amaru II and José de San Martín were avid readers of the *Comentarios*). However, more often than not, critics have rendered Garcilaso's disjunctive organization, his lies about the Inca empire,[7] and his inexplicable

---

[7] Garcilaso's representation of an orderly, civil primogeniture succession of Inca monarchs has come under a great cloud of doubt since María Rostworowski persuasively developed the notion that in the Inca empire it was the principle of duality that governed social organizations, including the highest positions leadership. In her *Historia del Tahuantinsuyu*, she writes: "Las guerras fratricidas entre Huáscar y Atahualpa, entabladas después del fallecimiento de Huayna Cápac, no fueron un fenó-

silences and contradictions readable by paying almost exclusive attention
to either his stated politics of reconciliation between the two nations or
his brilliant use of Renaissance rhetorical practices. But closer attention
to the constitution of a subaltern subjectivity could reveal a less-smooth,
grainier, more cunning, and also confused, Garcilaso.

In as much as Guamán Poma also starts out by offering his idealized
reader—the kings of Spain—his services, *El primer nueva corónica* inserts
itself in the crevice of the double subalterity of the colonized subject. But,
like Garcilaso's *Comentarios*, Guamán's services comprise mainly writing. He writes to the king, not only to supplement the information he is
getting, but also to correct it and thus affect the kind of knowledge from
which the king and his laws proceed. But Guamán Poma is no longer sure
that the writing he has spent half a life on can actually bring about a
change in the king's consciousness. To accomplish his purposes Guamán
Poma concludes that he must actually invert the relations of the subject of
his writing equation. The king must receive instruction and learning from
Guamán Poma. The kings must occupy the position of the subaltern and
Guamán Poma should impart the knowledge that the king does not pos-
sess. For the king to come upon the possession of useful and complete
knowledge, he must give himself over to the power/knowledge of the
Andean, only then will he "know" what questions to ask. At this point
the illusion of representation, the world of things, the world of mimesis,
has come to a complete halt. A new world is about to be born from the
ground up in the dialogic, sea-sawing engagement between king and subaltern subject. A sort of diatopic (post-modern?) learning would ensue
from Guamán's call for new relations in the constitution of knowledge. If
the king were to adopt the subject position prescribed to him by Guamán
Poma, then the world would have been truly upside down, for the subaltern would have been heard.

meno extraño ni único en la historia andina. Al contrario se trataba de circunstancias
que se repetían al final de cada gobierno. Esta situación de anarquía se debía a las costumbres sucesorias y a la lucha por el poder que estallaba con menor o mayor intensi-
dad a la muerte del Inca. El motivo principal de los alborotos era la ausencia de una ley
sobre herencia del poder, agravado por el hecho de que varios miembros de un grupo
de deudos del Inca fallecido podían aspirar al mando y gozaban de iguales derechos y
prerrogativas" (137). She adds, "los mismos cronistas desmienten sus afirmaciones
[respecto al mayorazgo] y proporcionan datos contradictorios cuando se trata de casos
concretos" (137).

However, Guamán Poma does not get to this scene without having, like Garcilaso, engaged in a polemic of his own with colonial discourse. Much more at the margins than Garcilaso, with apparently a lot less financial means than the *mestizo* at Montilla, Guamán Poma too seems to have been an avid reader and consumer of all forms of colonial discourse. Guamán Poma stays away, as much as possible, from naming his sources. It has taken the painstaking work of Rolena Adorno (*Guaman Poma: Writing and Resistance in Colonial Peru*, 1986) to reveal the full extent of the hidden polemics of this subaltern subject. Adorno states that the "presence of hidden polemic informs and explains the compositional principles of his discourse; it is responsible for the respective roles that history writing, oratory and fiction play in structuring his work" (6). In his polemics, drawing from Andean memory and existing praxis, Guamán Poma flatly contradicts some of his Spanish sources. He also rewrites them. For instance, departing from the Spanish claim that the Virgin performed a miracle and stunned the Indians so that they would not fight against the Spaniards, he proceeds to argue that "no hubo conquista." Therefore, the Andeans should not be treated under the law as if they had been vanquished *inimicus* of Spain.

What is more, the work of both men go even beyond the polemicizing with the misrepresentations made of Andean culture and Amerindians in general. Beyond correction and commentary the aim of both texts is to fill the empty space left by the claims of difference and construct difference as they saw it. To write culture they needed to erase, re-inscribe, overwrite, and they especially had to write from the borders, from the edges. Their location, as Garcilaso readily metaphorized it with his parental doubling is the space where doubling occurs. In-between past and uncertain present what takes is doubling of both times. Not in-between languages, but a palimpsest of languages. Not in-between symbolic systems, but rather their rearticulation and redistribution. In-between identities, themselves daily interrogated by the flux of social and ideological change,[8] turn into multiple identity positions.

Finally, as fragmentary and palimpsestic texts, both the *Comentarios* (1609-1616) and *El primer nueva corónica* (1615) continue, from their

---

[8] In *The Location of Culture*, reading from Guillermo Gómez-Peña's rasquache texts Homi Bhabha sees the relevance of the in-between to the study of subaltern subjectivities. "They provide the terrain for elaborating strategies of self hood" (6).

location, to question the powers of representation and thus avoid a reenactment of the relations of domination which require a reliable, full knowledge of the other that can take the place of closure. Both men understood the deployment of culture in its duplicate and duplicitous sense: representation and place of enunciation. Having understood culture as an epistemological and enunciative problem, Guamán Poma and Garcilaso, as subaltern subjects, manage to speak, and to question us, from their interrogating position, and even when surrounded by "theoretical" conditions of impossibility.

Originally published in *Dispositio/n* No. 46. (1994) (Issue dedicated to: Subaltern Studies in the Americas), 229-244.

Works Cited

ADAM, Ian and Helen TIFFIN, ed. *Past the Last Post.* Calgary: University of Calgary Press, 1990.

ADORNO, Rolena. *Guaman Poma: Writing and Resistance in Colonial Peru.* Austin: University of Texas Press, 1986.

ASHCROFT, Bill. "Excess: Post-colonialism and the Verandahs of Meaning." In *De-Scribing Empire: Postcolonialism and Textuality.* Ed. Chris Tiffin and Alan Lawson. London: Routledge, 1994. 33-44.

BHABHA, Homi K. *The Location of Culture.* London: Routledge, 1994.

CASTRO-KLARÉN, Sara. "Autores indígenas americanos: escritura, poder y conocimiento." In *Escritura, transgresión y sujeto en la literatura latinoamericana.* México: Premiá Editora, 1989. 159-176.

—. *The History of Sexuality.* New York: Pantheon Books, 1978.

HERNÁNDEZ, Max. *Memoria del bien perdido: conflicto, identidad y nostalgia en el Inca Garcilaso de la Vega.* Lima: Instituto de Estudios Peruanos, 1991.

HULME, Peter. *Colonial Encounters: Europe and the Native Caribbean, 1492-1797.* London: Methuen, 1986.

KADIR, Djelal. *The Other Writing.* West Lafayette: Purdue University Press, 1993.

MIGNOLO, Walter. "Colonial Situations, Geographic Discourses and Territorial Representations: Towards a Diatopical Understanding of Colonial Semiosis." *Dispositio* 1989: 93-140.

PRATT, Mary Louise. *Imperial Eyes: Travel Writing and Transculturation.* London: Routledge, 1992.

RABASA, José. "On Writing Back: Alternative Historiography in *La Florida del Inca.*" In *Latin American Identity and Constructions of Difference.* Ed. Amaryll Chanady. Minneapolis: University of Minnesota Press, 1994. 130-145.

ROSTWOROWSKI DE DIEZ CANSECO, María. *Estructuras andinas del poder. Ideología religiosa y política.* Lima: Instituto de Estudios Peruanos, 1983.

SPIVAK, Gayatri. "Can the Subaltern Speak?" In *Colonial Discourse and Postcolonial Theory: A Reader.* Ed. Patrick William and Laura Chrisman. New York: Columbia University Press, 1994. 66-112.

TYLER, Stephen A. "Post-Mordern Ethnography." In *Writing culture: The Poetics and Politics of Ethnography.* Ed. James Clifford and George E. Marcus. Berkeley: University of California Press, 1986.

WHITE, Hayden. *Tropics of Discourse.* Baltimore: Johns Hopkins University Press, 1978.

WILLIAMS, Patrick and Laura CHRISMAN. *Colonial discourse and Post-colonial Theory: A Reader.* New York: Columbia University Press, 1994.

YOUNG, Robert. *White Mythologies: Writing History and the West.* London: Routledge, 1993.

CHAPTER 7

Garcilaso's Cuzco: Space and the Place of Knowledge

I. HUMANISM AND RENAISSANCE

Scholars have written volumes on the influence of Humanism and the European Renaissance on the intellectual formation of Inca Garcilaso. At the same time, Garcilaso's *particular* affinity for the Italian Renaissance has gone largely unnoticed; and this, despite the fact that his first intellectual production was a Spanish translation (1590) of *Dialoghi d'amore* (1535) by Yehudá Abravanel, better known to Hispanists as León Hebreo. Critical analyses have tended to circumscribe Garcilaso's relationship with Humanism and the Renaissance, limiting his engagement with the two great European intellectual movements to their local manifestations in Spain. Ignoring the geographical reach of Garcilaso's library, this approach assumes that, because Garcilaso lived in Spain and wrote in Spanish, his most significant sources and influences had to have come from contemporaries' writings in Spanish. For this reason, scholars like Luis A. Arocena, Aurelio Miró Quesada, and even José Durand spend so much time tracing names and trying to identify contacts that Garcilaso had or might have had with the "learned circle of Andalusian Humanists."[1] There is, of course, an historical explanation for the singular focus

---

[1] I refer here to José Durand's foundational work on Garcilaso, to Aurelio Miró Quesada's well-documented Prologue to the Biblioteca Ayacucho's edition of the *Royal Commentaries*, to the work of Luis A. Arocena and to the careful and erudite study by Margarita Zamora. Even though Arocena, moved by Valcárcel's strident declaration, does admit to the influence of the Italian Humanists, his study nonetheless

on Spanish Humanism to the exclusion of the obvious, pervasive, and I believe determinative relationship that Garcilaso had with Italian Humanism; when studies of Latin American literature began to emerge in the nineteenth century, they were appropriated by the "discipline" (*à la* Foucault) of Hispanism. Among all the Garcilaso scholars, it is worth noting that only Luis E. Valcárcel has privileged Garcilaso's debt to the Italian Humanists. Indeed, after inventorying Garcilaso's library and registering references scattered throughout Garcilaso's writings, Valcárcel declared unequivocally that "in his approach to cultured Europe, [Garcilaso] prefers the Italians" (Valcárcel "Garcilaso Inca," cited in Arocena: 23).

The tendency to enclose the Latin American colonial *imaginaire* within Spain's cultural orbit and brand all colonial writing with the stamp of Hispanism is especially surprising in the case of Inca Garcilaso. Not only was the cornerstone of Garcilaso's intellectual production a text related to Italy, as I have already mentioned; but throughout the entire corpus of his writings, Garcilaso leaves abundant evidence of his decisive contacts with, and fundamental interest in, the culture of the Renaissance outside of Spain, a Renaissance culture that was, you might say, exotic to Spain. Garcilaso scholars have explored his Neo-Platonism, recognizing the influences of Ficino and Castiglione, of Byzantine and Italian novels, and of Giovanni Botero and Ariosto. They have also compiled lists of the Roman histories in Garcilaso's library, including Plutarch's *Parallel Lives*, Suetonius' *The Twelve Caesars*, Polibius' *History of Rome*, and the *Commentaries* of Julius Caesar. To this day, however, there are no com-

---

privileges the influence of a Renaissance Humanism largely defined by Marcelino Menéndez y Pelayo in texts bequeathed to Hispanism; texts which Arocena reproduces at length. Such a reading reduces Renaissance Humanism to a narrow and Hispano-centric intellectual space. In this sense, Arocena's work merely echoes previous arguments made by Marcel Bataillon and Américo Castro about the influence of Erasmus in Spain, the ideal of intellectual renewal in Juan Luis Vives, and the heterodoxy of Juan Valdés. Arocena does grapple creatively with Menéndez y Pelayo's well-documented argument that Garcilaso produced a utopian novel in the style of Thomas More. Perhaps the most important fact that Arocena contributes (30) to this discussion is that Thomas More and his circle of utopian thinkers met and befriended Rafael Hitlodeo, the Portuguese man who had sailed with Amerigo Vespucci and whose accounts of the Amerindian societies he encountered were widely read. In any case, it is Silvio Zavala's work, which Arocena cites but fails to engage, which introduces ideas capable of breaking new ground in the study of Garcilaso and the European Renaissance. In this regard one would also need to consult the work of O'Gorman (see bibliography).

parative studies that examine Garcilaso's representation of the Inca empire as a creative Romanization, a portrayal made possible by a Renaissance in the process of inventing itself through the reinvention and appropriation of the world of antiquity.[2]

The meticulous study of José Antonio Mazzotti ("The lightning bolt") breaks apart the neo-colonial enclosures of traditional Hispanism, expanding the range of possible rhetorical sources for Garcilaso to include Quechua oral traditions and practices. Scholars have long questioned the validity of Garcilaso's sources, and indeed of Garcilaso himself as a reliable source for historians, archaeologists, and others interested in the Inca Empire. This persistent historiographical critique, it seems to me, has given rise to the kind of study which is content to compare empirical data from Garcilaso's text with evidence found in the writings of other well-known "chroniclers" such as Blas Valera, Polo de Ondegardo, José de Acosta, Las Casas, and Cieza de León. While limited and deficient in many ways, such studies do suggest the rich and complex vision of cultural recovery and renewal embedded in Garcilaso's text. However, to reach an even greater appreciation for the scope and complexity of Garcilaso's writings (as well as those of Guamán Poma), scholars would do better to explore the notion of "colonial semiosis," as elaborated by Walter Mignolo.[3] The present generation of Garcilaso scholars is fortunate in that the established canon of literary criticism has all but ignored Garcilaso's relationship with Italy and the Italian Renaissance. Of particular interest to me is the way that Garcilaso, ensconced as he was in the Renaissance world, was able to take advantage of the rediscovery of Rome and the ancient Mediterranean in order to speak of—or better yet,

[2] In his incisive reading of Garcilaso's representation of the walls of Saqsawaman, Mazzotti (see "The lightning bolt") shows how Garcilaso, in making the thunder an instrument of the sun, adapts Incan iconography to the image of Jupiter carrying his lightning bolt. Mazzotti takes note of the same process of Cuzcan "Romanization" which I elaborate in this essay.

[3] Mignolo ("Afterward," "Colonial") formulates the concept of "colonial semiosis" to encompass the processes of transculturation that occur beyond the limits of discourse and are intimately related to the systems of European writing. The concept of "colonial semiosis" expands the area of cultural contact to include not only the responses of the Amerindian to the challenges of European culture, but also and importantly, the adaptation and transformation of Amerindian and European symbolic systems by colonial subjects like Garcilaso.

to write—his own lost empire. His was an empire in ruins, but an empire that marked the starting point, the origin, for the present; a present that, as David Brading has suggested, could be understood (in utopian terms?) as a *new* holy empire (Brading 255-272).

Given the confines of this essay, the best I can do is to begin to flesh out some aspects of the representation of Cuzco in the *Royal Commentaries* (1609). To a certain extent, my concerns have been fostered by the debates over the representation of space that characterizes much of contemporary Postcolonial Studies. What I find particular interesting are the issues involved in naming and the construction of colonial spaces in pursuit of new subjectivities. In the case of Garcilaso in particular, the idea of space as a gnoseological place is of central importance. In the pages that follow, I hope to demonstrate that the "Cuzco that was another Rome" (*Royal Commentaries* 5) figures in the *Royal Commentaries* as a sacred place; a city whose very architecture inscribes a shared commitment to the necessary knowledge, both religious and practical, for the construction of an Andean state.

II. CUZCO AND HUMANISM

In his now-classic *Meaning in the Visual Arts,* Erwin Panofsky reminds us that the term *humanitas* historically "had two clearly distinguishable meanings, the first arising from a contrast between man and what is less than human; the second between man and what is more. In the first case *humanitas* means value, in the second a limitation" (Panofsky 4). Cicero believed that *humanitas* was the quality that distinguished *homo humanos* from the barbarians and vulgar peoples who lacked all sense of *pietas*. Human mores and education were twin aspects of the notion of *urbanity*, a notion defined as the opposite of *nature* (Panofsky 2).

The Renaissance notion of *humanitas* revived the classic antithesis civilization vs. barbarism (*feritas*) and superimposed it upon its medieval counterpart *humanitas* vs. *divinitas*. Marsilio Ficino defined Man as a rational soul of divine intelligence contained (trapped) within a human body. It is this kind of ambivalence about *humanitas* that would give birth to Renaissance Humanism. Humanists reject authority, but respect tradition (Panofsky 3). Thus they are able to differentiate between the sphere of culture and the sphere of nature. Unlike nature, which is always accessible to the human senses, culture is only visible or only accessible to consciousness in the "records left by man" (Panofsky 5). Only objects created by the hand and intelligence of Man contain and represent ideas that are separate and distinct from the objects of material existence. The cultural object both contains relations of meaning, and evokes the perception of those relations; in other words, the cultural object allows us to distinguish the expressed idea from the means used to represent that idea. As Panofsky writes "to perceive the relation of construction is to separate the idea of the function to be fulfilled from the means of fulfillment [...] man's signs and structures are records because, or rather in so far as, they express ideas separated from, yet realized by, the process of signaling and building" (5).

Writing within this Humanist framework, Garcilaso lays down his own historical cornerstone in "The Founding of Cuzco, the Imperial City," the narrative which occupies Chapters XV and XVI of Book I, Part I of the *Royal Commentaries*. Here Garcilaso establishes the meaning of his narrative through a fundamental separation of culture from nature; a separation that eventually brings about a rational (as opposed to a "bestial") order, re-presented in the urbanity of Cuzco. In this well-known recounting of Cuzco's mythical foundation, Garcilaso introduces and then reproduces the voice of his ancestral uncle to recount how the hill of Huanacauri, or "the wild mountain" (38) as it was called, dominated the valley of Cuzco prior to the arrival of Manco Inca, later known as Cápac, or "the generous and magnificent one." From this space of "hills and bramble," inhabited but not yet humanized, Manco Cápac and Mama Ocllo singled out some families who would later be converted into citizens and certain rocks which would be converted into cities. Secondly, the founders ordered their chosen ones to construct houses and huts, with "the Inca showing them how they should be made" (38). From its very beginning then, Cuzco was designed as an imperial city and a model for all future cities in the empire. Garcilaso presents Manco "the generous and magnificent," the first Inca ruler, as "the grand architect of Andean cities" (40). Garcilaso thus constructs the city of Cuzco and its surrounding hinterlands as sacred space, having been tread upon and configured by the founders themselves. Because Cuzco was designed by the Incas, it is a divine city, perfect in form from the outset, product of the superior intelligence of the civilizing Inca couple. Unlike the creation process described in the *Popol Vuh*, the Inca city did not evolve through a series of failed experiments improved upon by time and successive divinities. In the very design of its architecture, Cuzco expressed and inscribed the social and political ideals of Inca governance. For this reason, its Inca remains constitute a monument of "records" that give meaning to the past, humanize time, and convert that time into a preamble for the present and the future. The city's design is like an entelechy that prefigures its eventual role as an imperial center, but at the same time embodies the passage of time, that is, history. In the words of the ancestral uncle:

> In this way our imperial city began to be populated; a city divided into two halves called *Hanan* (Upper) Cuzco and *Hurin* (Lower) Cuzco. This division of the city was not ordained so that those of one half could take advantage of the other through exemptions and privileges; instead, all were to be equal like brothers. (40)

The uncle's description reveals the fundamental concept animating the design of Inca urban space: to inscribe the social order and social practices in the architectonic structure. Here it seems to me that Garcilaso is conjoining his version of the foundational logic of Cuzco to the ideals of urbanism found in Italian Humanism. To return to the description of the ancestral uncle, he states that "[t]he Inca only wanted this division in the population and the different names of the upper and lower halves so that there be a perpetual reminder that the King had called forth some followers and the Queen had called forth the others" (40). In other words, and as the narrator Garcilaso will suggest a few pages later, Inca urbanism constitutes a kind of writing, a systematic symbolization of socio-religious and gnoseological practices (108).

Later in this essay I will explore Garcilaso's images of Inca urban space in greater detail, but for now let me offer some other preliminary thoughts. In reviewing the existing literature on the Incan imperial city, it is evident that the images that remain to this day coincide or are based upon Garcilaso's portrait of the city as drawn in the *Royal Commentaries*.[4] The later chapters are clearly most influential in this regard, for

---

[4] For a brief introduction to the recent bibliography, see Angles Vargas (*Historia*), Miño Garcés, Agurto Calvo, Gasparini y Margolies (*Arquitectura inca* and *Inca Architecture*), Hyslop (*The Inca* and *Inca Settlement*), and of course the fundamental work of Tom Zuidema (*The Ceque* and *Inca Civilization*).

there one finds descriptions of the design of the city, its many buildings, and the different uses made of its architecture. Garcilaso's vision-version of the city persists even in the midst of the raging historiographical debates; debates which, on the one hand question the accuracy of his information, and on the other, revalidate his authority based on evidence garnered from archeological excavations (such as those Valcárcel undertook in relation to the underground base of the towers at Saqsawaman [see Valcárcel "Saisawaman"; Angles Vargas *Sacsayhuaman*]). Within his *Royal Commentaries*, Garcilaso repeatedly imagines Cuzco as the scene of the grand entrances and departures of the Inca armies (read Roman legions), and center of the many ceremonies which marked the Incan calendar. The descriptions of these scenes and ceremonies constitute the bulk of the long "narrative" in the first volume of the *Royal Commentaries*. In fact, the rhetorical function of Cuzco as the center of Garcilaso's narrative is a whole other topic deserving of attention; for the purposes of this essay, however, it is enough to recognize the place of Cuzco as a foundational and ceremonial space in Inca history.

III. A PROBLEM OF KNOWLEDGE AND METHOD

An obvious methodological problem comes immediately to the fore. Thanks to recent works by Santiago Agurto Calvo (*Cuzco, la traza urbana de la ciudad inca*, 1980), R. Tom Zuidema (*Inca civilization in Cuzco*, 1990), Víctor Angles Vargas (*Historia del Cuzco incaico*, 1989), Gasparini and Margolies (*Arquitectura inca*, 1977), and Leonardo Miño Garcés (*El manejo del espacio en el imperio inca*, 1994), we now understand very clearly that the Incas envisioned and utilized Cuzco and its environs as a kind of sacred space. However, in historicizing the modern notion of "sacred cultural space" within an Inca universe whose experience and ordering of the sacred was so different from the modern, scholars have had to rely upon the descriptions of places and social relations handed down from the chroniclers, among whom Garcilaso figures prominently. For example, the description of the temple of *Acllahuasi* with its central plaza, its surrounding chambers, and the streets extending out from the chambers, comes directly from Garcilaso, who for his part, quotes extensively from Cieza. The resulting palimpsest is therefore inevitable. In fact, all modern readings of Garcilaso have already been informed and influenced by descriptions from the *Royal Commentaries* which have filtered into studies on Andean architecture, ethnography, and history. In any case, the factual accuracy of Garcilaso's vision-version of Cuzco and Inca history is not what matters most here; it is the work itself that is of fundamental importance, not only because of its having been written by someone born and raised in the city, a member of an important *panaca,* and a resident of one of the city's palaces, but also because of the foundational nature of its writing on the Incan Empire.

IV. OUR KNOWLEDGE OF CUZCO

At this point, what we know for certain is that the city of Cuzco, as well as its surrounding hills and mountains, were sacred places for veneration and pilgrimage for the Incas. According to the foundational story, Manco Inca staked his famous staff into the center of a marshy area, and his followers, after conducting drainage and landfill, converted this area into a plaza, or central open space, "around" which they erected the grand buildings that we now call "Inca Palaces." They drained the marsh by rerouting the water into two irrigation canals which they equipped with beds of crushed stones and covers. This exhaustive labor, whose purpose was to provide water for the city, is yet another manifestation of the sacred and cultured (in the Humanist sense of the word) character of the Inca's vision for the city. As Miño Garcés (25) points out:

> Water, whose preponderance in the geography of the Valley of Cuzco is evidenced by its rivers, springs, irrigation canals and rainfall, was of primordial importance in Incan culture. In fact, it is amazing how many streams and springs Cobo (1964, Chs. XIII to XVI) enumerates in his account of the valley's *ceques* and *huacas*. Zuidema (1989, 353) corroborates this number in his own mapping of Cuzco's *ceques*.

At the same time, it is clear that the most important reason for the Incas having chosen Cuzco as the seat of their empire is its strategic location, facilitating the movement of people and goods between different ecological zones. The city's altitude places it in the heart of the Quechua temperate zone, in the very center of a variety of ecological niches that could easily be accessed and controlled by the Inca (Miño Garcés 27).

As Miño Garcés points out, Cuzco is situated "at the axis of multiple meanings: isothermal, geographic, ethnographic, agrological, and climatological" (29). Clearly the choice of place was not at all fortuitous, but rather the product of an ancient and profound knowledge of the environmental conditions of the Andean region. What is most striking about the meaning of Cuzco, however, is that its very being congeals an epistemology that envisions the systematic integration of knowledge. In this respect, modern works of ethnohistory confirm what the ancestral uncle recounted in the foundational myth of Cuzco; that is, that not only was the selection of place deliberate, but so too was the particular structure and organization of the city, consciously planned and carried out in conjunction with, or as the concrete realization of, the central categories that regulated Inca culture: upper and lower, bipartition and quadripartition. It comes as no surprise, then, that the foundational myth should encompass the conjoining of all "divine" knowledge, while at the same time declaring the magnanimity and wisdom of Manco Inca in the scene where he is named, or invested, with the title "Cápac."

The location of *Coricancha*—Temple of the Sun—constitutes another example of the intersection of different kinds of knowledge. The Incas chose this spot in accordance with astronomical criteria, and it thus became both an expression of astrological knowledge and the center point of the map of pilgrimage routes. Garcilaso repeatedly states his own understanding that the Incas chose the asymmetrical locations of Cuzco's buildings for complex reasons involving both practical knowledge and religious expression. These two elements, moreover, were mutually constitutive. For example, in his discussion of the Inca calendar and the store of knowledge the Incas possessed about the movement of the stars, Garcilaso claims that the arrangement and architecture of the city's buildings corresponded to a complex of knowledge realms that went beyond the merely residential. He states that the solstices were "left written" by the Incas with "grand and notorious signals which are the eight towers" (104).[5]

According to Zuidema ("Cuzco, Quipu"), the choreography of Incan dances and their occurrences at specific times within the calendar

---

[5] Miño Garcés (80-87) complains that existing studies on Cuzco have tended to be functionalist in approach, and as such, have divided and compartmentalized a complex and highly-integrated reality. He calls for a more integral vision, one that recognizes Incan space as a conjunction of multiple knowledges (astronomical, cosmological,

expressed the bipartite and quadripartite system of Incan organization; and at the same time, the performance of the dances allowed people to experience the structuring nature of reality. The physical space of Cuzco was integrated into the cosmological system of the *ceques*, while the asymmetrical and quadripartite network of *ceques* determined the hydrological system and the roads (Hyslop, *Inca Settlement* 67). The axis of this entire complex of knowledge was the *Coricancha*—Temple of the Sun—from whose heights the ruling Inca, equipped with the *quipus*, *ceques*, and ceremonial calendar, could gaze upon the organization of the empire as one would an open book. In this sense, Garcilaso's comment is quite accurate inasmuch as they "wrote" with their towers and solar observatories.

Keep in mind that when Miño Garcés insists upon the need for more complex approaches to this integral knowledge from the perspective of the social sciences, this contemporary sociologist finds himself confronted with the same problems of cultural translation that Garcilaso faced. It was in the writing of the *Royal Commentaries* that Garcilaso attempted to resolve these problems, commenting alternatively from the perspective of one culture then the other, constructing texts and subtexts that oscillate between coherence and contradiction. Through this kind of writing, Garcilaso was able to create the possibility of reading dialogically. In the foregoing, I will show how Garcilaso lays out the social meanings embedded in Cuzco's Inca buildings, illuminating their social materiality through the referential framework of a Renaissance Humanism that exalted the study of the past. For Renaissance Humanists, history constitutes the knowledge of the records of human endeavor, and it is this knowledge that ennobles us and differentiates us from "natural man."

V. THE "PLAN" OF CUZCO

Today we have abstract models visualizing not only the irregular layout of Cuzco (which some scholars claim the Incas designed to resemble the figure of a sacred puma), but also the size and shape of the city's buildings and even the mysterious niches in its stone "canvasses" or walls. For the

practical) that mutually bestow meaning upon each other. Miño believes that Zuidema's research and methodology are capable of illuminating the complexity of Cuzco's structural layout, its kinship network of *panakas* and its system of *ceques*.

first three centuries after the Conquest, however, not a single blueprint or illustration of Cuzco appeared. As Gasparini and Margolies have pointed out, all we have from that period are verbal descriptions, although these did, for their part, inspire several drawings of the city from a bird's eye perspective. The two authors of *Arquitectura inca* do not hesitate to qualify these illustrations as pure fantasy, as nothing more than European reworkings of Ramusio's 1556 formula which the Spaniards first used to design their American cities and which was recreated for centuries thereafter. "This widely disseminated 'scene never seen' first appeared in the book of Antoine de Pinet (1564) with the legend 'Il cuscho città principalle della provincia del Peru'" (Gasparini and Margolies, *Inca Architecture* 63). The city appears to be made entirely of stone and completely rectangular. The streets are straight and have irrigation channels running through the middle of them. In the distance there is a wall that surrounds the city with towers and a great palace crowned with an enormous turret. This Cuzco is none other than the representation of the Renaissance ideal of urban structure and order. It was not until 1812 that Pentland would produce the first drawing of Cuzco's layout based on scientific instrumentation (63).

VI. Cuzco and the Problem of Knowledge

In the opening pages of the *Royal Commentaries*, Garcilaso argues that his work addresses problems, not so much of content, but of knowledge and the translation of gnoseological categories. In recognizing different modes of knowledge authenticated by their very practice, one could argue that Garcilaso anticipates Lévi-Strauss' notion of the science (logic) of the concrete, even though the renowned French anthropologist was referring specifically to a type of knowledge by analogy that existed among the Amerindian cultures of the Amazon.[6] It is not that Garcilaso posits a system of knowledge by analogy in Incan society; what is important to note, how-

---

[6] See Lévi-Strauss, "Totemism and the Savage Mind." We know that in his study on totemism, Lévi-Strauss argues persuasively that in "primitive" societies one finds a richness of biological and zoological knowledge working through systematic characteristics that challenge the knowledge of modern societies. "Every investigation into social organization, religious life, ritual activity and mythical thought demands a thorough acquaintance with ethno-minerology, ethno-zoology, ethno-botany" (32).

ever, is that he clearly proposes the *validity* of *another* mode of knowledge, one that is equally humane and productive. In doing so, he first grapples with what he sees as the problem of language, in terms of both the unreliable and misleading translations of Quechua into Spanish and the issue of naming. He argues that because the greater Cuzco region is such an ancient site of human habitation, that is, because the human "records" of the place are so numerous and complex, an inability to decipher this Andean topology is the first great obstacle to acquiring knowledge about the space-place itself and the culture that articulates it. This explains why Garcilaso always begins his chapters on Cuzco by interpreting the meanings of the names of the places he describes. Cuzco, for example, means "navel" in the Incas' secret language (what scholars today believe was Puquina). However, learning the literal meaning of the name is not enough; one also needs to know the reason for the name since there is no material determinant for the nomenclature (it does not function as a natural sign). Cuzco does not mean marsh, mountain, spring, or any of the other natural elements that characterize the place. According to Garcilaso, Cuzco is "the navel" because the city, with its oblong and tapered configuration that mirrored the shape of the Inca empire itself, was located in the very center of the imperial territory, just as the navel is centered in the human body (43). Garcilaso's analogy suggests that the Incas, with their system of knowledge, possessed the necessary instruments to both measure distances and conceptualize those distances in geometric forms. After deciphering the meaning of Cuzco, Garcilaso presents a portrait of an imperial administration organized entirely through a decimal system, one used by the Incas to keep accurate registers, census counts and up-to-date information on the expanding empire. In other words, the decimal system became the means for the Inca to merge their understanding of spacial organization, their maps, with the possibility of acquiring, accumulating, and expanding their stores of knowledge. Counting numbers enabled the Incas to measure, and measuring distances seems to have been the primordial means of knowing and organizing. Measuring enabled them to find correlatives; to separate and differentiate.

As part of his constant preoccupation with validating Inca knowledge, Garcilaso explores the state of scientific inquiry among his maternal ancestors and asks how it was that they attained their stores of knowledge without having access to writing. In spite of their "rusticity, the Incas managed to correctly chart the movements of the sun, the solstices and the equinoxes." This knowledge, writes Garcilaso:

was left written in grand, notorious signs, which are the eight towers they constructed to the east of the city of Cuzco and the eight towers to the west. [The towers] were arranged in groups of four, with the two smaller ones, each a little more than the height of three men, standing in-between the two larger ones. The smaller ones were set *eight or twenty feet* apart from each other and the same distance apart on either side from the two larger towers, which were much bigger that the watchtowers of Spain. The large towers were used to protect and monitor occurrences at the small towers. Upon rising and setting, the sun passed directly through the space between the two small towers, and this space was the point of the solstices. The towers of the east corresponded to those of the west depending upon whether it was the spring or summer solstice. (105, my emphasis)

Although he does not state so explicitly, Garcilaso is clearly determined to present Cuzco as a ceremonial and astronomical observatory, very different from the Renaissance city whose "cityscape" would communicate a different use of space, a different type of human habitation, a different value system. Since the Incas themselves had resided in the city, they too, that is, their bodies, were part of the sacred structure. Garcilaso explicitly depicts the sacred character and inscription of those bodies in the scene in which Manco Cápac mandates that royal Incas be differentiated from other Incans by their haircuts and the size of their earlobe holes (51). Further reiterating Cuzco's status as an astrological and sacred observatory, Garcilaso notes that "in order to confirm the solstice, an Inca would position himself in a certain spot at sunrise and at sunset to observe and make sure it was so" (105).

In terms of the order in which he presents Cuzco, Garcilaso does not proceed along a spacial continuum describing each Cuzcan building in turn; rather he lets the categories of Incan knowledge chart his course. In fact, the next topic he introduces is the Incan calendar, its division into lunar months and solar years, and Incan understandings of the relationship between these two.

The sequential logic of Garcilaso's discourse proceeds from the towers that enable the observation of the solstice, to the calendar, and then to Cuzco's rectangular center where the Incas placed elaborately-carved stone columns to trace and verify the equinox. As Garcilaso explains:

In order to verify the equinox, they had columns of elaborately-carved stone placed in the temples or plazas in front of the temples of the sun. Each day the priests [...] carefully observed the shadow cast by the column. They had the columns placed in the center of a large enclosed circle that occupied the entire width of the plaza and patios. Through the middle of the circle, from east to west, they draw a line using a cord. Based on their long years of experience, they knew from what point to the other the cord had to be tied. By the shadow the column cast over the line, they were able to see the equinox approaching [...]. When no shadow was cast on any part, they claimed that day as the equinox. At that point, they adorned the columns with all the flowers and fragrant herbs they could find and placed a throne atop the columns for the sun; for on that day, they said, the sun was seated upon those columns in all its glory and radiance. (106)

Garcilaso makes it evident that for the Incas, space was an empty page of sorts upon which to inscribe their social organization: the designation of upper and lower communities (*hanan* and *hurin*), the allotment of spaces for the palaces of the different *panaca* and their descendents (even designating empty spaces for future *panaca*), and the placement of astrological observatories in all the plazas and in front of all the temples of the sun throughout the empire; temples that the Incas built in likeness to the one in Cuzco—the model city/book. This notion of space does not allow for the idea of a "landscape." In fact, a thorough examination of the representation of Cuzco in the *Royal Commentaries* shows that Garcilaso humanizes all Cuzcan spaces ("humanizes" in the Ciceronian sense as much as the modern) by presenting these spaces as the scenes of rituals, ceremonies, and dances. In other words, he always presents Cuzco's buildings and plazas in terms of their institutional and collective uses; these are imperial spaces in majesty, conception, and usage. It would seem that Garcilaso coincides with Zuidema inasmuch as both attempt to demonstrate, using totally different methodologies of course, the complex integration of knowledge in the Andes and the emblematic representation of that integration in Cuzco.

Garcilaso's representation of Cuzco—the place where Inca knowledge is concentrated and made manifest—is carved into monumental pieces, each deserving of a chapter of its own. Nowhere in the *Royal Commentaries* is there a systematic or overall description of the physical-spacial aspects of the city. The description of *Acllahuasi* comes the closest to what might be considered a totalizing (or bird's eye) view of the city. Here it is possible "to see" the layout of its streets, plazas, roads, royal chairs, dams, and buildings. However, Garcilaso keeps interrupting his description of the rest of the city in order to redirect attention to the interior of the Temple of the Sun and to recount once more the details of its destruction and the ponder the fate of the golden disc that represented the sun. Clearly, it is not ocular vision that determines the sequence of Garcilaso's presentation, but gnoseological vision and memory. The description is not determined by the gaze; instead Garcilaso integrates various themes: the gods, their meanings, the cult of their worship, the calendar, agriculture, the armies, and the *panaca*. From the altar of the sun, Garcilaso proceeds to the chamber of the moon and contemplates its painted image of a woman's face; and from there he proceeds to the chamber of Venus and the stars, where he calls attention to the ornamental ceiling with its many renderings in silver of "the large and small stars like those of the starlit sky" (160). After gazing at the stars, Garcilaso enters the chamber of *Illapa*, where he takes the opportunity to clear up a common misconception, explaining that the tripartite nature of *Illapa* (as lightning, thunder, and lightning bolt) should not be confused with a divine trinity in the Christian sense (162). Because only Incas with the largest earlobe holes were allowed into the temple of the sun, Garcilaso visualizes all these chambers as empty. In contrast to the plazas crowded with people involved in various ceremonies and dances, these chambers emerge from memory as mute and even ghostly.

At only a few moments in this remembered reconstruction of Cuzco does Garcilaso color his description with the subjectivity of the one remembering. He expresses sentimental feelings towards the spaces he evokes only when comparing the grandeur of a monument with its actual state of ruin or neglect. Melancholy pervades his evocation and detailed description of the golden gardens of the Temple of the Sun, for example, upon finding them transformed into the primitive and under-watered vegetable patches of the Dominican friars. Sorrow weighs heavily upon him as he recalls fountains with golden pipes that watered those gardens, gardens in which everything, even the hoes, were made of gold, but gardens that now bore barely a trace of their springs. "And I could find only one of [those springs] [...] the others had been lost for lack of knowledge about where they originated [...] because they found no Indian who could say where the waters of that fountain had come from nor where they had gone" (168).

If there is anyone who constructed and wielded a functionalist (*à la* Malinowski) and at the same time integrated vision of Cuzco, it was Garcilaso. His descriptions in the *Royal Commentaries* divide Cuzco into a series of buildings, each endowed with its own institutional and cognitive function. What differentiates one building from another was not its size or the particular historical moment when it was constructed, for although the stonework might have been different, there was no variation in style. Garcilaso's Cuzco was an eternal city and functioned as a model for all the others. Descriptions of events related to private histories and subjectivities have no place here; rather, the city is imaged as the scene of grand entrances and exits by Incan armies. It is a city of collective and institutional acts. From a Humanist perspective, these "records" left by others from the past are what made those others human; and in just the same measure, knowledge of the past constitutes our own humanity and finds its parallel in the Incan notion of keeping "records" by inscribing space with buildings that embody both cultural practices and stores of knowledge. The cause of Garcilaso's melancholy is not so much the loss of physical grandeur as it is the loss of knowledge. His lament for a Cuzco in ruins is so profound because with the murder of Atahualpa and the subsequent massacres carried out by the Spaniards, all the royal Incan lineages were tragically decimated and "[t]he teachers and priests that had existed in that republic were no more" (168). This void made it impossible for Cuzco to ever be again the city/book that it had been when those who knew how to "read" it could understand its logic and meaning. Garcilaso's fragmented, yet foundational description is the only counterpoint to the Spanish occupiers who did not know how to recognize the city as a seat of knowledge, that is, as another Rome, the city whose rediscovery would give Europe its splendid Renaissance.

Originally published in Spanish as "El Cuzco de Garcilaso: el espacio y el lugar del conocimiento" in *Asedios a la heterogeneidad cultural*. Eds. José Antonio Mazzotti and U. Juan Zevallos Aguilar. Lima: Asociación Internacional de Peruanistas, 1996. 135-152. Translated by Barbara M. Corbett. Reproduced with permission of José Antonio Mazzotti.

Works Cited

Angles Vargas, Víctor. *Historia del Cusco incaico.* Cuzco: Angles, 1989, 3 vols.

—. *Sacsayhuaman: portento arquitectónico.* Cuzco: Angles, 1990.

Arocena, Luis A. *El Inca Garcilaso y el humanismo renacentista.* Buenos Aires, 1949.

Brading, David. *The First America: The Spanish Monarchy, Creole Patriots, and the Liberal State 1492-1867.* Cambridge: Cambridge University Press, 1991.

Gasparini, Graziano and Louise Margolies. *Inca Architecture.* Patricia Lyon, tran. Bloomington: University of Indiana Press, 1980.

Hyslop, John. *Inca Settlement Planning.* Austin: University of Texas Press, 1990.

Lévi-Strauss, Claude. *Anthropology and Myth.* Roy Willis, trans. New York: Basil Blackwell, 1987.

Mazzotti, José A. "The Lightning Bolt Yields to the Rainbow: Indigenous History and Colonial Semiosis in the *Royal Commentaries* of El Inca Garcilaso de la Vega." In *Modern Language Quarterly* 57, 2 (1996): 197-211.

Mignolo, Walter. "Afterward: From Colonial Discourse to Colonial Semiosis." *Dispositio* 36-38 (1989): 333-337.

—. "Colonial and Post-colonial Discourse: Cultural Critique or Academic Colonialism?" *Latin American Research Review* 128 (1993): 120-131.

Miño Garcés, Leonardo. *El manejo del espacio en el imperio de los incas.* Quito: CLACSO, 1994.

Panofsky, Erwin. *Meaning in the Visual Arts.* Chicago: University of Chicago Press, [1952] 1982.

Valcárcel, Luis E. "Garcilaso Inca." *Revista del Museo Nacional* VIII, 1 (1939): 3-60.

—. "Saisawaman redescubierto." *Revista del Museo Nacional* IV, 2 (1935): 161-203.

Vega, Inca Garcilaso de la. *Comentarios reales de los incas.* Aurelio Miró Quesada, ed. Caracas: Biblioteca Ayacucho, 1976, 2 vols.

Zuidema, R. Tom. "Cuzco, Quipu and Quadrant." *XXVI International Congress of the History of Art*, Washington DC, 1986, Ms. 18 pp.

CHAPTER 8
Pedagogies Baroque

I. SOR JUANA, SIGÜENZA Y GÓNGORA, AND A QUESTION OF METHOD

In this essay I explore the relationship of Jesuit pedagogy put in place in the colonial *colegios* of New Spain, and the transference of classical humanist culture to the colonies for the purposes of forming local intellectuals. I also discuss the role played by Jesuit education on the basis of the *Ratio Studiorum* (1599) and the circulation of knowledges and aesthetics that played an important part in the peculiar "Baroque" creations of Sor Juana Inés de la Cruz (1651-1695) and Carlos de Sigüenza y Góngora (1645-1700). Jesuit education and aesthetic interests are credited with many of the signal achievements of colonial culture: religious "syncretism," the architectural and pictorial baroque, a proto-nationalist imaginary, and in the case of Mexico, the two towering intellectual figures of the colonial period. Both Sor Juana Inés de la Cruz and Carlos de Sigüenza y Góngora are figures closely associated with the intellectual climate founded and promoted by the Jesuit philosophy of education. However, although the influence of Jesuit pedagogy lasted well into the nineteenth century—and it may have even extended into our day—as of now we do not have a clear idea of what were the assumptions and practices that constituted the pedagogy that shaped most of the members of the colonial elites and the wider public that came into contact with either the schools themselves or their alumni between 1572, when the Jesuits founded their first *colegio*, and 1773 when they were expeled from Ibero-America.

Intrigued by the figure of Sor Juana, by her vast contact and manipulation of an archive of symbols, allegories, and rhetorics distant and alien to Mexico a mere one hundred and fifty years by the time of her birth, I asked myself: what were the means of archival transfer and translation available and used during this period of colonization? What specific means of implantation of the European archive were in play so as to bring about the seemingly "natural" emergence of this young woman as a subject of knowledge? During the cultural formation of this one hundred and fifty years, what colonizing forces were at work which, on the one hand, exhibit Sor Juana and Sigüenza y Góngora as the chief promontories of a geological formation, and on the other, cover over the layers of rock, minerals, detritus, and gems that make up the two towering figures?

Identified and consolidated by her interpreters as a Baroque poet, Sor Juana's texts have been the object of a myriad of studies during the twentieth century, the century that organizes the Latin American cultural past into periods and sets of delayed, anachronistic or avant la lettre correspondences with Spain at first, and Europe later. Indeed one can safely say that the figure of Sor Juana as the Baroque writer par excellence has been the creation of the twentieth century's own invention of the Baroque. In *Constructing the Criollo Archive: Subjects of Knowledge in the "Biblioteca Mexicana" and the "Rusticatio Mexicana"* (2000), Anthony Higgins challenges the construction of the Baroque that twentieth century scholars have elaborated. Higgins makes two key points. He first questions the homogeneity that the concept of the Baroque confers to a whole and very long moment of cultural formation in Mexico. The Baroque as deployed by Mariano Picón Salas, Pedro Henríquez Ureña, Irwin Leonard, José Lezama Lima, and Roberto González Echevarría operates, according to Higgins, as "a homogenizing master sign" that renders the multiplicity of heterogeneous cultural practices of coloniality invisible (xii). Higgins's second point deals with the teleological position of critics who, like Lezama Lima and González Echevarría, establish the Baroque not only as a point of origin for all Latin American cultural productions, but see in it the metaphor for the very conditions of possibility for discursive formations in Latin America. Despite Higgins' objections to the deployment of the term, it is not hard to see how this sense of the Baroque as a discursive space that enables the joint appearance of contradictions has proved appealing to scholars who, with a critical apparatus inherited from a European epistemology that sees its own master history as a single developmental thread, have had to face the contentious multiplicity of coloniality.[1]

Posited as an insatiable appetite for the inscription of every space available, as an irremediable anxiety before the void of uncertainty that accompanied the religious wars in Europe and the changes brought about by the expansion of Capitalism, the Baroque appears as the space for the joint appearance of contradictions. This notion posits the birth of the Baroque in Europe and assumes its transplantation to America, where once rooted, it bears splendid fruit (Maravall). This story line precludes any possible American origins. It leaves out the Colonial American religious wars of evangelization and extirpation of idolatries. It passes over the trauma of the conquest, the anxiety of coloniality lived by both the defeated Amerindian societies and the colonizing order struggling to establish a reproduction of European culture as the dominant. The celebration of the Baroque as the quintessential Latin American modality in its twisting and turning of every sign within its orbit is a notion that one can see imbedded at the core of many a metaphor devised to encompass the non-dialectical heterogeneity that occurs in Latin America (Cornejo Polar). It informs the recent deployment of transculturation, and it may even provide the fertile ground on which "hybridity," as envisioned by Néstor García Canclini and Homi Bhabha, despite the differences between them, flourished as only a flower acclimatized to its new environment can do.

In this genealogy of the baroque as a space of mixtures and contradictions in Spanish America, it is worth going back to the 1993 book by Katheleen Ross on Sigüenza y Góngora. Ross establishes a distinction between the interpretative categories implicit in Irvin Leonard's views of "Old Mexico" and the critics coming from Latin America. As constructed by Leonard, the concept of the Baroque owes much to the system of oppositions that anchor Heinrich Wolfflin's *Principles of Art His-*

---

[1] Walter D. Mignolo speaks of the colonial difference as "the space where the coloniality of power is enacted... where the restitution of subaltern knowledge is taking place and where border thinking is emerging" (ix). He adds that "the colonial difference of the modern/colonial world is also the place where Occidentalism as the overarching imaginary of the modern/colonial was articulated" (ix-x). The coloniality of power is likened to a machine that incessantly transforms differences into values and produces value-laden classifications and reclassifications of the peoples and cultures of the world from a Eurocentric perspective in which Europe is always already normative.

tory (1950), while for Picón Salas, writing in 1944, Wolfflin offers a questionable model for understanding the colonial formation that is baptized as the "Barroco de Indias" (Ross 20). Where Leonard had seen "estrafalario" (wild, extravagant) prose and verse, Picón Salas, along with Alfonso Reyes, find a local "vitality" expressed in complex sets of contradictions. This vitality, in turn, constitutes the climate where the search for an American identity can begin to grow and eventually flourish (Ross 27). Later in the century José Lezama Lima (1910-1976) will read in the variegated interests and multiple prose and verse experiments authored by Sigüenza y Góngora as a kind of subversion, not unlike the labyrinthine subversive poetics of his own prose in *Paradiso* (1966).

Indeed, Ross makes a further distinction between idealist and materialist interpretations of the seventeenth century. The idealist approach encompasses everyone from Leonard to Octavio Paz (1914- 1999), while the materialist school is championed in *La cultura del barroco* (1975) by José Antonio Maravall, a book that accrues not only the macro politics of Europe at the time but a great of discussion about the circumstances of everyday life. Despite this macro/micro approach, Maravall is almost silent about the events, political and cultural, in Spain's colonies. Ross moves on to place the work of John Beverley under the Maravall umbrella in as much as both critics see the artists and intellectuals of the period overwhelmed and in consonance with the regime of absolute power emanating from the Crown. It would thus seem that we do not really have an agreement, and much less a "homogenizing" view of the period that goes by the label of "Baroque" in Spanish America. In this regard, Mabel Moraña vigorously states that "el gongorismo lejos de ser en todos los casos la lengua muerta del poder imperial, dio a muchos intelectuales del barroco de Indias un motivo de lucimiento en el proceso de conformación de la identidad hispanoamericana" (242). It appears that the Baroque as a critical term continues to be the object of much controversy. It also appears that the Baroque as the label for a historico-cultural period remains much in dispute, and part of this dispute can in turn be located in relation to the geographical and geopolitical location of the critics thinking about it. There are those who write from a Latin American location (Picón Salas, Lezama Lima, González Echevarría, Moraña, Paz) and there are those who write from other (outside) locations (Irvin, Beverley, Ross, Higgins).

If the Baroque, as an intellectual and stylistic construct, is the invention of the twentieth century (it is the work of twentieth century art critics, literary critics, and intellectual historians,) the relations that establishes this invention must be dialogical, in the sense that neither the "I" nor the "Thou" are consolidated entities but rather unstable and porous sites of enunciation. The great Spanish poet Luis Cernuda used to say that the Spanish poets of his Civil War generation broke with the immediate sterile past of Spanish poetry that they had inherited through a rediscovery of the poetry of Luis de Góngora. Cernuda used to add in his poetry seminars, which I attended as a graduate student, that the task of his generation was not only to create a new Spanish language for Spain but to devise a hermeneutics for reading the Spanish Baroque poets and in doing so reinvent Góngora for modernity. A fresh look at the period when Sor Juana writes might keep that idea in mind: to re-invent an important part of the past for our post-modernity.

Octavio Paz, always keenly aware of the creative power of the reader in the textual equation, opens his magnificent *Sor Juana Inés de la Cruz o las trampas de la fe* (1982) by crediting a poet, Amado Nervo (1870-1919), with the modern re-making of Sor Juana. In distancing his own reading of Sor Juana from the recent revival staged by feminism, Paz dates the origins of his own book to the 1930's and flatly states that *Juana de Asbaje* (1910) by Amado Nervo sets in place the hermeneutics by which "la poesía de Sor Juana ha dejado de ser una reliquia histórica para convertirse en un texto vivo" (11). For Paz, it is the poets of the Contemporáneo group in Mexico, especially Xavier Villaurrutia (1903-1950), who produced Sor Juana as the poet that would intrigue and fascinate the modernist Paz who, like Cernuda and Góngora, claims the Mexican nun not only as his predecessor but indeed as his contemporary. For Paz, Sor Juana is nothing less than a dear predecessor in Borges's sense of the term, and thus a "living text" (11).

However, Sor Juana, as the master intellectual of the period, does not appear for Paz as such until 1971, when Harvard invites him to teach there and, without hesitation, he decides to teach a course on Sor Juana. He then reads Sor Juana within the intertextuality of the period made available to him by the collections on music, numerology, hermeticism, Egyptian mysticism, neo-Platonism, Luis de Góngora, and many other living and arcane topics available in the Harvard Library. It is at the Harvard Library that Paz is able to delve, and recreate if you will, Sor Juana's archive. Armed with a sense of the archive available at the time in Mexico City, Paz proceeds to create a period piece. As scholar, but more to the point, as a Mexican public intellectual, Paz writes on the Baroque and Sor Juana, as he puts it, in order to restore to Mexico one of the most significant parts of its history, a formative period, forgotten and desiccated into the ruins of the past by the secularist ideology of the Enlightenment and independence and the need to break with Spanish colonialism. In the first chapter, significantly entitled, "Una sociedad singular," Paz argues that

> no tenemos una idea clara de lo que hemos sido... Nuestra historia es un texto lleno de pasajes escritos con tinta negra y otros escritos con tinta invisible. Párrafos pletóricos de signos de admiración seguidos de párrafos tachados. Uno de los periodos que han sido borroneados y enmendados con más furia ha sido el de la Nueva España... esa deformación no es sino la proyección de nuestras deformaciones. (23)

The colonial period was made invisible and scratched over, Paz argues, by the exigencies of linear history which demands that epochs and periods succeed each other in a series of more or less clean cuts and significant breaks. A more informed sense of the historical canvas, one that would place less emphasis on the transformative power of time, would, for Paz, produce a figure of Mexico's past and present made of blurred ruptures and continuities of uncertain durations. Paz further erodes the linear model when, like Michel Foucault, and Cornejo Polar later, he speaks of layered and uneven movements of space-time configurations. "Más que de continuidad debe hablarse de superposiciones... deberíamos ver [la historia de México] como una yuxtaposición de sociedades distintas... Las rupturas no niegan una continuidad secreta, persistente" (26). The author of *The Labyrinth of Solitude* (1950), the author who rejected the inauthenticity of the border culture of the *pachuco*, offers here a historiographical model that emphasizes a non-dialectical, heterogeneous model for the formation of a period. Thinking of the Baroque did indeed involve quite a shift in Paz's thinking about the past and present.

Thus, not unlike Amado Nervo, but taking on a much larger project, Paz performs a restaging of the period for us forgetful moderns. And this is so despite the fact that one of the most frequent criticism made of Paz's study of Sor Juana is that it is a book that foregrounds the period at the expense of Sor Juana. Such a complaint can be justified only if we think that the singularity of the person or the "literature" that she wrote over-shadows the historical moment or the historiographical problem. My recent experience with *Las trampas de la fe* cannot confirm this assessment. Without understanding what we mean by the Baroque we cannot hope to have a serious understanding of the appearance of writing such as Sor Juana's. Such an approach leaves out the historicity of the "Baroque" as the central conceit in the making of "literature" as the object of the disciplining discourse of literary criticism.

I found the Paz book fascinating precisely because it deals with the now forgotten epistemological problematic of period, the lifestyles and modes of knowledge of the upper and lower classes, the court culture of the viceroyalty, the formation of the colonial intellectual block, the issues and debates that mattered in the power plays that involved Sor Juana, the learned nun, as a marginal and yet a paradoxically powerful player. I found three chapters of particular importance for the topic that concerns me here: "Una literatura transplantada," "El mundo como jeroglífico," and "La madre Juana y la diosa Isis," for when thinking about pedagogy in colonial situations the question of transference, the gaps and sutures that occur in the process of translation and implantation of an archive, prove fundamental.

The epistemological problems wrapped up in her figure as a Baroque poet open the way for a number of questions. Some are direct questions: how did a woman, a doubly subaltern subject, living in a place where there were no sanctioned avenues nor institutional venues for the education of women or other subaltern subjects, come into contact and make available to herself the immensely varied body of knowledge which Paz details in the three chapters mentioned above? The body of works and ideas alluded to by the scholars who reconstruct the intertext in which she thought and wrote would take many years to master today, a task made harder by the absence of a friendly guide or proper interlocutors. How did a colonial subject in Mexico salvage the distance—physical and spiritual—encompassed between the Renaissance rediscovery of the Greek and Roman Classics and Mexico? Did the distance facilitate the encounter? How was it possible for Sor Juana to assume a body of inter-preters capable of deciphering all the hidden (to them and to us) clues and allusions imbedded in the "Arco Alegórico de Neptuno"? How large was this community of interpreters and how did they come about? How well versed in the mesh of allegories that she conflates in the "Neptuno

Alegórico" were those present in the plaza that particular day? Or, was the Arco and its very ungraspable composition an object intended to preclude a certain type of communication, an object intended to assert knowledge as a distant and secret, but nevertheless magically powerful tool available to the initiated (colonials)? If so, how did this community of interpreters come about? In looking at the pedagogy implanted in the Jesuit schools we should be able to provide some of the answers to these questions.

Paz's disentangling reading of the "Neptuno Alegórico" is overwhelming. It foregrounds not only an archive that has been forgotten by modernity but a set of relations between symbols and allusions which systematically eludes explicitness. Obscurity and ambivalence is posited as a chief value. The "Neptuno" is indeed ciphered, and its meaning can be deciphered only if we go back to the current of hermetic syncretism of the Renaissance left in the dust bins of modernity (now being revived by the fiction of Daniel Brown and his best selling *The DaVinci Code,* 2003). Most modern readers lose patience and fare very poorly before *Hieroglyphica* by Piero Valeriano, *Los emblemas* by Aliciato, Vicenzo Cartari 's *Le imagini de i dei de gli antichi,* or Atanasio Kircher's *Oedipus Aegyptiacus* (Paz 235-237). The ciphered and arcane route by which Sor Juana makes Neptune a descendant of Isis marches over many occult passages of the Renaissance fascination with Egypt and especially the work of the Jesuit Atanasio Kircher, whose legacy on Egyptology would eventually constitute the basis of later Masonic iconography. In unraveling this mystery Paz's research points to a key but forgotten connection between the now hidden faces of the Renaissance and the only too visible aspects of the Baroque in Mexico. Instead of the established rupture or even opposition between the two periods, what emerges in *Las trampas de la fe* is a clear, differential colonial connection that lets us see both "periods" as overlapping, as superimposed layers animated and connected by gaps and empty spaces which allow for unique and untested fusions and amalgams, unevenly distributed over a remapped space of composition.

In this regard, Paz suggests that Sor Juana herself, in borrowing the Renaissance method of the mythographers, understood the possibilities offered by the cultural palimpsest. Paz observes that:

A Sor Juana le interesaba sobre todo subrayar los nexos entre Neptuno y la sabiduría. Para convertirlo en hijo de Isis se vale del mismo método de Sigüenza y Góngora, un método universalmente empleado por los mitólogos del Renacimento y de la Edad Barroca. Sor Juana señala que Cartario [Vicenzo Cartari] se equivoca—o sea confunde, funde—a Minerva y a Isis, en verdad ambas diosas son la misma que no es otra que aquella. (229)

The method of fusion or equivalency—"funde, confunde"—makes it possible for Sor Juana to posit in the arch of the "Neptuno Alegórico" that all the goddesses of knowledge go back to, or are the same as, Isis, and that in turn Isis "se transforma en una suerte de emblema secreto—aunque proclamado a voces—de la madre Juana Inés de la Cruz... la monja letrada insigne" (232). Here, as Octavio Paz brilliantly points out, we can see that colonial subjects like Sor Juana devise, out of the anthologizing and castigating of the texts of the classics and ancients, a method that allows for gaps and empty spaces which let them speak from their locus of enunciation. This is not simply a fascination with the occult. Rather it constitutes a method that allows for the combination of original and new linguistic, social, and imaginary elements. If Sor Juana and her community of interpreters could find pleasure in deciphering and unraveling all the hidden messages packed in the emblems that articulate the arch that she constructs, the question to explore then is how did this community of interprets become so competent? How and where was all this learning about Europe's antiquity available, why would these colonial subjects learn and retain this body of knowledge, and how was it so effectively transferred, assimilated and deployed in the public—not secret—rituals devised to affirm the power of the distant and most Catholic and Serene monarch? Paz himself holds to the view that Kircher's work contained the architecture for syncretism and that as such it enclosed the invisible roads in the map of the secret passages between the Renaissance and the Baroque. Paz sees in Kircher's work an "extraordinaria amalgama [de elementos contradictorios] de saber y delirio razonante, su obra fascinó al siglo XVII" (238). It seems quite certain that Sigüenza y Góngora was an avid reader of Kircher. The Mexican savant made use of the same Renaissance mythographic method of fusion and equivalency in his own arch, where he dared propose the Aztec emperors as models for the good government for Christian colonial monarchs. The work of the German Jesuit could be found in the libraries of the Jesuit schools in Mexico, and, indeed, it was part of Sigüenza y Góngora's fabulous collection of books, Aztec manuscripts, and art (238). In this sense Kircher and his method were available directly to the *letrados*, but in an oral culture it may have traveled long and well by word of mouth.

In his foreword to Jacques Lafaye's *Quetzalcoatle and Guadalupe: The Formation of Mexican National Consciousness 1531-1813* (1976), Octavio Paz is preoccupied with the task of the historian and especially with the question of period or epoch, that is to say with the manner in which we can understand both historical continuity and change. How does a historical formation arise? What sustains it through time? How do we, in looking upon the past, ascertain that a given formation comes about and has indeed passed? Paz is certainly aware of the fact, perhaps in the wake of Edmundo O'Gorman's challenge to empiricism (*La idea* and *La invención*), that historical periods do not come about as a result of inhuman historical laws but are actually a discursive phenomenon as Hayden White had already argued in his *Metahistory: The Historical Imagination in Nineteenth Century Europe,* (1973). And yet, Paz admits that it is "perfectly clear that each society, each epoch, is something more than an ensemble of disparate facts, persons, realities and ideas" (Lafaye ix). For Paz, this unity arises from the collision of contradictory tendencies and forces: "Each epoch is a community of tastes, needs, principles, institutions and techniques" (ix). The historian, as in the case of Lafaye's book on Guadalupe and the rise of Mexican national consciousness, searches for "coherence—a modest equivalent of the order of nature—and this search relates him to the scientist. But the form that this coherence assumes is that of the poetic fable: novel, drama, epic poem" (ix). For Paz, Lafaye's hermeneutics of Mexican history, his delving into the history of belief rather than ideas or state recording of surface political eventualities, constitutes the disinterment of a corpse buried in the backyard.

Here Paz is already putting forth the central thesis of his later book on Sor Juana: the colonial period is not the othered past, but rather the point of origin of modern Mexico. As such, it travels in a movement of discontinuities, superimpositions, negations, and contradictions. For Paz, the much celebrated syncretism of the Catholic world and the Amerindian societies does not appear once and already formed, but rather, at least in the colonial period, makes two separate and distinct appearances. Paz points out that it is a phenomenon that first "appeared at the base of the colonial pyramid" (xiii). In a second appearance, "Syncretism, as a deliberate speculation designed to root Christianity in the soil of Anahuac and uproot the Spaniards,... appears later, in the seventeenth century, and does not reach its apogee...until the eighteen century" (xiii). I am aware of the problems that have been leveled against the concept of syncretism, but this is not the place to take up that discussion. Thus, for Paz, the transformation of Quetzalcoatl into Guadalupe shows that "New Spain wishes to be the Other Spain: an empire, the Rome of America" (xii). For Paz this is a contradictory proposition, for New Spain wishes to be the realization of Old Spain, and "this implied the negation of the latter" (xii). The consummation of Old Spain requires that the New becomes another Spain in a Phoenix-like transformation. This desire is best encapsulated in Sigüenza y Góngora's double-headed articulation of Saint Thomas-Quetzalcoatle the Phoenix of the West, which Paz calls "An unfathomable mystery: it is other, yet it is the same" (xii).

II. The Jesuits and the Humanist Paedeia

It is widely asserted that the central figure in this unfathomable mystery (it is other, yet it is the same) is the labor of the Jesuits and their project for creating an ideology of colonization that would not reject the Indian past, but find instead spaces to insert it. Soon after their arrival in New Spain (1572), the Jesuits were in a position to claim pedagogical hegemony in colonial education. Lafaye's *Quetzalcoatl and Guadalupe* probably makes the most daring and persuasive argument regarding the "cultural revival" that the Jesuits brought about in New Spain, an enterprise that was based on "broad popular support," and upon which "the clergy were to elaborate a new ideology that broke not with the ancient Indian beliefs but with those of the first [Franciscan] missionaries" (61).

If the Franciscan utopia failed in part because of the friars' intransigence with Amerindian religion and costumes, what system of knowledges, what conception of education and subject formation enabled the Jesuits to achieve the admired, or denigrated as the case may be, cultural formation of imagining Anahuac as an Other Imperial Spain/Rome? In order to examine the genealogy of the Jesuit subject formation in Mexico we need to go back, not to the Calmecac, but to the "mitigado" humanist pedagogical understandings that the Jesuits put in place in their schools.

The Jesuits arrived in Mexico in 1572, but before that they had been setting up schools for the European elites in Italy, Germany, France, and Spain. The Colegio Romano opened in 1551.[2] They were never able to penetrate England where they were regarded to be a species next to the devil himself. El Colegio de San Pedro y San Pablo was the first college that they set up in Mexico (1574), and it immediately attracted the attention and support of the authorities and the *criollo* families of the entire territory of what was then called New Spain. Most of the students were borders, but some went home at the end of a hard day of work in which most of the instruction, and indeed the interaction among pupils and between teachers and students, was in Latin. In order to understand the curriculum and pedagogy implanted in the Jesuit schools it is necessary to go back to the formation of the humanist pedagogical revolution of the Renaissance.

With the fall of Constantinople in 1453 many Greek scholars migrated to the West. They brought a profound and uninterrupted familiarity with the Ancient Greek and Roman texts newly rediscovered in Italy. These Greek scholars emphasized the notion that governing was indeed a work of art and that the prince should therefore be an educated man trained in the art of government. Humanist learning meant the cultivation and disciplining of talents and the ways of being human. Such a pedagogy, indeed the very idea of shaping learning and thus shaping man, went back to the Greek idea of paedeia and the gymnasium. The close imitation of Greek and Roman ideals and curriculum was then deemed absolutely necessary. Aulo Gelio defined the humanities in terms that have survived to our day: "Una educación cuyo objeto son las artes liberales, porque estas hacen humanísimos a los que las comprenden íntegramente y entran a fondo en ellas" (Gómez Robledo 16-17). Literature, sculpture, music, history, mathematics, and philosophy were to bring forth the Greek ideal of being (male) human. Aulo Gelio clarifies that "'humanitas' fuera no lo que el vulgo cree, y que entre los griegos se llama filantropía, y significa cierta cortesía y bondad para con otros hombres indistintamente; si no que llamaron 'humanitas' a lo que los griegos llaman paidea y nosotros una educación cuyo objeto son las artes liberales" (16-17). Gómez Robledo argues que the

---

[2] See O'Malley. Chapter 6 offers a detailed description of the founding of the first schools in Messina and Rome and their further expansion, with papal favor. Over the course of two centuries the Jesuits established more than 800 schools.

Renaissance studied the classics in order to produce something new in politics (20). Historians read Cicero, for instance, to learn how to write history, to imitate the model and to get closer to Rome itself. Latin was revived as the language of learning and thinking. While the printing press helped disseminate the Roman texts, they were nevertheless not easily available, so that oral reading and recitation of passages from the classics became common place. There developed, as it later did in Mexico, a great taste for hearing Latin speeches, and epic and lyrical poetry. The cult and the cultivation of Latin dovetailed with the Roman ideal of the orator (25).

In this regard, Anthony Grafton and Lisa Jardine, in *From Humanism to the Humanities: Education and the Liberal Arts in Fifteenth- and Sixteenth-Century Europe* (1986), write that the earlier acquisition of Greek culture by the Roman intellectual elite entailed a systematic and thought-out program of incorporating a whole and alien textual corpus and pedagogy into Roman education (4). Quintilian searched for the education that could produce the man who could perform best as a Roman citizen, and both Greek and Roman teachers insisted that literary training would ensure the foundation of the well-rounded and active citizen (5). Thus we can see that the Romans wanted an educational program that would produce great statesmen, just like the Renaissance wanted to produce the prince by means of the Humanities, and the Jesuits wanted to produce educated and loyal intellectuals for the administration of the nascent empire, also by means of classical education.

Grafton and Jardine also point out that until recently the history of education had not been taken seriously by social historians. New questions have been asked and the results have been striking in particular for our understanding of Early Modern Europe (xi). Nothing less than an educational revolution took place between 1450 and 1650. This revolution entails the rise of the classical curriculum and the downfall of scholasticism (xii). However, the triumph of humanism cannot simple be explained by an intrinsic worth or practical utility. Grafton and Jardine write:

> On the contrary, the literary education of the humanists displaced a system far better adapted to many of the traditional intellectual and practical needs of European society. Scholasticism was very much a going concern... It offered literacy in Latin to thousands of boys. It provided a lively and rigorous training in logic and semantics. It equipped students with complex skills and fitted them to perform specialists' tasks ... The liquidation of this intellectual sys-

tem was clearly the murder of an intact organism, not the clearing away of a disintegrated fossil. (xiii)

In contrast with scholasticism a humanist education offered a rigorous empirical investigation and codification of grammar and syntax, rigorous exercises in prose and composition, the art of allusion, and the mastery of metaphor, all of which proved invaluable for the rise of modern literatures in the vernacular. But, according to Grafton and Jardine, these solid merits alone did not win humanism the battle over scholasticism. The success of humanism can better be explained in the fact that "the new system fitted the needs of the new Europe that was taking shape, with its closed governing elites, hereditary offices and strenuous efforts to close debate on vital political and social questions" (xiii-xiv). It conferred upon the more prominent members of the new elite an indelible cultural seal of superiority, and

> it equipped lesser members with fluency and the learned habit of attention to textual detail and it offered anyone a model of true culture as something given, absolute, to be mastered, not questioned—and thus fostered in all its initiates a properly docile attitude toward authority. The education of the humanists was made to order for the Europe of the Counter-Reformation and of late Protestant Orthodoxy. And this consonance between the practical activities of the humanists and the practical needs of their patrons, we argue, was the decisive reason for the victory of humanism. (xiv)

In retrospect one could say that scholasticism, with its emphasis on logic and the dialectic, fostered an independent attitude. Thinking about our present pedagogical conditions, Grafton and Jardine remark that "in the Renaissance as in other periods, the price of collaborating in the renewal of art and literature was collaboration in the constrictions of society and polity" (xiv). Grafton and Jardine show that the humanist curriculum, the unshakable faith in the Greek and Roman letters, was not immune to ideologies of mystification, to a process of naturalization that could, ultimately, be turned into the space for grounding unquestionable authority and imitative habits of mind.

It appears that the Renaissance invention of human learning forgot that the miracles of Roman education—Cicero and Quintilian—had been the result of a conscious emulation of a foreign ideal and the transposition of an oral tradition into a written archive. As in Rome, the Jesuits colleges in Mexico also forgot that the "Greek program had evolved in the course

of a gradual conversion of Greek culture from oral to written form"
(Grafton and Jardine 4). Aware of the bilingual problems that arose from
this wholesale implantation of the Greek curriculum in Rome, the Greek
teachers during the time of Quintilian modified it and fashioned an
approach to the mastering of skills that was clearly suited to the groom-
ing of political spokesmen and lawyers (4). Rome adopted the literature
of an alien culture in a foreign language but this adaptation would involve
a method of anthologizing the Greek legacy (14). This importation of
Greece into Rome as duplicated by the humanist further meant that the
student was not expected to develop original ways of thinking or independent ideas. Nor was he encouraged to express his own emotions or to
deviate from the manner in which any given topic was conceived. Instead
the student was expected to "commit to memory a set or rhetorical loci
where subject matter may be classified according to the key kinds of topics needed to make a case ('virtue', 'usefulness', 'pleasure,' 'goodness').
These he must draw upon in his theme, not because he has thought the
matter through and decided that they are appropriate, but because they
were the proper loci for the theme. He is to be a virtuoso at writing by
number" (Grafton and Jardine, 17-18). Guarino himself practiced this
sort of exercise in Italy. Guarino's schools were created so that the students would learn to write pure Latin, master the web of classical allusions, the mythology of the ancients, and become comfortable with a
huge lexicon of quotations (13). As in the schools later in Mexico, the students were offered a large stock of factual information, a large selection of
texts and glosses, and careful instruction in rhetoric. Guarino's pupils,
like the students at San Pedro y San Pablo, learned to speak ex-tempore
on any subject in Latin. They prepared for careers as ambassadors, secretaries in high offices, lawyers and priests, and especially preachers.

For Grafton and Jardine this kind of humanist education fostered
obedience and docility (20-24) rather than the growth of the individual's
subjectivity endowed with critical skills that could free the student from
received dogma and authority. Perhaps for that reason, Lorenzo Valla in
1450 began advocating another kind of humanist education. He developed a critical approach to the writers of antiquity and conceived of textual analysis as a means of exploring problems rather than the rote imitation of the masters. Vallas method and approach was not welcomed in the
Catholic countries. But the revival of Cicero was adopted and made a
centerpiece of Jesuit pedagogy despite certain reservations.

Differing from Dante, Valla thought that the classics could be studied on their own, without reference to Christianity, a proposition that would have been unacceptable in the colonial schools. Indeed, the study of Cicero was perceived by many as a direct challenge to the Bible because the moral message to be taken from Cicero stood in direct conflict with the Bible. The fundamental challenge of the pagan writers to Christianity was never too far away as the pagans endorsed Stoicism and Skepticism. It was indeed "dangerous" to offer an education based on the classics in the colonies, and thus the *castigado* method seemed most appropriate. However, Cicero's concern with public life as the highest aspiration of the model citizen is indeed well represented in the Jesuit curriculum. Students were encouraged to aspire to the "glory" of winning a public oratory or poetry contest. Reciting without error in perfect Latin from the texts of the classics was indeed considered a high achievement. Such accomplishment would eventually lead, as they did in Rome, to the glory of the Mexican nation and its wise rulers. O'Malley writes that not only Ignatius but the whole Jesuit order recognized the value of education in governance and with it basic accord with humanists program based on the reading, explication, and imitation of the classics (209). Grafton and Jardine think that because the humanists actually produced docile subjects and emphasized the ready-made nature of knowledge, they went from forming the back bone of the Jesuit colleges to establishing the foundation of the Protestant Academies, such as the Strasburg Academy (171). This capacity to produce docile citizens may also account for the success of the Jesuit schools in the eyes of the authorities.

III. PEDAGOGIES BAROQUE

It is clear that the return to the Ancients, the creation of learning sites outside of the Universities proper, did not guarantee independent thinking or the rise of secular human learning in Europe. The humanist methods for shaping the individual into a learned and human man were indeed co-opted and reshaped by those who feared a full and free exploration of the writing ideology and world of the Pagans. The humanist ideal of the Greek paideia was thus checked by the "mitigado" approach, a form of censorship of the texts of the Ancients exercised in Catholic countries. It is important to note that the love for the Greco-Roman world was never intense in Spain (Gómez Robledo 25). Nevertheless, the revival of Latin as the language of the master texts and the language of schooling, thinking, and literary expression flourished and came to form the backbone of the "Instaurario Studiorum" not only in Italy but also in the Colegio de San Pedro y San Pablo in Mexico. There, as in Rome and Messina, the preparation of Latin oratory pieces consumed a great deal of the student's time and was the occasion of prideful display before the great colonial authorities and the satisfied parents who could think of their sons as the correlatives in Europe (Gómez Robledo 21). It is clear that the Latin period—Latin as the chief language of instruction and thinking—lasted much longer in Mexico than it did in any European country, where the birth of modernity had taken different directions and expressions.

Latin was even more important in the frequent theatrical staging at the Colegio. It appears in a discursive series—church building, religious painting, luxiourious European clothing, elaborate court ritual, public display of wealth—that metonymically expresses the power and the new, extraordinary wealth of conquest. The writing and enacting of hundreds of plays in Latin ("hablar y escribir elegantemente el latín," Gómez Robledo 59) does not attest in Colonial Mexico to the realization of the humanizing ideals of the Greek paedeia. Instead, the staging of plays written in Latin by the students of the Colegio seems to have taken a meaning quite different from what the humanities and critical thinking intended. The plays "aparecen siempre como parte principalísima del lujo de trajes, las sedas, los brocados y las piedras preciosas. Esto era lo que en gran parte conmovía a las gentes" (23). People were moved not by the content of the plays in Latin, but rather by the spectacle of the performance of a splendidly sumptuous public act in which they could participate as an audience. Somehow, occupying the place of the audience, that is to say of the interpreter, of these plays acted out in Latin brought on great deal of satisfaction and delight to the colonials who understood very little of what was being said. Paradoxically then, the study of Latin, the imitation of the Roman and Greek ideals of critical thinking and freedom, had turned into an instrument of hierarchy, into a display of difference which, in another twist of Paz's unfathomable, held the power to move the colonial's sense of pride and pleasure. As if to mitigate his own disbelief in the face of the paradox that he just uncovered in his research, Gómez Robledo asks his reader to consider if the affective achievement of the plays does not count as one of the achievements of the Jesuit pedagogy: "¿No nos cuentan acaso que en las fiestas que se hicieron en México para la beatificación de San Ignacio, la multitud derramó abundantes lágrimas cuando las imágenes de los Santos, movidas por goznes, se saludaron y se abrazaban?" (24).

Contrary to the thesis advanced by Grafton and Jardine, Gabriel Méndez Plancarte, in his pioneering study of Humanism in Mexico, *Humanistas mexicanos del siglo XVI* (1946), and almost of all other scholars who have written after him see an exceptionally democratizing and socially liberating force in the way Mexican intellectuals handled Humanism. These Mexican scholars hold to the idea that Humanism indeed taught a universal human understanding and a respectful regard for all things human, irrespective of the individual's race or social status (Gómez Robledo 29). As proof, these scholars offer the work of the many evangelists, from Bartolomé de Las Casas (1474-1566) to Diego Vasco de Quiroga (1477-1565), who came out in the defense of the Indian's humanity. But of course Méndez Plancarte and the other scholars forget, that the humanist legacy in the thinking of these evangelists, all born and trained during Spain's short lived climate of Humanism, has nothing or little to do with the much later system of pedagogy in the Jesuit's schools and architecture which is especially designed to overcome the approaches of the Dominicans and Franciscans to Amerindian subjects. Scholars such as Gómez Robledo and Ramón Kuri Camacho go as far as to see in the Jesuit deployment of humanistic learning in Mexico the interrupted birth of an "alternative modernity" (Kuri Camacho 99-110). How the facts of conquest and the presence of the Nahuatle population were negotiated by the students of the Jesuits is a story that we still do not quite understand. Indeed, for Lafaye, the syncretism of belief that congeals in the figure of Guadalupe is not possible without the agential presence of the Indian population, but how that presence penetrated, dislodged, or displaced the strict and yet mitigated Greco-Roman curriculum of the Jesuit schools is an area that needs further exploration, especially in view of how the schools were run and what they taught.

The Jesuit pedagogy emphasized the student and not the teacher. It demanded that the student acquire a solid foundation in Grammar before he could move on to the more advanced courses in the Humanities and Rhetoric. It ordinarily took three years of memorizing Latin grammar, repeating out loud selected passages and composition excursus. Students did three hours of grammar in the morning and two more in the afternoon (Gómez Robledo 59-63). Gómez Robledo further states: "Ejercicios de memoria, repeticiones, preguntas, concertaciones, composiciones en prosa y verso, declamaciones oratorias o dramáticas, concursos poéticos, en fin todo lo que se podía imaginar en cuestión de ejercicio" (60). The objective of the courses taken by the students was, as in Europe, to learn to speak, read, and write Latin. Students enrolled in the schools as they turned ten years old and stayed till they graduated at sixteen. The entire six years were divided into three parts, each dedicated to grammar, rhetoric, and the mastery of the Roman classics with a special emphasis on the study and emulation of Cicero, Virgil, Horace, Ovid, and Quintilian (39-61, 100-110). The supreme objective was the achievement of perfect oratory.

Students at these Jesuit schools attended five hours of class everyday. There was no study of Spanish or any other mother tongue. All instructional and even organized recreational activities such as poetry recitals, staging of plays, and even games (spelling bee any one?) were in Latin. The *Ratio Studiorum*, a curriculum put together by Ignatius himself at about 1599, was the central piece in the intellectual and artistic formation of the pupils at schools such as San Pedro y San Pablo. It was Ignatius' desire that all Jesuit *colegios* follow the same plan and achieve the same objectives. The guiding pedagogical ideas included the notion of constant drilling and repetition. A student could not move on unless he had mastered the previous course. Textual study began with the professor reading out loud a very short passage and proceeding to explain all the possible stylistic and cultural references present in the text. The text's depth and singular perfection was indeed regarded as sacred. Its complex pleating and unfoldings of meaning were revealed so that the students would better learn to imitate its power and authority (Gómez Robledo 103-107). In fact, the Jesuit manual states that "toda prelección de Cicerón debe constar de dos partes: una, la explicación del pasaje y, la otra, la observación del mismo encaminada a la imitación; la primera es como cuerpo; ésta es el alma de la prelección" (Gómez Robledo 113).

Jesuit education stressed the idea of competition among the students, as it was designed to prepare intellectuals ready to engage with and win in the combat of ideas and discursive power struggles going on in the world. Most examinations, oral or written, were public. Special attention was given to the exercise of oral skills, and to the mastery and imitation of the Roman texts (Gómez Robledo 97; O'Malley; 214-217). In New Spain, public examinations were but one of the many rituals and jousts in which these organic intellectuals displayed their oratory and polemicizing skills. The Viceroy, the Inquisition, the Real Audiencia, and many members of his court attended the plays, poetry and essay competitions, and even graduation examinations. Often two virtual armies competed in these events called "concertación." In emulation of the military organization of the Order, the struggle began with soldier interrogating soldiers, and it moved all the way up to the generals. The competitors would be asked to conjugate verbs, decline a noun, recite and provide etymologies, parse an analogy, explain a poem, unfold a metaphor, interpret an emblem, or decipher an enigma. The public experienced particular delight in competitions that included the deciphering of emblems, enigmas, and "empresas" (Gómez Robledo 133) The "empresa" required exquisite abilities based on specific hermeneutics designed for the deciphering of icons and symbols in paintings which depended on ciphered verbal icons and figures. No doubt Sor Juana attended many such a joust in court during the years she spent there as a *protégé* of the viceroy and the dotting vicereigns who so loved her talent for wresting current meaning out of the arcane set of references then in circulation. The emblem, one of the nun's favorite modes of encoding, was more easily accessible to a wider audience, for it was an epigraph that contained a ciphered meaning to be disentangled. Such public displays of the oratory and interpretative verbal skills of the students trained at the Jesuit schools spread to the training of students in schools run by the other educational orders, since they did not want to left behind in the competition set up by the Jesuits. Also, and most important, such public display created a relatively large community of interpreters and practitioners beyond the sphere of the schools and the court. Sor Juana, given the circumstances of her birth as a commoner and her gender, could not, of course, attend a Jesuit school, but her exposure to such a classical education at court and her own learning allowed her not only to compose in ciphered ways but also to have an audience capable of interpreting her very public "Neptuno Alegórico."

Hers was not the only "arco triunfal" ever composed in Mexico. The students at the Jesuit schools composed many arches before and after Sor Juana's. The San Pedro and San Pablo school made one such arch in 1578. It reached 70 feet in height. It was designed by the famous Genovese architect Juan Francisco Base (Gómez Robledo 73-81). The arch was adorned with a combination of flowers, hangings, statues, rabbits, birds, Latin inscriptions, paintings depicting a colloquy of angels, and allegorical paintings that showed a German (Luther) in opposition to an Indian (the catholic Mexican people). Such ciphered complexity and excessive arrangement of visual symbols and signs delighted the audience trained for the exercise of such interpretative capacity. There was a great deal of pride in this achievement. It is thus not surprising that a generation later both Sor Juana and Sigüenza y Góngora proceeded with confidence in the composition of their arches and the ability of their audiences to delight in the performance of a correct reading of all the ciphered messages. Both the historian and the poet manipulated a rich semiotic arsenal, which was not limited to a few intellectuals and *letrados*, but was rather available to a larger part of the population due to the program of instruction at the Jesuit schools and the public, competitive philosophy of education that underscored it.

However, the Jesuit schools' "success" with the *Ratio Studiorum* was not a simple question on method for the transportation and acquisition on Roman letters and values as noted above. The emphasis on exercises and question and answer memorization was the legacy of the system at the University of Paris where Ignacio de Loyola had studied. This system was perfected at the Colegio Romano, one of the first colleges founded by the Jesuits and where the mitigado method was born. Intellectually, the *Ratio Studiorum* represents the harnessing of the pedagogical philosophy of the Humanities, as put in place by the Italian Renaissance for the invigoration of the scholastic method developed at the University of Paris where Ignatius had learned the value of disputation, public examination, and publication of the results of one's scholarly labors. Basically, Ignatius understood with all clarity the force and place of education as yet another way of political struggle. In the *Ratio Studiorum* he brought together two methods for achieving the best education possible in the defense of the values he thought were necessary to compete in the evergoing struggle for discursive dominance.

The mitigation of the secular learning that the Humanist program entailed meant the inclusion of theology, the advocacy of a Christian teleology and the preservation of the scholastic method of reasoning. At the Roman College, and in Mexico, humanistic learning was centered on the work of Cicero and Virgil. In the early stages of the colleges Erasmus and Valla were included but soon their texts were banned as we have discussed above. The Jesuit co-option of the humanist curriculum and method into an addiment of Scholastic education is indeed confirmed by Mauricio Beuchot:

> En el siglo XVI había ciertamente ideales humanistas renacentistas, pero el andamiaje filosófico que les daba una base de recepción era la escolástica. Casi podría decirse que en México hubo una escolástica humanista, una escolástica hermetizante y una escolástica modernizada según el siglo del que se tratara, y por supuesto hubo una escolástica ajena a influencias y cambios. (65)

Clearly, what moves forward in Mexico, in several overlapping waves of adaptation, is the scholastic matrix of argumentation.

The Jesuit colleges in Mexico had their own press and there they printed, in expurgated version, the Roman authors as well as other selections from the Renaissance archive. Gómez Robledo (221) reports that at the turn of the century one could still see in circulation copies of the *Emblemas de Alciato* (1577), *Elegías de Ovidio* (1577), and *Gramática de Álvarez* (1569), all edited at the San Pedro y San Pablo by the Italian Humanist Ricciardi. In a permit given to Ricciardi to print books in Mexico we can see: *Fábulas*, Catón, Luis Vives, *Selectas* de Cicerón, *Bucólicas* de Virgilio, *Églogas* de Virgilio, *Elegancias* de Lorenzo Valla, *Cartas* de Cicerón, Marcial Purgado, and "tablas de ortografía y retórica" (Gómez Robledo 63). Reading and imitating the *castigado* classics was not regarded as a private act of cognition, for such reading was destined to public display in the competitions and the plays. These performances of the classical archive no doubt reached many more than the students at the schools and the very select public at the ceremonies held within the school's walls.

Only two years after their arrival in Mexico (1572), the Jesuit order decided to hold a great spectacle of learning in Mexico. They held a public examination of their pupils. The Bishop, the Viceroy, and the entire nobility attended the event at San Pedro y San Pablo. The walls of the schools were adorned with great hand written poems authored by both the classic masters and the precocious Mexican pupils. The entire city celebrated such display of effective learning. And the Jesuits presented it as proof of the efficacy of their method of memorization. A year later the school put on plays written by the students. They decried the offenses that the heretic Christian sects inflicted upon the Roman Church. This too was an instant success.

The Jesuit schools had manufactured an amazing amalgam of learning and indoctrination. The study of Cicero did indeed train the pupils in public oratory. It also conferred lessons dealing with the good citizen and the organic intellectual. The Roman republican ideals were then mitigated, or rather disciplined, by two powerfully bending forces: purgation of passages considered inconsonant with the teaching of the Church, and scholasticism, that is to say, a logic of reasoning that the Italian Humanists and Erasmus himself considered inimical to the purposes of fostering critical thinking, the pivot of the Greek paedeia. What was put in place at San Pedro y San Pablo (let us not pass over the emblematic name of the school) was indeed a baroque teaching machine in which repetition and indoctrination, the production of docile organic intellectuals, reigned as the reason d'etre of learning. We could say that the success of the Jesuit education in the colonies, like the success of humanism in Europe, was in great part due to the easy fit between and ideology for the production of docile, learned subjects for the new colonial order. To this effect, Beuchot reminds us that while: "el humanismo surge como oposición a los escolásticos, pugnando por el método histórico y filológico en contra del método especulativo de los primeros" (74). Where humanism and scholasticism seem to coincide is on the emphasis of the method based on question and argument, and it is at this point where the *Ratio* performed a blending of methods. In this regard, Beuchot points out that scholasticism

fue una filosofía muy argumentativa, los escolásticos eran grandes argumentadores, por eso sus tratados nos parecen a veces sobrecargados de argumentos; había argumentos para casi todo y aun probaban y volvían a probar las premisas y fundamentos en los que apoyaban las conclusiones o tesis... eso podría darle un tinte de vacía y hueca acuciosidad. (56)

Ramón Kuri Camacho, not unlike other students of the period, sees in this superimposition a first and seminal feat of syncretism, a syncretistic move that in his view extends its reach beyond the blending of pedagogical philosophies and allows for the resolution of the many historical and cultural contradictions inherited from the fact of conquest: "El sincretismo jesuita y su eclecticismo filosófico serán un principio esencial del mestizaje profundo, que en la nación mexicana alcanzará hasta el siglo XX... El esfuerzo vital de los jesuitas por abrirse a otras culturas apenas tiene paragón" (105). For Kuri Camacho, such an ability represents nothing less than "fórmula [para] llevar a la práctica una modernidad alternativa (104).

Leaving aside the question of an alternative modernity, it is important to point out that the idea that a syncretist approach to culture could arise out of an education under the guidelines of the *Ratio* would need a greater attention to specifics. For one thing, the *Ratio* regulated and classified everything, leaving, it seems to me, little room for the holding of two contradictory propositions, feelings, or attitudes at once. The *Ratio* organized not only the curriculum and method of learning, but also the organization of the school's administration in very strict terms. There were rules for everything. The Prefect of Studies saw that the rules for examinations, prizes, and academies were enforced universally. Latin permeated all intellectual activities, and it excluded the use of the mother tongue as an instrument of learning. Such an exclusion can hardly be said to constitute an act consonant with a philosophy of syncretism where new American forms could occur.

On the other hand, if grammar means the perfect acquisition of the Latin language, rhetoric implied the training in perfect eloquence. The entire method depended on disciplining the mind by means of the stickiest memorization and disciplining the political subject under the codes of the honor principle. It was not, as Irwin Leonard has stated, a superfluous and idle education destined only to adorn the language or literary skills of the students. It did provide adornment, as Grafton and Jardine also note in the case of Humanism in Europe, but the adornment was not superfluous. To the contrary, it was like all luxury items, revealing and confirming of the subject position occupied by the students in the power-knowledge grid. It was an education that absorbed all the physical, mental, and emotional energies of the students in seeing, understanding, and manipulating a world object paradoxically distant and yet so intimately close to their experience and success as students and members of a socio-political class. It must also have been an education fraught with uncertainty, for the connection between the ancient Roman writers and the patterns of life outside the walls of the school must have seemed unfathomable, to use Paz's felicitous term for the period in question. And yet as Jacques Lafaye and others have written, the last quarter of the sixteenth century "saw the appearance, in large part under Jesuit inspiration, of aspects of cultural revival hitherto unknown in New Spain" (61). For the French historian, this was the result of the

> confluence of the Christian sense of the marvelous with Ancient Indian beliefs. Because the mendicant orders had failed to eradicate idolatry, a half century later Christian images had been substituted for Indian idols at the cite to which Indian pilgrimages were made. Along with these material substitutions there developed syncretism beliefs and pious legends. (61)

IV. BENDING PEDAGOGIES

But one phenomenon is not to be conflated with the other. What happened at the Indian sites of pilgrimage seems entirely divorced from the regiment of subject formation unfolding at the Jesuits colleges, even though the Jesuits were present in both. In one site the descendants of the Aztec cultures appear as the subaltern agents of a colonial formation which engages the Jesuit's project of Christianization. At another site, there appear the *criollo* as subaltern agents in a colonial formation which engages the Jesuits in a pedagogical project of transferring the scholastic adoption of the Greek and Roman educational program used in the production of political elites. It would thus seem that these two different and even perhaps contradictory pedagogical sites operated at the same time, and, at certain key conjunctures, cross each other's paths. When that crossing occurred something other than what was intended took place. Is it fair to say that the differential in the equation is the participation of the descendants of the Aztec world? Are they, then, the architects of the force that bent the Jesuit project out of shape?

Or perhaps the reverse could be posited, that is to say that learning about the Greco-Roman world, its political thought, its mythological system, and its oratory tradition furnished a historiographical scaffolding within which the Aztec world could be rescued at the level of the *letrados* from the condemnation of the Franciscans and the Requerimiento. Could it be said that at both sites, via the mitigado familiarity with the Greek and Roman world of myth, literature, history, and art, the legacy of the Aztec world could be saved and reinvented, made consonant, appear metonymically foliated with the revered Mediterranean ancients? Was this a palimpsest or archeological move facilitated by the Renaissance's own interest in the civilized Pagan universe? In other words, the Humanist repetitious study of the ancients as ancestors, who in many ways surpassed the culture of the day as models of learning and virtue, could be transferred to the study (not the revival) of Mexico's own Pagan ancestry. Garcilaso de la Vega certainly saw the possibility for this move when he stated that his interest was the history *and* "fábulas" "de ese Cuzco que fue otra Roma" (35). What happens then in the Jesuit schools is *both* the success and the failure of transference. The immovable memorizing of certain Roman texts and thinkers and the mastery of the Latin language allows for mastery of key tropes and topoi, which, detached from their original classical matrix, in time served as the unquestionable and naturalized scaffolding where a repertoire of ideas and topoi rendered *similar* by force of exclusion of the marks of difference could be articulated as part and parcel of a syncretic logic. The very narrowness of the range of the topoi allows the fitting of the Aztec rulers as mere examples of good government in Sigüenza's arch. The Aztec princes enter the stream of the series stripped of the cultural specificity that the Franciscans rejected when they deemed the whole of Aztec culture as incompatible with the Christian logos and ethos.

The pedagogical transference and transculturation that occurs in the Jesuit colleges cannot, then, as Lafaye would have it, be conflated with the Virgin of Guadalupe phenomenon for several reasons. First, the Sigüenza y Góngora appropriation of the Greco-Roman world is the conscious act of a studious individual who produces an object of political importance in the public sphere destined to persuade the church-state machine of colonial power of the possibility of a certain similarity between two sets of ancient cultural topoi. In contrast, the appropriation of the saints into the Aztec world of the divine occurs at the level of the *multitudes*, the rhythms of daily life, and the realm of worship, that is a space that blurs the distinction between private and public but which is nevertheless not comparable with the space of the official, public reception accorded by the viceroy and the Inquisition to the subaltern but *letrado* students of the Jesuits. Second, Sigüenza y Góngora, and Sor Juana with her "Arco de Neptuno Alegórico," display their learning in a Baroque manner in an act of loyalty and obedience to the power of the colonial authority whose entrance into Mexico City reenacts Cortés' own conquest of the Aztec empire. Sigüenza y Góngora's reach for equivalence or similarity appears from the start in the trench of ambiguity provided by imperial discourse to the subaltern colonial.

His arch is offered as one more fruit of the land (*frutos de la tierra*). It is an offering from the subaltern to the majesty across the Ocean and as such it does nothing other than to acquiesce to the notion that the Aztec world is dead for ever. The Aztecs can be understood but never resuscitated, just like the Romans can be read, but they will be always *mitigado* and disciplined by the Catholic Church. This final relegation of the Aztecs to a past that has no hope of continuity is the product of the pedagogy of San Pedro y San Pablo, one which Sor Juana had also assimilated quite well in her own "Arco de Neptuno Alegórico" which, in contrast with her poetry, does not constitute a living text.

Third, these public acts/offerings by two organic intellectuals stand at a great distance from the cult to the saints/Aztec gods, for this cultural object is created in an effort to continue and preserve the Aztec world from the destruction of the Franciscan pedagogy of uncompromising rejection and subjugation. The masking of the Saints and of Quetzalcoatle/Guadalupe imbricates knowledge upon a structure of feeling and, indeed, action. Politically the direct appropriation of the Saints by the populace itself is chiefly an affective, and thus most effective, move. In contrast, both Sor Juana's and Sigüenza's immense intellectual feats, precisely because of their subtlety and elite arcane learning, eschew the affective and the political and remain corralled within the walls of the epistemology of San Pedro y San Pablo, that is to say faith and argument, both modes of knowledge that complemented rather than subverted or challenged the Imperial power.

One must thus conclude that, contrary to Paz's nostalgia for the arcane world of Sor Juana, the Criollo dreamers of Mexican independence were correct in rejecting such an origin (as constructed by Paz) as the foundational past of the modern nation that they aspired to create, and were only too clever in wrapping themselves in the flag of the local Virgin of Guadalupe in order to mark the colonial difference. Even the Pope is aware of that distinction for he acknowledged it in his decision to canonize Diego, the fictional "indito," to whom the Virgin supposedly gave her message.

This essay was written in 2002 for a Conference on the Baroque held at the University of Wisconsin, Madison.

WORKS CITED

BEUCHOT, Mauricio. *Estudios de historia y filosofía en el México colonial.* México: Universidad Nacional Autónoma de México, 1991.

CORNEJO POLAR, Antonio. "Una heterogeneidad no dialéctica: sujeto y discurso migrante en el Perú moderno." *Crítica cultural y teoría literaria latinoamericana. Revista Iberoamericana,* 176-77. Ed. Mabel Moraña. 1996. 837-44.

GRAFTON, Anthony and Lisa JARDINE. *From Humanism to the Humanities: Education and the Liberal Arts in Fifteenth- and Sixteenth-Century Europe.* London: Duckworth, 1986.

GÓMEZ ROBLEDO, Xavier. *Humanismo en México en el siglo XVI: el sistema del Colegio de San Pedro y San Pablo.* México: Editorial Jus, 1954.

HIGGINS, Anthony. *Constructing the 'Criollo' Archive: Subjects of knowledge in the 'Biblioteca Mexicana' and the 'Rusticatio Mexicana'.* West Lafayette: Purdue University Press, 2000.

KURI CAMACHO, Ramón. *La Compañía de Jesús, imágenes e ideas. Scientia conditionata, tradición barroca y modernidad en la Nueva España.* Puebla: Benemérita Universidad Autónoma de Puebla, Plaza y Valdés Editores, 2000.

LAFAYE, Jacques. *Quetzalcoatl and Guadalupe: The Formation of Mexican National Consciousness, 1531-1813.* Chicago: University of Chicago Press, 1976.

MARAVALL, José Antonio. *La cultura del barroco: análisis de una estructura histórica.* Madrid: Ariel, 1975.

MORAÑA, Mabel. "Barroco y conciencia criolla en Hispanoamérica." *Revista de Crítica Literaria Latinoamericana* 14:28 (1988): 229-51.

PAZ, Octavio. *Sor Juana Inés de la Cruz o las trampas de la fe.* México: Fondo de Cultura Económica, 1982.

ROSS, Kathleen. *The Baroque Narrative of Carlos de Sigüenza y Góngora: A New World Paradise.* Cambridge: Cambridge University Press, 1993.

CHAPTER 9
The Nation in Ruins: Archeology and the Rise of the Nation

> Hasta ti, Macchu Picchu.
> Alta ciudad de piedras escalares
> por fin morada del que lo terrestre
> no escondió en las dormidas vestiduras.
> En ti, como dos líneas paralelas
> la cuna del relámpago y del hombre
> se mecían en un viento de espinas.
> Madre de piedra, espuma de los cóndores.
> Alto arrecife de la aurora humana.
> Pala perdida en la primera arena.
> Esta fue la morada, éste el sitio
>
> Pablo Neruda,
> "Alturas de Macchu Picchu"

> "Present resemblances enable us to resuscitate dead recollections"
>
> Marcel Proust, *La Prisonnière*

I. THE RIDDLES OF IMAGINED COMMUNITIES

The idea and ideology of the nation has recently been the subject of intense inquiry. I do not have space here to review that corpus of literature. Suffice it to say that the two most prominent arguments that will play a role here are the idea of the invention of tradition as advanced by Hobsbawm and Ranger, and Benedict Anderson's thesis on the determining relationship between the growth of print and the spread of nationalism in the New World, Europe, and other areas of the world. Anderson has stressed the idea that "nation-ness, as well as nationalism, are cultural artifacts of a particular kind" (4).[1] He adds that the particular ways in which they came into being account for the profound emotional charge associated with their sense of legitimacy (4). These artifacts, he

---

[1] See Benedict Anderson, *Imagined Communities: Reflections on the Origin and Spread of Nationalism*.

argues, once created, at the end of the eighteenth century in the New World, "became modular, capable of being transplanted with various degrees of self-consciousness, to a great variety of social terrains" (4). On the whole, Anderson's major contribution to the discussion on nationalism devolves on the brilliant design of his concept of "imagined community," an idea that easily travels from one terrain of analysis to another. For that reason it is worth quoting here at length and especially because it in fact was already advanced by Ernest Renan in his (1882) definition of nation as cultural artifact. For Anderson the "nation is an imagined political community—and imagined as both inherently limited and sovereign"(6). It is imagined "because the members of the even smallest nation will never know most of their fellow members... and yet in the mind of each lives the image of their community"(6). Anderson is keen on stressing that nationalism is "not the awakening of nations to self-consciousness: it invents nations where they do not exist"(6). By inventing Anderson means creating in the sense of making.

However, his chapter on Latin American Movements of Independence (47-65) registers a number of unresolved problems which Anderson himself calls "riddles" (50). The "riddles" are the result of the fact that his theory cannot account for the multiple specificities at play in the processes of independence in Latin America. Despite Anderson's attention to the picaresque novels by José Joaquín Fernández de Lizardi, all published after 1826 and still unavailable in English translation, and his attention to the Creoles's frustration with their exclusion from high office in the colonial administration, it is clear that neither his thesis on the spread of print—in the form of novels and news papers—nor his elaboration of the "modal journey of pilgrimage" (57) provides a sufficient explanation for the homegrown nationalisms of the Latin American Movements of Independence.

Anderson has little to say on the question of local intellectuals and homegrown discourses of independence in print, iconography, and other modes of encoding and circulating memory. It is indeed remarkable to see that in the case of Mexico he places his focus on the post-1810 picaresque novels of Lizardi while the whole question of the Virgin of Guadalupe and the low-level clergy that headed the movement for Mexican independence is left out. As Jacques Lafaye has shown, the cult to the Virgin of Guadalupe and its indissoluble link to Mexican national consciousness was neither built by, nor did its spread rest on the dissemination of, print (Lafaye). Likewise, Anderson ignores the historical work of the Jesuit Francisco Javier Clavijero (1731-1787) and his attempt to anchor the Mexican nation on a history of Mexico's antiquities. The thesis of "imagined communities" leaves out also, and almost by necessity, what Carlos Fuentes refers to as "el sacrificio de los pobres párrocos que encabezaron el único levantamiento de la gleba india y campesina, armada con palos y picos [que] dejaba la independencia al azar de un acuerdo entre guerreros" (Fuentes 132).

How Anderson deals with Mexico is simply an example that can be multiplied in regard to many other, equally important, discursive specificities. When these are brought into play in the consideration of nation building in Latin America they present a serious challenge to Anderson's modular traveling thesis. Latin American nation building and the nationalisms of the Independence period require more complex explanations, themselves based on detailed analysis of the criss-crossing of many more discrete discourses and historical forces than just newspapers and novels or Creole inability to journey up the bureaucratic stream of colonial institutions.

In this chapter I explore certain key continuities and breaks in well-established local knowledges and memory systems which exceed the limits of print in the Andes and Mexico. The conjunction of established local knowledges with the appearance of new knowledges, especially archeology, in the national imaginary of Mexico and the Andes provide fertile ground for the examination of the deployment of particular historical forces active in the rise of nations out of the evolving colonial grid.

I focus here on three significant moments in the making of the nation as a cultural artifact linked to a "people" who claim immemorial occupation of the land. These moments of emergence in Mexico and Peru have been chosen because the materiality of culture that constitutes them exceeds the bounds of print media as well as writing, and especially novels. For example, the body of knowledge that enables and constrains the Túpac Amaru II rebellion relies on a memorial art based on iconography, dance, dress, and ritual. The daily viewing of and interrogation posed by the ancient ruins in the case of Mexico led Clavijero in the late eighteenth century and Eduardo Mariano Rivero (n.d.) in the early nineteenth century in Peru to the exploration, drawing, and writing of the ruins left by the Aztecs, Incas, and Mochicas. In these cases, the study of archeology stretches the timeline of the nation and creates immemorial "ancestors" for the postcolonial nation. In these two instances, archeology allows a mapping of the nation that reconfigures territory by privileging forgotten or even forbidden sites of memory.

In examining the rise of archeology in rooting modern, postcolonial nations into the land, I do not intend to establish empirical relations of cause and effect, for my concern is with discursive formations and my approach is genealogical. It is important to emphasize here that genealogy, inasmuch as it points to discontinuity, destroys the illusion of linear development. But genealogy also allows the identification of deeper, hidden continuities which are the product of sequences of transformations and combinations. The three moments discussed here do indeed exhibit sequences of transformations in the deployment of deviations, incomplete reversals, and reappearances. A genealogical approach to the rise of archeology in the nascent postcolonial polities does not, as Michel Foucault would put it, "pretend to go back in time to restore an unbroken continuity that operates beyond the dispersion of forgotten things" (Foucault, *Language* 146). On the contrary, Foucault states that genealogy, as it follows the complex course of descent, maintains "passing events in their proper dispersion" (146).

In what follows I keep in mind Walter Benjamin's sense of the writing of history from the urgency created by the crisis of the present. I think that Benjamin's emphasis on a perspective informed by the sense of a present crisis illuminates not only the task of the archeologist "then" but also the endeavor of those who examine the past today. Writing history in order "to seize hold of a memory as it flashes up at a moment of danger" (Benjamin 255) is different from the impossible articulation of the past as it "really was."[2]

If indeed we can only write the past from the sense of one's own the present, in examining the discourses that construct the nation in Latin America, it is important today not to loose sight of the recent challenges

[2] In "Theses on the Philosophy of History" Benjamin writes: "To articulate the past historically does not mean to recognize it 'the way it really was' (Ranke). It means to seize hold of a memory as it flashes up in a moment of danger. Historical materialism wishes to retain that image of the past which unexpectedly appears to man singled out by history at a moment of danger. The danger affects both the content of the tradition and its receivers...convinced that even the dead will not be safe from the enemy if he wins" (255).

made to European historiography, especially with regard to the Hegelian single and universal timeline. Michel Foucault's challenge to the idea of history that assumes a living world "actually" moving on a single plane of homogeneous space and time is particularly useful here, for if there is a heterogeneous history sustained by parallel, asymmetrical, contradictory and yet contemporary epistemologies, that indeed is the case of the post-conquest Andes. After the conquest, linear, Christian time neither meshed nor absorbed Andean concepts of time-space (*pacha*). Moreover, the colonial world set as a remote outpost of the center and its self-ascribed homogeneous time produced its own "backward" time location. Questioning the assumption of a homogenous historical and lived time-space is even more relevant here, for such homogeneity is claimed by Anderson to be the result of the spread of print and the subsequent con-struction of imagined communities. I therefore look into the fractures and limits that mark the differences between subsequent or parallel ideas of nationhood founded each in turn on sign systems other than writing and the spread of print. On the whole my chief concern here will have to do with the deployment of memory and its often labyrinthine paths in the making of history and nation. I take history to mean both the lived experience entwined in the appearance of events and the writing or recording of the event by a series of mnemonic devices.

II. MAPPING THE NATION

In *History and Memory* ([1977] 1992), writing before Anderson advanced his arguments on the New World origin of nationalist discourses, Jacques Le Goff states that the idea of the nation dates back to the French Revo-lution" (151).[3] He decidedly differs from Federico Chabord for whom the idea of the nation dates back to the Middle Ages (Le Goff 151). In this regard, Anderson's distinction between the nation as an imagined com-munity and the nation-state is as pertinent as it is illuminating. Boyarin

---

[3] Le Goff's collected essays on the topic of history and memory first appeared in Italy in 1977 under the title *Storia e Memoria*. His arguments on the origin of the mod-ern nation did of course not benefit from Anderson's arguments as to the New World origin of nationalism and nation. Anderson's critique of the ailing and determining Eurocentricism present on almost all of the literature on nationalism and nation is indeed well taken.

makes another further and useful distinction between an ethnic nation and the nation-state. The ethnic nation or the medieval idea of nation is a concept grounded on a genealogically defined people who hold on to a memory of common origins or common birth. In this sense the idea of nation is closely linked to the Latin *nasci* from which it derives (Boyarin 1-38), but it does not mean an imagined community in Anderson's sense of the term.

Le Goff's notion of the nation as a new divinity or as sacred fatherland establishes a profound link with the writing and reading of history, for it is in the practices of memorialization of the dead and the shape and features ascribed to the father's land where the nation both appears and is sustained.[4] However, the link between the practices that memorialize the dead—writing of history, erection of statues, tombs, public ritual, poetry and novels, museums—and the territory designated as the "fatherland" have not always been self evident.

Ernest Renan launched a radical questioning of the constitutive series of ideas that had come to compose the nation: shared immemorial occupation of a territory, common religion, language, traditions, and race. Renan delivered his influential lecture "What is a Nation?" at La Sorbone in 1882. He bluntly asked: "Upon what criterion... should one base... national right? By what sign shall we know it? From what tangible fact can one derive it?" (13).

It is worth going over Renan's concerns here, for each and every one of the principles that he questions as the proper foundations of the nation pertain to ideas that prove crucial to claims for "national" autonomy in the colonial situation. For instance, Renan's preoccupation with national legitimacies is not restricted to the legal question. He is also concerned with problems of unity and homogeneity in and of the population. At the core of the legal problem lies the question of permanent occupation of the land, to wit, the most obvious tangible sign. Renan puzzles over the

[4] Le Goff notes that until the nineteenth century history was not regularly taught in schools in France. Aristotle had excluded it from the sciences and medieval universities did likewise. With the French Revolution the teaching and writing of history received a new impetus. It is taught in primary, secondary, and university education. The nineteenth century ensured the diffusion of historical culture among the masses (Le Goff 152). See also Benedict Anderson on Jules Michelet and the emplotment of French national history (197-199). Of course the key text here is Hayden White's *Metahistory: The Historical Imagination in the Nineteenth Century*.

republican challenge to the idea of right by dynastic (conquest) rule. If after the French Revolution dynasties can be deemed illegitimate and therefore dynastic rule can no longer provide the basis for either right nor unity, does the "permanent" occupation of a territory by a given "race" confer upon the people "primordial right"? Renan considers the substitution of the divine right of kings for what he calls the "ethnographic principle" a "grave error"(13) for it could eventually destroy European Civilization. The principle of the "primordial right of races" could give legitimacy to the autonomy claims of numberless ethnic groups at the time already subsumed under the existing European nation-states. Instead of tangible evidence of territorial occupation he opts for a vague and somewhat mystical culturalist model in which besides and beyond anthropological specificities there are universal "things" such as reason, truth, and beauty (25).

Surprisingly, Renan also tries to dismantle the link between nation and language. As if abiding by the opening statement of his essay—nations are forged as much by the operation of forgetting as they are by the work of memory—the French historian states that France "has never sought to earn unity of language by coercive measures" (16). In this statement Renan forgets the on going process of turning peasants into Frenchman (Weber).[5] However, what Renan has in mind for his critique on the language-nation sequence is the work of comparative philology and its links to archeology, which together bring back the ethnographic principle. If languages are to be regarded as signs of race, Renan reasons, then linguistic theory carries within it the same disabling dangers as the ethnographic claims. He reasons that neither the specificity of language or religion nor the idea of "the people's" occupation of the territory in question are sufficiently safe grounds on which to establish the claims of the nation.[6]

[5] Homi Bhabha in "DissemiNation: Time, Narrative, and the Margins of the Modern Nation" points out that Renan's thesis on forgetting does not apply uniformly. Subaltern groups are invited to carry out the heavier part of the forgetting. Such forgetting leads to a homogenization of memory and the writing of history. This is especially relevant in colonial situations in which power asymmetries constitute the foundation of the lived world: "Non-hegemonic sectors of society are obliged to forget" (311).

[6] Anthony D. Smith shows that the European intelligentsias of the late eighteenth and nineteenth century, in inventing the nation, had to breathe life into the past, to create a truly living past. This life-like construction was not achieved by simple antiquarianism. Smith points to the key role played by modern, scientific disciplines—philology,

Renan thus posits the nation as an almost mystical amalgam of "body and soul." Anticipating Anderson, Renan claims that the glue that binds the community is the "sentimental side" (18). Nationality's affect is capable of uniting the soil, as the field of struggle and labor, with the soul, that element that only the spirit (memory?) can furnish. In the end for Renan "man is everything," that is to say culture, in the formation of this sacred bond of nationality. The nation is a *spiritual principle*, the outcome of the "profound complications of history" (19). Eliding his early emphasis on the forgetting that goes on in the making of memory, the constituting principle of nationality turns out to be the possession in common of a rich legacy of memories and the desire to live together (19).

Thus, if the nation is constituted not by territory commonly held, nor by shared language or religion but rather by the possession of common memories about the past, and its being is predicated on the profound imbeddedness of the complications of history, it follows that the nation cannot be improvised, there cannot be "new" nations. The nation, in fact, is the lived (reiterated) memory of the past and it relies on the deployment of the arts or memorializing the dead as Le Goff has pointed out.

For colonial peoples facing the task of establishing a discourse capable of legitimizing not only self-rule but also the repossession of the territory lost to the colonizing powers, the complications of history and the reiterated memory of the past are not so simple. Renan's views pose a challenge rather than a possibility. A reiterated memory of the past is a task of deliberate construction in a colonial and postcolonial situation. The same can be said for elucidating the complications of history. Renan's two

anthropology, history, sociology, folklore and archeology—in the translation of the "idealized images of the ethnic past into tactile realities" (180). Smith makes a distinction between the work of "returning intelligentsias" and "secular intelligentsias." It would seem that Renan's rejection of the ethnic principle and the rooting work of philology arises, in part, as a critique of the Romantic interest in ruins and landscape prevalent in the desire to build ethnic nations in Europe as well as the interest in archeology and philology that followed in the wake of the Napoleonic invasion of Egypt. Smith observes "how this desire for physical tangibility and verisimilitude invaded European intellectual and aesthetic consciousness"(181). This resulted in "a growing awareness of the differences between heritages and pasts that had previously been conflated. From the 1760s a controversy raged between partisans of the 'Roman past'.... and the purer, linear Greek aesthetic heritage" (181). Philology and even lexicography were "pressed into service by the 'returning intelligentsia' with its vision of a didactive past and of history as a salvation-drama" (181).

claims assume an always already shared and homogeneous "history" and "memory" in part induced by forgetting. But the given of a colonial situation is that the memory of the past is disputed, contradictory, multiple, and contestatory. Thus the very issues that Renan wishes to banish from the discussion on the construction of nations and nationalism—primordial right to territorial occupation, ethnographic principle, linkage between language-nation and "race"—are to be found playing key roles in the discourse on the nation in postcolonial situations. Here, archeology provides the discursive space where these issues unfold as the "new," but rather old, postcolonial nations rise from the ruins of conquest.

III. IMPERIALISM, NATION AND ARCHEOLOGY

Implicit in both Le Goff's and Renan's idea of the nation is the operation of mapping a narrative (history) onto a territory (fatherland). This narrative anchored onto concepts of origin, agency, population, self-identity, memory of dead ancestors, and heroes takes hold onto a territory that is delimited as the scenario of lived space.[7] Conceived as a "real place," the space in which we live, the set of social relations which bounds us, the nation becomes the stage upon which a people who hold onto a tradition and deploy a force onto the past in order to establish cultural boundaries. The modern concept of nation, predicated on a single line of homogeneous time, responds to the notion of a "sharply bounded, continuously occupied space, controlled by a single sovereign state, comprising a set of autonomous and yet essentially identical individuals" (Boyarin 2).[8]

Boyarin points out eighteenth-century views on "space" and "time," as cognitive categories, are fueled by the West's colonialist project of "mapping the world" (6). This project holds time as a dynamic and energy-loaded (history) arrow that traverses "dead" and static space (6-7). This very emphasis on geography is taken up by colonized peoples as they

[7] "Lived space" is a term introduced by Henri Lefevre to mean a socially created spatiality. Lived space is not far from Foucault's sense of "real place," that is, the space in which we live, the set of social relations, the heterogeneous spaces of sites and relations, the heterotopias that constitute every society. See Soja (142-143).

[8] Gramsci observed that "in France the meaning of the 'national' already includes a more politically elaborated notion of the 'popular' because it is related to the concept of 'sovereignty': national sovereignty have, or had, the same value" (208).

embark on the struggle for emancipation. Demarcating the ground of the nation, stamping the lived spaces with the time of origin and durability of the colonized ground, demanded that the nationalist claims reconnoiter the possibility and potential of geographic discourses.

For Boyarin, when collective consciousness was articulated in the context of a struggle against European imperialism, colonials adopted the notion that collective identity, and hence both loyalty and legitimate exercise of power, was determined by spatial relations. "By the end of the nineteenth century, then, the contest was for control of space rather than its definition" (Boyarin 9).

If geographic expeditions, with the scientist-explorer at the center, produced the "known" world for Europe and its "others" at the end of the eighteenth and throughout the nineteenth centuries, archeology and its close links to comparative linguistics, remapped the globe with a countervailing wind. The force of archeology acted counter to the spatial dissemination of navigation in the hands of exploration. Geographic mapping of territories allowed colonials to stake foundational grounds on which to build the house of the future nation.

However, the future alone is never enough. For the future to acquire direction and become the shared will to "live together" as Renan put it, a shared past is the necessary and indispensable condition. Archeology proved crucial for colonial peoples engaged in the endeavor of "inventing" a nation and indeed in deploying the ethnographic principle as a positive force on which to base their claims to legitimate struggles for self-rule. Archeology had the capacity to literally "dig" the people into the ground and thus establish an inalienable link to the past as lived space. In doing so it also proves the unbelonging of the colonizer.

Perhaps even more important than the material link to the land, archeology, for the peoples "without history," enables the conversion of collective memory into tradition and maybe even into history.[9] Tradition—the transmission of collective memory from generation to generation—in the sight of archeological monuments can attempt to close the generational gap, the rupture between father and son, which makes of tradition the lesser of the arts of memory. Tradition in the sight of archeology comes

[9] Let us not forget that the keeping of written records of the past has been, since Herodotus' expedition onto the Scythians, the West's requirement for parity with its "others."

closer to the production of the smooth and homogeneous timeline of history. In *The Ethnic Origin of Nations* (1986), speaking of the European deployment of archeology in the nineteenth century, Anthony D. Smith points out that "Archeology has been perhaps the most useful of disciplines in recovering communal pasts... The material remains uncovered bring home to us, as only tactile objects can, the physical immediacy of former eras and archaic peoples, lending vivid substance to the records of chronicles and epics" (180-181). For the (modern), postcolonial nation, archeology—sites in place—spatializes on the surface of a re-reconnoitered and rationalized territory, clearly demarcated by linguistic and immemorial boundaries, the place of the communal past and present.

But nothing in the vagaries of mapping the world or the rise of nationalism is actually that simple. While the globe was being both expanded and contracted by faster and better means of communication, it was also being "compressed and controlled by the growth of capitalism" (Harvey 240). The new knowledges brought along by explorers and scientists such as Humboldt and Darwin, in the cases of Spanish America had the effect of setting forth a number of local knowledges and forces that, in time, would partially shift intellectual production and control to the formerly colonial (objects) subjects.

The processes involved in the production of power-knowledge were not always unidirectional, that is to say from Europe to America. As with Garcilaso de la Vega, Inca, the undisputed founder of nationalist ideology in the Andes and perhaps for all of Spanish America (Brading 255-273, 483-491), colonial subjects proved capable of managing the imperial power-knowledge machine in order to contest oppressive discourses and identities spewed out of the colonizing archive. Before Humboldt brought to Europe's attention the importance and grandeur of Inca and Aztec engineering and architecture the Jesuit Francisco Javier Clavijero (1731-1787), taking up Sigüenza y Góngora's (1645-1700) earlier interests in Aztec antiquities, wrote his *Historia antigua de México* (1780). For Clavijero, Aztec codices, maps, sculpture, and ruins were not just eloquent historical sources but the living presence of the past. It is interesting to note however that while Humboldt's visit to Peru in 1802 fueled an already existing interest in ruins and the pre-conquest past, the text that constitutes Humboldt's own guide as he makes his way down the cordillera from Quito to Lima is none other than the *Comentarios reales* by Garcilaso de la Vega, Inca (Núñez, *Alexander* 69-71, 106, 127, 192-198). Nevertheless, and despite his secondary interest in the Amerindian past, Humboldt's visits and descriptions of ruins in Mexico and Peru validated and promoted the incipient curiosity in local intellectual circles.[10]

IV. ANDEAN SITES OF MEMORY

In the fourth part of this essay I want to examine and compare the making of the so-called proto-nationalist project of Túpac Amaru II with the rise of national history and its link to archeology in the two decades immediately after independence. I will argue that the difference between the terms of the Andean Utopia expressed in the Túpac Amaru II movement and the later archeological vision of the nation as inalienable territory entails a paradigm shift. Such a shift is, on the one hand, grounded on the specificity of the lived local Andean knowledges, and, on the other, on its finely attuned and yet dissonant concordance with a growing sense of the past as "other" during the long nineteenth century.

The deployment of the sites of memory will serve me as a pivotal point around which I will seek to establish the shift. In the case of the national construction entailed in the Túpac Amaru II movement I find memory practices embodied in the lived organic discourse that ties the present to the past as the living memory that guides everyday practices. The past as present is immediately perceptible; it is in sight of the whole Andean collectivity and fills the coordinates of the lived space. That is why the ideal of restoration is possible. The social memory of the past registers a sense of presentness. It is the living past that enables subjects to engage in testimonies that preserve memory as a seamless web with the lived world. Memory, after the defeat of Túpac Amaru II and the cruel and inhuman punishment imposed on his followers, momentarily orients the thinking on the nation towards the future exclusively inasmuch as memory of the past enters into the silence of trauma and the full crisis of independence. Contemporary Andean historians register this cut from the lived space of the past with as a significant silence in the making of the nation's history. That resounding silence was brought about by the strict

[10] See Humboldt. See also Chapter Four, "The Age of Reason" in Bernal. See also Poole.

censorship imposed by the Spanish authorities after the execution of Túpac Amaru II.[11] The national subject would seem to lack a place from where to speak the self in either time or space. Porras Barrenechea writes that the writing of national history during the early decades of the republic was given almost no attention. The message of the aboriginal cultures, Porras Barrenechea says, seems now far away, and indeed postponed indefinitely. And the republican present did not seem important. The nation's history was not taught either in schools nor at the universities (Porras Barrenechea 437). Not until the appearance of *Paisajes peruanos* (1912; 1955) by José de la Riva Agüero, will the nation emerge as a continuous time-space construct. In this regard it is not insignificant that the first "history" of the Peruvian past is authored by a foreigner. William Prescott's *History of the Conquest of Peru* (1847) remains unrivaled until the end of the nineteenth century. The silence of history will find in antiquarian collections, field trips, and emotional but unsystematic exploration of ruins the point of enunciation for a new discourse on the nation as past and present and the link between the dead and the living.

The deployment of memory and the constitution of the past/present during the Age of Andean Insurrection (1720-1790) has been studied and clarified in the work of path-breaking ethno-historians.[12] Both José Gabriel Condorcanqui (1738-81), better known as Túpac Amaru II, and Juan Santos Atahualpa (n.d.), based their claims to authority and leadership on the idea of direct descent from the Incas (ethnographic nation). The underlining assumption was that the rebels would restore the cosmological as well as the social, economic, political, and affective order of the past. The contract between the rebel "Incas" and their followers, be they the Cuzco aristocracy or the peasantry at large, came about on the basis of a shared, living memory. The sense of place, the space of lived social relations, the heterotopic[13] character of the Andean memory con-

---

[11] In *Fuentes históricas peruanas* Raúl Porras Barrenechea writes that: "Se dio poca importancia a la historia nacional en las primeras décadas de la república. Rotas las tradiciones que nos unían con España, lejano y pospuesto el mensaje de las culturas primitivas se concedió poca importancia al presente republicano... La historia no ocupa un puesto en la inquietud cultural ni en los programas de los colegios y universidades" (473).

[12] See Flores Galindo *Túpac Amaru II-1780* and *Buscando un Inca*. See also Burga.

[13] See Foucault on heterotopia in "Of Other Spaces."

stituted the conditions of possibility for the restorative ambition of the Neo-Inca projects.[14]

For John Rowe the "going back" in the dressing fashion of the *curacas* indicates, in a thesis contrary to the claims made by the *Invention of Tradition*, that "es notable la autenticidad del estilo inca de los trajes" and that "la tradición inca [permanecía] auténtica y viva" (23). Manuel Burga has documented the sites of memory—ritual processions, clothing, insignia, food, language, altars, theater—deployed by the Neo-Inca revival of the Andean elites. These were visual spaces that competed with alphabetic memory, for they also bore the capacity to retain and disseminate the narrative of Inca ancestry well beyond the limits of print media. Around the middle of the eighteenth century "a veritable cult of Inca antiquity flourished in the old Inca capital. Public ceremonies, *curacas* dressed as Incas, flags, conch shells and symbols of the sun" (Klarén 116) were regularly displayed in view of a public which comprised all sectors of society, including the Spanish clergy which, for reasons of their own, chose to look the other way.

Inspiration for Neo-Inca revivalism is attributed almost unanimously[15] to the republication and wide circulation of Garcilaso de la Vega's *Comentarios reales* (1609) in 1722. While in this case one could cite the power of print, reading, and orally disseminating the multiple contents and rhetorics of Garcilaso's long, complex, and heavy book stands a long way from the print effects of newspapers, the serialization of novels and pamphlets. The reading of Garcilaso proved "incendiary" among the Indian gentry (Brading 490). Túpac Amaru II carried the book with him as he travelled the Andes with his mule trains. It is thus not farfetched to imagine the easy passage and mixing of the contents and affects of the *Comentarios reales* into the mainly oral and visual culture of the period.

---

[14] John Rowe in "El movimiento nacional inca del siglo XVIII" argues that after three generations of Jesuit education the *curacas* had forgotten Inca religion (21). However, "donde se nota más la fuerza de la tradición cultural inca es en el traje... En estos cuadros se nota algo sorprendente; se ha dado un paso atrás en la adopción de las modas europeas y se muestran los nobles incas con vestidos más tradicionales que los que aparecen en los dibujos de Guamán Poma" (22).

[15] See Brading; Flores Galindo; Burga; Klarén.

In fact the Bishop of Cuzco, Juan Manuel de Moscoso y Peralta, attributed directly the force and restorative clarity of the rebellion to the reading of the forbidden book. The Bishop reasoned that "if the *Comentarios* of Garcilaso had not been the reading and instruction of the insurgent... Túpac Amaru would not have embarked on the detestable audacity of his rebellion" (Brading 491). But the moment of revelation for the Bishop was not yet over. Under the urgency created by the present, the Bishop suffered yet another illumination. In his letter to the *corregidor* Arreche and during the siege of Cuzco (1781) the Bishop realized that he had been blind to the meanings of the cultural space he had been "sharing" with the Andeans under his tutelage. The Bishop had not been decoding the Andean colonial sites of memory—dress, food, Quechua theater, ritual dance, even landscape and architecture—which for a reading- and writing-centered sense of culture and communication must have seemed nothing other than silent objects not worth an intellectual's attention.

Incendiary as the *Comentarios* may have been, it alone could not have created the possibilities for insurgency. It is actually its convergence with the constant sight of Inca portraits and costumes that kept alive the Inca past that enabled the insurgents to imagine the past as a Golden Age. In retrospect Bishop Moscoso grew more and more disturbed at the Spaniard's oversight. It was a blunder to allow the Indians to make and publicly display their fabled ancestors in no lesser place than the Jesuit Colegio de San Francisco de Borja, for "the Indians are a species of rational beings who are more impressed by what they see than by what they are told" (Brading 491).

It would seem that the Bishop of Cuzco, even in his retrospective wisdom, forgot the events of the Taqui-Oncoy (Millones), as well as the campaigns for the extirpation of idolatries that consumed the Andes in the fires of evangelization only a century before his watch. Both the Taqui-Oncoy and the confessions made to José de Arriaga by the priests of the *huacas* in the Lurín valley, better known today as the *Myths of Huarochirí*, remain as telling documents on the Andean resistance to the extirpation of local memory. However, the memory of the injury to the colonial state by the priests and *curacas* of the sixteenth century proved to be only too well and alive. The colonial state followed the execution of Túpac Amaru II and the destruction of his family with the *quintado*, that is the execution of every fifth able-bodied male in every one of the tupamarista villages (Klarén 191). This measure was meant put an end to all local intellectuals. The Europeanized and highly educated Indian elite withered. It was silenced. Túpac Amaru's proto-nationalist and counter hegemonic insurgency came to an end with the physical disappearance of the bodies of the *curacas* who, by rule of descent, constituted a site of memory and thus provided, like the king's body in France, a link with the past of the nation as a set of indivisible biological and cultural relations in space and time.[16]

In a more present-oriented study, Flores Galindo in *Buscando un Inca* (1987) examines the survival of the millennial (oral) narrative tradition of the Incarrí and the ritual dances which themselves relate the past in conjunction with an understanding of the present world of each community, the ritualization of food, drink, and dress as expressive vehicles of subject identities. I would add that at stake in this massive display of ritual is the production of time and space as a set of bridges over repeated fractures. These are strategies which enable Indians to think out of their own knowledges and practices the "right" to occupy and use the land. While this memorialization of tradition does not make use of the alphabet and as a whole has been deemed "oral," upon closer reflection it is obvious that it is neither oral nor subterranean as Flores Galindo characterized it (*Buscando* 90, 93). It is in fact a visibility coded in signs and systems of signification which go well beyond the power of alphabetic memory sites such as books, novels, and newspapers.

With the exception of the narrative of Incarrí, all the other sites of memory examined by Galindo and Burga represent forceful visual and oral forms of encoding memory and subjectivity which, at any time, can be deciphered and re-encoded into linguistic constructs of different kinds and genres. Ritual dance does indeed tell stories but its deployment is not by linguistic means until another form of cognition interpellates it. It involves codification of body movements, costumes (color and design) in conjunction with music (sound and rhythm) which acquire meaning as they come together in a dynamic combination, publicly displayed on a specific day of the calendar that organizes the passage of time for the community of interpreters. The linguistic dimension accompanying ritual

---

[16] Despite the fact that the nineteenth century is also a very long century in the Andes, it is beyond the scope of this essay to examine the sites of memory in the more than 100 Indian rebellions of the Age of Andean Insurrection and the many others that were to follow into the twentieth century. See Flores Galindo, *Buscando un Inca*.

dancing is of course in Quechua, itself a constant presence linking the past to the present. The same can be said of all other performances—dress, food, medicine. They represent a coherent overlapping of many cultural codes which, when decoded in the power of language, represent powerful passages between past and present.

In contrast with print culture, these spacio-temporal passages involve the theatricalization of belief and practice. Like Inca and post-Inca *tablas* (*quicllas*) and plays, they encode a memory that requires an ever-renewed and flexible community of interpreters who can at once produce the same text and adapt it to the changing re-interpretative conditions. However these visual (linguistic+) representations of the past cannot in any way be considered subterranean as Flores Galindo stated, for they need the light of day and the participation of the whole interpretative community to ensure their validity and survival. On the contrary, it is print culture with its demand for individual and silent operation of the interpretative act that is more likely to produce a subterranean world of knowledge and feeling. The non-alphabetic, public Andean traditions which converged in the Túpac Amaru II rebellion produced a visibility in Foucaultian terms.

The force of the event was dispersed with the *quintado* and re-absorbed into the practices of everyday (Quechua) life, but it, like the Inca or the Incarrí, did not disappear. Food and dress rituals continued. Dances and commemorations repeated themselves with the regularity of the seasons. Above all, the land, dotted as it was with *chacras, apus,* and *huacas* remained as "silent" but signifying sites in which the connection with the past was re-elaborated. The heterotopic character of Andean space-time was not smoothed over by the defeat of Túpac Amaru II, but it did pull apart the convergence of memory sites that made the rebellion thinkable.

V. LOCAL KNOWLEDGES AND PARADIGM SHIFTS

After the execution of Túpac Amaru (1782) the/a "national" project centered in Cuzco had spent all its force, and the idea of the nation reappeared, in a shift, with the Amantes del País in Lima. The young creoles witnessed with disquiet a new twist in the colonizing process. The age of scientific exploration was re-positioning the time-space they inhabited. From a place valued for its mineral wealth, Peru was now seen in the metropolis as a place plentiful in the data necessary for the completion of the global mapping of the world undertaken by a swiftly modernizing Europe. Under the Enlightenment's new knowledge requirements and its new conception of the past, the colonials' incipient vision of the past suffered yet another complication and entered more decidedly than ever into new zones of uncertainty and contradiction from those already capitalized in Garcilaso's struggle with historiography.

Neither the cooperation nor the permission of the creole elite was necessary for the new science to enter (in Edward Said's sense) the land. In fact, visits to Lima by the new explorers and scientists, left the creoles with the distinct impression that they were "behind" in the homogenous time-space that Anderson posits as the horizon for the "creole pioneers." Their knowledge warehouse regarding their "own" land appeared indeed empty and the place where they would fill it was not the local scene but rather where the scientists came from. Intellectually and emotionally underequipped to begin to reconnoiter the multiple dimensions of the time-space which they had dubiously understood but undoubtedly inherited, they began their own voyage in the opposite direction. New knowledges—geography, physics, botany, mineralogy—were the goods sought by the Lima elite.

It is well known that the Enlightenment brought an "*aliento nacionalista.*" Its interest in geography, fauna, and flora did not fail to inspire an interest in the past in people like the members of the learned society Amantes del País. According to Porras Barrenechea, *the Mercurio Peruano* "se inquieta por desentrañar el pasado espiritual del Perú" (473). In 1816 the Viceroy Rodríguez de Mendoza puzzled over the absence of historical and geographical knowledge. Ignoring or forgetting the orders issued by Charles V prohibiting the writing of history and of the Indian's "*antiguallas,*" the Viceroy interpellates no one and everyone at the same time when he asks: "Y qué razón hay para ignorar la geografía e historia del suelo en que pisamos?" (Porras Barrenechea 473) It seems also that the Viceroy's questions gloss over the fact that with the expulsion of the Jesuits in 1767 there occurred a "loss of management and entrepreneurial efficiency [intimately connected] to the Jesuits establishment of teachers colleges, schools and universities in Lima and Cuzco" (Klarén 101) as well as an incipient but strong interest in the writing of local "American" histories.

VI. Mexico: A Case in Point

The most salient loss in geography and history was of course the departure of the exiled Jesuit Clavijero (1731-1787) who had begun to write his *Historia antigua de México* (1780) while still in Mexico and expecting to be appointed to the newly created chair in Antiquities at the Real Pontificia Universidad (Bernal 14). Clavijero laments the loss of the sources that Sigüenza y Góngora (1645-1700) had so lovingly accumulated on Mexican antiquity. The Jesuit sees himself following in the footsteps of the foundational gestures of the first "mexicanist".[17] Like Sigüenza y Góngora, and also in emulation of Garcilaso, but in contrast with the Amantes del País, Clavijero states that his "desire is to advance the claims of both strands of inheritance" (Bernal 52). For Clavijero, Mexico's glory and possible nationhood meant the relation of the ancient past (Aztec) to the present (postcolonial).

In this regard Ignacio Bernal points out that "Mexican patriotism saw itself as a cultural and not a political matter" (54). Anticipating Renan, for Sigüenza y Góngora, Clavijero and the Nahuatl scholar Augustín de Vetancourt, culture and nation were not only equivalent but in fact depended on each other (Bernal 54). For them, as in the case of the Cuzco elite, the sites of culture-nation were the original Indian records, books (*códices*), "maps," sculptures, calendar stones, temples and pyramids, "myths," and accounts of the past. The fortuitous but consequential presence of Leonardo Boturini, who arrived in Mexico in 1736, contributed strongly, if strangely, to further the equivalence between nation and culture.

Boturini's affection for and obsession with Sigüenza's papers and collection of antiquities led to the catastrophic confiscation of the collection by the Spanish authorities in Mexico. The collection continued to suffer important losses even later in Spain where Boturini had sought refuge for and with what he salvaged as he fled Mexico persecuted by the colonial authorities. His *Idea de una Nueva Historia General de la América Septentrional* (1746), largely based on Giambatista Vico's ideas on history, reopened the question of the origins of the American Indians and

---

[17] The "Sociedades Económicas de Amigos del País" which proved crucial to the development of Spanish American intellectuals at the time of the Enlightenment, owe their origin, partly, to the stress that the Padre Benito Jerónimo Feijóo (1676-1764) placed on experience and direct observation in learning (Bernal 72).

the problems involved in thinking of history in universal (homogeneous time-space) terms.[18] Although Boturini's work met with something less than success, it prompted Clavijero's sense of urgency about his own project. It clarified the need for the institutionalization of the study of the Mexican past, conceived as a line which led directly to the origins of the Amerindian peoples. Ignacio Bernal notes that when the hearing of Boturini's case regarding his unauthorized stay in Mexico and the possession of parts of the confiscated collection was over in Spain, the Consejo de Indias recommended the founding in the capital of New Spain of an Academia de la Historia de México (Bernal 61).

No such thought ever crossed the minds of the Spanish authorities who put down the Túpac Amaru II rebellion, despite the fact that many of the measures taken in the aftermath of the rebellion implicitly and explicitly recognized the culturalist nature of the nationalist thinking now recognized as "ahead" of its time. Perhaps the fact that Boturini was an Italian working with Vico's ideas and the fact that he seemed to be dealing mainly with alphabetic encoding of memory records weighed on the minds of the Spanish authorities and caused them to think of Boturini's history as an enterprise of their own. Perhaps even more important in the reception of Boturini's work by the Spanish authorities was the fact that the French Revolution had not yet occurred.

At any rate, the Amantes del País in Peru did not pass in silence the racist and anti-American views of the Enlightenment. Like Clavijero, in trying to bring forth the evidence that would sustain their claims regarding the intelligence and accomplishment of Amerindians, the Amantes del País wrote in 1791 an entire edition of the *Mercurio Peruano* dedicated to Peruvian antiquities, ruins, and monuments (Porras Barrenechea 57). They took special notice of Cornelius de Pauw and the generally negative judgements on the Peruvian and pre-Columbian past consigned in the *Encyclopedia*.

Ignacio Bernal points out that many of the Jesuits exiled in Rome, informed by their many years of residence in Ibero-America, were infu-

---

[18] It is well known that Boturini's idea of history as a time construct derived from Vico's (1668-1744) *Scienza Nova* (1725), itself based on the study of Roman law. Following Vico's division of the temporal line Boturini envisions three breaks as a way of organizing his knowledge of Mexico's past: a divine world (the time of the Gods), a heroic world (the time of the heroes) and a time of man (Bernal 59).

riated by the thesis on American inferiority developed by the towering intellectual figures of the time (David Hume, Buffon, Hegel etc). Clavijero wrote especially to counter-attack the work of the Encyclopedist de Pauw in his *Recherches Philosophiques sur les Américaine* (1768) (Bernal 68-74). Because Clavijero was in Italy, he based his work mainly on papers and Aztec paintings. But he could not emphasize strongly enough the importance of ruins and monuments for history writing as well as the need to preserve them as the chief evidence of the nation's glorious past. Thus the connection of the nation to the ruins of past remains is already established by Clavijero.

VII. THE EMERGENCE OF AN ARCHEO-SPACE

It is significant to remember that the first history of Mexico appears before the Wars of Independence, while in the case of Peru the nation will have to wait for a whole century before the thinking of the past achieves a disposition which permits the emergence of a line, jagged and broken as it may be, of causes and effects. The past, as the time of the dead ancestors, will first appear in the discourse of the nation as the work of archeology. The nation then slowly emerges as an archeo-space that both marks and erases the distance from the past. A new archeo-space is born where the landmarks bear names such as Pachacamac, Chavín, Tiahuanaco and Chan-Chan.[19]

[19] Archeology has recently been the object of a postmodern critique. Finding meaning in the past is no longer a simple and transparent objective act of knowledge for archaeologists. The interpretation of material culture is now being carefully examined in its practices and history. Henrietta Moore in "The Problems of Origins: Poststructuralism and Beyond" examines the sensitive link between archeology and origins and points to the fact that "narratives in archeology and anthropology often mislead, and they mislead because they present themselves as concerned with beginnings"(51). She warns that "our stories of the past must end with the present... our representations of the past are shaped not by what we know to be true of the past, but by what we believe to be true of the past" (51). I have already pointed out that I was going to treat the many approaches to the construction of the past that the writing of history entails in a Benjaminian way, inasmuch as the past is always approached from the urgency of the present. Moore's concerns dovetail with my own genealogical approach. In this regard, Ian Hodder's questions on context and the reading of material culture as a text are also important for any study dealing with archeology and its hermeneutical power. See Hodder.

One could argue that the defeat of the proto-nationalist project had a paralyzing effect on the thinking of the nation. As in the case of the French revolution, the Túpac Amaru II rebellion produced a breach with the immediate past which in some ways began to be seen as "other." In France, as the country began to change from a rural society into a place of urban dwellers, there occurred a "massive disruption of traditional forms of memory... [and] the past begins to look like a foreign country" (Terdinan 5). The institution of memory, and thus the question of history, became a critical preoccupation. Intellectuals began an inquiry into what was to be called the "modern" as distinct from the past. No greater contrast could be drawn than with the bleak historical scene in Peru in which the sequence of two great breaks with the past produced the incontestable silence of the nineteenth century.

At issue is the conception of the past. If memory is the key agent in the construction of the past, the would-be historian in Peru encounters immediately the disquieting lack of transparency of the written and unwritten records of the past. The facts of conquest made the recording of memory always already a problematic modality for access to the past. Instead of establishing records, narratives, and subjects, memory in the plural seems to breed controversy, alternative knowledges, and disputed accounts. Something more solid and less plurivocal and contestable than the accounts of the Spanish chroniclers is needed in order to provide the foundations on which the house of the nation can be built.

It is widely acknowledged that the father of modern, scientific archeology in Peru was the German scholar Max Uhle, whose long residence and undisputed authority in and on Peru was encapsulated in the fact that between 1906 and 1912 he was the director of the Museo Histórico de Lima (Porras Barrenechea 73). Uhle's scientific studies (measuremts of monuments and sites in combination with stratigraphic excavation and regional chronology) (Bahn 195-196) of ruins and other archeological monuments is not without important precedents. In fact, it is almost impossible to separate the history of archeology in Peru during the first half of the nineteenth century from the history of scientific travel and exploration.

In his search for historical sources, Porras Barrenechea lists only one prominent local collector of antiquities: the opulent *limeño* businessman Pedro Bravo de Lagunas (n.d.). Another person mentioned by Porras Barrenechea is Llano Zapata who apparently wrote a memoir in which he described "restos incaicos de templos, acueductos y caminos" (Porras Barrenechea 57). As a landscape configured by ruins, as a territory of interest because of its connection to antiquities, as an archeo-space, Peru begins to make brief but repeated appearances in the travelogues of scientists and explorers. In these texts the past is not only "other," due to its remoteness in time, but it is also other because of its remoteness in spatial distance from Europe and its cultural distance from both the past and modern times in European time-space. The ruins stand out in their grandeur but their allure is underscored precisely by the neglect and even remoteness with which the local intellectuals regard them. "Hieratic" and "hermetic" are the preferred adjectives intended to describe the monuments. Upon a closer look it is clear that both "hieratic" and "hermetic" speak more accurately of the scientist's sense of his own incapacity to read the monument that of the monument's own semiotic status. However this very sense of labored or impossible interpretation is what makes depicting the ruins irresistible especially to the explorer who includes in his retinue a good draftsman, as Humboldt did.

The French traveler and botanist José Dombey (in Peru between 1778 and 1785) left perhaps the most lasting impression among Peruvians (Riviale).[20] Dombey was the first "scientist" to venture beyond Lima. In *Imagen francesa del Perú: siglos XVI-XIX* (1976) Pablo Macera[21] indicates that most of Dombey's originals were lost in the fire that he set to his papers after returning to France. Nevertheless it is known that he kept a

---

[20] Writing from a French point of view, Pascal Riviale says that the first eye-witness information about Peru to arrive in France is the product of the commercial route opened by the merchants of Saint-Malo at the beginning of the eighteenth century. This was followed by the reports of educated travelers such as Feuillée in 1714, Frézier in 1716, and Le Gentil in 1727. He adds that "Las instrucciones 'etnográficas' remitidas por el Abad Barthelemy al botánico Joseph Dombay constituyen una interesante ilustración de las modificaciones sobrevenidas tanto en la percepción que se tenía del Perú y de las fuentes documentales útiles como en la manera de enfocar éstas" (24).

[21] According to Macera, until the publication of the results of Charles-Marie de la Condamine's expedition (1751) most of what the French knew about Peru was derived from the *Comentarios reales*. Slowly ideas derived from the Spanish chronicler began to be displaced by the knowledge amassed by the explorations to America (30-34). Dombey's works follow in the foot steps of La Condamine although it is important to remember here that most of Dombey's work is lost (41). Nevertheless, he is the first naturalist who travels to the interior of Peru and also the first to attempt a close examination of Pachacamac (44-45).

botanical and an archeological diary. He visited and measured Pachaca-mac, and upon his return he took some fine Paracas textiles and 400 *hua-cos* intended as gifts for Louis XIV.[22] Macera says that "hasta Dombey la arqueología no existía en el Perú" (59).

Humboldt's arrival in 1802, his admiration for the "simplicity, sym-metry, solidity and consistency" (Porras Barrenechea 58) of Inca archi-tecture[23] closes the eighteenth century's views on archeology, leaving one puzzling message to the incipient groupings of intellectuals in Peru.[24] Despite the disparaging views expressed by the Encyclopedists, the rem-nants of the pre-Columbian past were the subject of interest and even admiration to those who actually did come and experienced sensorially the scope and features of the territory.[25] If archeological preoccupations were the province of the travelers, digging was still in the hands of the *huaqueros* with the notable exception of a "peruano aireado en Europa"

---

[22] Macera writes that while in Peru Dombey was physically attacked by the Span-ish members of the Ruiz and Pavón expedition with the intention to rob him of his research. The botanist Ortega coveted Dombey's botanical collection and in fact mod-eled the *Flora Peruviana* on the method and classification grid brought by Dombey. When Dombey returned to France in 1785 he was, at the age of 43, in broken health. "Calvo, con escorbuto, sin dientes, resentido con su gobierno y con la corte de Madrid, se retiró a Lyon casi loco y en un momento de desesperación quemó los orig-inales de la obra que pensaba dedicar a Luis XVI" (59).

[23] Humboldt attributed all architecture, roads, and aqueducts in Peru to the Incas. His imagination did not encompass the existence of other highly sophisticated pre-Inca cultures.

[24] In 1839 the French scientist Alcide d'Orbigny (1802-1857) published his *L'Homme Américaine* in which he proposed a new classification of Amerindian "races." The American physiologist Samuel George Morton had just published his *Crania Americana* (1839). Based on cranial measurements taken from his world-wide skull collection, Morton concluded that there was not a single human species but sev-eral, each with a separate origin. D'Orbigny, basing his arguments on data collected during his stay in Bolivia (1830-1833), proved Morton incorrect. These two studies opened the nineteenth century's debates on the origin and diversity of the Amerendian peoples. Despite the fact that d'Orbigny spent only a couple of months in Peru and was unable to visit any major archeological site, the long-standing debate of the origin of Amerindian peoples is very much in Rivero's mind and research. In his book he gives a detailed account of the latest episodes in the debate and contests any view that posits separate origins. For more on d'Orbigny, see Riviale (22-54).

[25] Porras Barrenechea ratified this state of affairs when he writes that "durante la primera etapa republicana la curiosidad arqueológica es tan solo patrimonio de los huaqueros, [y] algunos coleccionistas empíricos" (53).

(Porras Barrenechea 58). Both Porras Barrenechea and Estuardo Núñez consider Mariano Eduardo Rivero (n.d) "el precursor de nuestra moderna ciencia arqueológica" (Porras Barrenechea 59). This Peruvian, "aired out in Europe," is simply left to desiccate on page 59 of Porras Barrenechea 's own collection of sources for writing the History of Peru. Virtually nothing is available on the life and/or work of Rivero.

VIII. NARRATING THE NATION'S ARCHEO-SPACE

The story of the book Rivero wrote is not only interesting but germane to the matter at hand, for it encapsulates the guiding idea of this chapter: the redefinition of the idea of the nation after the Túpac Amaru II rebellion in light of the establishment of an inextricable timeline between the nation and an archeo-space made possible in "modern" in Peru by the new science of archeology.

The life and work of Mariano Eduardo Rivero appears indelibly intertwined with the life and research of Johann Jakob von Tschudi (1818-1889), the German scholar who arrived in Peru in 1838 with a degree in medicine, but ended up making a major contribution in Quechua linguistics and archeology. Like Dombey, Tschudi was also a naturalist who devoted equal attention to the fauna, flora, geography, and the language of the native people. Despite the fact the Tschudi's major work would eventually result in a study of Quechua and especially of its literary forms and the *Ollantay*,[26] at the time of his arrival in Peru a clear distinction between nature and history still operated in the mind of most explorers and travelers. The "native" people, their costumes and other remnants of their past belonged to the *nature* side of the divide. Language and city building, two instances of collective and individual consciousness, failed to be included on the *history* side. Such a division continued the logic inaugurated with the conquest based as it was on the denial of coevalness.

---

[26] *Apu Ollantay* is one of the Quechua dramas popular in the eighteenth century. It is a Quechua drama written in the pre-conquest Wanka traditional composition style of enacting historical deeds. After the Túpac Amaru II rebellion, the Spanish authorities banned the secular Quechua language theater. The suppression of this drama tradition offers proof of the force that such theater retained for the indigenous sense of identity. For further discussion of the origins and history of Quechua drama in the Andes, see Echevarría (55, 262, 406).

The challenge for Rivero, Tschudi's good friend, guide, and colleague, was to find the knowledge apparatus that would allow him to reverse the ideological assumptions imbedded in the naturalist's episteme. Thus far, ruins had testified not to the past as present but rather to the past as distinct and disconnected from the present.[27] The task of linking the glorious but ruined past to the rising nation fell not to history (documentary and archival) but rather to archeology (visible, tactile and measurable, non-alphabetic). The immediate and unmediated presence of the ruins, like the fauna and flora, appear ready to be taken by the naked eye or by instruments newly designed by science, all of which mimic the visual structures of perception of the eye unfettered by the letter.

Mariano Eduardo Rivero was born in Arequipa and studied in Europe during the first quarter of the nineteenth century (Porras Barrenechea 62). His field of study was mineralogy. It is fair to surmise that his education in Europe was probably aimed at the acquisition of up-to-date knowledges in mining and chemistry. By 1826, the year when Bolívar departed from Peru, Rivero was named the first Director of the Museo Nacional by the Libertador himself. The mining engineer was obviously well connected in the high spheres of Peruvians fighting for control of the state, for he was chosen to lead one of the most self-referential institutions and key sites of memory in the nation-state.

Rivero's interest in antiquities was obviously shared by an influential sector of the elite. Two years after his inauguration (1828) he wrote an article on Peruvian antiquities. It eventually became the book-length study which he published with Tschudi's help in Vienna. *Antigüedades peruanas* (1851) was published under an ambiguous authorial connection with Tschudi.[28] It was the first book authored by a Peruvian to be pub-

---

[27] The challenge remained throughout the nineteenth century and continued into the twentieth century. In the case of d'Orbigny, whose work showed France that Peru was much more than fauna and flora, his views of the people and society were nevertheless disparaging and negative. "Con las opiniones políticas de d'Orbigny... el Perú descendía a la categoría de una tribu en contraste con su pasado histórico y sus recursos naturales. Las dos imágenes no parecían coincidir" (Macera 116).

[28] Estuardo Núñez in *Viajes y viajeros extranjeros por el Perú*, says that Tschudi is "uno de los más típicos viajeros románticos que asoman por el Perú" (325). But he does not detail the reason why, for him, Tschudi's work is "romantic" other than to speak of his delight in life and his sense of adventure. Núñez does make a distinction between the "romantic traveler" and the later scientific explorers (325). However,

lished with a very large number of color plates on the many mummies, cranial remains, *textiles*, *huacos*, maps, and monuments studied in the text. According to Porras Barrenechea, the rather lengthy book "despertó la curiosidad arqueológica. . . y es hito de partida para todas las investigaciones de este género surgidas en el siglo XIX" (61). The book has often been attributed to Tschudi, but Porras Barrenechea unhesitantly states: "el autor verdadero es Rivero... [es] una buena síntesis de los conocimientos históricos y arqueológicos del Perú a mediados del XIX" (60). Tschudi himself, in the prologue, endorsed the book without reservations and gave all the credit to Rivero.[29]

One of the most important changes to arise with scientific travel literature was the appearance of a sort of double vision as the pages of the books grew richly illustrated with black and white sketches and color plates. Rivero was familiar not only with the work of scientific travelers to Peru such as Dombey and La Condamine, he was also a student of the work of other botanists and ethnographers who made extensive use of illustrations. He was also aware of the new scientific methods and technologies introduced by Humboldt. The impact of Humboldt's method and descriptive vision can be better assessed in light of the systematic publication of his beautifully and abundantly illustrated 35 volumes published between 1807 and 1839 in Paris. Drawings, sketches and plates figure as key elements in the configuration of knowledges that Rivero sought to bring together in his *Antigüedades*.

Antigüedades peruanas presents the object of cognition in the conjunction of the writerly with the graphic. The "reader"/viewer takes in the linguistic description informed by the graphic "illustration." The travelogue aspects of Rivero's book coordinates what the author sees with his own eyes with what the reader sees on the page. This doubly-

---

Núñez states that the *Antigüedades peruanas* is indeed the first work of scientific archeology on Peru (329), and that Tschudi understands the entire work to be Rivero's with the exception of the chapters on language which is of course what Tschudi himself says in the introduction to the *Antigüedades*.

[29] Tschudi himself is credited with having initiated serious philological work on the Quechua language and its textual realizations. Núñez writes that "frente al poco rigor filológico de [Clements Robert Markham (1830-1916)] Markham, Tschudi señaló el rumbo en la investigación filológica del drama" (332). Shortly before his death he published in Leipzig a collection of his works on the Quechua language which include essays on "historia cultural y lingüística del Perú antiguo" (332).

mediated seeing, nevertheless, inscribes the value of the direct experience of the present as if it were a totally new perspective onto the world. The travelogue of the scientist relies also on the conceit of the new. Rivero takes advantage of the idea that scientific traveling configures a totally "new" America as it is apprehended by new methods and perspectives. Macera sustains that the modern and scientific thrust of the explorer bolsters his claims to knowledge and authority with the powerful innovation of the graphic impact of maps, charts, views of the land, the fauna, the flora, volcanoes, and human types on the land. Rivero's rendition of ruins, skulls, ceramics, and people on the land profit from the "visual methodology" inaugurated by Humboldt.[30]

The traveler archeologist joins to his scientific descriptions the emotional experience of the encounter with the object of his desire. The thrill of being for the first time in front of an "unknown" landscape is brought back by the traveler to share with his audience back home. The historical operation of the travelogue is to produce at once, as de Certeau showed in the case of Jean de Léry (Certeau 209-243), the ruin as a virtual object immediately available to the pleasures of the reader and at the same time mark the difference and distance between the reader's experience in his chair and the object in real time and space, out there, in America. The object disposition of the travelogue creates a flat surface in which the objects appear in the memory dimensions and dynamics of the traveler.

However, in the case of Rivero, the objects remain in the immediacy of the land, "el suelo que pisamos," as Bishop Rodríguez indicated. The distancing of the travelogue genre requires a re-disposition in the narrative of the national. The writing-sketching dynamics of the travelogue, of the "noticias del imperio," thus plays only a minimal part in the work Rivero wrote in conversation with Tschudi. The Swiss scholar, it is important to say here, by reason of his contact with Quechua as a living language, also altered his initial plans and ended up moving Quechua into the side of

---

[30] Although centered on the "vision" of "race," Deborah Pool's discussion of the traveler's gaze lays the ground for future considerations in further studies on the intersection of archeology and other topics in nation building and imaging. See especially Chapter Three, "An Economy of Vision" in *Vision, Race and Modernity*. In reference to Humboldt, Pool remarks that "It was his interest in migration that fueled Humboldt's study of New World archeology, for it was in the mute stones and hieroglyphs of the Andean and Mexican archeology that he hoped to read America's "racial" history" (76).

ethno-history in the nature/history divide.[31] Rivero's chief interests and perspectives are actually historical, for the archeo-space of Peru that he develops is more concerned with the age of the object than with the characteristics of the space. Thus Rivero's work on "antigüedades" establishes the indissoluble link between history and archeology, between the "hieratic" monuments and the discourse that renders them into an ongoing history. To this effect he writes that "Among all the sciences which are involved in the study of history, none exceeds in importance archeology, or the knowledge of the monuments and antiquities; a science which has proceeded to tear the veil which covered the past ages, synthetically to reconstruct the events of remote periods, and to supply the scarcity and total absence of chronicle and tradition" (1).

I have not been able to secure the edition in Spanish of *Antigüedades peruanas* (1851). However I was surprised to find out that less than two years after its publication in Vienna and the solemn presentation that Rivero made of it to the Peruvian Congress, an English edition was already circulating in the United States. German and French translations also appeared the same year (Núñez, *Viajes* 338). The English translation carries a reduced number of plates and only in black and white.[32] Although most of the sketches appear as part of the last chapter entirely dedicated to the description of the ancient monuments, the title-page is faced with a long, complex view of the sizeable architectural remains and landscape of the "Palace or temple of the island of Coati, in Lake Titicaca." The sacred island in the Titicaca is one of the presumed places of origins of the Incas.

According to Francis L. Hawks, the English translator, the immediate translation and publication of the book was undertaken in view of the popularity achieved by Prescott's *History of the Conquest of Peru* (1847). Rivero's book is also judged to offer "much that did not fall within the design of [Prescott's] admirable work" (Prescott n.p). Indeed Rivero's organization of knowledge reveals a plan to incorporate the apparatus and discourses of the new sciences into a thorough and vast probing. He had two aims in mind: first the re-examination of the Spanish chroniclers in search of (hard) data

---

[31] Back in Vienna and especially during the later part of his life Tschudi kept corresponding with his "Amigo entrañable de la juventud, Mariano Eduardo Rivero" (Núñez, *Viajes y viajeros extranjeros por el Perú* 328).

[32] The English translator indicates that the Spanish original has 58 large plates, "most of them colored and all beautifully executed" (xi).

and second, to bring to bear on the subject the latest developments in Europe and the United States in anthropological (physical and cultural), archeological and linguistic studies. Rivero was indeed working on the figure of man as it was beginning to emerge in the incipient social sciences.

Perhaps ahead of his time, Rivero's foundational project calls for a comparative method. "We are not of the number of those blind admirers of the ancient Peruvian culture... [neither do we consider] the narratives of the old Spanish chroniclers... mere fables." (xiii) His is then a research project that does indeed live up to the "conscientious comparison of these narratives with the remains of Peruvian antiquity" (xiii). Although he is one of the first Americanists to plough systematically through the writings of José de Acosta, Cieza de León, Fray Marcos de Niza, Fernando de Montesinos, and many others together with the archival records used by Prescott, Rivero relies heavily if not on the data, then certainly on the vision of Garcilaso de la Vega, Inca. Rivero does deal with what he calls Garcilaso's "partiality" (47-49), and he warns the reader to take Garcilaso with a grain of salt. However when it comes to what Renan later would call the "spirit of the nation," Rivero cannot resist the seduction structured by Garcilaso's voice, style, elegant nostalgia, and subtly contestatory historiography.

If Garcilaso's effort in attempting a convergence of knowledges that somehow would bring into a single world (see part 2, chapter 2 in this volume, "Mimicry Revisited"), Andean knowledges with Renaissance epistemologies and historiography was monumental and almost in-human, the task Rivero sets for himself is in a way even more daunting. Rivero faces the infinite expansion of European knowledge operating together with the ever-fading Andean crafts of knowledges and memory. Much of Rivero's book is taken up, like the *Comentarios reales*, with correcting the myriad, old and new, accounts and inventions of the origin of the Amerindian peoples, the origin and chronology of the Incas, etc. Like Garcilaso he corrects by showing the contradiction active in the knowledges that figure the "fabulous," and often dehumanizing accounts of the people and their culture. He also marshals the contemporary scientific evidence available—cranial measurements, observation and description of mummy bundles, temporal estimates on the antiquity of the ruins, and comparative studies on Old World religion and linguistics. Unlike Garcilaso, who longed to return to Peru so that he could have better sources and the privilege of first-hand observation and collecting, Rivero has at his disposal two key fields of memory and depositories of information: language and ruins.

Tschudi claims authorship for Chapter V of the *Antigüedades*, the chapter dedicated to the Quechua language and literary compositions. It is clear that both men, unlike Renan, recognize the intimate relation of language to the historiographical operation and most especially to the archeological project. They find it strange that "even those who have studied the archeology of [Peru and Bolivia] have passed by the study of the idioms spoken by their independent and powerful inhabitants in earlier times. Without doubt language is the chief archeological element, the sole monument of reconstruction [for] the entire essence of a people" (93).

In his preface Rivero considers that the study of history is important to the present of the republic inasmuch as it can be instructive of how past societies "prepare a people for the enjoyment of national liberty" (1*). In other words, the study of ancient Peru is neither part of a Romantic curiosity nor is it an addition to the cult of exoticism. If "modern" nations found the possibility of a future on the idea of the rational exercise of liberty, then the government envisioned and practiced by the Incas, on the very same land on which the Peruvian nation-state tittered in the wind of uncertainty, had something relevant to say. Like Garcilaso, and the Túpac Amaru II rebellion before him, Rivero understands that "the code which governed the Ancient Peruvian nation, dictated by its founder, Manco Capac.... laid the foundations of that public happiness, of which for some centuries his descendants have been deprived" (1*).

He adds that his plan is to study the beneficial institutions "on the very spot where they existed," to examine their archeological monuments, "to obtain an exact knowledge of the language, laws, science, religion and costumes". All of this is to be done by complementing archival and library knowledges with travel and first-hand material observation, for he has traversed "the land of the Incas" (x).

IX. The Ethnographic, Territorial Nation

Rivero's discourse articulates three key notions in the discourse of the nation: ethnographic priority and descent, territorial permanence, and originary language. Rivero, contrary to Renan, affirms the primacy of these three components in the making of nation. These are the very notions that Renan took up some forty years later in "What is a Nation?" and which remain alive in today's discussion of the making of imagined communities. In *Antigüedades peruanas,* by way of establishing the scientific permanence of the ruins, Rivero performs an inverse historical operation to Renan's and Anderson's reading of the invention of the nation. Like Garcilaso, he *joins together* what the conquest and European historiography had set apart. The present geography of Peru, mediated by archeology, is indeed claimed as the same land (landscape) as the one crafted and transformed by the Incas. Temporal distance is thus narrowed or even sutured so as to produce the "same," continuous in time and space. Therefore human events happened on the "same" territory and the people today are indeed the descendants of the Inca empire. Today's people long, and in fact have embarked on a search, for public happiness (the rational exercise of liberty) under the banner of a nation-state which actually did exist before.

While Rivero's line of descent is clear, from the Incas to the current nation-state, the identity of the descendants appears at best ambiguous and blurred precisely because he wants to produce a national subject beyond the existing distinctions between Indians, mestizos and criollos. He also wants to produce a subject beyond the anthropological debate on cranial measurements and diverse human origins. It is not easy to determine if Rivero also labors under the contradiction encapsulated in "Incas sí, indios no" as was later the case with the aristocratic historian José de la Riva Agüero (1885-1944). Descriptions of the Inca's craft of religion, architecture, road building, medicine and other knowledges and arts do not stay confined to the past in Rivero's narrative, for he brings ethnographic findings to illuminate the remnants of the past. His present observations and considerations on language, theater, and poetry are used to round out or penetrate our understanding of the past. Archeology, the observation, dating, assessment and interpretation of ruins, is the one branch of knowledge and modality of presentation of the past which overwhelms the past/present divide by which the "modern" republic is unquestionably turned presently into the "land of the Incas." The archeological perspective transforms the nation's territory into a field of memory. Andean topography acquires a new disposition. Its borders and delineations reflect the location and size of the cultural areas identified around the chief ruins of temples, administrative centers, cities, roads, and aqueducts. Tiahuanaco, Huánuco viejo, Pachacamac, Chan-Chan, Chavín, and Paramonga constitute the new lexicon that names the archeo-space of the nation.

X. Conclusions

Fortunately for Rivero's foundational enterprise—raising the nation from the ruins of the past—language, line of descent, territory, tradition, and an archeo-space were available to him as both empirical experience and epistemological categories. Despite Renan's disqualifiers, they have remained the foundational blocks of the nation's narrative. Memory, as in the case of Garcilaso, weaves a myriad of fables that connects and intertwines linkages between territory and human occupation in time and space. The telling of narratives yields the "spirit" of the nation.

However, the spirit of the nation, that indispensable surplus, arises in Peru at the confluence of myriads lines and sites of memory and forgetting. It is clear that the Túpac Amaru II movement had kept and dynamized a memory and narrative of the nation well outside of the bonds of print and the print culture of the Creole elites. Nevertheless the rebellion's memory and its modes of inscription left in its wake a sense of the (ethnographic) nation as a place and people connected with the pre-conquest past still present in ruins and language. Archeology, throughout the nineteenth and twentieth century, enlarges the territory of the archeo-space first put in book form by Rivero. With the growth of the archeo-space of the nation the time gap between past and present narrows. And thus the Chilean poet Pablo Neruda feels at ease claiming Machu Picchu as the cradle for all "American" past and present "nations." Finally, the Peruvian archeologists Luis Lumbreras at the closing of the twentieth century in his epilogue to the secondary school manual *Visión arqueológica del Perú milenario* (1990) can confidently write on the relation of man, land, and knowledge: "La tierra creció en nuestras manos y nuestra sabiduría... Fuimos aprendiendo los secretos que nos hicieron grandes, con mucho trabajo, nuestros *amautas* los fueron guardando cuidadosamente y cada campesino tenía las manos cargadas de historia" (323). Lumbreras's understanding of the relation between archeology and the nation's present and future articulates the space where the national subject appears consolidated in a plural "nosotros"— the descendants of the pre-conquest Andeans—and "nuestros" which Rivera could only posit as a utopic subject on and in the "land of the Incas." That subject stands the test of time for it is the object of the safe keeping of the *amautas* now reconfigured, by the power of archeology, into the ancestors of a long, if often broken, line of intellectuals thinking the nation in ways and manners that exceed the narrow epistemology of the written word and its printed dissemination.

A slightly different version of this chapter was originally published as Sara Castro-Klarén, "The Nation in Ruins: Archeology and the Emergence of the Nation" in Sara Castro-Klarén and John Charles Chasteen, editors' book, *Beyond Imagined Communities: Reading and Writing the Nation in Nineteenth-Century Latin America*, pp.161-195. © 2003 Woodrow Wilson International Center for Scholars. Reproduced with permission of The Johns Hopkins University Press.

Works Cited

ANDERSON, Benedict. *Imagined Communities: Reflections on the Origin and Spread of Nationalism.* London: Verso, 1983.

BAHN, Paul G. *The Cambridge Illustrated History of Archeology.* Cambridge: Cambridge University Press, 1996.

BHABHA, Homi K. "DissemiNation: Time, Narrative, and the Margins of the Modern Nation." In *Nation and Narration.* Ed. Homi Bhabha. London; New York: Routledge, 1990. 291-323.

BENJAMIN, Walter. "Theses on the Philosophy of History in Illuminations." In *Illuminations.* Ed. Hannah Arendt. Trans. Harry Zohn. New York: Schoken Books, 1969.

BERNAL, Ignacio. *A History of Mexican Archeology.* London: Thames and Hudson, 1980.

BOYARIN, Jonathan. "Space, Time and the Politics of Memory." In *Remapping Memory: The Politics of Timespace.* Ed. Jonathan Boyarin. Minneapolis: University of Minnesota Press, 1994.

BRADING, David. *The First America: The Spanish Monarchy, Creole Patriots, and the Liberal State 1492-1867.* Cambridge: Cambridge University Press, 1991.

BURGA, Manuel. *Nacimiento de una utopía: muerte y resurrección de los incas.* Lima: Instituto de Apoyo Agrario, 1988.

CERTEAU, Michel de. *The Writing of History.* Trans. Tom Conley. New York: Columbia University Press, 1988.

FUENTES, Carlos. *Los cinco soles de México: memoria de un milenio.* Barcelona: Seix Barral, 2000.

GONZÁLEZ ECHEVARRÍA, Roberto and Enrique Pupo Walker, eds. *The Cambridge History of Latin American Literature.* Vol. I. Cambridge: Cambridge University Press, 1996.

GRAMSCI, Antonio. *Selections from Cultural Writings.* Cambridge: Harvard University Press, 1985.

HARVEY, David. *The Condition of Postmodernity: An Enquiry into the Origins of Cultural Change.* Cambridge: Blackwell, 1989.

KLARÉN, Peter. *Peru: Society and Nationhood in the Andes.* New York: Oxford University Press, 2000.

LAFAYE, Jacques. *Quetzalcoatl and Guadalupe: The Formation of Mexican National Consciousness, 1531-1813.* Chicago: University of Chicago Press, 1976.

LE GOFF, Jacques. *History and Memory.* Trans. Steven Randall and Elizabeth Claman. New York: Columbia University Press, 1992.

LUMBRERAS, Luis G. *Visión arqueológica del Perú.* Lima: Milenario, 1990.

MACERA, Pablo. *La imagen francesa del Perú, siglos XVI-XIX.* Lima: Instituto Nacional de Cultura, 1976.

MILLONES, Luis, ed. *El retorno de las huacas: estudios y documentos del siglo XVI.* Lima: Instituto de Estudios Peruanos, 1990.

MOORE, Henrietta. "The Problems of Origins: Poststructuralism and Beyond." In *Interpreting Archeology: Finding Meaning in the Past.* Ed. Ian Hodder. London: Routledge, 1995. 51-53.

NERUDA, Pablo. "Alturas de Macchu Picchu from *Canto General.*" *Literatura hispanoamericana: antología e introducción histórica.* Ed. Enrique Anderson Imbert. New York: Holt, Rinehart and Winston, 1960. 686.

NÚÑEZ, Estuardo. *Viajes y viajeros extranjeros por el Perú.* Lima: Conacyt, 1989.

—. and George Petersen, eds. *Alexander von Humboldt en el Perú: Diario de viajes y otros escritos.* Lima: Banco Central de Reserva del Perú, 2002.

POOLE, Deborah. *Vision, Race, and Modernity: A Visual Economy of the Andean Image World.* Princeton: Princeton University Press, 1997.

PORRAS BARRENECHEA, Raúl. *Fuentes históricas peruanas.* Lima: Instituto Raúl Porras Barrenechea, 1963.

PROUST, Marcel. "La Prisonnière." Quoted in *Present Past* by Richard Terdiman. Ithaca: Cornell University Press, 1993. 3.

SMITH, Anthony D. *The Ethnic Origins of Nations.* Oxford: Blackwell, 1986.

RENAN, Ernest. "What is a Nation?" *Nation and Narration.* Ed. Homi Bhabha. Trans. Martin Thom. New York: Routledge, 1990. 8-22.

RIVERO, Mariano Eduardo de and Juan Diego de Tschudi. *Antigüedades peruanas.* Viena: Impr. Imperial de la Corte y del Estado, 1851.

RIVIALE, Pascal. *Los viajeros franceses en busca del Perú antiguo (1821-1914).* Lima: Instituto Francés de Estudios Andinos, 2000.

ROWE, John. "El movimiento nacional Inca del siglo XVIII." In *Túpac Amaru II-1780*. Ed. Alberto Flores Galindo. Lima: Retablo de Papel, 1976. 11-53.

SOJA, Edward. "History: Geography: Modernity." In *The Cultural Studies Reader*. Ed. Simon During. London: Routledge, 1993. 135-150.

TERDINAN, Richard. *Present Past*. Ithaca: Cornell University Press, 1993.

WEBER, Eugen. *Peasants into Frenchmen: the Modernization of Rural France, 1870-1914*. Stanford: Stanford University Press, 1976.

CHAPTER 10
The Ruins of the Present: Cuzco Evoked

PREAMBLE

In the previous chapter, I argued that Benedict Anderson's case—in which he links the emergence of national imagined communities to the rise of print and the spread of literacy—did not quite obtained in Latin America, because in both the case of Venezuela and Mexico, which he gives as his examples, the rates of literacy were too low for print to carry the force and weight Anderson assigns to it. In the case of the Andes, where literacy rates were even lower than in Mexico, print-dependant communication faced two even greater challenges: the geographic and historical fragmentation of the territory, as well as the qualified and precarious "hegemony" of Spanish over Quechua.

However, being a reader of Garcilaso de la Vega, Inca, Guamán Poma, and José María Arguedas, as well as modern interpreters of Andean culture—Tom Zuidema, Manuel Burga, Flores Galindo—something told me that memory and the sense of community was tied not only to ritual dance and theater, to a rich oral culture, but especially to the Andean cosmo-vision in which the land constitutes a sacralized space that memorializes mythical, historical, and present events. The myth of Huarochirí showed me how each stone and stream represented and told over again the story of the origins of each *ayllu*. It is now well understood that Andeans claim descent from *huacas* who in turn are visible features of the landscape—rivers, streams, caves (*pacarinas*), lakes, mountains, great trees—something that both Garcilaso de la Vega and José María

295

Arguedas frame and reframe in rendering their representations of Andean cognitive horizons and modalities.[1]

In doing research for that chapter, I was inspired by the work of Clavijero, the Mexican Jesuit, who in conceiving of writing the first history of Mexico, develops a project which by necessity has to modify the then established historical period table. Clavijero reconfigures the history of Mexico as a new world polity whose time starts with the Aztecs, or even before, perhaps with the Olmecs. He then rejects the Spanish conquest as the place from which Mexican time flows. The official imperial chroniclers are thus contested. Clavijero justifies his historiographical move on the basis of his own experience as a Mexican subject living under the shadow and light of the Aztec ruins and the desire that such ruins have always instilled in him for greater knowledge of that past inscribed on the land, if nowhere else.

In my search for a comparable figure in Peru, I found, of course, the incipient work of the Amigos del País and their excursions to ruins near Lima and elsewhere in the coastal valleys. But it was not until I found the work of Mariano Rivero that I was able to postulate the notion that in ancient polities such as the Andes and Mesoamerica the sacralized space where the original inhabitants lived becomes a sort of archeo-space, a text that can, to a greater or lesser extent, be read everyday in its full or limited historical dimension by most subject-members of a community. Thus arose the idea of studying ruins and deciphering their meaning and place in the construction of communities, be they national or microscopic. However, as it is obvious from the foregoing, ruins are not inert piles of stone. They are the work of generations past. To a great extent, they are sites of abandonment from present-day use and meaning, and in this regard it is necessary to consider how the local memory and interpretation of these sites intersect with the discourse of archeology, a discipline that posits itself as separate and other from the knowledges of the local community residing *now* in the location of the/their *past*. According to the old practices of archeology the locals have almost no access to this knowledge, having, presumably, *forgotten* the history and meaning of the place, precisely because of their "inadequate" non-western literacies, or low levels of literacy altogether.

---

[1] For more on the question of memory and alternative modes of inscription to print culture, see chapter 9 of this volume "Nation in Ruins."

At some point it would be interesting to have a book on the archeo-logical poetics of the construction of the nation in the Andes. I believe that my very incipient study on Rivero and Johann Jacob von Tschudi is a beginning, especially a beginning that allows us to see the complexity of the project. Much more needs to be done on Rivero, his forerunners, and the situation in Peru once the German and American archeologist began going to the Andes with serious and well-funded research projects that intersected with the efforts of local intellectuals busy trying to map the archeo-space of the nation. I am of course thinking of Julio C. Tello, a most influential archeologist in Peru and an Andean specialist who nev-ertheless never published a book.

In what follows I will offer a textual analysis, of the archeological poetics of evocation, one of the chief narrative modes and rhetorical con-structs in the representation of ruins. I am going to focus on Sir Clements R. Markham's—1830-1916—*Cuzco: a Journey to the Ancient Capital of Peru, With an Account of the History, Language, Literature, and Antiq-uities of the Incas, and Lima; a Visit to the Capital and Provinces of Mod-ern Peru,* published in London in 1856 and reissued by Kraus Reprint in Millwood, New York, 1973.[2] In my analysis of Markham's text, I show that a lettered cultural memory shapes Markham's eyewitness experience of the ruins and determines the narration he produces. The cultural imag-inary operating on the witness becomes more salient in the act of evoca-tion than the actual experience of being in the presence of ruins. Ruins, in Markham, evoke the memory of what he has already encountered by reading various texts, especially the Inca Garcilaso de la Vega's *Comen-tarios reales* (1609). This already-known cultural memory is in turn rid-dled with its own obsessions and nostalgias, a sort of cultural memory *en abyme.* However, before I delve into Markham's journey to Cuzco I need to frame a little further the questions of the nascent archeological poetics about and in Peru.

The emergence of disciplines such as history and archeology in nine-teenth-century Latin America exacerbated the question of national ori-

---

[2] In 1878, the Hakluyt Society issued a translation in two volumes of the *Comen-tarios reales de las incas* by Clement R. Markham. The publisher was Bart Franklin in New York. Markham also translated and introduced the first part of the chronicle of Peru by Pedro Cieza de León (1532-1550) as *The Travels of Pedro Cieza de León.* It was also published by the Hakluyt Society in London in 1864.

gins insofar as historical knowledge, until then, had been linked exclusively to lettered culture. The absence of alphabetic script in the preconquest Amerindian cultures propelled the hermeneutic of ruins to the forefront of the inquiry on national origins. This is the moment that marks the emergence of the archeo-space of the nation and its myriad disciplinary complications. For instance, Rivero's archeological findings appeared intertwined with the linguistic work of Johann Jacob von Tschudi on Quechua grammar and literature. The original intention of the Swiss doctor's journey to Peru was to discover medicinal herbs and learn about Inca medical knowledge in general. However, as a result of his journey, Tschudi became aware of the need to become a linguist first and an archeologist later. While in Peru, Rivero's archeological knowledge had proven indispensable to Tschudi. When the doctor returned to Vienna, having written the first modern grammar of the Quechua language, he became the principle sponsor of Rivero's archeological work and of the eventual publication of his *Antigüedades peruanas* (1851), which was quickly translated into English as *Peruvian Antiquities* (1853). Tschudi's scientific journey to Peru taught him three things, none of which would be lost on Markham: that the criollo intellectuals in Lima knew little about native Andean medicine or any other matter dealing with Andean civilizations, that the chief impediment to learning about this ancient knowledge for them and for him was the ignorance of Quechua, and that the *Comentarios reales* were an excellent guide to his questions and objectives.[3]

In recognizing the importance of the Quechua language for ethnobotany, archeology, and ethno-history, Tschudi anticipates the discovery that the Maya epigraphers eventually made in the twentieth century: that the current speakers of Maya posses knowledges (*saberes*) that are indispensable to the reconstruction and understanding of the pre-conquest knowledges and cognitive modalities. We cannot hope to understand the meaning of a ruin if we do not know the name of the place in the original language. We cannot know the full import of the marketplace on each ninth day of the moth in Cuzco if we do not know that the place was

---

[3] Despite Rostworowski's disparaging remarks regarding the value of the Inca Garcilaso's work as a source on Andean civilizations, recent work on archeology, architecture, and *quipu* has tended to validate the Inca as a source. See, for instance, Miles.

called *kusipata*, which in Quechua means the "the place of joy." Ironically, in the middle of the nineteenth century, we find that Tschudi makes the same claims to authority as Garcilaso first did for the writing of his seminal *Comentarios reales*: language is the storehouse that contains all possibilities. It is not a prison, but rather the *kolk'a* ("storehouse" in Quechua). Such claims to authority based on knowledge of the language of those who built the present ruins are exploited to great advantage by Markham in his sections on Quechua literature and especially on the play *Ollantay*.

Postmodern archeologists are keenly aware of the difficult interpretative discursive conditions in which their discipline operates. In *Interpreting Archeology: Finding Meaning in the Past* (1995) Michael Shanks and Ian Hodder pull away from "processual" or positivist archeology and state that the only archeology possible today is the interpretative kind. The archeologist needs to be aware of his subject position in relation to the past and of the fact that the discourse he generates is at once creative and critical. Hoddar and Shanks write that we can thus "expect a plurality of archeological interpretations suited to different purposes, needs and desires" (5). Taking their theoretical position of discourse from Foucault, they call for an awareness of how the technique and style shape how archeology "designs and produces its pasts" (24). Such a shift from validation to signification, "from anchoring our accounts of the past itself to the ways we make sense of the past by working through artifacts" (25), is what Shanks and Hodder call an archeological poetics. With this framework in mind that accounts for both the poetics of archeology and the arrival of archeology as a new science in the Andes, let us now turn to Markham.

Markham, like the English translator of Rivero's and Tschudi's works, introduces his book by reference to William H. Prescott's (1796-1859) histories of the conquest of Peru (2 vols., 1847) and Mexico (3 vols.,1843), excellent and understudied books in the re-writing of the Amerindian societies and the conquest. Prescott was born in Salem, Massachusetts to a prosperous old-line family. He studied at Harvard, but was blinded in one eye and wrote with a special "writing-case" that enables him to write without seeing. He learned several languages, and had a secretary to read to him and find necessary materials. By the mid 1820s, he decided to write a three volume *History of the Reign of Ferdinand and Isabella the Catholic* (1837), based on many books and manuscripts received from Spain. This original research, based on other sources, won Prescott considerable praise and esteem as a historian and, in a way, set a new benchmark. Although he makes no reference to the works of Rivero and Tschudi in his introduction—he may have read them upon his return to England—in his later chapters Markham relies heavily on the veracity of the information in both books for many of his claims about Quechua literature.

In his "Introduction," Markham attempts to command the reader's attention with promises of tales of great adventure, no less-marvelous or less-true than the stories told by the now famous and well-regarded Prescott. It is not clear whether Markham knows that Prescott is blind. It is nevertheless obvious that he thinks that nothing surpasses the accuracy of the eyewitness' personal account, although he is drawn, too, to the high adventure of medieval epic. The young Englishman is convinced that tales of the conquest fuse together several types of narrative and are thus superior to all other accounts of marvel and adventure: "Surpassing in wonder the tales of Amadis de Gaul, or Arthur of Britain, yet histori-cally true, the chroniclers of the conquest of the New World, the volumi-nous pages of the Inca Garcilaso, and the simple record of the true-hearted old soldier, Bernal Díaz, are the last and not the least wonderful narratives of medieval chivalry... But in the eager search for information with regard to the conquest of America, the deeply interesting history of its anterior civilization has been comparatively neglected; and the blood thirsty conquerors have been deemed more worthy of attention that their unfortunate victims" (2).

Markham is not only all set to correct this mistake in the selection of the subject of history, but he is prepared to go even further. As if reproaching Prescott for having relied exclusively on the chroniclers and other archival material when the thing to do in the traveling-obsessed context of the nineteenth century would have been, like John Lloyd Stephens and Frederick Catherwood with *Incidents of Travel in Central America* (1841) and *Incidents of Travel in Yucatan* (1843), to go see for one's self the place and the people, Markham announces that his book is based on an extensive visit and visual exploration of Peru and the Inca ruins. These students of the Spanish chroniclers, Markham says "have never themselves gazed with rapture on the towering Andes, nor exam-ined the native traditions of the country described, nor listened to sweet but melancholy [sic] Inca songs, nor studied the beautiful language in which they were written" (3). From the four points that Markham

makes—first hand visual experience, examination of native understandings of the world, knowledge and appreciation of the language and of its
artistic manifestations—we can clearly see that the American explorer
and archeologist had profitably assimilated the historiographical lesson
taught by Garcilaso, lessons that where lost neither on Rivero or Tschudi.

Moreover, Markham points out, of all the people who have recently
written on Peru "none had visited once the imperial city of Cuzco" (3).
Markham offers not only a novelty, but also the exclusive claims to the
kind of first-hand knowledge and visual perspective that his text presents.
His "visit to the actual scene of the deeds of the Incas, by one who would
be at pains to undertake such a journey" (3) would thus surpass anything
that historians could craft. The new science that Markham is presenting
to his new audiences combines the information that history can offer
with the confirmation and amplification that only first hand exploration
and actual contemporary sighting of the "scene of the deeds" can com-
bine. The disposition to travel and the will to undertake arduous treks
away from the comforts of libraries or archives is what singles out the
new knowledge modeled, of course, on Humboldt's own accounts of his
expedition to the "New World."

When Markham sailed from England in August of 1852 (3) he passed
through New York and Panama on his way to Peru and reached Lima
some four months? later (9). His travel account moves quickly through
Lima in order to open the second chapter with the "Journey to Cuzco."
The first stop on his ascent to Cuzco is Chilca, and he is quick to remark
that "it is inhabited by a race of Indians, who thus isolated in a small oasis
surrounded by the sandy wilderness, have preserved much of the spirit of
freedom and independence" (21). From the following paragraph it is clear
that Markham had already had some ideas about the interaction between
Indians and Spaniards, and far from the first scene being one of abjection,
as it is with the arrival to Cuzco of Ernesto and his father in *Los ríos profundos* (1958), in Markham's "scene of the deeds" he easily finds evidence
of the Indians' resistance to Spanish oppression. Markham understands the
importance of resistance for the portrayal of 'authenticity." "An instance
of their determined resistance of oppression occurred the morning after my
arrival: when, my soldier having given the syndic of the village a blow with
a butt-end of a pistol, the whole population assembled in a state of the
utmost excitement, and insisted on the fellow being sent back a prisoner for
trial in Lima. So careful were the Indians of their rights…" (21).

In an even smaller village, in Asia, consisting of no more than ten mud huts, the savvy traveler finds another longed-for gem: "At this wretched little place I found and Indian who possessed a copy of the *History of the Incas* by Garcilaso de la Vega, and who talked of their deeds as if he had studied its pages with much attention" (23). Markham's descriptions are crisp. His details are always telling since they are the result of very keen observation and an excellent background on the socio-economic history of the country. Having spent the night in Cañete he observes that the proprietors of the estates are "an excellent class of country gentleman, upright, hospitable and kind to their slaves and dependants" (25). He then provides his reader detailed information on the haciendas in the valley, their names, the names of the owner, the crops, the number of workers and families on the land. In this "joyful arrangement" he does not fail to mention if there is a priest or a chapel on the land and notes all the different products available in the area. Like all European travelers in the nineteenth century, Markham does not fail to see with a commercial eye, and knows that his readership is as interested in a good adventure tale— the history of the Incas and the great ruins of Cuzco—as they are in knowing about the possibility of setting up business in the area. Peru does emerge as an archeo-space, but it is never just that, as the eye of the traveler reconnoiters the archeo-space the topography of commercial value. In doing so Markham produces a curious kind of palimpsest, for he layers over the old Andean sacred agricultural space the transformed space of the *encomienda* and the *hacienda*, which itself is colored by the traveler's perception of future commerce and profit.

But of course Markham is true to his promise. He takes the reader to the "scene of the deeds." As he passed through Pachacamac, the traveler uncovers the previous identity and meaning of the place. This the great Chimú, "conquered by the Incas, in the time of Pachacutec, whose son the renowned Prince Yupanqui proved the superiority of the arms of the Sun, in many fierce battle with Yunca Indians" (30). Nothing less and nothing more than a page taken from the accounts of King Arthur. He does not fail to note that in the "*huacas*, or burying places, many curious relics of this period have lately been dug up, including specimens of Inca pottery, stone canopas [sic], or household gods, golden earrings, and silver ornaments for various kinds" (31). Markham does not make mistakes. His knowledge of Inca and pan-Andean culture is accurate, as his chief source is Garcilaso.

If his knowledge of pan-Andean culture is always there to inform the land that he traverses with a sense of the past, he shows that he is just as versed on the events of the conquest in spotting places where battles took place, or where people camped or made significant stays. As he reaches the gates of the hacienda Larán, he informs us that the place is said to have been the boundary between the territories granted to Pizarro and Almagro. The narrator in Markham steps forward to install in this otherwise meaningless spot on the earth a meaning drawn from the past. Although now quite forgotten, the battle remains loaded with significance, as it unleashed the civil wars that were to plague Peru even more harshly than the conquest itself. "It was there that Marshall Almagro established his headquarters, when returning from Chile in 1537; he proceeded to the Coast, to claim from Pizarro his share of the territories of Peru. The stormy interview between these two fierce adventurers at Mala, led to the retreat of Almagro into the interior, and his final overthrow in the bloody battle of Salinas" (33). Oh, yes the battle of Salinas, the battle so well chronicled and studied by Garcilaso, as the battle itself cost his father his good name and a fall from the Crown's graces, from which neither the father nor the son would ever recover.

The growing anticipation that Markham's narrative has built in his journey of ascent to Cuzco finally peaks when the traveler meets the splendorous object of his desire: Cuzco. First imagined and caressed in the fantasies encountered in the narratives of Garcilaso, Cieza de León, and of course Prescott, Cuzco is now a present reality to be taken in by all his senses. Cuzco evoked! Cuzco as the magnet that pulled him away from England into the rarely visited Andean mountain range is finally before the traveler's eyes in the unforgettable morning of March 18, 1853. With his fine memory of the topography of the Tahuantinsuyo, Markham reports that he crossed the Apurímac river and entered the territory that "Once composed the empire of Manco Capac, the first Inca of Peru" (94). From there, the traveler retraces the imagined steps of both the Incas in battle or in conquering marches, and Spaniards marching through Inca roads and sleeping over in royal tambos as they reconnoitered the sociospace over which they claimed domain. Markham's narrative makes visible scenes of antiquity by weaving inseparable strands of imagined memory with present sensory perceptions. As he *sees and feels* the living ruins of the Inca Empire, he imparts upon each stone, each hanging bridge, each flowering tree, each solar clock, an aura of nostalgia and a patina of its past appearance.

This is a narrative done in pentimento style, in which palimpsest play is incessant. It is as if he had been there before. As he writes, he evokes the sense of parting from the beloved space while at the same time registering the excitement and joy of actually being there with his own body. His foundational text, Garcilaso's own nostalgia for Cuzco and the beloved mother country, pours out of the pores of Markham's prose. He captures and reproduces to a fault the Inca's own oxymoron: the enthused laments for unimaginable originality and intelligence that created the now extinct and yet ever-present empire.

Markham's ascent to Cuzco in February 1853 predictably follows one of the Inca's famous routes. Small villages and agricultural fields appear and disappear as the road winds through the majestic mountains. At every turn, the traveler spots ruinous fields and walls that at once situate him in the present and transport him, via evocation, to a Peru before the conquest's destruction. Although pre-conquest Peru is now in ruins, *as ruins* the walls and fields bear witness to the bursting of life and beauty that existed before the Spaniards' arrival. Ruins and wildflowers are juxtaposed in Markham's descriptions to emphasize the conquest's destruction. "Slopes covered with lupin, heliotrope, verbena, and scarlet salvia" (53) frame his reenactment of the battle between a young Almagro and the viceroy Vaca de Castro in 1542. Markham writes: "The battle was long doubtful; but at length Castro was victorious, and out of 850 Spaniards that Almagro brought into the field, 700 were killed. The victors lost about 350 men..." (61-62). No more is said about the soaking blood that must have run over the Hatun Pampa that day. No mention is made of the thousands of Indian men and women soldiers who made up the armies against whom the Spanish fought.

Cuzco functions in Markham as an omnipotent object of desire that dictates the inclusion and exclusion of subject matter. Asia, Cangallo, and Ayacucho are just stops along the way to Cuzco. After Ayacucho, the narrative focuses on the particularities of the deep rivers that must be crossed to approach Cuzco, the difficulty of the terrain, and the marvel of the hanging bridges. The reader is reminded of the landscapes drawn by José María Arguedas in *Agua* (1935) and *Los ríos profundos* (1958). Reversing Markham's route, Arguedas' young men walk the same ascending and descending paths, arrive at similar *abras* (passes), and view deep rivers as they move away from Cuzco and Ayacucho in pursuit of their destiny in coastal cities like Nazca and Lima. On March 18, 1853,

Markham crosses the Apurímac River, intensely aware of the fact that the river's name means "Apu that speaks," and that in crossing this river he has emulated Manco Cápac, his cultural hero.

The English traveler is overcome with emotion. To know that he is standing on the same ground on which Manco Cápac stood as he came upon the Cuzco region is simply overwhelming. The traveler has anticipated this moment for many years, and the desire inspired by the reading of histories overwhelms the real, lived moment. Historical (i.e., textual) memory overtakes lived experience, which can only be rendered in terms previously set forth in writing by his inspirational tutor, Garcilaso de la Vega. He is not yet in Cuzco, but he imagines Manco Cápac (via Garcilaso) thinking about securing the site and deciding to construct four fortresses: Ollantay-tambo to the north, Paccari-tambo to the south, Paucar-tambo to the east, and Lima-tambo to the south. Soon thereafter, the historian-traveler snaps out of his textual indulgence and returns to the present time of this travel account to provide the reader with a splendidly vivid scene of the dangers and travails of reaching the bridge before finally crossing over it to see Cuzco.

The march to the city continues. Two great pampas still remain to be traversed before Markham can see Cuzco from the summit of the last pass. At the end of the day, when he finally arrives, Markham boisterously exclaims and invokes the city no fewer than four times: "Cuzco! City of the Incas! City, where, in by-gone times, a patriarchal form of government, was combined a with state of civilization... Cuzco! The hallowed spot where Manco Cápac's golden wand sank... Cuzco! Once the scene of so much glory and magnificence, how art thou fallen!" (95). It is in this last evocation that the text undeniably signals Markham's intertextual location as well as the incessant construction of the Garcilasian palimpsest on which the book relies.

He must let the splendor of the past precede the present image of ruin. The ruin can never stand alone, it must be always represented in pentimento with its past glory. As we can see, the four invocations of Cuzco focus on the city's historical nature and aura. We read in Markham the Cuzco that Garcilaso textualized rather than the Cuzco that the traveler's own eyewitness gaze configures. The object of his desire is in plain sight, but it comes across in his book as shrouded by the memory of images that first arose from reading Garcilaso's prose—images which themselves came from remote, youthful memories of the Inca who surveyed the city and its lost splendor. Viewing Cuzco as a living ruin, then, entails a constant interplay among images that appear in the here-and-now of the traveler's gaze and images previously stored in the mind's eye.

The Cuzco that continues to unfold before Markham's eyes is a site of knowledge, ceremony, and glory. As the traveler continues to evoke Cuzco, we find not a description of the Inca architectural ruins, but rather an evocation of splendid rituals and ceremonies that filled *plazas* and streets with theatrical dances, joyous offerings to the sun and the moon, and, as in imperial Rome, the march of armies back to Cuzco after the conquest of the great Chimor or Pachacamac. Cuzco's imperial character fascinates the English traveler, and while comparisons to the grandeur of imperial China and India are not missing, also implicit is an allusion to imperial England and its world colonies.

Perhaps wanting to outshine Tschudi's recent achievements as an expert in Quechua (172), Markham seems to be thinking about a subsequent journey to Urubamba from his earliest days in Cuzco, where he hears that Don Pablo Justiniano, the priest of Laris and a descendant of the Incas, has in his possession the only known copy of the originally transcribed play *Ollantay*. Markham also hears that Don Pablo has some full-length portraits of the Inca. In the nineteenth-century race for knowledge and imperial acquisitions, these "ruins" and treasures would be any traveler's crowning jewels.

Either before departing for Peru or after his return to England, Markham read the *Ollantay* carefully. The account of his journey to Urubamba and his contemplation of the ruins at Ollantaytambo are interlaced with the play's love story. Ollantaytambo's ruins become a multilayered and dynamic palimpsest infused with the play's drama. Markham preserves the human dimension of the place at the forefront of his text such that the reader is never just looking at ruins, but is rather always aware of the Incas' history as actors in space and time. Like Cuzco before, Ollantaytambo now comes alive with Markham's own narrative rendition of lovers' adventures, army battles, and an enamored rebel who risks it all for the forbidden Ñusta's love.

Markham closes his journey into the past, his passage among the ruins, with generous translations from the *Ollantay* and heartfelt praise for the richness and sweetness of the Inca language. In so doing, he does not quote Garcilaso, his master text and guide, but he does stress the notion that knowledge of the language of the (living) culture in ruins is indispensable to seeing and that seeing is wrapped in language. Cuzco, as it is evoked in Markham's intertextual world, a world in which place and memory interact incessantly, appears less as a ruin and much more as a powerful, living, speaking scene of history—an indelible memory, an Apu-rimac with a poetics all its own.

An earlier version of this essay was published in Michael J. Lazzara and Vicky Unruh (eds.): *Telling Ruins in Latin America*, 2009, New York: Palgrave MacMillan, 77-86. Reproduced with permission of Palgrave Macmillan.

BIBLIOGRAPHY

MARKHAM, Clements R. *Cuzco: a Journey to the Ancient Capital of Peru, With an Account of the History, Language, Literature, and Antiquities of the Incas, and Lima; a Visit to the Capital and Provinces of Modern Peru.* London: Chapman and Hall, 1856.

MILES, Susan A. *The Shape of Inca History: Narrative and Architecture in an Andean Empire.* Iowa City: University of Iowa Press, 2002.

ROSTWOROWSKI DE DÍEZ CANSECO, María. *Historia del Tahuantinsuyu.* Lima: Instituto de Estudios Peruanos, 1988.

SHANKS, Michael, et al, eds. *Interpreting Archaeology: Finding Meaning in the Past.* London: Routledge, 1995.

PART II

DEBATING POST-COLONIAL THEORY

"I have faith in being strong/Give me,
armless air, give me leave/to galloon
myself with zeros on the left".
César Vallejo. *Trilce* XVI

CHAPTER 1
Mimicry Revisited: Latin America, Postcolonial Theory, and the Location of Knowledge

I. MAPPINGS OF THE GLOBAL

The exploration of the epistemological relations between theory, as produced in the metropolis, and literature or culture, as a second order of production which takes place in the periphery, has been taken up with new vigor in light of the ongoing debate on postmodernism. It has been noted that a key aspect of the center-margin relationship interprets, redefines, and locates novels and poems from the periphery "in-theory" and in the center and then returns them to the peripheries destined and packaged for (value added) consumption. Such operation also conveys literature to classroom for use in subject formation, the construction of national and cultural identities. Such practices in metropolitan theory have produced hierarchical canonical criteria by which, for example, Borges becomes part of a universal (value added) canon taught in English departments, Rigoberta Menchú appears in courses on "Third World Literature" or women studies, César Vallejo never makes it outside graduate seminars in departments of "Spanish," and Luisa Valenzuela is adopted as part of comparative women's literature courses.

Seen from this perspective, "theory" can provide a determining force in the conceptualization of cultural and literary histories, and in the writing of self by both metropolitan and colonial subjects. As theory claims larger and deeper knowledge zones, as it globalize its reach, it places a new urgency on a debate whose outline I cannot even begin to trace here. Nevertheless, I intend to make a few preliminary points in order to use them as signposts for a more local inquiry into the relations of postcolonial theory and our understanding of Latin American intellectual production.

Before the challenge of postmodern theory, Latin Americans and Latin Americanists debated, embraced, examined, liked, doubted and/or rejected Marxist aesthetic theory. But relations between art and society were never sufficiently explained. *The Political Unconscious* (1981) by Fredric Jameson, with its incorporation of poststructuralist theory into a general historical theory of narrative as a socially symbolic act, provided a passage between the aesthetic and the political realms, between the individual and the collectivity inasmuch as, and according to Jameson, the "aesthetic act entertains always an active relationship with the real. It draws the real into its own texture" (81). For the hermeneutics of the political unconscious, texts were artifacts opened to multiple meanings, to successive rewritings and over-writings. Allegorical readings, of the kind Jameson delineates, transform the texts into a machinery for ideological investment (30). Jameson's own reading of Conrad's *Nostromo* (1963) and *Lord Jim* (1968) provide us with a masterful display of allegorical reading within the paradigms of Euro-American history. Jameson's hermeneutical model however, cannot account for narrative the world over. The universalist outlook implicit in the Marxist master code evidenced its own its limits when it became clear that the allegorical rewriting of Balzac and Conrad could not be stretched so as to account for the difference(s) posed by García Márquez, Borges, José María Arguedas, Derek Walcott, or Soyinka. Nevertheless, the existing cartographic system allowed the elaboration of an epistemological category which corresponded to the global division of labor and power: "Third World Literature." But this new reductive category also proved insufficient, for, as Jameson himself pointed out, "the purpose of the canon is to restrict our aesthetic sympathies, to develop a range of rich and subtle perceptions which can be exercised only on the occasion of a small but choice body of texts"("Third World Literature" 65) and therefore, "Third World Literature" by definition falls outside the limits of aesthetic sympathies engendered and nurtured by the canon.

Validating but not really accounting for the difference, Jameson's concept of "Third World Literature," itself a forerunner of the globalizing tendencies of postcolonial nomenclature, has elicited criticism from Indian and Latin American intellectuals. They argue that the "Third

World" designation of the southern part of the earth is itself a projection of Eurocentric epistemology in collusion with the forces of globalizing capital (Ahmad 95-122). Aijaz Ahmad writes that "Third World Literature" is a term with no theoretical status: "At best it represents yet another instance in the construction of ideal types" (97). Inasmuch as the vast majority of literary texts from the southern continents are

> unavailable in the metropolis....literary theorists who set out to formulate 'a theory of cognitive aesthetics of third world literature' will be constructing ideal types, in the Weberian manner, duplicating all of the basic procedures which Orientalist scholars have historically deployed in presenting their readings of certain traditions of 'high' textuality as the knowledge of a supposedly unitary object which they called 'the Islamic civilization.' (97)

In another modality but still in the same left theorizing quarters, a great deal has been said about the ambiguous relationship of the terms "postmodern" and "Latin American literature." On the one hand, John Barth, in his characterization of a symptomatic "literature of exhaustion," quickly incorporated Borges and García Márquez into an *avant-la-lettre* postmodern fiction,[1] that is to say, the canon. The left, on the other hand, questioned, on good ground and with open hostility, the wholesale adoption of postmodern rhetorical markers as the only elements that the center validated in the texts wrought in the periphery. Moreover, the implications in the prefix "post," just as in postcolonial theory, are particularly troublesome. It could be descriptive of a continental history which had not yet even completed its own modernization

---

[1] See Barth, *The Literature of Exhaustion and the Literature of Replenishment.* In this essay, almost completely devoted to Borges, Barth argues that the work of the argentine author of "fictions" "May paradoxically turn the felt ultimacies of our time into material and means for his work—*paradoxically*—because by doing so he transcends what had appeared to be his refutation, in the same way that the mystic who transcends finitude is said to be enabled to live, spiritually and physically, in the finite world....Whether historically the novel expires or persists seems immaterial to me; if enough writers and critics feel apocalyptic about it, their feeling becomes a considerable cultural fact, like the *feeling* that Western civilization, or the world, is going to end soon" (10-11). By the same author also see "Post-modernism Revisited." Roberto González Echevarría points out, however, that the identification of postmodernism and the boom is in fact asymmetrical because postmodernism questions the very notions of "great author" and "master" (unified) text. See González Echevarría.

phase(s).[2] Journals have devoted whole issues to the question of modernity/postmodernity in Latin America, wondering whether: "¿Puede hablarse de postmodernidad en América Latina?"[3]

Contrary to Nelson Osorio's strictly developmental model and Klor de Alva's exceptionalist claims, Nicolás Casullo thinks that the critique of modernity leveled by postmodern theory is intrinsically relevant to Latin America. He feels that "si la crisis de lo moderno o de la aparición de lo postmoderno... [se da] cuando ya no hay coincidencia entre lo que podríamos llamar el avance de lo social y económico, y la cultura que da cuenta de ese avance en Occidente... [ya no sólo] hay un descentramiento total sino que ya miras desde un descentramiento."[4] The Argentine sociologist looks upon postmodernism as a set of discursive dispositions which challenge the notion of a centered unitary subject in possession of a hegemonic unitary set of knowledge/power. If that is the case, then one could agree with Casullo and argue that Latin American writing has always already been "post"-modern, that is to say a site of contested hegemonies. For the outlook from the colonies stemmed from a de-centered and de-centering questioning subject.[5] Latin American cultural production, as Casullo notes, can be seen as a representation of modernity's permanent crisis, a crisis always deeper and harder in the periphery. Like other more recent interventions in the debate, Casullo's position does not reject the theoretical apparatus of post-structuralism. Instead he, like other theorists, garnishes it and incorporates it into a local(ized) intellectual tradition conversant and deft in the arts of de-centering.[6] This is not to forget, however, that as Jameson argues in *Postmodernism, or,*

---

[2] See Osorio Tejeda. John Beverley feels that the bibliography on the subject has "become unmanageable" (157).

[3] See *Nuevo Texto Crítico* (1990, Nos. 6,7), *Revista de Crítica Literaria Latinoamericana* (1989, No. 29), *Boundary 2* (1993, No 20). For further aspects of the polemic on postcolonialism see Klor de Alva. Peter Hulme feels that Klor de Alva's argument is flawed because rather than difference for Latin America he seems to be claiming exceptionalism in the processes of independence from Spain and Portugal. See Hulme.

[4] See interview with Nicolás Casullo by Claudia Ferman, in Ferman (30). See also Casullo.

[5] See chapters 2 and 6 in this volume.

[6] In a similar vein John Beverly in *Against Literature* (1993), José Rabasa in *Inventing America: Spanish Historiography and the Formation of Eurocentrism* (1993), and Walter Mignolo in "Human Understanding and (Latin) American Inter-

The Cultural Logic of Late Capitalism (46), postmodernism is not to be understood as a style among others but rather as the cultural dominant of late capitalism. As such, it does not constitute a break in a modern/postmodern dichotomy but it is rather "the form taken by the authentically modern in our period, and a mere dialectical intensification of the older modernist impulse toward innovation" (59).

It is within the scope of this general relocation and harnessing of "post" theorizing, as distinguished from the notion of a consolidated "theory," that I plan to look at the possible intersections between some positions in the paradigm of postcolonial studies, the study of Latin American cultures, and the self-representations that Latin American intellectuals have made (imagined) for themselves and their writing practices.

II. ERRORS AND THE TORRID ZONE

Problems regarding the interfacing of power/knowledge and margin/center were already in the mind of Garcilaso de la Vega, Inca (1539-1616) when, late in the sixteenth century, he tried to settle the question as to whether there were two worlds—an old and a new—or only one. The geographic problem, the Inca thought, could be settled on the basis of sensory perception, personal experience, and common sense (the sedimentation of received knowledge). However, the fact that he had to invoke ancient and contemporary "modern" authorities in order to be credited with knowledge of the sensory obvious is but a metaphor for the cultural disposition by which Europe had already consolidated its repression and occlusion of its Amerindian other in the constitution of its one knowledge.[7] Neither Garcilaso nor his contemporaries could have imagined the kind of distance and (self-) critical perspective which now enables us to understand time and space not as natural categories but as

ests: The Politics and Sensibilities of Geocultural Locations," harness, with caveats, post-structuralism, and its branching postcolonial arm, into the service of a revisionist discourse of the Latin American Left (Beverly 109).

[7] In "Modernism and Imperialism" Fredric Jameson, following Jacques Berque's thesis, points out that colonized peoples suffer a "dépossession du monde." "Its effects are representational effects, which is to say systematic block on any adequate consciousness of the structures of the imperial system....since the colonized other has become invisible" (*Nationalism* 10-11).

cultural constructs, and yet that is exactly what was at issue in the truth claims made regarding the impermeability of the northern from the southern hemisphere.[8] Frustrated with the refusal to accept empirical proof from the lips of a colonial and most especially about whether one, as a material and cultural being, could pass from the torrid zone to the temperate zone, Garcilaso, grasped at the fringes of religious thinking and concluded his argument with the hope that their "error" and "heretical imaginings" about the impermeability of the north from the south would be corrected in hell, a utopian time-space which held the promise of complete and utter revelation of the truth. Aware that he was being dispossessed of his knowledge—the double knowledge of a colonial subject—aware that the argument about the blockage of the torrid zone was false, Garcilaso insisted on the geographical continuity of the two zones, a continuity which metaphorically stood for that of his bicultural formation. And so he wrote from the irreducibility of his experience:

> And to those who doubt if it is flat or round may be satisfied by the testimony of those who have gone around it... And to those who say that of the five parts of the world called zones only the two temperate are inhabitable and that the midmost is excessively hot.... maybe assured that I myself was born in the torrid zone, in Cuzco... that I have been in the temperate zone south... and that to reach this other northern temperate zone, where I am writing these words, I passed through the torrid zone. (9-10).

The scene of writing that Garcilaso stages in the *Commentaries*, places him, a native of Cuzco, "writing back," as in *The Empire Writes Back* (1989), in his house in Córdoba, Spain.[9] However, similar to so many other moves Garcilaso made in his work, while in his house in Córdoba, writing

---

[8] In *Postmodernism, or, The Logic of Late Capitalism*, Jameson goes further and points out that "neither space nor time are 'natural' (as ontology or human nature alike): both are the consequences of projected afterimages of a certain state or structure of production and appropriation, of the social organization of productivity" (367).

[9] The delicious phrase "writing back" belongs to Salman Rushdie. I make reference here to one of the central books in postcolonial studies, *The Empire Writes Back* (1989) by the Australians Bill Ashcroft, Gareth Griffiths and Helen Tiffins. Postcolonial studies as postulated in the topics, methodologies, and ideological positions taken in this book I believe comes quite close to an emancipating program for knowledge. As such it could be a good point of departure for a dialogue project about Latin America which shares a similar goal.

for him implies a reversal and an equivocation of the center periphery relation, for the center in Garcilaso's commentaries is either occupied by
Cuzco and not Córdoba or it becomes a mobile point of reference.

In his preamble to his massive *Royal Commentaries* (1609) Garcilaso
tries to refine, "theorize," or ask critical questions of the rules of discursive
formations which shut out the knowledge which the other possesses, a
knowledge which he wants and needs to bring to bear on the European discussion (invention) of America, on the construction of its ancient civilizations as the work of "primitive" subjectivities. He attains a low level, a
sotto voce mode of theorizing, detectable only to those with finely trained
senses, attuned to the issues at hand. In many ways the work of the Inca, his
whole oeuvre, from the translation of the dialogues of León Hebreo from
the Italian to the Spanish, to his commentaries, could be regarded as precursor to the problematic outlined in *The Empire Writes Back*.

But Garcilaso could stake out an epistemological position from which
to theorize openly by appropriating directly for himself the discourses of
either political theory, philosophy, or theology. In Spain all forms of dissent had become heretical ("sus heréticas imaginaciones") and the son of
an Inca noblewoman was very aware of his doubled (ethnic and religious)
vulnerability. Moreover, the impossibility of theorizing was also part and
parcel of the discursive rules under which he "choose" to write so as to be
published.

First, he chose to *correct by means of completion* of the record rather
than questioning directly the truth of the "false" statement. According to
Garcilaso statements made by Spanish chroniclers and historians were
false because they were incomplete, and they were incomplete because
the Spanish chroniclers, not knowing Quechua, did not understand the
culture which, for Garcilaso, is primarily given in/with language. Garcilaso's appreciation of the indivisibility of culture from language is his
great achievement, one which strikes as astonishingly modern and which
has not received sufficient attention. However, in selecting completion as
a contestatory move Garcilaso is implicitly saying that European reason
once completed, once made into *one* can be fully sufficient to account for
itself and its others. So he "chooses" to carry out his enterprise within the
standing discursive rules. To do so, as an outsider, he must *imitate, seem
to imitate*, or *be seen imitating* in order to write the *complete(d)* truth.

Second, if his enterprise was to render Andean knowledge in its own
different ("authentic") pre-contact symbolic forms, then he was bound to

fail in his desire to engage authoritatively the attention of his European readers. "Authority," as Foucault has shown and feminist criticism has further demonstrated, devolves on rhetoric, consensus, and power canonizations. Further, as the Peruvian ethnohistorian María Rostworowski has argued, the stark originality of the Andean culture rendered key parts of it incommensurable with current European modes of cognition and imagination.[10]

Third, as Rostworowski writes, those who entered Andean territory and reported on its society and culture registered *unbelievable* mistakes and errors:

> En las crónicas no solo se manifiestan errores, *conscientes o no* en la interpretación de la religiosidad indígena, sino también en las referencias políticas... [Los cronistas] se mostraron parciales y dieron informaciones tendenciosas, defectuosa[s]. Muchos de nuestros errores se inician en las referencias dadas por los cronistas, *yerros incomprensibles*. ¿Podían acaso los cronistas aquilatar y transmitirnos la experiencia andina? (13)

The answer to the ethnohistorian's question was already given by Garcilaso in his remarks on the discursive impossibility of writing Andean civilization without knowledge of the language and further impeded by the positionality of the *cronista*-conqueror as historian or eye-witness.

Fourth, "theorizing" on the very reason that ruled over topics that needed radical overhaul in themselves and which the "discovery" and conquest of America made only more controversial and dangerous—the origin of man, the nature of knowledge, the Edenic myth of creation, the divinity of Christian rule—was a task beyond the power of any individual. Thus, in view of the set of impossibilities he encounters, Garcilaso, cleverly, slyly,

---

[10] See Rostworowski. Tom Cummins, comparing the ways and degrees to which European systems of representation could accommodate themselves to—code, re-code, encode—states that the difference in the forging of more Aztec and less Andean texts or images immediately after contact has to do with the fact that for the Andean to be represented visually to a European audience the Andean system of representation was subject to a greater form of transformation. "The Peruvian system of representation could not even be used to depict idolatry to interested Europeans, because the Andean art did not correspond in any way to European notions of representation" (189-190).

opts for the one discursive form porous enough to let him try out a number of short term strategic challenges which, when viewed as a totality, amount to a protracted and debilitating guerrilla warfare on the discursive castle he needs to crack in order to insert another knowledge and even, as Mazzotti argues, another rhetoric ("Subtexto andino"). Such a form is narrative. Narrative understood as poliglossia. Narrative as Bakhtin, in *The Dialogic Imagination* (1981), has shown it to be constituted by the constant appropriation of discourses which claim specific and latest purchase on the real. As the Inca writes back, he stresses and develops the fragmentary and polysemic potential of narrative subgenres. This is so even when he chooses, due to another set of strategic reasons, to call his work "commentaries." In composing a massive and meandering narrative with no fixed subject matter and with an oscillating subject of enunciation, Garcilaso provides for himself the occasion, the gap, from which to challenge, as Julio Cortázar later does in *Rayuela* (1963) the theory of genre and subject (myth, history, fiction, chronicle, philosophy, ethnography) that at once limits and cancels the knowledge of the subaltern colonial subject. So that when he "corrects" by completion he destabilizes, when he mixes mythic and mimetic modes he shows the constructedness of their separation, when he changes his name he questions the identity relation (legal, authorial) between experience, autograph, and lineage.

With his manifold narrative Garcilaso intends to filiate his story to history. While adopting strategies confined to fiction he also draws his distance from the "fictive" by showing that the Spanish *cronistas* were more prone than even ordinary, illiterate Andeans to confuse reality with "imaginings." The strategy of "correcting" by bringing in detailed differing and accurate information, quite different from Said's strategy in *Orientalism* (1985), enables Garcilaso to show the *reason* in and of Andean culture. Further, his choice of commentary, in the tradition of the eyewitness commentary that Caesar inaugurated in his polemics with the state's historians in Rome, and St. Jerome's ambivalent use of the term (Christian Fernández 6-7)[11] allows the colonial subject to revise the history being institutionalized as well as to deconstruct, as in today's usage,

---

[11] Christian Fernández (6-7) shows that Garcilaso was more than conversant in the use and theory of commentary during the Renaissance. According to Fernández, Garcilaso's deployment of commentary is an appropriation of St. Jerome's theory on commentary as exegesis.

the unified authorial voice of the Spanish chroniclers who copied and certified each others' incomprehensible errors. In view of the Inca's positionality: a colonial writing in the metropolis in one of the several European languages that he, as a Renaissance humanist, knew; a colonial
writing from the inside of the discursive dispositive that casts him as an
immature human being with very limited capacity for the use of reason
and yet writes to challenge these very dispositions; a colonial writing
mostly given to sly commentary woven trough with delicate irony and
devastating scholarship. Indeed one is very tempted to portray Garcilaso
as the first postcolonial intellectual, and thus stretch Jameson's line of
postmodernist genealogical precursors even further back. He imitates, he
even mimics, the costumes of his betters. In doing so Garcilaso would
seem an exemplary figure for the characterization that Homi Bhabha
makes of the postcolonial intellectual today.[12]

Are we then positing a postmodern postcolonial discourse *avant la
lettre* which pushes back the dates far beyond the English civilizing "voyage out" to India, Africa, Australia, Canada, U.S.? Are we simply demonstrating the universality of Bhabha's own intuition when he takes Foucault's notion of counter-modernity ("What is Enlightenment?") and
suggests that:

> In general terms, there is a colonial counter-modernity at work in the eigh-
> teenth and nineteenth centuries' matrices of Western modernity that if
> acknowledged would question the historicism that analogically links, in a lin-
> ear narrative, late capitalism and the fragmentary, simulacral, pastiche symp-
> toms of post-modernity. This linking does not account for the historical tra-
> ditions of cultural contingency and textual indeterminacies (as forces of social
> discourse) generated in an attempt to produce an 'enlightened' colonial or
> postcolonial subject. (173)

The linkage between the Inca's position and Bhabha's claim about a
colonial counter-modernity already inscribed within modernity devolves
on the very large "if" of the phrase "if acknowledged." What the project
and strategy of Garcilaso slyly and yet stridently stated is the paradoxical

---

[12] See Bhabha. See especially the essays on mimicry (85-93) and the postcolonial
and the postmodern (140-175). For further details on this proposition see Schelonka.
Garcilaso's case would then stretch back the "astonishing genealogical [line] of precursors that Jameson outlines for postmodernism" (Jameson, *The Political* 3-6, 15, 367).

desire for a single history that would acknowledge rather than sublate colonial alterity. Nevertheless, neither Garcilaso in Córdoba then, nor the postcolonial critic in England now, find it possible to disentangle the desire for acknowledgement as subjects (other) of the metropolitan discourse from the need to write alterity as cultural difference without falling into a galloping cultural relativism or endless plurality. It seems that Bhabha, following Franz Fanon[13] closely, and preceded by Garcilaso, faces the impossibility of being at once at the center and yet speaking from another location. It is indeed true that Garcilaso too registers then the postcolonial condition of unhomeliness but differing from Bhabha the Inca *inverts its meaning* and develops the possibility of the syncretic (doubled, not hybrid) figure of *mestizaje*.

Furthermore, the Inca and Bhabha would seem to agree on the notion that the recognition of cultural alterity is predicated on translation[14] and that therefore it is "from this hybrid location of cultural value—the transnational as the transnational—that the postcolonial intellectual attempts to elaborate a historical and literary project" (Bhabha 173). Bhabha postulates today what the Inca and Guamán Poma knew and practiced some four hundred years ago. Basically, when conquest and cultural encounter call for deep levels of translation and negotiation between different discourses and cultural practices, writing subjects engage the problematic of signification and judgement: aporia, ambivalence, indeterminacy, closure, the threat to agency, the status of intentionality, the challenge to "totalizing" concepts. They thus anticipate the problematic of contemporary theory.

Without knowing it, Homi Bhabha lists (173), as part of the ambivalence of the colonial subject, most of the rhetorico/ideological traits and subject positions which we have learned to recognize in the Inca's oeuvre. It would follow then, as Bill Ashcroft has claimed, that the postcolonial condition is not a post-independence phenomenon but rather an effect of

[13] Extending Fanon's notion of the colonial subject's desire for mutual recognition Bhabha argues that wile subordinate peoples need to assert their indigenous cultural traditions and retrieve their repressed histories, we need to be aware of the fetish of fixed identities. He stresses instead the unhomeliness, the condition of extra-territoriality that is "paradigmatic of [the] colonial and postcolonial condition" (9, 40-65).

[14] For the work of the Inca as cultural translation see the excellent work of Susana Jakfalvi-Leiva.

the imperial process from the moment of colonization to this day (2). And this is inasmuch as the study and the production of "literature" became a privileging norm, "a template for the denial of the value of the 'peripheral,' and the 'marginal,' the 'uncanonized.' Literature was made as central to the cultural enterprise of the Empire as the monarchy was to its political formation" (3). Such deployment of literature, Ashcroft asserts, has caused many writers—Henry James, T.S. Elliot—to want to deny their origins in an effort to be more English than the English (4).

However, we know of course that the Inca, unlike T.S. Elliot, went out of his way to claim, recover, and proclaim his *double* origins. Unlike Said and Bhabha, he made some very specific and different claims to local knowledge. It is this recovery and claim of local knowledge that not only needs to be acknowledged in this debate but should indeed be restored to its proper place without defacing deformations or a totalizing overhauling into postcolonial generalities. It therefore seems pertinent that, although I cannot take up the matter fully here, a few more remarks on postcolonial theory and our understanding (teaching) of Latin American culture and literature be made. But before I do so I believe it important to clear up, a bit, not only the meaning of "post" but especially the uses of "modernity." Surely, the very notion of a Latin American postmodernity calls into question the kinds of modernities we may have in mind.

III. Emancipatory Projects at Large

Deploying Latin American writing as either postmodern *avant la lettre*, as Casullo and others do, or postcolonial before the "post," as I have shown that it can be done, is a question that needs careful discussion. For my purposes here I want to set my limits between David Harvey's *The Condition of Postmodernity* (1989) and Enrique Dussel's *The Invention of the Americas* (1995) because both attempt a study of modernity that could enable us to rescue the liberating forces within it. Inasmuch as modernity was conceived as an emancipatory project to set us free from ignorance, intellectual obscurity, and tyranny, it is important to see what went wrong and identify what can be salvaged before the whole enterprise is discarded as some postmodernist opinions would have it. In such an appraisal it is always useful to keep in mind Ihab Hassan's contrast between modernity and postmodernity (Hassan table 1). It articulates the postmodern critique of modernity in a nutshell, but it does not, as we shall see, take into account the first critique of modernity which Dussel attempts to delineate in his most recent work, nor does it show the disunity of modernity itself.

In his chapter on "Modernity and Modernism" David Harvey examines Baudelaire's thesis on modernism (1863). In it the poet conjoins the ephemeral and fleeting with the eternal and the immutable as the sense of modernity (Baudelaire). Harvey notes how modernism, thus conceived, has the capacity to "swing around in meaning until it faces the opposite direction" (10). It can, simultaneously, hold conflicting meanings and feelings of mastery and vulnerability (10). The tension and conflicting meanings thus imbedded in Baudelaire's notion of modernism account for the different and contradictory meanings attributed to modernism.

Modernism stands for a feeling of joy, powerfulness, adventure, and transformation which is underlined by a sense of impending chaos, fragmentation, and destruction. Modernity is then "a paradoxical unity, a unity of disunity; it pours us all into a maelstrom of perpetual disintegration and renewal, of struggle and contradiction, of ambiguity and anguish. To be modern is to be part of a universe in which, as Marx said, 'all that is solid melts into air'" (11). In some ways, it would seem that postmodernity is but a radicalization of one of the Janus faces of this unity of disunity.

Paramount in Baudelaire's model is a sense of contingency and fragmentation, a feeling that the transitoriness of things, as in *Dom Camurro* (1890) by Machado de Assis and *Rayuela* by Julio Cortázar, overtakes us in a sea of constant change. It nullifies any possibility of viewing biography or history as continuity. And yet as Harvey points out, *the project* of modernity, as it goes back to the Enlightenment, would disavow any such set of uncertainties and contingencies. It thus follows that on the illuminated side of its own (hidden) doubleness, the project of the Enlightenment was a movement to secularize and demystify knowledge and social organization in order to liberate all human beings from the oppression of ignorance. Knowledge, the most distinctive characteristic of *Homo sapiens*, was to provide objective science, universal laws based on universal morality, and autonomous art. At the center of the project of modernity rested the ascendancy of autonomous thinking subjects who, empowered by knowledge, would carry on a general emancipatory project. It would release the human species from the abuse of arbitrary power and its own

dark and sinful nature. This desideratum was called progress. Harvey
points out that the Enlightenment thinkers saw the maelstrom of change
and the transitoriness of things as the necessary condition through which
the modernizing project would be achieved (13).

So it would seem that the project of modernity as it stems from the
Enlightenment, not unlike Baudelaire's sense of the modern, allows for a
dual formulation from its inception. What brings about the disillusion
with the project of modernity is not its unity in disunity nor the change
and destruction "necessary" to its protean processes as Europe spread to
all corners of the globe "modernizing" it, but the unanticipated events
that turned the destructive power of science and progress upon Europe
itself. Whether the project should be abandoned completely, as postmodernist thought would have it, or salvaged in part, depends on how we
explain and how we identify the *dark side* of the project and it has had its
deployment in world history. The question Dussel and Harvey ask is
how do we now understand, that is intervene, in the knowledge/power
game so as to erase the fascism within its constitution?

Both Harvey and Dussel, although coming from very different intellectual traditions, present genealogies of Enlightenment thought which
attempt to isolate dormant elements within the project of modernity that
already contain the makings of fascism. Dussel pushes his examination of
the killing-fields of modernity all the way back to the "discovery" of
America. The Argentine philosopher argues that the holocaust of the
conquest constitutes the pivotal side of European modernity. I will take
up Dussel's thesis later, but for the moment I want to continue to examine other relevant aspects of Harvey's view on the kind of modernity
which postmodern thinking sets up for the purposes of the constitution
of its own difference.

While the Enlightenment erects fixed categories necessary to its own
claims of universality, necessary to the challenge that its reason will pose
to ecclesiastical power, it also masks a contradiction inasmuch as it allows
the artist an autonomous (aesthetic) realm of cognition beyond reason
itself. Exactly who possessed the claim to "superior" reason seemed, if
not doubtful, at least ambiguous. On the one hand, Francis Bacon, in his
utopian *New Atlantis* (1620) envisioned and "elite but collective male,
white wisdom" (Harvey 14), while others, like Rousseau, radicalized
feeling and proposed a different strategy for achieving the emancipatory
hopes which the Enlightenment placed on the "great minds."

The concept of the artist's exceptionality, however, proved malleable to yet another way. Enlightenment reason could not easily account for the art treasure which was pouring into imperial Europe. Thus Europe's second empire conceives of a separate aesthetic realm in an effort to accommodate the *objects* (cultures and other knowledge) which daily arrive into the coffers of queens, collectors, museums, archives, merchants, and scholars. The heart of Europe, the place where philosophy has *its home*, makes room, sets up a separate chamber—the aesthetic mode of cognition—to deal with the unexpected results of cultural contact and conquest.

In doing so the Enlightenment was of course reiterating the stipulations by which Amerindian thought, once separated from gold ornaments, came to be represented by the evangelizing reason of Spanish intellectuals, as the work of the devil. As such it was confined not to a separate mode of cognition but more radically to the realm of the dark and sinful irrational, while Christian theology and desire served as the basis for the claims to "natural" dominance in a "rational" and "civilizing" order.[15] In this division of labor we can see an anticipation of Carl Pletsche's modern division of epistemological labor: Europe (First World) produces knowledge, that is philosophy and science, the Second World produces ideology, that is false knowledge, and the Third World produces "culture," objects and peoples which can be studied as if they were "autonomous" from the society (knowledge) in which they emerge (Pletsche).

Aesthetics arouse as an autonomous field, Harvey argues, also out of the recognition of the "difficulty of translating Enlightenment principles of rational and scientific understanding into moral and political principles appropriate for action" (19). It was, Harvey states, in this gap that Nietzsche was able to insert his powerful and devastating message: art and aesthetic feeling have the power to beyond good and evil (19). A radicalization of Harvey's argument, in light of the already discussed effects brought about by cultural contact, would lead us to propose that the recognition of the difficulty in translating "rational and scientific" principles into "universal political principles" is a recognition driven *home* by the contradictory experience of empire and its "civilizing mission" or rather the imposition of one local (universal) cultural ethos over other systems of rationality such as the

[15] For a concise discussion of the Spanish intellectuals who fashioned such reason, see Brading.

Aztec, Andean, or Hindu. So that we can read Nietzsche radical subjec-
tivism itself as a response to the challenges posed by other rationalities
which he *represented* and figured in his encounter with and restoration of
the (home) cult of Dionysus.

With the uplifting of aesthetics above science and philosophy, the unified and fixed reason of the Enlightenment registered yet another unfore-
seen vulnerability to *other* realms of cognition, even when, as in the case
of Nietzsche and Freud, the knowing subject labored under the belief
that it *alone* was pushing the logic of reason beyond its very (*home*) limits. To know otherwise, to know beyond good and evil, even in the case
of the postmodern critique of modernism has not yet acknowledged the
possibility of knowing from the reason of the other, for the other when
recognized, has always been domesticated under the label of "culture,"
"myth," "Cubism," and more recently "magic realism." Until the assault
staged by postmodernism Europe has not dared to know, as Kant
required of reason to do, the reason of radical alterity. In other words,
Europe's various versions of modernism—fleeting or eternal—, as well as
postmodernism, have yet to acknowledge the shape of their own formation as subject in contact with other cultures.

In his introduction to the recent reprinting of the translation into English of Fernando Ortiz's *Contrapunteo cubano* (1940) (*Cuban Counterpoint*, 1995) Fernando Coronil rightly points out that the work of the
Cuban anthropologist stands as a critique of this imperial occlusion, for
"Ortiz shows that the constitution of the modern world has entailed a clash
and disarticulation of peoples and civilizations together with the production of images of integrated cultures, bounded identities and inexorable
progress" (xiii). Moreover, from a peripheral perspective and thus with a
different accent from Baudelaire's, Ortiz puts forth the idea that a world
forged by the violence of conquest and colonization makes defining the
boundaries of the West and its Others, an always risky proposition.[16]

For yet another genealogy—as opposed to a fixed point of origin—for
an examination that shows even deeper errors, false beginnings, greater
disparity, radical invention, and imagined appraisals of self consistency,[17]

---

[16] See Ortiz (ix-lvi). Important in this debate are also Coronil's views on Bronis-
law Malinowski's sly introduction of Ortiz's original cultural model.

[17] Michel Foucault differentiates history from genealogy in that the latter is not
"the erecting of foundations." Instead it "disturbs what was previously considered

we now turn to Dussel's revision of the conquest of the Amerindian civilization and the role it played in the constitution of European self-centered identity. For a consideration of the possible role of the emancipatory power of modernity in a global future we need to consider Dussel's discursive configuration in which Europe's modernity would not occlude but rather face its corresponding other: Latin America.

Dussel contends that a "myth lies hidden in the emancipatory concept of modernity" and that Eurocentrism and its concomitant component, the "development fallacy," become the central issue once the existence of this myth is acknowledged (19-20). Modernity's myth, its hidden false origin in Descartes' dictum "I think therefore I am," the imaginary quality of its own self consistency, has to do, in Dussel's argument, with a misreading of its origins. Such a misreading lies hidden and yet animates the implications of the despotism imbedded in Kant's "What is Enlightenment?" (1784). Here Dussel reads Kant at slant from Foucault's own influential reading of the same text. The Argentine philosopher links instantly Kant's views of emancipation from a "state of immaturity" (69)[18] to Hegel's developmental philosophy of history. While both Foucault and Dussel focus on Kant's notion that enlightenment (*Aufklärung*) means the "exit of humanity by itself from a state of culpable immaturity" (Dussel 117), there is soon a parting of ways over the genealogy and meaning of "immaturity."

On the one hand Foucault argues that "exit" does not mean a heralding of a new era but rather a difference that *today* introduces with respect to yesterday and that "immaturity" refers thus not to a period but rather to a certain state of our will that makes us accept someone else's authority to lead us to where the use of reason is called for. Thus, "Enlightenment is defined by a modification of the pre-existing relation linking the will, authority and the use of reason" (Foucault, "What is Enlightenment?" 34). From this interpretation of Kant's phrase Foucault goes on to argue that Enlightenment constitutes a "dare to know" and not the dawn of a new period in history. Dussel, on the other hand, reads Kant's statement *more*

---

immobile, it fragments what was thought unified; it shows the heterogeneity of what was imagined consistent with itself" ("Nietzsche, Genealogy, History" 82).

[18] Michel Foucault's essay "What is Enlightenment?" takes its title from the piece Kant published as a response to a newspaper inquiry on the subject in 1784. See Kant. The quotation here comes from the version quoted by Dussel in (20).

fully, or with a different stress. He focuses on the meaning of the whole phrase in which immaturity is modified by *culpable.* Altogether, Kant speaks of a culpable immaturity anchored in "laziness and cowardliness" which are "the causes [that] bind great parts of humanity in this frivolous state of immaturity" (Dussel 33). Foucault may have missed, or failed to recognize, the origin of such views and phrases, but for Dussel they are objects of instant recognition for they belong to none other than Gonzalo Fernández de Oviedo y Valdés (1478-1557), the Spanish humanist who in his denigration of the inhabitants of the New World advanced the notion that the Indians bore the blame for their conquest and enslavement. The slave owner Humanist-*cum-encomendero,* in his *Historia general y natural de las Indias* (1535), let the world know that "This people [are] by nature lazy and vicious, of little faith, melancholic, cowardly, of low and evil inclinations, liars and of little memory or constancy... In the same way in which their skulls are thick so is their understanding, beastly and ill-inclined" (Fernández de Oviedo y Valdés, qtd. in Brading 40; 677). Foucault's forgetfulness or ignorance leads to one reading. Dussel's archival detection leads in quite another direction. His linkage between Oviedo's justification for conquest and holocaust with Kant's hidden genealogy of meanings and Hegel's developmentalism is unavoidable from the Latin American intellectual perspective.

Dussel makes a further connection and shows how Kant's views on immature cultures provide the ground for a full-blown theory of Eurocentric exceptionality, as David Brading shows in his *The First America,* an idea already posited by Fernández de Oviedo and Ginés de Sepúlveda as the ground for the justification of Spanish domination of the Amerindians even when and after evangelization had turned them into "good" Christians (Brading 79-101). Such exceptionalism is of course contained in Hegel's philosophy on the works of the Spirit in, for, and from the heart of Europe. Dussel reminds us that Hegel's developmental views produced the American peoples, even the fauna and the flora, as examples of primitive, monstrous, degenerate weaklings (21). Such views are of course not far from the "descriptions" that Fernández de Oviedo, the Italian educated owner of *encomiendas,* offered Europe in the middle of the sixteenth century. Both Europeans built the case for the Amerindians to be always *constitutionally behind* or outside Spirit.

Thus one could argue with Dussel that Enlightenment reason did not in fact *dare to know (sapere aude).* Actually, it denied and repressed a substantial part of its own knowledge (of the other) in order to construct its own exceptionality. However, in an awkward but not so distant way, Dussel's arguments concerning this "dare to know," which Kant calls the Enlightenment, could in fact be bolstered by other aspects of Foucault's analysis of Kant's text. The French theorist stresses how the contradictory ways in which the play of obedience and dare to know, the play of private and public reason in Kant's views on the Enlightenment, end up in a *contract of rational despotism* which Kant proposes to Frederick II, and which by extension underline modernity's occlusion of the rationality of the Other.

In order to better appreciate my point on Foucault and Dussel and Dussel's own thesis on the occlusion of the reason of the Other, let me here review Foucault's analysis of the play of reason in the drama by which humanity would *exit the state of immaturity*. According to Foucault, Kant defines two essential conditions under which mankind can escape from its immaturity. This requires making a distinction between the realm of obedience from the realm of the use of reason. Humanity will reach maturity when it is no longer required to obey and it will use reason for reason's sake, that is to think as one pleases (so long as one obeys as one must?). This brings in the distinction between the private and public use of reason. Reason would be free in its public use and submissive in its private (daily?) use. Kant's proposal then comes down to a political problem in which individuals would have the audacity to exercise reason freely in public while they obey as scrupulously as possible in private (Foucault, "What is Enlightenment?" 37). The best guarantee for this contract with rational despotism is the idea of the public and free use of *Autonomous reason*, for such use guarantees obedience, on the condition that the political principles to be obeyed conform with universal reason (37). Foucault here notes that both terms—universal and humanity—offer even further problems, but he stays with the freedom/obedience contradiction or aporia.

It is here that Dussel's argument can be used to radicalize the problematic that Foucault sees in "What is Enlightenment?" This radicalization is possible because Dussel's thinking is elaborated from a different locus of enunciation, and that is the Latin American intellectual tradition, which, as David Brading points out, occurs by "reason of its engagement with native history and American reality" and is thus "idiosyncratic, regionally diverse, and distinct from any European model" (1). As Europe always already knew from its long experience in conquest and cultural contact, but particularly after contact with the Amerindian civilizations and the great debate between Las Casas and Sepúlveda, there is no "universal" (political) reason to be stipulated, much less one that can guarantee or be compatible with *Autonomous reason*. Therefore the contract could not be made "universal" by relying on the notion of a reasoning "humanity." Implicit in the formulation of the contract is the need for domination, obedience, and violence. As Dussel puts it, it is the need for this violence onto those constructed as being in a state of "culpable immaturity" that constitutes the myth of modernity and development.

IV. DUSSEL AND MUTUAL RECOGNITION

Despite the fact that or precisely because such a devastation of Enlightenment's reason is now possible in Europe itself, but especially because Dussel, like other Latin American intellectuals have *another* subject and history in mind, *The Invention of the Americas* does not completely give up on the emancipatory forces of the project of modernity or reason itself. The project Dussel proposes, not unlike Garcilaso's own some four hundred years earlier, is to salvage reason from the killing violence of the Spanish warrior class and its intellectuals, the despotic violence imbedded in the Enlightenment contract and the implicit irrationality in the postmodern critique of modernity's myths. Dussel's project entails, like Garcilaso' own, the destruction of the opposition between self and other as constitutive of the process of self-identity. It calls for the mutual recognition of the reason of the respective other. Such a project would mean the end of a Europe/Latin American hierarchical opposition. Out of this destruction there would emerge a sense of coexistence. Such a project was made impossible by a modernity that came to be constituted on the basis of the *requerimiento*, characterized by Brading as a:

> cynical piece of legal gibberish which proved a source of much merriment both to its author and the conquerors. In effect it announced that God, the creator of the first men, had chosen St. Peter and his successors in Rome as monarchs of the world, superior in authority to all earthly princes. A latter-day pope had conferred possession of the Indies on the king of Spain. In consequence the Indians were *commanded to recognize his authority and to become his free, Christian subjects*. Any denial or delay in accepting these demands would entail

instant war, rendering them liable to death or enslavement as rebels. Perhaps the most remarkable feature of the *requerimiento* was the absence to any reference to Christ, his place in the theoretical scheme allocated to St. Peter or the Papacy. (81, my emphasis)

Dussel's argument that the myth of modernity perpetrates a gigantic *inversion* in which the innocent victim becomes culpable, and the culpable victimizer becomes innocent, is clearly founded in the theoretical scheme that the Spanish humanists Ginés de Sepúlveda and Juan López de Palacios Rubios fashioned in the *requerimiento*. Not unlike Ginés de Sepúlveda, modernity lapses into irrationality by advocating violence as the means for including, or rather subsuming, the other.

One of the cornerstones of the project by which reason may be rescued out of the ruins of modernity entails a radical reexamination of the earliest formation of modernity in order to recover, uncover, and acknowledge the violent reason of conquest and oppression. Forgetting the past will not do and a new and fresh (postcolonial?) critique of it is again necessary in order to establish a reasoning conversation among "equally" posited subjects. To this effect Dussel will not criticize reason as such. He differs from the postmodern theorists, although he does accept their critique of reason as dominating, victimizing, and violent. "I will not deny universalist rationalism its rational nucleus, but I do oppose the irrational elements of its sacrificial myth... I affirm the reason of the Other as a step toward a transmodern worldhood" (26).

One of the chief points that *The Invention of the Americas* seeks to make in the modern/postmodern debate is that the reason of violence, fundamental to the first European expansion by conquest, already holds within it the despotic contract of the Enlightenment. However, the purpose of Dussel's argument is not simply to push back the genealogy to Spanish humanists such as Ginés de Sepúlveda, but rather, like Garcilaso, to reposition the reason of the Other and thus *complete* the works of reason as such. This is accomplished in two moves which bear keen relevance to the problematic deployed in the notion that inspires the title of *The Empire Writes Back*.

First, Dussel makes a distinction between the despotic thinking of Ginés de Sepúlveda, who defends the right to conquest on the basis of Luke 14: 15-24, and one of the first critiques of modernity in Gerónimo de Mendieta's (1525-1606) utopian *Historia eclesiástica indiana* [ms 1596, facsimile 1870] (68).[19] Although the Franciscan favored waging war against the indigenous people, if they opposed evangelization, he nevertheless recognized the rationality of Amerindian peoples and cultures and the need to preserve them both. It is only Bartolomé de Las Casas however, who among the intellectuals of his time, is able to *surpass* modernity's own sense of criticism as represented by Mendieta and Vitoria and later Kant (69).

In his own daring to know, Las Casas exposed the logical contradictions, the intentionally false rendering of Amerindian practices and beliefs, and the humanist invention of a culpable immaturity. As he sees it, in Las Casas' political theory there already operates a model for the trans-modern dialogue that he seeks with the people like Habermas. Dussel states that the Bishop of Chiapas

> appropriated modernity's emancipatory meaning without partaking of its irrational myth, which attributed culpability to the Other. He denied the validity of any argument sanctioning violence in order to *compel* the other to join the community of communication... Las Casas's concern focused on how the other should enter the community and begin to participate in it. (69-70)

Therefore, Las Casas is the first and only (post-colonial?) European to insist on the rationality of the other and on the inescapable need for a dialogue on the basis of reason. It is interesting here to note that David Brading singles out Las Casas in a similar manner and credits him with having redefined the political theory of papal authority over the Amerindian possessions (96) as well as having developed the theoretical basis for a comparative ethnography (90-92).

The second move that Dussel makes is to reposition reason. He harnesses what we *now* know—the difference that the present makes upon the past—about the rational conditions of the knowledge which articulated Guarani, Aztec, or Andean societies. He, like Garcilaso in his *Comentarios*, shows (even if Descartes and Derrida ignored them) that "before there

---

[19] Dussel is not only hard on Sepúlveda's Spanish humanism but he also demands greater coherence of the contemporary critics of modernity. He feels that "modern humanist [such as] Ginés de Sepúlveda shared the conquistadors frame of mind, as do contemporary rationalists who anticipate an easy dialogue or does Jürgen Habermas who has yet to develop a theory of the conditions of the possibility of dialogue" (87).

being a *cogitatum*" this other (Amerindian) was already a distinct (*distincta*) subjectivity and not merely different in postmodern terms (74).

In his chapter "Amerindian in a Non-Eurocentric Vision of World History," Dussel both re-inscribes Garcilaso, even if he hardly makes mention of him, and attempts to *surpass* the sixteenth-century project of the Inca's two-fold *mestizaje*. Assuming a truly de-centered world and a radical deconstruction of Europe's reason, Dussel attempts to establish the theoretical possibility for a conversation in a community of equals which begins with the recognition of the Other not as *projection*, and not measured and evaluated in Europe's own discursive terms. The trans-modern project calls for a "bonding [which] occurs not via negation, via subsumption from the viewpoint of alterity" (138). Only then, when the viewpoint of alterity has occupied the place (home) of the discursive apparatus will the possibility of transcending Eurocentrism be actual and the emancipatory promise of modernity be regarded as a serious possibility. And here is where I see the half move that neither Garcilaso nor Kant's Enlightenment, not even Baudelaire's sense of the ephemeral and the fleeting, ever made towards emancipation: to put up the works of Christianity and its links to empire on the table for a radical historicizing project.

I believe that Dussels trans-modern project, a project that links up with Las Casas and Garcilaso's critique of modernity's "I conquer therefore I am," a project that stems from the specificities of Latin America's geo-cultural formation, should be conceived as one of the two arms of a pincer-like movement onto a Eurocentric reason not yet ready to acknowledge its constitution in empire. The other arm would be the Anglophone postcolonial theorizing of projects such as *The Empire Writes Back* together with the orchestral assembly of *Colonial Discourse and Post-Colonial Theory* edited by Patrick Williams and Laura Chrisman (1994).

V. Empires and the Pleats of Mimicry

Nevertheless, in proposing a pincer-like movement onto the single-minded constitutionality of European reason, the question of imitation or mimicry needs to be cleared up, for it is essential to the idea of dialogue between imperial subject and its relational subaltern. In the postmodern postcolonial debate, as it pertains to Latin America, there are several propositions floating about which need examination. First there is the notion that the internationally famous repertoire of recent Latin American fiction makes up an ensemble of postmodern texts *avant la lettre*. Such a projection, like Osorio's refusal to accept the "post" without a previous, full-fledged modernity, postulates a single, all-encompassing line of development and locations. Second, we have the arguments advanced by the notion of the "shock of recognition" (Stonum) which makes it possible to think of North American and Latin America's discursive formations, due to their marginal and contestatory geocultural beginnings and locations, as always already postmodern. Third, of course, there is the case of Borges, not often enough theorized as a precursor of Europe's postmodern theory[20] but somehow always acknowledged as having something to do with it. Fourth, since so many of the topics in the discursive problematic of postcolonial theory seem to be but a repetition of problems faced earlier by Latin American writers and intellectuals, it seems logical to see in figures such as Garcilaso de la Vega, Inca, a postcolonial writer (theorist) *avant la lettre* (see chapter 6, "Writing Subalternity," in this volume). Fifth, both the claims made generally by postmodern and postcolonial theory for Latin American letters are gestures which simply re-inscribe Latin America's elites' cultural dependence on outside theorists. In the case of postcolonial "theory," the theorists are former colonials of the English empire, and they have gotten far ahead of the Latin Americans even if the Spanish-speaking folks may have gotten started earlier. Gayatri Spivak, Chandra Mohanty, Homi Bhabha et al. have *purchase* at the center in a way in which no Latin American intellectual has ever had. It is the challenge of *Orientalism* (1985), *The Location of Culture* (1992) and *In Other Worlds* (1988), among others, which bring renewed questions for intellectual history, historiography, and cultural criticism.

Altogether these claims and propositions would seem to engage in a surface play of images on mirrors held at an angle from each other. Are we before a nomenclature game, or do have something more concrete in this game which would seem to devolve on the question of *imitation* or maybe even mimicry, that is "the wearing of a linguistic mask, speech in a dead language" (Jameson, *Postmodernism* 16-17). It would seem as if Borges's own beginning in "Tlön, Uqbar, Orbis Tertius" (1944): "Debo

---

[20] For an excellent examination of the topic, see Toro.

a la conjunción de una enciclopedia y un espejo...." (Borges 431) were unfolding in this consideration of Latin American intellectual traditions and postcolonial theorizing.

Taking his concept of mimicry from Lacan,[21] Homi Bhabha has put into circulation the idea that the colonial subject rearticulates in mimicry "the representation of identity and meaning along the axis of metonymy" (90). Bhabha goes on to quote Lacan and say that mimicry is like camouflage, "not a harmonizing or repression of difference, but a form of resemblance, that differs from or defends presence by displacing it in part, metonymically" (89). Its threat, Bhabha believes, stems from the prodigious and strategic production of conflictual, fantastic, discriminatory "identity effects" in the play of "a power that is elusive because it hides no essence, no itself. And that form of resemblance is the most terrifying to behold" (90). Thus, in a colonial (postcolonial?) situation we are before a metonymy of presence (89) and what emerges between mimesis and mimicry is *writing*, a mode of representation (87).

Though Bhabha's thesis on mimicry starts out by locating the strategy of mimicry in the forked, "though not false," tongue of Lord Rosebery and other English subjects involved in the colonization of India, Bhabha makes a point of showing how the metonymy of mimicry in the colonial situation is in fact double. Mimicry constitutes the hallmark of the subjectivity produced by the English colonial education (Bhabha himself?). The Indian critic takes his cue from V.S. Naipaul and his novel *The Mimic Men* (1967): "Mimic man raised 'through our English schools' [...] is the effect of a flawed colonial mimesis, in which to be Anglicized is *emphatically* not to be English" (87). For a Latin American, the resemblance and repetition between Naipaul's "discovery" of turning out to be "almost the same, but not quite (white)," *written* originally by Garcilaso and then by countless other Latin Americans is only too obvious. But, do we have here yet another doubling, in which the English ex-colonials take the subject position of Lord Rosebery and the Latin American intellectuals occupy the Naipaul-Bhabha position, or do we posit our own first *writ-*

---

[21] Lacan writes: "Mimicry reveals something in so far as it is distinct from what might be called an itself that is behind. The effect of mimicry is camouflage... It is not a question of harmonizing with the background, but against a mottled background, of becoming mottled—exactly like the technique of camouflage practiced in human warfare" (99; qtd. in Bhabha 85).

ing and theorising for the Anglophone ex-colonials to mimic? Are we, as the Lacanian Bhabha claims, locked in the endless chain of fear and paranoia of the self-same? Or is there another way to interpret the colonial mimicry, a more Andean way to resolve the displacement of self identity upon the face of difference?

Leaving such English and Spanish colonial resemblances and repetitions aside, let me note that Bhabha makes two more important points in his figuration of mimicry as a postmodern reading of subject formation in colonial settings which are important for our discussion here. First he argues, in the language of psychoanalysis and based on capital insights borrowed from Franz Fanon, that the logic of mimicry—almost the same but not quite (white)—produces not only ambivalent discourses but also gestures which destabilize colonial authority.[22] Mimicry and imitation deploy a *partial and incomplete presence* for both the master and the subaltern subject. It is this partial presence, this metonymy, that turns resemblance into a threat. It is none other than the *"guachafo*, crudely and wisely expresses in the popular 'Aunque se vista de seda la mona, mona se queda.'"[23] One cannot help but note the obvious similarity in situations of mimicry ("representation of a difference that is itself a disavowal," 86) between Latin American and Indian instances of colonial writing. Such have occurred in Latin American texts, first in relation to Spanish and Portuguese canonical rules and tastes, and later in differential representation of class and ethnic identities (Arguedas, Parente Cunha, Eltit, L.R. Sánchez) in countless instances. However, I think that in a comparison between postcolonial (West and East) Indian writing and the Latin America's on going critique of modernity and Eurocentrism (Garcilaso, Guamán Poma, Fray Servando Teresa de Mier, Las Casas, Borges et al.), Latin America subjects *resemble* but do *not mimic* the ambivalence por-

[22] Bhabha does not distinguish between the colonial subaltern subject and the colonizer subject when he speaks of "colonial" subject or discourse. This may be because he believes that mimicry is a two-way street isasmuch as "mimicry emerges as the representation of a difference that is itself a process of disavowal. Mimicry is thus the sign of a double articulation" (86).

[23] Resemblance into a threat describes Unamuno's reception of Darío in Spain when he said after personally meeting the Nicaraguan poet: "Todavía se le ven las plumas." Another good example of the threat of the partial presence of imitation is the well known syndrome of the "guachafo" in Peru which Vargas Llosa has amply employed in his novels beginning with *Pantaleón y las visitadoras* (1973).

trayed in Bhabha's agonistic and deterritorialized own narrative of mimicry. And I think that this difference has to do with Bhabha's exaggeration of the deterritorializing force of migration from the torrid to the
temperate zones. Moreover, I think that the Indian critic overestimates
the historical and universalizing power of the Lacanian subject theory
with which he invest his reading of Naipaul. In fact, with his own arguments but to a different effect I would say that *similar* is, precisely, *not the
same,* nor does it need to be.

Because mimicry repeats, Lacan says, it threatens with the notion that
there is no original (nothing behind). It follows, according to Bhabha,
that there is no essential Englishness, culture, history, and correspondingly no authentic Indian culture. Mimicry, as repetition of a non-origi-
nal, does indeed translate Naipaul's own geo-cultural location. But does
it translate Garcilaso's, Arguedas' or Borges's in comparable terms of
uprootedness? Lacan's split subject in Bhabha's hands duplicates end-
lessly without ever finding a *home,* a behind or a place of origeneity. For
Naipaul's mimic men there is no geo-cultural location, no ground, no history. For mimic men history turns into a farce. Naipaul chooses to be
English (use of the English language, schools, publishers, residence)
while the Inca, though marooned in Spain, chose to be part of a collectivity of others, who for historical reasons, did or would *resemble his own*
developing identity. Above all, the Garcilaso de la Vega, Inca, Arguedas,
Borges et al. chose the materiality of a place, a location that, despite a condition of uprootedness (unhomeliness) could be mapped into a *home,* a
place from which to speak. Starting with the Inca, Latin American intellectuals have looked upon the inevitable situation of mimicry and transformed its threat of endless splitting into the will to coexist, that is to
occupy both places at once. That is why Garcilaso, with an Andean ideology of complementarily in mind—*hanan* and *hurin*—*chooses the excess of
both* rather than the part in the metonymic game of presence. Naipaul's
"almost but not quite" therefore falls short of Garcilaso's use of the Spanish language to say "porque soy indio y me precio de ello."

Let us remember here that the Andean ideology of complementarity
postulates the confrontation and reciprocity of opposing forces. Duality is
the principle that structures the religious and social dimensions of the
Andean world. Bodily symmetry is the model for duality (Platt). Dyarchy
was the principle of organization for army command as well as for provincial administration (*curacas*). The Andean idea of duality is also expressed

in the mirror symmetry attributed to the male gods. The great divinities—Tunapa, Viracocha and Pachacamac—were not only marked by doubled characteristics and opposite attributes but they were also ruled by the principle of *hanan* and *hurin* (above and below). María Rostworowski explains that "Cada divinidad poseía su doble llamado "hermano" por los naturales. Tenían la idea de que todos los dioses disponían de una réplica, del mismo modo que cada Inca poseía su *huaque* o hermano" (22). Thus, these Andean dual and cuatripartite models differ markedly from the binary models Levi-Strauss postulates for the Amazonian societies he studies. It is these very binary models, and not the complimentary Andean duality, which inform Derridian and Lacanian theorizing, that is to say the fountainhead for Bhabha's "colonial" mimic men.

What is more, the logic of complimentarity assumed by Garcilaso in his desire to *be both* in his writing in order to double the meaning-making processes holds within the capacity for the figuration of that which is dissimilar. Rostworowski points out that "el espejo reproduce la imagen como un duplicado y la palabra *yanantin* expresa la simetría corporal que se traduce en las piernas, pies, brazos, manos, orejas, ojos, senos, testículos. Entre ellos son *ichoc-allauca*, la izquierda y la derecha; mientras la boca y el ano son lo alto y lo bajo" (22). In opposition to symmetrical objects, the word *chhulla* indicates that which comes without a pair, by itself, that is uneven. "La idea de *chhulla* complementa la dualidad de *yanantin* para formar la tríada" (22). Thus *hanan* (masculine and above) and *hurin* (feminine and below) express the complimentary cuatripartition with which Garcilaso "theorizes" the sets of oppositeness and exclusions that the colonial system imposes. Dyarchy among the Incas allowed the possibility of thinking in terms of simultaneous existence of two Incas, one in Hanan Cuzco (older bother) and the other in Hurin Cuzco (younger brother) This notion of duality and simultaneity has nothing to do with the metonymy of mimicry. Garcilaso makes clear reference to this cuatripartite division in his narration of Cuzco's foundational myth.[24] Furthermore, Tom Zuidema also shows that the Cuzco genealogical model provides for the adoption of enemies in the role of

---

[24] In his *Inca Civilization in Cuzco* (1990), Tom Zuidema points out that the Inca model of administration derived from the Cuzco origin myths proposes a genealogy in which the enemies are adopted in the role of ancestors. This genealogical model allowed for assimilation at all levels, including the highest.

ancestors and that such assimilation can take place at all levels including the level of "Inca by privilege."

Thus we see that Garcilaso, having within his arsenal of discursive possibilities an epistemology of complimentarity and assimilation by privilege, is able to formulate his theory of *mestizaje*—a doubling—as a response to the colonial formation of difference. This *mestizaje*, which at once completes and complements, is very far from the paranoia of the "self-same" which underlines the mimicry that Bhabha postulates. With Garcilaso before Bhabha, and with Dussel before Foucault, we find ourselves situated in genealogical points which are tied to specific and different localities. The close examination of both Garcilaso and Dussel show that genealogies of local knowledge not only yield specific but very different intellectual formations. Such differences clearly limit the power of homogenization inherent in the seduction of all postmodern theorizing, postcolonial theories included, and caution us on the need to continue to historicize our subjects-objects of knowledge.

Again we have here a question of different and specific genealogies, themselves locked in step to the specificities of place and "history."[25] Without devoting attention to specific genealogies and to integrated knowledge of particular phases in global history, we run the risk of privileging colonialism as the supreme event in history and homogenizing the multiple processes of othering as well as resisting otherness.[26] In order not to fall into versions of postmodern or postcolonial theory that

[25] A. Ahmad's critique of postcolonial theory and its aggrandizement with global claims at the expense of time-space specificities is well taken. Mimicry is one of those terms undergoing an inflationary purchase. Moreover, Ahmad feels that postcolonial theory suppresses the explanatory power of Marxist theory. For Ahmad the axis colonial/postcolonial creates more problems than it solves and therefore "we need to produce integrated knowledge of a particular phase in global history ("Postcoloniality: What is a Name" 28).

[26] See Benita Parry, "Problems in Current Theories of Colonial Discourse", *Oxford Literary Review* 9 (1&2), 1987. See also Aijaz Ahmad, "Third World Literature in the Era of Multinational Capital", in *Theory: Class, Nations, Literatures*. London: Verso, 1992. A more recent argument on the need to study distinct genealogies can be found in Juan Poblete, "Homogeneización y heterogeneización en el debate sobre la modernidad y la post/modernidad". *Revista de Crítica Literaria Latinoamericana*. Año XXI, No. 42. Lima, 1995, 115-30. Poblete writes "la paradoja de la postmodernidad es entonces, que, a este nivel, se constituye, necesariamente, en una homogeneizante afirmación de la heterogeneidad" (121).

become, paradoxically, homogenizations of mimicry, hybridity, subversion, and cultural cross-crossing, we need to engage specific local(ized) genealogies, narratives, and representations in order to identify the nodal points in the becoming of each. We need to learn to build alternative strategies which make it still possible to claim reason, a minimal rationality for a truly emancipatory project to be imagined.

As we have seen, Dussel's formulation of a Latin American critique of Europe's first project of modernity ("I conquer therefore I am") and his restoration of the reason of the Amerindian cultures to the human legacy constitute one such alternative genealogy. And of course there are others. I am thinking of the work carried out recently by ethnohistorians and several "literary critics." His formulation follows in the footsteps of Garcilaso' project of co-existence. Such a project of mutual recognition within and outside the subject becomes then the basis for Dussels transmodern project of emancipation which not only includes but stems from the reason of the dominated in whatever hierarchical pair they may appear. In this regard I believe that the authors of *The Empire Writes Back* make a very important point for Latin Americanists to bear in mind: in colonial situations the writers-poets, playwrights, and novelists have been the theorizer inasmuch as other, more serious, and less porous modes of representation were unavailable to them. "Writers" challenged colonial discursive authority from specific geo-cultural locations: the Maori and the Irish in Australia, the Canadians in the English commonwealth, the East Indians in Trinidad, and the African-Americans in the Caribbean.

In this vein Walter Mignolo in "Human Understanding and (Latin) American Interests: The Politics and Sensibilities of Geo-cultural Locations" offers a genealogy of Latin American meditation on self as self-constitutive. Mignolo goes beyond the notion that our discursive modes are constituted by, as well as represent, a historically given heterogeneity.[27] The Argentine critic attempts to radicalize notions of location, migration, and deterritorialization in post-colonial theorizing in order to operate a transformation in our understanding of the histories of colonization, imperialism, and globalization.

---

[27] See Perus. There she argues that Cornejo Polar's thesis on the constitutive heterogeneity of Latin American discursive modalities drawn from the imperial evidence antecede, correctly, Bakhtin's dialogics.

In trying to get past the debate on the possible correlation between postmodern theory and Latin American letters Mignolo states that "Postcolonial theories and cultural histories are not an alternative to postmodern theories and cultural analyses, but rather a complementary critical relocation of the epistemological grounds and historical allocation of cultures that we now identify with the modern period of Western European History" (101). Mignolo feels that the distinctiveness and complimentarity of Latin American intellectual production needs to be reassessed, now that territoriality and location are at once floating and fixed, now that people cross nationalities and languages and can no longer think fixed national or cultural identities. Identities are now thought of as a process which devolves upon loci of enunciation and imaginary constructions. Since Latin America entails the emergence of culture(s) out of the ruins and discontinuities of other which the conquest wrought, Mignolo, following Dussel, proposes a pluritopical hermeneutics as the appropriate grid for understanding and ascribing fitting value to the various decolonizing constructions of cultural identity which Garcilaso's *mestizaje*, Ortiz's transculturation, and Silviano Santiago's hybrid or discourse in between have elaborated. All these are examples of writing against the self-same, they are re-locations of the loci of enunciation (112).

Building with the remnants, writing against the grain, dismantling the violent reason of modernity, relocating the loci of enunciation, relocating the place of imperial languages, doing the work of transculturation in music, poetry, narrative, legitimizing ancient knowledge, and dismantling the supremacy of philosophy by showing that its undergirth is but a narrative are all intellectual operations known in the metropolis as postmodern and practiced in Latin America as part and parcel of a local knowledge marked by its geo-cultural location. However, in Latin America, such practice *cum* theory has remained nameless. It is simply what we do, oddly. Besides making claims as to our discoveries *avant la lettre*, we students of Latin America, need to go beyond claiming the rightfulness of a co-existence with Europe, beyond establishing a pluritopical hermeneutics in which the reason of the other is allocated its proper place in the communication community, we need to attempt a complete, pluritopical rewriting of our intellectual history not as mimicry but as co-existence. In such a new historicist history the first thing we must do is get rid of a periodization steeped in mimicry and which derails the necessary consideration of non-canonical texts for a *complete* accounting of our practices. In doing so we need to write a double-stranded genealogy of Europe and Latin America, one which would account for our crucial presence in its own construction as subject, for we are not others to ourselves "los indios, mestizos y criollos (del Perú)." This needs to be done now, for the process of othering is still very much at work within our "nations" and in the world at large. Only then can we wrest a subject position in a reconstructed emancipatory project of transmodernity.

Originally published in *El debate de la postcolonialidad en Latinoamérica: una postmodernidad periférica o cambio de paradigma en el pensamiento latinoamericano*. Eds. Alfonso de Toro and Fernando de Toro, 137-165. © 1999 Madrid: Iberoamericana; Frankfurt am Main: Vervuert. Reprinted by permission.

WORKS CITED

AHMAD, Aijaz. *In Theory: Classes, Nations, Literatures.* London: Verso, 1992.

—. *Postcoloniality: What is a name?* Unpublished manusrcipt, n.d.

BARTH, John. *The Literature of Exhaustion and the Literature of Replenishment.* Northridge: Lord John Press, 1982.

BEVERLEY, John. *Against Literature.* Minneapolis: University of Minnesota Press, 1993.

BHABHA, Homi K. *The Location of Culture.* London; New York: Routledge, 1994.

BORGES, Jorge Luis. "Tlön, Uqbar, Orbis Tertius." In *Obras completas 1923-1972.* Buenos Aires: Emecé Editores, 1974. 431-443.

BRADING, David. *The First America: The Spanish Monarchy, Creole Patriots, and the Liberal State, 1492-1867.* Cambridge: Cambridge University Press, 1991.

CUMMINS, Tom. "Representations in the Sixteenth Century and the Colonial Image of the Inca." In *Writing Without Words: Alternative Literacies in Mesoamerica and the Andes.* Eds. Elizabeth Hill Boone and Walter D. Mignolo. Durham: Duke University Press, 1994.

DUSSEL, Enrique. *The Invention of the Americas.* New York: Continuum, 1995.

FERNÁNDEZ, Christian. *The Concept of Commentary in the* Royal Commentaries. Washington, D.C.: Unpublished Paper: Modern Languages Association, 1996.

FOUCAULT, Michel. "Nietzsche, Genealogy, History." In *The Foucault Reader.* Ed. Paul Rabinow. New York: Pantheon Books, 1984.

—. "What is Enlightenment?" In *The Foucualt Reader*. Ed. Paul Rabinow. New York: Pantheon, 1984. 32-51.

HARVEY, David. *The Condition of Postmodernity: An Enquiry into the Origins of Cultural Change*. Cambridge: Blackwell, 1989.

HASSAN, I. "The Culture of Postmodernism." In *Theory, Culture and Society* 2.3 (1985): 119-32.

JAMESON, Fredric. *Nationalism, Colonialism and Literature*. Belfast: A Field Day Panflet, 1988.

—. *The Political Unconscious: Narrative as a Socially Symbolic Act*. Ithaca: Cornell University Press, 1981.

—. *Postmodernism, or The Cultural Logic of Late Capitalism*. Durham: Duke University Press, 1991.

—. "Third World Literature in the Era of Multinational Capitalism." In *Social Text* (Fall 1986): 65-88.

LACAN, Jaques. "The Line and the Light." In *Four Fundamental Concepts of Psychoanalysis*. Ed. Alan Sheridan. London: The Hogart Press and the Institute for Psychoanalysis, 1977. 91-105.

MAZZOTTI, José. *Subtexto andino y discurso sincrético en los Comentarios reales del Inca Garcilaso de la Vega*. Princeton: Pd.D. Dissertation, 1993.

NAIPAUL, V.S. *The Mimic Men*. New York: Macmillan, 1967.

ORTIZ, Fernando. *Cuban Counterpoint; Tobacco and Sugar*. Durham: Duke University Press, 1995.

PLATT, Tristan. "Symétrie en mirroir." In *Annales* 33 anné (septembre-decembre 1978): 1081-1107.

ROSTWOROWSKI DE DIEZ CANSECO, María. *Estructuras andinas del poder. Ideología religiosa y política*. Lima: Instituto de Estudios Peruanos, 1983.

STONUM, Gary Lee. "Undoing American History." In *Diacritics* 11 (September 1981): 45-61.

VEGA, Garcilaso de la. *Royal Commentaries of the Incas and General History of Peru*. Vol. I [1605]. Trans. Harold V. Livermore. Austin: University of Texas Press, 1966.

CHAPTER 2
Literacy, Conquest and Interpretation: Breaking New Ground on the Records of the Past

I

The stimulus provided by the plural commemorations surrounding the 500th anniversary of the first recorded arrival of European subjects to America (1492) continues to bear fruit. The unexpected conjunction of the postmodern and postcolonial challenges to received historiography and the "rediscovery" of the conquest of America have brought a number of important works which revise our understanding of European imperial expansion. Works such as Peter Hulme's *Colonial Encounters* (1986), Stephen Greenblatt's *Marvelous Possessions* (1991), Djelal Kadir's *Columbus and the Ends of the Earth* (1992), and Gordon Brotherston's *Book of the Fourth World* (1992), among others, have questioned the epistemological assumptions which until recently have guided the study of the "new" world from the matrix of its "invention" in Europe. Several recent publications further such scholarly renovation.

Understanding the past is of course always linked to the perspective that the present affords us. Our ability to read the records of the past is not only tied to the amount or quality of the "data," but it also involves our cultural capacity to recognize and interpret systems of recording information which are not our own. Both Patricia Seed's *Ceremonies of Possession* (1995) and Richard C. Trexler's *Sex and Conquest* (1995) delve deeply into sources that can be deciphered by the grammar of our conventional understanding of "writing." Patricia Seed looks at what English, French, Dutch, Spanish, and Portuguese subjects did in order to legitimate, for themselves, taking possession of the "new" land. She does not discuss how the Amerindian subjects understood such rituals nor how the Europeans reported that the Amerindians understood them. Riding on the shoulders of Spanish conqueror-observers, *Sex and Conquest* crosses the Atlantic in order to review the records left by the Spanish soldiers, bureaucrats, and missionaries on the matter of sodomy and transvestism (2). Walter D. Mignolo's *The Darker Side of the Renaissance* discusses many topics found in cultural histories, but its main project is to break with current cultural genealogies which posit the classical tradition as a justification for colonial expansion. In so doing it introduces a conception of history as a coexistence of clusters in which the darker side of the Renaissance, played out in the Americas, interacts with Other and eventually othered systems of knowledge.

After reviewing an impressive number of sources on Mediterranean antiquity Richard Trexler feels confident that he has laid the ground for arguing that "far more than intimacy in microrelationships, the primary and pre-ordaining social fact regarding male homosexual behaviors in the societies under review was the threat of *punitive* gendering of foreign and domestic enemies to show them as akin to women" (14). Thus, homosexual rape, according to Trexler, was viewed in ancient Mediterranean cultures, as "the violation of an outsider, like a foreigner, an animal and, indeed, like a woman"(17). Trexler describes how Herodotus recounts, for instance, that on conquering the Ionian cities, the Persian king had all the most favored boys emasculated. In ancient Norse society castration was also the common humiliation inflicted on losers (18). But the most striking visual record is to be found in connection with Egyptian military life. Egyptian written records include inventories of Libyan penises gathered after victory. Trexler also reminds us that Saul, in the Old Testament, required 100 foreskins of enemies from David as a price for the hand of his daughter. David brought in twice the number. In Jerusalem, a Hill of Foreskins bore witness to the covenant with Yahweh himself (18).

The connection of homosexual rape to the mutilation of male sexual organs allows Trexler to go back and forth between instances of rape after conquest, the reduction of conquered populations to sexual servitude in conquering armies and the institution of the berdache—the permanently traversed, passive male—in Islamic Spain. Trexler's main purpose in reviewing the evidence available in Europe up to the time of the Spanish conquest of Mexico and the Andes is to say that homosexual rape is an instance of asymmetrical power relations on which patriarchy is founded. He describes a world in which both men and women were born into a system of penetrative penality (7). For Trexler, military pederasty, as Spartan practice illustrates, is the way in which "these one-on-one homosexual unions emerge as fundamental parts of the process of creating, articulating and maintaining political power in ancient society, just as the later heterosexual marriage helped articulate institutions of property" (25).

Taking a cue from Michel Foucault, Trexler underscores his awareness of the dangers of projecting our modern sense of homosexuality (individual desire) onto the sodomitic practices of the past (6). He circumscribes the building of his case—the relation of punitive anal penetration to the emergence of patriarchal political institutions—to male anal penetration and/or of the sexually mutilated male's "passive" body.

In the case of Medieval Spain, the evidence marshaled by Trexler shows that despite the Christian abomination and prohibition of the "pecado nefando"—King Alfonso of Portugal decreed death by burning to the sodomites in 1446—pederasty was actually a common practice in the peninsula (52). Reasoning that widespread pederastic practices cannot appear one day and be gone the next, Trexler argues that one "simply must expect certain sexual practices within certain social formations" (59). Therefore, the soldiers who came to America grew up in a culture in which homosexuality was encountered in the political and public humiliation of the lawbreaker, the cloister, the cathedral schools, the berdache, the harems, and the armies before it surfaced as part of their own individual development (62). "They knew of men who dressed as women for life, they knew that homosexual activities were common when women where not available and they knew that homosexual activities were widespread across Iberia among the natives and not just the visitors"(62).

With this background on the Iberian conqueror—the sources for future historical and anthropological writing of Amerindian societies—Trexler turns his eyes to the Americas where he finds, as anticipated, multiple reports of transvestism, berdache, and pederasty. While writing on Europe, Trexler's awareness of the dangers of projection cautioned his assessment of sodomy and its relation to modern homosexuality. However, in the case of the Americas Trexler is more inclined to assert that "berdaches were to be found in almost all American tribes, North and South" (9). Given the diversity of Amerindian cultures among themselves, and the cultural distance from the European "model," more rather than less caution would seem necessary. Unfortunately such is not the case in *Sex and Conquest*. The reports filed by the Spanish soldiers, missionaries, and historians are not submitted to close scrutiny in view of the differences that marked the Taino, Aztec, Moche, Cherokee or "Sioux" cultures.

What is more, in his review of his sources Trexler finds the writing of the "mestizo" historians an obstacle (155). Taking Garcilaso de la Vega, Inca as his prime example, Trexler feels that *mestizo* historians "recognized that they would have to deny their female side, so to speak, a central part of their human definition, if they were ever to be able to forget their conquest and claim their (illusory) equality with the conquerors" (155). By focusing on Garcilaso's own report on the Inca laws against sodomy Trexler writes that "the fabled Incas were not, as Garcilaso would have it, haters of sodomy" (157). The case, as Trexler builds it, is quite to the contrary.

Relying on the scattered but constant Spanish reporting of pederasty among the different and diverse Amerindian societies, Trexler is able to conclude that transvestism, pederasty, and even berdache could be found anywhere from the Caribbean to the Mississippi, from Mexico to Panama, from Pachacamac to Chile. The intentionality of the reporting on sodomy—justification for the cruelty exercised by the Spanish soldiers and the evangelizers—does not weigh much in Trexler's discrimination of sources. The conditions under which "facts" were observed—battlefield, scorched earth marches, destruction of temples where gold was to be found, accusations before church authorities—are not brought into consideration for contextualization of the reports. Without paying attention to the asymmetrical linguistic and power relations of the confessionary and the evangelization campaigns, Trexler tells that he considers the writing of the missionaries the equivalent of "thick description." Further, the incommensurability of the Spanish own self-understanding with that of the diverse Amerindian cultures is not brought into this mapping of eunuchs and anal penetration in temples, warrior women in battle, or military captives in servitude. In contrast, in *Sexo y conquista* (1994) Araceli Barbosa Sánchez says that while the recent revision of the question of pederastic practices in this hemisphere indicates that it was a widespread phenomenon (62-64) it is still of capital importance to retain a critical attitude in the face of reports whose chief purpose was to justify the conquest and to defame and slander the Amerindians. Barbosa reminds the reader that Amerindians were often accused of sodomy in order to justify setting the dogs on them. Vasco (de Balboa) in Cuarecua set the dogs ("aperrear")on the Indians because the Spanish had found several men in the cacique's house wearing "women's" clothing and "dispuestos a usos licenciosos" ("predisposed and ready to engage in licentious customs"). These men were in fact wearing their customary cotton robes and face and arm jewelry (58-60).

Barbosa insists on reminding us that the reports of the Spanish *cronistas* and even the interpretation that Peter Martyr constructed "estaba plagado de mendacidad" (were saturated with mendacity) (61). Moreover, the reporting of the *cronistas*, even in the case of the intelligent and discerning Cieza de León, was mediated by European categories. In the case of the myth of the giants of Pueblo Viejo, Barbosa uses Cieza's introduction of the figure of the archangel St. Michel as an example of such mediation, whereas Trexler, commenting on the same myth, feels that Cieza's introduction of the archangel is "innocent" (143). However, Barbosa, like Trexler and Bernardo Ellefsen in *Matrimonio y sexo en el Incario* (1989), feels that there is enough reliable information which allows for further investigation of the question of ritual, religious homosexuality in temples in the Andes and Mexico. Differing from Trexler's thesis on the relation of male anal penetration and the power articulations of patriarchal state building, Barbosa asserts that both the institution of the *cuiloni* in Mexico and the *castrati* and sterile priests found in Andean temples have their origin in magico-religious rites and the general celibacy imposed in the temples. There is no question that much more research is needed before we can say anything definitive about male anal penetration in pre-modern Europe or in the Americas before and after Europe's western expansion.

As recent studies on the Andes have allowed us to gain a better sense of pan-Andean cosmologies and religious practices their connection to the state is also being understood in a more coherent manner. In the case of religious practices pertaining to the deployment of the body—dressing as "women," sexual mutilation, not dressing at all, food rituals—a thorough understanding of at least Quechua, if not also Aymara, has revealed, once again, the incommensurable dimensions of Andean cultures. Like the Spanish conquistadors and other early "observers" of Amerindian cultures, Renaissance scholars generally lack such linguistic competence. Such is not the case, however, with the work of María Rostworowski, whose many books on Andean religiosity and state building are not cited in *Sex and Conquest*.

Taking into consideration the extensive vocabulary for body parts, sensory terms and their articulation in Quechua and Aymara, Constance Classen, in *Inca Cosmology and the Human Body* (1993), writes that the body was held as a symbol of the principle religious tenet in Inca society. It was the junction of the principles of balance and reciprocity. The principles of *inti* (the sun, structure, clarity, and fertilizing male energy) interacted in complimentary relations with *quilla* (the moon, fluidity, obscurity, and female fecundity). *Yanantin* is the word for the concept of pairing, complementariness, for male and female pairs as well as eyes and arms. Just as there could not exist a body without a left and a right side there cannot exist a man without a woman. Male and female are essential to each other (12-13). The concept of the "conjugal pair" as a fundamental unit is expressed by the term *karihuarmi* (man-woman). The human body is itself the symbol of wholeness and integrity in the Andes (13). However, these antonyms are relative to their context. Water, generally conceived of as feminine, can become male when associated with the idea of semen fertilizing the earth. "Even human bodies are not unequivocally one sex or the other. The Incas for instance would send women's cloths to men they deemed to have failed in their masculine role." This was so because war was a male task (13).

In her analysis of Pachacuti Yamki's diagram of the cosmos, Classen says that the human couple at the center represents the basic concept of the *karihuarmi* and that Viracocha can then be said to embody the ideal original integration of male and female. "This union of male and female was also expressed in the hermaphrodite sculptures worshipped at various sites in the Tahuantinsuyo" (22). Thus gender ideology in the Andes is based on concepts of reciprocity, complementariness, and parallelism. What is more, culture is the product of the fruitful collaboration of woman and man. While premarital sex was tolerated, homosexuality and masturbation were punished under Inca law because they "wasted seed." Both subverted the *karihuarmi*. Homosexuality threatened the order and the integration of the dualistically ordered cosmos (60-61). In contrast, sibling incest was in keeping with the ideal *karihuarmi*. The Inca (The Sun) and the Coya (The Moon) together embodied the cosmos. Because culture is the weaving of duality, an unmarried person stands as non-culture. Such tight social and cosmological complementariness of the male and female principles calls into question Trexler's universalizing thesis on the military "origin" of institutionalized pederastic practices.

On the matter of homosexual priests in the temples, María Rost-worowski in *Estructuras andinas del poder: ideología religiosa y política* (1983) writes that the Incas maintained an elaborate priesthood with different kinds of priests specializing in different functions. Chief in this division of labor was divination. Villac Umo (the priest who tells) held a great deal of power and was elected to office by the Inca nobility. The other major activity belonged to the priests who heard confession. Inca priests were usually men, but it was not unusual for women to have priestly functions at the local *wak'as*. This was especially true when temples were dedicated to the moon. There were also the doctors and the philosopher-diviners. Classen points out that, like the *acllas*, the diviners were outside the normal social order. They went naked, roaming the most desolate parts of the empire, always looking directly at the sun. They lived alone and in complete austerity. For Classen, the diviners constituted a third class in the savage/civilized Inca social dichotomy (67). They did not wear clothes, they did not live in towns and they did not practice agriculture. Their naked bodies served as conduit for the divine, a practice which entailed great dangers. Ordinary subjects could not look directly onto the *wak'as*, nor onto the sacrificial procession of the *capacocha*, and the priest could not look on the face of the divinities either. This is perhaps one reason why they approached Pachacamac, as Cieza de Leon, Garcilaso, and Cobo report, walking backwards as they waited for the oracle to speak "en una postura indecente y fea" (in an ugly and indecent posture) (Cobo qtd. in Ellefensen 324).

Tom Zuidema, in *Inca Civilization in Cuzco* (1990), has linked ritual homosexuality to the kinship conceptualization by which the older son is a "son" and the younger son is a "nephew." This distinction leads to the opposition between lord and priest, or that between lord and servant, in the public services in the temples. Zuidema speculates that public ritual homosexuality of the lords with the priests seems to be connected with agricultural rituals in which the men spoke in a female voice (31) or with the temporary calendrical function of a younger brother who officiated, dressed like a woman, during specific agricultural ceremonies (31-32).

It is interesting to note that María Rostworowski does not address the question in either *Estructuras andinas del poder* nor in her more recent *Pachacamac y el Señor de los Milagros* (1992). Perhaps her silence means that the concrete, hard, ethnographic and archeological data beyond the written record left by the chroniclers is not yet there to venture into speculation or interpretation. Nevertheless, as we can see from just a brief glance into the social and cosmological complexity in the Andes, our understanding of homosexual practices in either societies of great antiquity or modern communities is enhanced when we look at them as local, regional historical phenomena.

II

By tracing the ceremonies of possession enacted in America by English and French colonists to their medieval origins, Patricia Seed makes "sense" of the otherwise seemingly absurd English ceremony of planting and cultivating a garden (30-32) in order to claim possession of American land, or the French parade in order to assert having entered into an alliance with the Indians who then "permitted" the French to settle onto Indian lands (63). Although Seed casts an anthropological eye on her study of the ceremonies of possession, she relies, of course, on the written record in order to identify and trace their ideological matrix. Thus Seed demonstrates that the Portuguese claims to territory "discovered" as a result of their advanced nautical and astrological expertise are spurned and considered nonsensical by the English sovereigns who take possession to mean nothing less than physical occupation of the land (102). Seed shows that the Portuguese felt that by putting to practical use the astronomical knowledge developed by Islamic science and translated for Christendom by the Jewish scholars employed by the Portuguese kings, they had an inalienable right to the lands to which they provided the sailing route. Seed delves deeply into the work of the Jewish scholars, who "composed at least fifteen known original treatises on instruments of observation and created the first scientific literature written in Hebrew," (117) financed by the Christians kings. The case of the astrologist Zacuto illustrates many of the points Seed makes regarding the partnership between the Jewish scholars and the expansionist ambitions of the Portuguese state. In 1484 Zacuto published his *Rules of the Astrolabe*, thus providing Master John the means to reach distant shores, keep reliable records of the sailing routes, establish the latitude of their location, and thus lay the claims of finders keepers.

Patricia Seed's account of the transposition of Babylonian and Islamic science by Jewish scholars into the coffers of the Portuguese kings contains within it yet another story of the making of the supremacy of the alphabetic writing in the Mediterranean on the eve of the Iberian conquest of this hemisphere. Her chapter on the archeology of the Requirement (*requerimiento*)—the supreme ceremony of possession enacted by the Spanish conquerors—furthers our understanding of the peculiar role that alphabetic writing played in the deployment of power and colonization in the Americas.

Although it has been well known that the Spanish idea of holy war was a calque—Americo Castro, *The Structure of Spanish History*, (1954)—of the Islamic jihad, Seed's examination of the ritual and religious dimensions of Islamic legal life throws new light on the juridical status of the jihad as an antecedent of the requirement. The jihad was conceived in Islam as a summons sent to the enemy in order to announce one's intentions of conquest (47). It also bore the "good" news of the new religion to non-Muslims (75). "The task of the Islamic messenger was to deliver a very specific demand. According to Averroes, the envoy must first 'summon them to conversion to Islam.' The word summons in Arabic (da'a) means 'invite,' 'call for,' 'implore,' 'demand.' Its Spanish translation means *requerir*.

Beyond showing that the idea and deployment of the requirement had its origins in the frontier situation between Islam and Christianity, Seed argues that the future status of the

Indians as tributaries of the Crown had also its origin in Islamic patterns of conquest and administration of agricultural non-Islamic peoples. In most schools of Islamic jurisprudence, *jizya* was collected from believers in monotheistic religions—peoples of the book. On the Iberian peninsula *jizya* was imposed on Christians and Jews (79). But another school of jurisprudence, the Ma-lik-i, allowed believers in non-Muslim faiths to also pay tribute and hence avoid servitude or slavery. Therefore, any people subdued by Muslims fighting a jihad could be required to pay a poll tax (80). Thus Spain, unlike all other colonial powers, established a capital tax on its Indian subjects. Seed also shows that the *aljama* was also calqued onto the administration of Indian subjects (85). Amerindians were not to be slaves. Like the *aljama*, they were guaranteed life, liberty, and a modified sense of property if they submitted to the requirement. Within this perspective Seed also shows that the New Laws of 1542, and especially the idea of creating "republicas de indios" within which indigenous law was allowed to operate, date back to the first Caliphs in Spain

(86). Américo Castro, whose work is surprisingly absent from the pages of *Ceremonies of Possession*, would have been very pleased to see this expansion of his thesis—the Islamic cultural deep-structure of Iberian institutions—into the realms of science and jurisprudence. With meticulous research and careful, linguistically sensitive reading of many new sources, Seed's study makes explicit the unstated but often determinant and highly significant local traditions and systems of meaning imbedded in the symbolic actions with which Europeans created colonial authority.

Reconstructing the archeology of European ceremonies of possession shows once more the differences between the localized European traditions of conquest and possession. It also underlines the conjunction between European imperial expansion and literacy. Scriptural authority allows the English to create rights for themselves to lands that they had neither "discovered" nor conquered. But perhaps the most telling instance of the concatenation of raw military power to literacy is encapsulated in the narrative of the *requerimiento*. The idea of reading out loud a document to people who could physically not hear the spoken words nor understand the language, and much less grasp the meaning of the ceremony involved, indicates the degree of mystification with which reading and writing had been endowed by both the tradition of the jihad and the use of Latin as the hieroglyph of knowledge and power.

Drafted in Spanish, the new imperial language, the *requerimiento*, was nevertheless intended as a summons, a demand to acknowledge the new or the new order. It was not meant to communicate the contents of the text but rather the violence that would ensue from not acquiescing to the capacity for destruction that the reading of the writing contained. As David Brading has put it in *The First America, 1492-1867* (1991), the *requerimiento* was a cynical document. Delving into the archeology of seemingly absurd ceremonies does not change the fact that, as instruments of conquest, these ceremonies were invested with meanings and consequences which facilitated "in good conscience" the rapid destruction of the Amerindians and their cultures.

In Juan López Palacios Rubio's decision to calque the ceremony of reading the *requerimiento* to people who could not have been remotely expected to understand Castillian, there is a radicalization of the calque of the jihad. The refusal to accept the message was thus always already built into the ceremony. It was assumed that the peoples "without writing," peoples not of the book, would be incapable of responding "appropriately" to the message. Thus, as the document itself announced, they deserved to be destroyed. The story of the Renaissance's misreading (pun intended) of American graphic systems of communication is only now beginning to be addressed. It transports our focus away from European actions and records of their actions and observations to the dynamic of action and intellectual interaction that ensued on both sides of the Atlantic after 1492.

III

In her introduction to *Writing Without Words* (1994) Elizabeth Hill Boone shows how the tendency to think of alphabetic writing as visible speech has eclipsed other forms of graphic record keeping and communication. The idea that alphabetic writing transcribes language and that language constitutes the supreme instrument of thought and cognition has made possible an evolutionists view of graphic systems in which pictorial systems of communication, such as the Aztecs had developed, came to occupy one of the lowest rungs, or simply be disqualified from the scale of "writing." Boon finds this hierarchical classification of "writing" limiting. It does not allow for the idea that for "Indigenous American cultures *visible speech* was often not the goal... art and writing in Pre-Columbian America are largely the same thing" (3): "Tlacuilolitztly" means both to write and to paint. The Nahuatle graphic system was capable of keeping and conveying knowledge by presenting ideas in a notational system which did not necessarily relied on the transcription of linguistic forms.

Boon indicates that in order to break out of the limiting Mediterranean legacy (9) which conceives of writing as speech made visible, we need to reach a broader definition of writing (3-4), one which "allows us to consider both verbal and non-verbal systems of graphic communication" (4). In order to break out of the fundamental difficulty of speaking about writing without tying it to language, it is important to remember the long acknowledged shortcomings of alphabetic writing in transposing and transcribing the full import of speech. Writing leaves out tone, pitch, and the gestural context of oral communication. Boon marshals new and important evidence for thinking of alphabetic writing as only one among many other successful notational systems, such as musical scores, algebraic notation, and chemical formulae. Drawing on the work of Stillman Drake, we can see that ordinary language cannot express the full import of scientific relations and other notational systems succeed where language cannot because of the human ability to "grasp certain relationships visually at a glance but not to describe them in words with anything like equal precision" (Drake 136, qtd. in Boon 9).

Structures, as in chemistry or the Inca ceque system, are more efficiently depicted than described. Pictorial notations are valuable in physics and extremely useful in chemistry for they diagram and render visible the invisible. The present proliferation of new forms of visual communication also constitutes evidence of the fact that alphabetic writing is but a partial rendition of speech, and only one of the possible systems of notation. In view of the above, Boon feels that it is time to get away from the Mediterranean ethnocentric view of "writing," to look at the complete graphic catalogue and to conceive of writing as "the communication of relatively specific ideas in a conventional manner by means of permanent, visible marks" (Sampson 15). Such a definition of writing would lead us to reconsider not only Aztec systems of communication but also the Andean quipu as "writing," and it would decouple the notion that acts of cognition and feeling can only be recorded in alphabetic writing. Systems such as chemistry formulae and the quipu can hold and convey knowledge separate from language. Quipu notation, Boon writes, is like mathematics and scientific notation, or somewhat like musical notation (21-22).

The preeminence of alphabetic writing as the most perfect and "natural" instrument for acts of cognition and the organization of knowledge is an idea which rises to hegemony within the Renaissance philosophy of language and, in conjunction with the European "encounter," with the incommensurability of the Amerindian cultures. The story of the colonial semiosis—the study of the interactions between the layered and various systems of communication and representations within or between cultures—that has taken place during the two main waves of colonization of the Americas is taken up in *The Darker Side of the Renaissance*. Mignolo's archeology of Humanism uncovers the hidden layers of Renaissance thinking about language, its origins and the ties of language to state building, the relations of language to dominion over territories, the seemingly inseparable links of alphabetic writing to the nature and organization of knowledge; the ties of language and the deployment of colonial rule; the status of language and the place of the colonial subject and, above all, the exclusion of Amerindian knowledge and subjects from the instances of colonial power created by the place accorded to alphabetic writing.

The Darker Side of the Renaissance is a rare example of truly interdisciplinary scholarship. The book's project calls for serious grounding and practice in linguistics, semiotics, philology, hermeneutics, history of ideas, and literary criticism. The demands of Mignolo's topics—literacy, territoriality, and colonialism—together with the comparatist approach that he chooses make for a focused but at the same time wide ranging analysis on questions of "writing systems," map making, and the collusion of writing with colonialism. This is indeed a book with a tremendous scope. It is founded on enormous learning, and it is crafted with unusual intelligence. It will have a strong impact on colonial studies for years to come in part because Mignolo does not exhaust, could not exhaust, the magnitude of the topics that he recasts in the light of our current understanding of discursive issues and subaltern interventions in the organization(s) of knowledge.

The first major section of *The Darker Side of the Renaissance* delves into the Renaissance philosophy of language as articulated by the Spanish humanists Antonio de Nebrija and Bernardo José Aldrete, and the consequences that their ideas had on the colonial policies that classed the Maya "books," Aztec "codices," and the Andean quipus as "primitive" or even diabolically inspired objects. The second part deals with the colonization of memory. Most of it is dedicated to developing a new understanding of the work of Bernardino de Sahagún. His massive effort to acquire, reorganize, and "translate" Aztec knowledge by means of alphabetic script and knowledge genres and categories imbedded in Latin and Spanish understanding of culture and civilization (202) is questioned as it is found to contain the colonial apparatus by which Amerindian knowledges are either occluded or rendered into a plane of continuity with the Renaissance. While the work of Sahagún has recently been studied by Jorge Klor de Alva in *The Work of Bernardino de Sahagún: Pioneer Ethnographer of Sixteenth Century Aztec Mexico* (1988), shinning light on the Aztecs' "informants" and scribes employed by Sahagún, Mignolo emphasizes the discontinuity in Renaissance culture that the encounter with Amerindian cultures inaugurates. This discontinuity of the classical tradition marks, for Mignolo, the beginning of the counter-modernity that signals Latin American cultural production from its inception (202-217).

One of the least known chapters in the writing of Latin America's cultural history is the story of the Italian knight Bernardo Boturini Benaducci. Inspired by Gianbatista Vico's model of a universal history of mankind, Boturini laid down the foundations for our "modern" understanding of the Mexican manners, customs, and systems for recording the past (143-163). With his *Idea de una historia general de la América Septentrional fundanda sobre el material copioso de figuras, símbolos, carácteres y jeroglíficos, cantares y manuscritos de autores indios últimamente descubiertos* (1746), Boturini began the re-discovery of the Aztec past by reformulating its records into three ages: the age of the Gods, the age of the heroes and the age of men. This reformulation corresponded with Vico's own ideas on the three linguistic stages of evolution in human kind (144).

Vico's notion that "every nation spoke by writing," *in lettere volgari* (146), contests the Renaissance philosophy of language that celebrated the alphabet. Vico makes it possible for Boturini to perceive what the Spanish missionaries missed (read), namely that the Amerindians, prior to the arrival of the Europeans, had their own ways of writing (146). According to Mignolo, Boturini's recognition of the Aztec system for recording the past as "writing" reveals "the connivance between alphabetic writing and history [as] a regional invention of the West" (147). The section on Boturini illustrates one of Mignolo's major points: the complicity during the imperial age between historiography and empire building, between subject and object of investigation.

In accord with Edouard Glissand's critique of history and literature as instruments of Western empire which have served to "suppress and subjugate other forms of recording the past and finding means of interaction for which literature became the paradigm" (126-27), Mignolo sees in his own examination of the darker side of Humanism and its myth of Modernity an effort to recast historiography as we know it. Existing historiography should thus be understood as a regional Western invention (127) which has allowed the West to think that other peoples did not have means to record their memory of the past.

The question of how to read *other* records remains caught in the snare of the reader's own hermeneutical practices. For those born and bread in the "reading" conventions of the West, "reading" a Mixtec "text" represents a daunting challenge. Even reading Maya glyphs calls for the acquisition of new skills which extend beyond learning the Maya code. Precisely because of the occlusion of Amerindian cultures fostered by colonialism, reading postcolonial texts such as Guamán Poma's *El primer nueva corónica i buen gobierno* (1616) or *The Chilám Balám Book of Chumayel* require a good deal of learning and perspicacity.

The Darker Side of the Renaissance points to these texts from a theoretical point of view, but it does not offer extensive or new readings of the many texts and maps that it considers in the development of its comparative semiosis. For detailed, exhaustive, technical, and often dazzling readings of Amerindian "texts," "maps," and "writing," the reader should see Gordon Brotherston's *Book of the Fourth World: Reading the Native Americans Through their Literature* (1992). Brotherston's study of the technique and knowledge of the *tlacuilolli*, the writer-painter of the Aztec screen folds, explains in detail the principle of multiple reading (58) highlighted by both Mignolo and Boon. Brotherston writes that in precortesian screen folds, the capacities of the *tlacuilolli* are perceptible even to a greater degree, thanks to the finer calligraphy of line and dot, lexis of color, appeal to embedded data, and multiple readings. "The complexity of the statement that is made as a result, especially in the works of certain length like the *Tepexic Annals* (fifty two pages) so far exceeds the limits of verbal language as to render transcription an unending task" (Brotherston 50-60).

But of course it cannot be forgotten, especially in the plurotopic reading proposed by Mignolo, that it was the "natives" who learned Latin and Spanish in order to translate their world and answer the questions posed by Sahagún or Durán in Mexico and José de Arriaga or José de Acosta in the Andes. They, and later the *mestizo* historians, were the only masters of two worlds. Bicultural people like Jacinto Cunil, who provided the nexus between contemporary "Maya" and the classical Maya of the glyphs, and Gloria Alzandúa, are featured in this narrative of cultural exchange, appropriation, occlusion, discontinuity, and power.

The third part of *The Darker Side of the Renaissance* deals with the omphalos syndrome (227). The aim of this section is to bring to the fore coexisting territorialities which had been repressed by the Renaissance mapping of the city, the earth, and the cosmos. The fundamental question concerns the various systems and technologies available, at the time of the Spanish conquest, for the ordering of space. In this section of mapping and the institutionalization of cosmographies, Mignolo aims to show, by studying Mateo Ricci's understanding of Chinese maps and López de

Velasco's attempt to produce a general and universal cosmography based of his questionnaire (*Relaciones geográficas*, 1574), that cartography does not suddenly emerge as a rational enterprise from previous ethnic and irrational organizations of space based on the perception of the body as the model for the cosmos. Neither do geometric organizations of space necessarily replace ethnic ones. Instead, several organizations of space can and do coexist as has been the case in the Andes and in China, where Western cosmographies did not actually displace "native" organizations of space (258).

For Mignolo, the *Relaciones geográficas*, which were the answers assembled in America in response to the fifty questions prepared in the *Instrucción y memoria* (244) that López de Velasco sent to the colonies, illustrates the distinctive role that writing, together with mapping, played in the colonization of memory and space. "It implied a configuration of a new game directly related to territorial control and the transformation of humanist men of letters into notaries public and men of the law" (283). This chapter also examines the post-colonial Amerindian instances of "mapping." However, the status of these "maps," those which have survived, remains uncertain for we do not yet have the means to decipher them.

This part, like the two previous ones, offers the reader a plethora of information seldom gathered together. The particulars in themselves will not surprise specialists in the different fields brought together. What is keen and important in *The Darker Side of the Renaissance* is the myriad of new relations and the overall changed perception of the canvas of the organization of knowledge that Mignolo's comparatist method and "pluritopic hermeneutics" brings about. It is the theoretical and ideological move made by this scholar—"to carve a locus of enunciation from which to look at the European Renaissance from the perspective of colonial and post-colonial worlds"—that will make this book obligatory reading. Therefore I will say a few more words about this intended reversal in historiographical perspective and the foundations that Mignolo lays for understanding *otherwise*.

Two terms figure largely in the construction of Mignolo's method and project: semiosis and pluritopic hermeneutics. In dialogue with current postcolonial theorizing, Mignolo insists that his book is as much about understanding the past as it is about speaking the present (5). Aware that scholarly discourses now, as before, acquire their meaning on the grounds of their relation to the subject matter as well as the audience, the "locus" of enunciation from which one speaks (Foucault's *mode d' enunciation*) contributes to changing or maintaining systems of values and beliefs. Institutional foundations of discursive formations are thus foregrounded not only as subject matter—cosmographies by the Royal Council of the Indies, Sahagún's Nahuatl scribes learning and writing Latin—but also as challenge for today postcolonial scholars.

The study of colonial situations calls for further redefinition of the scholar's locus of enunciation. Colonial situations by definition imply a multiplicity of traditions. There is no "natural tradition." In order not to repeat the past—the universalization of a regional epistemology—present day scholars need to question the assumptions of any naturalized tradition which has no room for asking: how does the Chinese or the Amerindian perspective understand its others? Monotopic hermeneutics proves insufficient for the understanding of colonial situations. A pluritopic hermeneutics is thus more suitable, for it calls, by definition, for a comparative methodology.

Mignolo finds the concept of "text," as it has been developed in literary studies, confining. Text and even discourse seem to be too heavily associated with alphabetic writing. They call to preeminence the very philosophy of language that he has sought to de-center. Thus for Mignolo "colonial semiosis" points to a trend in colonial studies, discussed in the essays in *Writing Without Words*, for example, in which many other signs systems—art, graphic communications systems, oral traditions and performances, tactile and musical notations—are recognized as manifestations of feeling, memory, and cognition.

Finally, Mignolo offers a look at the Renaissance from the possible vantage point of the colonized. He thus attempts to reverse a historiography which, with notable exemptions, has dominated colonial studies. In doing so, he also makes a theoretical proposal that will have lasting influence on the field not so much because it is new but rather because Mignolo lays the theoretical foundation for a pluritopic epistemology. Making clear distinctions in relation to his theoretical background Mignolo is careful to show that his critique of alphabetic writing and the spread of Western literacy neither departs nor coincides with Derrida's positions in "Writing before the Letter" (*Of Grammatology*). In Derrida's argument, the complicity between alphabetic writing and knowledge is not deconstructed. Instead, it is assumed. Further, Mignolo, in contrast with Derrida, seeks to mark the discontinuities with the classical tradition that colonization implies. Such concerns are not present in Derrida. The concerns guiding *The Darker Side of the Renaissance* have their origins in the work of Jack Goody on alphabetic writing, Franz Fanon on colonization, and Antonio Gramsci on *Letteratura e vita nazionale* (1952) and *Gli intelletuali e l'a organisazione della cultura* (1955). Ultimately, it is the role of the intellectual in the organization of culture which drives the overall design of the inquiry undertaken by Mignolo. He sees scholars today as heirs of the humanist legacy—both as observant and participant in the process of colonization. He feels that scholars today have the ethical obligation to describe incommensurable conceptual frameworks while at the same time to reestablish the lost equilibrium between alternative systems of knowledge that the underside of the Renaissance swept away.

WORKS CITED

BARBOSA SÁNCHEZ, Araceli. *Sexo y conquista.* México: Universidad Nacional Autónoma de México, 1994.

BOONE H. Elizabeth. "Introduction: Writing and Recording Knowledge." In E. Boone and W. Mignolo, *Writing Without Words: Alternative Literacies in Mesoamerica and the Andes.* Durham: Duke University Press, 1994: 3-26.

BROTHERSTON, Gordon. *Book of the Fourth World: Reading the Native Americas Through Their Literature.* Cambridge: Cambridge University Press, 1992.

CLASSEN, Constance. *Inca Cosmology and the Human Body.* Salt Lake City: University of Utah Press, 1993.

DRAKE, Stillman. 'Literacy and Scientific Notations." In *Towards a New Understanding of Literacy.* Eds. Merald E. Wrolstad and Dennis F. Fisher. New York: Praeger, 1986. 135-155.

MIGNOLO, Walter. *The Darker Side of the Renaissance: Literacy, Territoriality and Colonization.* Ann Arbor: The University of Michigan Press, 1995.

ROSTWOROWSKI DE DÍEZ CANSECO, María. *Estructuras andinas del poder. Ideología religiosa y política.* Lima: Instituto de Estudios Peruanos, 1983.

SEED, Patricia. *Ceremonies of Possessions in Europe's Conquest of the New World 1492 1640.* New York: Cambridge University Press, 1995.

TREXLER, Richard C. *Sex and Conquest: Gendered Violence, Political Order and the European Conquest of the Americas.* Cambridge: Polity Press, 1995.

ZUIDEMA, R. Tom. *Inca Civilization in Cuzco.* Tran. Jean Jacques Decostes. Austin: University of Texas Press, 1990.

CHAPTER 3

"Writing with his Thumb in the Air:" Coloniality, Past and Present[1]

In *España, aparta de mí este cáliz*, as the savage Spanish civil war drew to an end, César Vallejo wrote on the death and resurrection of the soldier Pedro Rojas. A short version of the first line of the poem, "Solía escribir con su dedo gordo en el aire," appears as the title of one of the last books written by Antonio Cornejo Polar, *Escribir en el aire: ensayo sobre la heterogeneidad socio-cultural en las literaturas andinas* (1994). I return to Vallejo's idea of writing in the air with a pen made of flesh ("pluma de carne"), with the thumb, in the absence of pen and paper, because the image of "escribir en el aire" bears an emblematic relevance to the cultural and ethical conundrum affecting the study or rather the writing of colonial situations, past and present.[2]

Vallejo's poem is not a farewell to arms. If anything it establishes an inescapable and concrete link between past and present. The image of Pedro Rojas, writing in the air, memorializes the undying will to perdure in solidarity, for his finger, spelling "viban" as if it were living speech, writes over and over again: "¡Viban los compañeros!"

Pedro Rojas passes on, but the passage that configures his death is fraught with ambiguity, for the poem doubly inscribes the meaning of "¡Pasa!" In the couplet: "Papel de viento, lo han matado: ¡Pasa!/ Pluma

---

[1] This part of the title corresponds to my translation of the lead line in César Vallejo's poem "Pedro Rojas," also known as poem III in *España, aparta de mí este cáliz* (1939). See Vallejo 261-263.

[2] I write this essay in memory of Antonio Cornejo Polar, unexcelled colleaguage, brilliant critical intelligence and compatriot.

de carne, lo han matado: ¡Pasa!"; "¡Pasa!" could be understood as either
an exclamation shouting the death of Pedro Rojas or as a coded dialogue
between the sentinel and the voice of the man reciting the secret word in
his search for safe passage. The poem seeks to stand as a living memory to
the struggle. It refuses the esstrangement of the past, it writes the past as
a living present for Pedro Rojas, "después de muerto,/ se levantó, besó su
catafalco ensangrentado,/ lloró por España/ y volvió a escribir con el
dedo en el aire:/ '¡Viban los compañeros! Pedro Rojas.'"

This essay, in a way flows from Vallejo, for the intent is to problema-
tize the question of the past for us, the living. Can/should, students of
colonial Latin America afford to think of the past as a foreign country?
What does it mean to employ textual strategies for reading the artifacts of
the past as if the conditions of textual production imbedded in or side-
skirted by the texts themselves were over and done with and thus the
texts free float in time and space until they reach our desks for "literary"
interpretation? What similarities exist between colonial texts, or modern
texts, for that matter, and Vallejo's two scenes of writing? Is our task as
intellectuals concluded after the appreciation (added value) and celebration of the semi-literate Pedro Rojas, the man who writes the memory of
his engagement in the Spanish civil war with his own flesh? Or do we
enlarge the scope of our gaze to consider the second scene of writing, the
moment when Pedro Rojas, already dead, writes again, lest his life be forgotten, the same verse that took him to his death?[3] To a very large extent
both Gustavo Verdesio and Álvaro Félix Bolaños, in questioning the relationship of past to present in the existing approaches to colonial studies,
are in fact raising the problem of solidarity, that is, the political position
of academic intellectuals in the world today as a system of forces constituted by the past.

---

[3] It is important to remember that the story of Pedro Rojas is based on real life stories of executions of railroad workers, who had been incarcerated, and on the crum-
pled piece of paper ("Abisa todos compañeros y marchar pronto/nos dan de palos bru-
talmente y nos matan/como lo ben perdío no quieren sino/la barbaridá") found in the
pocket of a poor *campesino* buried in a cemetery in Burgos. For further connections of
Vallejo's poems with the lives of combatants in the Spanish civil war see Cornejo
Polar's last chapter in *Escribir en el aire* (228-239), as well as Ruíz Vilapana 38-39.

I. THE PAST AS A PRESENT PROBLEM

Gustavo Verdesio's question: "What is the use of our work?"[4] is indeed far reaching. It raises the fundamental and increasingly vexed question of use value in literary and Cultural Studies. As such it is not a question that emerges specifically or attains exclusively to colonial studies. It spans over the entire scope of academic work in the humanities, and it links with several of the theses developed by Bill Readings in *The University in Ruins* (1996). According to Readings, literary culture has been disengaged from its connection to the national subject. It has lost its raison d'etre as constituted in the nineteenth century (75). Literature is no longer the language of national culture in the United States. Readings argues that the "general notion of culture... as the organic synthesis that acts as both the totality and the essence of particular knowledges," (75, 81) without which there can be no essence and no center, which appeared fully articulated in Bishop Newman's *Idea of a University* (1878?)[5], is no longer in place. In this framework for liberal education, and more specifically for the study of literature, the humanities were situated in opposition to practical knowledge and the principle of utility. The study of literature became an end in itself. The unity of knowledge sought by the liberal education was the imminent principle of intellectual culture, and academic knowledge was produced by an assemblage of learned men in the pursuit of intellectual culture. Intellectual culture applied both to the production of knowledge (truth) by means of the various disciplines and to the teaching of individuals. This inherited understanding of the place of literature in the production of intellectual knowledge and the production of the national subject has now dissipated (Readings 77). However, its force wanes unevenly. It grinds with intensely jarring sounds in the context of *colonial* studies where the clashing and brimstone of cultural struggles, contesting subjects, and general conditions of yet unexamined heterogeneity twirl and swirl in fascinating and frustrating movements.

To a large extent Verdesio's question is prompted by the pervasive and unacknowledged reading practices of New Criticism present in most of

---

[4] This question comes from a letter from Gustavo Verdesio to me inviting me to write this essay.

[5] See Newman. In that volume also see, Castro-Klarén, "The Paradox of Self in *The Idea of a University*," 318-339.

the scholarship dedicated to Latin American colonial texts and its connection to the institution of literature built in this century by the idea of liberal education in conjunction with the production of the national subject. Anchored on the idea that the (autonomous) text itself suffices as the terrain of intellectual operations to be engaged by the (autonomous) liberal subject, New Criticism, in its many transformations, continues to authorize the separation of the "aesthetic" object from its conditions of historical production. In this regard, Readings observes that in the United States, the idea of literary culture was structured on the notion of the canon rather than on the idea of an ethnic tradition. This shift allowed for the minimization of the weight of ethnicity and elitism of the English model in both Newman and F. R. Leavis (83-84). However, as Wendell V. Harris reminds us, "canons are made up of readings, not of disembodied texts" (110). And reading practices return us to questions of generalized cultural understandings, to the power negotiations implicit in the constitution of academic knowledges and the construction of normative criteria.[6]

Part of the work of New Criticism was to construct the criteria for the Masterpieces series. But the paradox that New Criticism conceals in its move to establish a canon of masterpieces is that, despite its divorce from historical context and historical scholarship in establishing a canon, it in fact calls for continuity and rupture criteria and thus introduces history through the back door. The historical criteria that inhabits the pleats of New Criticism performs its work silently. It organizes the canon within a historical perspective which in fact goes unexamined. The ensuing tension between reading strategies designed to address the purely "aesthetic" (autonomous) nature of the "literary" text, but which in fact conceals the historical grounding of the texts together with the problem of periodization, leaves relatively superficial marks when it deals with highly modernistic, linguistically self-reflexive texts. However, colonial intertextualities, frontally engaged, as they always are, with the knowledge/power question, unavoidably point to the gaping

---

[6] In "Canonicity" Harris notes that the operation of canonicity entails license for infinite exegesis of certain texts. He affirms the play of criteria which Alastair Fowler noted when he distinguished at least six kinds of canons in simultaneous general use in the institution of literature. According to Harris the six kinds of canons (potential, accessible, official, personal, cortical, and pedagogical) could indeed be expanded if we recognize that the ultimate function of canon formation is to compete (118) in a constant process of texts selection informed by selection criteria which itself is subject to change.

impasses implicit in the "aesthetic" approach to literature and culture. This can be readily seen in Bolaños's article on *El carnero* as well as the very mixed critical reception of *testimonio* texts. In these colonial textualities the national subject is either cleansed, absent, contested, or mistaken[7] but seldom, if ever, reaffirmed.

The crisis of the literary model is compounded when the "national" subjects implicit in the reading protocols of the critic, and the critic, as a historical individual, do not coincide in the same socio-historical location. This awkward and unacknowledged lack of fit between reading practices and national subjects appears not only marked by the dynamics of the teaching machine but also inscribed by a special relation of distance, by affects interdicted by "lejanía." Such is the case of many Latin American intellectuals working in the North American academy[8] and of Euroamerican subjects studying Latin American texts.

Yet another type of distance which affects the interpretation of Latin American culture also occurs in the North American academy. The cultural battles over the canon, the demonstration that the canon is "an ethnocentric and non-representative basis on which to ground the kinds of claims that have been historically made for literature" (Readings 85), has left the study of literature in a position that is "neither practical nor ethically defensive" (85). This paradoxical situation arises from the changing "status of knowledge inherent in the disciplinary problematic in the contemporary university"(86). In a world in which all choices are good, the ethical relation of the academic intellectual to the production and reproduction of knowledge is indeed blurred and ethically fragile.

Because the link between literary studies and the formation of the citizen has been broken, literature has lost its once privileged position. It is now a field among others. The canon has lost its sacredness and it has come to

---

[7] For a discussion on the problems of constituting a Latin American postmodern cannon *avant la lettre* see Larsen 155-163.

[8] In his critique of the work that deconstruction and Cultural Studies have performed on the study of Latin America, Román de la Campa takes up the question of distance (*lejanía*). He proposes the introduction of a "cartography of comparative frames" for the study of Latin America. "Me refiero a una configuración que reconozca la condición transnacional de lo latinoamericano y sus practicantes—*latinoamericanistas* de diversos estilos, ideologías y modos de subsidio—que permita también re-significar una nueva relación entre las disciplinas de lo social dirigidas hacia la investigación empírica y las nuevas humanidades orientadas hacia descalces discursivos" (78).

function as one of several other forms of delimiting the field. Literature is now an archive that stores all kinds of texts occupying roughly similar niches. It is not the (selective) museum that once housed the treasures of the nation. This archive no longer amounts to an organic vision of national literatures or cultures, "nor does anything within the system of knowledge require that it should" (86). This battle over the canon may be new in the United States, but I venture to say that it is the very stuff of which the history of Latin American letters is made, for the criollo national subject and its coincidence with the rise of literature has been a phenomenon of very short and precarious duration. Disputes which questioned the limits and criteria that organized divisions between a potential versus an official canon, a personal as opposed to a pedagogical canon, an accessible as opposed to a critical canon, have fueled the pages of "Latin American Literature" since the Lunarejo's (Juan de Espinosa y Medrano) defense of the baroque aesthetic, onto Andrés Bello and Domingo Faustino Sarmiento, and of course José Carlos Mariátegui, Jorge Luis Borges, and more recently feminism.

To some extent a parallel story could be told in relation to the study of "Latin American Literature" in the departments of Spanish, Romance, and Foreign Languages in the United States. Without glossing over the history of the peripheral and conflicted position that the study of Spanish (with its own inner breaks and contradictions) occupies in the United States academy, it can nevertheless be observed that the decoupling of the national subject from the study of literature in the English departments, made visible at the annual meetings of the Modern Language Association, and the emergence of the archive as multiple and inorganic, has had a direct impact on the question of use, that is to say the (ethical) justification of the discipline for all scholars in the field of literature. The conservative detractors of the postmodern shift vociferously brought it up year in and year out with their ridicule of the titles of the MLA panels. Finally the ferocity of their attack found in the reception of Rigoberta Menchú the sublime object of their discontent. In this debate, history entered, once again, mutilated and disguised, but in full force, through the back door of the cultural wars over postmodern (hybrid) subjects, narratological appreciations, academic locations, archival orders, and authentic subjects. But it failed to address fully and ethically the fact that the Menchú text, like Vallejo's poem, is a narrative about war. As such the hermeneutics deployed on testimonial texts which deal with the trauma of war, a war that has never stopped since its Spanish colonial inception, demand an approach that far exceeds the confines of the literary and which return us to history, to the fullness of experience. Spanish departments, as the authors of the introduction suggest, need to take a long look at the literary practices that adorn the walls of their treasured (prison) houses (Jameson).

Before the moment when the authority of the literary canon began to unravel, the assumption in place held that "Latin American Literature" was the museum where the monuments of high culture and spirituality of each nation were put on exhibit. It was the equivalent of an international centennial exposition. The use value hinged on the manifest proof of literary achievement and the "expression" of a culture-language constituted in its difference. Once the museum doors were opened passed the front exhibit halls and into the *fondos* or archival records—residues, shards, sedimentation, protoformations, fragments of wholes, fragments of series—the whole question of canonicity and representation (use) gave way.[9] Stimulated by the changing desires and seductive agendas of Cultural Studies, a whole other corpus of hidden, forgotten, and even concealed jewels appeared strewn in the many layers of the *fondos*. But for many, the use value of these texts was still governed by evolutionist, aesthetic, and modernist criteria—the chronicles seen as proto-novels or proto-ethnography, the nun's diaries as proto-feminist textualities.

However, I do not want to leave the impression that the doors that opened vistas beyond the canonical front exhibit halls were opened by either Cultural Studies in the United States or simply the loss of centrality suffered by literature. One could configure other narratives on the voyage to the *fondos*, a word which in Spanish means "archival storage," "financial solvency," as well as the "depths." The most important point to note here is that the gaze into the long past and into indigenous and provincial cultural realms neglected by the modernist canon was never allowed rest or self complacency. It was always disrupted by writers who, like José María Arguedas or Augusto Roa Bastos, kept in the forefront of consciousness alternative stories, narrative modalities, and ethics of knowledge. Their work demanded reading strategies that reached deep

[9] I am aware and I agree with Neil Larsen's argument that explains the rise of *testimonio* and other less-canonical texts as an exhaustion of the critical approaches put in place by the boom of the Latin American novel in the United States and other international markets (1-24).

into the colonial and pre-Columbian past and rhetorical *fondos*. In their unflinching historical gaze they delved into the production of subjects other than the national subject as constituted by a narrative of ever modernizing (Eurocentric) Latin American literatures. The appearance of testimony and the force of ethnohistory, as well as the issues in self-reflexive anthropology, all contributed to the non-centering of the purely literary modes of interpretation of Latin American culture and literature.

The idea of "colonial literature" is clearly no longer viable. A nominalist switch to "colonial discourse" only compounds the problem, for as Neal Larsen has argued, this switch conceals a misconception regarding the category of the aesthetic, conceived narrowly as a kind of formalism that excludes the social and the material as "extrinsic" content.[10] There is no text that is not aesthetic, for the aesthetic is always part and parcel of all communication. To separate the aesthetic from colonial texts is to grant exclusive rights over the domain of the aesthetic to Eurocentric categories—gender modalities, certain kinds of tropping, conceits, and language games. It is to deny the aesthetic dimension in the communications dynamics of the colonial archive and pre-Columbian textualities. The real problem, as Larsen points out, is not historicism, but rather "a perplexity over how to interpret the uniquely and profoundly tragic historical outcome of the epoch of conquest and colonization" (107).

In this regard, and if I may be permitted a personal note, I must say that it was Julio Cortázar's epistemological challenge to the aesthetic of the "realistic" novel and to the modernist subject—cronopios, *Ubu Roi* and 'pataphysics—that opened the way for me to become a reader of Guamán Poma and other "dishevelled" colonial texts. The key to a decolonizing enterprise does not reside in any particular "literary approach," nor is it sufficient to call for a non-Eurocentric mindset, for, as José Rabasa has pointed out, "Eurocentrism is a pervasive condition of thought" and not simply an uncritically held cultural ideal (Rabasa,

---

[10] In his chapter "Aesthetics and the Question of Colonial 'Discourse'" Neil Larsen shows that the idea of counter-posing literature as the domain of the "aesthetic" to the historico-material creates a false dualism. Larsen argues for "the necessity of taking up aesthetic categories precisely so as to be able to break with colonizing frameworks"(104). The uncritical rejection of aesthetic criticism in the case of colonial texts, ratifies, rather than challenges, the traditional colonizing perspective, "in effect granting to 'Eurocentricism' the exclusive right to make aesthetic judgements" (105).

Inventing America 18). Decolonizing knowledge and subjectivity assume rather a relentless attention to the writing of history, that is to say the mounting of a critical approach to historiography, in the broadest sense of the term. And in order not to fall into the trap of self-transparency, self-vigilance goes hand in hand with an open and critical commitment to the question of ethics.

When "colonial discourse," that "system of statements that can be made about colonial peoples, about colonizing powers, and about the relationship between these two; that system of knowledge and beliefs about the world within which acts of colonization take place... [that system of statements that] works to constitute reality... for the subjects who form the community on which it depends" (Ashcroft 42), is mistakenly taken for an amplification of "colonial literature," the field of colonial studies begins to suffers strong distortions, tensions, and contradictions. Many of them seem to be the prompters for the concerns discussed in the essays of the editors of the volume. However, it seems that the differences in approach and results between the old study of "colonial literature" and "colonial discourse," or for that matter postcolonial theory, cannot be sufficiently stressed.

In *Inventing America: Spanish Historiography and the Formation of Eurocentrism* (1993), José Rabasa succeeds in getting beyond the problems imbedded in "colonial literature." Rabasa's critique of "colonial discourse" takes up and pushes beyond Edmundo O'Gorman's study of the chronicles as epistemological and rhetorical presuppositions. Departing from Michel Foucault's concept of discursive formation and Edward Said's *Orientalism* (1978), Rabasa shows, for instance, that the "generic differences between histories, chronicles, and *relaciones* (accounts) corresponds to rules that not merely reflect aesthetic formulas but define who has the authority to speak and what is legitimate knowledge" (5). Not unlike Said, Rabasa is less concerned with correcting the factual mistakes incurred into the making of "colonial discourses" than in detecting and analyzing the tropes and epistemological operations by which "America" is produced as a "new" and subordinate world in relation to a Europe that from the moment of "discovery" on will be able to conceive of itself as the center. It is in this vein of inquiry that Rabasa's critique of colonial discourse shows that the "production of America is coterminous with the formation of Europe and its Others'"(6) as well as with the colonization of subjectivities otherwise known as a globally extended Eurocentric epistemology. For Rabasa, destabilizing the ground of factuality entails, as it did for Said, a critique of representation, a permanent awareness of the rhetorical moves that produced and continue to produce them now, and effect the real. Thus, any sense of referential plenitude underscores the colonial writing of the world which subjugates Indian and other subaltern knowledges (9-10).

From the following, it is clear that the term "colonial discourse," as it has been pressed into accelerated and multiple general uses, needs to undergo critical examination if it is to maintain the edge once given to it by Said. Understood as a form of discourse and not as a form of description of a "reality" out there, "colonial discourse" pointed to the operations of knowledge and power—military, scientific, political, artistic, documentary—by which Europe produced the non-European world as difference. As Rabasa points out "colonial discourse" managed to graft "colonial situations and cultural artifacts into the analysis of discourse" (10), a move which did not exclude the colonized from breaking through the gaps of the hegemonic thrust of colonial discourse. It follows then, that for critics interested in the decolonization of knowledges, it is necessary to go beyond a description of the colonizing forces put in place by colonial discourse and the resistances it encountered as it fanned its forces around the globe. It is necessary to join those Latin American subjects who have written alternative histories and alternatives subjectivities as they went about deconstructing the modes of subjectivation that they encountered in different lived colonialities. In this regard, Rabasa asserts that "the history of Latin America can be read as the constant construction of alternative histories and subjectivities" (14). I think that his emphasis on the positive side of the construction rather than on the negative side of the resistance needs now further exploration in the field.

Indeed, I see Bolaños and Verdesio calling for such a critical reappraisal in the current situation in colonial studies. Their move is not to be confused with a desire to restore literary studies to their former place in the academy. The questions they ask address the problem of the production of knowledge in a deeply historical sense.

II. PARADIGM SHIFT

The omnivorous category "Latin American Literature" is no longer, if ever it was, a stable construct. One of the destabilizing factors has been the irruptive introduction of the colonial archive which has forced a reconsideration of questions of origin, constructions of teleological canons, and, of course the national, public intellectual as the subject of the production of knowledge in the various regions and time-zones of Latin America. The "aesthetic" core, as constructed by formalist and modernist theories of canon formation, has been unable to resist the pressure exerted by all the disheveled texts (colonial and modern) which exhibit alternative knowledges, (aesthetic) configurations and demand reading strategies of their own.

In conjunction with other forces, the study of literature gravitated towards the study of "culture." Culture appeared as a more encompassing concept. Endowed with the legacy of modern anthropology, culture was conceived as the complex whole of life patterns and practices of belief and feeling. Beyond Levi-Straussian myth reading and all its attendant problems, there lay the promising notion that the study of culture was "only apparently the study of custom, beliefs, or institutions [and that in fact it was] fundamentally the study of thought" (Geertz 352).

Insufficient attention was paid however, to the fact that the anthropological definition of culture, as James Clifford points out, emerged as the liberal alternative to racist classification of peoples and human diversity. "It was a sensitive means for understanding different and dispersed 'whole ways of life' in light of colonial contexts of unprecedented global interconnection" (234-35). Cultures in the plural pointed beyond the original Eurocentric evolutionary value as originally drawn by José de Acosta in his *Historia natural y moral de las Indias* (1590). Culture in this sense was not too distant from Matthew Arnold's own concept of "high" culture, for cultures now were conceived as stable, enduring, syncretic, and ahistorical. Clifford notes that culture thus appears as "a process of ordering and not of disruption. It changes and develops as a living organism" (235). Valentine Daniel has clarified the normalizing assumptions embedded in the idea of culture as total system. It leaves no outside that can resist it. The work of culture thus conceived, Daniel points out, is to "colonize, convert and conquer", to normalize "fugitive elements that may drift within their expanding semeiosic field," leaving no space for counterpoints that cannot be subsumed or tamed by the power of culture (68-69).

As a whole, the field of colonial studies remained distant from the postmodern critique of anthropology. Only a handful of scholars in the field began testing the concept of culture as a semeiotics in which human behavior is understood as symbolic action. Clifford Geertz's view of culture as an "interworked system of construable signs, [as] a context, something within which there can be intelligibility" (14) that is thickly described, began to open the horizon of colonial studies beyond a narrowly conceived textuality and put in place the idea that "colonial" studies were not circumscribed to the "chronicles."[11]

Cultural semiosis offered the possibility for a clear reference to the totality of signs, for an approach to the ceaseless exchange and negotiation of symbolic systems and subjects in tension. Cultural semiosis seemed particularly attuned to the problems of colonial struggles. It proposed, for instance, a way of thinking about the engagement between alphabetic cultures and pictographic and knotting modes of recoding the past and producing knowledge. Keenly aware of the conceptual and locational inadequacy of "literature" as a discipline, and coming from an intellectual tradition which owed more to anthropology and the philosophy of history than to "literary" studies in the United States, Walter Mignolo called for a fundamental shift,[12] often referred to as a "paradigm shift."

---

[11] E. Valentine Daniel takes issue with Geertz's sense of culture as a system capable of offering meanings for all levels of human activity. He prefers to think of culture as a "dense cluster of semeiotic habits" (67). For Daniel, the hermeneutic power of culture is due to the protean nature, to the "absolute dynamism" of the term (68). Human life is shot through with that dense cluster of signs. Daniel goes on to argue that human beings themselves are but dense clusters of signs. Thus, "to be is to be significantly" (80). Individuation is then brought about by a dense clustering of signs just as much as culture is the result of dense clustering which gives the appearance of essence (80). Daniel concludes that "it is the semeiotic concordance brought about by habit "that gives human beings a sense of coherence and integrity from which the ability to act is born" (81).

[12] See Walter Mignolo's "Afterword: On Modernity, Colonization and the Rise of Occidentalism" in his *The Darker Side of the Renaissance*. He notes there that the purpose of his book is to undo the Renaissance's foundational Eurocentrism (315). He reviews his intellectual formation in Córdoba, Argentina. Mignolo states his differences with Derrida on the question of writing and literacy and notes that Jack Goody and Ian Watt's article "The Consequences of Literacy," published a few years before *On Grammatology*, were in fact more influential on his thinking on the relation of the spread of literacy and the West's systems of colonial domination (321). Antonio Gramsci, Frantz Fanon, Edward Said, Edward Glissant, Edmundo O'Gorman, and

If what is meant by paradigm shift what is something like Thomas Kuhn's thesis in *The Structure of Scientific Revolution* (1962), a revolution that overthrows the older paradigm and replaces it with an incompatible framework,[13] such an event, has not yet taken place in the study of colonialities. And Verdesio, who seems to be calling for such a shift, does well to remind us of this fact. Such a shift seems not only ambitious but daunting. It implies a complete re-hauling of the field of Latin American Studies and the humanities in general, not just literature. What is more, as José Rabasa reminded me in a recent conversation (October 1, 2000), a paradigm shift in Kuhn's sense takes place behind the backs of the subjects working in a given period.

As I understand it, the shift that Mignolo has in mind entails massive new learning, mastering of a multidisciplinary bibliography that spans both sides of the Atlantic and a thorough, critical theoretical reorientation. The project far exceed the confines of the work possible inside the monolingual confines of "Spanish" departments, loaded as they still are with the remnants of New Criticism and philology. In view of the fact that "Spanish" failed to develop into a modern intellectual language in Europe, the monolingual measure severely curtails the possibilities of stepping out of the ideologies and epistemologies already inscribed in the "Spanish" configurations of knowledge, some of which we see decried in Verdesio's analysis of the reception of the new-historical novel and which fly contrary to the work of Latin American intellectual history. "Spanish" monolinguism runs counter to the long standing Latin American project of decolonization, which began with recognizing the insufficiency of the monolingual Spanish intellectual tradition, and sought, from its earlier manifestations—Garcilaso de la Vega, Inca, on to the Modernistas, Mariátegui, Borges, Mansilla, Arguedas, and Cortázar—to furnish its arsenal with learning available in any language whatever. A fundamental shift entails breaking out of the confines not only of literature and its correlation with national subjects, but it also means breaking

Giambattista Vico figure prominently in Mignolo's formation in the philosophy of history an intellectual quest at best distant from the program of studies in "Spanish" departments.

[13] For a brief characterization of Kuhn's thesis on change in scientific knowledge see the entry for "paradigm" in *The Cambridge Dictionary of Philosophy* (1999), 641-42.

out of, or reconfiguring the intellectual and linguistic confines of "Spanish" departments in the United States.[14]

A fundamental shift implies critical and systematic delearning of the paradigms that sustain the inertia of the field. It should not prove surprising that *The Darker Side of the Renaissance* (1995) comes immediately to mind as one of the best examples of the fundamental change that Mignolo has called for. In their effort to map new routes for colonial studies, several of the scholars writing in this volume cite the work of José Rabasa, Antonio Cornejo Polar, and Mabel Moraña. Despite key theoretical differences, the work of these critics is highlighted here for their keen interest in historicizing the study of the past, relocating the locus of enunciation of the scholar, and redirecting the gaze of the critic towards the self-deployment of subaltern subjects pleated in the narrative of the criollo-national subject. Seen under this light, Cornejo Polar's emphasis on the cultural heterogeneity of Andean literary legacies is not too far away from Rabasa's inquiry into the colonial ordering and subordination of the *tlacuilos*' ways of knowing. Such a family resemblance or shared adjacency[15] points to the urgent need for comparative studies between the history of Mesoamerican and Andean colonialities. It also holds the promise for opening up new ground and furthering a shift that in time may be recognized as paradigmatic.

It is perhaps not too risky to say, that despite the perception of differences in research agendas which have to do more with the originary place of some scholars working in the field rather than with the stated desired destination, a fundamental shift is indeed at work. The problematic outline by the Latin American Subaltern Studies Group is a call for radical change which in many ways dovetails with Mignolo's earlier essay. Reading against the grain has indeed cleared out the underbrush in the forest.

---

[14] English departments are open to the whole of European intellectual traditions as well as to Third World texts provided they are in English, because, due to their hegemony, they do not bother to read in other languages. Roughly the same can be said for French. But that is indeed not the case with the Spanish language and yet the departmental configuration is predicated on a notion of equivalence that is just not there.

[15] Paul Bové in *Mastering Discourse: The Politics of Intellectual Culture* (1992) writes of the influence of the history of science by George Canguilhem on the work of Michel Foucault. Canguilhem traced the ways in which some sciences extended—like vectors—throughout culture. He showed how they thus open new spaces for new forms of knowledge production. Sciences thus *cohered*, they *shared adjacency* (7).

But a fundamental shift will not be in place until a genealogical look into history cuts through vast swaths of growth in the forest of standing "truths." In order to dismantle the assumptions which allow the invisible continuity of colonialist knowledge practices such as the uncritical approach to the canonizing formulas that end up performing the "cleansing operation" that Bolaños so forcefully demonstrates in his consideration of Arciniegas, Colombian historiography, and *El carnero* read as a colonial picaresque, the field needs to track down the way in which discourse constitutes objects and makes them available for study.[16]

A shift to a genealogical approach requires scholars to sustain ambitious and long-term projects, to become historians (see Rabasa, "Pre-Columbian Pasts") or philosophers of entire systems of thought. One of the major obstacles, it seems to me, stems not from the differences among those calling for a shift, but rather from the trendiness in the field. The demand that legitimates research with the value of novelty runs counter to the huge investment in learning that needs to be made in order to break out of the old paradigm. Slow, consistent, and solid accretion may turn out to be a good method for producing changes in epistemological assumptions. Instead of books on trendy subjects read by the very few, we may have to rely on far-reaching articles capable of making a material difference; that is to say articles whose publication does not allow for things to remain the same.

In this regard, the recent article by Lindsay Waters, the Executive Editor for the Humanities at the Harvard University Press, is most relevant. In a way the title says it all: "A Modest Proposal for Preventing the Books of the Members of the MLA from Being a Burden to Their

---

[16] It is important to remember here, especially after having cited Neil Larsen's critique of the idea of replacing literature with discourse, that "discourse," as analyzed by Foucault, gets shortchanged in these two communications. Paul Bové reminds us that to give a definition of "discourse" would by itself amount to yet another essentialist move. Nevertheless we understand that language is discourse, an enduring flow made visible by "tracing the genealogy of discipline as a series of events existing as transformations of one another" (6). Discourse is "the organized and regulating, as well as the regulating and constituting functions of language that it studies." "Discourse produces knowledge about humans and their societies but the truths of these discourses are relative to the disciplinary structures, the logical framework which they are institutionalized, they can have no claim on us, except that derived from the authority and legitimacy, the power granted to or acquired by the institutionalized discourse in question" (9).

Authors, Publishers, or Audiences." Waters basically argues that scholarship in the humanities would be better served if we returned to the publication of substantial and path breaking articles of interest to audiences beyond the disciplinary tenure committees who require a book, no matter how slim, marginal, repetitious, or self centered. Scholars of Latin American letters seldom consider in which ways their work modifies the existing knowledge in other disciplines. If we are concerned with the decolonization of knowledge and with breaking out of the restrictions built around us by colonial discourse, one of our major objectives should be to establish dialogue with other disciplines—anthropology, historiography, English, political theory—as well as other area studies.

III. Globalization, the National Subject and Latin Americanism

On a previous occasion I have written on the disarray, the plethora of approaches with no center or direction, that passes for a field of study. In "Interrupting the Text of Latin American Literature: Problems of (Missed) recognition" I argued that part of the problem of disarray in the field, and especially the situation of the locus of enunciation of the critic, has to do with the unsettling problematic of identity in a globalized world. What each of us thinks and does is inevitably bound up with who we think we are. This not to say that the personal is the political. But it is to acknowledge that the dynamics of self-recognition imply a consciousness of the bounds of identity which in turn tie up the questions of ethical responsibility that we consider paramount in the exercise of critical practices.

Although we have come to realize that identities, even when hegemonic, are never solid, organic, or stable, this is not the same as saying that they do not exist nor that they have ceased to be constructed. The question then devolves not on whether we respond to single and hegemonic identities or to multiple (heterogenic) subject positions, but how we go about constructing identities and how we negotiate different subject positions, for the construction of identities bears heavily on practices of interpretation, from the every day to the philosophical. The problem of identity orients the authorization of protocols of entanglement and makes possible the assemblage of observation and enunciatory positions.

Globalization has only exacerbated questions of identity, for it has at once clarified and complicated the problem of positionality. The new mode of production of wealth has displaced the territorial states. It has redefined the role that they once played in the world's imperial division of (intellectual) labor. This has brought about the awareness that "[se] exige un cambio radical de las representaciones culturales que América Latina ha generado sobre sí misma" ("A radical change is needed in the cultural representations of itself that Latin America has generated") (Castro-Gómez and Mendieta 8). This radical change affects three chief categories: the territorial nation, the identity of national (*criollo*) intellectual, and historiography. As the post-nation condition gains ground over the international order, there appears the diasporic intellectual (Martiniquean, Indian, Nicaraguan, Jamaican, Argentine, Peruvian, Australian, Cuban, Vietnamese, Algerian) as an actor in the metropole. He/she navigates alongside, but not in place of, the ship of the national intellectual, who is no longer always at home either. The dynamics of de-territorialization and re-territorialization in the knowledge/ power production animate the complex, vexed, and indeed fruitful debate over a Latin Americanism from and about Latin America.

Questions of identity overflow into questions of solidarity. Can the national intellectual transport his originary "*punto de mira*" (perspective) without suffering the impact of the forces of de-territorialization? Are these national agendas any more liberating, emancipatory, or ethical than the agendas generated in the diaspora? As Bolaños and Restrepo show, writing the nation, in the case of Colombia, has meant a monumental job of erasure of subjects and concealment of violences which could easily compete with any other "outside" colonizing force now. Or are the forces of globalization such that all enunciatory positions have become diasporic, bound ineluctably for the borderland?

Perhaps it is too early to tell. Perhaps the nation-state, already missed by some (Sarlo), will manage to make a come back as the best point of articulation for meeting the demands for (economic and cultural) justice the world over. For the interests that produce globalization as universal democratization and equal access to markets are, in fact, local and not at all neutral. As Santiago Castro-Gómez and Eduardo Mendieta put it: "Todos hoy viven en una situación de riesgo, por lo tanto es necesario un protagonismo (agency) sobre la vida propia al nivel cognitivo, hermenéutico y estético" (11). However, as things stand now, theoretically, with the big fear of essentialisms and representation, "la respuesta no puede venir marcada por representaciones de tipo esencialista que establecen diferencias orgánicas entre pueblos y territorialidades" (12). The problem is not Latin Americanism, as some would have it, for Latin American Studies has built a field of knowledge which, despite its northener gaze and interests, has provided us with a treasure of knowledge about Latin America and with positions and positionalities in the world's academies. The question for the de-colonizing agenda is how to marshal that knowledge to the service of a fundamental shift; how to muster agency and how to establish solidarian ties[17] without re-establishing forms of domination based on false identitarian politics; how to provide, from an ethical position, a critique of colonialism-globalization?

On a previous occasion,[18] reflecting on the challenge of Cultural Studies to "literature" and on the irritation with which some of the better-known propositions of Cultural Studies have been received in Latin America (Beverley; Sarlo; Yúdice, "Postmodernity" and "Cultural Studies"), I proposed that the pursuit of a critical pluralism capable of leading to emancipatory movements needed to find a way of escaping the endless decentering relativism rampant today. An ethical inquiry would have to come to grips, as I said above, with the question of identity and modes of subjectivation.

As we now understand the question there is no identity that is natural or extra-political. Judith Butler (*Gender Trouble*) argues that the radical strategy for feminism is not so much to improve the condition of women, for that goes without saying, within networks of power that subject, but to subvert the constitution of women's identity within the patriarchal paradigm. Within this logic it follows that the advocacy for a coalition politics in which women, constituted as resisting subjects, would *maintain* rather than overcome their differences in the form of a series rather

---

[17] Solidarity, as Laclau and Mouffe point out, needs to be rearticulated away from the homogeneous nation of class and into the concept of a series of equal and cooperative struggles trying to overcome domination and achieve liberty (182). It is important to keep in mind that "equivalence is always hegemonic in so far as it does not simply establish an alliance between given interests, but modifies the very identity of the forces engaging in that alliance" (183-84).

[18] In the foregoing arguments concerning the agonal subject I am rephrasing parts of chapter 5 in part 2 of this volume, "Interrupting the Text of Latin American Literature: Problems of (Mis)Recognition."

than an amalgamation, as Laclau and Mouffe also propose. The contradiction implicit in the idea of a coalition of resisting subjects, is lessened, if we posit, as William Connolly proposes, not natural, unified and coherent subjects, but rather *agonal subjects* for whom power is both constraining and enabling (*The Ethos* xv-xix), a notion not too distant from the practices on colonial subjects such as Garcilaso de la Vega, Guamán Poma, Sor Juana Inés de la Cruz and others.

For the agonal subject, as distinct from the Augustinian subject,[19] respect for others, that is, for difference, is based on one's own resistance to attempts to govern their conduct.[20] Liberty is itself the practice of, rather than the absence of, power. Because identity is constituted in difference, it is then the irreducibility of the other (Guamán Poma's project) to one's own strategy that teaches one to respect others as free subjects, precisely because they are different.[21]

---

[19] In the *Augustinian Imperative: the Politics of Morality* (1993), William Connolly shows that to this day Euroamerican political theory and practices remain under what he calls the "Augustinian Imperative," that is "the insistence that there is an intrinsic moral order susceptible to authoritative representations" (xvii). This imperative makes its pursuit obligatory and thus opens the quest to "move closer to one's truest self by exploring its inner geography" (xvii) through confession and submission to the higher authority of God, himself produced by confession (44) and the need to ward off the anxiety of death (81). As he examines the birth of difference in Augustine, an analysis reminiscent of Borges on the heresiarchs, Connolly posits that for Augustine to consolidate the Christian self there had to be heresies to denounce and demote. Connolly asks: "What price have those constituted as pagans, infidels, heretics and nihilists throughout the centuries paid for this demand to confess an intrinsic moral order?" (81). Many histories rush to detail the answer to this question, but none is better known to students of Latin America than the Spanish and Portuguese evangelization of Mexicans, Andeans, Mayas, Tupinambas, etc., etc.

[20] It is ironic and very fitting, as we speak of colonization past and present, to verify how much in common the Andean ethic of "respect" has with the ethics of the agonal subject proposed by Connolly at the opening of the second millennium of European imperialism. For a close study of the ethic of respect—*respeto*—see Bolin. It is interesting to note that Marisol de la Cadena, in her postmodern and very worthy approach to the history of *indigenismo* in Cuzco, rediscovers *respeto* as the key cultural formation elaborated by the market women in their search for empowerment in a neo-colonial and still racist historical environment. De la Cadena, however, fails to see the Andean, pre-contact roots of this cultural formation.

[21] Bartolomé Álvarez's "memorial" to Philip II, *De las costumbres y conversión de los indios del Perú* [1588] complains and registers the impossibility of the colonial-evangelizing logic for understanding the Andeans' reason and desire for holding onto

In a globalized world in which power is distributed asymmetrical and neo-colonization processes are still very much under way, the agonistic subject, the subject attendant to *respeto,* would seem to represent a good place for both resistance as well as coalitions in plurality. *Respeto* in Chillihuasi means indomitable pride in one's culture. Respect and politeness towards all living things—nature, people—is exercised in utter self-confidence and in memory of the ancestors (Bolin 5). *Respeto* also means solidarity, itself imbued with the Andean ideals of reciprocity and love for the *pachamama* on which all living things depend (8-10).

Here in the metropolis William Connelly has developed intensely and extensively the political consequences of Foucault's agonistic subject as well as those flowing from the care of the self (as other) for the constitution of a radical liberal democracy.[22] If identity is conceived as a set of limits of density that enables selves to choose, think, and act—and if identities can only be maintained in the face of that from which they differ—then the formation of particular identities becomes inevitable. This means that no matter how aggressively national and regional identities come under fire by globalizing or neo-globalizing projects, identities such as Argentina, or Latin America, or the diasporic intellectual situated in the metropole, are always in the making. The question is, then, not how to contain or foster the formation of identities, but rather how to keep them from becoming congealed, naturalized, and potentially violent to the (evil) other. Only *respeto* or agonistic identities can keep one from uttering again: "Quisiera tener entendimiento raso y estilo curioso para dar a entender la pena que siento de daño tan irremediable, si el cielo no viene al remedio (Álvarez 143)... que quisiera quemarlo por dogmatizar a él y a su hermano, que tiene el ídolo de su padre escondido" (137).

In the face of galloping globalization a reworking of pluralism by positing an agonistic subject, *respeto,* capable of *reciprocal recognition,* offers a way out of the particularisms that Beatriz Sarlo decries, as well as

---

the two religions on parallel tracks of respect under colonial domination. He writes that in "la dureza de sus corazones y la torpeza de sus entendimientos" (142) "entre otras razones que dicen o hallan para acreditar su intento [los malos evangelistas], es darles a entender que nosotros somos unas gentes diferentes de ellos y ellos son otras diferentes de nosotros; y así para ellos [los indios] dicen ser la doctrina de sus padres y pasados, y para nosotros la nuestra; y que los sacerdotes los engañamos, y que a ellos no les conviene lo que les enseñamos" (134).

[22] For a discussion of the radicalization of Foucault by Connolly, see Simons 95-126.

the breached communication circle postulated by some readers of *testimonio*. Within an epistemology of reciprocal recognition, the subaltern[23] does not only speak but is in fact also heard. He/she is not burned for keeping in hiding his/her father's (idols) knowledge. His knowledge is acknowledged not as the voice of the marginal but in dialogic situation, for pluralism, as Connolly points out, is not sufficient to stem the reemergence of congealed subjects. Tolerance, as predicated by multiculturalism in the United States, is an "undeveloped form of critical responsiveness" for it relies on mis-recognition. In contrast, the critical responsiveness engaged by agonal subjects does not appropriate or assimilate, for it departs from the idea that identities are both differential and collective (Connolly, *The Ethos* xv).

Critical responsiveness thus "opens up a cultural space through which the other might consolidate itself into *something* that is not afflicted by negative cultural markings" (Connolly, *Augustinian*, 29) as the subaltern has been when he/she is posited in the Hegelian master/slave dynamic. For Connolly, the subaltern does not need to be thought of as negativity, for difference is not reduced to a pre-existing code (as in "Can the subaltern speak?"). In this new political space strangeness in oneself and others can be engaged without resentment or panic, for "freedom resides in the spaces produced by such dissonant junctures" (xx).

In this vision of agonist democracy, in this culture of *respeto*, the self is not robbed by difference, the self is instead difference. Thus the ethics of agonistic engagement call for studied indifference, the ceremonial politeness and distance of Chillihuasi, rather the fake familiarity of the Television multicultural village. In a world of contending identities, collaboration can only be selective (Connolly, *The Ethos* xviii). The point within the contest of Latin American Studies and the past and present colonialities is that there is no need to establish a north/south gnoseological opposition nor a literature/cultural or colonial studies /postcolonial theories studies one. What is necessary is to transform the way in which we experience difference and the many ways in which the several imperial legacies have produced differences that divide and impede the work of their dismantling.

---

[23] Ileana Rodríguez ("Hegemonía y dominio") has shown that the subaltern is a category which designates subjects located in the interstices of power. They live in constant negotiation, "agenciándose" (making it) within the networks of knowledge/power.

IV. CONCLUSIONS

Instead of summarizing the arguments presented above I would like to conclude by taking up two moves which, placed side by side, begin to yield an agenda for specific directions into a/the new paradigm. José Rabasa speaks of producing an inventory for a decolonizing colonial studies. For his part, Walter Mignolo, in "Posoccidentalismo: el argumento desde América Latina" (1998), argues for a fundamental break with "el relato histórico de América debido a la cuestión étnica y por lo tanto al sujeto de la historia" (40).[24]

I think that there is general agreement on the need to break with evolutionist historiography which of course includes the history of literature; to move beyond the ideological constraints and assumptions of the reading practices and criteria for canon formation authorized by New Criticism; to break with the existing Eurocentric periodization which produces terrible distortions in the constitution of objects of study. A good example of such a challenge is Higgin's study (*Constructing the Criollo Archive*) which moves alongside the colonial baroque, the colonial sublime, thus complicating our understanding of the production of poetry before the independence movements and illuminating a little more the determining role played by Jesuit intellectuals throughout out the colonial period. *The Shape of Inca History* by Susan A. Niles (1999) offers an excellent example of how to read culture beyond the alphabetic

---

[24] The meaning of "posoccidentalismo" in Mignolo's article goes had in hand with Fernando Coronil's development of the term. In his call for a move beyond occidentalismo, conceived as the mirror image of Edward Said's orientalismo, Coronil writes: "Lo que caracteriza al occidentalismo, tal como lo defino aquí, no es que moviliza a las representaciones estereotipadas de sociedades no-occidentales, ya que la jerarquización etnocéntrica de diferencias no es privilegio exclusivo del mundo occidental, sino que dicho privilegio está íntimamente conectado con el despliegue del poder global del Occidente... Como sistema de clasificaciones que da expresión a formas de diferenciación económica y cultural en el mundo moderno, el occidentalismo está inseparablemente ligado a la constitución de asimetrías internacionales suscritas por el capitalismo global... retar al orientalismo requiere que el occidentalismo sea desestabilizado como un estilo representacional que produce concepciones polarizadas y jerárquicas del Occidente y sus otros y las convierte en figuras centrales de la narrativa de la historia global y local" (131). For an English version of this article see "Beyond Occidentalism: Toward Nonimperial Geohistorical Categories." *Cultural Anthropology* 11(1): 51-87, 1996.

sources and how to produce views into the past which are shaped by the epistemologies of the conquered.

A break with existing periodization, an example of the annexation of Latin American history to the European production of the world, will require much learning across many fields of inquiry. It is a task beyond the capacity of a single scholar and that is why it perhaps remains enveloped in the inertia that organizes the field. It goes without saying that collaborative work is an urgent need, and in that regard the new volume *Rethinking Literary History* that Mario Valdés, Linda Hutcheon and Jedlal Kadir are organizing promises to be a keystone in the construction of a new paradigm.

Whether the term is used or not, there seems to be an agreement on the need to adopt a genealogical approach to time and space. A genealogical approach could also provide the ground for the multiplicity of time and cultural formations to come up to the surface of Latin American history. Rabasa is indeed very firm on the need to deconstruct antiquarian historiography in order to reveal the ways in which the pre-Columbian past has been and continues to be organized and appropriated by past and present colonial enterprises.

Essential, it seems to me, is the long postponed need to develop a lexicon of terms that lifts away the Eurocentric loads of concepts such as "Indians," "Indies," "America," and even "Latin America." Perhaps adopting Guamán Poma's false (true) etymology could be one way of beginning to signal the force of another perspective. Instead of continuing to write "Indians" after Columbus, why not write, "In-dia," after Guamán Poma. Such a gesture would begin to signal an assumed critical perspective onto the object of discourse. A remapping of critical consciousness should entail developing a toponymy that makes semantical the relations that articulate the spaces mapped.

Most, if not all of these moves dovetail with Mignolo's proposal for an over-arching post-occidentalist approach, in as much as under occidentalism Europe has assigned to itself the exclusive capacity to know different times and cultures. In a sweeping re-periodization of his own, Mignolo proposes to enter into the realm of three key moments of occidentalism in Latin America in order to lay them bare and produce new ground for understanding the epistemological work of imperial legacies. He considers the first moment to be the annexation and conversion of the "Indians," the second would be the birth and expansion of anthropology and the production and annexation of the "primitives," and the third would be the Humboltian moment when science annexes once again the territories and peoples of "America" to a Eurocentric scientific grid of knowledge.

To gain an understanding of each of these moments and the repercussions of such annexations in our day a great deal of new research is needed. We are only beginning to understand the problematic of evangelization with the work of Luis Millones and others on the Taqui-Oncoy and the Huarochirí narratives in Peru, the work of López Austin and Serge Gruzinski in Mexico. Less is known, from a genealogical optic, of similar processes of colonization in Paraguay and Brazil, for instance. Even if all this genealogical work were at hand, to begin to have any sense of completeness demands comparative work. Its absence considerably hampers colonial and modern studies.

In "Rethinking the Colonial Model," Walter Mignolo writes a genealogy of vast scope on the constitution of the "colonial difference" first, and the constitution of the "imperial difference" afterward. There he emphasizes the "irreducible difference between talking "about" the colonial difference and talking "from" it" (158). For Mignolo, this distinction is all important, for without it, "knowledge would remain in the desincorporated world of universal categories. The irreducible category shall be maintained" (158-159). Otherwise one risks, once again, the very absorption of which Eurocentrism was made. The article is enormous and it elaborates on the making and transformation of the colonial difference from the sixteenth century on (60). It refuels the debates on the colonial difference as well as literary history/the history of literature. It especially opens up new perspectives on how to distinguish spacio-temporal moments which can take the place of the present Western periodization.

Finally, in our consideration of the agonal subject and the possibility of solidarian coalitions we must take into account the conditions of the Latin American diaspora. The current United States census estimates that there are now approximately 40 million "Hispanics" living north of the Rio Grande. The borderland conditions of de-territorialization and re-territorialization dovetail only too neatly with the problematic of conquest and coloniality to be ignored here. Gloria Anzaldúa's *Borderland/La frontera*, proposes the generation of a border epistemology. Both Walter Mignolo and José Saldívar ("Las fronteras") see in the concept of the borderland the ground that might propitiate recognition and alliances between Chicanos and Latin Americans. The diaspora could be regarded as a productive space in which to overcome oppositional thinking. However, in order for the borderland not to become yet another bloody trench we need to posit the agonistic subject, or better yet the Andean cultural category of *respeto*, for had it been left in place by the waves of occidentalization, "otro sería nuestro cantar" (we would be singing a very different song).

In conclusion, to say that other (colonial, subaltern, feminine, Indian) rationalities have much to contribute to our understanding of the present as a legacy of the past is not to write out of nostalgia. It is to dig into the *fondos* of the archive as Bolin did in *Rituals of Respect* or Niles does in *The Shape of Inca History* and find "new" solutions stemming from that which has been forgotten by the imperial gaze but kept still in the pleats of the complex and never-ending colonial situation. It is then, in the wake of Vallejo, a refusal to accept either the estrangement of the past or its annexation to single, colonialist reason.

Originally pulished in *Colonialism Past and Present: Reading and Writing About Colonial Latin America Today*. Ed. Alvaro Félix Bolaños and Gustavo Verdesio, 261-288. © 2002 Albany: State University of New York Press. Reprinted by permission.

WORKS CITED

ÁLVAREZ, Bartolomé. *De las costumbres y conversión de los indios del Perú. Memorial a Felipe II*. [1588]. Madrid: Polifemo, 1998.

ASHCROFT, Bill, Gareth GRIFFITHS, and Helen TIFFIN. *Key Concepts in Post-Colonial Studies*. London; New York: Routledge, 1998.

BEVERLEY, John. *Against Literature*. Minneapolis: University of Minnesota Press, 1993.

BOLIN, Inge. *Rituals of Respect: The Secret Survival in the High Peruvian Andes*. Austin: University of Texas Press, 1998.

BOVÉ, Paul A. *Mastering Discourse: The Politics of Intellectual Culture*. Durham: Duke University Press, 1992.

CASTRO-GÓMEZ, Santiago and Eduardo MENDIETA, ed. *Teorías sin disciplina, latinoamericanismo, poscolonialidad y globalización en debate*. México: Porrúa; San Francisco: University of San Francisco Press, 1998.

CASTRO-KLARÉN, Sara. "Interrupting the Text of Latin American Literature: Problems of (Missed)recognition." *Nuevas perspectivas desde/sobre América*

Latina: el desafío de los estudios culturales. Ed. Mabel Moraña. Santiago de Chile: Editorial Cuarto Propio/Instituto Internacional de Literatura Iberoamericana, 2000. 387-405.

CLIFFORD, James. *The Predicament of Culture: Twentieth Century Ethnography, Literature, and Art.* Cambridge: Harvard University Press, 1988.

CONNOLLY, William E. *Augustinian Imperative: the Politics of Morality.* Newbury Park: Sage Publications, 1993.

—. *The Ethos of Pluralization.* Minneapolis: University of Minnesota Press, 1995.

CORNEJO POLAR, Antonio. *Escribir en el aire.* Lima: Editorial Horizonte, 1994.

DANIEL, E. Valentine. "The Limits of Culture." *In Near Ruins: Cultural Theory at the End of the Century.* Ed. Nicholas B. Dirks. Minneapolis: University of Minnesota Press, 1998. 67-91.

GEERTZ, Clifford. *The Interpretation of Cultures: Selected Essays.* New York: Basic Books, 1973.

HARRIS, Wendell V. "Canonicity." *PMLA* 106.No. 1 (1991): 110-121.

JAMESON, Fredric. *The Prison-house of Language: A Critical Account of Structuralism and Russian Formalism.* Princeton: Princeton University Press, 1972.

LACLAU, Ernesto and Chantal MOUFFE. *Hegemony and Socialist Strategy: Towards a Radical Democratic Politics.* London: Verso, 1985.

LARSEN, Neal. *Reading North by South: On Latin American Literature, Culture, and Politics.* Minneapolis: University of Minnesota Press, 1995.

MIGNOLO, Walter. *The Darker Side of the Renaissance: Literacy, Territoriality and Colonization,* Ann Arbor: The University of Michigan Press, 1995.

—. "Posoccidentalismo: el argumento desde América Latina." *Teorías sin disciplina, latinoamericanismo, poscolonialidad y globalización en debate.* Ed. Santiago Castro-Gómez and Eduardo Mendieta. Mexico: Porrúa; San Francisco: University of San Francisco Press, 1998. 31-58.

—. "Rethinking the Colonial Model." *Rethinking Literary History: A Dialogue on Theory.* Ed. Linda Hutcheon and Mario Valdés. Oxford/New York: Oxford University Press, 2001. 155-193.

RABASA, José. *Inventing America: Spanish Historiography and the Formation of Eurocentrism.* Norman: University of Oklahoma Press, 1993.

—. "Pre-Columbian Pasts and Indian Presents in Mexican History." *Colonialism Past and Present: Reading and Writing About Colonial Latin America Today.* Eds. Álvaro Félix Bolaños and Gustavo Verdesio. Albany: State University of New York Press, 2002. 51-79.

READINGS, Bill. *The University in Ruins.* Cambridge: Harvard University Press, 1996.

RODRÍGUEZ, Ileana, "Hegemonía y dominio: subalternidad, un significado flotante." *Teorías sin disciplina, latinoamericanismo, poscolonialidad y globalización en debate.* Ed. Santiago Castro-Gómez and Eduardo Mendieta. México, D.F.: Porrúa; San Francisco: University of San Francisco Press, 1998. 102-119.

RUÍZ VILAPLANA, Antonio. *Doy fe....un año de actuación en la España naciona-lista.* Paris: Éditions Imprimerie Coopérative Étoile, 1937?

SARLO, Beatriz. *Escenas de la vida posmoderna.* Buenos Aires: Ariel, 1994.

VALLEJO, César. *Poemas en prosa. Poemas humanos. España, aparta de mí este cáliz.* Ed. Julio Vélez. Madrid: Cátedra, 1988.

YÚDICE, George. "Cultural Studies and Civil Studies." In *Reading the Shape of the World.* Eds. Henry Schwarz and Richard Dientz. Boulder: Westview, 1996. 50-67.

—. "Postmodernity and Transnational Capitalism in Latin America." In *On Edge: the Crisis of Contemporary Latin American Culture.* Eds. Jean Franco, Juan Flores, and George Yúdice. Minneapolis: University of Minnesota Press, 1992.

CHAPTER 4
The Recognition of Convergence: Subaltern Studies in
Perspective

In what follows I adhere in a general way to the questionnaire that Gustavo Verdesio has prepared as the point of departure for a reflexion on the work that the initiative of the Latin American Subaltern Studies group has performed in the various fields that constitute Latin American Studies and the disciplinary knowledges that conform to it. Obviously I cannot address all the questions that Verdesio poses. This is partly because more space and effort would be needed than what is possible here. Parts of the questions asked have been addressed already and in different moments by some of the founding members of the group.

I am thinking for instance of the "Introduction" that John Beverley writes to his recent *Subalternity and Representation: Arguments in Cultural Theory* (1999) where he takes up at length the crisis of Marxism and the epistemological thrust of Subaltern Studies in conjunction with the polemical reception accorded to it by both some historians and literary critics in the field of Latin American Studies. In "The Im/possibility of Politics: Subalternity, Modernity, Hegemony" Beverley discusses amply the relation of Cultural Studies to Subaltern Studies. Likewise in the "Introduction" to *The Latin American Subaltern Studies Reader* (2001) Ileana Rodríguez provides the reader with a brief intellectual history of the Latin American Subaltern Studies group, a discussion that spells out how Subaltern Studies appears in a canvas of epistemological crisis in which it was necessary to "Find ways of producing scholarship to demonstrate that in the failure to recognize the poor as active, social political, and heuristic agents reside the limits and the thresholds of our present hermeneutical and political condition" (3). Another founding member of the group, José Rabasa, has written recently on the conjunction of postcolonial theory and subaltern studies in order to establish a ground for dialogue between scholars who investigate the colonial past in Latin America and the postcolonial initiative which coming from the periphery of the former British empire dates colonialism to the eighteenth century, traces its epistemological roots to the Enlightenment and erases both the Spanish colonial past and its impact on the very formation of modernity (16-20). Finally, Walter Mignolo has written repeatedly and amply on a good deal of the problematic outlined in Verdesio's questionnaire. Suffice it here to make reference to his recent *Local Histories/ Global Designs: Coloniality, Subaltern Knowledges, and Border Thinking* (2002). In a shorter form I addressed earlier the overlapping of, as well as the divergences between, the "new" colonial studies—inflected by discourse theory, semiotics, and *testimonio* theory—and key questions in postcolonial theory as presented in the work of Homi Bhabha and Bill Ashcroft (interview with Zevallos-Aguilar).

Given that I am not one of the founding members of the group, and that I did not participate in the writing of the group's manifesto, I think that it might be of interest to attempt a brief narrative of how I came to participate in the group's third meeting in Puerto Rico in 1996, then attended the meeting at William and Mary, then at Duke University, and finally the meeting at Rice University. In a way this narrative might illustrate the fact that not all scholars who find Subaltern Studies a productive and promising theoretical and political vantage point depart from the same location, sense of crisis, or search, nor, once in dialogue with Subaltern Studies in its South Asian or Latin American modality, walk in the same exact path or towards a universally agreed goal. After all, one of the salient features of Subaltern Studies is the attempt to secure a democratic and more self-conscious field of enunciation. For me, tracing the different genealogies of the interlocutors in the Latin American Subaltern Studies Group or in Subaltern Studies at large constitutes one of the most significant learning experiences that group formations can afford in an otherwise academic environment designed for isolated and insolating intellectual work.

My early work on José María Arguedas, the author of beautifully crafted novels, had left me with more questions than answers. I chose to write on Arguedas at a time when neither *Los ríos profundos* (*Deep Rivers*)

(1958), nor Arguedas' ethnographic essays had achieved canonicity. Outside Peru, Arguedas was indeed regarded as a provincial writer and some of the claims made by the authors of the "nueva novela," later called the boom—Vargas Llosa and Carlos Fuentes—came nothing short of writing Arguedas' epitaph. In the United States academy it was clear that Arguedas could not be compared to Alejo Carpentier, for the Cuban writer had been wrapped in the prestige of the "barroco de Indias," a label in which critics teaching at major United States universities and writers such as Lezama Lima had invested a great deal of historiographical acumen. I often wondered why artists and intellectuals who came from areas of Latin America where the colonial baroque had not produced the great architectonic feats of the Jesuits churches in Mexico or the Andes, nor the paintings of the Cuzqueño School, or the sculpture of the Alejaidinho or the Guaraní, took such pains to identify cotemporary writers like Severo Sarduy and Lezama Lima with a "barroco de Indias," but that is material for another discussion. In comparison to the "barroco de Indias" Arguedas was not only associated with the lowly and eccentric Indigenismo, but to complicate matters further, he had criticized Indigenismo from a position of "authenticity," claiming that Indigenismo presented a false portrayal of Andean social formations. He was particularly keen on questions of representation, both in the modern and the postmodern sense of the term. Arguedas' critique of Spanish as his possible literary language was an indication that our current understanding of the conquest and the colonial period called for thorough revision. The problems that Arguedas' fictional ethnography posed for the question of culture in colonial situations and the construction of the speaking subject under conditions of epistemological dominance resisted the then available tools of analysis.

This seemed especially true when Arguedas himself rejected the harnessing of his reflex ion for the various political struggles of the time. When he finally came out and said "no soy un aculturado" in response to Ángel Rama's efforts to include "ethnic" narratives into a globalizing theory of Latin American literature, it seemed perfectly clear that his work exceeded the existing paradigms. Once again Arguedas rejected the explanatory power of a universalizing ambition of the concept of "acculturation" indicating that the local could be, ought to be, a place for theorizing.

At the time the field of study called Latin American Literature offered, as two oppositional sides of the same coin, a text-centered hermeneutics sometimes called New Criticism, and or (but mostly or), a sociology of literature. This latter approach often blurred with dependency theory. Critics felt that the aesthetic or "literary quality" of canonical works was being compromised by the contextual emphasis of both methods of interpretation. It followed that if the singularity of the objects of inquiry ceased, so would the place of the discipline that interpreted them. Increasingly the question devolved around problems of interpretation rather than the particulates of each enthroned text or author. Master texts and master authors began to lose their explanatory powers. Barthes' thesis on the "death of the author" weighted heavily right at the very time when scholars working in departments of "Spanish," that is literary critics, had begun claiming for literature texts that had before been considered "crónicas," eyewitness reports, letters to the king, reports, and even state sponsored narratives of conquest. Moreover, few pointed out the connection between Barthes' theoretical assumptions at the base of his claim on the death of the author and Borges' own deconstruction of the author in his "Biblioteca de Babel" and "Tlön Uqbar Orbis Tertius," to name only two of his devastating texts. But the seeds that Borges planted had begun to germinate even if perhaps the kind of tree that they would grow into had not yet been envisioned. Foucault's critical essay "What is an Author?" both clarified the question as well as exacerbated the construction of the debate in oppositional terms. If some of the differences between the two approches were perceived as inimical it was in part because the epistemological object "literature" was already in question and there was a general denial about this eclipse. It was also because such formulation had not yet come to the fore with full visibility as it would a decade later when in the field of English New Historicism and Cultural Studies overtook the crisis and moved to establish it as the very place of innovative thinking.

The Modern Language Association's publication of *Redrawing the Boundaries: The Transformation of English and American Literary Studies* edited by Stephen Greenblatt and Giles Gunn in 1992, put the Good Housekeeping seal of approval on the transformation that interdisciplinary initiatives, together with "deconstruction, cultural materialism, gender studies, new historicism" (1) and subaltern studies had already brought about. The anxiety and discomfort that Subaltern Studies causes in some areas of the fields of study dedicated to Latin America today is not unlike the discomfort that literary critics and social scientists felt as the impact of postmodern theory dismantled boundaries and introduced new methods and perspectives in the study of English. Above all it redefined the object and its relation to the subject. Some of this anxiety is also related to the fact that SUBALTERN STUDIES with capital letters has been perceived as the sole initiative of historians and that as an "originally" South Asian theoretical move it is thought to be incompatible with the standing cognitive map that assigns certain types of intellectual labor to certain areas of the globe. There is no problem, or less of a problem, with French theory. However, this anxiety could be better understood in relation to the formation of the grid that Aníbal Quijano and Walter Mignolo call the coloniality of power.

But I have skipped over what for me was really the key portal to finding a way out of the prison house of literature conceived as a series of aesthetic objects located in a space of splendid isolation. What begun to open the way out of the dilemma was the reading of Julio Cortázar and his groundbreaking questioning of the categories which constituted the aesthetic as the beautiful, and the bourgeois subject and literature as an expression of " the nation" or the "national" or the psychological depth of the "author." Of course Borges had already done much of that, but Cortázar's displaced and gyrating subjects unfolded the cognitive problematic. In Cortázar, the "death of the author" was already indeed the crux of the matter. His call for more a compatible reader underlined the problem of interpretation and put into undeniable question the arbitrary separation of texts into genres whose lines could not be traversed lest we as readers transgressed what turned out to be short lived but naturalized cultural agreements. There was nothing essentially novelistic about any particular narrative, nor was philosophical reflexion on culture necessarily divorced from narrative form.

What is more, the author of *Rayuela* (1963) took me into a journey through French speculative anthropology, surrealism, and several of the maudit writers in whose work, as it turns out, Michel Foucault was also finding paths that lead outside of the established boundaries (see Miller, especially the chapters "The Death of the Author," "Waiting for Godot," and " The Castle of Murders"). The *cronopios* and the "modelos para armar" showed me the corrosive power of laughter before the self-appointed seriousness of "literature." *Rayuela* gave me the gift of the fragment and underscored the crisis of continuity as a principle of meaning. It took me to Gaston Bachelard and his *The Philosophy of No* (1938), to the idea of a counter-history of science that would enable me to read Michel Foucault once I started attending the Dartmouth Faculty Seminars on Theory.

At the time I was not so much concerned with the general dimensions of an epistemological, and thus a political, crisis, as both Ileana Rodríguez and John Beverley state that they were. I was more concerned with the growing idea that the discussion in the seminars on "theory"—Bakhtin, Kristeva, Lyotard, Derrida, Foucault—implied a serious and irreversible turn in the way we had understood our received history of Latin American Culture. Feminism was of course already in full bloom and its challenge to the sovereign subject of patriarchy dovetailed into the inquiry that Cortázar had provoked by requiring that in order to find out what was going on in *Rayuela* his reader trace every lead he put out and situate every name he dropped in and out of the vast intertext that he manipulated to produce an unhinged text.

Arguedas had of course introduced the question of the past not only as a problem for historiography but also as an unresolved and inextricable part of the living present in his approach to the portrayal of Andean culture. From very different perspectives and locations it seemed to that both Arguedas and Cortázar were questioning the linearity of time that thus far had governed our efforts to make sense of the past—the writing of history. Cortázar was in search of a narrative theory that would abolish the distances created by Western time and psychology. His narrative signals a search for simultaneity, for multiple and diverse presences and performances in a single moment. His interest in jazz and its structural capacity to abolish time and even authorship did not seem that far from Arguedas' own search for a seamless connection between present and past in the music of the Andes. The question of the representation of the past, or rather of the impossibility of the representation of the past as inherited in current cognitive structures and academic thinking, was only exacerbated for me with the reading of Guamán Poma. Like my first reading of *Rayuela* from a modernist understanding of literature, *El primer nueva corónica y buen gobierno* (1615) appeared as a total chaos. Once again Cortázar's gift of the mobile fragment, of the restless puzzle that is forever trying to achieve form only to unravel once more, opened an avenue by which to enter a world in which the clash and struggle of epistemologies and paradigms sets every object previously fastened and subjected adrift. Postmodern theory began to fall into place as a *relocated* ground from which to formulate questions on the received narratives of the past that would not repeat the modernist teleology.

In *The Political Unconscious* (1981), Fredric Jameson's emphasis on the idea that we never apprehend a text in all the freshness of the thing-in-itself but rather that "text's come before us always-already-read... through the sedimented reading habits and categories developed by those inherited interpretative traditions" (9) seems to seed the path for a reconsideration of a historiography that had always already written principles of dependency, imitation, and copying into our understanding of the formation of Latin American cultures. Jameson's objective to restructure the problematics of ideology, of representation, of history and of cultural production "around the all-informing process of narrative" (9) allowed the passage from novel to "crónica" and from "crónica" to most colonial texts. While the question of agency appeared ever more complicated, Foucault and de Certeau, with their notions of spatiality, locus of enunciation, discourse, and especially the dismantling of the Western modern subject as the only subject of knowledge, seem to dovetail into epistemological concerns that I now had to consider to represent the core of a Latin American thinking, coming from below, which started with the attempt by both Garcilaso de la Vega, Inca and Guamán Poma to wrestle with history, or rather with the appropriation of the past by Spanish historiography.

With those concerns in mind I made the acquaintance of José Rabasa. He had moved to the University of Maryland and I had gone to Johns Hopkins University. There, Judith Butler, whose *Gender Trouble* (1990) I had devoured, was offering a seminar on postcolonial theory. Her Foucauldian assault of the sovereign subject spelled out uncanny connections with the French artists and philosophy that I had read to get a hold of Cortázar. This time, the topics to be treated in the syllabus of postcolonial theory seemed oddly familiar. However, not a single Latin American intellectual was in the list of readings. And yet the sense of recognition was unmistakable, especially when it came to Franz Fanon. As it turned out, Rabasa and I spoke of having a reading group. I missed the Dartmouth seminar experience and learning of Rabasa's writing on historiography the idea of a reading group in the Washington area seemed propitious. This convergence of concerns entailed a shared sense that in certain domains of what was generally postmodern theory one could find a selected basis for asking questions about the construction of "other" that did not entail an acceptance of negativity about the dominated nor an alienation about the subaltern, and much less a reinscription of "orientalism." The dialogue that started in this reading group led to an invitation to join the Latin American Subaltern Studies Group.

In writing an incomplete but highlighted narrative of how I came to attend the third meeting of the Latin American Subaltern Studies group, I am responding to Verdesio's question on the genealogies of Latin American Subaltern Studies, Cultural Studies, and Postcolonial Theory in the United States. Having read similar and perhaps more self-conscious accounts on the genealogy of their epistemological situation by Ileana Rodríguez, John Beverley, and Walter Mignolo, the latter in the "Afterward" to his *The Darker Side of the Renaissance: Literacy, Territoriality and Colonization* (1995), I have come to the conclusion that as individuals we have indeed been walking in different paths, but moving, as Guha puts it, towards a "shared horizon that each can recognize as his own" (37). It is clear that some of the founding members felt a particular urgency and recognized with unusual clarity the crisis that ensued for the Left after the defeat of the Nicaraguan revolution and communism at large. Others, as I have pointed out in the chapter "Writing With His Thumb in the Air," had already embarked in an inquiry that interrogated history as writing, that is to say as a problem of representation. Anthropology's own postmodern crisis—the predicament of culture—had brought the question of the "other," "oral cultures," and the construction of "peoples without history" into critical focus. Methods of inquiry and styles of writing, together with Eurocentric assumptions on the normativity of alphabetic writing and the subsequent intellectual deficiency marked by its absence, were now the hot topics of discussion. For a student of colonial cultures, this debate seemed to have the events of the Spanish conquest of Aztecs, Mayas, and Andean at its very core. Ethnohistorians were also grappling with problems of representation and agency as they "wrote" in the matrix of the discourses that allowed and validated their disciplinary formations the self-representations of the dominated. *Testimonio* was only one of the many areas of cultural production where subjects' agencies and representations were contested. The problem of subaltern knowledges in the Americas tested the limits of the paradigms of knowledge. Moreover, these debates were not exclusively given in the North American academy as part of the polemic over postmodernism and subaltern studies might lead one to believe. No less strident, they were also, and continue to be, a part of the Latin American intellectual tradition that, while strongly critical, did not and does not necessarily see itself as "other" from Europe's own critical avant-garde, for in constructing these genealogies we must not forget that Latin America and Europe are constitutive of each other.

Thus when Ranajit Guha writes in the opening paragraphs of *Dominance Without Hegemony: History and Power in Colonial India* (1997), that his inquiry intends to take up the question of "history as writing" (xiii), one does not so much have a sense of revelation but rather the exhilarating feeling of recognition. Guha's key question: "who writes the history of the subjugated people?" was indeed already broached some five hundred years ago by Garcilaso de la Vega, Inca in his *Comentarios reales* (1609). Likewise, when Guha delves into the language question and cogently argues that in asking "who asks the question: 'who is the king of Bengal?'" (xiv). there is already a historiographical move that leads to critique of the epistemological categories that inform "history," we can hear a clear sounding of the same note in the *Comentarios*. Indeed the case made by Garcilaso on the question of Quechua as the seat of categories for thinking and understanding the Andean social and cosmological organization is more subtle and stylistically sophisticated than Guha's take on the hierarchical relation between English and Bengali. Five hundred years apart, both the Inca and Guha write on historiography in order to wrestle with the conqueror's appropriation of a past. Both argue that once the past is rendered in European categories it no longer coincides with the memory that the dominated had for it is interrupted when questions like "Who is the King of Bengal?" or "How did the Incas win this kingdom?" demand a reshuffling of what had sedimented in the "before." Guha mounts a formidable attack on what he calls Liberal historiography in order to dispel the myth of ideological neutrality (6). Garcilaso de la Vega, Inca constructed a subtle intertextuality but equally a devastating attack on Spanish historiography by pointing out that in not knowing the language, language as categories of thinking, the Spanish asked the wrong questions, got the wrong answers and thus wrote the accounts of the past that conquest and epistemological violence allowed. Despite the differences forged by a distance of five hundred years and the experience of two different types of coloniality, one cannot but see that in both cases colonialism entails the "pathos of a purloined past" (xiv). The question here is not as much restitution as it the effort to clear the ground for the understanding of the power of writing and its historical legacy for "postcolonial" subjects.

It would seem that the South Asian critique of nationalist and bourgeois history has as its objective halting the writing of India's history as a
"pedestal on which the triumphs and glories of the colonizers [...] could
be displayed" (3). This move dovetails only too well with the preoccupations over a historiography that had constructed Latin America as a savage, "other," or backward periphery. Both challenges to a Eurocentric
way of establishing the world's past, of making other people's past inaccessible outside of the forms given by English or Spanish (175) seek to
advance an epistemology that is not merely imitative or derivative of its
colonial center. Not unlike Arguedas, Guha aims to show that the colo-
nialized also construct versions of their past, and they do so for purposes
quite different from those who dominate them; they do so with their own
discursive rules (3). However, the reclamation of the Indian past, of both
the time "before" British colonialism as well as the time of the Raj, is not
a simple move to the "before." It demands a deeply complicated move
which comes down to the expropriation of it from England's previous act
of expropriation (194). For the author of *Dominance Without Hegemony*, the questions finally devolve on the matter of power, for "No historiography of colonial India would be truly Indian except as a critique of
the very fundamentals of the power relations which constitute colonialism itself" (195), a position very close indeed to Aníbal Quijano's own
sense of the coloniality of power.

One could discuss many other points of convergence between a Latin
American reflexion on the power-knowledge connection, the question of
dominance, and the work of Dipesh Chakrabarty, Gyan Prakash, and
other Indian historians associated with the South Asian Subaltern Studies
Group. The point here has been to show that what we have is a conver-
gent inquiry into coloniality. For that convergence to go beyond the
point of recognition it would be necessary, as Dipesh Chakrabarty has
put it many times in personal conversations, a sharing of archives. That is
a formidable task. I think that the fact that Guha writes so insightfully
into the question of colonial historiography as a question of dominance
without hegemony without ever having even heard of the *Royal Commentaries* by Garcilaso de la Vega, Inca constitutes an excellent example
of the work of coloniality[1] and the magnitude of the task of sharing

---

[1] When Guha expand his inquiry into the question of an English education for
India's intellectuals he brings in Bernal Díaz del Castillo and his account of the con-

archives. The dismantling of the legacy of coloniality will first of all require the recognition of a shared location in the vast intersections of the power-knowledge machine.

Originally published in *Dispositio* 52 (2006): 95-106.

WORKS CITED

GREENBLATT, Stephen and Giles GUNN, ed. *Redrawing the Boundaries: The Transformation of English and American Literary Studies.* New York: Modern Language Association of America, 1992.

GUHA, Ranajit. *Dominance Without Hegemony: History and Power in Colonial India.* Cambridge: Harvard University Press, 1997.

JAMESON, Fredric. *The Political Unconscious: Narrative as a Socially Symbolic Act.* Ithaca: Cornell University Press, 1981.

MIGNOLO, Walter. "Subaltern Studies: Projects for Our Time and Thier Convergence." *The Latin American Subaltern Studies Reader.* Ed. Ileana Rodríguez. Durham: Duke University Press, 2001. 35-47.

RABASA, José. *Writing Violence on the Northern Frontier: The Historiography of Sixteenth Century New Mexico and Florida and the Legacy Of Conquest.* Durham: Duke University Press, 2000.

RODRÍGUEZ, Ileana, ed. *The Latin American Subaltern Studies Reader.* Durham: Duke University Press, 2001.

quest of Mexico (175-177). It is not clear to me what Guha learned about either the Spanish language policies of the period of conquest or about the language map of pre-conquest Mexico.

CHAPTER 5
Inter-rupting the Text of Latin American Literature: Problems of (Mis)Recognition

> "Se pedía a grandes voces:
> -Que muestre las dos manos a la vez.
> Y esto no fue posible.
> -Que piense un pensamiento idéntico, en el tiempo
> en que un cero permanece inútil.
> Y esto no fue posible.
> -Que entre él y otro hombre semejante a él se interponga
> una muchedumbre de hombres como él.
> Y esto no fue posible".
>
> (César Vallejo, "Nómina de huesos")[1]

I. ENTANGLEMENTS

To say that the field, as we received it in Anderson Imbert's anthology (1960), has changed is to understate the obvious. But to begin to describe how it has changed, why it has been receptive to certain transformations and not to others, who and what have played leading roles in the bulldozing of the received meaning of the canonical literary legacy is quite another matter. I do not wish here to describe nor analyze the characteristics or the forces which have wrought such transformations. I refer to the changed topography of the field of Latin American Literature merely to frame my discussion on recognitions and missed-recognitions of identities, for I believe that the challenge of Cultural Studies to "Latin American Literature" pivots on the question of the multiple deployments of subject identities. Paramount in this discussion are not only the effects of the de-centering of the subject, exacerbated by the global situatedness of processes of subjectification, but also questions pertaining to subject location in plural or pluralizing cultural and political environments.

---

[1] It is interesting to point here to the play of knowledge/identities that Guillermo Gómez-Peña operates when he speaks of the processes of demexicanization and misunderstanding that constitute the border-crossing that defines him and his work. See the radio interview with Guillermo Gómez-Peña, quoted in Yúdice, *On Edge* 41. See also Gómez-Peña.

A diversity of approaches—dependency theory, feminism, marxism, psychoanalysis, postmodern theory—have brought about expected as well as unanticipated and even unwelcome developments. For instance, the emergence of Colonial Studies in the context of postmodern theory has opened up multiple possibilities for revamping our understanding of an unfortunately neglected and all-important formative period. But the parallel neocolonization of the Latin American canon by a new totalizing deployment of Spanish-language literature in Spanish departments, which takes advantage of the dismantling of "national" literatures, is a disturbing development.[2] It encourages the facile passing from one geo-cultural space to another. It trivializes the idea of in-depth knowledge of a given field. It enables a-historical blending and misguided homogenization.

Like any changing panorama, the field has registered enormous unevenness. There has been strong continuity of the biographical, intentional, patriarchal, and national approach mixed in with postmodern nomenclature and trenchant theoretical renovation. These multifarious currents at work have produced a "field" in which an all-purpose but faintly direct growth has proliferated. However, a plethora of approaches, a much enlarged choice of "authors" and problems, several cutting edges, and no sense of center or generalized purpose does not in any way resemble the protocol of entanglement—"a methodological tactic that construes objects and phenomena always in relation to complex temporal and spatial contiguities and proximity, and sees artifacts and events in linkage to regimes or reason"[3] (Leitch 146)—intended by Cultural Studies. Breaking out of the binding and uncritically reproduced habits of "lite-

---

[2] The author of the *Comentarios reales* (1609) is now re-figured in English as a curious, sort of obscure, but quaintly interesting Golden Age writer. A young assistant professor describes herself in the Web in the following terms: "I have just finished my dissertation on the Inca Garcilaso de la Vega, a rather unique Golden age writer....Garcilaso attempts to write a history of the Incas and make it comprehensible to a Spanish audience—a task similar to that of an undergraduate student making a last minute term paper comprehensible to his professor—a big challenge" (Heid).

[3] In his discussion of the Birmingham School of Cultural Studies, Vincent B. Leitch explains that the protocol of entanglement "conditions not only the objects selected for study, but the parameter set upon cultural inquiry" (146). Drawing upon Dick Hebdige's *Hiding in the Light: On Images and Things*, Leitch says that to determine the "cultural significance" of an object involves the awareness that neither the product, nor its consumption or status gains the analytical center for "nothing stands beyond culture" (146-148). There are of course examples of excellent work informed

rary analysis" will take much more than a free mixing and matching of authors and periods.

The field of study known as Latin American Literature, that space where things occupy places as the expression of an architecture of knowledge, has probably never existed. Nevertheless, the chronological order of periods and master/minor writers has been transformed into a tangle which does not seem to offer the possibility of direction or justification. This assessment is not the expression of nostalgia. Neither is it to be confused with a fear of not being one of the "withits" (Lindenberger). It is not a wish to return to any of the meta-narratives, but rather it springs from the conviction that a complete free-for-all, a limitless relativism, offers problems and dangers, both intellectual and ethical, that need to be addressed. It is not a question of finding a new grid to be imposed from powerful academic sites. It is rather the need to identify a way of finding terms and terrains which would allow for a general discussion of what it is we as academics, in search of understanding and explaining Latin American culture in the United States, and by extension to the publics encompassed in global English, do. What we do, in this location, is of course bound up with who we think we are, for even in the age of suspicion, we have come to realize that identities, and their on-going construction, are inevitable. The question then devolves not on whether we respond to a single hegemonic identity or to multiple subject positions, but on how we go about constructing them, for the construction of identities is paramount to the practice of interpretation, to the authorization of protocols of entanglement.

Of course this concern over practices of interpretation is shared with many other critics. Beatriz Sarlo, renders a harsh and pessimistic report on the conditions of postmodern culture in a globalized Argentina. Among other things, she is interested in the play of identities that the games fostered by an electronic non-nationally produced culture circulate in newly deterritorialized social spaces. The national subject appears to be checkmated. Beyond the new asymmetry of material resources and cultural powers available now to literate culture (the school system is in shambles) in relation to mass media culture (50 channels broadcast 24 hours a day), Sarlo questions, wearily, the culturalist position which holds that a galloping pluralism offers greater and better prospects for

by the convergence of cultural and literary studies in "our" field. John Beverley's scholarship is a case in point.

democracy than a social organization in which public intellectuals play a critical role or see themselves as an avant-garde.

Moreover, Sarlo is not at all persuaded that the proffer of an unexamined hybridity of mass and literate cultures can be considered the place of emergence for new subversive and thus emancipatory cultural formations.[4] It would seem that from another angle and from a different location, Sarlo coincides with the ongoing critique of hybridity (128) as earlier deployed by both Cultural Studies and Homi Bhabha. Summarizing the debate on hybridity in postcolonial theory, Bart Moore-Gilbert observes that: "The celebration of cultural hybridity can all too easily mask a new system of hierarchies—or rather the continuation of the old system in a new guise" (194). Moore-Gilbert also notes that one of the most enthusiastic advocates of global hybridization happens to be the *Harvard Business Review*. Like Sarlo in Argentina, the Tanzanian critic further cautions on the uncritical theorization of hybridity. This uncritical embrace of hybridity as taken insufficient account of the historical deployment of the concept to the advantage of the colonizer, as the case of Matthew Arnold would readily illustrate. So that "in this sense there may be a direct continuity between some conceptions of hybridity employed in colonial discourse and in the current (neo)colonial dispensation... [for] the hybrid and multiple nature of the subject social formations was used to legitimate the imposition of central power as a 'unifying' force" (194). Furthermore, theories of hybridity seem to erroneously conceive of the center as a unified whole. They thus lose sight of the fact that the "center is just as heterogeneous and unstable, in terms of its class, gender and even (now) ethnic identities as the periphery" (194). What is more, today, the number of subject positions that one can occupy have become potentially infinite. Any group or individual

---

[4] In *Escenas de la vida posmoderna. Intelectuales, arte y videocultura en la Argentina*, Sarlo refutes George Yúdice's thesis on the "rearticulation of tradition" which he attributes to the popular classes in Latin America now facing the onslaught of an American media which globalizes the earth with its cultural products. Yúdice writes that "If we dispose with [the] evolutionary model, however, and seek other premises, it is possible to construe a positive account of Latin American cultural practices that does not lapse into knee-jerk affirmations of authenticity or despairing laments over an ersatz ontology. A new generation of cultural critics has put forth such concepts as 'transculturation,' 'cultural rearticulation,' and cultural 'reconversion' to account for the ways in which the diverse groups that constitute Latin America negotiate their cultural capital" ("Postmodernity" 18).

can at any time be part of the 'center,' or the 'periphery,' or simultaneously be located in both places, as Guillermo Gómez-Peña theo-satirizes.

In view of the perils which nest at the heart of hybridity theory as well as the fading of the writerly culture with which the nation arose into processes of self-identity and cultural sovereignty over its claimed territory, from the south and in dialogue with the north, Sarlo points to a "necesidad urgente de una discusión general de ideas [que] no puede ser considerada una vanidad de intelectuales de viejo tipo, ni supervivencia ilegítima de hegelianos o marxistas clandestinos que juegan su poder simbólico" (193). The author of *Escenas de la vida posmoderna* warns that without a general perspective, pluralism, of which hybridity is a subcategory, rather than a signature of tolerance, tends to become the practice of particularisms that isolate and stand in the way of dialogue (191). The way out of this paradox imbedded in the heart of postmodern fragmentation and pluralism resides, for Sarlo, not in more dissemination and more "estallidos de los sentidos" (194), but rather in the search for a common project capable of reinstating ties with the past so that the present can be lived as a project linked to the future (194). I, like many of us, have never been able to resist the seductiveness of a common project. However, a common project can only become truly common if we share identities, goals, values, and practices, and above all if we avoid the danger of mis-recognitions. The problem of mis-recognitions arches over many of the impasses of hybridity theory, nomadism, diaspora, and border theory. It constitutes the key for the exploration of a general discussion of ideas as well as a common project.

The cultural marketing that Sarlo explores and decries is not unlike the tangling proliferation of discrete studies that in accumulation make up our "field" of study. Restricting the scope of one's focus considerably, one can detect a similar silent marketing force operating in the baroque budding and branching out that marks the study of Latin American literature and culture in the North American academy. In order to establish the ground for a general discussion and determine the ways in which a *common* project might be fashioned, one would first need to interrupt the mindless marketing-studying of Latin American "literature" in the setting of academic pluralism.[5] For if the mis-theorization of hybridity can in fact be

---

[5] George Yúdice in "Cultural Studies and Civil Society" criticizes Sarlo's position regarding the penetration of public spaces by the mass media. In search, not of a com-

shown to be complicit with both the old and the neo-colonization of the world, then the values of a mis-recognized pluralism, by displacing blindly previous authorizations in the production of knowledge and mis-placing it randomly in an unexamined and overvalued pluralism, can be expected to have the effects of hiding in the light. The task before us is not to revert to the production of hegemonies—Jacobin or otherwise—by the appropriate subjects of progressive views of history but rather to find the cultural means by which to pluralize pluralism so that we may envision a radical democracy based on the refusal to dominate.[6] If culture is the sphere in which ideologies are diffused and organized, in which "hege-mony is constructed, broken and reconstituted" (During 186) then current crisis could offer the conditions of possibility for a breakthrough away from the failure of old forces which failed because they were tied to a "narrow, abstract... or castle-like" humanism (Gramsci 211).

II. INTER-RUPTING LITERATURE

John Beverley, in *Against Literature* has already proposed the idea of interrupting the flow of "literature" and diverting it into the larger and more complex problematic of Cultural Studies. One of Beverley's purpo-ses was to break with the confines of the subject of textuality and ques-tion the power/knowledge grip which had constructed the canon of the "literary." Taking "literature," as the Birmingham School of Cultural Studies did, to be too wedded to the historical cultural production-domi-nation of bourgeois elites, Beverley went so far as seeing in *testimonio*

---

mon project, but of civil society, Yúdice writes that "Sarlo has substituted a political for a communicational optimism, entrusting to the state... the unlikely outcome of a disinterested and critical culture" (54).

[6] In *Hegemony and Socialist Strategy: Towards A Radical Democratic Politics* (1985) Ernesto Laclau and Chantal Mouffe argue that in view of the de-centering of the subject, the end of teleological narratives, the porosity and historicity of all identities, democra-tic politics not only has to mean a radical and *plural* democracy in which democratic equivalences mean *respect* for others—however those others may be constituted—but also entails the refusal to dominate (176-193). They conclude that "It is clear that a Left alternative can only consists of the construction of a different system of equivalences, which establishes social divisions on a new basis... The Left [should locate] itself fully in the field of democratic revolution and [expand] its claims of equivalents between the dif-ferent struggles against oppression" (176). Thus a radical democracy would not only entail plurality of equals but would have as its corollary the *refusal to dominate.*

texts the dawning of new hybrids in which the "popular" impulses of oral, subversive, and subaltern positions came to coalesce.

But of course one cannot, and should not, forget that in the formulation of this position—to swing wide open the doors of the castle-like classrooms to "*testimonio*"—what fundamentally mattered was not the Birmingham School of Cultural Studies, which had not ever dreamed of a text like Rigoberta's, but rather the wars that the Latin American states waged against peasants and urban guerrillas. Despite the complexities of the textual mediatization of its birthing scene, *testimonio* ushured in another subject, the popular subject. The convergence of forces that made visible the point of no return, the point where one could enunciate phrases such as "against literature" or "postliterature," appears as a molar formation in which the entanglement of cultural productions within an intervened Latin America and the conditions of the export journey of the cultural objects and events wrought there requires a study of its own and of course exceeds what I can do here. But at least it is obviously clear that the northern love-affair with *testimonio* did not register a parallel fascination in Latin American academic literature programs, that is to say, the place from which Sarlo speaks.

Despite the cogent criticism that Beverley deploys on the national-patriarchal constitution of the Latin American canon, of which Anderson Imbert's anthology is perhaps the crowing glory, it might be fair to say that attention to *testimonio* signaled more the critical exhaustion in the United States' academy of the boom rather than the enthronization of a Cultural Studies perspective into the making of the Latin American culture object. In part that is why the mere title of Beverley's book awakens fear and resistance in the "nostalgia" crowd.[7]

Grounded in certain aspects of the problematic of Cultural Studies, but insufficiently critical of their own "ethnographic turn," students of Latin American culture propelled Rigoberta's text into the culture wars being fought in the United States academy. The fact that those wars were fought, as both Charles Taylor and James Davidson Hunter have shown, on a turf defined more by religious struggle than strictly canonical disputes[8] does

---

[7] See Lindenberger's "Teaching and the Making of Knowledge."

[8] Hunter understands the culture wars in the United States as conflict based on "political and social hostility rooted in different systems or moral understandings...They are not merely attitudes that can be changed on a whim but basic commitments and

not seem to have been computed in the equation. The net effect was for Rigoberta's life story to appear cast against the horizon of local United States identity politics. Rigoberta's struggle for political and discursive space was both misunderstood and mis-recognized by students who read the events of her story as one more example of the exotic-atrocious. *Testimonio* traveled through the networks and processes of domestication into the multicultural complex of the metropole by which the outside of the system is incorporated into its vast reaches. *Testimonio* studies did not insert the problematic of Cultural Studies into the study of literature as a serious and critical point of no return. Most of the criticism written on it responded to narratological frames of textual study. The wars to which *testimonio* bears witness and the twisting thread between events and discursivity which *testimonio* problematizes were, by and large, left out by the "literary" concerns and even the anthropological turn.

If, as Cultural Studies holds, culture has specific political functions in the construction of hegemonies,[9] and the production of docile subjects, then the inclusion of Rigoberta's pathos in the multicultural canon seems only too appropriate. But if, on the other hand, the objective is to interrupt the operations of governability by introducing disruptive textualities in the cultural formation of the subject in the North American classroom, then the subject of discussion should have been, an "I," (contingent subject) Rigoberta, and not Rigoberta the ethnographic object of the academic subject of knowledge. What should be put in play is the reading of Rigoberta (an intended conflation of the text and the referent which emerges from the reading) as a cultural formation at the

---

beliefs that provide a source of identity, purpose and togetherness for the people who live by them" (42). Thus the cultural wars can be traced "ultimately and finally to the matter of moral authority. By moral authority I mean the basis on which people determine whether something is good or bad, right or wrong, acceptable or unacceptable, and so on" (42). See also Castro-Klarén.

[9] I do not wish to homogenize the theoretical diversity within Cultural Studies. Stuart Hall has recently reminded us of the fact that "Cultural studies has multiple discourses; it has a number of different histories... It always was a set of unstable formations. It was 'centered' only in quotation marks... It refuses to be a master discourse... There was never a moment when cultural studies and Marxism represented a perfect theoretical fit" (278). From the beginning there was "always already the question of great inadequacies both theoretically and politically "(279). However, Hall ends by noting the "astonishing theoretical fluency" achieved by Cultural Studies now (278).

crossroads of serious interdisciplinary analyses, itself capable of questioning the very disciplines which are constituted in the practice of academic analysis. Thus the object of the ethnographic turn should be constituted by the event of placing Rigoberta in the readings lists of the North American academy during the period of the Cultural Wars. The academic critic would then have to practice a bit of auto-ethnography him/her self. The appearance of such an event or cultural artifact would be closer to the heart of Cultural Studies, and it would refrain from reducing the "reading" of *I, Rigoberta Menchú* to academic credit.

III. RETREAT OF WRITERLY CULTURE

In what follows I will take up the positive charge of the challenge of Cultural Studies to the existing disciplinarity of "literary" studies. But before I do that I want to delve into two points that both Sarlo and Beverley make about the crisis of the public intellectual in Latin America and the retreat of the writerly culture in which he/she and the "national public" operated. It is important to note the links that they establish between this cultural crisis in Latin America and the consequences it may have in the study of Latin American culture in the North American academy.

Both Beverley and Sarlo elaborate the notion that the writer-hero, in the style of Sarmiento and Bello, has now waned. It is part of a finished and over-with past. Massive historical change accounts for the fact that the discourse of the fathers of the motherland no longer resonates. Incisively, Beverley points out that a transference took place in the study of the humanities in the Latin American universities, whereas national identities emerged bound in the writerly practices of these founding intellectuals. This cultural *arielismo*, this ideology of the *ciudad letrada*, is for Beverley no longer sustainable as the organizing principle of either a canon or as a set of guiding principles by which to understand Latin American culture. In *Against Literature*, both Ariel and Calibán are no more, for the Calibán of Fernández Retamar appears now interdicted by the mass media phenomenon. Calibán no longer needs to learn the master's language in order to curse him, for the master appears to have vanished with all the other solid modern things that have melted into the airwaves. Implicit in such interdiction is the notion that massive as well as personal communication, presences of absences, have now been detached from writing.

Audio-visual media have ushered a new democratic access to information and to entertainment which should empower subjects previously excluded from the power-knowledge circuits of the letter. Certainly Rodó never had such a scene in mind. The speed with which mountains of information are now made instantly available would exceed even Sarmiento's wildest pedagogic dreams. In view of the disintegration of the model of the Republic of Letters, Beverley proposes that we replace literature as our object of study with culture and cultural politics. For him, "the decisive terrain today is the mass media" (8).

Looking at the crisis of the public intellectual from the perspective of a political history of the last fifty years, Sarlo takes stock of the historical mistakes intellectuals have made when, in emulation of the founding fathers, they fashioned themselves as representatives of the choices and sacrifices the "people" would make within a historical scenario which postulated a future resolution. Given the mistaken political advocation of many, the complicity of some with regimes of terror, and the loss sustained by others in the war against dirty wars, the confidence the public may have had in the political discourse and agency of intellectuals has, like the hegemony of a lettered culture, simply vanished. Sarlo explains that now the lettered intellectuals themselves see a choice of cultures upon which to comment but not necessarily intervene:

> Lo que se consideraba en el pasado cultura letrada ya no organiza la jerarquía de culturas y subculturas. Los letrados eligen entre dos actitudes. Lamentan el naufragio de los valores sobre los cuales se funda su hegemonía como letrados. Otros celebran que los restos del naufragio hayan llegado a la costa y van armando un artefacto para explicar en que consisten las nuevas culturas... Los segundos son los nuevos legitimistas... instalan su poder como decifradores de lo que el pueblo hace con los restos de su propia cultura. Las cosas se han invertido para siempre: los neo-populistas aceptan una sola legitimidad, la de las culturas producidas en el cruce entre experiencia y discurso audio-visual. (120-21)

Both Sarlo and Beverley perceive the same phenomenon: the crisis of the lettered city, the subsequent de-centering of literature and the overwhelming importance of mass media culture. However, they have different interpretations regarding the types of forces involved in the emergence of the phenomenon. They therefore also register variances in their engagement strategies. They diverge in their evaluation of the role mass media can play in a given society, the particular way in which each can interact with what is left of the lettered city, and in the orientation that the irremediable adoption of Cultural Studies can take in the face of this cultural mutation.

As literature is de-centered, mass media becomes hegemonic and thus dominant in the shaping of the future. Neo-populist critics, in emulation of Hoggart's move (*The Uses of Literacy*), would argue that a certain type of "literary critical analysis can be applied to certain social phenomena... (popular arts, mass communications) so as to illuminate their meanings for individuals and their societies" (Hoggart, "Literature and Society"). This move would seem to opt for the neo-populist choice Sarlo finds insuffi-cient, and indeed dangerously naive.[10] It gives up on the responsibility of the intellectuals to discern categories and values and to mount a critical dis-course of the present. It leaves the fields of culture and politics open to the creativity and resourcefulness of the "people" without taking into conside-ration that "the people" are always already caught in multidimensional asymmetries of power. "The people," facing the loss of critical literacy, as the public school system is dismantled, must also device the intellectual grid and tactical response necessary for the affirmation and defense of a cul-ture in which their own best interests could be represented. Prying open "the people" from the national intellectuals seems like a high price to pay for both the "people" and the intellectual in the name of a global symbolic democratization staged elsewhere. For Sarlo, the neo-populist move of the Cultural Studies model, especially its assumption of a high/low, old/new, literacy/audio-visual hybridity, in conjunction with an a-historical exten-sion of "literary modes of analysis," is itself part of a postmodern paradox that fosters false oppositions and identity conflicts. The availability of new cultural goods to the masses does not necessarily guarantee a "popular" capacity for agency in the transformation of the received messages emana-ting from the global centers of cultural production which remain an outside to the "national" community. Furthermore, the sweeping marketing of

[10] Writing on the Cultural Studies extension of the method developed by Roland Bar-thes to reveal the normally hidden codes that organize society, Dick Hebdige explains that the hope was that the semiotic method would at once render meaningful and make disap-pear the gulf between the intellectual and the "real" world. He adds that: "Under Barthe-s's direction semeiotics promised nothing less than the reconciliation of the two conflicting definitions of culture upon which cultural studies was so ambiguously posited—a marriage of moral conviction (in this case Barthes's Marxist beliefs) and popular themes: the study of societies total way of life" ("From Culture to Hegemony" 361).

audio-visual cultural products creates a retreat of the culture of literacy from all fronts, especially the school, thus creating a disturbing asymmetry between the lettered culture, in which the terms of nation identity were forged, and the audio-visual production of a global "citizen" (consumer) identity. In view of this intertwined asymmetry which bends and twists forces of cultural production and cultural consumption in Argentina, and by extension in all of Latin America, an asymmetry which by definition cannot be liberating or democratic, there appears a demand for another way out of the paradox of cultural agency and cultural politics.

Rather than falling into an unwarranted celebration of the popular and their postulated capacity to rework global culture into sites of local and even subversive cultural productions of their "own" national communities, Sarlo calls for a reparation, a reconstruction, a refurbishing of the lettered culture. In such a scenario intellectuals would play a critical and discerning role. Sarlo sees the role of the intellectual as both indispensable and unavoidable, because:

> una cultura debe estar en condiciones de nombrar las diferencias que la integran. Si ello no sucede la libertad cultural es un ejercicio destinado únicamente a realizarse en los espacios de las elites estéticas o intelectuales... [La libertad] cultural necesita de dos fuerzas: estados que intervengan equilibrando al mercado cuya estética delata su relación con el lucro; y una crítica cultural que pueda librarse del doble encierro de la celebración neopopulista de lo existente y de los prejuicios elitistas que socavan la posibilidad de articular una perspectiva democrática. (197-98)

She thus concludes that "una crítica humanística [repudiated by Cultural Studies] puede ser defendida como necesidad y no como lujo de la civilización científico-técnica" (196).

IV. INTER-RUPTION AND DILEMMAS

Despite Sarlo's call for a recapturing of the values of a humanist criticism, the question of the public intellectuals and their intervention in society within the cultural mutation operated by the revolution of electronic communication remains as only one of the many dilemmas of our time. Problems in defining culture as deployed in Cultural Studies—"culture is the sphere in which ideologies are diffused and organized, in which hegemony is constructed and can be broken and reconstituted" (Forgacs 186),[11] or "culture means the actual grounded terrain of practices, representations, languages and costumes of any specific historical society" (Hall 5)—as well as the intervention of Cultural Studies in the larger social terrain of power interactions has been the subject of heated and repeated theoretical discussions from within Cultural Studies itself.

Almost ten years ago Lawrence Grossberg, in "The Circulation of Cultural Studies," expressed his concern for the "fact that cultural studies increasingly, and in new ways, is being commodified and institutionalized" (178). The dilemma for Grossberg resides in the fact that Cultural Studies has been "highjacked by an alliance between the apparent demands of the intellectual work" (178), which require a taking up of "fixed" positions, the exigencies of the distribution of its work, which have erased the internal differences within Cultural Studies, and its "own success as a politically committed and theoretically sophisticated body of work" (178). One of the consequences of success has been the assimilation of Cultural Studies into an ambiguous and more general notion of cultural criticism[12] so as to effect a dispersal which erases how the political and intellectual history of Cultural Studies had offered a particular way of engaging questions of culture and power (179).

According to Grossberg, Cultural Studies has attempted to grapple with this dilemma by positing itself as an ever changing body of theoretical work committed to a radical challenge to disciplinary knowledges. Positing culture as the site of complex relations with other practices in specific social formations and as an overall project aware of a constant need of rephrasing and reconstruction, Cultural Studies extends and stretches theory in order to respond to the emergence of new historical

[11] Forgacs discusses the linkage Gramsci makes between the formation of Italian culture and literature during the Renaissance and the absence of national-popular movement (186). He further notes that the national-popular designates not a cultural content, but the possibility of an alliance of interests and feelings between different social agents which varies according to the structure of each national society" (187).

[12] In the preface to his *Cultural Criticism, Literary Theory, Poststructuralism*, Vincent Leitch writes that "Within the long tradition of cultural criticism, the relatively recent formation of cultural studies....constitutes a significant moment of flowering and institutionalization, but one not without problems. The practice of cultural critique increasingly challenges the taboo of cultural inquiry, revealing a shift of interest in ethics, politics and social activism" (xi).

articulations (Grossberg 180-181). Seen from Grossberg's perspective, Cultural Studies "refuses to define its own theoretical adequacy in academic or narrow epistemological terms. Theory is measured in relation to its enablement of strategic interventions into the specific practices, structures and struggles" that characterize its place in the contemporary world (179). Also, it mounts an effort to clarify its own local, historical specificity, within which cultural struggles function. Following Grossberg one must therefore remember that the relations between culture and society, or between culture and power, are always historically constituted. Thus, Cultural Studies examines how specific practices, such as the massive deployment of audio-visual media in Argentina, are placed between the social structures of power and the lived realities of every day (Grossberg, in passim, 181).

If we attend to Grossberg's rearticulation of Cultural Studies as practices which interrogate the production of knowledge attendant to historical specificities, and we severely prune the "celebratory populist" project that Sarlo criticizes, then Cultural Studies and Sarlo's call for a reconfiguration of the "neo-humanist" approach to an understanding of "culture" would appear to be in relative proximity. This would seem even more so in light of Grossberg's desire to correct the perception that Cultural Studies represents a galloping "anti-humanism."[13] For him, cultural studies neither denies real people nor doubts their agency, but it does historicize them and does not admit to any intrinsic human nature or identity. And yet, precisely because Grossberg recognizes the historical boundaries of cultural formations, both his position and Sarlo's still conceal perils of missed-recognition, for the question of subject identity—its formation in difference with the other and subsequent deployment in the political realm—remains hidden in the light.

---

[13] "Cultural studies does not deny real people, but it displaces them in equally real and over-determined historical realities. What they are as individuals and human beings is thus not intrinsic to them. Our practices produce our identities and our humanity, often behind our backs... Anti-humanism does not deny individuality, subjectivity, experience, or agency; it simply historicizes and politicizes them, their construction and their relationships. If there is no essential human nature, we are always struggling to produce boundaries, to constitute an effective human nature, but one which is different in social formations. In other words, human nature is always real but never universal, singular or fixed" (183).

Grossberg's re-articulation of Cultural Studies extends yet another bridge to perhaps the major contention in Sarlo's critique of the populist hybridity model that she reads in Cultural Studies. Sarlo is not merely concerned with the idea of giving proper weight and place to the local scene in cultural analysis. She is actually more interested in exploring the ways in which an Argentine intellectual may mount a perspective adequate to the panorama he/she is to "see." She thus asks Cultural Studies to respond to the question: "¿Cómo armar una perspectiva para ver?" from Argentina (10). The emphasis placed in Grossberg's re-articulation of cultural studies on culture as a localized formation together with a revitalization of conjuncture as a methodological commitment to specificity should leave the field open for a particular Argentina, Aymara, or California re-articulation to the historical phenomenon in which the letter, the book, and the literary culture built upon it are displaced by massive electronic means of communication and all the attendant consequences of the re-configuration of the social.

However, one must remain weary of replicating the *arielista* wedding between literature and the patriarchal intellectual that Beverley discloses. Just like the populist model causes irritations and fissures when imported into Argentina, neither the terms nor the dilemmas of the Argentine discussion can be wholly transported into the halls of the North American academy. While solidarity with our cohorts in Latin America is indeed a very desirable thing, we can probably achieve more effective results if we start by recognizing that the North American academy in the United States is, first of all, situated elsewhere, and second, it does not correspond to either what is left of the Argentine academy nor to the social formation in which public intellectuals such as Sarlo, David Viñas, Ricardo Piglia, or Diana Bellesi perform. For the kind of critical Cultural Studies called for by Sarlo to have resonance in the United States, *we*, here, would have to begin by recognizing this crucial locational difference. Recognizing differences does not necessarily imply a loss, for, as William Connolly argues, identity is constituted by a set of limits or density that enables selves to chose, think, and act. The paradox of identities is that they can only be constituted and maintained in relation to that from which they differ (*Identity\Difference* 9, 64, 94). It is thus important to interrupt the assumption of contiguity between northern and southern intellectuals and to move to a logic of identity\difference by which identity is understood as contingent, unstable, porous, and capable of entering into a plurality of contingent and yet ethical negotiations and allegiances. Identities are nei-ther intrinsic nor inevitable. It is no longer necessary to abide by the Augustinian imperative whose claims to deep, true, and moral identity, which determine the immorality of others,[14] have been shown to proceed from the specificity of Augustinian anxiety on death and thus the inven-tion of salvation (see in Connolly's *The Augustinian Imperative* chapter 4, "The Genesis of Being").

An impulse to solidarity[15] from the north with certain Latin Ameri-can subject positions will be better grounded when this differential in location is taken into critical account, when we understand that the point is not to stick Rigoberta into the "literature" canon (as was done at Stan-ford) but rather to read the story of the war against the Quiché as history and an object\event that cuts into the real. Such practices would eliminate the risk of banality lately associated with Cultural Studies.

V. Deviating the Flow

The assumption of such locations in space and time curtails the reach, as well as modifies the shape, of many of the key provisions of Cultural Stu-

---

[14] In *The Augustinian Imperative: A Reflection on the Politics of Morality*, William Connolly shows that to this day Euroamerican political theory and practices remain under what he calls "the Augustinian Imperative," that is "the insistence that there is an intrinsic moral order susceptible to authoritative representations"(xvii). This impe-rative makes its pursuit obligatory and thus opens the quest to "move closer to one's truest self by exploring its inner geography" (xvii) through confession and submission to the higher authority of God, himself produced by confession (44) and the need to ward off the anxiety of death (81). As he examines the birth of difference in Augustine, in an analysis reminiscent of Borges on his heresiarchs, Connolly posits that for Augustine to consolidate the Christian self there had to be heresies to denounce and demote. Connolly asks: "What price have those constituted as pagans, infidels, here-tics, and nihilists throughout the centuries paid for this demand to confess an intrinsic moral order?" (81). Many histories rush to detail the answer to this question, but none is better known to students of Latin America than the Spanish evangelizing conquest.

[15] Solidarity, as Laclau and Mouffe point out, needs to be re-articulated away from the homogeneous notion of class and into the concept of a series of equal and coope-rative struggles trying to overcome domination and achieve liberty (182). However, "equivalence is always hegemonic insofar as it does not simply establish an alliance between given interests, but modifies the very identity of the forces engaging in that alliance" (183-84).

dies. A historicized Cultural Studies could articulate shared, "commonly differential" (north-south) projects in cultural politics. This requires recapturing the contemplative gaze and restricting the uncritical embrace of a distracted reception of subjects of "popular culture."[16] There then could ensue a practice that is less driven by purely theoretical considerations. An agenda more securely anchored on history would enable Cultural Studies to cope with the impossible complexity of its own historical context. I believe that a genealogical turn to history, as an investigation that loosens the necessary character of established truths, will not only enable us to avoid over-theorizing but also skirt the danger of falling into the atrociously fatal banal of Baudrillard (*Les Strategies Fatales*).

Therefore, it would also seem sensible that we not let go of the knowledge accumulated in the different academic disciplines. Instead, a genealogical revamping of religion, philosophy, history, and archeology, with particular emphasis on questions of everyday life as theorized by Michel de Certeau, would permit the possibility of *interrupting the flow* of the disciplines, including literature, and deviate their course into the investigation of terrains heretofore occluded from view. Genealogically historicized accounts of popular subjects enmeshed in the making of cultural heterogeneity would keep us away from the blinding light of incorrectly assumed commonalities and misrecognitions.

As Simon During explains in his introduction to *The Cultural Studies Reader*, the new mode of Cultural Studies no longer sees "popular" culture as a social formation against the state (1-25). Rather, influenced by feminist theory, it places emphasis on *affirming other* ways of life. Because society is conceived, like the subject, as a basically de-centered set of processes, Cultural Studies is particularly interested in sub-cultures, subalterns, and marginality. However, Cultural Studies has not figured out a logic by which to conceive of all these communities within some kind of communication circuit or relational coherence.

It is difficult to know to what extent the North American academy could be considered a sub-culture. Not too long ago it was called an ivory

[16] For a discussion of the narcissism embedded in the postulation of a popular subject without proper attention to the ideological investment made by the critic and the practice of "distracted reception" see Morris 158-59. Morris finds a more positive approach to the theorization of popular culture in recapturing the contemplative gaze from the work of Michael de Certeau, *The Practice of Everyday Life*.

tower in order to allegorize the myth of its isolation and thus its "independence" from the state. Studies on the role of literature and more especially on the formative function of literary studies have uncovered the fundamental roles that the ivory tower plays in the formation of docile subjects. As an institution, the academy organizes reading and writing as a form of governability. Thus, the terms of canon formation, the disciplinary and curricular norms which organize our teaching and research-publication need to be considered as if they were a molar formation—the linkage of an object of study with regimes of (un)reason.[17]

It therefore follows that if the United States has been exerting a growing hegemonic force in the formation of Latin American cultures and politics and there has been a concomitant growing northern might in the making of knowledge about Latin America, an interruption of our everyday practices is in order. The idea that "virtually everything produced on Latin America in the 1950s was profoundly shaped by the imperatives of the Cold War" (Berger 81) is indeed sobering. In literature, with virtually a handful of exceptions,[18] nothing has been written on the ongoing project of reading the south from a perspective mounted from the north.

The notable exception is the recent *Reading North by South* (1995) by Neil Larsen. He writes that the self-authorization of the north as reader of the south continues to derive from "the same wellspring of colonial common sense" that authorized Bernal Díaz to "quote" Montezuma in order to authorize his own narrative of the conquest. Larsen then asks: "What is and has been the history of this reading?...What have been the modes of self-authorization evoked by metropolitan 'readers' of Latin America, both in its texts and as 'text'?" (2). Larson answers this question in terms of a brief autobiography of encounter and self-transformation of the knowing subject. He narrates the anti-colonialist sympathies that produced the canonization of the boom (5) and posits that such canonization of high modernist

[17] Vincent Leitch in *Cultural Criticism, Literary Theory, Poststructuralism*, argues that a key task of cultural criticism is "to link objects with regimes of (un)reason," for the text is always entangled in regimes of reason "embodied in the languages of the 'nation,' the specimen text is regimented in two senses: first it is embedded in regimes and, second, it is so embedded, methodologically speaking, through a process of calculated analytical accretions" (7).

[18] See for instance Amy K. Kaminsky's efforts to analyze texts written by Latin American women from a perspective drawn from the texts themselves. The chapter on "translating gender" (1-13) is of particular interest.

texts as *One Hundred Years of Solitude* and *Hopscotch* could have occurred despite their very specificity. "Taking this line of thinking to an extreme, one might suppose that the specific kinds of literary qualities associated with the boom... were in fact irrelevant" (5). For Larsen, the cultural logic involved in the negotiation of canonicity is indeed complex. For one thing, the opening offered to the Latin American texts was part of a design to prolong the legitimacy of the modernist canon itself (6). Such suspicion leads Larsen to point out that while Latin America may be accorded *literary parity* based on a universalizing aesthetic standard embodied in modernism, such parity only occludes "its conservative if not regressive side" (7).

Larsen also finds in the critical events surrounding the entrance of *testimonio* into the North American academy a good example of the problems in reading the south from the perspectives mounted in the *local* North. Severely taking to task the readings of *testimonio* as counter-canonical textualities, Larsen shows that the "self-exclusion" required on the interdicted reader—knowing subject—of Rigoberta's secrets is but a symptom of the crisis of the New Left which tends now to place all political agency in a romanticized "Third World" (14-15). Ironically, the gesture of canonical decolonization which started out with a move towards inclusion of the boom writers ends up theorizing its own *incapacity* to read Rigoberta, who, having molted out of her ethnographic subject position, now stands as an unbridgeable other. As such Rigoberta cannot, exactly, be excluded or constituted into a new outside. She simply corresponds to the northern reader's self-exclusion from a communication circuit that would encompass both the Quiche woman and the North American scholar. Somehow, the workings of "theory" have produced northern and southern subjects situated in a breached communication circuit.

The story that Larsen reconstructs is basically correct and grave. Its telling constitutes a pioneering and almost solitary thread in the genealogical tapestry that needs to be woven with many other colors and thicknesses. Our understanding of the production of Latin American culture-literature will always be distorted if we do not seriously consider the anomalous place and history of "Spanish" departments in the North American academy.[19] The marginality of "Spanish" is only too obvious in comparison with the centra-

---

[19] For example both Roberto González Echevarría and Jean Franco have repeatedly complained about the silence that surrounds their voices when they speak for those outside the field of "Spanish."

lity of English language texts and criticism. Such marginality further compli-
cates relations with Latin American intellectuals whose subject position, as in
the case of Beatriz Sarlo in her own country, is only comparable to that of a
chaired Professor of American Literature here. There is an undeniable and
complex asymmetry, almost an inversion, between the knowing subject in
the Latin American academy (central in a globally marginal location) and
his/her counterpart here (marginal in a globally central location). However,
we need to ask, is this asymmetry unbridgeable, is it destined to produce mis-
recognition, to prefigure the impossibility of dialogue?

I think that the possibility of dialogue and even coalition can be explored in a reframed, genealogical approach to culture. It could achieve better focus on questions of localization and subject identities. The historicizing perspective would enable the grasping of the shards and wastes of
every day life dispersed in the networks of the past leading up to the present.[20] The discards of history would serve as talisman around which new
visions of the past, and thus the present, can be configured. In such a project Faucaultnian notions of spatialization would coincide with de Certeau's recommendations on the tactical uses of history (de Certeau, *The
Capture of Speech* 158) and temporality. The "lost places of the past" can
then be turned into "active spaces of fiction capable of being reinvented
over and over again" (158). They would yield not *other* but simply forgotten subjects, who like Guamán Poma or the warrior-archangels of the
School of Cuzco,[21] act as a magnetic force which enables us to repopulate
and reconfigure the map of the making of Latin American identities and
knowledges. Relics and remnants remain loaded with irruptive power.
But this power cannot be garnished by cultural historians without engaging in extensive and exhaustive empirical research that will provide the
threads and looms for a genealogical Cultural Studies.

---

[20] In *The Practice of Everyday Life*, de Certeau aims to find the relics of the past,
the discards of the discourse of history in order to use them as magnets around which
a creative swarm of forgotten and repressed absences might congregate and configure
new versions of the past.

[21] The famous archangels painted by the disciples of the School's founder, Tito
Cusi, owe their iconography and proliferation to the fact (shard) that the Jesuit order
in charge of evangelization in the Andes did not yet have Saints to offer to the Andeans as life role models. In order to compete with the Augustinian and the Dominicans,
the Jesuits encouraged the Indian painters of the School of Cuzco to feast their imagination in the warrior qualities configured in the iconography of the archangels.

If we are to displace literature for Cultural Studies the first step is to revamp the criteria by which we have thus far constituted "texts" and "discourses." The developmental and organic criteria which informed the literature canon ought to give way to the constitution of molar formations, sites, and other spatio-temporal configurations that could eventually constitute culture in the plural. Only when we are in the possession of massive "new," or rather forgotten or buried, information can this sort of re-drawing of history and historiography be possible. It follows then that the prevailing notion of relevant texts has to be generously reworked in the awareness that this is not yet another enterprise of culture collecting (Clifford).

The convergence of Cultural Studies with a new historicity would enable us to bypass the obstacles implicit in the problematic of post-colonial studies as developed from the former English speaking colonies. A new historicity would open up new vistas to the spatio-temporality of everyday life with its irreducible and incompatible sites. Foucault called this superimposition of incompatible and tension-filled piling up of sites a heterotopia.[22] These layered but non-coincidental spaces are held together by air vacuum zones that create a space of illusion. The gap between the layers creates a space that is other, the unthought. Although Foucault could, from a Eurocentric point of view, only speculate that colonies may have functioned as heterotopias of compensation for Europe ("Of Other Spaces"), students of Latin American cultural history understand that colonial power relations function, by definition, as air vacuum zones of entanglement, as local heterotopias. A reframing of the tension and difference implied in heterotopia could open the way for a new historiographical approach to the formation of Latin America's cultures and subjects of identity and political history.

Finally, the kind of critical pluralism implicit in de Certeau's idea of emancipation, Sarlo's call for a new humanism, and Beverley's manifesto in favor of Cultural Studies as a way of displacing the elite subject of literary studies with a more "popular" one, enclose a call for an *ethical inquiry* that has so far escaped the relentless relativism of a de-centered universe. Key to the question of culture in the plural is the question of identity and of modes of subjectification, for, as we now understand it, there is no identity that is

[22] For an actualization of Foucault's concept of heterotopias, see Soja.

natural or extra-political. Judith Butler (*Gender Trouble*) argues that the radical strategy for feminism is not so much to improve the condition of women, for that goes without saying, within networks of power that subject, but to subvert the constitution of women's identity within the patriarchal paradigm. She advocates a coalition politics in which women, constituted as resisting subject, would *maintain* rather than overcome their differences. The contradiction implicit in the idea of a coalition of resisting subject is lessened if we posit, as William Connolly proposes, not unified and coherent subjects but rather agonal subjects for whom power is both constraining and enabling (*The Ethos* xv-xix).

For the agonistic subject, respect for others, that is, for difference, is based on resistance to attempts to govern their conduct. Liberty is itself the practice of, rather than the absence of, power. Because identity is constituted in difference, it is then the irreducibility of the other to one's own strategy that teaches one to respect others as free subjects, precisely because they are different. In a globalized world in which power is distributed asymmetrically—North American academy/Latin American academies, mass media/lettered culture—the agonistic subject would seem to represent a good place for both resistance as well as coalition in plurality.

In the face of galloping globalization a reworking of pluralism by positing an agonistic subject capable of *reciprocal recognition* offers a way out of the particularism that Sarlo decries, as well as of the breached communication circle postulated by some readers of *testimonio*. Pluralism based on tolerance, Connolly points out, is not sufficient to stem the re-emergence of congealed unitary subjects. Because tolerance is an "underdeveloped form of critical responsiveness," it relies on mis-recognition. In contrast, the critical responsiveness engaged by agonal subjects does not appropriate or assimilate, for it departs from the idea that identities are both differential and collective (Connolly, *The Ethos* xv). "Critical responsiveness opens up a cultural space through which the other might consolidate itself into *something* that is not afflicted by negative cultural markings. Moreover, within the critical or agonistic political framework, the other, the subaltern, does not need to be thought of as negativity, for difference is not reduced to a pre-existing code (as in "Can the subaltern speak?). In this new political space strangeness in oneself and others can be engaged without resentment or panic, for "freedom resides in the spaces produced by such dissonant junctures" (Connolly, *Augustinian* 29).

In Connolly's vision of agonistic democracy, the self is not robbed by difference, self is instead difference. Thus the ethics of agonistic engagement call for studied indifference, critical responses, selective collaboration, and contending identities (Connolly, *The Ethos* xviii). The point in an agonistic democracy as a world order is not to abolish difference as in north/south, or in literature/Cultural Studies, but rather to transform the way in which we experience difference in order to be able to form collective identities across difference and liberate us from the type of individualism that is linked to the state. Agonistic democracy, like a Cultural Studies mindful of its goals, cultivates a politics of disturbance which does not abolish differences and thus would keep us from the violence of mis-recognition.

A Spanish version of this chapter was originally published in *Nuevas perspectivas desde/sobre América Latina: el desafío de los estudios culturales*. Santiago de Chile: Editorial Cuarto Propio/Instituto Internacional de Literatura Iberoamericana, 2000. 387-405.

WORKS CITED

BERGER, Mark T. *Under Northern Eyes: Latin American Studies and US Hegemony in the Americas 1898-1990*. Bloomington: Indiana University Press, 1995.

BEVERLEY, John. *Against Literature*. Minneapolis: University of Minnesota Press, 1993.

CERTEAU, Michel de. *The Capture of Speech*. Minneapolis: University of Minnesota Press, 1997.

—. *The Practice of Everyday Life*. Trans. Steven Rendall. Berkeley: University of California Press, 1984.

CLIFFORD, James. "On Collecting Art and Culture." In *The Cultural Studies Reader*. Ed. Simon During. London: Routledge, 1993. 49-73.

CONNOLLY, William E. *Augustinian Imperative: the Politics of Morality*. Newbury Park: Sage Publications, 1993.

—. *The Ethos of Pluralization*. Minneapolis: University of Minnesota Press, 1995.

—. *Identity\Difference: Democratic Negotiations of Political Paradox*. Ithaca: Cornell University Press, 1991.

DURING, Simon, ed. *The Cultural Studies Reader*. London: Routledge, 1993.

FORGACS, David. "National-popular: Genealogy of a Concept." In *The Cultural Studies Reader*. Ed. Simon During. London: Routledge, 1993. 177-193.

FOUCAULT, Michel. "Of Other Spaces." *Diacritics* 16 (1986): 22-7.

GRAMSCI, Antonio. *Selections from Cultural Writings*. Cambridge: Harvard University Press, 1985.

GROSSBERG, Lawrence. "The Circulation of Cultural Studies." In *What is Cultural Studies?* Ed. John Storey. London: Arnold, 1996.

HALL, Stuart. "Cultural Studies and its Theoretical Legacies." In *Cultural Studies*. Eds. Lawrence Grossberg et. al. New York: Routledge, 1992.

HEBDIGE, Dick. "From Culture to Hegemony." In *The Cultural Studies Reader*. Ed. Simon During. London: Routledge, 1993. 357-368.

—. *Hiding in the Light: On Images and Things*. London: Routledge, 1988.

HEID, Pat. *Spanish Department, Colby College*. <http://www.colby.edu/spanish/pat.html>.

HOGGART, Richard. "Literature and Society." *The American Scholar* 35. 277-89.

—. *The Uses of Literacy*. New York: Oxford University Press, 1958.

HUNTER, James Davison. *Culture Wars: The Struggle to Define America*. New York: BasicBooks, 1991.

LACLAU, Ernesto and Chantal MOUFFE. *Hegemony and Socialist Strategy: Towards a Radical Democratic Politics*. London: Verso, 1985.

LARSEN, Neal. *Reading North by South: On Latin American Literature, Culture, and Politics*. Minneapolis: University of Minnesota Press, 1995.

LEITCH, Vincent B. *Cultural Criticism, Literary Theory, Poststructuralism*. New York: Columbia University Press, 1992.

LINDENBERGER, Herbert. "Teaching and the Making of Knowledge." *PMLA* 113:3, May 1998: 370-378.

MOORE-GILBERT, Bart. *Postcolonial Theory: Contexts, Practices, Politics*. London; New York: Verso, 1997.

SARLO, Beatriz. *Escenas de la vida posmoderna*. Buenos Aires: Ariel, 1994.

SIMONS, Jon. *Foucault and the Political*. London; New York: Routledge, 1994.

VALLEJO, César. "Nómina de huesos." In *César Vallejo. Obra poética*. Paris: Archivos, 1988. 325.

YÚDICE, George. "Cultural Studies and Civil Studies." In *Reading the Shape of the World*. Eds. Henry Schwarz and Richard Dientz. Boulder: Westview, 1996. 50-67.

—. "Postmodernity and Transnational Capitalism in Latin America." In *On Edge: the Crisis of Contemporary Latin American Culture*. Eds. Jean Franco, Juan Flores, and George Yúdice. Minneapolis: University of Minnesota Press, 1992.

CHAPTER 6
Lima: A Blurred Centrality

Lima is located on the banks the Rímac river. In Quechua, the general language of the Inca empire (1400-1532), Rímac means "the one who speaks." However, the earliest archeological records indicate that the people who built the Lima culture (A.D. 200-800) may be of Aymara origin. They may have come from Coquimbo in Chile and Tucumán in Argentina (Augurto Calvo 82). The Lima culture, to judge by the pottery samples in archeological sites, was in permanent communication with other cultures of the Central Andes: Moche, Nazca, Recuay, and Wari (Lumbreras 119). The pyramid of Maranga in the Rímac valley shows structural similarities with the greater pyramids of the Moche valley. Polychrome murals have been found at most of the Lima pyramids. An estimated million tons of handmade adobes went into the construction of the Huaca Juliana, the Huaca Trujillo, and the Maranga pyramid, all of which are still standing in what is today the metropolitan radius of the city of Lima (Lumbreras 1990: 258-270).

Pachacamac, to the south in the Lurín valley, constitutes one of the most spectacular centers of Lima culture. This adoratory to the maker of the universe, later encompassed in the Inca cult to the Sun by the Inca Túpac Yupanqui (1471-1493), remained as the center of pilgrimages until the Spanish conquest. The great complex faced the ocean and the entire edifice was painted in vermillion. The old temple enshrined the famous oracle of Pachacamac represented in a bifrontal (back to back) deity. One side holds an ear of corn, and his name is Vichama, god of daylight. The other holds feathers, and he is Ichama-Pachacamac, the god of darkness.

Hernando Pizarro destroyed this statue in 1533, but others, scattered in the region, survived (Silva Sifuentes 69-170; Watanabe 329-332; Agurto 145-50, 153). Pachacamac shared many of the constitutive features of Wiracocha, the Wari deity posited as the maker of the universe, and it is for that reason that the temples in Pachacamac became a powerful center in Andean cults and pilgrimages (Agurto l06). According to María Rostworowski, the cult to Pachacamac as maker of the world associated with earthquakes maintained its force through the colonial campaigns of extermination of Andean religions. Pachacamac is in fact the deity inscribed within the popular contemporary cult to the Señor de los Milagros. It is Peru's pan-deity.

I. Colonial Semiosis

The arrival of the Spanish conquistadors in the Lima region on January 18, 1535, represents a second Andean urban foundation. It dislocates Cuzco's centrality but it does not eclipse the former "navel" of the Inca Empire. Lima's centrality, anchored on the power of the institutions that writing deployed, will constitute itself in a struggle for hegemony with other urban centers in the former Inca empire. The Spanish colonial political system, resting on the concept of private property, sees the foundation of the city as the enactment of a ceremony by which the land is emptied out of all previous cultural practices and made ready for the inscription of the land use specified in the Spanish urban grid. Surrounding the plaza, and as if facing each other, the four major instruments in colonial rule—church, judiciary, executive, pillory or *picota*—claimed land and built their edifices around the *plaza de armas*. The streets which flowed out of the grid into the countryside and the "Indian towns" harbored the huge land grants made to the early conquistadors and the different and competing evangelizing orders. An immense cathedral, great houses, meandering convents and opulent churches built by Indian labor and decorated by carvings and paintings flowing out of the hands of European, *mestizo*, and Indian artists reconfigured the landscape of the Rímac valley.

Despite the fact that the *quipu* were widely and universally used throughout the Inca empire, alphabetic writing displaced all Andean systems of recording memory and notation in official discourses (Millones

90). The Church's systematic destruction of the *quipu*, together with the priestly and administrative class who used them, did not eradicate their use in daily life. In practice it remained advantageous to continue using the *quipu* because is proved indispensable in the collection of tribute, taxes, as well as sins in the confessional. Nevertheless, writing in this colonial situation, not only sustained the Spanish institutions founded upon its deployment but also produced a new class of Andean—*mestizo*, Indian, mulatto, *criollo*—intellectuals. The two towering local intellectuals who stemmed from Andean families, Garcilaso de la Vega, Inca (1539-1609) and Guamán Poma de Ayala (c. 1534-1615) used alphabetic writing not only to write in Spanish, but as in the case of Guamán Poma, to also record his writing in Quechua and Aymara. The fact that neither Garcilaso nor Guamán Poma were residents of Lima speaks of the contested centrality of Lima.

After Pizarro's founding of Lima, the new urban space was often the site of military and murderous struggle for power among the conquistadors themselves and the several Crown officials dispatched from Spain with orders to establish a colonial organization in which the Spanish Crown would play the paramount role. While the Spaniards fought for control of the unimaginable wealth and spoils of conquest, the Andean population faced the compounded effects of invasion: endemic war, famine, rape, forced labor, loss of "property," forced relocation, inducement into the *encomiendas* and *repartimientos*, organizational breakdown, and cultural disruption. The consequences of conquest were disastrous and the holocaust the Andeans lived was expressed in Guamán Poma's refrain: "Dear God keep us from extinction" ("Que no nos acabemos"). Historians estimate that the Andean holocaust involved a population decline from approximately 9 million inhabitants in 1531 to one million by the time of the New Laws reached Peru in 1543 (Klarén 49). By 1620, a few years after the death of Guamán Poma, the census registered a total of 700,000 Indians in the viceroyalty of Peru (Bakewell 151).

In order to supply the coastal *repartimientos*, *encomiendas*, and the great houses in the Spanish towns with labor for sugar and wine making as well as domestic service, African slaves were imported in large numbers. By 1586 Lima boasted four thousand African slaves, a number which increased to fifteen thousand by 1640 (Millones 83). In comparison, Lima's non-African population was two thousand in 1580 and nine thousand by 1630. Lima was not only the seat of a large slave population but also of run away and free slaves mixed in with the thousands of vagabonds, beggars, and *pícaros* of all ethnic backgrounds. The colonial administration was hard pressed to "classify" this multitude for taxing and tribute collecting purposes. They devised the grid of the *castas* by which all "mixtures and their offspring were obligated to pay tribute" (Millones 83). The reality of an uncontrollable *mestizaje* eventually gave the lie to a racist nomenclature developed as a control mechanism for fixing the population in geographical space as well as in rigid social and economic niches.

In 1529 Charles V offered the Viceroyalty of New Spain (Mexico) to the Count of Oropesa, Don Francisco Álvarez de Toledo. He turned it down. Almost sixty years later, one of his younger sons, Francisco de Toledo, arrived in Peru (1569) in order to organize the colonial administration of the former Inca empire. During his years in Peru (1569-1581), Viceroy Toledo chose to travel and reconnoiter the country in order to "pacify" it, dispose of the last Inca descendants and all possible leaders of Indian or *mestizo* rebellions. On September 24, 1572, forty years after the foundation of Lima by Pizarro, Toledo had the last Inca, Túpac Amaru, executed in the great Plaza of Cuzco. This was only one of the many actions that Toledo took in order to "prove" that the Incas were "tyrants" and as such could not aspire to self-rule or joint rule with the Spanish. Toledo's purpose in decimating the Inca nobility was twofold: to destroy them physically in order not to have to negotiate with anyone, and to invalidate Bartolomé de Las Casas's claims of Inca legitimacy as "señores naturales." With the execution of Túpac Amaru, Cuzco was decentered and all eyes in the viceroyalty had to turn to Lima as the condensation of a new power game.

During his inspection the viceroy traveled with a phalanx of 70 men— jurist and clergy—whom he deployed into several tasks and whose reports and *crónicas* constructed a good part of what we now both know and ignore about life and the history of the Andes. Toledo had been raised at the courts of Charles V and Philip II and he knew how to identify and motivate (with economic, social, and psychological rewards) talented men whom he brought into his service. Among the people who collaborated with him stand the names of intellectuals such as José de Acosta, Polo de Ondegardo, linguists and translators such as Diego González de Holguín, extirpators of idolatries such as Cristóbal de Albornoz, adventurers such as Pedro Sarmiento de Gamboa, and warriors such as Martín de Loyola.

Even though he did not spend most of his time in Lima—his general inspection took five years to complete (1570-1575)—Toledo did set down the foundations for what was to evolve into an urban administrative center, with an important courtly life in which Spanish jurists, clergymen, low level intellectuals, poets and plastic artists mixed with an ever-increasing number of *mestizo* and even Indian clergy, lawyers, teachers, sculptors and painters. With the establishment of the printing press (1583), Toledo gave impetus to San Marcos University (1551). He also approved the establishment of the Jesuit College for the sons of the Inca nobility and the building of the Franciscan, Augustinian, Dominican, and Mercedarian monasteries. Lima began to acquire the physical and social capital necessary to fashion itself at the center of the Viceroyalty of Peru.

Toledo's labor legislation, based on *Gobierno del Perú* (1567) by the Spanish jurist Juan de Matienzo (1520-1575), provided the ground rules for a colonial exploitation which would make possible or impossible the cultural life of Lima as a space of intense, and more often than not, asymmetrical cultural contact. The idea of "reducing" the Indians into "repúblicas de indios" where they could be controlled by the *corregidor* and supervised by the *curaca* not only broke with the agricultural pattern of Andean population settlement but it also gave rise to the Indian towns. These became new social spaces in which Andean culture would embark on an evolutionary post-contact process of its own, marked by the paramount presence of the Church and seared by the campaigns for the extirpator of idolatries. In 1609, driven by zealotry and personal interests, the clergyman Francisco de Ávila began making it public that through confession in towns near Pachacamac he had learned that many Indians, and especially *curacas* and Andean priests, continued to worship the *huacas*. He proposed and won approval to conduct a campaign to discover the *huacas*, identify and bring to trial, under the auspices of the Holy Inquisition, the leaders of the "idolatries" (Millones 113). With the "reducciones de indios" Toledo created a cultural contact situation which he did not anticipate: the possibility of governing the Indies had been left in the hands of the evangelizing clergy, for they acted as the sole agents of cultural transformation. The priests did not only make use of public ceremonies but they had also at their disposal the sacraments, all of which marked key moments in the process of legitimization of the Andean peoples as subjects of the Crown.

The entire lifecycle of an Andean person was traversed by the sacraments. However, and despite the powerful tools at the clergy's disposal, the Andeans resisted the loss of their gods and rituals and more often than not the post-extirpation clergy decided that it was better to pretend to be unaware of the andeanization of Christianity. As the colonial process unfolded, it became evident that the persecutions and destruction of Andean priests (*hechiceros*), which began as early 1565 with the persecution of the Taqui-Oncoy (dancing sickness) movement, did not benefit anyone (Millones 243-266). When, at the end of the eighteenth century, the *curacas* were replaced with "alcaldes de indios," named by the Spanish authorities, the power of the *hechiceros* had not diminished. The new leaders also needed the *huacas* in order to govern effectively (Millones 118).

Toledo also reconfigured the *mita* in order to have enough labor for the mines. From then on the Andean world revolved around the new centers of mineral production: silver in Potosí and mercury in Huancavelica. Lima's bureaucrats and traders benefitted from the legislation that gave them control over the export of these minerals to Europe. Lima's cultural activity was dominated by the departure of the armed fleet during the months of April and June. Slowly, Lima gained the fruits of a *pax colonial* marked by an intense ceremonial life. The objective was to construct for the American subjects a visible sense of the power of the metropolitan center which, from a great distance, ruled their lives. A calendar with more 150 celebrations was devised. The arrival and departure of viceroys, bishops, and other important figures in the colonial regime was marked by lengthy parades and other public acts. Often, the colonial order celebrated events in Spanish life that had already taken place some three to six months past. Invariably the *plaza de armas* was chosen as the appropriate space for such state sponsored spectacles of self affirmation and continuity.

The Spanish authorities understood fiestas as an effective mode of mass communication in a society in which they needed to show the effects of their power as often as possible in order to conserve it. Visitors from all over the viceroyalty were simply owed by the pomp and pageantry and especially by the everlasting nature of the ceremonies and celebrations. The concentration of surplus, the extravagant expenditure of precious resources, the seemingly co-extensive space with the metropolis constituted an image of the glory of power. In this sense Lima concentrated and irradiated a great cultural and political power over the rural areas of the empire.

But the notion that the center of the Viceroyalty of Peru settled into a life of comfort dominated by a court of splendor is today challenged by new scholarship on the subject. The tropical climate was unhealthy to the many who lived in cramped quarters in a city without running water or sewerage. The hospitals, on the whole run by the charitable orders, were in fact centers for the spread of disease and death. Major earthquakes shook the city in 1655, 1687, and 1746 destroying several of its architectonic jewels. Pirates and corsairs regularly raided the port of Callao. Such insecurities accentuated the intense ritual life already fostered by the many centers of religious life. Convents, monasteries, and schools absorbed and channeled almost all of the intellectual energy of the colonial city. These institutions were practically the only avenue for literacy and learning for *mestizos* and one of the few places were mulattos, *castas*, and women could escape a life of grinding physical labor and endless poverty. "Spiritual" life of all kinds found its way, to run risks of its own, into the several institutions offered by the Church, from family worship and Sunday mass to *cofradías*, monastic contemplation, and even higher education. It is thus not surprising that the colonial period produced more saints and holy people than secular intellectuals. Doña Inés Muñoz, wife and later widow to Martín de Alcántara, Pizarro's half-brother, founded in 1573 a sumptuous monastery consecrated to the Virgin of the Immaculate Conception. The daughters and sisters of the encomenderos joined in droves. By 1688 the convent had 309 religious, 14 novices, 18 lay women, and 27 *donadas* (servants).

Rosa de Lima (1586-1617), the first American saint, was one of the many holy men and women who, during their own life, became objects of cults which attributed to them the power to perform miraculous cures. Santa Rosa's contemporary and counterpart in popular devotion was the Dominican barber and servant Martín de Porras. The daughter of Spanish parents, Rosa de Lima was quickly canonized (1671) while the humble mulatto had to wait until the second half of the twentieth century to become the first "black" saint. Today they are revered as a pair and their procession constitutes one of the largest public ceremonies in modern Lima.

Towards the end of the seventeenth century the population of Lima had grown to 37, 234 people and twenty percent belonged to some type of religious organization. The Holy Office of the Inquisition, in Peru from 1569 to 1820, made sure that any deviation was met with severe discipline and punishment. Furthermore, the Church was not always happy with its saints. They represented a thorny problem. On the one hand, their faith, life of sacrifice, and especially their Christian death, could be construed as a monument to the success of the evangelizing mission and the transplantation of Spanish counter-reformation culture in the American dominions. On the other hand, that very same faith, and especially their mystical raptures, indicated the possibility of direct communication with God. The Church coped with its possible displacement by requiring all men and women embarked in the holy life to confess all visions, dreams, or revelations. Further, all the faithful were under strict orders to denounce anyone suspected of heresy or heterodox practices. Even under such tight strictures, it was not always possible for the holy men or women to report visions that conformed to the Church's beliefs, and many were tried, tortured, and burned at the stake (Millones 185). Such was the case of Francisco de la Cruz (1530-1578) who studied in Valladolid between 1558 and 1561 under the tutelage of Las Casas.

Born Isabel Flores de Oliva, the purposeful and delicate Rosa took it as her mission to help the destitute Indians and blacks who came to die unmercifully in the Lima Hospitals. But it was the deadly fasting and excruciating mortification of her young and beautiful body that made her famous in Lima and beyond. Rosa too was associated with a circle of mystics, but when the Inquisition questioned her she responded by claiming complete ignorance and incapacity to understand what her visions meant. Her untimely death at the age of 31 allowed her to escape a full dressed inquiry by the Holy Office. Her death was one of the great events of Lima history: her body had to be moved several times in order to prevent members of her cult from cutting a finger or some other part of her sacralized body to keep as holy relic.

Writing, confession, belonging to devotional circles, preaching, and thinking were all very dangerous acts to engage in within the confines of a colonial regime anxious about protestants, Jews, and Indians which, together, were used to represent the projection of the fears, insecurities, and self doubts of the colonial enterprise. In this climate of oppression and repression it is not surprising to find literary expression confined to anonymous satirical verse, *autos sacramentales* (mystery plays), and sermons. In fact, neither of the two great texts of the this period were written in Lima. The *Comentarios reales* by the *mestizo* exile Garcilaso de la Vega, Inca, was published in Lisbon in 1609-1617 and the *El primer nueva corónica y buen gobierno* finished in 1615 by Guamán Poma, lost until 1908 when the Americanist Richard A. Pietschmann found it in the Royal Library in Copenhagen, was published in Paris by Paul Rivet in 1936 (see chapter 6 in this volume).

The colonial semiosis which began in Cajamarca with the scene in which the Inca Atawalpa throws the Bible on the ground as a way of showing his displeasure with the Spanish claims that the Bible spoke the word of God, continued with the counter reformation politics of evangelization. Visual representations—paintings and particularly *estampas* or prints—played a great a role in the colonization of the Andean imaginary as writing did in the establishment of discursive formations which organized thinking and feeling. The printing press brought to Lima in 1583, in conjunction with the three *Concilios* of Lima (1565, 1567,1583) were instrumental in the establishment and advancement of a cultural colonial policy which was two-pronged: the propagation of Christian belief by means of *estampas* or prints, etchings and paintings together with the indoctrination of the catechism. The publication of *Doctrina christiana y catecismo para la instrucción de los indios* (1584) and the *Confesionario para los curas de indios* (1585), together with the arrival of master Flemish and Italian painters, were key moments in the development of two of the most productive and original colonial arts: painting and religious transculturation.

The Council of Trent (1545-63) policies recommended the conversion of heretics through the use of visual texts. The Jesuits, leaders in the Catholic counter-offense against Protestantism, took up enthusiastically the idea of conversion in the Indies by means of the visual arts. Philip II gave them ample dominion over the education of the Indian elites and often recognized the special aptitude of the newly founded order for the evangelization of the American Indians (López-Baralt 174). The development of the colonial schools of painting—Cuzco, Lima, Chuquisaca, and Quito— as conveyors of the Christian themes selected as appropriate for catechization, responded strictly to the policies adopted in Trent. Painting is thus born in intimate relation with a didactic and highly ideologized purpose and, as such, it will move within very closely watched strictures.

Íñigo de Loyola, a Spanish painter, arrived in Cuzco in 1545, in order to populate with images the enormous churches being built all over the viceroyalty. However, his main mission was to train Indian and *mestizo* men of talent to produce images in the European manner. Other Spanish painters followed under the same conditions and the Cuzco School of painting was born out of the transculturated learning that the local artists produced in the several workshops of the Andes. Seventy percent of the painters associated with the School of Cuzco, founded by Diego Quispe Tito (1611-1681), were Indians (Gisbert 104). But not all the paintings done had religious themes. Many were also portraits of prominent Spaniards and their families. And the rich *caciques* also paid to have their portraits done in either Spanish or post-Inca vestments. The *caciques* often paid to have paintings which recorded great ceremonies or *fiestas* (Fane 144-155, 171-180). These canvases remain a rich source of ethnographic data.

The iconography of the European counter-reformation suffered important alterations in the hands of the Indian and *mestizo* painters of the School of Cuzco. All topics pertaining to Mary were taken up with fruition. The theme of the Immaculate Conception and the Mother and Child dominated. Scenes in the life of the Child Christ adorned the walls of almost every church. The return from Egypt was a particulate favorite. Scenes from the crucifixion in which the torture of the flesh is powerfully depicted found a market in churches as well as in domestic altars. Despite the fact that the theme of the Trinity was excluded from the preaching done to the Indians for fear of misinterpretation and confusion with the Andean trinity composed of father, son, and brother (Gisbert 88), it was a topic *mestizo* and Indian artists and their patrons found appealing. The God with three faces or three manifestations captured the imagination of the Andean who deployed their very own readings of this iconography. Thus the Madonna became the outer casing of the great *Apus*—snow-capped mountains, sources of spring water—and Santiago was revalidated as a manifestation of the *Illapa*, the thunder god. Of course the most original and celebrated creation of the Cuzco School are the effeminate and delicate archangels armed with muskets, whose military uniforms were in consonance with models depicted in French military manuals (Bayón 742). The abundance of this delicious creature is associated with the special place the Jesuit conferred upon angels as they catechized the Indians. The Jesuits were a newly created order and had no saints of their own, so they used the angels in military garb as an emblem of Christian conquest and divine predilection for Spain (Gisbert 87)

In Lima, the Italians Bernardo Bitti (1548-1610) and Angelino Medoro (157?-1631) taught the basic techniques of European painting and cemented a Mannerist style and iconography (Mesa and Gisbert 9-

10) that would be used practically until the end of the colonial period (Stastny 32-34). In 1588 the Italian painter and engraver Mateo Pérez de Alesio (1547-1616) arrived in Lima with a huge amount of prints of etchings and "libro de dibujos" by Durer (Mesa and Gisbert 64-68). Alesio was not the only painter to have arrived with an ample collection of prints which he used not only for instructive purposes but also as a type of archive which contained models—clouds, trees, flowers, legs, faces, wings—which could quickly be put to the service of composition and rendition of any request made of the workshop. Baltasar de Figueroa in Colombia left six books of prints (*estampas*) of lives of saints and some 1800 other parts and motifs (Stastny 35).

Along with the presence of these Italian artists, the iconographic and thematic archive of colonial painting was well stocked by the printing presses and export houses of Amsterdam. By the middle of the seventeenth century the export of paintings, etchings, prints, and fine furniture to America, and the import of raw materials from Spanish America, accounted for a fundamental transformation in the art business and the processes of transculturation on both sides of the Atlantic. It is thus not surprising to find in colonial churches and private collections works by Zurbarán, Rubens, and other Flemish and Spanish masters (Stastny 34).

In the late sixteenth century, the *Academia Antártica*, a group of Spanish and creole poets, imitated the Academies which existed in Spain. Juan de Miramontes Zuazola (-1614), Amarilis, and the Anónima, given their neo-platonic orientation, are associated with the poetics of the *Academia Antártica*. The programmatic collection *Discurso en loor de la poesía* (1608) is attributed to Amarilis, the woman poet who also wrote a long love letter to the Spanish poet and playwright Lope de Vega. The *Discurso*, like much of the work of the poets of the *Academia Antártica*, indicates a close association with Spanish Petrarchism (Adán 23-46).

Life in the colonies during the seventeenth century was characterized by corruption and contraband. Almost any office or title was for sale. The outcome of any encounter with the law was subject to games of influence and bribes. Some *criollos* were able to take advantage of the situation but, in general, they lost out to the Spanish-born elite which controlled all the sites of power in all the major institutions associated with writing. Personal advancement was virtually impossible. The sense of claustrophobia with which people lived was intensified by the Peninsula's own disillusionment after Spanish imperial ambitions suffered the major blow of the loss of the Armada to England. The full swing of the counter-reformation and the onset of the Baroque in the metropolis had specific and very local manifestations in the colonies. Obligated to keep silent by virtue of the many royal decrees and the cultural policies of the Inquisition, the upper-class colonial intellectuals who were not permitted to write novels or histories of the Indian peoples took up the tortuous route of baroque prose and satirical verse (Costigan 29).

Charted by Charles V in 1551 at the request of the Spanish colonists who wanted their sons to receive university titles in order that they may be eligible for positions in the high bureaucracy, San Marcos University, modeled after Salamanca, by the 1570's boasted sixteen academic chairs, including one in Quechua. It maintained its place as the premier colonial university offering training in the five major faculties necessary to rank as a major university: arts (philosophy), theology, medicine, civil law, and canon law. By 1678 it offered mathematics but Quechua had been suspended. Although secularly endowed, the religious orders, who run *colegios* with college level instruction at the sites of their own convents and monasteries, also offered at San Marcos instruction in the writings of their most prominent theologians—St. Thomas Aquinas and St. Augustine. They thus gave the scholastic tradition in Spanish America a foundational role. But only San Marcos could confer baccalaureates, masters, licentiate and doctoral degrees. San Marcos remained the focus of intellectual life for the colonial elites. Until the end of the eighteenth century it used the same texts books approved for use (censored) in the entire Hispanic world and in doing so it contributed to the creation of a bifurcated pattern of cultural contact with Europe, for what the Spanish authorities put in the list of the forbidden—novels, philosophy, science, history—came into the colonies by way of a substantial book contraband.

The number of men and women who lived in monasteries and nunneries during the seventeenth century in colonial cities was very large indeed. The population inside the monasteries included not only the friars or nuns of the order, but also novices, *legos*, students, *donados*, servants, slaves, and artisans. By 1621 the Lima Audiencia estimated that there were 1,053 friars in the monasteries of the Franciscans, Dominicans, Mercedarias, Jesuits, Benedictines, and Augustinians. By far the Jesuits had the largest number of students (170) while the Dominicans had 30 *donados*. The monasteries had grown not only in size (they often occupied more than a square block), but in intellectual, social, and economic importance. Their quarters often boasted beautiful architecture, patios tiled in the Seville style, splendid churches decorated with the best of the colonial baroque wood carvings, Cuzqueño or Lima school paintings, orchards, and of course legendary kitchens (Durán Montero 118-22). However, male monasteries and schools paled in comparison with the women's convents and *beaterios* housed lay women who took simple vows under the rules of the Third Order of the Franciscan Rule and other similar societies. Elementary schooling was offered to various classes of girls (Lavrin, 165-95, Bakewell, 246). In 1625 a petition was made before the Audiencia to create a new convent of Santa Catalina in Lima. One of the reasons given was the population saturation in the existing convents and the unabated growth in new vocations. Such numbers, contrary to what might be expected, were perceived to be a problem. Charles II indicated his desire to see the number of women in convents curtailed because he had learned that the servants who, on the whole were *mestizo*, mulatto and black, were women of very "bad and despicable habits". They made it impossible to really keep cloister from the world (Durán Montero 123).

The Lima convents of women were also disruptive to the Spanish city grid. As they extended to harbor the social formation taking place within the walls of their domain, they expanded, often occupying several city blocks. And indeed their efforts to extend over larger spaces were predicated on the fact that the crowed condition in which they lived caused many of the residents to die of tuberculosis (Durán Montero 124). The impossibility of entering the convents, either because of lack of space or the inability to pay the necessary dowry, saw the multiplication of the *beaterios*. These communities offered an ordered and simple life of prayer, routine, and spirituality. Many of this *beaterios* channeled their energies into social work and took in orphans, abused women, repentant prostitutes, and even Indian women inspired by a true vocation. The austerity of the *beaterios* contrasted with the luxury of some of the private cells in the cloistered convents. Relatively well-read nuns often disputed the meaning of the rule of their order and other interpretative matters with the Bishop. The case of María Antonia Lucía del Espíritu Santo (1646-1709), founder of the Descalzas, is today as notable as it was then notorious (Bermúdez-Gallegos 25-28). Hagiography reading, writing, and commentary constituted the mainstay of conventual imaginary. All convents belonged to the contemplative orders. None belonged to the teaching orders. The latter would not appear until the end of the eighteenth century (Bakewell 247).

The impact of an official world organized by a set of enclosures, fixed hierarchies, and censorship is most visible in the effects it had on the elite (*criollo*) colonial intellectual. Pablo Macera understands baroque culture as a cultural formation traversed by imperative ideas, forms, and rules for action and belief (in Costigan 36 and Macera 2: 400) which leave little room for alternate forms. In the scholastic atmosphere of the period the colonial intellectual had to hide his frustration and often wasted his/her energies contributing to the pageantry of ceremonies, poetry jousts, panegyrics, and other forms of court poetry. *Gongorismo*, with its vocabulary and universe of reference steeped in Greek and Roman myth, history, legend, and literature, was then in vogue in Spain. Paradox, antithesis, inversion, and parallelism comprised the rhetorical preferences of *Gongorismo*. The bulk of the baroque poetry written under this circumstance was but an extravagant exercise of verbal technical pyrotechnics. Scholastic arguments, euphuistic poetry failed as a means for reflexivity or for the inscription of lived reality. *Gongorismo*, named after the Spanish poet Luis de Góngora, was practiced more as a instrument for ideological control than as a poetic form suitable for the exploration of subjectivity or the imaginary. Before this impasse, the solution adopted by many was to distance themselves from privileged discursive forms. Their work came to constitute a kind of baroque counter-culture (Costigan 39) practiced by itinerant and certainly part-time writers. John Beverly points out that what characterizes *Gongorismo* in America is the way in which it is utilized in order to mystify, through its powerful stylistic and metaphorical alchemy, the Indian labor which is the real basis of wealth and of consumer goods (90). Satirical verse, as in the case of *Diente del Parnaso* (Ricardo Palma 1837) provides a good example of disenchanted distance but not of what we understand as modern critique. To a certain extent, colonial satire recovered the ironic perspective of the general populace onto the illusory games of the official truths. Satire also began the work of incorporating colonial language use and lexicon in a referential move intended to record and represent the local universe. The idea of a "new" American literary system begins to emerge. Whether the poems were addressed to the members of the high court or the populace, the fact that they expressed dissent and disbelief in the official and pompous cultural forms offered a way to explore the incorporation of new historical subjects—*pícaros*, pimps, whores, cardsharps, cuckold husbands, fake virgins—into colonial discursive formations.

The case of Juan de Espinosa Medrano (1629-88), better known as "el Lunarejo" is pertinent here even though he did not live in Lima. He was an illegitimate child. His racial parentage remains in doubt. What matters is that he wrote some of the most accomplished poetry in Góngora's style, and achieved fame with the sermons he delivered in the Cuzco cathedral. "Lunarejo" was one of the most learned men of his time and he is usually remembered for his *Apologético en favor de D. Luis de Góngora, Príncipe de los poetas líricos de España* (Lima, 1662) which he wrote in order to defend the Spanish poet as well as baroque aesthetics. "Lunarejo" argues that Góngora is quite entitled to write a poetry given to the beauty of rhetorical complication rather than to transcendental themes because Góngora's poetry is not epic or religious. Known also as the Doctor Sublime, Medrano was also highly regarded for his vast knowledge of the classics and the dramas and comedies that he wrote in Quechua and Spanish. "El Lunajero" studied in the Universidad de San Ignacio de Loyola in Cuzco and received his doctorate in 1654. In the *Apologético,* Medrano expresses a clear self-identification with the New World and with men of letters who wrote *from* America. He questions the common-place idea that someone from the Indies could not be considered a good writer capable of pleasing the Europeans and he rejects the idea that satirical poetry is the only venue possible for an American: "Pero, que no puede haber bueno en las Indias?....Sátiros nos juzgan, tritones nos presumen, que brutos de alma, en vano se alientan a desmentirnos máscaras de la humanidad" (qtd. in Chang-Rodríguez 118) ("What is this? There cannot be good writers in the Indies? They think us satyrs, trytons, brutes. In vain they encourage themselves to paint us as mere human masks").

In the long run, in the development of Latin American letters, the questioning of the Eurocentric literary value system voiced from Cuzco would be more influential and long lasting than the satirical move of the poets associated with Lima's cultural milieu or the *Academia Antártica*. In the context of the life of Medrano it is important also to underscore the role played by the sermon as a cultural form which mediated between certain types of orality and the more established written genres. Both the sermon and the theater, the principle colonial verbal manifestations, assume the participation of a larger and more heterogeneous public than poetry or the essay do, despite the fact that the euphuistic sermon seduced a public which did not fully understood it. The seduction worked precisely because, as Antonio Gramsci might put it, the public found it too difficult to understand and therefore judged to be good (Rodríguez-Garrido 154-55).

The "Barroco de Indias" refers to the *mestizo* architectural style that shaped every building and adorned the facades of temples and houses. Exuberant in size, color, and decorative motifs, the Spanish American Baroque of the highlands in contrast (Kubler and Soria 96) was heavy and imposing. The requirements of tremendous loads of local stone affected the Baroque in Lima which had no nearby quarry. Most of the decoration was reserved for the gold leaf alters and *retablos* or niches inside the churches and the private chapels of the very wealthy. Art historians have demonstrated the clear imprint of Indian artisan traditions as well as Pre-Columbian iconography in Potosí, Pomata, Juli, and Arequipa (Kubler; Murillo).

II. LOCAL KNOWLEDGE AND THE EFFECTS OF THE ENLIGHTENMENT

The eighteenth century is often regarded as a period of transition in colonial rule from the Hapsburg to the Bourbons (War of Spanish Succession 1700-1713) and the subsequent Bourbon reforms which brought, albeit slowly, great changes in the intellectual and artistic horizon of the Spanish American colonies. The Bourbons adopted a policy of increased independence from the Papacy. They also limited many of the privileges (*fueros*) previously granted to the Church and the clergy. They loosened the grip of scholasticism and fostered the expansion of knowledge in the natural sciences and economic change. By 1723 the medical faculty in San Marcos accepted the scientific explanation of the circulation of blood.

The process of positive reception of the Enlightenment was launched by the Jesuits. Descartes, Newton, and Leibnitz were being taught in the Jesuit colleges and it was Francisco Javier Clavijero (1731-1787) who, in Mexico, launched the most powerful attack of scholasticism. The Jesuits were expelled from Spain and its colonies in 1767; in Lima, San Marcos stepped in to fill the vacuum left by the Company. Attention was also paid to the idea of creating a system by which education would be available to the general populace. The idea of accumulating and propagating scientific and economic knowledge lead to the creation of many *Sociedades económicas* or *Amigos del País*. The teaching of science found many obstacles—from religious orthodoxy to lack of trained teachers. The *Sociedad de Amigos del País* published the *Mercurio Peruano* between 1791 and 1793. The best minds of the high culture of Peruvian enlightenment wrote for the *Mercurio* on economics, science, geography, philosophy, history, and even novels and theater. Contact with French intellectual and artistic life was intense and formative. The ample and lasting embrace of France in the intellectual and plastic arts began with the *afrancesados* of this period. Perhaps the life of Pablo de Olavide (1725-1803) and his close association with Diderot, who wrote a biography of the Peruvian exile, serves as an example of the French connection.

On the whole, the eighteenth century is best characterized by the scientific expeditions which brought with them several of the new natural sciences—physics, botany, chemistry, archeology, and history. Scientific expeditions alidated the local intellectuals' desire to know about themselves and their own territories and societies. Contact with cosmopolitan circles of men of knowledge was for the first time available directly to individuals. The French expedition to measure the geographical degree of latitude than began in 1735 resulted in a comprehensive description of Peru. Jorge Juan and Antonio de Ulloa, the two Spanish scientists in the expedition, produced a comprehensive and critical report of the viceregal administration. Ecclesiastical visits also gathered social and economic information. During six years of continuous visitations the Bishop of Trujillo, Baltasar Jaime Martínez Campañón (1735-1797) gathered an enormous collection of paintings depicting with great accuracy the daily life of his parishioners. The Spanish doctor Cosme Bueno (1711-1798) published the *Descripciones geográficas del Virreinato del Perú* in a series of Lima almanacs (1763-1772 and 1774-1778).

Historiography under the Bourbons lifted the censure over the writing of local history. The urban and regional *petites histoires* made their appearance. Illustrious native sons engaged in the description of their region in order to advance economic and educational interests. Archeological expeditions began the rediscovery of the Inca and pre-Inca ruins. Guides were published. These dry descriptions provide a wealth of ethnographic information on the daily life of Indian costumes and religious belief. Of course the most important single expedition (and personality) to explore Spanish America was that of Baron Alexander von Humboldt (1769-1859). The impact in both Spanish America and Europe of his *Personal Narrative of Travels to the Equinoctial Regions of the New*

Continent during the years 1799-1811, and his *Ensayo político sobre el reino de la Nueva España* (1807-1811), bridged in one single stroke the "fissure that had opened between the European Enlightenment and American reality" (Brading 517).

Because of the great rebellion lead by José Gabriel Condorcanqui (1738-1781) or Túpac Amaru II in 1780 the *ilustrados* did not engage in the writing of Indian histories as Sigüenza y Góngora did in Mexico (Brading 483-91). This absence does not mean that Indian and *mestizos* were not writing local history. As Luis Millones has demonstrated, the parades and theatrical presentations in town squares and *plazas* were deployed as the texts on which Andean *petites histoires* were being memorialized. Indeed, forms of Andean pre-conquest theatrical representation survived until the end of the eighteenth century. The Spanish authorities associated the success of the Túpac Amaru II rebellion with abundant and regular staging of Andean dramas in Quechua. After the execution of Túpac Amaru II, secular drama in Quechua—plays such as *La tragedia del fin de Atahualpa*— were banned. But Quechua drama, such as *Ollantay*, continued to be composed and represented as late as 1780.

Clearly, in Lima, a city which interiorized a Spanish self-identity, the most popular form of theater was the *sainete*, a short satirical piece which poked fun at local types and vices. *Sainetes* were performed in open air theaters or *corrales* and, later, in the larger coliseums with night lighting. Its most famous *limeña* actress was no doubt Micaela Villegas (1739-1819), better known as the Perricholi. Her seductive dance and passable *sainete* performances gained her the devoted attention of Viceroy Manuel de Amat y Juniet. The theater, together with Sunday mass and the parades and other public *fiestas*, remained as the chief cultural texts, despite the growth of print culture and the greater voice of local public intellectuals (Castro-Klarén, 1996: 87-99). The lettered city to which Ángel Rama assigned so much importance in the development of Latin American culture, at the end of the eighteenth century, was a very small affair indeed.

Pablo Macera writes that education during the eighteenth century remained stratified. It was a question of class privilege. Communication between the various educational sectors was at a standstill. An aristocratizing concept of culture informed those who saw themselves as illustrated reformers. While colonial universities and colleges had no difficulty recruiting instructors—there was a surplus of doctors—school teachers were very hard to find. Primary school instruction was rudi-

mentary. The Provision of 1789 required reading, writing, basic arithmetic, and catechism (Macera 2: 219-22). Complaints on the quality of
the teachers, the low salary offered, and the poverty of the school conditions were endemic. Until the end of the eighteenth century, the sons of
the *caciques* could, as boarders, receive relatively good schooling in the
Colegio de San Borja in Cuzco and El Colegio del Príncipe in Lima.

The cost of this education was obviously exorbitant and the state did
not provide any subsidies. However, the common Indians and the sons of
the *curacas* were not the only sector of the population who had almost no
access to education. Like all colonial cities, Lima lived around the *plaza*,
the market, and the church, not the school house. It is estimated that by
the end of the eighteenth century there were 5,000 people enrolled in primary school (Macera 2: 258), of which only twenty percent received a
good education and most belonged to the nobility. Neither the middle
class nor the masses could aspire to any education.

The state of books and printing presses in Peru at the end of the eighteenth century is indeed telling. Despite the fact that there were twenty-
eight presses available, the book was mainly an imported object. These
presses worked only partially and never managed to stay in business for
very long. On the whole, the material conditions for the productions of
books in Peru were missing: paper had to be imported. At times books
were torn apart in order to reuse the paper. However, trade in books was
a good business and they were sold in the same shops were nails and ribbons were offered. But the best libraries in Lima were not built on such
local commerce. Books came into collector's hands by way of direct
order from Europe. The most famous collector was the precocious intellectual and wealthy aristocrat José de Baquíjano y Carrillo de Córdoba
(1751-1817), who during the wars on Independence remained loyal to the
Spanish crown (Burkholder and Johnson).

Nevertheless, Lima, because of the import monopoly of the port of
Callao, became the largest depository of books in the South American
colonies. From Lima, Spanish books traveled to Santiago, Quito, and La
Paz. The private libraries in Peru could easily compete with their Spanish
counterparts. However, the notion of public libraries was a long way off
and this affected directly the habit of reading and the possible number of
readers (Macera 2: 283-95). For the most part, the colonial aristocracy did
not read for pleasure. The best personal collections of bureaucrats and
clergymen did not surpass 300 volumes. Among the best libraries of the

period is one with 1,190 books bought by Hipólito Unanue (1755-1833) in 1798. The libraries in the monasteries far outweighed any private collection. Learning was more a desire than a possibility. The foundation of two provincial universities—San Agustín in Arequipa in 1828 and the Universidad Nacional "La Libertad" in Trujillo in 1824—went a long way to turning desire into reality.

III. INDEPENDENCE

In the past historians taking Lima to be the center of events in Peru had argued the Independence movement in Peru as a late arrival, forged in the end by the converging armies of San Martín and Bolívar. Historians now map a more complex, fragmented, and regional picture in which the Túpac Amaru II rebellion (1780) plays a decisive precursor role. Satirical verse, the *pasquín,* or "libelous pamphlet," expressed early nationalistic feelings (Bacacorzo 16-26). Arequipa's Mariano Melgar (1790-1815) wrote the most important civic poetry of the period. His progressive radicalism and concern for the oppressed Indian masses anticipated the several waves of the *Indigenista* movement. More than a poet, Melgar lived his life as a Romantic icon. His "Marcha patriótica" celebrated the entry of the revolutionary forces of Mateo Pumacahua in Arequipa in 1814. The Spanish authorities summarily executed the poet for his participation in the rebellion. His popular poems and patriotic struggle turned him into a martyr of Independence. "Carta a Silvia" heralded a new, pre-Romantic sensibility. It should be associated with the *yaraví* (*harawi*), the popular, pre-Hispanic love songs adopted for the guitar. Melgar's *yaravíes* mark an important step towards a genuinely emancipated literature (Higgins 56- 61).

In the absence of a book-buying public or a flourishing book industry (Higgins 63), it is not surprising that the journalistic form of the *costumbrista* sketch came to dominate the cultural scene in Lima. The high-born Felipe Pardo y Aliaga (1806-68), in his short-lived satirical journal *El espejo de mi tierra* (1840), adopted a radical critical attitude towards the society of his day. He directed his satire against the *criollo* upper classes whose hereditary shortcomings—ignorance and indolence—disqualified them to rule the chaos that the republic, with its democratic rhetoric, had brought about. Pardo y Aliaga was not alone in conceiving of the theater as a pedagogical tool in the formation of a national literature concerned with local realities. His contemporary, Manuel Ascencio Segura (1805-71), from the perspective of his own middle-class origins, with his "Catecismo para el pueblo," wrote biting satires of every aspect of the country's political and cultural organization. Like most of the criticism voiced in satire, the Republican theater expressed its disillusionment in moral terms and continued the love of gossip and scandal which eventually produced the *Tradiciones peruanas* (1880, 1888) by Ricardo Palma (1833-1919).

A frustrated historian working in a cultural milieu where the idea of a nation had not yet emerged and in which historiography had not yet taken its first steps, Palma's love of the document as a shard of the past, together with his satirical and yet subservient laughter and his mastery of the piquant phrase, lead him to compose his *Tradiciones*. Palma began as a derivative Romantic poet, but later his interest in the scandal of the recent past led him to his *Anales de la Inquisición de Lima* (1863), the source for much of the information embodied in his *Tradiciones*. One again, like the *sainete*, the *costumbrista* theater, and the *yaraví*, Palma's *Tradiciones* honed in on the local event, the crafting of a distinct language of immediacy. Palma's awareness of being on the brink of something new was best captured in his linguistic work, the *Neologismos y americanismos* (1896), *Papeletas lexicográficas* (1903), and his indefatigable institutional work to have the Spanish Academy of the Language recognize his own work and American Spanish as true, if different, peers.

In marked contrast with the polished and amusing prose of the *Tradiciones*, the amateurish novel *El Padre Horán* appeared in serialized form in the Lima newspaper *El Comercio* in 1848. Its author, Narciso Aréstegui (1826-69), was a *cusqueño* who studied in the Colegio Nacional de Ciencias y Artes founded by Simón Bolívar. Set in Cuzco, *El Padre Horán* narrates the seduction and the murder of the daughter of liberal land owner by her confessor. It is based on the actual murder of a young girl from a well-to-do Cuzco family. Aréstegui anticipates several themes for the *indigenista* novel that was to come: the Church's hypocrisy, the central government's unwillingness and failure to stimulate local industry and agriculture, and the general disregard for the welfare of the nation's citizens. His ideas were consonant with the polices of the Government of President Ramón Castilla (1797-1867) in office at the time of the publication of *El Padre Horán* (Kristal 44).

Clorinda Matto de Turner (1852-1909), the founder of the *indigenista* novel, had done her literary apprenticeship with her own refashioning of

Palma's work in *Tradiciones cuzqueñas* (1879). In 1883 she traveled to Arequipa where she worked as chief editor of the newspaper *La Bolsa* and published her historical tragedy *Hima-Sumac* (1892) and a text book for teaching literature to the "fair sex" (Delgado 89). In 1886 she returned to Lima where she found open doors in the principle journals of the period: *La Revista Social* and *El Perú Ilustrado*, which eventually she headed. She became a member of the *El Ateneo* and *El Círculo Literario*. With *Aves sin nido* (1889), a novel squarely placed in the realist tradition, Matto de Turner overcame some of the rhetorical and aesthetic difficulties of *El Padre Horán*. The novel focused attention on the abuse of authority by the political superstructure but it did not analyze the relationship of authority with the powerful economic interest which authority served. It seems to suggest that the appointment of enlightened and humanitarian officials would be enough to resolve the problems of the social and economic formations of the Peruvian highlands (Higgins 76). The vision that Matto de Turner gave of the Indians was external, from an urban, centralist, perspective.

In the aftermath of the War of the Pacific (1879-1883) Peru faced a profound and general upheaval. New institutions fostered the formation of Peruvian intellectuals whose ties to the socioeconomic hegemonic groups were neither solidaristic nor markedly dependant. These intellectuals proposed a thorough modernization of Peru; in the field of commercial and cultural affairs, they called for more contact with the outside world. Regarding the Indian question in the hinterland, they advocated establishing the Indian ownership of the land that they worked. But this did not mean that Indians were to participate in national politics: they were considered an inferior race to be kept under the tutelage of an enlightened intelligentsia.

Much of this national project emerged from the *Club Literario* founded by the *Amigos de las Letras* in the 1860's and their journal *La Revista de Lima*, of which González Prada was the leading figure until 1886. In opposition, Ricardo Palma blamed the Indians for loosing the war and the politicians in the Partido Civil for causing it (Kristal 98). President Andrés Avelino Cáceres, a general in the Peruvian resistance, explained the defeat of Peru by the Chilean army and navy in terms of political disarray, underscoring the work of the Peruvian collaborationist. He did not attack the landed oligarchy, the target of the *indigenista* novel and González Prada's circle. Both Ricardo Palma and

González Prada would spend a good part of their lives rebuilding the national library that the Chilean occupation burnt.

As a dissenter, González Prada, together with other intellectuals, founded the *Círculo Literario*. Eventually this group became the political party La Unión Nacional (Kristal 108). Concurring with the general positivist thesis that ignorance and servitude arrest industrial progress, González Prada, in his famous *Politeama* speech of 1888 argued that Peru lost the war with Chile because the Indians, who comprised the majority of the country's population, felt no compelling reason to fight for a nation which in fact had never incorporated them as citizens and had mindlessly exploited them. In *Pájinas libres* (1894) he thundered: "Chile's hands mangled our flesh and crushed our bones, but the real weapons of the enemy were our ignorance and our system of servitude" (44). He identified the judge, the governor, and the priest as the "trinity of [Indian] brutalization"(44). Education, especially science and other forms of secular learning, would set free not only the Indian, but the other equally ignorant classes that made up the Peruvian polity. In many ways, González Prada delineated the paths that the *indigenista* and the regionalist novel followed until the middle of the twentieth century.

Somewhat forgotten but straddling the period between the monumental work of César Vallejo and the dismantling of the old order carried out by González Prada, stands the figure of Ventura García Calderón (1886-1959). Like other influential Peruvians he spent most of his life in Europe. There he combined a career of diplomacy with journalism. He wrote fiction in Spanish—*La venganza del cóndor* (1924)—and in French—*Danger de mort* (1926) and *Couleur de sang* (1931). Embracing all three geographical regions of Peru his stories attempt to recover roots (Higgins 113). However, his influence in the formation of a national literature is more closely connected to his work as influential literary critic and his right-wing politics. His racists views were constantly contested by the provincial intellectuals who founded new literary circles and journals: *Atusparia* in Huaraz, *Boletín Kuntur* in Sicuani, *Warakú* in Arequipa, *Boletín Titicaca* in Puno, *La Sierra* and *La revista universitaria* in Cuzco. These provincial intellectuals put forth a project for Indian literacy in a newly negotiated citizenship contract. In 1938 the government of Peru asked him to edit the twelve volume *Biblioteca de Cultura Peruana*, which has ironically played a normative role in the writing of twentieth-century histories of Peruvian literature.

The history of painting during the Republican period begins with the diaspora of two generations of painters following the War of the Pacific. They went to Europe to improve and acquire technical knowledge. Often they worked successfully and even attained recognition in Paris or Rome (Lauer 34). Their pictorial language and topics tended to be "universal" or, rather, Eurocentric. Great painters such as Ignacio Merino, Francisco Laso, Carlos Baca Flor, and Daniel Hernández lived, worked, and died in the metropolis. Their strong suit was portraiture: it is said that the most famous Parisian actresses posed for Reynaldo Luza. A generation later, Felipe Cossio del Pomar became famous as a painter of sumptuous, half-naked *gringas* or the famous "Vargas Girls." Mirko Lauer argues that one of the important effects of the diaspora was to break the dependency of the artist from the Limeño and provincial oligarchies (36) and to "free" the imaginary of painting from the received colonial norms and tastes. However, despite this move to migration and residence in Europe, there was also a current of local painters whose work captured, in portrait and murals, the lived experience of the nineteenth century. Pancho Fierro's watercolors offer an example of such popular painting destined to be enjoyed by the same subjects depicted in the composition.

IV. THE TWENTIETH CENTURY

In 1870 the walls that protected Lima from Indians and pirates were demolished by the American engineer Henry Meiggs under contract with the Peruvian government. Lima's elites were dreaming of an elegant and open city in the modern French style. They wanted avenues, circular *plazas*, parks, and boulevards. Lima was enlarged and beautified. The passing from a Spanish spacial order into a modern urban complex is captured in the nostalgic *Una Lima que se va* (1921) by the *cronista* José Gálvez (Elmore 23-25).

In his *Lima la horrible* (1964), the poet Sebastián Salazar Bondy (1924-1965) finds that the *conspiración colonialista* (23-33) which Palma constructed, despite the dismantling work of José Carlos Mariátegui (1895-1930), remained alive in the myths that sustained the centrality and sophistication of Lima's lifestyle: to flatter fawningly, to please, to homogenize. For Salazar Bondy the myth of a colonial arcadia on which Lima based its claims to hegemony rest in the cultural cycle of *sátira-*

lisura-huachafería, (satire—the fleetingly malicious phrase—the pastiche) (Salazar Bondy 69-73). The task of getting through this culture of deception and amusement in order to uncover the realities which formed the country was to be the work of a variegated but always multiplying cadre of intellectuals and artist coming from all areas of Peru to participate in a construction of the national center—a process which has, of course, not yet ended.

In a manner of speaking, the construction of a real center for a real country began with the publication of Peru's first literary history. José de la Riva Agüero (1885-1944) argued in *Carácter de la literatura del Perú independiente* (1905) that in responding to the question "Is there a Peruvian Literature"? the answer had to be in the negative. For him, Peruvian literature, just like Latin American literature, was already irremediably inscribed within the borders of Western culture and thus Peruvian writers could not aspire to originality. They could only hope to achieve a certain accent or peculiarity (Delgado 7).

At the same time that Riva Agüero wrote in Lima, intellectual activity in the provincial universities was producing irreversible changes in the production of knowledge and national subjects in Peru. The Universidad de San Antonio Abad in Cuzco led the way in university reform. The reforming students in Cuzco, inspired by the rediscovery of Machu Picchu in 1911 threw out the old-fashioned authorities, held elections for the first time, and chose the U.S. citizen Albert Giesecke as rector of the university. It is said the Cuzco and Arequipa were closer to Buenos Aires and its spirit of modernity than to Lima. European magazines, newspapers and books arrived directly and in great numbers to southern Peru. Many key cultural groups emerged at this time: "Resurgimiento" in Cuzco, "Orkopata" in Puno and "La Bohemia" in Trujillo. Neither the recently founded School of Engineering (1896) nor the Agronomy School (1902) could accommodate all those who sought technical degrees. Many middle-class men and women went to Chile and Argentina in search of a better college and university education.

Lima was to be the recipient of these forces of renovation and innovation emerging from the different regions of the country. A few names make the point: Julio C. Tello (1880-1947), archeology (Huarochirí); Abraham Valdelomar (1888-1919), journalism, fiction (Ica); César Moro (1903-1956) and Carlos Oquendo de Amat (1899-1936), poetry (Puno); Alberto Hidalgo (1897-1967), poetry; Percy Gibson (1908-1969), theater (Arequipa); Jorge

Basadre (1903-1980), history (Tacna); José Carlos Mariátegui (1894-1930), political theory; Luis E. Valcárcel (1891-1987), history (Moquegua); César Vallejo (1892-1938), poetry; Víctor Raúl Haya de la Torre (1895-1979), political theory, politician (La Libertad); Enrique López Albújar (1872-1966), narrative, journalism (Lambayeque); and Mariano Iberico (1892-1974), medicine (Cajamarca) (Burga and Flores Galindo 169). There were also many readers of newspapers and magazines; the latter increased from 167 in 1918 to 473 in 1928. Most of the intellectuals mentioned above contributed regularly to magazines and news papers. The fact that Mariátegui published extensive portions of his *Siete ensayos de interpretación de la realidad peruana* (1928) in journals is evidence of the confidence placed in the intellectual sophistication of the public (Manrique, 215-219). Intellectuals writing in Lima or abroad expected now to have a national audience. The proliferation of intellectuals identified with liberal positions and strongly affected by both the Mexican and the Russian revolutions set off a reaction on the part of the old oligarchy in conjunction with the Catholic church. In 1917 they founded the Universidad Católica as a focus of resistance.

By 1928 there were 2,290 university students in the country, and 1,849 were enrolled in San Marcos. In 1919 an alliance of labor and intellectuals brought university reform to San Marcos. More than two thirds of the students enrolled at San Marcos were born in the provinces. An unexpected great transformation was about to take place. These intellectuals were to enact a second modern national foundation, one in which Lima would take a central but always contested hegemony.

Contemporary Peruvian painting begins with a formal break made with academic painting. The professional plastic arts are now local in inspiration. However, both the market as well as the institutions connected with the valorization and circulation of art were incipient in Peru. The Museo de Historia Nacional directed by Max Uhle and the *Academia Concha* were in the 1920's the two major institutions concerned with art (Lauer 48). The Escuela Nacional de Bellas Artes would not have been possible without these two pioneers. Local painters, with their local landscapes, began to foster the idea of paintings as objects of domestic decoration.

Daniel Hernández was asked to direct the Escuela Nacional de Bellas Artes in 1919. Within three years the school roster showed among its students the group of painters that would create modern Peruvian painting: Julia Codesido, Elena Izcue, Ricardo Goyburo, Alejandro González, Emilio Hohkpler, Carlos Quíspez Asín, and Jorge Vinatea Reynosa

(Lauer 67). The influence of the *indigenista* José Sabogal was, however, the factor that would give the avant-garde its determining characteristics. The rediscovery of pre-Hispanic art, the arrival of nationalism, and the "isms" of the avant-garde mean that developments in painting parallel those in literature. The cultural nationalism of the 1920's can be summarized in Mariátegui's dictum "Let us make Peru Peruvian" (Lauer 81). However, no other artist embodied all the contradictions of this period better than José Sabogal. His work is not so much *indigenista* as a dedication to the rural town. With their colorful houses and *patios*, for the first time human figures of all classes and phenotypes (Lauer 103) were depicted. Sabogal did not like the *indigenista* label for his work. He thought of the school he headed as a movement towards a rediscovery of Peruvian humanity (Lauer 113).

After the World War I Europe was thought to be bankrupt, and artists and intellectuals, while not being parochial, turned their gaze to their immediate intellectual surroundings. During the nineteenth century, localized Romanticism, Naturalism, and especially Positivism had accumulated a vigorous legacy in Latin America. In Peru the initiator of the regional, realistic novel was Abraham Valdelomar (1888-1919) whose short fiction attached a new emotive value to the evocation of simple and sunny provincial life. The recovery of the presence of the Indian continued with *Cuentos andinos* (1920; *Andean Stories*) and the novel *Matalaché* (1928) by Enrique López Albújar (1872-1966). His narratives painted a wide and colorful canvas of rural life. Oral tradition and bilingual *mestizo* lore were skillfully woven in the representation of everyday life. This regionalist trend in fiction was also shaped by the consequences of the students' movement for university reform.

In *Perú: problema y posibilidad* (1931), the historian Jorge Basadre (1903-1980) wrote that the Indian question and the problem of national identity had become indistinguishable. National identity transcended territorial and juridical problems and instead it came to be understood as a negotiation of a series of contradictions (Elmore 100). Thus the electoral project labelled *La Nueva Patria* which swept Augusto B. Leguía (1863-1932) into the presidency responded to the demands made by, or in behalf of, the long neglected indigenous majority of Peru. Leguía created an Office for Indigenous Affairs, headed by the distinguished sociologist Hildebrando Castro Pozo (1890-1945). The dedication of an official holiday to the commemoration of the Indian (*el Día del Indio*) signaled the institutionalization of the assimilation of the largely rural indigenous population into the official and mainstream life of the nation.

In history, sociology, anthropology, the arts, and politics the concept of the "Indian," as a suppressed national subject, functioned as a pivotal locus for the re-elaboration of self and national identities. Nevertheless, in literary salons, poetry readings and Sunday literary pages, it was the noisy and sentimental verse of José Santos Chocano (1875-1934) which received official acclaim. The symbolist verse of José María Eguren (1874-1942) was accorded a muffled and truncated reception and its impact would not be felt until after the change in sensibilities which emerged after the World War II.

The publication of *Los heraldos negros* (1918; *The Black Heralds*) by César Vallejo (1892-1938) constitutes the major watershed in modern Peruvian literature and a major shift for poetry in the Spanish language as a whole. The *Colónida* group of poets had already distanced itself from *modernism*, emphasizing a simpler and more direct rhetoric. Alberto Hidalgo (1897-1967) had burst into the scene with his avant-garde poetics in *Arenga lírica al Emperador de Alemania* (1916). But the full extent of the crisis of the old epistemology was not revealed until Vallejo began to publish. He depicted a numbed and bewildered humanity in the face of unceasing and senseless pain synthesized in the title poem: "Hay golpes en la vida, tan fuertes ... Yo no sé." This young provincial Peruvian, operating from a remote corner of the world, pursued a radical inquiry into language and metaphysics and he established that Spanish American artists no longer needed to emulate European models before finding the caliber and horizon for their own thinking.

Vallejo was born in Santiago de Chuco, an isolated Andean village in northern Peru. But the geographical distance separating Santiago de Chuco from Lima and even Paris had already been shortened in both time and space. By the time Vallejo arrived in Lima in 1917 he had studied literature and law at the National University in Trujillo and he had already fielded fully the challenge that modern science and philosophy posed for Romanticism and Christianity. Among the books that Vallejo received as university prizes in 1913 and 1914 we find Hippolyte Taine's *Nineteenth-Century French Philosophy* (1857), Max Müller's *History of Religion*, Ludwig Gumplowitc's *Social Philosophy* (1910), Gérard's *Attic Eloquence*, and Ernst Henri's *The Riddle of the Universe* (1900) (Franco 9). The shattering effect that evolution theory had on Vallejo's concept of the poet and man's place in this crazed universe is evident in *Los heraldos negros* (1919).

During his years in Trujillo, and as a member of the Trujillo Bohemia, which had its counterpart in many other provincial cities, Walt Whitman, Maeterlinck, Emerson, Unamuno, Rodó and an anthology of French symbolism poetry were avidly read and discussed. Spanish and French literary magazines placed in Vallejo's hands a good sampling of the intellectual and artistic effervescence created by Aragon, Apollinaire, Tzara, Duhamel, and Claudel in Paris. *Claridad, Proa*, and other Argentinean magazines were also regularly received all over Peru. Contact with these liberating projects and practices made living in the colonial atmosphere of Trujillo only more claustrophobic. In 1917 Vallejo, like thousands of other provincial intellectuals of the period, embarked for Lima. There he found a job as a school teacher. In the elegant and snobbish Lima of the time, he was lucky enough to be admitted to the literary circle of the Conde de Lemos, Valdelomar's literary pseudonym (Franco 15).

Vallejo's questioning of the Romantic myth of the poet deepened while in Lima. However, his interview with González Prada, now Director of the National Library, proved encouraging. Vallejo felt reassured in his iconoclastic search for radical originality and regeneration. The fame he had gained with *Los heraldos negros* was not enough, however, to guarantee him employment or provide him with an adequate community of readers. When the absolutely genial and radically different *Trilce* appeared in 1922 the reception ranged from hostile to frigid. Influential reviewers deemed the book "incomprehensible," or weird (Franco 25). By the time he wrote *Trilce*, Vallejo had not only digested Kant, Rousseau, Spinoza, and Henri Barbusse, but he knew that philosophy furnished inadequate explanations to the problem of self and knowledge in a godless universe. If Vallejo cited the names of modern philosophers it was not to authorize his thought on their work but rather to make a parodic on the insufficiency of their discourse.

Trilce proved to be a revolutionary book devoted to the radical exploration and sub-version of language. It embraces and wrestles with the results from the fall of the individual self and the impossibility of knowledge. Vallejo's quest for an authentic language annihilates the possibility of the "I" type of enunciation: the individual's voice in blurred into the regularity of nature's rhythms and man can no longer claim a privileged place in the workings of the universe. *Trilce* denies all possibility of transcendental design and purpose and the poet is left, as Jean Franco has put it, with the "puzzle of his own motivation" (81). Already with *Los heraldos negros*,

Vallejo had understood the destabilizing possibilities of ungrammatical or in-human language. In many ways *Trilce* was ahead of its time and heralded the Derridean theory of language. Vallejo wrote against the grain: he roughened language, the idea of expression, and the aspiration to making sense. This prescient discovery was perhaps linked to his knowledge of Quechua and the untranslatability of linguistic forms.

Vallejo produced exploding and yet dense and resisting texts (Franco 91), in striking contrast with the poetry that preceded and surrounded his work. His dismantling of the received poetics together with the elaboration of his own horizon constituted the appearance of the personal as the foundation in the national-universal and would be regarded as such by all who wrote after him.

Despite Vallejo's monumental status, literary history cannot ignore the several other major poets whose profoundly innovative work made up the many layered legacy of the avant-garde in Peru. Like much of the Latin American avant-garde, Alejandro Peralta (1899-1973) in *Kollao* (1934); Carlos Oquendo de Amat (1905-1936) in *Cinco metros de poemas* (1927) (*Five Meters of Poems*), Emilio Adolpho Westphalen (1911) in *Abolición de la muerte* (1935) (*Abolition of Death*), and César Moro's (born Alfredo Quíspez Asín, 1903-1956) in his Surrealist verse (written almost entirely in French), produced contestable texts which were simultaneously international and autochthonous. The avant-garde, stimulated and observed by José Carlos Mariátegui's critical eye, came to constitute a wide spectrum in artistic production; it cannot be regarded as the arbitrary appearance of genius but rather as the emergence of a cultural formation long in the making.

La casa de cartón (1928; *The Cardboard House*) is the narrative masterwork of the avant-garde. Written by the brilliant poet Martín Adán (1908-1985, born Rafael de la Fuente Benavides), this version of the artist as a young man story relies on broken rhythms, sketchy character portrayal, and neologisms. It has no plot. The forty prose fragments (Unruh 105) evoke, with a mixture of humor and nostalgia, the relationship of the young man to his upper-class surroundings. Easy pleasure is mixed with the despair of the cultural desert in which his class navigates. The narrator is familiar with foreign writers and feels anxious about his easy but fragile acquisition of European culture. Tempted by the familiar option of a trip and even residence in Paris and despite the family's pressure to give up his artistic aspirations, the narrator decides to stay in Lima and accept his artistic vocation. The world of literature, the cardboard house, remains as his only possible world. This manifesto for an interior exile found very few readers, remaining only a literary curiosity. The influence of the recluse Martín Adán was to skip a generation.

The growth of capitalism with its concomitant destruction of the ancient Andean economies and ways of life aggravated the conditions of the Indians' life both in the cities, the haciendas, and the small towns which dot the Andean mountain ranges. Thus the Indian problem continued to command the attention of the intellectuals. A radical *indigenista*, Luis E. Valcárcel (1891-1987), argued that the ancient Andean cultures were not dead, that the Indians' indigenous culture had survived the brutal process of conquest and colonization, and that it was now poised to descend onto the more Hispanized coastal towns and cities and reconquer the country. Although such a thesis seemed to exaggerate the vitality of the Indian culture, the demographic explosion and migration to the coastal cities that began in the 1930's, in a way, made good Valcárcel's prediction. This thesis connected with the findings made by archeology, anthropology, and history. The rediscovery of Machu Picchu in 1911, the work of Julio C. Tello (1880-1947) on the pre-Inca Paracas and Chavín civilizations, and the excavations of the city of Chán-Chán in Trujillo began to point to a very long and ancient history which needed to be dealt with as intellectuals struggled with the question of national identity. Uriel García (1884-1965), author of *El nuevo indio* (1929), remarks on the intersection of the indigenista movement in the 1930's and their contact with *The Decline of the West* by Oswald Spengler (Flores Galindo 43). There appeared to be a coincidence between Spengler's exultation of the order of rural life and its sublime relation to the environment with the *indigenists'* own sense of a beneficent and ordered rural world. Neither Henri Bergson, Nietzsche, nor Keiserling was absent from this panorama of the doubled construction of the autochthonous (Elmore 41).

José Carlos Mariátegui (1895-1930) and Víctor Raúl Haya de la Torre (1895-1979) formed part of this political and intellectual ferment which was in turn spurred by both the Mexican (1910) and the Russian (1917) revolutions. The possibility of constructing new societies, free of the exploitation of humanity by humanity that was implicit in capitalism, had spread around the world. While in Italy, Mariátegui observed and analyzed European culture with an ethnographic eye. He read in German, French, English, and of course Italian. For him, as with many other Peruvians—Pablo de Olavide, Ventura García Calderón, César Moro—to be *afrancesado* or intensely

Europeanized was a way of being creatively Peruvian. Deep knowledge of all things European provided the critical distance for emancipation from the Eurocentric *religión del progreso* (Flores Galindo 42-44). Upon his return from Italy, drawing on his experience with Antonio Gramsci's work, Mariátegui founded the newspaper *La Razón*, and with it he inaugurated analytical journalism. His critique of the fundamental assumptions by which the dominating classes had understood and ruled Peru was immediately perceived as a threat. Mariátegui disagreed with Leguía's project of assimilating the Indian "masses." He thought that the Indian cultures should have a chance to stand discreetly on their own. Leguía closed *La Razón*; Mariátegui then founded the journal *Amauta* (1926-30) in whose pages were to collaborate the most distinguished Peruvian and Latin American thinkers and artists of the period. The impact of *Amauta* lasted well beyond the years of its publication. It created a new climate of opinion, a new concept of how Peru should be viewed within the context of the modern world. With the publication of *Siete ensayos de interpretación de la realidad peruana* (1928) (*Seven Interpretative Essays on Peruvian Reality*, 1991) Mariátegui was recognized as one of the most important political and cultural theoreticians of the twentieth century.

Mariátegui's analysis of Peruvian reality devolved on the relation of economic to social and cultural structures. For the first time the colonial feudal landowning oligarchy was seen as the force that held back modern development of the economy and the society as a whole. Among other things, Mariátegui concluded that the necessary emancipation of the Indian peasantry was to be achieved as part of a general agrarian reform which would restore the land to the Indians who worked it. He also analyzed literature in terms of its role in the formation of the nation-state and found the Peruvian panorama deficient. Furthermore, in one of his most important essays, "Arte, revolución y decadencia," Mariátegui argued that Ortega's views on *La deshumanización del arte* (1925) were fostering a misunderstanding about the nature of modern art in the Spanish-speaking world. For Mariátegui the concept of dehumanization corresponded to modern art's detached (decadent) spirit which carried the kernel for engaged and revolutionary artistic practices (Unruh 25). Mariátegui called for a synthesis of technical innovation and critical engagement.

Like Mariátegui, Haya de la Torre also thought that the struggle for modernization and emancipation centered on a fight against capitalist imperialism. He found his defining moment during the university student marches and protests against the government and the calls for university reform. Haya emerged as a charismatic speaker capable of leading the emerging urban masses. In 1924, while in exile in Mexico, he founded the political party APRA (Alianza Popular Revolucionaria Americana) and began his lifelong ambition to revolutionize the political and social structures of life in Latin America. In 1927 he published his influential *Por la emancipación de América Latina* (*For the Emancipation of Latin America*). His later *El antiimperialismo y el APRA* (1935; *Anti-Imperialism and the APRA*), offered a synthesis of his political thought and program for Peru. He spent a good part of his life in exile and his presidential ambitions were forever thwarted.

APRA played an important role in the life of many artists and intellectuals in Peru. Magda Portal (1903-1989), like many other *apristas*, suffered prison and exile, defining a new profile for women as a politician and writer. As a feminist she called attention to the precursor role of Flora Tristán (1803-1844) and wrote a biography of the Franco-Peruvian socialist. However, it is her autobiography *Ser mujer en el Perú* (1979; *Being Woman in Peru*) that is of greater interest today. Ciro Alegría (1909-1967), the father of the modern Peruvian novel, author of the prize-winning *El mundo es ancho y ajeno* (1941; *Broad and Alien is the World*), was for many years an APRA party member. José María Arguedas (1911-1969), considered the greatest of all Peruvian novelists, expressed a lack of confidence in APRA and its aspirations to represent the interests of either the working classes or the Indians in the haciendas and *ayllus* (Indian communities).

Writing a few years after the World War II, Arguedas mounted a serious critique of *indigenista* writers. He felt that they spoke about a phantasmagoric Indian who in fact did not exist. The Indian of novels such as *Huasipungo* (1934) by Jorge Icaza (1906-1978) was an abject being, deprived of all subjectivity and intelligence. This Indian was both hopeless and false, and his advocates did, in Arguedas's mind, more harm than good. In contrast, Arguedas's fiction did capture the Indian perspective on the world, and in doing so, offered a sophisticated and rich tapestry of feeling, complex thought, and self-understanding heretofore unknown by those outside the Indian world. Arguedas's narrators are not outside observers of the Indian's suffering, joy, or tactical struggles. They either partake of Indian consciousness or struggle to sympathetically share visions and concerns in a mutual defense for life and cultural survival. In his first collection of short stories *Agua* (1935; *Water*), as well as his masterwork *Los ríos profundos* (1958; *Deep Rivers*), Arguedas narrates from within the density of the rural world.

Many, if not most of these intellectuals, came to Lima from the provinces in one or another of the successive migratory waves by which Lima was to lose its viceregal and "hispanic" mythical character. Lima became the site of *cholo* (the not quite sophisticated or modernized subjects) occupation. During the 1940's Lima saw the arrival of 218,955 people from the provinces (Elmore 147). In the 1950's the city's population swelled by one third (364,000). Arequipa, Trujillo, and other coastal cities suffered a corresponding influx of migration from the highlands. This demographic revolution has not yet come to a halt and the economic, social, political, and cultural consequences have been unimaginable. Salazar Bondy in *Lima la horrible* had already pointed out that Lima's own cultural essence was inauthenticity. The *kitsch* style of superficial and false imitation was in fact Lima's chief characteristic before the popular migrations. With the migratory waves Lima passed quickly from a false viceregal demeanor to the style of the squalor and hopelessness of a Third World capital. Lima's population at the start of the millennium exceeded seven million (Klarén 434, Table 3).

During this period the writing of history became more institutionalized. Raúl Porras Barrenechea (1897-1960), professor and diplomat, left behind a host of disciples. Though he never wrote a major work himself, his method of archival research trained many of the superb historians that were to come a generation later. Luis Alberto Sánchez (1900-1994) authored many books on Peruvian literature and taught for many years at several universities. He controlled the pages of several literary supplements as well as access to fellowships for study abroad. However, the most comprehensive, intelligent, and objective account of the formation of the nation was written by Jorge Basadre (1903-1980) in his ten volume *Historia de la república del Perú* (1949; *History of the Republic of Peru*) (Delgado 127-128).

Fiction in Peru grew thickly with the contributions made by a host of excellent novelists who focused on the teeming urban centers. Enrique Congrains (1932-2009) and Julio Ramón Ribeyro (1929-1994) captured the gray tones of Lima, the decaying odor of the old oligarchy, the daily erosion of the very order that Mariátegui had wanted to dismantle, the despair of the middle classes. There appeared no horizon beyond the routine frustration of marginal work, boring love making, and the eternal duration of the spiritual fog that engulfs Lima's life. Carlos Eduardo Zavaleta (b. 1928), Luis Loayza (b. 1934), Oswaldo Reynoso (b. 1932) have also finely examined the intricacies of a sad and subtly violent Limeño life.

With the accelerated crisis of the agricultural sector, social and political conflict overwhelmed all other orders of perception. Landscape, nature, and family receded into the background. The generation of 1950, marked by the Cuban Revolution and the Cold War, responded in several different ways to both the aesthetic and political challenges before them. Anchored in the minuscule splintering of the Left, the social sciences produced towering figures such as Luis Lumbreras in archeology, Alfredo Torero in linguistics, Julio Cotler and Aníbal Quijano in sociology, Pablo Macera and Carlos Araníbar in history, and Luis Millones, Manuel Burga, and Tito Flores Galindo in ethno-history. Abimael Guzmán, the leader of *Sendero Luminoso* (The Shining Path), together with other intellectuals and artists who sought revolutionary change in Peru, also belong to this generation

The cosmopolitization of poetry blurred the opposition between the pure poetry and the politically engaged poets. Washington Delgado observes that there seems to be an alternating current in Peruvian literary practices. Periods of fecund poetry writing seemed followed by explosion in novelistic innovation. In the 1960's the blending and distancing of pure poetry with socially committed verse in the work of Jorge Eduardo Eielson (1924-2006), Sebastián Salazar Bondy (1924-1965), Javier Sologuren (1921-2004), Blanca Varela (1926-2009), Washington Delgado (1927-2003), and Juan Gonzalo Rose (1928-1988) achieved a radical revitalization of poetic form and language. Their poetics mark a high point in the tradition of skeptical lucidity. Carlos Germán Belli (1927) with *Oh! Hada cibernética* (1961), *El pie sobre el cuello* (1964), and many other collections represents this generation's return to a classic and yet colloquial language capable of articulating themes of universal import in humble and mundane settings. James Higgins thinks that this is indeed a remarkable generation of poets whose standards are unmatched anywhere in Latin America (293). Younger poets such as Antonio Cisneros (1942) with *Los comentarios reales* (1964; *The Royal Commentaries*) and *El libro de Dios y de los húngaros* (1978), and Rodolfo Hinostroza (1941) with *Consejero del Lobo* (1965; *The Wolf's Adviser*), and, of course the mourned guerrilla Javier Heraud (1942-1963), cultivated a matter-of-fact and yet lyrical language which expressed deep political commitment (in the line of César Vallejo) together with a serious inquiry into a poetics for a perilous and uncertain world.

This period also saw a greater professionalization on the part of the artist. The presence of Kafka, Joyce, Huxley, and Faulkner (in translation) became generalized in the university literature curriculum. At the same time, an iconoclastic push for innovation and even radical change was once again emerging from the provincial sector. The "Grupo Renovador Alkamari" in Cuzco, the "Avanzada Sur" in Arequipa, the "Peña del Mar" and "Bahía" in Trujillo, the "Raíz de Piedras" in Huancayo, mobilized great political and cultural energies at a very high level of sophistication (Gutiérrez 49).

Three Peruvian fiction writers achieved international acclaim and financial success. The first to jump onto the presses of international marketing was Mario Vargas Llosa (b. 1936) with his technically innovating, wrenching, and captivating *La ciudad y los perros* (1963; *Time of the Hero*). Almost a decade later Alfredo Bryce Echenique (1939) with *Un mundo para Julius* (1970; *A World for Julius*), with a light prose and profound humor, would portray the happy ending world of the Peruvian ancient regime. Manuel Scorza (1928-1983) died soon after a long residence in Europe which launched his fiction onto the international market. His most notable achievement is the narrative cycle of five novels which began with *Redoble por Rancas* (1970; *Drums for Rancas*) and ended with *La tumba del relámpago* (1979; *Lightning's Tomb*). Differing from Vargas Llosa, who strongly criticized *indigenismo*, and especially Arguedas for holding onto the vision of an archaic utopia, Scorza renacted *indigenismo*, while revising the traditional assumptions of realism.

This was a very fecund period in Peruvian letters, music, theater, and art. The work of painters such as Fernando de Szyszlo (b. 1925), Armando Villegas (b. 1926), Víctor Humareda (1920-1986), and Tilsa Tsuchiya (1936-1984) achieved international recognition. Because Peruvian presses do not distribute internationally nor market their publications outside Peru, the fiction of many excellent writers remained at home: José Adolph (b. 1933), José Antonio Bravo (b. 1939), César Calvo (1940-2000), Eduardo González Viaña (1941), Miguel Gutiérrez (b. 1940), and Edgardo Rivera Martínez (b. 1934). The phenomenon of exile or simply migration began to show in the publication of novels written about Peru by writers who left during their formative years. For the first time Peruvians of African ancestry broke into the mainstream of publication. Antonio Gálvez Ronceros (b. 1931) and Gregorio Martínez (b. 1942) were highly praised for the transgressive humor and linguistic play of their prose.

The towering figure of the period is Mario Vargas Llosa. He brought literary renovation to a stale realism. He has maintained an astonishing rhythm of publication. Like other Peruvian intellectuals, he has lived all his adult life in Europe. He has achieved bestseller status not only in Spanish but in many of the other languages into which his novels and journalism have been translated. Despite the editorial success of novels like *La tía Julia y el escribidor* (1977; *Aunt Julia and the Scriptwriter*) his most important novel is *Conversación en la Catedral* (1969; *Conversation in the Cathedral*). There, he couples his brilliant novelistic technique with his deepest reflection on human motivation and its relation to violence as a social organizing principle. His characters struggle naively, unknowingly, against a historically imbedded chain to the past that devastates their lives. In his later novels Vargas Llosa switches tone and attitude. The discrepancy between the character's capacity to face the crushing forces of life and their insufficient awareness of their tragic circumstances is no longer set in a tragic mode. Now, the effect is one of humor. Like Miguel Gutiérrez in *La violencia del tiempo* (1991; *The Violence of Time*), Edgardo Rivera Martínez in *País de Jauja* (1993; *The Land of Plenty*), Vargas Llosa in his absorbing *La guerra del fin del mundo* (1981; *The War of the End of the World*), participated in the marvelous revival of the historical novel in Peru and Latin America.

The last two decades of the twentieth century have been a period of profound change in Peru. Twelve years of military dictatorship ushered in a panoply of long overdue and inexpertly carried out reforms. The agrarian reform that resulted in the peasants leaving the land and joining the urban poor brought forth a parallel informal society; change was deep, disturbing, and chaotic. As the country moved back into the game of electoral politics the guerrilla *Sendero Luminoso* (Shining Path) intensified its terrorist campaign against the state, especially in Lima. Plagued by uncertainty, wage depression, protracted and deep unemployment, the death of thousands of its poorest citizens, and the inept and untold corruption of the Alan García administration, the country plunged into economic and social collapse. In 1987 Vargas Llosa, wrapped in the prestige conveyed upon him by his brilliant international success as a writer of novels, decided to run for the presidency. The winner of the elections of 1990 was the then unknown Alberto Fujimori.

As the country collapsed and massive shifts of power and identity were taking place in the heart of darkness, artistic and intellectual production did not, as one would have expected, come to a halt. In a disenchanted assessment of the loosely grouped generation of 1950, Miguel Gutiérrez questioned the social and historical analysis provided by historians, social scientists, and even poets of his generations in reference to the revolutionary struggle that defined Peruvian history during the latter part of this century. Writing during the height of the terror, Gutiérrez felt that the much-admired Pablo Macera acted as a free shooter during the years when the generation split apart into several irreconcilable partisan sectors (Gutiérrez 207) which denied the country appropriate political and intellectual leadership. He is equally critical of the uses that Aníbal Quijano makes of Mariátegui. In the midst of the terror in the streets and the massacres carried out by the state in prisons and villages, Peruvians of all classes migrated to Europe, the United States, Canada, and even Australia.

However, among those who stayed, there emerged compact groups of younger generations of fiction writers, poets, and playwrights. In popular music, *chicha*—a blending of Andean rhythms and *cumbia*—and salsa invaded the country's airwaves and dance halls. Short, galvanizing plays were staged in the multiple theater houses in Lima and other cities. Television journalism began to play an important role in the shaping of the citizen's awareness of the country's disastrous situation and the lack of future prospects. Many new national subjects made their entrance into the main stream of Peruvian public spheres: working-class women, peasants, youth leaders, shanty town leaders, women journalists, judges, *guerrillas*, terrorists, new *beatas*, and saints.

More recently, the publication of thousands of poems in short-lived literary magazines, university gazettes, and literary journals has acquired a greater intensity with the return to democratic forms of political expression. Poetic movements such as *Hora Zero* (1970-73) and *La sagrada familia* (1975) rang iconoclastic bells. Carmen Ollé (b. 1947), the most respected feminine voice, is associated with the aesthetics of *Hora Zero* which, in a way, evoke the concept of *écriture* explored by Roland Barthes in his epoch making *Writing Degree Zero* (1965). Very young women poets coalesced around the notion of *zafarrancho*—bricolage, makeshift work—as the appropriate description of the kind of writing possible at the end of a century in which everything seems to have been tried and lived. Titles such as *La rosa fálica* (1983; *Phallic Rose*) by Sui Yun (b. 1955) and *Ese oficio no me gusta* (1987; *I Don't Like that Job*) by Rocío Silva Santisteban (b. 1963), capture the desire to write, together with the discomforting idea of being a poet.

Theater, in the last thirty years, has centered around very small stages like *Cuatrotablas*. The entire work tended to be collective. The *Grupo Yuyachkani* with their play *Los músicos ambulantes* (1979; *Itinerant Musicians*) has been enormously successful. This theater has been very timely. It stages plays with plots built around current important debates in national life and in that way it competes successfully with the immediacy of radio and television. Because of its simultaneous appeal to various modes of perception, theater garnishes the talent of painters, musicians, writers, actors, and producers, and thus it plays an increasingly important role in galvanizing large groups of artists and intellectuals—a role which the more solitary exercise of writing or painting had not been able to play. University theater production (San Marcos, the Universidad de Lima, the Universidad Católica) also played an important role in popularizing experimental theater (Higgins 300-304). Film in Peru had its beginnings in the twenties with *Luis Pardo* (1927), directed by Enrique Cornejo Villanueva, and like theater, it has recently achieved national and international success with the adaptation of historical themes—*El caso Huayanay* (1981) and *Túpac Amaru* (1984)—or classical novels such as *La ciudad y los perros* (1984) and *Yawar fiesta* (1986).

Radio has played a capital role in the conservation and the dissemination of Andean languages and music. Radio and television has served to disseminate the work and personalities of writers actors, singers, dancers, politicians, historians, and even literary critics. Radio has stimulated the production and consumption of *huayno* and *yaraví* in the coastal cities and *marinera, cumbia, chicha, tondero,* and waltzes in the Andes. Both *criollo* and Andean music have produced a plethora of composers, musicians, singers, and dancers who perform with various degrees of commercial success.

Just like in music, painting, political theory, and the social sciences, the arts and crafts in the twentieth century in Peru have experienced the impact of the provincial and lower classes at the previously dominant center. The result has been an unimaginable multiple enriching of the intellectual and artistic life of a sleepy and remote colonial region of the world in which vast creative powers of all races have transformed and continue to change the national cultural legacy.

This chapter was originally published in *Literary Cultures of Latin America: a Comparative History* edited by Valdes & Kadir (2004) Chp.39 "Lima: A Blurred Centrality" by Castro-Klaren © Oxford University Press, Ltd. By permission of Oxford University Press.

WORKS CITED

ADÁN, Martín [Rafael de la FUENTE BENAVIDES]. *La casa de cartón*. Lima: Talleres de Impresiones y Encuadernaciones Perú, 1928.

AGURTO CALVO, Santiago. *Lima pre-hispánica*. Lima: Finanpro, 1984.

BACACORZO, Javier. "El pasquín y su trascendencia en la lucha libertaria nacional." In *Literatura de la emancipación*. Lima: Universidad Nacional Mayor de San Marcos, 1972. 16-26.

BAKEWELL, Peter. *A History of Latin America: Empires and Sequels, 1450-1930*. Cambridge: Blackwell Publishers, 1997.

BAYÓN, Damián. "The Architecture and Art of Colonial Spanish America." *CHLA*, 2: 709-45.

BAYÓN, Damián and Marx Murillo. *History of South American Colonial Art and Architecture*. New York: Rizzoli, 1992.

BERMÚDEZ-GALLEGOS, Marta. *Poder y transgresión: Perú, metáfora e historia*. Lima: Latinoamericana Editores, 1996.

BEVERLEY, John. *Una modernidad obsoleta: estudios sobre el barroco*. Caracas: Fondo Editorial A.L.E.M., 1997.

BRADING, David. *The First America: The Spanish Monarchy, Creole Patriots, and the Liberal State 1492-1867*. Cambridge: Cambridge University Press, 1991.

BURGA, Manuel and Alberto FLORES GALINDO. *Apogeo y crisis de la república aristocrática*. Lima: Rikchay Perú, 1979.

BURKHOLDER, Mark A. and Lynman L. Johnson. *Colonial Latin America*. New York: Oxford University Press, 1998.

CASTRO-KLARÉN, Sara. "El siglo XVIII: sujetos subalternos y el teatro de la Perricholi." In Ed. Francisco La Rubia Prado and Jesús Tordecilla, *Razón, tradición y modernidad: re-visión de la ilustración hispánica*. Madrid: Tecnos, 1996. 87-99.

CHANG-RODRÍGUEZ, Raquel. "La subversión del barroco en *Amar su propia muerte* de Juan de Espinosa Medrano." In Ed. Mabel Moraña. *Relecturas del Barroco de Indias*. Hanover: Ediciones del Norte, 1994. 117-148.

COSTIGAN, Lúcia Helena. *A sátira e o intelectual criollo na colônia: Gregorio de Matos e Juan del Valle y Caviedes*. Lima: Latinoamericana Editores, 1991.

DELGADO, Washington. *Historia de la literatura republicana: nuevo carácter de la literatura en el Perú independiente*. Lima: Ediciones Rikchay, 1980.

DURÁN MONTERO, María Antonia. *Lima en el siglo XVII: Arquitectura, urbanismo y vida cotidiana*. Sevilla: Diputación de Sevilla, 1994.

ELMORE, Peter. *Los muros invisibles: Lima y la modernidad en la novela del siglo XX*. Lima: Mosca Azul, 1993.

FANE, Diana. Ed. *Converging Cultures: Art and Identity in Spanish America*. Brooklyn: The Brooklyn Museum, 1996.

FRANCO, Jean. *César Vallejo: The Dialectics of Poetry and Silence*. Cambridge: Cambridge University Press, 1976.

GISBERT, Teresa. *Iconografía y mitos indígenas en el arte*. La Paz: Gisbert y Cia., 1980.

GONZÁLEZ PRADA, Manuel. *Pájinas Libres*. Lima: Thesis, 1966. [1894].

GUTIÉRREZ, Miguel. *La generación del 50: un mundo dividido*. Lima: Sétimo Ensayo, 1988.

HIGGINS, James. *A History of Peruvian Literature*. Liverpool: Cairns, 1987.

KLARÉN, Peter. *Peru: Society and Nationhood in the Andes*. New York: Oxford University Press, 2000.

KRISTAL, Efraín. *The Andes Viewed from the City: Literary Discourse and Political Discourse on the Indian in Peru 1848-1930*. New York: Peter Lang, 1987.

KUBLER, George and Martín SORIA. *Art and Architecture in Spain and Portugal and their American Dominions, 1500-1800*. Baltimore: Penguin Books, 1969.

LAUER, Mirko. *Introducción a la pintura peruana del siglo XX*. Lima: Mosca Azul, 1976.

LÓPEZ-BARALT, Mercedes. *Icono y conquista: Guamán Poma de Ayala*. Madrid: Hiperión, 1988.

LUMBRERAS, Luis G. *The Peoples and Cultures of Ancient Peru*. Trans. Betty J. Meggers. Washington D.C.: Smithsonian Institution Press, 1974.

—. *Visión arqueológica del Perú*. Lima: Milenario, 1990.

MACERA, Pablo. *Trabajos de historia*. (4 vols.) Lima: Instituto Nacional de Cultura, 1977.

MARIÁTEGUI, José Carlos. *Siete ensayos de interpretación de la realidad peruana*, Lima: Amauta, 1928.

—. *Seven Interpretative Essays of Peruvian Reality*. Trans. Marjory Urquidi. Austin: University of Texas Press, 1971.

MESA, José de and Teresa GISBERT. *Holguín y la pintura virreinal en Bolivia*. La Paz: Editorial Juventud, 1977.

Millones, Luis. *Nuestra Historia: Perú colonial*. Lima: COFIDE, 1995.

MORAÑA, Mabel, ed. *Relecturas del Barroco de Indias*. Havoner: Ediciones del Norte, 1994.

MORO, César [Alfredo Quíspez Asín]. *La tortuga ecuestre*. Lima: Ediciones Tigrondine, [1939] 1957.

OQUENDO DE AMAT, Carlos. *Cinco metros de poemas*. Lima: Editorial Decantar, 1927.

ORRILLO, Winston and Eduardo Congrains Martin, Eds. *Antología general de la prosa en el Perú*. (2 vols.) Lima: Encoma, 1971.

PERALTA, Alejandro. *Kollao*. Lima: Talleres de la Cía de Impresiones y Publicidad, 1934.

PORTAL, Magda. *Ser mujer en el Perú*. Lima: Topaku, 1979.

RIBEYRO, Julio Ramón. *Crónica de San Gabriel*. Lima: Ediciones Tawantisuyu, 1960.

—. *Los geniecillos dominicales*. Lima: Populibros Peruanos, 1965.

RODRÍGUEZ-GARRIDO, José A. "Espinosa Medrano: la recepción del sermón barroco y la defensa de los americanos." In Ed. Mabel Moraña. *Relecturas del Barroco de Indias*. Hanover: Ediciones del Norte, 1994. 149-172.

SALAZAR BONDY, Sebastián. *Lima la horrible*. Lima: Populibros, 1964.

SILVA SIFUENTES, Jorge. *Nuestra historia: el imperio de los cuatro suyos*. Lima: COFIDE, 1995.

STASTNY, Francisco. *Breve historia del arte en el Perú: la pintura precolombina, colonial y republicana*. Lima: Editorial Universo, 1967.

UNRUH, Vicky. *Latin American Vanguards: the Art of Contentious Encounters*. Berkeley: University of California Press, 1994.

WATANABE, Luis K. *Nuestra historia: culturas preincas del Perú*. Lima: COFIDE, 1995.

CHAPTER 7
Posting Letters: Writing in the Andes and the Paradoxes of the Post-colonial Debate

> "The universal, ecumenical road we have chosen to travel, and for which we are reproached, takes us ever closer to ourselves."
> José Carlos Mariátegui, *Seven Interpretative Essays on Peruvian Reality* (1928)

I. COLONIALITY AT LARGE

The postcolonial debate irrupted in the North American academy in the 1980's. At this time the field of Latin American Colonial Studies was being revamped in light of the questions prompted by the generalized reading of Guamán Poma's *El primer nueva corónica y buen gobierno* (1616?), Edmundo O'Gorman's *La invención de América. El universalismo en la cultura de Occidente* (1958), and the general opening in interpretation occurring as a result of structuralism first and post-modern theory later. The reading of Guamán Poma and Edmundo O'Gorman, widely separated in time but not in their hermeneutical thrust, inaugurated a thoroughgoing inquiry into the modes and consequences of Western historiography. They pushed the field beyond its standing empirical and philological parameters. Read in conjunction with new developments in semeiotics and French theory, both Guamán Poma and Edmundo O'Gorman posed questions that went far beyond the untrustworthiness of the Spanish chroniclers and their narratives of conquest in Mexico and the Tahuantinsuyo.

In very different languages and styles both the Andean Indian writing a letter to the king of Spain and the contemporary Mexican historian, understood that the problem of writing history rested in the occlusion of the epistemological assumptions underlining and regulating this narrative mode as an imperial modality of thought. Their focus on narrative rhetoric and the politics of writing—how is authority constituted, under what conditions has the information been gathered, from what power-knowledge

469

perspective is the narrative constructed, what is the author's locus of enunciation, who is the ideal reader of the narrative, what modes of persuasion
are being deployed in the construction of the truth of the narrative—placed
Guamán Poma and Edmundo O'Gorman at the center of unprecedented
scholarly discussions that shook our received understanding of the "colonial period." [1] The subsequent revision of the colonial period entailed deep
consequences for the whole of the study of Latin America. In the field of
"literature" the challenge posed by Borges's intertextual theory and the
undermining of the high-culture literary canon by the emergence of *testimonio* had begun an "internal" process of repositioning of period, genre,
and cultural boundaries that implied a thorough and profound movement
of all the existing posts and signs that allowed for the constitution of
objects of study.

It should thus not be surprising to see that the appearance of *Orientalism* (1979), by Edward Said, received a mixed reading. On the one hand
the thesis advanced in *Orientalism* seemed similar to the claims made in
O'Gorman's own thesis on the "invention"—the non-referential disposition of the epistemological object—of America by the historiography of
the sixteenth century. Said's sweeping inquiry was a brilliant investigation of Europe's invention of the Orient as its nineteenth-century other,
and it rang surprisingly familiar themes for scholars in the Latin American field. Reading *Orientalism* produced in students of Latin America
"the shock of recognition," an effect that, postcolonial theory claims,
takes place in the consciousness of postcolonial subjects as they asses
their experience of coloniality in comparison with the memory of other
colonial subjects. Said's daring reconnoitering of Europe's construction
of its other at once went beyond and also confirmed O'Gorman thesis
and insight into the nature of the writing of the history of empire and its
hierarchical impulses. Informed by Antonio Gramsci's views on culture
and Michel Foucault's discourse theory, Said, not unlike José Carlos
Mariátegui in his *Seven Interpretative Essays on Peruvian Reality* ([1928]
1971), brought under his scope not just historiography but also literature
and the human sciences to show the regulatory power of ideology. How-

---

[1] In part 2, chapter 3 of this volume "Air: Writing with his Thumb in the Air," I
develop at greater length the process of change in the field of colonial studies. As in this
chapter, I show there the reconfiguration of the field due to changes brought about by
Latin American scholars working in Latin America and high French theory at large.

ever, *Orientalism* provided yet another shock to students of colonial
Latin America. This time it was a shock of misrecognition, for Said's
imagination seemed to equate the history of colonialism exclusively with
Europe's penetration of the "Orient." Thus, his inquiry ignored the
Spanish conquest, the avatars of colonialism, and the inception of modernity in Ibero-America. Moreover, it seemed wholly unaware of the
thinking that Latin American intellectuals—from Garcilaso de la Vega,
Inca (1539-1616) onto Javier Clavijero (1731-1787) and César Vallejo
(1892-1938)—had been doing on the epistemological violence of the conquest and the subsequent subalternization of the knowledge of the other.

The purpose of this chapter is to map out the points of intersection
and of divergence between the most salient and influential aspects of
postcolonial theory, its paradoxes and thinking in the Andes on the questions of empire and coloniality. Since the span of thinking in the Andes is
as wide as it is fractured and as deep as it is heterogeneous, my effort
herein can thus only be preliminary. However, in going over the different
ways in which this mapping could begin to place some posts and markers
on the surface in order to sketch some lines and directions, I have found
that the inquiry undertaken by Mariátegui on the question of the discourse of colonialism is indeed paradigmatic; I therefore focus on his
main theses as points of departure. In short, I try to place Mariátegui's
inquiry into the workings of colonialism and the cultural force that it
deploys in dialogue with key topics and themes in postcolonial theory.
But first a word on coloniality and another on postmodern theory.

II. COLONIALITY

Coloniality is a concept put in circulation by Walter Mignolo. In his recent
*Local Histories/Global Designs: Coloniality, Subaltern Know ledges and
Border Thinking* (2000) Mignolo offers a sustained and ample treatment of
coloniality. Based on Aníbal Quijano's own conception of the coloniality
of power as the innermost chamber of capitalism, as an energy and machine
that transforms differences into values (14, 27-38), Mignolo conceives of
coloniality as a world-system that constitutes the underside of modernity
and whose duration has yet to reach its limits. For Mignolo, the colonial
difference is the space where the coloniality of power is enacted, where the
confrontation of local histories, displayed in different spaces and times

across the planet, takes place (*Local Histories* ix). The coloniality of power implies a fractured locus of enunciation as the subaltern perspective takes shape in response to the colonial difference and hegemonic discourse (x). Together with Quijano, Mignolo sees the constitution of the coloniality of power through the following operations:

1. The classification and reclassification of the planet's population, an operation in which the concept of culture (primitive, stages of development, Europe as the norm) plays a key role.
2. The creation of institutions whose functions is to articulate and manage such classifications (state institutions, universities, church, courts).
3. The definitions of spaces appropriate to such goals.
4. An epistemological perspective from which to articulate the meaning and the profile of the new matrix of power from out of which the new production of knowledge could be channeled (17).

This idea of coloniality of power as a world-system intersects in many areas with several of the main postulates of what has been configured as postcolonial theory in the work of scholars who write on the discursive characteristics of the imperial expansion of Europe over South East Asia, Australia, Canada, and the Middle East. One of the chief tenets in the concept of the coloniality of power is that the point for the inception of the modern/colonial as a world-system has to be set back to the time of the Spanish conquest of Amerindian societies and cannot assume, as postcolonial theory does, the Enlightenment to be the point of origin of Janus-like modernity. Consequently "post-colonial" theory, with its orientalist perspective, is repositioned. It is not the canvas. Rather it takes the place of an item within the larger canvas of struggles that 1492 brought about for the entire planet. Coloniality of power overcomes postcolonial theory in its temporal and spatial reach. Nevertheless, it is interesting to see that in the entry for "imperialism," the editors of *Key Concepts in Post-Colonial Studies* (1998), relying mainly on Said's later *Culture and Imperialism* (1993), write that "for post-colonial theory there was a continuous development of imperial rhetoric and imperial representation of the rest of the globe from at least the fifteenth century" (126).

Moreover, the idea of "coloniality at large" makes it easier to understand how within the evolving colonial distribution of tasks and hierarchies over the world's cultures and peoples, it was possible for *Orientalism* to ignore the history of Latin America in the making of a postcolonial world, if by postcolonial we understand all developments after contact between Europe and its othered or subalternized civilizations. One of the effects of the coloniality of power has been the production of hierarchies and differences among the colonized. The imperial English-speaking world, even at the fringe location of its colonial out-posts, has considered itself a notch "above" Latin America in the tree of knowledge. This perspective is itself the result of the imperial struggles between Spain and Northern Europe, a story much too complex to even allude to here, but one which is critically entwined with the rise of modernity and the location of Latin America in the mapping and distribution of knowledges. The coloniality of power had classified Amerindian and all subsequent knowledges forged in Latin America as subaltern and alien to the preoccupations of scholars like Said or Gayatri Spivak. They understood knowledge and power to reside at the seat of the colonizer, the subject position occupied by definition by the interlocutors of their writing. Much as Guamán Poma addressed his letter to the king of Spain, these English writing and speaking postmodern thinkers address their inquiry to the northern Euro-American academy.

Despite the fact that we do not yet have a south-south dialogue between, let us say, South East Asian scholars and Latin American scholars, a dialogue which was one of the objectives of the Latin American Subaltern Studies Group, concepts such as the coloniality of power, elaborated by Latin American scholars and certain claims made by postcolonial theory make it possible to think of a critical, plurotopic approach to cultural theory. A plurotopic approach would be more fitting with the critique of hegemony imbedded in postcolonial theory than monolingual, isolating, north-south two way dialogues between imperial and "former" subaltern subjects who, because of the accidents of history, share the same colonial language. In other words, a lot could be gained if Latin American scholars established a dialogue with scholars like Said or Homi Bhabha in order to come across the divide established by coloniality itself. If that where the case, a plurotopic space of debate could be inaugurated. Of course a predisposition to listening, on both sides, would be necessary. It is important to remember here that such a plurotopic dialogue is not without precedent. We are not inventing the wheel. The postcolonial hermeneutic of the modern/colonial world-system that the Spanish conquest inaugurated was already rendered plurotopic by Garcilaso's maneuvering of the Renaissance.[2] What follows in this chapter is thus not a search for unanimity but rather a mapping of convergences, differences, and paradoxes projected onto an uneven ground that shares a common horizon as this planet is enveloped by the vapors and flows of the power of empire.

III. COLONIALITY AND THE BATTLE FIELD

There are various ways of approaching a discussion of the terms of coloniality in the Andes and a possible intertextual and inter-subjective conversation with postcolonial theory across English, Spanish, Portuguese, and Amerindian languages such as Quechua and Aymara. Before beginning in any of the possible ways available to the analysis of the problem it is important to remind the reader that just as coloniality is marked by an intense heterogeneity so is the series of claims and topical discussions that "postcolonial theory" entails. Bart Moore-Gilbert in *Postcolonial Theory: Contexts, Practices, Politics* (1997) wrestles with the distinction and hostility between postcolonial theory and postcolonial criticism (5-17). He notes the emphasis on resistance in postcolonial criticism. Scholars and intellectuals who see the sign of postcolonial thinking as resistance to colonial discourse also express a persistent hostility to postcolonial theory which they find too closely associated with postmodern theory, a critique suspected of complicity with the very modernity that it deconstructs. As inaugurated by Edward Said, postcolonial theory entails "an approach to [colonial discourse] analysis from within methodological paradigms derived... from contemporary European cultural theories" (Moore-Gilbert 16). Moore-Gilbert discusses amply the various critiques that have been leveled to "postcolonial theory" as it appears in the work of Edward Said, Homi Bhabha, Gayatri Spivak, and Bill Ashcroft. Any reader of the works of these influential theorists knows that the differences between them are enormous, as each is closely associated with different and competing currents in European philosophy and theory. To

[2] There is no reader of Garcilaso de la Vega, Inca who does not immediately detect his command of Renaissance letters and the brilliant maneuvers to harness the Renaissance recovery of classical Greece and Rome in order for him to make the Inca civilization understandable to Europe's first modernity. See Durand; Zamora; Rabasa.

read Bhabha is to never forget Lacan and to follow Spivak is to always be more than aware of Derrida, Marx, and the ins and outs of the controversies in philosophy and literary theory in the United States academy. Postcolonial theory is by no means a set of coherent and integrated approaches, assumptions or methods in cultural analysis, but it has been an exceptionally important institutional development in the English speaking world. Moore-Gilbert emphasizes the "elasticity of the concept 'postcolonial.'" He thinks that its capacity to change directions and to appropriate situations and concepts has brought it to the point that it is "in danger of imploding as an analytical concept with any real cutting edge" (11).

For me what is important in postcolonial theory has do with the fact that postcolonial theory, in all its heterogeneity and ambition, redeploys key aspects in postmodern theory—opacity of language, de-centering of the subject, suspicion of authority, demolition of epistemological and cultural universal claims, relocation of subjects—in order to show the complicity of "knowledge" and systems of imperial domination. In this sense I find a great deal in postcolonial theory to run very close to Foucault's own discourse theory and its implications for historiography.[3] That move, it is true, runs the risk of invigorating and universalizing even more the epistemological power of the imperial centers, but like many aspects in postmodern theory (and, Marxism earlier and the avant-guards earlier, and romanticism earlier), postcolonial theory has a liberating potential when engaged in *critical dialogue*, as Mariátegui did with Marxism and Garcilaso de la Vega, Inca, did earlier with Spanish historiography, for nothing is autochthonous and insular or pristine after contact. Postcolonial theory articulates, like Latin American critiques of empire do, a double and/or multiple set of critical languages, trying often but not always succeeding in mounting a challenge to hegemony, saying always with Ranajit Guha that the state of colonial affairs amounts to: "domination without hegemony."

---

[3] See the entry on "discourse" in *Key Concepts in Post-colonial Studies*. There the editors note that discourse as used in postcolonial theory is "specifically derived from Foucault" (70). The entry goes on to say that "for Foucault discourse is a strongly bounded area of social knowledge, a system of statements within which the world can be known. The key feature of this is that the world is not simply 'there' to be talked about, rather it is through discourse itself that the world is brought into being... It is the 'complex of signs and practices which organizes social existence and social production'" (71).

Thus, what behooves the student of colonialism, not unlike Foucault's own enterprise or for matter the sense of discovery that Michel de Certeau practices and theorizes, is to look and act in the cracks and crevices of the system in order to break open the homogeneous surface that power/knowledge is always smoothing over. Postcolonial theory, once inflected as a dialectical and critical investigation of the myriad ways in which the coloniality of power constructs the center-periphery relations does not have to be seen as entirely divorced from the work of Latin American intellectuals. Much of the thinking carried out in the "Latin" south entailed finding forms and ways of material and epistemological challenges, creating spaces and subsequent freedoms from the domination of empire. This struggle has not been brought to end by any of the "posts" for the colonial outposts everywhere continue to post messages and letters that seem new only to those readers who are unfamiliar with the past and "other" colonial histories. It is important here not to forget, as Darcy Ribeiro remarked, that the legacy of empire has not only been deeply damaging but it is still very much with us. Ribeiro reluctantly points out that even high-ranking Latin America intellectuals, "[have seen] themselves as occupying subaltern positions" (qtd. in Mignolo, *Local Histories* 21). Starting with Garcilaso de la Vega, Inca, the same can probably be still said of many a diasporic intellectual today, even those who seem most successful. It thus follows that occlusion is not the Achilles tendon of the center alone, it can also occur in the periphery as well as to diasporic intellectuals.

To offer a proper account of the avatars of the critique of imperial hegemony in the Andes one would need a much deeper revision of the historiography of thinking in the Andes, one that is not available to us now. I will therefore take some shortcuts and weave my way back and forth between the seminal essays authored by José Carlos Mariátegui in the first quarter of the twentieth century, the challenge to the Spanish conquest in the work of Garcilaso de la Vega, Inca, and Guamán Poma.

IV. PARADIGMS ON TRIAL

In his *Seven Interpretative Essays* Mariátegui captures the essence of the gearing of problems that at once constitute coloniality in Peru and stand in the way of understanding their meaning as a space for possible critique and action. Mariátegui, like Garcilaso de la Vega, Inca, develops a discourse that allows him to keep track of two or more lines of trends and locations in the devolution of events within coloniality. This move has little to do with Homi Bhabha's concepts of hybridity or mimicry, for the latter stresses the idea of *"mimando"* or clowning, of imitation and mockery, of copy that denies the idea of an original (Bhabha 85-92). This Bhabhian sense of mimicry, as a copy that denies the sense of an original, is of course not new to readers of Latin American texts, for the conceit appears in the early Borges, in the Borges of "Tlön, Uqbar, Orbis Tertius" (1941). Mimicry, it is true, produces an ambivalent subject, not unlike the oscillating Garcilaso. But Garcilaso was not so much undecided and *ambi-valent* (as in mimicry) about his values or his terrain as he was trying to occupy both sides in the duality of worlds brought about by the conquest. The ambition of his dual or doubling operation was to deploy an ambidextrous cultural competency that allowed him to roam freely and firmly in both worlds and not to feel, as V.S. Naipaul does, that no matter how English he becomes, he still is not "quite white." Naipaul, the model for Bhabha's concept of colonial mimicry, is therefore always left with a feeling of insufficiency, itself the hallmark of mimicry. This is not to say that mimicry is not a condition given in coloniality. It may even be the general condition of colonial subjects. Such a feeling of fraudulent imitation and inflictive mockery is best captured in the Peruvian word *huachafo*. The novels of Mario Vargas Llosa are filled with *huachafos*. But that is not at all the case to be found in the enterprise of Mariátegui who follows in the line of Garcilaso's ambition to occupy fully both cultural traditions.

Perhaps anticipating Foucault, Mariátegui sees Peru, and by extension the scope of Andean history, as an uneven space of alternating and transformative ruptures and continuities. The conquest and the rule of coloniality mark and deploy in every possible way—economic system, legal system, domination by direct and epistemological violence, linguistic break—the irreparable break that Garcilaso de la Vega, Inca and Guamán Poma recognized and tried to suture and repair in their own different ways. But the land itself, the territory made by man, and the "problem of the Indian" lead Mariátegui to understand the presence and force of deep economic and cultural continuities that, although denied, arch over the rupture of the conquest and haunt the idea of the modern (European-like) nation. The opening paragraph of the book holds the key to the Mariátegui's break with positivist historiography and also with the Hegelian model of history, a move that postcolonial theory offers as its operational ground. Mariátegui's salvo against idealist history declares,

The degree to which the history of Peru was severed by the conquest can be seen better on an economic than on any other level. Here the conquest most clearly appears to be a break in continuity. Until the conquest, an economy developed in Peru that sprang spontaneously and freely from the Peruvian soil and the people. The most interesting aspect of the empire of the Incas was its economy... The Malthusian problem was completely unknown to the empire. (3)

Mariátegui opens up three major problems for thinking history in the Andes. First, contrary to the established Eurocentric perspective initiated by the Spanish chronicles and later affirmed by the rest of European historiography (coloniality of power), Mariátegui posits a break in Peruvian history because he introduces the radical notion that the temporality of Peruvian history has its origins and indeed achieves its formative structure during the long duration of Andean civilizations. The nation's past therefore belongs outside the parameters of European historiography which at best can make room for the "peoples without history," but cannot account for their devolution in their own time. This elsewhere delineates a timeline that is not coincidental with Europe's view of its own single temporal development. Thus, on this point Mariátegui's thinking interrogates, as do postcolonial theory and subaltern studies, the question of historical agency and the homing/homelessness of history. The Peruvian theorist is here proposing that history in the Andes, to be properly understood, must stretch back and perhaps even forward in a temporality of its own. In order to do so it must recognize other peoples and other sectors of the nation's peoples as historical actors. Mariátegui thus follows in the wake of the challenge to European historiography already started by Garcilaso de la Vega, Inca, and by Guamán Poma. While his interest in the land and the economic structure shows the importance of Marx for Mariátegui's radical inquiry into time and agency, it is just as important to see that his radical thinking comes from a long line of rerouting and rerooting European thought into the matrix of colonial living and thinking to produce a difference capable of conveying the sense of life in the Andes. This difference, I argue, has little to do with either hybridity or mimicry as understood in postcolonial theory.

The second point made by Mariátegui in the opening paragraph questions the universality and predictive capacity of European models for understanding human action in the world. For if the Malthusian problem did not develop within the structure of Inca economy then it follows that one has to question the explanatory and predictive power of Malthus's demographic theory. To what extent is Malthus's "discovery" then no longer an economic "law" affecting all human stages of demographic change, but simply an inspired analysis of a local situation in Europe's capitalist and imperial development? Do these three moves in Mariátegui—multiple historical temporalities, replacement and repositioning the subject of history, and refusal of European modes of historical explanation—not "provincialize" Europe in a manner similar to the one developed by Dipesh Chakrabrty's brilliant *Provincializing Europe: Postcolonial Thought and Historical Difference* (2000)? Mariátegui in Peru in the 1920's, with the epistemological tools available at the time—Gramsci, Marx, Schopenhauer, Nietzsche, Garcilaso de la Vega, Inca, archeology in Peru, fieldwork in Peru—engages three operations fundamental to postcolonial theory, the latter writing in the wake of postmodern theory.[4]

V. Changing the Subject

In the second chapter of the *Seven Essays*, Mariátegui addresses "the problem of the Indian." This "problem" is one created by criollo state-building historiography in its attempt to build a national history that "mimics," in Bhabha's sense of the word, the history of the old European nations, such as France or England. The problem of the Indian, Mariátegui shows, is colonialism itself. He turns the problem on its head. He argues that the Indian is not the problem. Rather the Indian is the bearer of the system of economic and cultural exploitation that holds colonialism in place. The Peruvian state does not know how to resolve this problem inasmuch as it is an apparatus that is at once colonial and "modern." As Quijano later theorizes, Mariátegui argues that colonialism, in order to exploit and continue suppressing the labor force that the Indian represents, has put in place a complex set of institutions that reproduce *coloniality at large*. No amount of schooling and republican "modernization" in general can unglue this complex, for colonialism as the foremost

---

[4] Of course the problem of the writing of history entails many more concerns that the three touched on here and both Mariátegui and postcolonial theory address them in complex and multiple ways, many of which have yet to be explored fully and which of course I cannot even begin to list here. The above is just a brief example of the work that remains to be done.

expression of capitalism does indeed constitute the underside of modernity. In order to free the Indian from racist and economic oppression, a whole new system of land tenure, one that challenges the notion of private property that thus capitalism itself, would be necessary.

Striking a blow on nineteenth-century pieties that predicate the improvement of the "uncivilized" or subalternized peoples of the globe, Mariátegui writes:

> The tendency to consider the Indian problem as a moral one embodies a liberal, humanitarian, enlightened nineteenth-century attitude that in the political sphere of the Western world inspires and motivates the 'leagues of human rights.' The antislavery conferences and societies in Europe....are born of out this tendency, which always has trusted too much of its appeals to the conscience of civilization. (25)

Once again, Mariátegui offers a critique of Eurocentric thinking, even when it appears to be sympathetic to those suffering the ill effects of imperialism, for Mariátegui's thinking seems founded on the capacity and the will to think otherwise under any and all circumstances. As many have pointed out, postcolonial theory is part and parcel of the age of suspicion inaugurated by Marx, Nietzsche, and Freud. As such it must be careful not to allow itself to be complicit with the liberalizing forces in theory which in fact mask the continuation of coloniality, as Mariátegui points out.

Mariátegui is obviously aware of such a trap. The trajectory of his thought, as seen in his indictment of literature, describes a constant radicalization and self-vigilance. This merciless critique was inaugurated in Peru by Manuel González Prada (1844-1918). This iconoclastic and fearless critic of the embrace of coloniality/modernity is recognized by Mariátegui and other radical thinkers of his generation as the "maestro." Mariátegui's suspicion of the good intentions of liberalism will of course be reinscribed in José María Arguedas's own critique of *indigenismo*, of transculturation theory, and of anthropology itself. Such suspicion is also at play in the reception that postcolonial theory has been accorded in Latin America in general. Invested with the prestige of the new, with the glow of the promise of liberation, situated at the center of the newest imperial power, postcolonial theory nevertheless often seems to be sounding themes and approaches developed in Mariátegui's analysis and thus already well known to Latin Americans.

VI. Education, (Non)Learning, and Ideology

In his essay on "Public Education" Mariátegui investigates the forms in which education in Peru has been complicit with the establishment and prolongation of empire despite the fact that independence from Spain and national republican educational reforms were supposed to produce a national subject capable of thinking and solving the problems of the nation. Of course Mariátegui knows, as postmodern theory later posits, that the nation is a construct. He calls it an "illusion," a "myth." But he nevertheless understands it to be a necessary construct for the accomplishment of other important human goals, goals which without a nation could perhaps never be achieved. He sees the lettered city inaugurated by Spanish colonial rule with its universities and colleges in the hands of various clerical orders and its almost exclusive emphasis in the humanities as "factories for the production of writers and lawyers" (79). These institutions of learning are, in fact, an impediment to learning, to critical thought, and to the formation of the nation. *Letrados*, like in Spain before, by virtue of their expertise in hallow and baroque linguistic games have continued to manage and advance the interests of the coloniality of power. Up to the very day when Mariátegui writes, education remained a privilege, its democratizing potential always restricted and limited by the very class of *letrados* whose real aim was to reproduce themselves in the institutions controlled by their elders.

Mariátegui himself was not the product of any great university or Ph.D. program. He was a self-taught man who, while in exile in Italy, continued his education reading voraciously but judiciously. He developed a very keen mapping system that enabled him to quickly determine what could fit into his general project of economic, political, and intellectual liberation. He made extremely careful choices and was quick to drop out fads and even classics when he determined that their thought was not liberating in the Latin American context, as is the case with Marx's thought on religion. He found that Antonio Gramsci, Benedetto Croce and George James Frazer, for instance, opened widely the avenues for thought that he had already begun clearing as a result of his own previous ample reading in European philosophy, empirical observation, and the work of many other minor but important local intellectuals. The footnotes in *Seven Essays* offer a singular bibliography, for it not only lets us see what European and American cultural thinkers and philosophers

Mariátegui was reading but also how he was noticing, selecting, and absorbing the work of local intellectuals. Here his approach and method differs considerably from Said's, Bhabha's, and Spivak's, diasporic intellectuals who hardly ever draw on the work of "oriental" or other local intellectuals.

Latin America was at the time awash in cultural magazines, and it seems that Mariátegui, the editor of the epoch making *Amauta*, received and read them all. Indeed, Southern Peru, with its historical ties to Argentina, never missed an issue of *Prisma, Babel, Claridad, Martín Fierro*, or *Sur*, much less the cultural pages of the great newspapers from Buenos Aires or Mexico City. Mariátegui, in turn, was a regular contributor to *La vida literaria*, edited in Buenos Aires by Samuel Glusberg (Tarcus). Radical thinking and abundant publishing in seemingly remote locations like Cuzco, Puno, and Arequipa was the order of the day. This is probably one of the strongest and key differences between the overall configuration of postcolonial theory and Latin American radical thinking. The first seems to be the work of isolated, highly educated diasporic intellectuals situated in prestigious academic positions in the United States. Their work is mainly in reference to the discursive dimensions of the colonial encounter, as conceived in the matrix of postmodern theory, while Latin American intellectuals like Mariátegui or Arguedas or even Borges for that matter, come from long traditions of "their own" that entwines, as a matter of course, the ongoing colonial encounter with a locally established critical discourse. Mariátegui's footnotes freely and unselfconsciously mix citations from the work of Emilio Romero, a Cuzqueño historian, with Gramsci. He considers Benedetto Croce's aesthetic in relation to Abelardo Gamarra's poetics and finds the Cusqueño poet as insightful as the Italian critic. Mariátegui was a Marxist but that did not keep him from finding food for thought in Waldo Frank's comparative approach to the cultural formation of the English-speaking American colonies and the legacy of the Iberian conquest. What is more, he tried to put in dialogue with the cultural theory of the Mexican José de Vasconcelos with Frank's cultural interpretations. Mariátegui's liberated vantage point is, by implication, the result of an education that, like a via negativa, gained its freedom by virtue of having been denied entry into the institutions that perpetuate the coloniality of power. Mariátegui sits comfortably on both sides of the Atlantic and takes it for granted, like Borges did at the same time in Buenos Aires, that he, as a Peruvian intellectual, is free to roam in all libraries and archives. Likewise he is free to debate any of the views extant in the extensive intertext in which he navigates. His critique of the colonial legacy in Peruvian education addresses precisely the educational system's cultivation of closure, omission, learning by rote and its penchant for establishing repressing thinking and academic authority.

   Drawing on Waldo Frank's *Our America* (1919), Mariátegui indicts the energy-sapping Spanish education and compares it, unfavorably, with the "energy and strength available in the culture of the Puritan and the Jew, who, in settling the territory that was to be the United States, directed their energies to utilitarian and practical ends" (81). Citing his Peruvian contemporary César A. Ugarte, Mariátegui, a Marxists, offers a psycho-cultural interpretation of Peru's marginal position in the world of capital:

> The Spaniard of the sixteenth century was not psychologically equipped to undertake the economic development of a hostile, harsh, unexplored land. A warrior... he lacked the virtues of diligence and thrift. His noble prejudices and bureaucratic predilections turned him against agriculture and industry, which he considered to be occupations of slaves and commoners. Most of the conquistadores were driven only by greed for easy and fabulous wealth and the possibility of attaining power and glory. (in Mariátegui, 85)

What is more, this psychological interpretation for Mariátegui does not necessarily exclude religion. In fact he credits Puritanism with the economic development of the English colonies. He even asserts that "Spanish colonization did not suffer from an excess of religion" (83), for Mariátegui, reading Frazer has developed a totally new concept of religion and its role in social formations. This consideration of psychology together with religion and only next to economy as historical forces, shows that Mariátegui, like Arguedas later, and Guamán Poma and Garcilaso earlier, is not always ready to throw out the baby with the bath water. Culture for Mariátegui is indeed the matter at hand and not simply hallowed books in authorized libraries. The long held practices of debate, selection, and appropriation of ideas coming from the imperial centers are taken for granted as a naturalized mode of operation by Mariátegui, who does not evince anguish and fear, as in the mimicry model, but rather seeks the foundation for a definite break with the coloniality of power in a deeply historicized critique of the power of discourse, institutionalized education, and other sites of ideological deployment. This postcolonial move offers much more than just resistance—the hallmark of postcolonial criticism according to Moore-Gilbert (16). It is, and it calls for, creative thinking on a grand scale.

However, appropriation has its limits and holds many dangers. It is a neutral tool that can be put to the service of both progressive, de-colonizing forces as well as reactionary recolonializing drives. That is why Mariátegui, a keen reader of French philosophy and literature, condemns the anachronistic educational reform that the Peruvian universities underwent when they adopted the French model. He bases his assessment on two legs: an examination of French education in France at the time, its own reactionary tendencies; and the discursive and political places or receptors where such a philosophy of education falls as it is imported into Peru. With his eyes always on the local play, Mariátegui draws from the work of French intellectuals who are critical of the system put in place by Napoleon, a system that gutted the democratizing thrust of the educational model created by the French revolutionaries. The Napoleonic reforms, intent on the training of bureaucrats, prolonged, like the colonial system inhered in Peru, the ignorance of the educated classes "for there was nothing to awake intellectual freedom" (84). According to Mariátegui, Edouard Herriot in *Creer* (1919) outlines the major ills of the French educational system. They amount to a failure to have created a primary and secondary school system capable of offering technical training. Moreover, Mariátegui observes that the "Third Republic has been able to break with this [Napoleonic] bondage, but it has not been able to break away completely from the narrow concept that tended to isolate the university from the rest of the nation" (85). For Mariátegui, the recent Peruvian reforms, based on the North American system, go a long way in remedying the distance between learning and the interests of the nation at large. There would have been a great stride forward were it not that they have been thoroughly sabotaged by the reactionary forces stationed in the faculty system of sinecures and other privileges. But the most important failure of this reform rests on the fact that it leaves the study of economics outside the core curriculum and is indifferent to the "indigenous element" (86).

Taking public education as a microcosm of coloniality Mariátegui is able to show how coloniality reproduces itself in layers and layers of imperial expansion. His analysis points out how under each attempt to reform there lies, as Foucault would later show with his archival and geo-logical metaphors, in deep and truncated air pockets, discourses always ready to reemerge. Thus it is clear that the thrust of Mariátegui's analysis of public education in both the imperial centers and ex-colonial spaces shows that the sense of a "real" postcolonial situation is only a temporary and precarious condition. This sense of overcoming the past can never be definitive. It can only be maintained in constant struggle. It cannot be totally overcome, not even with the wars of independence, for the system tends to its own reproduction. Mariátegui's theory of cultural change and intellectual freedom is not, therefore, that far away from Gayatri Spivak's own advocacy of the notion that liberation struggles cannot, now that there is nothing outside the text and that there is no sovereign subject, construct bounded subjects of resistance or impregnable counter-histo-ries. Instead, what is possible for both cultural theorists is the construc-tion of temporary but strategic critical perspectives, "strategic essen-tialisms," and provisional resisting subjects.

Mariátegui, of course, wants to go beyond a critique circumscribed to the halls of the academy. The academic nature of French education is pre-cisely his dissatisfaction with the adoption of the French model. "Strate-gic" and "provisionary" for Mariátegui mean the recognition of the inad-equacies of thinking in the world both at the center and at the margins. Above all, Mariátegui is thinking of culture as the realm of political strug-gle where there is nothing more certain than change. As an engaged intel-lectual, he and his comrades having spent time in jail and suffered exile, Mariátegui always already knew that all epistemological and political positions can only be contingent. Thus his study of public education in Peru evinces many of the key items in the problematic of the subaltern group of historians in Southeast Asia, as well as some of the hallmarks in postcolonial theory.[5]

The universities' links to society concern Mariátegui because of their inextricable connection to the question of formation of the national subject and the uses and places of knowledge in the political arena. In a sharp dif-ference with postcolonial theory, even with the postulates of the "teaching

---

[5] I do not have the space here to enter into the question of suppressed languages and subalternized knowledges in relation to education and the formation of the national subject but I think that some aspects of the problematic will at least be touched on at a glance in the section on literature.

machine" in Gayatri Spivak's work, Mariátegui looks on the intellectuals as a sector of society called upon to provide "intellectual guidance" to the working classes (95). Today, with the university in ruins, as Bill Readings has shown, we have a clearer perspective on the relationship of the humanities and the formation of the national (bourgeois) subject. We view with suspicion the deployment of the study of literature as a discursive formation integral to shaping of national (bourgeois) subjects. But at the time when Mariátegui was writing, the connection between the teaching of the humanities and the formation of national subjects was scarcely ever made. Mariátegui was writing at the margins a full fifty years before Readings takes up the question at the center. The liberation of knowledges and of the knowing subject was paramount for Latin America as its societies entered the heated battles of modernity and the universities seemed then, as they still do today, to offer the best vehicle for breaking the walls of ignorance constructed by coloniality. Mariátegui recognizes that education, *malgre lui*, is instrumental in the formation and identity of the national or international, bourgeois or revolutionary, reactionary or liberated subject. This cannot be changed and the question at hand is, once again, not to throw out the baby with the bath water, but to harness education for the project of national liberation and construction of national identity that is not oppressive.

Mariátegui's examination of the student-led university reform that started in Córdoba, Argentina, in 1919, and spread throughout Latin America, culminating in the International Congress of Students in Mexico City (1921), is prompted by the urgency to understand this socio-political movement at the microlevel. Moreover, Mariátegui feels that this "new generation" of Latin Americans holds the key to a continental union, the cherished Bolivarian dream that Mariátegui also considers indispensable in the struggle against colonialism. Again, Mariátegui's vision is focused on the local, concrete effects of thinking. He takes up topics whose examination will yield radical departures from the established understanding of the world. His intent is to compel changes in thinking. The poetics of César Vallejo and José María Arguedas later share in Mariátegui's sense of thinking in and for the world, a sensibility and conviction only exacerbated by the urgency of the lived.

But his is not the same as saying that Mariátegui was after short-term results only. Quite to the contrary, his interest in changing the world entailed a radical search that destabilizes the certainties that underpinned colonialism itself. For that reason, he is also critical of the student movement. He asserts that the failure of the student movement had to do with confusing enthusiasm with carefully studied, long-term plans. A reader of José de Vasconcelos, the Mexican cultural critic, Mariátegui points to the underside of the wide-open appropriation and indiscriminate undertaking of projects whose dimensions are not properly understood. He agrees with Vasconcelos's assessment when he writes that one of the gravest dangers in Latin American culture is the lack of follow through: "The principle weakness of our race is its instability. We are incapable of sustained effort and, for that same reason, we cannot execute a project. In general we should beware of enthusiasm" (Vasconcelos, qtd. in Mariátegui, 109). Mariátegui thinks that the student reform movement has been erratic and unstable, with vague and imprecise goals themselves prepared and underscored by a rhetorical and pseudo-idealistic education which has not yet understood the value of science and the stimulus that it provides to philosophy (110).

However, the best of the student spirit of reform flourishes not in Lima, still the center of colonialist reaction, but in Cuzco, where the project for a great center of scientific research evidences Mariátegui's conviction that "civilization owes much more to science than to the humanities" (120). And the Cuzco intellectuals have understood another key step in the intellectual liberation that university education ought to entail: to erase the distinction between "superior" and "inferior" cultures, because such distinction is false and ephemeral. It stands to reason that "there could not be high culture without popular culture" for the definition of one depends on the other (119). It would take an entire monograph to explain how the Cuzco intellectuals came to this understanding in 1919. Nevertheless one cannot but be tempted to say that due to their daily and concrete contact with the suppressed indigenous culture and the centuries-old struggle between Spanish hegemonization of the cultural space and the local intellectuals attempt to occupy that space, they came, on their own, to a very similar conclusion to that of Cultural Studies. That is to say that as a result of merging Marxism and the postmodern critique of the sovereign subject Cultural Studies began to dismantle the differences established between high and low culture as constructed in the work of Mathew Arnold at the end of the nineteenth century and which owe their construction to the specificities of English history. Mariátegui recognizes that any distinction between high and low culture is tied in colonial situations to the consequences of conquest and that as such they are inexorably tied to the construction of race. In the Andes this and other differences made their first

appearance with the Spanish chroniclers as they began establishing the difference between Europe and its conquered civilizations.[6]

In his concluding remarks Mariátegui stresses the fact that his intent
has been to "outline the ideological and political basis of public education
in Peru" (121). He places little hope in the liberating power of literacy, for
literacy is not a neutral value. The letter carries a heavy ideological burden. Furthermore, in Mariátegui's estimate, it is not possible to liberate
the mind of the Indian without liberating his body and the practices of
every day life that enchain them both. Liberating the Indian is not just a
pedagogical project, for "the first step to his redemption is to free him
from serfdom" (122). Thus, Mariátegui lays the fundamental ground for
Quijano's later theory on coloniality. Mariátegui's thesis on the coloniality of power is crystal clear when he writes that "Our Spanish and colonial heritage consists not of a pedagogical method, but of an economic
and social regime" (121). This statement echoes through the chambers of
Foucault's own power/knowledge theory. By implication, academic
freedom is thus but an illusion if it does not interact with the struggles in
the society at large. Perhaps here we have a true point of divergence with
what until now has been called postcolonial theory. This separation of
theory and practice is an argument leveled against postcolonial theory by
many a contemporary Anglophone critic, as a cursory review of *Colonial
Discourse and Post-colonial Theory. A Reader* (1994) would indicate.[7] It
is also one of the points of resistance to postcolonial theory in Latin
American circles.

---

[6] For an in depth study of intellectuals in Cuzco at the time when Mariátegui
writes, see Tamayo Herrera. For a history of *indigenismo* in Cuzco in the twentieth
century, see Cadena. For an assessment on the survival and transformation of indigenous culture in Peru, see Flores Galindo and Burga. See also chapter 9 in part one of
this volume, "The Nation in Ruins: Archeology and the Rise of the Nation."

[7] See specially Parts III and IV where in separate essays many critics such as Jenny
Sharp, Vijay Mishra and Bob Hodge, Ann McClintock and Anja Looma take up the
apparent disconnection and disregard of certain aspects of postcolonial theory and the
need for liberation from oppression of colonialism in the world.

VII. Religion

Mariátegui's reading of George J. Frazer's *The Golden Bough* (1890)
enables him to set up a perspective on religion that allows him, as cultural
criticism later would, to turn the gaze fixed on the rituals and beliefs of
the West's others onto its own normative religion: Judeo-Christian theology and practices. This is indeed a bold and daring step, for it levels the
previously established hierarchy between "true religions" or monotheistic creeds and the rituals and beliefs of polytheistic peoples. Mariátegui
thinks that now that the concept of religion has been broadened by
anthropology and myth studies, religion can be understood as much
more or much less than considerations on the institution of the church,
theology, and sacraments. Mariátegui sees the possibility of investigating
religion as one more dimension of the ideological formation of subjects.
Cast in this fashion, religion permits him to delve into and compare the
formation of the Puritan subject to the Catholic subject, and these two in
turn to the indigenous subject. The examination of religious practices and
beliefs, Mariátegui thinks, could perhaps hold the key for the understanding of indigenous subjectivity. Mariátegui uses anthropology to
lend legitimacy to Indian religion itself. In doing so he operates a complete reversal of the colonial claim to monopoly and hegemony over the
sacred and subjectivity. This move will of course not be lost on Arguedas,
who in his peerless novel *Los ríos profundos* (1957) will ask: how can the
force of religious belief be turned into political action in the modern
world, and how do men become both paralyzed and moved to action by
the force of belief? This investigation into the constitution and the force
of belief in the lives of illiterate, colonized people was also Gandhi's own
great question and finding in India's struggle for freedom from British
colonialism. It remains a fruitful question in subaltern historiography.

Reading Waldo Frank's popular *Our America* (1919), Mariátegui
brings to bear a Nietzschean slant onto the American journalist's comparative approach to the cultural differences separating the Americas.
Mariátegui concludes that the Puritan protest in England was rooted in
the will to power (125). Desiring power in England and finding it impossible to acquire it, the puritan developed a self disciple by which he turned
the "sweets of austerity" into a power over himself and later onto others.
The frugal and self-denying life released energy far better than any other
self-discipline. This energy accounts for all the characteristics of subject

formation associated with the agents of United States capitalism. The question is then, what forms of self-discipline permit the formation of channels that release positive energy into the body politic? If religion is one of those channels then one needs to ask: how does the Catholic superimposition of rites over indigenous beliefs constitute the subjective energies of the Indian population and how can they be released to the benefit of the Indian and the nation?

Although, like the Inca Garcilaso with the Spanish chroniclers, Mariátegui also must correct Frazer's idea that the original religion of the Incas was similar in its "collective theocracy and materialism" (126) to the Hindu religion, he nevertheless finds the operations of the study of religions in comparative perspective productive and liberating. The comparative study of religion opens the way for a new thinking on how Inca religion actually worked in the Andes. Mariátegui here disputes the established notion that the priesthood preceded the formation of the state in all cultures. For him, Andean culture has to be accorded its own space and specific modes of continuity. To try to understand it under the guidance of "universal" laws only contributes to and perpetuates ignorance of the particulars. The examination of Andean religion that he configures, based on the many works of the *indigenista* intellectuals of the Cuzco group, leads him to assert that "state and church formation were absolutely inseparable; religion and politics recognized the same principles and the same authority" (126). Thus, like the Greco-Roman identification of the political with the social, the Inca religion could not outlive the demise of the state. "It was a social and not an individual discipline" (127) and as such it was ready to accept another ritual without changing its beliefs.

Citing Emilio Romero's pioneering work on the system of deity substitution in the Andes, Mariátegui moves quickly past the problems in Frazer's misunderstanding of Andean religion and its encounter with the Catholic calendar and ritual. In Romero's "El Cuzco católico" Mariátegui, finds that, as Arguedas would later narrate, "The Indians thrilled with emotion before the majesty of the Catholic ceremony. They saw the image of the sun in the shimmering brocade of the chasuble and cope, they saw the violet tones of the rainbow woven into the fine silk threads of the rochet" (134). Examining the cultural process of negotiations, borrowings, transpositions, and transformations that would later be called "transculturation" by the Cuban anthropologist Fernando Ortiz, and indeed later built into one of the constitutive points of postcolonial theory (Ashcroft et al,

233-234), Mariátegui clarifies that "the missionaries did not instill a faith, they instilled a system of worship and a liturgy, wisely adapted to the Indian costume" (135). This point would have shocked Garcilaso who did believe in the possible and complete substitution of Andean religion with Christianity based on the idea that one ethical code was not all that distant from the other and on his own comparison of Roman and Inca religion. Guamán Poma, who always claimed that Andean religion was indeed more consistent and straight forward in the relationship between belief and behavior, would have been gratified to read Mariátegui's analysis, for in many ways it coincides with his own diagnosis of what was going on in the Andes during the campaigns for the extirpation of idolatries circa 1600. Mariátegui inflects Frazer, like Garcilaso bended the entire Renaissance to read Andean matters, like Homi Bhabha inflects Lacan and Renan to read and reposition the "location of culture."

VIII. LITERATURE ON TRIAL

Mariátegui begins the last of his seven essays by clarifying that "trial" is here used in a legal sense, for he will make the institution of "literature," as the maximum expression of the coloniality of power, responsible for the work it has performed through the centuries. In this scenario an intellectual like Mariátegui is a witness for the prosecution. He regards his seventh essay as an open trial on the colonialist mentality that has ruined the past: "My responsibility to the past compels me to vote against the defendant" (183). Cultural critique is thus a question of conscience, not a mere exercise in analysis or a display of rhetorical games. The indictment of the *letrado* culture that follows could not be stronger or more to the point, and it is not surprising to see that it contains the seeds for Ángel Rama's later *La ciudad letrada* (1984).

At the outset, and as usual, Mariátegui, aware of the impossibility of absolutely objective knowledge in an always political cultural milieu, warns the reader that he does not pretend to be impartial (183), although such admission of positionality does not necessarily mean the negation of universal human aspiration or solidarity. He regards admitting to positionality as part and parcel of the individual's ethical and political responsibility. His politics, he says, are philosophy and religion, not Marxism or scientific materialism (183). While Mariátegui poses the problem of national literature, he does not see that the aesthetic aspect of literature is divorced from the politics. Quite to the contrary, he regards the one as intrinsically related to the other.

In a definition of nation that surprises us for its similarities with the theses of Benedict Anderson and Homi Bhabha, Mariátegui advances that for him "the nation itself is an abstraction, an allegory, a myth that does not correspond to a reality that can be scientifically defined" (188). The similarity might be due to a common reading of Ernest Renan's essay "What is a Nation?" (1882) where the French philosopher advances the thesis that the nation is not a territory, not a language, and not a religious tradition but rather a cultural construct woven in the loom that entwines memory with forgetting. Therefore it follows that, for Mariátegui, the idea of an autochthonous and authentic national literature is an illusion. Only the Chinese, he says, if they had managed to achieve their desired total isolation, could then claim a "national literature." Mariátegui takes cultural contact and transformation as a given. Consequently he has no trouble in stating that Quechua grammar and writing are the work of the Spaniards. Quechua literature more properly belongs to bilingual men of letters like " El Lunarejo" (Juan de Espinosa Medrano (1632-1688), or to the appearance of Inocencio Mamani, the young author of *Tucuipac Manashcan* (in Mariátegui 184), a comedy written under the influence of the contemporary bilingual poet Gamaniel Churata. Mariátegui's view of this perennial exchange is not unlike the transculturation theorized by Ortiz, and it does not imply a one-way street with the colonized always doing the assimilation of forms and forces emitted by the center. This point appears with greater clarity in his essays on César Vallejo.

Mariátegui goes on to characterize the colonial following of Góngora and other Spanish fashions as servile imitation. When carefully considered today, Mariátegui's assessment of the colonial imitation of Spanish literary fashions has a great deal in common with Homi Bhabha's own sense of mimicry. However, as it was argued above, that servile imitation, that is to say mimicry, has little to do with the double or triple cultural competency to be found in Garcilaso's writing practices.[8] Garcilaso's

---

[8] For an extensive discussion of how Homi Bhabha's concept of mimicry as quite other from Garcilaso's idea of cultural mestizaje and sense of a post-conquest navigation in a double registry which does not necessarily imply the Lacanian idea of self betrayal, fear, and suspicion of the other, see part 2, chapter 1 in this volume, "Mimicry Revisited."

work along with Mariátegui's or Vallejo's must be considered the creative and capable model of a postcolonial discourse that claims agency, competency, and the power of inflection that the discourse of colonized can have upon the knowledges of the center as any history of the reception of Garcilaso's work in Europe can attest.

The cultural "dualism" that constituted Peru since the rupture of the conquest has obfuscated the need for a critical perspective on European modes of analysis. According to Mariátegui, a questioning of the methods and assumptions in the exegesis of metropolitan literatures is in order, for when they are uncritically assumed as a hermeneutic they alter the object of study. Thus they have to be either radically altered or abandoned (188). Owing to the shape of their own historical situations, colonial, bicultural literatures prove refractory to methods that assume a unified national subject or language. With the exception of two writers—Garcilaso de la Vega, Inca and "El Lunarejo"—literature written during the colonial period was for Mariátegui a "servile and inferior imitation" (188) of Spanish practices and models. These bombastic and empty texts had no understanding or feeling for the Peruvian scene. These bad imitators, even when satirical, sustained only by the force of imitation, lacked the imagination necessary for a reconstruction of the pre-conquest past and therefore failed to ground their discourse on anything concrete. They were incapable of establishing ties with the common people (190-193). For Mariátegui, satire and sarcasm are not necessarily critical or subversive positions. They can in fact be part and parcel of the same servile imitation that blocks the way, dilutes the paths of confrontation, and shrink the possibilities of imagining a world in which the relationship of master and slave does not predicate all relations. It is not until the appearance of Ricardo Palma (1833-1919) in the late nineteenth century that satire and mockery acquire a sharper edge due to Palma's interest in the colonial past. In disagreement with most of Palma's political critics, Mariátegui's sharp eye detects the fact that Palma's is not a nostalgia of the viceroyalty, as many had argued, but rather a distancing from it by the effect of a laughter that ridicules, a snickering that reveals the hypocrisy of the master as well as the consent of the slave and thus levels down the authority that supports claims to power and rule.

In his interpretation of the colonial and republican literature in the Andes, Mariátegui advances several key theoretical positions later developed by Antonio Cornejo Polar, Ángel Rama, and postcolonial criticism and theory. Mariátegui posits the heterogeneous discursive practices given in a plurilingual and pluricultural environment as he distinguished between texts written in Spanish or Quechua by bilingual subjects, texts written in either Spanish or Quechua by monolingual subjects. He also establishes a difference between servile imitations and texts written in Spanish which are nevertheless connected to the "Andean scene" and speak of the lived experience in the colonial world. He further distinguishes between complicit and critical satire. Mariátegui thus lays the ground for the debate on transculturation that Ángel Rama's thesis, based Ortiz's own analysis of the formation of culture in Cuba, will bring about in the consideration of Latin American culture as a whole, a debate that has been a dominant force in cultural and literary theory during the last thirty years.

It is important to note here that while Ángel Rama chooses the work of José María Arguedas as one of the prime examples of transculturation, some critics have uncritically deployed the idea to explain myriad aspects of Latin American culture in a celebratory move. Others, like Antonio Cornejo Polar, have warned that this re-dressing of the *mestizaje* metaphor hides within it the same potential for oppressive homogenization hidden in *mestizaje*. Others have even pointed out that transculturation also occludes the hierarchical difference implicit in all colonial situations and it itself could be considered a deployment of the same *letrados* who erected the colonial teaching machine. Arguedas himself never embraced transculturation as a proper description of either his work or cultural dynamics in the Andes. As it is well known, in his acceptance speech of the Inca Garcilaso Prize (1968) Arguedas rejected the notion that he was an *"aculturado"* (Arguedas; Rama, *Transculturación*; Moreiras). I think that he would also have rejected the notion of transculturation if by that we mean a one-way flow of cultural goods from the colonizer to the colonized, and an appropriation process going on exclusively at the colonized end in which either the remnants or the jewels of the imperial center are recycled. This latter notion of cultural exchange has little to do with "exchange" between two asymmetrical and contending subject positions and much to do with the notion of bricolage. This notion of one-way cultural flow, is not what Mariátegui has in mind either when he speaks of cultural exchange or when he analyzes the work of César Vallejo, for Mariátegui argues that Vallejo brings about the definitive rupture with the colonial legacy. Thus his "creative" and original poetics would be beyond processes such as transculturation whether this is read in a celebratory or suspicion mode. Arguedas's vocation as a writer was defined and transformed by his reading of Mariátegui when as an insecure and impoverished Andean youth Arguedas first came to reside in Lima. The author of *El zorro de arriba y el zorro de abajo* (1971) (*The Fox Up Above and the Fox From Down Below*, 1998) writes fully informed by Vallejo's poetics.

Positing the problematic of duality of Peru's culture as a foundational concept for the understanding of all colonial formations, including literature mostly written in the colonizer's language, Mariátegui's cultural theory is not at all far from the impacting discoveries of postcolonial theory. Given the constrains of space, as en expeditious memory exercise I will simply list the topics in *Key Concepts in Post-Colonial Studies* (1998) and highlight the areas of discussion of mutual concern to Mariátegui, his generation, and postcolonial theory: indigenous people/colonizer, agency, ambivalence, anti-colonialism, appropriation or catachresis, binarism, center/periphery, class and post-colonialism, colonial discourse, colonial desire, contrapuntal reading, counter-discourse, cultural diversity/cultural difference, decolonization, dependency theory, essentialism/ strategic essentialism, ethnicity, ethnography, Eurocentrism, hegemony, hybridity, imperialism, *mestizaje*, mimicry, nation and language, national allegory, orality, *testimonio*, transculturation.

Mariátegui's negative assessment of colonial literature acquires greater depth in light of the figure of César Vallejo, the author of the epoch making *Los heraldos negros* (1918) (*The Black Heralds*, 1990), and *Trilce* (1928) (*Trilce*,1973), and now widely recognized as the greatest poet of the Spanish language in the twentieth century. Vallejo's radical inquiry into language and the world won Mariátegui's immediate admiration. Writing at a time when most of the established critics rejected Vallejo's departure from romanticism and symbolism, Mariátegui praises Vallejo for ushering "poetic freedom and autonomy" and for bringing in "the vernacular in writing" (250). Vallejo, according to Mariátegui, does what the entire colonial period failed to do: "For the first time indigenous sentiment is given pristine expression... he creates a new style, ...a new message and a new technique" (250). Mariátegui astutely recognizes that the novelty, originality, and force in Vallejo's poetry are truly beyond commentary. In order to convey a sense of the compactness of Vallejo's poems and the arresting effect of the poems on the reader, Mariátegui compares it to music: "Indigenous sentiment has a melody of its own and

[Vallejo] has mastered its song" (250). It is interesting to note that Arguedas also uses music as the metaphor for capturing the sense of sublime expression.

For Mariátegui, Vallejo has overcome the dualism of form and substance as well as the dualism that the conquest created. He has achieved the total integration of language, form, and meaning that allows the poem to speak the world. Vallejo has also overcome the problem of description, the rhetoric that underscores the distance between language and the world. Vallejo offers a critique of what we would call today "representation" and uses the word instead to close the gap between the world and the word. Vallejo's poetry is above all genuine. It is at one with itself. "Vallejo does not explore folklore. Quechua words [when they appear in his writing] are a spontaneous and integral part of his writing... he is not deliberately autochthonous. His poetry and language emanate from his flesh and spirit; he embodies his message. Indigenous sentiment operates in his art perhaps without his knowledge or desire" (252). Mariátegui is especially interested in pointing out that Vallejo's nostalgia is not a nostalgia of a specific past but it is rather a "metaphysical protest, a nostalgia of exile, of absence" (252). A homelessness, one might say today, but a nostalgia that "throbs with the pain of three centuries" of affliction and endurance (254).

Mariátegui is quick to point out, however, that Vallejo, even when he confronts God ("You have always been well") or when he feels God's pain, is neither a satanic nor a neurotic poet (254). I think that in Mariátegui's interpretation of Vallejo, which is amazingly on the mark, we find one of the key divergences and differences with postcolonial theory for the latter is truly a child of the age of suspicion and neither Mariátegui nor Vallejo, for all their devastating critique of the modes of knowledge/power of the colonial centers, really shared in the nihilist narcissism of some aspects of the West's modernity. Vallejo's sorrow is for the whole of humanity and even for God, and as Mariátegui points out, "Nothing in his poetry is egotistic [or] narcissistic" (257). On the contrary "he achieves the most austere, humble and proud simplicity" (257).

The same may said of Mariátegui's own cutting but always direct writing. It is well known that the style of some postcolonial theorists is rather baroque, that there is nothing austere or simple in their texts. In Vallejo Mariátegui finds not only beauty and a compelling critique of metaphysics but the much desired break with colonialism: "Today the rupture is complete" (287). Vallejo's art announces the birth of a new sensitivity, of a new world. Indeed Mariátegui feels satisfied with the yield of the trials he has conducted. He thus closes his book by asserting the productive side of the colonial paradox: "The universal, ecumenical road we have chosen to travel, and for which we are reproached, has taken us ever closer to ourselves" (287). This assertion stands in clear opposition to the fear, suspicion, and continuous mutilation of mimicry.

CONCLUSIONS

No doubt Mariátegui's singular and seminal analysis of coloniality in Peru had the theoretical power to reach well beyond the borders of the Andean nation and Latin America. But precisely because of the coloniality of power, his work, as well as the work of many other Latin American intellectuals, did not readily circulate beyond the borders of the Spanish language. Until the rise of the Spanish American novelists in the international cultural arena (the boom) Spanish remained a subalternized language. It was, as Walter Mignolo has argued, a European language subalternized in the quarters of the powerful second modernity of the Enlightenment, the time when the rest of the globe came under the aegis of the British empire and with whose Commonwealth postcolonial theory is most deeply and closely associated.

I have spent the greater part of this chapter showing how Mariátegui's radical thinking in many ways anticipates the preoccupations of postcolonial theory despite the fact that Mariátegui does not depart from a body of postmodern theory that in a way lays the basis for the postcolonial questioning and de-centering of the West's power/knowledge primacy. I have, I think, remarked repeatedly on the fact that Mariátegui, like Garcilaso de la Vega, Inca and Guamán Poma before him (although Mariátegui did not read Guamán Poma because his work was lost until basically the nineteen thirties) and José María Arguedas afterwards, never ceased to learn and to inform their thinking with and from local knowledges. In fact these four theorists could say that they think as they do, write as they do, and occupy the intellectual space that they do "porque soy indio" as Garcilaso wrote in his classic *Comentarios reales* (1609).

In this claim made by indigenous *mestizos*, rests, I think, the most important difference between one of the most easily embraced and fre-

quently deployed concepts in postcolonial theory and the radical decolonizing thinking of these four Andean intellectuals. It is the difference
between mimicry as originally developed in Homi Bhabha's *The Location of Culture* (1994) and the conception of *mestizaje* as a doubled layered, but not split, cultural competence of the colonial subject. When
Garcilaso, writing in Spain and hoping to pass the censors in order to
publish his commentaries on Inca history and society, writes that he disputes the portrayal of the Inca empire in the Spanish chronicles, and
states that he does so "porque soy indio," he is not contradicting himself.
He is already disputing the colonizing notion that the subject must be
culturally univocal and that therefore he chooses by suppressing part of
his lived experience and his multiple knowledges. Garcilaso is establishing the fact that postcolonial subjects walk on two legs, that they can
achieve cultural competence on both registers. Mutilation of the one of
his several cultural registers is not necessary in order to inhabit the postcolonial world. The bicultural colonial subject is a capable subject precisely because he can move from one side to the other, keep them apart,
bring them together, cross over, set them side by side in dialogue, struggle for complementary and reciprocity, or simply keep them at distance
depending on the play of the given moment. Garcilaso, who claimed
authority on things Inca by virtue of his knowledge of Quechua, nevertheless mastered Hebrew, Latin, and Italian in order to write in Spanish
the pre-conquest past. He posits the postcolonial subject as a subject who
must learn to occupy multiple strategic positions. This multiplicity does
not imply a schizophrenic subjectivity. Likewise Guamán Poma, who
wanted the Spanish to leave the Andes entirely, decided nevertheless that
keeping scissors and writing would be beneficial to the reconstitution of
the Andean world.

This Andean concept of doubling and multiplying cultural competen-
cies is indeed divorced from the concepts of mimicry and hybridity in
Bhabha. Coming from Lacan, as they do, they imply a sense of lack, fear,
suspicion, and perennial disencounter and joylessness. The camouflage
that takes place in mimicry, the dissembling that breeds suspicion and
pain in the colonial encounter that Bhabha so ably portrays does indeed
take place in Andean coloniality and it has no better representation than
in the empty imitators of Góngora that Mariátegui describes as part and
parcel of a servile literary production which does little to elucidate and
much to obfuscate the workings of coloniality. But such mimicry is not

universal and determining of all colonial situations and indeed the four intellectuals singled out in this chapter define the colonial struggle precisely as the capacity to achieve competence in all power/knowledge situations and thus stem the tied of mimicry, the paralyzing suspicion of inauthenticity, and the practices of thoughtless imitation.

This chapter was originally published in Coloniality at Large: *Latin America and the Postcolonial Debate*. Eds. Mabel Moraña, Enrique Dussel, and Carlos A. Jáuregui, 130-157. © 2008 Durham: Duke University Press. All rights reserved. Reprinted by permission.

Works Cited

Bhabha, Homi K. *The Location of Culture*. London; New York: Routledge, 1994.

Bill Ashcroft, Gareth Griffiths, and Helen Tiffin. *Key Concepts in Post-Colonial Studies*. London; New York: Routledge, 1998.

Guha, Ranajit. *Dominance Without Hegemony: History and Power in Colonial India*. Cambridge: Harvard University Press, 1997.

Mariátegui, José Carlos. *Seven Interpretative Essays of Peruvian Reality*. Trans. Marjory Urquidi. Austin: University of Texas Press, 1971.

Mignolo, Walter. *Local Histories/Global Designs: Coloniality, Subaltern Knowledges, and Border Thinking*. Princeton: Princeton University Press, 2000.

Moore-Gilbert, Bart. *Postcolonial Theory: Contexts, Practices, Politics*. London; New York: Verso, 1997.

Quijano, Aníbal. "The Colonial Nature of Power and Latin America's Cultural Experience." In *Sociology in Latin America (Social Knowledge: Heritage, Challenges, and Perspectives)*. Ed. R. Briceño and H.R. Sonntag. Caracas: Proceedings of the Regional Conference of the International Association of Sociology, 1998. 27-38.

Tarcus, Horacio. "Revistas intelectuales y formaciones culturales izquierdistas en la Argentina de los veinte." In *Revista Iberoamericana* Vol. LXX. Nums. 208-209. Julio-diciembre 2004: 794-772.

Vega, Inca Garcilaso de la. *Comentarios reales de los incas*. Aurelio Miró Quesada, ed. Caracas: Biblioteca Ayacucho, 1976, 2 vols.

BIBLIOGRAPHY

ABERCROMBIE, A. Thomas. *Pathways of Memory and Power: Ethnography and History Among an Andean People*. Madison: University of Wisconsin Press, 1998.

ACOSTA, José de. *Historia natural y moral de las Indias (1590)*. Ed. Edmundo O'Gorman. México: Fondo de Cultura Económica, 1979.

—. *Obras del padre José de Acosta*. Ed. Francisco Mateos. Madrid: Ediciones Atlas, 1954.

ADAM, Ian and Helen TIFFIN, ed. *Past the Last Post*. Calgary: University of Calgary Press, 1990.

ADÁN, Martín [Rafael de la Fuente Benavides]. *La casa de cartón*. Lima: Talleres de Impresiones y Encuadernaciones Perú, 1928.

ADORNO, Rolena. *Guaman Poma: Writing and Resistance in Colonial Peru*. Austin: University of Texas Press, 1986.

AGUIRRE BELTRÁN, Gonzalo. *El proceso de aculturación en México*. México: UIA, 1970.

AGURTO CALVO, Santiago. *Cuzco: la traza urbana de la ciudad inca*. Cuzco: Proyecto Per-39, 1980.

—. *Lima pre-hispánica*. Lima: Finanpro, 1984.

AHMAD, Aijaz. *In Theory: Classes, Nations, Literatures*. London: Verso, 1992.

—. *Postcoloniality: What is a name?* Unpublished manusrcipt, n.d.

ALBO, Javier and Joseph M. Barnadas. *La cara campesina de nuestra historia*. La Paz: Unitas, 1984.

ALEGRÍA, Ciro. *Broad and Alien is the World*. Trans. Harriet de Onís. London: Merlin P., 1941.

—. *El mundo es ancho y ajeno*. Santiago: Ediciones Ercilla, 1941.

ÁLVAREZ, Bartolomé. *De las costumbres y conversión de los indios del Perú. Memorial a Felipe II*. [1588]. Madrid: Polifemo, 1998.

ANDERSON, Benedict. *Imagined Communities: Reflections on the Origin and Spread of Nationalism.* London: Verso, 1983.

ANDERSON IMBERT, Enrique and Eugenio FLORIT, eds. *Literatura hispanoamericana.* New York: Holt, Rinehart and Winston, 1960.

ANGLÉS VARGAS, Víctor. *Historia del Cusco incaico.* Cuzco: Anglés, 1989, 3 vols.

—. *Sacsayhuaman: portento arquitectónico.* Cuzco: Angles, 1990.

ANZALDÚA, Gloria. *Borderlands: the New Mestiza = La frontera.* San Francisco: Aunt Lute Books, 2007.

ARGUEDAS, José María. "La agonía de Rasu Ñiti." In *Amor mundo y todos los cuentos.* Lima: Francisco Moncloa Editores, 1967.

—. *Agua.* Lima: CIP, 1935.

—. *Formación de una cultura nacional indoamericana.* México: Siglo Veintiuno Editores, 1975.

—. "No soy un aculturado." *El zorro de arriba y el zorro de abajo.* México: Colección Archivos, 1992. 256-58.

—. *Los ríos profundos.* Buenos Aires: Editorial Losada, 1958.

ARGUEDAS, José María and Pierre DUVIOLS, eds. *Mitos de Huarochiri: Narración quechua recogida por Francisco de Ávila* (1598?). Trans. José María Arguedas. Lima: Instituto de Estudios Peruanos, 1966.

AROCENA, Luis A. *El Inca Garcilaso y el humanismo renacentista.* Buenos Aires, 1949.

ARRIAGA, José de. *The Extirpation of Idolatry in Perú.* Ed. Clark Keating. Lexington: University of Kentucky Press, 1968.

ASCHER, Marcia and Robert. *Code of the Quipu: A Study in Media, Mathematics and Culture.* Ann Arbor: University of Michigan Press, 1981.

—. "The Quipu as Visible Language." *Visible Language* 9 (1975): 329-356.

ASHCROFT, Bill. "Excess: Post-colonialism and the Verandahs of Meaning." In *De-Scribing Empire: Postcolonialism and Textuality.* Ed. Chris Tiffin and Alan Lawson. London: Routledge, 1994. 33-44.

ASHCROFT, Bill, Gareth GRIFFITHS, and Helen TIFFIN. *The Empire Writes Back: Theory and Practice in Post-colonial Literatures.* London; New York: Routledge, 1989.

—. *Key Concepts in Post-Colonial Studies.* London; New York: Routledge, 1998.

AVENI, Anthony F. *Empires of Time: Calendars, Clocks, and Cultures.* New York: Basic Books, 1989.

BACACORZO, Javier. "El pasquín y su trascendencia en la lucha libertaria nacional." In *Literatura de la emancipación.* Lima: Universidad Nacional Mayor de San Marcos, 1972. 16-26.

BACHELARD, Gaston. *The Philosophy of No.* 1938.

BAHN, Paul G. *The Cambridge Illustrated History of Archeology.* Cambridge: Cambridge University Press, 1996.

BAKEWELL, Peter. *A History of Latin America: Empires and Sequels, 1450-1930.* Cambridge: Blackwell Publishers, 1997.

BAKHTIN, M. M. *The Dialogic Imagination.* Trans. Caryl Emerson and Michael Holquist. Austin: University of Texas Press, 1981.

BARBOSA SÁNCHEZ, Araceli. *Sexo y conquista.* México: Universidad Nacional Autónoma de México, 1994.

BARTH, John. *The Literature of Exhaustion and the Literature of Replenishment.* Northridge: Lord John Press, 1982.

—. "Post-modernism Revisited." In *Review of Contemporary Fiction* 8 (Fall 1988): 16-24.

BASADRE, Jorge. *Meditaciones sobre el destino histórico del Perú.* Lima: Ediciones Huascarán, 1947.

—. *Perú: problema y posibilidad.* Lima: F.y E. Rosay, 1931.

BAUDRILLARD, Jean. *Les Stratégies Fatales.* Paris: Grasset, 1983.

BAUDELAIRE, Charles. *Selected Writings on Art and Artists.* London: Cambridge University Press, 1981.

BAUER, Brian. *Astronomy and Empire in the Ancient Andes.* Austin: University of Texas Press, 1992.

BAYÓN, Damián. "The Architecture and Art of Colonial Spanish America." *CHLA*, 2: 709-45.

BAYÓN, Damián and Marx Murillo. *History of South American Colonial Art and Architecture.* New York: Rizzoli, 1992.

BENAVIDES, Rafael de la Fuente. *De lo barroco en el Perú.* Lima: Universidad Nacional Mayor de San Marcos, 1968.

BENJAMIN, Walter. "Theses on the Philosophy of History in Illuminations." In *Illuminations.* Ed. Hannah Arendt. Trans. Harry Zohn. New York: Schoken Books, 1969.

BERGER, Mark T. *Under Northern Eyes: Latin American Studies and US Hegemony in the Americas 1898-1990.* Bloomington: Indiana University Press, 1995.

BERMÚDEZ-GALLEGOS, Marta. *Poder y transgresión: Perú, metáfora e historia.* Lima: Latinoamericana Editores, 1996.

BERNAL, Ignacio. *A History of Mexican Archeology.* London: Thames and Hudson, 1980.

BEUCHOT, Mauricio. *Estudios de historia y filosofía en el México colonial.* México: Universidad Nacional Autónoma de México, 1991.

BEVERLEY, John. *Against Literature.* Minneapolis: University of Minnesota Press, 1993.

—. "The Im/possibility of Politics: Subalternity, Modernity, Hegemony." *The Latin American Subaltern Studies Reader.* Ed. Ileana Rodríguez. Durham: Duke University Press, 2001. 47-63.

—. *Una modernidad obsoleta: estudios sobre el barroco*. Caracas: Fondo Editorial A.L.E.M. 1997.

—. *Subalternity and Representation: Arguments in Cultural Theory*. Durham: Duke University Press, 1999.

BHABHA, Homi K. "DissemiNation: Time, Narrative, and the Margins of the Modern Nation." In *Nation and Narration*. Ed. Homi Bhabha. London; New York: Routledge, 1990. 291-323.

—. *The Location of Culture*. London; New York: Routledge, 1994.

BOLIN, Inge. *Rituals of Respect: The Secret Survival in the High Peruvian Andes*. Austin: University of Texas Press, 1998.

BOONE H. Elizabeth. "Introduction: Writing and Recording Knowledge." In E. Boone and W. Mignolo, *Writing Without Words: Alternative Literacies in Mesoamerica and the Andes*. Durham: Duke University Press, 1994: 3-26.

BORGES, Jorge Luis. "Tlön, Uqbar, Orbis Tertius." In *Obras completas 1923-1972*. Buenos Aires: Emecé Editores, 1974. 431-443.

BOUTURINI, Lorenzo. *Idea de una Nueva Historia General de la América Septentrional*. Madrid: Impr. de J. de Zuniga, 1746.

BOVÉ, Paul A. *Mastering Discourse: The Politics of Intellectual Culture*. Durham: Duke University Press, 1992.

BOYARIN, Jonathan. "Space, Time and the Politics of Memory." In *Remapping Memory: The Politics of Timespace*. Ed. Jonathan Boyarin. Minneapolis: University of Minnesota Press, 1994.

BRADING, David. *The First America: The Spanish Monarchy, Creole Patriots, and the Liberal State 1492-1867*. Cambridge: Cambridge University Press, 1991.

BROKAW, Galen. "Khipu Numeracy and Alphabetic Literacy in the Andes: Felipe Guamán Poma de Ayala's *Nueva córonica y buen gobierno*." *Colonial Latin American Review*, Vol.11, No 2 (2002): 275-303.

—. "The Poetics of *Khipu* Historiography: Felipe Guamán Poma de Ayala's *Nueva Corónica* and the *Relación de los quipucamayoc*." *Latin American Research Review* 38.3 (2003): 111-147.

—. "Toward Deciphering the Khipu." *Journal of Interdisciplinary History*. 35.4 (2005): 571-589.

BROTHERSTON, Gordon. *Book of the Fourth World: Reading the Native Americas Through Their Literature*. Cambridge: Cambridge University Press, 1992.

BROWN, Michael F. and Eduardo FERNÁNDEZ. *War of Shadows: The Struggle for Utopia in the Peruvian Amazon*. Berkeley: University of California Press, 1991.

BRYCE ECHENIQUE, Alfredo. *Un mundo para Julius*. Barcelona: Seix Barral, 1970.

—. *A World for Julius*. Trans. Dick Gerdes. Austin: University of Texas Press, 1992.

BURGA, Manuel. *Nacimiento de una utopía: muerte y resurrección de los incas*. Lima: Instituto de Apoyo Agrario, 1988.

BURGA, Manuel and Alberto FLORES GALINDO. *Apogeo y crisis de la república aristocrática.* Lima: Rikchay Perú, 1979.

BURKHOLDER, Mark A. and Lynman L. JOHNSON. *Colonial Latin America.* New York: Oxford University Press, 1998.

BUTLER, Judith. *Gender Trouble: Feminism and the Subversion of Identity.* New York: Routledge, 1990.

CADENA, Marisol de la. *Indigenous Mestizos: The Politics of Race and Culture in Cuzco, Peru, 1919-1991.* Durham: Duke University Press, 2000.

CAMPA, Román de la. "De la deconstrucción al nuevo texto social: pasos perdidos o por hacer en los estudios culturales latinoamericanos." In *Nuevas perspectivas desde/ sobre América Latina: el desafío de los estudios culturales.* Ed. Mabel Moraña. Santiago de Chile: Editorial Cuarto Propio; Instituto Internacional de Literatura Iberoamericana, 2000.

CARRILLO, Francisco. *Cronistas del Perú antiguo. Enciclopedia histórica de la literatura peruana.* Lima: Editorial Horizonte, 1989.

—. *Enciclopedia histórica de la literatura peruana. Vol. 1: Literatura quechua clásica.* Lima: Horizonte, 1986.

CASTRO, Américo. *The Structure of Spanish History.* Princeton: Princeton University Press, 1954.

CASTRO, Daniel. *Another Face of Empire: Bartolomé de Las Casas, Indigenous Rights and Ecclesiastical Imperialism.* Durham: Duke University Press, 2007.

CASTRO-GÓMEZ, Santiago and Eduardo MENDIETA, ed. *Teorías sin disciplina, latinoamericanismo, poscolonialidad y globalización en debate.* México: Porrúa; San Francisco: University of San Francisco Press, 1998.

CASTRO-KLARÉN, Sara. "Autores indígenas americanos: escritura, poder y conocimiento." In *Escritura, transgresión y sujeto en la literatura latinoamericana.* México: Premiá Editora, 1989. 159-176.

—. "Dancing and the Sacred in the Andes: From the Taqui-Oncoy to Rasuñiti." In Stephen Greenblatt, ed. *New World Encounters.* Berkeley: University of California Press, 1993: 159-176.

—. *Escritura, transgresión y sujeto en la literatura latinoamericana.* México: Premiá Editora, 1989.

—. "Escritura y persona en el Nuevo Mundo." *Escritura, transgresión y sujeto en la literatura latinoamericana.* México: Premiá Editora, 1989.

—. "Historiography on the Ground: The Toledo Circle and Guamán Poma." In Ileana Rodríguez. Ed. *The Latin American Subaltern Studies Reader.* Durham: Duke University Press, 2001:143- 171.

—. "Interrupting the Text of Latin American Literature: Problems of (Missed)recognition." In *Nuevas perspectivas desde/sobre América Latina: el desafío de los estudios culturales.* Ed. Mabel Moraña. Santiago de Chile: Editorial Cuarto Propio/Instituto Internacional de Literatura Iberoamericana, 2000. 387-405.

—. "Mimicry Revisited: Latin America, Post-colonial Theory and the Location of Knowledge." In Alfonso de Toro and Fernando de Toro, eds. *El debate de la postcolonialidad en Latinoamérica*. Madrid/Frankfurt: Iberoamericana/ Vervuert, 1999: 137-164.

—. "Ontological Fabulation: Toward Cortázar's Theory of Literature." *The Final Island: The Fiction of Julio Cortázar*. Ed. Jaime Alazraki. Norman: University of Oklahoma Press, 1976. 140-151.

—. "The Paradox of Self in *The Idea of a University*." In *The Idea of University* by John Henry Newman. Ed. Frank Turner. New Haven: Yale University Press, 1996. 318-339.

—. "El siglo XVIII: sujetos subalternos y el teatro de la Perricholi." In Ed. Francisco La Rubia Prado and Jesús Tordecilla, *Razón, tradición y modernidad: re-visión de la ilustración hispánica*. Madrid: Tecnos, 1996. 87-99.

—. *Understanding Mario Vargas Llosa*. Columbia: University of South Carolina Press, 1990.

CASULLO, Nicolás, ed. *El debate modernidad-postmodernidad*. Buenos Aires: Puntosur Editores, 1991.

CERTEAU, Michel de. *The Capture of Speech*. Minneapolis: University of Minnesota Press, 1997.

—. *The Practice of Everyday Life*. Trans. Steven Rendall. Berkeley: University of California Press, 1984.

—. *The Writing of History*. Trans. Tom Conley. New York: Columbia University Press, 1988.

CERVANTES, Fernando. *The Devil in the New World: The Impact of Diabolism in New Spain*. New Haven: Yale University Press, 1994.

CHAKRABARTY, Dipesh. *Provincializing Europe: Postcolonial Thought and Historical Difference*. Princeton: Princeton University Press, 2000.

CHANG-RODRÍGUEZ, Raquel. "La subversión del barroco en *Amar su propia muerte* de Juan de Espinosa Medrano." In Ed. Mabel Moraña. *Relecturas del Barroco de Indias*. Hanover: Ediciones del Norte, 1994. 117-148.

CHIAPPI, Mario, Moisés LEMLIJ, and Luis MILLONES. *Alucinógenos y shamanismo en el Perú contemporáneo*. Lima: Ediciones El Virrey, 1985.

CISNEROS, Antonio. *Los comentarios reales*. Lima: Ediciones de la Rama Florida, Ediciones de la Biblioteca Universitaria, 1964.

—. *El libro de Dios y de los húngaros*. Lima: Libre-1, 1978.

CLASSEN, Constance. *Inca Cosmology and the Human Body*. Salt Lake City: University of Utah Press, 1993.

CLENDINNEN, Inga. *Ambivalent Conquests: Maya and Spaniard in Yucatan*. Cambridge: Cambridge University Press, 1987.

CLIFFORD, James. "On Collecting Art and Culture." In *The Cultural Studies Reader*. Ed. Simon During. London: Routledge, 1993. 49-73.

—. *The Predicament of Culture: Twentieth Century Ethnography, Literature, and Art.* Cambridge: Harvard University Press, 1988.

COE, Michael D. *Breaking the Maya Code.* London: Thames & Hudson, 1992.

CONGRAINS, Enrique. *Lima hora cero.* Lima: Círculo de Novelistas Peruanos, 1954.

—. *No una sino muchas muertes.* Lima: Populibros Peruanos, 1957.

CONNOLLY, William E. *Augustinian Imperative: the Politics of Morality.* Newbury Park: Sage Publications, 1993.

—. *The Ethos of Pluralization.* Minneapolis: University of Minnesota Press, 1995.

—. *Identity\Difference: Democratic Negotiations of Political Paradox.* Ithaca: Cornell University Press, 1991.

COOK, Noble David. *Demographic Collapse: Indian Peru, 1520-1620.* Cambridge: Cambridge University Press, 1981.

—. *Born to Die: Disease and the New World Conquest, 1492-1650.* Cambridge: Cambridge University Press, 1998.

CORNEJO POLAR, Antonio. *Escribir en el aire.* Lima: Editorial Horizonte, 1994.

—. "Una heterogeneidad no dialéctica: sujeto y discurso migrante en el Perú moderno." *Crítica cultural y teoría literaria latinoamericana. Revista Iberoamericana,* 176-77. Ed. Mabel Moraña. 1996. 837-44.

CORONIL, Fernando. "Más allá del occidentalismo: hacia categorías geohistóricas no imperialistas." In *Teorías sin disciplina, latinoamericanismo, poscolonialidad y globalización en debate.* Ed. Santiago Castro-Gómez and Eduardo Mendieta. Mexico: Porrúa; San Francisco: University of San Francisco Press, 1998. 121-142.

CORTÁZAR, Julio. *Rayuela.* Caracas, Venezuela: Biblioteca Ayacucho, 1980.

COSTIGAN, Lúcia Helena. *A sátira e o intelectual criollo na colônia: Gregorio de Matos e Juan del Valle y Caviedes.* Lima: Latinoamericana Editores, 1991.

COX, Victoria. *Guamán Poma de Ayala: entre los conceptos andino y europeo del tiempo.* Cuzco: Bartolomé de Las Casas, 2002.

CROSBY, Alfred. *The Columbian Exchange: Biological and Cultural Consequences of 1492.* Westport: Greenwood Press, 1972.

CUMMINS, Tom. "Let Me See! Reading is for Them: Colonial Andean Images and Objects 'Como es costumbre tener los caciques Señores.'" In Elizabeth Hill Boone and Tom Cummins eds. *Native Traditions in the Postconquest World.* Washington D.C.: Dumbarton Oaks Research Library and Collection, 1998: 91-148.

—. "Representations in the Sixteenth Century and the Colonial Image of the Inca." In *Writing Without Words: Alternative Literacies in Mesoamerica and the Andes.* Eds. Elizabeth Hill Boone and Walter D. Mignolo. Durham: Duke University Press, 1994.

DANIEL, E. Valentine. "The Limits of Culture." *In Near Ruins: Cultural Theory at the End of the Century.* Ed. Nicholas B. Dirks. Minneapolis: University of Minnesota Press, 1998. 67-91.

DELEUZE, Gilles. *Foucault.* Ed. and trans. Sean Hand. Minneapolis: University of Minnesota Press, 1988.

DELGADO, Washington. *Historia de la literatura republicana: nuevo carácter de la literatura en el Perú independiente.* Lima: Ediciones Rikchay, 1980.

DERRIDA, Jacques. *Of Grammatology.* Trans. Gayatri Chakravorty Spivak. Baltimore: Johns Hopkins University Press, 1976.

DOMENICI, Viviano and Davide Domenci. "Talking Knots of the Inka: A Curious Manuscript that May Hold the Key to Andean Writing." In *Archeology* November-December 1996: 48-56.

DRAKE, Stillman. 'Literacy and Scientific Notations." In *Towards a New Understanding of Literacy.* Eds. Merald E. Wrolstad and Dennis F. Fisher. New York: Praeger, 1986. 135-155.

DREYFUS, Hubert L. and Paul Rabinow. *Michel Foucault: Beyond Structuralism and Hermeneutics.* Chicago: The University of Chicago Press, 1982.

DURÁN MONTERO, María Antonia. *Lima en el siglo XVII: Arquitectura, urbanismo y vida cotidiana.* Sevilla: Diputación de Sevilla, 1994.

DURAND, José. "La biblioteca del Inca." *Nueva Revista de Filología Hispánica* 3 (1948): 239-264.

—. *El Inca Garcilaso, clásico de América.* México: SepSetentas, 1976.

DURING, Simon, ed. *The Cultural Studies Reader.* London: Routledge, 1993.

DUSSEL, Enrique. *The Invention of the Americas.* New York: Continuum, 1995.

ECHEVARRÍA, Roberto González. *The Voice of the Masters: Writing and Authority in Modern Latin American Literature.* Austin: University of Texas Press, 1985.

ELLEFSEN, Bernardo. *Matrimonio y sexo en el incario.* Cochabamba: Editorial Los Amigos del Libro, 1989.

ELMORE, Peter. *Los muros invisibles: Lima y la modernidad en la novela del siglo XX.* Lima: Mosca Azul, 1993.

ESPINOZA SORIANO, Waldemar. *Los huancas, aliados de la conquista; tres informaciones inéditas sobre la participación indígena en la conquista del Perú, 1558-1560-1561.* Huancayo: Universidad Nacional del Centro del Perú, 1971.

FABIAN, Johannes. *Time and the Other: How Anthropology Makes its Object.* New York: Columbia University Press, 1983.

FANE, Diana. Ed. *Converging Cultures: Art and Identity in Spanish America.* Brooklyn: The Brooklyn Museum, 1996.

FARRISS, Nancy M. *Maya Society Under Colonial Rule: The Collective Enterprise of Survival.* Princeton: Princeton University Press, 1984.

FERMAN, Claudia. *Política y postmodernidad. Hacia una lectura de la antimodernidad en América Latina.* Miami: North South Center, 1994.

FERNÁNDEZ DE OVIEDO Y VALDÉS, Gonzalo. *Historia natural y general de las Indias* (1535). Ed. Juan Pérez de Tudela. Madrid: BAE, 1959.

FERNÁNDEZ, Christian. *The Concept of Commentary in the Royal Commentaries.* Washington, D.C.: Unpublished Paper: Modern Languages Association, 1996.

—. *Inca Garcilaso: imaginación, memoria e identidad.* Lima: Universidad Nacional Mayor de San Marcos, 2004.

FLORES GALINDO, Alberto, ed. *La agonía de Mariátegui: la polémica con la Komintern.* Lima: DESCO, 1980.

—. *Buscando un Inca: identidad y utopía en los Andes.* Lima: Instituto de Apoyo Agrario, 1987.

—. *Túpac Amaru II - 1780.* Lima: Retablo de Papel, 1976.

FOUCAULT, Michel. *The Archaeology of Knowledge.* New York: Pantheon Books, 1972.

—. *Discipline and Punish.* New York: Pantheon Books, 1977.

—. "Governmentality." In *The Foucault Effect: Studies in Governmentality: With Two Lectures by and an Interview with Michel Foucault.* Ed. Colin Gordon, Peter Miller, and Graham Burchell. Chicago: University of Chicago Press, 1991. 89-97.

—. *The History of Sexuality.* New York: Pantheon Books, 1978.

—. *History of Sexuality. Volume I: An Introduction.* New York: Random House, 1980.

—. *Language, Counter-Memory, Practice: Selected Essays and Interviews.* Ed Donald F. Bouchard. Trans. Donald F. Bouchard and Sherry Simon. Ithaca: Cornell University Press, 1997.

—. "Nietzsche, Genealogy, History." In *The Foucault Reader.* Ed. Paul Rabinow. New York: Pantheon Books, 1984.

—. "Of Other Spaces." *Diacritics* 16 (1986): 22-7.

—. *The Order of Things.* New York: Pantheon Books, 1970.

—. "The Subject and Power." *Michel Foucault: Beyond Structuralism and Hermeneutics* by Hubert L. Dreyfus and Paul Rabinow. Chicago: The University of Chicago Press, 1982.

—. "What is an Author?" *Language, Counter-Memory, Practice. Selected Essays and Interviews.* Ed. Donald F. Bouchard. Ithaca: Cornell University Press, 1977. 113-138.

—. "What is Enlightenment?" In *The Foucualt Reader.* Ed. Paul Rabinow. New York: Pantheon, 1984. 32-51.

FOURIER, Charles. *Design for Utopia: Selected Writings of Charles Fourier.* New York: Schocken Books, 1971.

FORGACS, David. "National-popular: Genealogy of a Concept." In *The Cultural Studies Reader.* Ed. Simon During. London: Routledge, 1993. 177-193.

FRANCO, Jean. *César Vallejo: The Dialectics of Poetry and Silence.* Cambridge: Cambridge University Press, 1976.

FRANK, Waldo. *Our America.* New York: Boni and Liveright, 1919.

FUENTES, Carlos. *Los cinco soles de México: memoria de un milenio.* Barcelona: Seix Barral, 2000.

GASPARINI, Graziano and Louise Margolies. *Arquitectura inca.* Caracas: Universidad Central de Venezuela, 1977.

—. *Inca Architecture.* Patricia Lyon, tran. Bloomington: University of Indiana Press, 1980.

GEERTZ, Clifford. *The Interpretation of Cultures: Selected Essays.* New York: Basic Books, 1973.

GIBSON, Charles. *The Spanish Tradition in America.* New York: Haper and Row, 1968.

GISBERT, Teresa. *Iconografia y mitos indígenas en el arte.* La Paz: Gisbert y Cia., 1980.

GÓMEZ-PEÑA, Guillermo. "Documented/Undocumented." In *Multicultural Literacy: Opening the American Mind.* Eds. Rick Simonson and Scott Walker. St. Paul: Graywolf Press, 1988. 127-34.

GÓMEZ ROBLEDO, Xavier. *Humanismo en México en el siglo XVI: el sistema del Colegio de San Pedro y San Pablo.* México: Editorial Jus, 1954.

GONZÁLEZ ECHEVARRÍA, Roberto and Enrique PUPO WALKER, eds. *The Cambridge History of Latin American Literature.* Vol. I. Cambridge: Cambridge University Press, 1996.

GONZÁLEZ PRADA, Manuel. *Pájinas Libres.* Lima: Thesis, 1966. [1894].

GORDON, Colin. "Governmental Rationalty: An Introduction." In *The Foucault Effect: Studies in Governmentality: with Two Lectures by and an Interview with Michel Foucault.* Ed. Graham Burchell et al. Chicago: University of Chicago Press, 1991. 1-50.

GRAFTON, Anthony and Lisa JARDINE. *From Humanism to the Humanities: Education and the Liberal Arts in Fifteenth- and Sixteenth-Century Europe.* London: Duckworth, 1986.

GRAMSCI, Antonio. *Selections from Cultural Writings.* Cambridge: Harvard University Press, 1985.

GREENBLATT, Stephen. *Marvelous Possessions: The Wonder of the New World.* Chicago: University of Chicago Press, 1991.

GREENBLATT, Stephen and Giles GUNN, ed. *Redrawing the Boundaries: The Transformation of English and American Literary Studies.* New York: Modern Language Association of America, 1992.

GROSSBERG, Lawrence. "The Circulation of Cultural Studies." In *What is Cultural Studies?* Ed. John Storey. London: Arnold, 1996.

GRUZINSKI, Serge. *The Conquest of Mexico: The Incorporation of Indian Societies into the Western World, 16th-18th Centuries.* Trans. Eileen Corrigan. Cambridge: Polity Press, 1993.

GUAMÁN POMA DE AYALA, Felipe. *Nueva corónica y buen gobierno.* Ed. Franklin Pease. 2 vols. Caracas: Biblioteca Ayacucho, 1980.

—. *El primer nueva corónica y buen gobierno.* Ed. John Murra and Rolena Adorno. México: Siglo Veintiuno, 1980.

GUHA, Ranajit. *Dominance Without Hegemony: History and Power in Colonial India.* Cambridge: Harvard University Press, 1997.

—. "Subaltern Studies: Projects for Our Time and Thier Convergence." *The Latin American Subaltern Studies Reader.* Ed. Ileana Rodríguez. Durham: Duke University Press, 2001. 35-47.

GUIBOVICH, Pedro M. "Nota preliminar al personaje histórico y los documentos." *El retorno de las huacas: estudios y documentos sobre el Taki Onqoy, siglo XVI.* Ed. Luis Millones. Lima: Instituto de Estudios Peruanos, 1990. 23-40.

GUTIÉRREZ, Miguel. *La generación del 50: un mundo dividido.* Lima: Sétimo Ensayo, 1988.

HALL, Stuart. "Cultural Studies and its Theoretical Legacies." In *Cultural Studies.* Eds. Lawrence Grossberg et. al. New York: Routledge, 1992.

HANKE, Lewis, ed. *History of Latin American Civilization: Sources and Interpretations.* Vol. 1. Boston: Little Brown and Company, 1973.

HARRIS, Wendell V. "Canonicity." *PMLA* 106. No. 1 (1991): 110-121.

HARVEY, David. *The Condition of Postmodernity: An Enquiry into the Origins of Cultural Change.* Cambridge: Blackwell, 1989.

HASSAN, I. "The Culture of Postmodernism." In *Theory, Culture and Society* 2.3 (1985): 119-32.

HAYA DE LA TORRE, Víctor Raúl. *El antiimperialismo y el APRA.* Santiago de Chile: Ediciones Ercilla, 1935.

—. *Por la emancipación de América Latina.* Buenos Aires: M. Gleizer, 1927.

HEBDIGE, Dick. "From Culture to Hegemony." In *The Cultural Studies Reader.* Ed. Simon During. London: Routledge, 1993. 357-368.

—. *Hiding in the Light: On Images and Things.* London: Routledge, 1988.

HEID, Pat. *Spanish Department, Colby College.* <http://www.colby.edu/spanish/pat.html>.

HEMMINNG, John. *The Conquest of the Incas.* New York: Harcourt, Brace, Jovanovich, 1970.

HERAUD, Javier. *Estación reunida.* Lima: La Rama Florida, 1961.

—. *El río.* Lima: Cuadernos de Hontanar, 1960.

HERNÁNDEZ, Max. *Memoria del bien perdido: conflicto, identidad y nostalgia en el Inca Garcilaso de la Vega.* Lima: Instituto de Estudios Peruanos, 1991.

HERNÁNDEZ, Max, Moisés LEMLIJ, Luis MILLONES, Alberto PÉNDOLA, María ROSTWOROWSKI. *Entre el mito y la historia: psicoanálisis y el pasado andino.* Lima: Ediciones Psicoanalíticas Imago S.R.L, 1987.

HERRERA, C. Augusto Alba. *Atusparia y la revolución campesina de 1885 en Ancash.* Lima: Ediciones Atusparia, 1985.

HIDALGO, Alberto. *Arenga lírica al emperador de Alemania*. Arequipa: Quiroz Hnos., 1916.

HIGGINS, Anthony. *Constructing the 'Criollo' Archive: Subjects of knowledge in the 'Biblioteca Mexicana' and the 'Rusticatio Mexicana'*. West Lafayette: Purdue University Press, 2000.

HIGGINS, James. *A History of Peruvian Literature*. Liverpool: Cairns, 1987.

HINOSTROZA, Rodolfo. *El consejero del Lobo*. Lima, 1965.

HOBERMAN, Luoisa SCHELL and Susan SOCOLOW. Eds. *Cities and Society in Colonial Latin America*. Albuquerque: University of New Mexico Press, 1986.

HOBSBAWM, Eric and Terence RANGER, eds. *The Invention of Tradition*. New York: Cambridge University Press, 1983.

HODDER, Ian. *Reading the Past: Current Approaches to Interpretation in Archeology*. Cambridge: Cambridge University Press, 1991.

HOGGART, Richard. "Literature and Society." *The American Scholar* 35. 277-89.

—. *The Uses of Literacy*. New York: Oxford University Press, 1958.

HOLGUÍN, Diego González. *Vocabulario de la lengua general de todo el Perú llamada Qquichua o del Inca*. [1560] Lima: Imprenta Santa María, 1952.

HULME, Peter. *Colonial Encounters: Europe and the Native Caribbean, 1492-1797*. London: Methuen, 1986.

—. "Postcolonial Theory and the Representation of Culture in the Americas." In *Ojo de Buey* 2.3 (Otoño) (1994): 14-25.

HUMBOLDT, Alejandro de. *Cartas americanas*. Caracas: Ayacucho, 1980.

HUNTER, James Davison. *Culture Wars: The Struggle to Define America*. New York: BasicBooks, 1991.

HYSLOP, John. *The Inca Road System*. New York: Academic Press, 1984.

—. *Inca Settlement Planning*. Austin: University of Texas Press, 1990.

ICAZA, Jorge. *Huasipungo*. Quito: Editorial Atahualpa, 1934.

JAKFALVI-LEIVA, Susana. *Traducción y violencia colonizadora: un estudio de la obra del Inca Garcilaso*. Syracuse: Maxwell School of Citizenship and Public Affairs, 1984.

JAMESON, Fredric. *Nationalism, Colonialism and Literature*. Belfast: A Field Day Panflet, 1988.

—. *The Political Unconscious: Narrative as a Socially Symbolic Act*. Ithaca: Cornell University Press, 1981.

—. *Postmodernism, or The Cultural Logic of Late Capitalism*. Durham: Duke University Press, 1991.

—. *The Prison-house of Language: A Critical Account of Structuralism and Russian Formalism*. Princeton: Princeton University Press, 1972.

—. "Third World Literature in the Era of Multinational Capitalism." In *Social Text* (Fall 1986): 65-88.

KADIR, Djelal. *Columbus and the Ends of the Earth: Europe's Prophetic Rhetoric as Conquering Ideology*. Berkeley: University of California Press, 1992.

—. *The Other Writing*. West Lafayette: Purdue University Press, 1993.

KAMINSKY, Amy K. *Reading the Body Politic: Feminist Criticism and Latin American Women Writers*. Minneapolis: University of Minnesota Press, 1993.

KANT, Immanuel. "What is Enlightenment?" In *On History*. Indianapolis: Bobbs-Muriel, 1963.

KLARÉN, Peter. *History of Peru*. New York: Oxford University Press, 2000.

—. *Peru: Society and Nationhood in the Andes*. New York: Oxford University Press, 2000.

KLOR DE ALVA, Jorge. "Colonialism and Post-colonialism as (Latin) American Mirages." In *Colonial Latin American Review* 1.1-2 (1992): 3-23.

—. "Spiritual Conflict and Accommodation in New Spain: Towards a Typology of Aztec Responses to Christianity." In *The Inca and Aztec States 1400-1800: History and Anthropology*. Ed. George A. Collier et all. New York: Academic Press, 1982. 345-66.

—. *The Work of Bernardino de Sahagún: Pioneer Ethnographer of Sixteenth Century Aztec Mexico*. Albany: Institute for Mesoamerican Studies, University at Albany, State University of New York, 1988.

KRISTAL, Efraín. *The Andes Viewed from the City: Literary Discourse and Political Discourse on the Indian in Peru 1848-1930*. New York: Peter Lang, 1987.

KRITZMAN, Lawrence D. Introduction. *Politics, Philosophy, Culture: Interviews and Other Writings, 1977-1984*. By Michel Foucault. Ed. Lawrence D. Kritzman. London: Routledge, 1988.

KUBLER, George and Martín SORIA. *Art and Architecture in Spain and Portugal and their American Dominions, 1500-1800*. Baltimore: Penguin Books, 1969.

KUHN, Thomas S. *The Structure of Scientific Revolution*. Chicago: University of Chicago Press, 1962.

KURI CAMACHO, Ramón. *La Compañía de Jesús, imágenes e ideas. Scientia conditionata, tradición barroca y modernidad en la Nueva España*. Puebla: Benemérita Universidad Autónoma de Puebla, Plaza y Valdés Editores, 2000.

LACAN, Jaques. "The Line and the Light." In *Four Fundamental Concepts of Psychoanalysis*. Ed. Alan Sheridan. London: The Hogart Press and the Institute for Psychoanalysis, 1977. 91-105.

LACLAU, Ernesto and Chantal MOUFFE. *Hegemony and Socialist Strategy: Towards a Radical Democratic Politics*. London: Verso, 1985.

LAFAYE, Jacques. *Quetzalcoatl and Guadalupe: The Formation of Mexican National Consciousness, 1531-1813*. Chicago: University of Chicago Press, 1976.

LARSEN, Neal. *Reading North by South: On Latin American Literature, Culture, and Politics*. Minneapolis: University of Minnesota Press, 1995.

LAUER, Mirko. *Introducción a la pintura peruana del siglo XX*. Lima: Mosca Azul, 1976.

LAVRIN, Asunción, "Female Religious." In Eds. Louisa Schell Hoberman and Susan Socolow, *Cities and Society in Colonial Latin America*. Albuquerque: University of New Mexico Press, 1986. 165-195.

LEAVIS, F.R. *English in Our Time and The University*. London: Chatto & Windus, 1969.

LE GOFF, Jacques. *History and Memory*. Trans. Steven Randall and Elizabeth Claman. New York: Columbia University Press, 1992.

LEITCH, Vincent B. *Cultural Criticism, Literary Theory, Poststructuralism*. New York: Columbia University Press, 1992.

LEONARD, Irvin A. *Baroque Times in Old Mexico. Seventeenth-Century Persons, Places and Practices*. Ann Arbor: University of Michigan Press, 1959.

LEVILLIER, Roberto. *Don Francisco de Toledo*. Buenos Aires: Biblioteca del Congreso Argentino, 1935.

—. *Gobernantes del Perú, cartas y papeles, siglo XVI*. Ed. Roberto Levillier. Madrid: Imprenta de Juan Pueyo, 1925.

LÉVI-STRAUSS, Claude. *Anthropology and Myth*. Roy Willis, tran. New York: Basil Blackwell, 1987.

LIENHARD, Martin. *Cultura popular andina y forma novelesca: zorros y danzantes en la última novela de Arguedas*. Lima: Latinoamericana Editores, 1981.

—. *La voz y su huella*. Hanover: Ediciones del Norte, 1991.

LINDENBERGER, Herbert. "Teaching and the Making of Knowledge." *PMLA* 113:3, May 1998: 370-378.

LOHMANN VILLENA, Guillermo. "Etude Préliminaire." To *Gobierno del Perú* by Juan de Matienzo, Paris: Institut Francais d'Études Andines, 1967.

LÓPEZ ALBÚJAR, Enrique. *Cuentos andinos*. Lima: Imprenta de la Opinión Nacional, 1920.

—. *Matalaché*, 1928.

LÓPEZ-BARALT, Mercedes. *Icono y conquista: Guamán Poma de Ayala*. Madrid: Hiperión, 1988.

LÓPEZ MARTÍNEZ, Héctor. *Rebeliones de mestizos y otros temas quinientistas*. Lima: Ediciones P.L.V., 1972.

LUMBRERAS, Luis G. *The Peoples and Cultures of Ancient Peru*. Trans. Betty J. Meggers. Washington D.C.: Smithsonian Institution Press, 1974.

—. *Visión arqueológica del Perú*. Lima: Milenario, 1990.

MACCORMACK, Sabine. "Pachacuti: Miracles, Punishment, and Last Judgment: Visionary Past and Prophetic Future in Early Colonial Peru." *The American Historical Review* 93.4 (1988): 960-1006.

MACERA, Pablo. *La imagen francesa del Perú, siglos XVI-XIX*. Lima: Instituto Nacional de Cultura, 1976.

—. *Trabajos de historia*. (4 vols.) Lima: Instituto Nacional de Cultura, 1977.

MANNHEIM, Karl. *Ideology and Utopia*. New York: Harcourt Brace, 1936.

MANRIQUE, Nelson. *Nuestra historia. Historia de la República.* Lima: COFIDE, 1995.

MARAVALL, José Antonio. *La cultura del barroco: análisis de una estructura histórica.* Madrid: Ariel, 1975.

MARIÁTEGUI, José Carlos. *Siete ensayos de interpretación de la realidad peruana.* Lima: Amauta, 1928.

—. *Seven Interpretative Essays of Peruvian Reality.* Trans. Marjory Urquidi. Austin: University of Texas Press, 1971.

MARKHAM, Clements R. *Cuzco: a Journey to the Ancient Capital of Peru, With an Account of the History, Language, Literature, and Antiquities of the Incas, and Lima; a Visit to the Capital and Provinces of Modern Peru.* London: Chapman and Hall, 1856.

MATIENZO, Juan de. *Gobierno del Perú (1567).* Ed. Guillermo Lohmann Villena. Reprint, Paris: Institut Francais d'Études Andines, 1967.

MAZZOTTI, José A. *Coros mestizos del Inca Garcilaso: resonancias andinas.* Lima: Bolsa de Valores de Lima: Otorongo Producciones; México: Fondo de Cultura Económica, 1996.

—. "The Lightning Bolt Yields to the Rainbow: Indigenous History and Colonial Semiosis in the *Royal Commentaries* of El Inca Garcilaso de la Vega." In *Modern Language Quarterly* 57, 2 (1996): 197-211.

—. *Subtexto andino y discurso sincrético en los Comentarios reales del Inca Garcilaso de la Vega.* Princeton: Pd.D. Dissertation, 1993.

MÉNDEZ PLANCARTE, Gabriel. *Humanistas mexicanos del siglo XVI.* México: Biblioteca del Estudiante Universitario, 1946.

MENDIZÁBAL LOSACK, Emilio. "Don Felipe Guamán Poma de Ayala, señor y príncipe, último quellcakamayoc," in *Journal of Latin American Lore* 5 (1961): 83-116.

MENESES, Teodoro, L. Ed. *Teatro quechua colonial.* Lima: Edubanco, 1983.

MESA, José de and Teresa Gisbert. *Holguín y la pintura virreinal en Bolivia.* La Paz: Editorial Juventud, 1977.

—. *Mateo Pérez de Alesio.* La Paz: Instituto de Estudios Bolivianos, 1972.

METREAUX, Alfred. "The Inca Empire: Despotism or Socialism." *History of Latin American Civilization.* Ed. Lewis Hanke. Boston: Little Brown and Company, 1973.

MIGNOLO, Walter. "Afterward: From Colonial Discourse to Colonial Semiosis." *Dispositio* 36-38 (1989): 333-337.

—. "Cartas, crónicas y relaciones del descubrimiento y la conquista." In *Historia de la literatura hispanoamericana. Época colonial,* ed. Iñigo Madrigal. Madrid: Cátedra, 1982. 57-116.

—. "Colonial and Post-colonial Discourse: Cultural Critique or Academic Colonialism?" *Latin American Research Review* 128 (1993): 120-131.

—. "Colonial Situations, Geographic Discourses and Territorial Representations: Towards a Diatopical Understanding of Colonial Semiosis." *Dispositio* 1989: 93-140.

—. *The Darker Side of the Renaissance: Literacy, Territoriality and Colonization*. Ann Arbor, The University of Michigan Press, 1995.

—. "Decires fuera de lugar: sujetos dicentes, roles sociales y formas de inscripción." *Revista de Crítica Literaria Latinoamericana* 21.41 (1995): 9-31.

—. "Human Understanding and (Latin) American Interests: The Politics and Sensibilities of Geocultural Locations." In *Poetics Today* 1995: 101-126.

—. *Local Histories/Global Designs: Coloniality, Subaltern Knowledges, and Border Thinking*. Princeton: Princeton University Press, 2000.

—. "Posoccidentalismo: el argumento desde América Latina." In *Teorías sin disciplina, latinoamericanismo, poscolonialidad y globalización en debate*. Ed. Santiago Castro-Gómez and Eduardo Mendieta. México: Porrúa; San Francisco: University of San Francisco Press, 1998. 31-58.

—. "Preamble: The Historical Foundation of Modernity/Coloniality and the Emergence of Decolonial Thinking." In *A Companion to Latin American Literature and Culture*. Ed. Sara Castro-Klarén. Oxford: Blackwell Publishing, 2008.

—. "Rethinking the Colonial Model." In *Rethinking Literary History: A Dialogue on Theory*. Ed. Linda Hutcheon and Mario Valdés. Oxford, New York: Oxford University Press, 2001. 155-193.

—. "Signs and their Transmission: The Question of the Book in the New World." In *Writing Without Words: Alternative Literacies in Mesoamerica and the Andes*. Ed. E. Boone and W. Mignolo. Durham: Duke University Press. 1994. 220-270.

—. "Subaltern Studies: Projects for Our Time and Thier Convergence." In *The Latin American Subaltern Studies Reader*. Ed. Ileana Rodríguez. Durham: Duke University Press, 2001. 35-47.

—. *Writing without Words: Alternative Literacies in Mesoamerica and the Andes*. Durham: Duke University Press, 1994: 3-26.

MILES, Susan A. *The Shape of Inca History: Narrative and Architecture in an Andean Empire*. Iowa City: University of Iowa Press, 2002.

MILLER, James. *The Passion of Michel Foucault*. Cambridge: Harvard University Press, 1993.

MILLONES, Luis. *Nuestra Historia: Perú colonial*. Lima: COFIDE, 1995.

—. *El retorno de las huacas: estudios y documentos del siglo XVI*. Lima: Instituto de Estudios Peruanos, 1990.

—. "Un movimiento nativista del siglo XVI: el Taqui-Oncoy." *Ideología mesiánica del mundo andino*. Ed. Juan M. Ossio A. Lima: I. Prado Pastor, 1973.

MILLS, Sara. *Discourse*. London: Routledge, 1997.

MIÑO GARCÉS, Leonardo. *El manejo del espacio en el imperio de los incas*. Quito: CLACSO, 1994.

MIRÓ QUESADA, Aurelio. *El Inca Garcilaso de la Vega*. Lima: Empresas Eléctricas Asociadas, 1945.

MONTAIGNE, Michel de. *Essays*. Ed. W. Carew Hazlitt. Trans. Charles Cotton. Chicago: Encyclopædia Britannica, 1952.

MONTOYA, Rodrigo, Edwin MONTOYA and Luis MONTOYA. *La sangre de los cerros, Urkukunapa Yawarnin*. Lima: Centro Peruano de Estudios Sociales, 1987.

MOORE, Henrietta. "The Problems of Origins: Poststructuralism and Beyond." In *Interpreting Archeology: Finding Meaning in the Past*. Ed. Ian Hodder. London: Routledge, 1995. 51-53.

MOORE-GILBERT, Bart. *Postcolonial Theory: Contexts, Practices, Politics*. London; New York: Verso, 1997.

Moraña, Mabel. "Barroco y conciencia criolla en Hispanoamérica." *Revista de Crítica Literaria Latinoamericana* 14:28 (1988): 229-51.

—. ed. *Relecturas del Barroco de Indias*. Havoner: Ediciones del Norte, 1994.

MOREIRAS, Alberto. "The End of Magical Realism: José María Arguedas's Passionate Signifier (*El zorro de arriba y el zorro de abajo*)." In *The Journal of Narrative Techinique* 27:1. 84-111.

MORGAN, Arthur E. *Nowhere was Somewhere: How History Makes Utopias and How Utopias Make History*. Chapel Hill: University of North Carolina Press, 1946.

MORO, César [Alfredo QUÍSPEZ ASÍN]. *La tortuga ecuestre*. Lima: Ediciones Tigrondine, [1939] 1957.

MORRIS, Meaghan. "Banality in Cultural Studies." In *What is Cultural Studies?* Ed. John Storey. London: Arnold, 1996.

MURÚA, Martín de. *Historia general del Perú*. Ed. Manuel Ballesteros Gaibrois. Madrid: Historia 16, 1987.

MURRA, John V. *Formaciones económicas y políticas del mundo andino*. Lima: Instituto de Estudios Peruanos, 1975.

NAIPAUL, V.S. *The Mimic Men*. New York: Macmillan, 1967.

NERUDA, Pablo. "Alturas de Macchu Picchu from *Canto General*." *Literatura hispanoamericana: antología e introducción histórica*. Ed. Enrique Anderson Imbert. New York: Holt, Rinehart and Winston, 1960. 686.

NEWMAN, John Henry. *Idea of a University*. Ed. Frank Turner. New Haven: Yale University Press, 1996.

NILES, A. Susan. *The Shape of Inca History: Narrative and Architecture in an Andean Empire*. Iowa City: University of Iowa Press, 1999.

NÚÑEZ, Estuardo. *Viajes y viajeros extranjeros por el Perú*. Lima: Conacyt, 1989.

—. and George PETERSEN, eds. *Alexander von Humboldt en el Perú: Diario de viajes y otros escritos*. Lima: Banco Central de Reserva del Perú, 2002.

O'Gorman, Edmundo. *La idea del descubrimiento de América: historia de esa interpretación y crítica de sus fundamentos.* México: Universidad Nacional Autónoma de México, 1951.

—. *La invención de América: la universalización de la cultura occidental.* México: Universidad Nacional Autónoma de México, 1958.

—. *The Invention of America.* Bloomington: Indiana University Press, 1961.

—. *La utopía de Tomás Moro en Méjico.* México: Alcancia, 1937.

O'Malley, John W. *The First Jesuits.* Cambridge: Harvard University Press, 1993.

Oquendo de Amat, Carlos. *Cinco metros de poemas.* Lima: Editorial Decantar, 1927.

Orrillo, Winston and Eduardo Congrains Martin, Eds. *Antología general de la prosa en el Perú.* (2 vols.) Lima: Encoma, 1971.

Ortiz, Fernando. *Cuban Counterpoint; Tobacco and Sugar.* Durham: Duke University Press, 1995.

Osorio Tejeda, Nelson. "Intervention in a debate at Dartmouth." In *Revista de Crítica Literaria Latinoamericana* 33 (1991): 146-48.

Ossio, Juan M. "Cultural Continuity, Structure, and Context; Some Peculiarities of the Andean Compadrazgo." In *Kinship Ideology and Practice in Latin America.* Ed. Raymond I. Smith. Chapel Hill: University of North Carolina Press, 1984.

—. "Guamán Poma: Nueva corónica o carta al rey. Un intento de aproximación a las categorías del pensamiento del mundo andino." In *Ideología mesiánica del mundo andino.* Ed. Juan M. Ossio A. Lima: I. Prado Pastor, 1973. 153-213.

—. *Ideología mesiánica del mundo andino.* Lima: I. Prado Pastor, 1973.

Pagden, Anthony. *The Fall of Natural Man: The American Indian and the Origins of Comparative Ethnology.* Cambridge: Cambridge University Press, 1982.

Panofsky, Erwin. *Meaning in the Visual Arts.* Chicago: University of Chicago Press, [1952] 1982.

"Paradigm." *The Cambridge Dictionary of Philosophy.* Ed. Robert Audi. Cambridge: Cambridge University Press, 1999.

Pauw, Cornelius. *Recherches Philosophiques sur les Américaine (Œuvres philosophiques vol. iii).* Paris: J.F. Bastien, An III, 1794.

Paz, Octavio. *Sor Juana Inés de la Cruz o las trampas de la fe.* México: Fondo de Cultura Económica,1982.

Pease, Franklin. *Las crónicas y los Andes.* Lima: Pontificia Universidad Católica del Perú; México: Fondo de Cultura Económica, 1995.

—. *Del Tahuantinsuyo a la historia del Perú.* Lima: Instituto de Estudios Peruanos, 1978.

—. *El dios creador andino.* Lima: Mosca Azul Editores, 1973.

—. *El pensamiento mítico. Antología.* Ed. Franklin Pease. Lima: Biblioteca del pensamiento peruano, 1982.

PERALTA, Alejandro. *Kollao*. Lima: Talleres de la Cía de Impresiones y Publicidad, 1934.

PERUS, Françoise. "El dialogismo y la poética histórica bajtinianos en la perspectiva de la heterogeneidad cultural y la transculturación narrativa en América Latina." *Revista de Crítica Literaria Latinoamericana* 21.42 (1995): 29-40.

PHELAN, John L. *The Millennial Kingdom of the Franciscans in the New World.* Berkeley: University of California Press, 1958.

PLATO. *The Dialogues of Plato: The Seventh Letter.* Chicago: Encyclopaedia Britannica, 1952.

PLATT, Tristan. "Symétrie en mirroir." *Annales* 33 anné (septembre-decembre 1978): 1081-1107.

PLETSCHE, Carl. "The Three Worlds, or the Division of Social Scientific Labor, circa 1950-1975." *Comparative Studies in Society and History* 23.4 (1976): 505-90.

POOLE, Deborah. *Vision, Race, and Modernity: A Visual Economy of the Andean Image World.* Princeton: Princeton University Press, 1997.

PORRAS BARRENECHEA, Raúl. *El cronista indio Felipe Guamán Poma de Ayala.* Lima: Ed. Lumen, 1948.

—. *Los cronistas del Perú (1528-1650) y otros ensayos.* Lima: Banco de Crédito del Perú, 1986.

—. *Fuentes históricas peruanas.* Lima: Instituto Raúl Porras Barrenechea, 1963.

PORTAL, Magda. *Ser mujer en el Perú.* Lima: Topaku, 1979.

POSTER, Mark. *Critical Theory and Poststructuralism: In Search of a Context.* Ithaca: Cornell University Press, 1989.

PRATT, Mary Louise. *Imperial Eyes: Travel Writing and Transculturation.* London: Routledge, 1992.

PRESCOTT, William. *History of the Conquest of Peru.* New York: Bradley Company, 1847.

PROUST, Marcel. "La Prisonnière." Quoted in *Present Past* by Richard Terdiman. Ithaca: Cornell University Press, 1993. 3.

QUIJANO, Aníbal. "The Colonial Nature of Power and Latin America's Cultural Experience." In *Sociology in Latin America (Social Knowledge: Heritage, Challenges, and Perspectives).* Ed. R. Briceño and H.R. Sonntag. Caracas: Proceedings of the Regional Conference of the International Association of Sociology, 1998. 27-38.

RABASA, José. *Inventing America: Spanish Historiography and the Formation of Eurocentrism.* Norman: University of Oklahoma Press, 1993.

—. "Pre-Columbian Pasts and Indian Presents in Mexican History." *Colonialism Past and Present: Reading and Writing About Colonial Latin America Today.* Eds. Álvaro Félix Bolaños and Gustavo Verdesio. Albany: State University of New York Press, 2002. 51-79.

—. "On Writing Back: Alternative Historiography in *La Florida del Inca.*" In *Latin American Identity and Constructions of Difference.* Ed. Amaryll Chanady. Minneapolis: University of Minnesota Press, 1994. 130-145.

—. "Of Zapatismo: Reflections on the Folkloric and the Impossible in a Subaltern Insurrection." In *The Politics of Culture in the Shadow of Capital.* Ed. Lisa Lowe and David Lloyd. Durham: Duke University Press, 1997. 399-431.

—. *Writing Violence on the Northern Frontier: The Historiography of Sixteenth Century New Mexico and Florida and the Legacy Of Conquest.* Durham: Duke University Press, 2000.

RAMA, Ángel. *La ciudad letrada.* Hanover: Ediciones del Norte, 1984.

—. *Transculturación narrativa en América Latina.* México: Siglo Veintiuno, 1982.

RAMOS, Julio. *Desencuentros de la modernidad en América Latina: literatura y política en el siglo XIX.* México: Fondo de Cultura Económica, 1989.

READINGS, Bill. *The University in Ruins.* Cambridge: Harvard University Press, 1996.

RENAN, Ernest. "What is a Nation?" *Nation and Narration.* Ed. Homi Bhabha. Trans. Martin Thom. New York: Routledge, 1990. 8-22.

RIBEYRO, Julio Ramón. *Crónica de San Gabriel.* Lima: Ediciones Tawantisuyu, 1960.

—. *Los geniecillos dominicales.* Lima: Populibros Peruanos, 1965.

RIVA AGÜERO, José de la. *Carácter de la literatura del Perú independiente.* vol. I of *Obras completas.* Lima: Pontificia Universidad Católica del Perú, 1962.

—. *Paisajes peruanos.* Lima: Impr. Santa María, 1955.

RIVERO, Mariano Eduardo de and Juan Diego de TSCHUDI. *Antigüedades peruanas.* Viena: Impr. Imperial de la Corte y del Estado, 1851.

RIVIALE, Pascal. *Los viajeros franceses en busca del Perú antiguo (1821-1914).* Lima: Instituto Francés de Estudios Andinos, 2000.

RODRÍGUEZ, Ileana, "Hegemonía y dominio: subalternidad, un significado flotante." *Teorías sin disciplina, latinoamericanismo, poscolonialidad y globalización en debate.* Ed. Santiago Castro-Gómez and Eduardo Mendieta. México: Porrúa; San Francisco: University of San Francisco Press, 1998. 102-119.

—, ed. *The Latin American Subaltern Studies Reader.* Durham: Duke University Press, 2001.

RODRÍGUEZ-GARRIDO, José A. "Espinosa Medrano: la recepción del sermón barroco y la defensa de los americanos." In Ed. Mabel Moraña. *Relecturas del Barroco de Indias.* Hanover: Ediciones del Norte, 1994. 149-172.

ROMERO, Emilio. "El Cuzco católico." *Amauta*, December, 1927.

ROSS, Kathleen. *The Baroque Narrative of Carlos de Sigüenza y Góngora: A New World Paradise.* Cambridge: Cambridge University Press, 1993.

ROSTWOROWSKI DE DÍEZ CANSECO, María. *Estructuras andinas del poder. Ideología religiosa y política.* Lima: Instituto de Estudios Peruanos, 1983.

—. *Historia del Tahuantinsuyu.* Lima: Instituto de Estudios Peruanos, 1988.

—. *Pachacamac y el Señor de los Milagros: una trayectoria milenaria.* Lima: Instituto de Estudios Peruanos, 2002.

ROWE, John. "El movimiento nacional Inca del siglo XVIII." In *Túpac Amaru II-1780.* Ed. Alberto Flores Galindo. Lima: Retablo de Papel, 1976. 11-53.

RUÍZ VILAPLANA, Antonio. *Doy fe... un año de actuación en la España nacionalista.* Paris: Éditions Imprimerie Coopérative Étoile, 1937?

SAID, Edward W. *Orientalism.* New York: Pantheon Books, 1978.

SALAZAR BONDY, Sebastián. *Lima la horrible.* Lima: Populibros, 1964.

SALDÍVAR, José. "Las fronteras de Nuestra América: para volver a trazar el mapa de los estudios culturales norteamericanos." *Revista Casa de las Américas* julio-septiembre 1996: 3-19.

SALOMON, Frank. *The Cord Keepers: Khipus and Cultural Life in a Peruvian Village.* Durham: Duke University Press, 2004.

SAMPSON, Geoffrey. *Writing Systems: A Linguistic Introduction.* Stanford: Stanford University Press, 1985.

SÁNCHEZ, Luis Alberto. *La literatura peruana: derrotero para una historia cultural del Perú.* (5 vols.) 5th ed. Lima: Mejía Baca, 1981.

SÁNCHEZ ALBORNOZ, Nicolás. *The Population of Latin America: A History.* Trans. W.A.R. Richardson. Berkeley: University of California Press, 1974.

SARMIENTO DE GAMBOA, Pedro. *Historia de los incas.* Ed. Ángel Rosenblat. Buenos Aires: Emecé Editores, 1943.

SARLO, Beatriz. *Escenas de la vida posmoderna.* Buenos Aires: Ariel, 1994.

SCHELONKA, Greg. *Garcilaso de la Vega, Inca, The First Postcolonial?* Unpublished manuscript. 1994.

SCORZA, Manuel. *Redoble por Rancas.* Barcelona: Plaza & Janés, 1970.

SEED, Patricia. *Ceremonies of Possessions in Europe's Conquest of the New World 1492 1640.* New York: Cambridge University Press, 1995.

SERULNIKOV, Sergio. *Subverting Colonial Authority: Challenges to Spanish Rule in Eighteenth Century Southern Andes.* Durham: Duke University Press, 2003.

SHANKS, Michael, et al, eds. *Interpreting Archaeology: Finding Meaning in the Past.* London: Routledge, 1995.

SHEPHERD, George. *José de Acosta: Reading the American Past and Programming the Future toward the Christianization of Amerindians.* Washington, D.C.: Diss. Georgetown University, 1996.

SILVA SANTISTEBAN, Rocío. *Este oficio no me gusta.* Lima: Ediciones Cope, 1981.

SILVA SIFUENTES, Jorge. *Nuestra historia: el imperio de los cuatro suyos.* Lima: COFIDE, 1995.

SIMONS, Jon. *Foucault and the Political.* London; New York: Routledge, 1994.

SMITH, Anthony D. *The Ethnic Origins of Nations.* Oxford: Blackwell, 1986.

SOJA, Edward. "History: Geography: Modernity." In *The Cultural Studies Reader.* Ed. Simon During. London: Routledge, 1993. 135-150.

SOLOGUREN, Javier. *Antología general de la literatura peruana*. México: Fondo de Cultura Económica, 1981.

SORIA, Martín S. *La pintura del siglo XVI en Sudamérica*. Buenos Aires: Instituto de Arte Americano e Investigaciones Estéticas, 1956.

SPALDING, Karen. *Huarochirí: An Andean Society under Inca and Spanish Rule*. Stanford: Stanford University Press, 1984.

SPIVAK, Gayatri. "Can the Subaltern Speak?" In *Colonial Discourse and Post-colonial Theory: A Reader*. Ed. Patrick William and Laura Chrisman. New York: Columbia University Press, 1994. 66-112.

—. "Can the Subaltern Speak?" *Marxism and the Interpretation of Culture*. Ed. Cary Nelson and Lawrence Grossberg. Urbana: University of Illinois Press, 1989. 271-313.

—. *In Other Worlds*. New York: Methuen, 1987.

STASTNY, Francisco. *Breve historia del arte en el Perú: la pintura precolombina, colonial y republicana*. Lima: Editorial Universo, 1967.

STAVIG, Ward. *The World of Tupac Amaru: Conflict, Community and Identity in Colonial Peru*. Lincoln and London: University of Nebraska Press, 1999.

STERN, Steve J. *Peru's Indian Peoples and the Challenge of Spanish Conquest: Huamanga to 1640*. Madison: University of Wisconsin Press, 1982.

—, ed. *Resistance, Rebellion, and Consciousness in the Andean Peasant World, 18th to 20th Centuries*. Madison: University of Wisconsin Press, 1987.

STONUM, Gary Lee. "Undoing American History." In *Diacritics* 11 (September 1981): 45-61.

TAMAYO HERRERA, José. *Historia del indigenismo cuzqueño, siglos XVI-XX*. Lima: Instituto Nacional de Cultura, 1980.

TARCUS, Horacio. "Revistas intelectuales y formaciones culturales izquierdistas en la Argentina de los veinte." *Revista Iberoamericana* Vol. LXX. Nums. 208-209. Julio-diciembre 2004: 794-772.

TAYLOR, Charles. *Multiculturalism and the "Politics of Recognition."* Princeton: Princeton University Press, 1992.

TELLO, Julio C. *La primeras edades del Perú por Guamán Poma*. Lima, 1939.

TENENBAUM, Barbara A., ed. *Encyclopedia of Latin American History and Culture*. Vol. V. New York: Charles Scribner and Son's, 1996.

TERDINAN, Richard. *Present Past*. Ithaca: Cornell University Press, 1993.

THURNER, Mark. *From Two Republics to One Divided: Contradictions of Postcolonial Nationmaking in Andean Peru*. Durham: Duke University Press, 1997.

TOLEDO, Francisco de. *Ordenanzas*. Ed. Roberto Levillier. Vol. 8 of *Gobernantes del Perú, cartas y papeles, siglo XVI*. Ed. Roberto Levillier. Madrid: Imprenta de Juan Pueyo, 1925. 14 vols.

TORO, Alfonso de. "Post-Coloniality and Post-Modernity: Jorge Luis Borges: The Periphery in the Centre, the Periphery as the Centre, the Centre of the

Periphery." In *Borders and Margins: Post-Colonialism and Post-Modernity*. Eds. Fernando de Toro and Alfonso de Toro. Madrid: Iberoamericana; Frankfurt am Main: Vervuert, 1995. 11-43.

TREXLER, Richard C. *Sex and Conquest: Gendered Violence, Political Order and the European Conquest of the Americas*. Cambridge: Polity Press, 1995.

TYLER, Stephen A. "Post-Mordern Ethnography." In *Writing culture: The Poetics and Politics of Ethnography*. Ed. James Clifford and George E. Marcus. Berkeley: University of California Press, 1986.

UNRUH, Vicky. *Latin American Vanguards: the Art of Contentious Encounters*. Berkeley: University of California Press, 1994.

URTON, Gary. *Signs of the Inka Khipu: Binary Coding in the Andean Knotted-String Records*. Austin: University of Texas Press, 2003.

—. *The Social Life of Numbers: A Quechua Ontology of Numbers and Philosophy of Arithmetic*. Austin: University of Texas Press, 1997.

VALCÁRCEL, Luis E. *Etnohistoria del antiguo Perú*. Lima: Universidad Nacional Mayor de San Marcos, 1959.

—. "Garcilaso Inca." *Revista del Museo Nacional* VIII, 1 (1939): 3-60.

—. "Saisawaman redescubierto." *Revista del Museo Nacional* IV, 2 (1935): 161-203.

—. *Tempestad en los Andes*. Lima: Editorial Minerva, 1927.

—. *El virrey Toledo, gran tirano del Perú*. Lima: Impr. del Museo Nacional, 1940.

VALDELOMAR, Abraham. *El Caballero Carmelo*. Lima, 1918.

—. *Los hijos del sol*. Lima: Ciudad de los Reyes: Euforion, 1921.

VALLEJO, César. *Los heraldos negros*. Lima, 1918.

—. "Nómina de huesos." In *César Vallejo. Obra poética*. Paris: Archivos, 1988. 325.

—. *Poemas en prosa. Poemas humanos. España, aparta de mí este cáliz*. Ed. Julio Vélez. Madrid: Cátedra, 1988.

—. *Trilce*. Lima: Perú Nuevo, 1923.

VARGAS LLOSA, Mario. *La ciudad y los perros*. Barcelona: Editorial Seix Barral, 1963.

—. *Conversación en la Catedral*. Barcelona: Editorial Seix Barral, 1969.

—. *La guerra del fin del mundo*. Barcelona: Editorial Seix Barral, 1981.

—. *La tía Julia y el escribidor*. Bogotá: Círculo de Lectores, 1977.

VARNER, John Grier. *El Inca: Life and Times of Garcilaso de la Vega*. Austin: University of Texas Press, 1968.

VARÓN GABAI, Rafael. "El Taki Onqoy: Las raíces andinas de un fenómeno colonial." In *El retorno de las huacas. Estudios y documentos sobre el Taki Onqoy, siglo XVI*. Ed. Luis Millones. Lima: Instituto de Estudios Peruanos, 1990.

VEGA, Inca Garcilaso de la. *Comentarios reales* [1609]. Ed. Aurelio Miró Quesada. Caracas: Biblioteca Ayacucho, 1976.

—. *Royal Commentaries of the Incas and General History of Peru*. Vol. I [1605]. Trans. Harold V. Livermore. Austin: University of Texas Press, 1966.

VERGER, Pierre. *Fiestas y danzas en el Cuzco y en los Andes.* Buenos Aires: Editorial Sudamericana, 1945.

VICO, Giambattista. *La scienza nuova, 1730.* Napoli: A. Guida, 2004.

VILLASEÑOR, Nicole. *Perú: cronistas indios y mestizos en el siglo XVI.* México: SepSetenta, 1957.

WACHTEL, Nathan. *Sociedad e ideología: ensayos de historia y antropología andina.* Lima: Instituto de Estudios Peruanos, 1973.

—. *Los vencidos: los indios del Perú frente a la conquista española (1530-1570).* Trans. Antonio Escohotado. Madrid: Alianza Editorial, 1976.

WATANABE, Luis K. *Nuestra historia: culturas preincas del Perú.* Lima: COFIDE, 1995.

WATERS, Lindsay. "A Modest Proposal for Preventing the Books of the Members of the MLA from Being a Burden to Their Authors, Publishers, or Audiences." *PMLA* May 2000: 315-317.

WEBER, Eugen. *Peasants into Frenchmen: the Modernization of Rural France, 1870-1914.* Stanford: Stanford University Press, 1976.

WESTPHALEN, Emilio Adolfo. *Abolición de la muerte.* Lima: Ediciones Perú Actual, 1935.

WHITE, Hayden. *Metahistory: The Historical Imagination in Nineteenth Century Europe.* Baltimore: Johns Hopkins University Press, 1973.

—. *Tropics of Discourse.* Baltimore: Johns Hopkins University Press, 1978.

WILLIAMS, Patrick and Laura Chrisman. *Colonial discourse and Post-colonial Theory: A Reader.* New York: Columbia University Press, 1994.

WOLFFLIN, Heinrich. *Principles of Art History.* New York: Dover, 1950.

YOUNG, Robert. *White Mythologies: Writing History and the West.* London: Routledge, 1993.

YÚDICE, George. "Cultural Studies and Civil Studies." In *Reading the Shape of the World.* Eds. Henry Schwarz and Richard Dientz. Boulder: Westview, 1996. 50-67.

—. "Postmodernity and Transnational Capitalism in Latin America." In *On Edge: the Crisis of Contemporary Latin American Culture.* Eds. Jean Franco, Juan Flores, and George Yúdice. Minneapolis: University of Minnesota Press, 1992.

YUN, Sui. *La rosa fálica.* Lima: Ediciones Loto, 1983.

ZAMORA, Margarita. *Language, Authority, and Indigenous History in the Comentarios reales de los Incas.* Cambridge: Cambridge University Press, 1988.

ZAVALA, Silvio. *Utopía de Tomás Moro en la Nueva España y otros estudios.* México, 1937.

ZEVALLOS-AGUILAR, Juan. "Teoría poscolonial y literatura latinoamericana: Entrevista con Sara Castro-Klarén." *Revista Iberoamericana.* LXII, 176-77, 1996: 963-971.

ZUIDEMA, R. Tom. *Inca Civilization in Cuzco*. Tran. Jean Jacques Decostes. Austin: University of Texas Press, 1990.

—. *The Ceque System of Cuzco: The Social Organization of the Capital of the Inca*. Trans. Eva M. Hooykaas. Leiden: Brill, 1964.

—. "Cuzco, Quipu and Quadrant." *XXVI International Congress of the History of Art*, Washington DC, 1986, Ms. 18 pp.

CREDITS

Permissions for the inclusion in this gathering of the following material has been graciously granted by the publishers and individuals indicated below.

Chapter 1.1
Reprinted from Sara Castro-Klarén: "Huaman Poma and the Space of Purity", in Raymond L. Hall (ed.): *Ethnic Autonomy. Comparative Dynamics. The Americas, Europe and the Developing World*, 345-370. © 1979 New York: Pergamon Press. This is an extensively revised version.

Chapter 1.2
An earlier and smaller version of this essay was originally published in Spanish as "El orden del sujeto en Guamán Poma" in *Revista de Crítica Literaria Latinoamericana* Año XX, No 41. Lima-Berkeley, 1995, 121-134. Another version was published in my *Escritura, transgresion y sujeto en la literatura latinoamericana*. Mexico: Premiá, 1989. This is a newly expanded and revised text.

Chapter 1.3
An earlier version of this essay was originally published as Sara Castro-Klarén: "Dancing and the Sacred in the Andes: From the Taqui-Oncoy to Rasu-Niti", in *New World Encounters*, edited by Stephen Greenblatt. © 1993 by the Regents of the University of California. Published by the University of California Press.

Chapter 1.4
Published in two parts ("Memory and 'Writing' in the Andes" and "Writing the Andes") in Sara Castro-Klarén (ed.): *A Companion to Latin American Litera-*

ture and Culture. © 2008 Oxford: Blackwell. It has been minimally revised. Reprinted by permission.

Chapter 1.5
An early version of this chapter was originally published in *The Latin American Subaltern Studies Reader*, ed. Ileana Rodríguez, 143-171. © 2001 Durham: Duke University Press. All rights reserved. Reprinted by permission.

Chapter 1.6
Originally published in *Dispositio/n* No. 46. (1994) (Issue dedicated to: Subaltern Studies in the Americas), 229-244.

Chapter 1.7
Originally published in Spanish as "El Cuzco de Garcilaso: el espacio y el lugar del conocimiento" in *Asedios a la heterogeneidad cultural.* Eds. José Antonio Mazzotti and U. Juan Zevallos Aguilar. Lima: Asociación Internacional de Peruanistas, 1996. 135-152. Translated by Barbara M. Corbett. Reproduced with permission of José Antonio Mazzotti.

Chapter 1.9
A slightly different version of this chapter was originally published as Sara Castro-Klarén, "The Nation in Ruins: Archeology and the Emergence of the Nation" in Sara Castro-Klarén and John Charles Chasteen, editors' book, *Beyond Imagined Communities: Reading and Writing the Nation in Nineteenth-Century Latin America*, 161-195. © 2003 Woodrow Wilson International Center for Scholars. Reproduced with permission of The Johns Hopkins University Press.

Chapter 1.10
An earlier version of this essay was published in Michael J. Lazzara and Vicky Unruh (eds.): *Telling Ruins in Latin America*, 2009, New York: Palgrave MacMillan, 77-86. Reproduced with permission of Palgrave Macmillan.

Chapter 2.1
Originally published in *El debate de la postcolonialidad en Latinoamérica: una postmodernidad periférica o cambio de paradigma en el pensamiento latinoamericano.* Eds. Alfonso de Toro and Fernando de Toro, 137-165. © 1999 Madrid: Iberoamericana; Frankfurt am Main: Vervuert. Reprinted by permission.

Chapter 2.3
Originally pulished in *Colonialism Past and Present: Reading and Writing About Colonial Latin America Today*. Ed. Alvaro Félix Bolaños and Gustavo Verdesio, 261-288. © 2002 Albany: State University of New York Press. Reprinted by permission.

Chapter 2.4
Originally published in *Dispositio* 52 (2006): 95-106.

Chapter 2.6
This chapter was originally published in *Literary Cultures of Latin America: a Comparative History* edited by Valdes & Kadir (2004) Chp.39 "Lima: A Blurred Centrality" by Castro-Klaren © Oxford University Press, Ltd. By permission of Oxford University Press.

Chapter 2.7
This chapter was originally published in *Coloniality at Large: Latin America and the Postcolonial Debate*. Eds. Mabel Moraña, Enrique Dussel, and Carlos A. Jáuregui, 130-157. © 2008 Durham: Duke University Press. All rights reserved. Reprinted by permission.

Volúmenes publicados en Nuevos Hispanismos

Vol. 1: Julio Ortega (ed.): *Nuevos hispanismos interdisciplinarios y trasatlánticos*. 2010

Vol. 2: Miguel Casado (ed.): *Cuestiones de poética en la actual poesía en castellano*. 2009

Vol. 3: José R. Valles Calatrava: *Teoría de la narrativa. Una perspectiva sistemática*. 2008

Vol. 4: Kathya Araujo: *Dignos de su arte. Sujeto y lazo social en el Perú de las primeras décadas del siglo XX*. 2009

Vol. 5: Rubí Carreño Bolívar: *Diamela Eltit: redes locales, redes globales*. 2009

Vol. 6: Jorge Carrión: *Viaje contra espacio. Juan Goytisolo y W. G. Sebald*. 2009

Vol. 7: Oswaldo Estrada: *La imaginación novelesca. Bernal Díaz entre géneros y épocas*. 2009

Vol. 8: Leila Gómez: *Iluminados y tránsfugas. Relatos de viajeros y ficciones nacionales en Argentina, Paraguay y Perú*. 2009

Vol. 9: Guido Rings: *La Conquista desbaratada: Identidad y alteridad en la novela, el cine y el teatro hispánicos contemporáneos*. 2010

Vol. 10: Magdalena Chocano, William Rowe, Helena Usandizaga (eds.): *Huellas del mito prehispánico en la literatura latinoamericana*. 2011

Vol. 11: Fernando Rivera: *Dar la palabra. Ética, política y poética de la escritura en Arguedas*. 2011